Hymnal
COMPANION

Prepared by
Churches in the
Believers Church Tradition

Joan A. Fyock, Writer / Compiler
Lani Wright, Editor

Brethren Press
Elgin, Illinois

Faith and Life Press
Newton, Kansas

Mennonite Publishing House
Scottdale, Pennsylvania

Hymnal Companion

Brethren Press, Elgin, Illinois
Faith and Life Press, Newton, Kansas
Mennonite Publishing House, Scottdale, Pennsylvania

Cover Design—Gwen Stamm
Typography—G. Schultz Publications Production, Aurora, Illinois
Printer—Quebecor, Hawkins Kingsport, Tennessee

Library of Congress Cataloging-in-Publication Data
Hymnal companion / prepared by churches in the Believers Church tradition.
p. cm.
Includes bibliographical references (p.719) and index.
ISBN 0-87178-388-6 (alk. paper)
1. Hymns, English—History and criticism. 2. Church of the Brethren—Hymns—History and criticism. 3. General Conference Mennonite Church—Hymns—History and criticism. 4. Mennonite Church—Hymns—History and criticism. 5. Hymns—Biography. I. Hymnal (Elgin, Ill.)
M2117.H984 1992 Suppl. 2
264'.06502—dc20 96-19633

Cover symbol: The lamb in the midst of briars is a traditional Anabaptist symbol. It illustrates the suffering Lamb of God, who calls the faithful to obedient service. Since in the past it has been used to represent unity among believers, it is an appropriate symbol for this cooperatively produced book.

1 2 3 4 5 6 7 8 9 10 05 04 03 02 01 00 99 98 97 96

TABLE OF CONTENTS

FOREWORD

Hymnals, like family albums, record in words and music God's walk with ordinary people in all parts of their lives. Hymnals tell of Christian experiences in a form that present and future generations can sing or recite, praising the God "in whom we live and move and have our being." Behind every hymn there is a story—how it was conceived, who inspired it, how it is used.

The hymnal, for which this volume is a companion, was developed by The Hymnal Project, made up of personnel from the Church of the Brethren, the General Conference Mennonite Church, the Mennonite Church, Churches of God (contributors), and Mennonite Brethren (contributors). *Hymnal: A Worship Book* was published in 1992. This *Hymnal Companion* tells stories about the hymns, tunes, and resources found in *Hymnal: A Worship Book* and includes biographies of the people who wrote them.

The Christian life is best understood through story. The Old Testament begins with a story of creation. Stories about Abraham and Sarah, Moses, Ruth, David, and Jeremiah teach us the nature of faithfulness. Jesus taught profound insights about God through parables. The story of Jesus' life, death, and resurrection becomes real to us. Stories of our saints, martyrs, leaders, parents, and friends attest to God's faithfulness and love in times of suffering, doubt, and joy. The Spirit, who brings forth poetry from writers and music from composers today, is revealed in those creative stories.

Hymnal Companion helps us see how the Spirit moves—unrestricted by gender, race, time, or place. The articles for both hymns and resources show us something about the writers' experiences that gave rise to the text or the music. From the biographies we are given the opportunity to see how God lived and moved in the lives of the writers.

Our hope is that *Hymnal Companion* will strengthen our sense of heritage with Christians past and present by allowing their stories to enrich our own stories of God's ongoing love and faithfulness.

Rebecca Slough, Managing Editor
Hymnal: A Worship Book

PREFACE

Hymnal:A Worship Book includes hymns representing a wide variety of times and places. *Hymnal Companion* is designed to enrich our understanding of these hymns. For the Church of the Brethren, its predecessors are a twelve-page leaflet, "Brethren Hymns, Hymnals, Authors and Composers," by William Beery (1945), and *Handbook on Brethren Hymns* by Ruth Statler and Nevin Fisher (1959), which provides thirty-nine biographies and information on forty-seven hymns and six musical worship resources from *The Brethren Hymnal* (1951). Mennonites have had at their disposal *Exploring the Mennonite Hymnal,* produced in two volumes—*Essays* (1980) and a *Handbook* (1983)—correlating to *The Mennonite Hymnal* (1969) and Lester Hostetler's *Handbook to the Mennonite Hymnary* (1949) for *The Mennonite Hymnary* (1940).

Written for ministers, lay people, music lovers, and teachers, *Hymnal Companion* provides insights into familiar hymns as well as helpful information about more recent hymns. It is academically sound and accessible to the interested lay person; it is both factual and anecdotal. This *Companion* will be a valuable reference in church, college, and seminary libraries, and I hope it will also enrich personal and family devotional use of hymns.

In the first section of this book, the articles on the hymns are arranged alphabetically. To locate an article by hymn number, a numerical index of hymns is provided. Data about the hymn is placed in two columns at the beginning of each article (see p. ix for Key to Using the *Hymnal Companion*).

The second section of the book provides information about selected worship resources that are of special historical or denominational significance. The reader will also find a number of helpful definitions or commentaries on terms related to music and worship.

The third section of the *Companion* alphabetically presents biographies of most of the authors, composers, translators, and arrangers who created the hymns and worship resources. When only scant biographical information was available, the name was omitted in this section and brief comments included in the hymn article.

While every effort has been made to be as accurate as possible, much of the research was limited to secondary sources. Where discrepancies of dates, names, or places occurred, a decision was most often based on the majority opinion of the sources consulted. A selected bibliography, along with a list of sources cited, appears as one of the indexes. Not listed there, but of invaluable aid, were pre-publication manuscripts for the companions to *Worship III*, *Psalter Hymnal*, and *The United Methodist Hymnal*. The original research in this companion was obtained primarily through correspondence with authors, composers, arrangers, and translators around the world, from the Philippines to Nigeria. Deep appreciation is expressed to those who provided important information in this way.

I gratefully acknowledge the people who assisted with the research and writing of this volume. Dr. John G. Barr of Bridgewater College, Bridgewater, Virginia, had an especially significant role. In addition, these people need to be recognized: Dr. Carl N. Shull, professor of music emeritus, Elizabethtown College (early American hymnody); Dr. K. Gary Adams, Bridgewater College, and Rebecca Slough, Richmond, Indiana (biographies); Dr. George Wiebe, Canadian Mennonite Bible College (chorales); Dr. Horace Fishback, professor of music emeritus, Fairleigh Dickinson University (chorale tunes); Hedwig T. Durnbaugh (Scandinavian and early Brethren hymnody); and Dr. Mary K. Oyer, professor of music emeritus, Goshen College (music of Taizé and non-western hymns). Special thanks go to Mary Louise VanDyke, *Dictionary of Hymnology*, and Lloyd Zeager, Lancaster, Pennsylvania, for their assistance in tracing elusive persons, dates, and details, and to Walter A. Keeney, Jr., Lancaster, Pennsylvania, for volunteering hundreds of hours of computer data entry. I also extend my gratitude to the Lititz Church of the Brethren, where I had office space for more than four years and whose members provided computer equipment and expertise, many hours of volunteer clerical help and proofreading, sources for research, and invaluable encouragement.

May the information in this *Hymnal Companion* increase our understanding and inspire our faith.

Joan A. Fyock
Writer/Compiler
Hymnal Companion

KEY TO USING THE *HYMNAL COMPANION*

The statistical data in *Hymnal Companion* is an expansion of the data found below each hymn in *Hymnal: A Worship Book*. Text information is in the left column and tune information on the right. Below is an explanation of the elements that might appear in one entry:

213[1]
Let all together praise our God[2]

Lobt Gott, ihr Christen alle gleich[3]
Nicolaus Hermann (ca. 1485-1561), ca. 1554[4]
Die Sonntags Evangelia über das gantze Jahr, 1560[5]
Tr. Arthur Tozer Russell (1806-1874)[6]
Russell's *Psalms and Hymns*, 1851[7]

LOBT GOTT, IHR CHRISTEN[8]

Nicolaus Hermann (ca. 1485-1561)[9]
Ein Christlicher Abentreien, 1554[10]
(Zahn No. 198)[11]
Harm. by J. S. Bach (1685-1750)[12]
Cantata No. 151, 1725[13]

1. Hymn number in *Hymnal: A Worship Book*
2. First line
3. First line in original language
4. Author with birth/death dates, including date piece was written
5. Earliest source of text
6. Name of translator with dates
7. Earliest source of translation
8. Tune name
9. Composer of tune with dates
10. Earliest source of tune
11. Number in Johannes Zahn's *Die Melodien der Deutschen Evangelischen Kirchenlieder*
12. Arranger or harmonizer with dates
13. Source of arrangement

Abbreviations:

Alt.	Alteration
Arr.	Arrangement or arranged by
St.	Stanza(s)*
Tr.	Translator
Harm.	Harmony or harmonized by

*Where reference to stanzas occurs in the body of the article, a number after the colon indicates the line number in the text. For example, "st. 1:2" refers to stanza 1, line 2.

All bold numbers refer to hymns and worship resources and their related articles in *Hymnal Companion*.

In addition to worship resources **806-861**, a number of others are based on scripture passages. The worship committee's working principle was not to alter the form or content of readings found in the scripture resource section. Where the *words* of scripture were used as worship resources, the form and wording were sometimes changed, usually to avoid numerous masculine references to God. Treating scripture in this manner is a practice of longstanding among Christians, beginning in the New Testament. Direct quotations and paraphrases of scripture have shaped the thought and imagery of public and private prayer for centuries.

Especially note worship resource **685**, "Blessed be the God and Father of our Lord Jesus Christ." Ephesians 1:1-14 is the basis for this reading, and it was arranged for the worship book because no other suitable readings of praise were found with these themes.

Various liturgical terms are described in the articles on worship resources. They are set off by a wider margin and introduced by a question.

In the biographies the first lines of hymns are italicized, tune names are all caps, and the first lines of worship resources are in roman.

HYMN ARTICLES

393

A charge to keep I have

Charles Wesley (1707-1788)
Short Hymns on Select Passages of Holy Scripture, Vol. 1, 1762

BOYLSTON

Lowell Mason (1792-1872)
The Choir, or Union Collection of Church Music, 1832

The two volumes of Wesley's *Short Hymns* . . . contain more than two thousand hymns based on biblical texts. Wesley based this text either on Leviticus 8:35 or on Matthew Henry's commentary on Leviticus: "We have every one of us a charge to keep, an eternal God to glorify, an immortal soul to provide for . . . " (Young 1993). The text could be paired also with other biblical passages to highlight its nearly militant call to service and alertness to Christ's return (Luke 21:36; Eph. 4:1; Josh. 24:15). Crafted around verbs as dynamic as the God it glorifies, this hymn presents unwavering faith and decisiveness about a Christian's priorities. It would be well suited to services centering on mission, commissioning, or ordination.

"A charge to keep I have," originally written in two stanzas of eight lines each, was a popular text at campground revival meetings where it was most often associated with Jeremiah Ingalls' tune KENTUCKY. Here the two stanzas become four in order to fit the tune BOYLSTON. The alteration in stanza 3, from "jealous" to "zealous," comes from *The Mennonite Hymnal* (1969). This maintains Wesley's original intent and is an example of how the meaning of words can change over time.

BOYLSTON is credited to Lowell Mason in his *Boston Academy's Collection of Church Music*, 7th ed. (1839). First published seven years earlier in *The Choir* . . . , the tune was used for various texts in Mason's collections. It also works with "Bless'd be the tie that binds" (**421**). Boylston is a section of Boston, Massachusetts, and a well-known street in that city. Scholars disagree as to which of these served as the source of the tune name. The tune is sometimes called MASON as well.

165, 329

A mighty fortress is our God

EIN FESTE BURG

Ein feste Burg ist unser Gott
Martin Luther (1483-1546), 1527-1529
Klug's *Geistliche Lieder*, Wittenberg, 1529, 1531
165, tr. Frederick Henry Hedge (1805-1890), 1852
Hymns for the Church of Christ, 1953
329, tr. *Lutheran Book of Worship*, 1978

Martin Luther (1483-1546), 1529
(same source as text)

Called by some the "Battle Hymn of the Reformation," this hymn was written by Luther sometime during the years 1527-1529, possibly in connection with the martyrdom of his friend Leonhard Kaiser (Young 1993). Its first publication may have been in Klug's *Geistliche Lieder* or Michael Blum's *Enchiridion*, Leipzig (1528-1529). No copy of either hymnal survives, however. This hymn has become truly ecumenical, translated into at least fifty languages; there are more than one hundred known English translations. The first one, made around 1535, came out in Miles Coverdale's *Goostly Psalmes and Spirituall Songes*. It contains some interesting poetic nuances:

> Oure God is a defence and towre,
> A good armoure and good weap[-]e;
> He hath been ever oure helpe and succoure,
> In all the troubles that we have ben in.
> Therefore wyl we never drede,
> For any wonderous dede
> By water or by londe,
> In hilles or the see do[-]se;
> Oure God hath them all in his hod.[1] (Young 1993)

This hymn is a powerful paraphrase of portions of Psalm 46; the first three stanzas seem more directly related to the psalm than the final one. Most North American hymnals favor this translation by Hedge, while the one by Thomas Carlyle, found in the *The Mennonite Hymnal* (1969), is most used in England.

It is assumed that this melody and text appeared together in Klug's 1529 collection; however, the earliest extant copies are A. Rauscher's *Geistliche Lieder*, Erfurt, and the *Kirchengesänge . . .* , Nürnberg, both dating from 1531. The straightforward metric form of the melody used in most hymnals dates from the time of J. S. Bach.

An earlier form of the melody, retaining the more vigorous rhythmic patterns of the Renaissance era, is included here as well, coupled with an English version of the text prepared by the Inter-Lutheran Commission on Worship.

1. A hod is a long-handled tray for carrying a load, often bricks or mortar.

598

A wonderful Savior is Jesus

KIRKPATRICK

Fanny Jane Crosby (1820-1915)
The Finest of the Wheat No. 1, 1890

William James Kirkpatrick (1838-1921)
(same source as text)

This hymn is one of many collaborations by Fanny Crosby and William Kirkpatrick, though Kirkpatrick wrote more than one tune dubbed KIRKPATRICK. The book in which the hymn first appeared was compiled by George D. Elderkin, R. R. McCabe, John R. Sweney, and Kirkpatrick. Although George B. Holsinger, a Brethren editor, included this hymn in his 1899 collection of *Gospel Songs and Hymns No. 1,* it is in only one Brethren hymnal (1925) and finds its revival here. Mennonites have learned it from the *The Mennonite Hymnal* (1969), *Church Hymnal* (1927), and *Life Songs No. 2* (1938).

426

Abide, O dearest Jesus

CHRISTUS, DER IST MEIN LEBEN

Ach bleib mit deiner Gnade
Josua Stegmann (1588-1632)
Suspiria Temporum, 1628
Tr. August Crull (1845-1923)
Evangelical Lutheran Hymn Book, 1892

Melchior Vulpius (ca. 1560-1615)
Ein schön geistlich Gesangbuch, 1609
(Zahn No. 132)

The words of the disciples "Abide with us," spoken to the risen Christ at Emmaus, lay the groundwork for this hymn. Stanzas 3 and 5 have been omitted. Widely used in the German, it was frequently the closing hymn for the school day among Mennonites in Russia. Each stanza focuses on a different aspect of Christ's person and work and builds to a strong congregational benediction appropriate for concluding a service.

This tune derives its name from the text first associated with it ("Christ, who is my life"). J. S. Bach based his chorale Cantata No. 95, *Christus, der ist mein Leben,* on this melody. The simplicity of the music suits the serenity of the text.

653

Abide with me

EVENTIDE

Henry Francis Lyte (1793-1847)
Remains of Henry Francis Lyte, 1850

William Henry Monk (1823-1889)
Hymns Ancient and Modern, 1861

This text first appeared in leaflet form in 1847 with a tune composed by the author, though the exact date of its writing has been debated. In 1850 it was published in the Remains of Henry Francis Lyte, which notes its allusion to Luke 24:29 where the Emmaus road travelers plead with Jesus to "abide" with them.

It may be more appropriate, however, to see the hymn as relating to the close of life. The "eventide" of stanza 1 refers not only to evening, but to the evening tide, or low tide, which is associated with death. Through the five stanzas, the prayer calls on Christ's abiding presence when earthly help fades (st. 1), when everything seems to change (st. 2), when there is temptation to rely on other power (st. 3), when sorrow and suffering start to overwhelm (st. 4), and when death approaches and heaven looms (st. 5). Bert Polman writes, "The phrase 'ills have no weight, and tears no bitterness' in stanza 4 is not intended to deny the reality of pain and agony, but to point out that God's love becomes a source of strength precisely amidst difficulties and suffering" (*The Worshiping Church* 1990, 1991). Three stanzas in the middle of the poem are usually omitted but are equal in intensity with the rest of the piece:

Not a brief glance, I beg, a passing word;
but as thou dwell'st with thy disciples, Lord,
familiar, condescending, patient, free,
come not to sojourn, but abide with me.

Come not in terrors as the King of kings,
but kind and good, with healing in thy wings,
tears for all woes, a heart for every plea—
come, Friend of sinners, and thus abide with me.

Thou on my head in early youth didst smile;
and, though rebellious and perverse meanwhile,
thou hast not left me, oft as I left thee,
on to the close, O Lord, abide with me.

EVENTIDE was written for this text by William Henry Monk in the original edition of *Hymns Ancient and Modern* (1861). There are conflicting stories about its composition. One account, a letter from Monk's widow, says it was written "at a time of great sorrow—when together we watched . . . *the glories of the setting sun" (Haeussler 1952).*

This well-loved hymn also may be read, which is, in fact, the way it was introduced to North America in 1855. Although it is associated with funerals and memorial services, it could also be used for a New Year's Eve service or as a morning hymn of comfort (especially st. 5).

Given its prevalent theme regarding the closing of life, it is curious to note its popularity with soccer fans of Wembley, England, who sing it at the Cup Final.

254
Ah, holy Jesus

Herzliebster Jesu
Johann Heermann (1585-1647)
Devoti Musica Cordis, Breslau, 1630
Tr. Robert Seymour Bridges (1844-1930)
Yattendon Hymnal, 1899, alt.

HERZLIEBSTER JESU

Johann Crüger (1598-1662)
Newes vollkömliches Gesangbuch, Vol. II, Berlin, 1640
(Zahn No. 983)

Heermann's *Herzliebster Jesu* is a paraphrase based on the fifteenth-century *Latin Meditationes,* long attributed to St. Augustine. This portion most likely was written by Jean de Fécamp in the eleventh century. Heermann's chorales are representative of the many great chorales born of the suffering of the Thirty Years War. Robert Bridges' English version not only captures the spirit of the Latin and German texts, but also succeeds in fitting the unusual meter of Crüger's tune for the German text. Stanza 1:2 is changed for the sake of clarity from "that man to judge thee hath in hate pretended?" to "that mortal judgment hath on thee descended?"

This is one of several hymns from collections harmonized with figured bass. These are usually called *cantionals.* Johann Schein was a leader in this field, and Crüger refined the style by placing the melody in the top voice. Crüger's 1640 publication was evidently "the first to arrange chorales as melodies with a figured bass accompaniment rather than as settings for several voices" (Sadie 1980).

HERZLIEBSTER JESU bears some resemblance to the setting of Psalm 23 in the sixteenth-century *Genevan Psalter* and to "Geliebter Freund" in Schein's *Cantional oder Gesangbuch Augsburgischer Konfession* (1627). Crüger had the good fortune to work first with Heermann and then with Paul Gerhardt, both prolific poets. In his "Synopsis musica" (1630, 1654), Crüger defines music as "the science of artfully and judiciously combining and inflecting harmonic intervals . . . *especially for the purpose of moving man to the glory of God" (Sadie 1980).* J. S. Bach used this melody as part of his *Passion According to St. Matthew,* and much organ literature has been based on it.

531
Ah, what shame I have to bear

Sōgo Matsumoto (1840-1903), 1895
Tr. Esther Hibbard (1903-), 1962

IMAYŌ

Japanese melody, 12th c.

By using the first-person singular, this text dramatically projects the singer into the misery and penitence of the prodigal son. The wide range of the melody musically portrays the "cry" in the text—from the depths of despair to the heights of "empty" and "foolish dreams." The melody comes from an ancient song, traditionally sung by an old person who goes into the wilderness to die.

The hymn appears in *Cantate Domino III* (1974) and in *Hymns from the Four Winds* (1983), a collection of Asian American hymns published under the auspices of the National Federation of Asian American United Methodists.

253
Alas! and did my Savior bleed?

MARTYRDOM (AVON)

Isaac Watts (1674-1748)
Hymns and Spiritual Songs, Book II, 1707-1709, alt.

Hugh Wilson (1766-1824)
Adapt. by Robert Archibald Smith (1780-1829)
Sacred Music, 1825

Watts published this well-known hymn in *Hymns and Spiritual Songs* where it is part of a group of Lord's Supper hymns. In his later editions, stanza 2 of the original six was bracketed to indicate that it could be omitted. Stanza 5 also is omitted here. The most frequently adopted text alteration occurs in the closing line of the first stanza where "such a worm as I" (a cliché of humility in Watts's time) is changed to "sinners such as I."

Numerous hymnal committees have argued with Watts's theology in the third stanza (original: "When God the mighty Maker died"), and a variety of options has resulted. This version, "When Christ, the mighty Maker died," avoids any inference that "God is dead."

Many Christians have attested to the convicting power of this hymn, crediting it with playing a part in their conversion. Fanny Crosby, who, though blind, was to become a prolific hymnwriter, had made fitful trips to the altar until this hymn was sung. She said, "[W]hen they had reached . . . 'Here, Lord, I give myself away,' my very soul flooded with celestial light." The wail of unhappiness, sets the tone for stanzas 1-3, which establish the contrast between God's grace and human sin and proclaim how Christ bridged the gap through his death on the cross. The final stanza reflects a proper response to such sacrifice: thankfulness made manifest by imitating Christ's life of love.

MARTYRDOM—also known as AVON, FENWICK, and DRUMCLOG—appeared in late eighteenth-century leaflets in duple meter. R. A. Smith set the "old Scottish melody" in triple time. Two years later it appeared in *The Seraph, a Selection of Psalms and Hymns* (Glasgow) where it was credited to Hugh Wilson, whose heirs brought suit to establish that Wilson was the copyright owner. However, an article in the *Choir,* July 1934, traces similarities in the melody to the Scottish tune "Helen of Kirkconnel." The tune appears to owe its life to all three of these sources.

159
All beautiful the march of days

FOREST GREEN

Frances Whitmarsh Wile (1878-1939)
Unity Hymns and Carols, rev. ed., 1911

Traditional English melody
Arr. by Ralph Vaughan Williams (1872-1958)
The English Hymnal, 1906

Wile's pastor, William Channing Gannett, asked her to write a hymn that would reflect the spiritual values of the winter season—waiting, the revival of life ("Life mounts in every throbbing vein"), and God's presence in both chill and warmth ("thyself the vision passing by in crystal and in rose"). One commentary notes, "The quiet mood and reverent spirit of the lines recall the pastoral charm of John Greenleaf Whittier's 'Snowbound' " (Ronander, Porter 1966).

FOREST GREEN is an arrangement of the English folk song "The Ploughboy's Dream." Vaughan Williams noted it down as it was sung to him by Mr. Garman of Forest Green, Surrey, in December 1903 (Kennedy 1982). Vaughan Williams also used this tune for "O little town of Bethlehem," a combination now traditional to British people. "All beautiful the march of days" was sung at first to various tunes, but the first known appearance of it with FOREST GREEN is in the *Pilgrim Hymnal* (1931).

48
All creatures of our God and King

LASST UNS ERFREUEN

Laudato sio Dio mio Signore
St. Francis of Assisi (1182-1226), 1225
Tr. William Henry Draper (1855-1933)
Hymns of the Spirit, 1926, alt.

Kirchengesangbuch, Köln, 1623
Harm. and adapt. by Ralph Vaughan Williams (1872-1958)
The English Hymnal, 1906

This hymn is derived from the famous "Canticle of the Sun," which is attributed to St. Francis of Assisi. It was written in 1225, about a year before Francis's death when he was suffering from pain and blindness. The straw hut where he sought refuge from the summer heat was occupied by a swarm of field mice, adding to his discomfort. Under these trying circumstances, he wrote this hymn of praise and devotion, possibly the oldest religious poem in the Italian language still in existence. It is a *lauda* (Latin for "praise"), a popular religious song associated with the revival influenced by Francis of Assisi.

The original prose places humanity on an equal footing with all creation. For example, stanza 3:

> Be thou praised, my Lord, of Sister Water,
> which is much useful and humble and precious and pure.
> Be thou praised, my Lord, of Brother Fire,

by which thou has lightened the night,
and he is beautiful and joyful and robust and strong.

The paraphrase by English clergyman William Henry Draper was used at a Pentecost festival in Leeds, England, sometime between 1899 and 1919. It retains the broad outline of the text, which compels all creation, humanity included, to praise the Maker and to do so even in the throes of suffering (st. 5). Even death is portrayed as an ally of God's plan for creation (st. 6).

The melody takes its name from its association with the Easter text *Lasst uns erfreuen hertzlich sehr* (Let us rejoice heartily). Possibly basing it on an earlier folk song, Ralph Vaughan Williams first arranged the tune as a setting for "Ye watchers and ye holy ones." The hymn also may be sung as a two- to four-part round, omitting the fermata at the end of the second phrase. Another option is to sing successive phrases antiphonally, either switching at every phrase or every two phrases, with everyone joining in the "alleluia" and "O sing ye." Stanzas 5 and 6 could be sung a little softer and slower, to reflect the text and provide contrast for the exuberant final stanza.

122
All glory be to God on high

ALLEIN GOTT IN DER HÖH

Allein Gott in der Höh
Nicolaus Decius (ca. 1485-ca. 1546), 1522
Müntzer's *Gesang Buch*, Rostock, 1525 (Low German version);
V. Schumann's *Gesangbuch*, 1539 (High German version)
Tr. Gilbert Everett Doan (1930-), 1978
Lutheran Book of Worship, 1978

Nicolaus Decius (ca. 1485-ca. 1546), 1522
Deutsche Evangelische Messe, 1524 (Zahn No. 4457)

The text was, according to Luther Noss in *Christian Hymns*, written by Decius in 1522, at least one year before Martin Luther's first hymn. It was published originally without music in the Low German version, reflecting the Reformation movement afoot to encourage full congregational participation in worship. A High German version followed in 1539. It was a prose version of a part of the Mass that was sung, *Gloria in excelsis Deo* (Glory be to God on high). Beginning with the triune God, the poem devotes a stanza to each person of the Trinity, providing ample cause for praise of each.

The melody for ALLEIN GOTT is derived from the tenth-century plainsong setting of the *Gloria* for the Easter season. Like many of the chorales, the melody is in bar form (A A B) commonly used by the German *Minnesingers* (medieval poet/musicians) or *Meistersingers* (a newer term for the same group). The melody appears in several of the cantatas and organ works of J. S. Bach.

237
All glory, laud, and honor

ST. THEODULPH (VALET WILL ICH DIR GEBEN)

Gloria, laus, et honor
Theodulph of Orleans (ca. 750-821), ca. 820
Tr. John Mason Neale (1818-1866)
The Hymnal Noted, 1851

Melchior Teschner (1584-1635), 1613
Herberger's *Ein andächtiges Gebet . . .*, 1615

This medieval hymn was written by Theodulph, probably during his imprisonment at Angers, France, around 820. Legend holds that from the very beginning this hymn was associated with the Palm Sunday processional. Although the story is unsubstantiated, it is said that Theodulph secured his release by singing this hymn from his prison window as King Louis I rode by.

From the original Latin text of thirty-nine couplets, numerous translations have been made, including two by John Mason Neale. The following stanza reportedly was in use up to the sixteenth century:

> Be thou, O Lord, the rider
> And we the little ass;
> That to God's holy city
> Together we may pass.

The refrain, derived from the first couplet, hearkens back to the medieval custom of a clergy/congregational procession through the town on Palm Sunday. The archaic language has been retained to remind users that the text is very ancient and to connect us with early Christian tradition. The Hebrew "hosanna" (Ps. 118:25-26) means "Save us," and according to the Gospel accounts, it was sung during Jesus' entry to Jerusalem just before his death.

The melody ST. THEODULPH was one of two five-part settings written by Teschner for Valerius Herberger's hymn of consolation *Valet will ich dir geben*. When it was associated with this text in *Hymns Ancient and Modern* (1861), it was given the name ST. THEODULPH, even though it is doubtful that Theodulph was ever canonized.

106

All hail the power of Jesus' name — CORONATION

Edward Perronet (1726-1792)
St. 1, Toplady's *Gospel Magazine*, November 1779; full text, April 1780
Rev. by John Rippon (1751-1836)
Selection of Hymns, 1787

Oliver Holden (1765-1844), 1792
Union Harmony, 1793

Perronet's text has been edited and revised frequently. The most important of the older editions is the one by John Rippon, which alters some stanzas and replaces others completely, confirming that the phenomenon of hymn altering is nothing new! Contemporary hymnals show a variety of combinations of the Perronet and Rippon texts, sometimes with alterations and additions to both.

This triumphal text does justice to John's great revelation of the hosts of heaven loudly proclaiming the risen Christ's lordship. Christ trades his crown of thorns for the "many crowns" of a worthy king (Rev. 19:12), all the ransomed recognize and exalt their Redeemer, and believers everywhere become part of the great coronation ceremony.

CORONATION is the tune most frequently associated with this text in the U.S. Written by Holden the year before its first printing in Boston, it may be the only early North American hymn tune in general use in all denominations today. The name is derived from the text, this time from the concluding line of each stanza, "And crown him Lord of all." This tune and DIADEM are deliberately placed in different parts of *Hymnal: A Worship Book* to point up a variety of possibilities for uses in worship.

285

All hail the power of Jesus' name — DIADEM

Edward Perronet (1726-1792)
St. 1, Toplady's *Gospel Magazine*, November 1779; full text, April 1780
Rev. by John Rippon (1751-1836)
Selection of Hymns, 1787

James Ellor (1819-1899), ca. 1838

For comments on the text by Perronet and Rippon, see "All hail the power of Jesus' name" (**106**).

James Ellor wrote DIADEM for this text when he was nineteen years old. This tune name is taken from the third line of the first stanza, "Bring forth the royal diadem." Ellor was director of music for a Wesleyan chapel in the English town of Droylsden, near Manchester, and a hat maker by trade. He took the tune to the factory where he worked, and his fellow workers sang it enthusiastically. The tune, typical of the florid style of the period, became well known in the area and was used frequently for festal occasions.

A third tune often associated with this text is MILES LANE, found in *The Brethren Hymnal* (1951).

42

All people that on earth do dwell — OLD HUNDREDTH

William Kethe (d. 1594), 1561
Version from *The Psalms of David in Meeter* (Scottish Psalter), 1650

Louis Bourgeois (ca. 1510-ca. 1561)
Genevan Psalter, 1551

William Kethe contributed this paraphrase of Psalm 100 to the *Anglo-Genevan Psalter* (1561), using the tune for Psalm 134 from the French psalters of the time. By virtue of its inclusion in a 1564 appendix to the *English Psalter,* it gained the name OLD HUNDREDTH—the tune for Psalm 100 in the "Old Version" of the psalter by Sternhold and Hopkins (Oyer 1980).

This hymn, the oldest of all English psalm versions now in use, predates the King James Version of the Bible by fifty years. It links Christians today with believers of the Reformation era and, even earlier, to the worship of Israel. The text itself attests to the ageless praise of God's unending mercy and truth (sts. 3-4). The pattern of the stanzas could also indicate dividing the congregation in two and alternating the calls to praise (sts. 1,3) with the rationale for the accolades (sts. 2,4).

Three text changes in common usage today came with the Scottish Psalter of 1650. In stanza 1:2 "Him serve with mirth" originally read "fear"; and in stanza 2:1 "Know that the Lord is God" was "The Lord ye know is God." In stanza 2:2 the word "flock" originally was "folk." Julian speculates that the change may have come about through a printer's error (Julian 1907).

This melody is "the only tune that has been preserved intact throughout the entire history of metrical psalmody, and as such it deservedly ranks at the head of all Protestant church music" (*The Hymnal 1940 Companion,* 1951 ed.). Composed or arranged by Louis Bourgeois, the tune was first used for the setting of Psalm 134. In later English books it appears with Psalm 100, with which it is most firmly associated.

21

All praise to our redeeming Lord

RESIGNATION (JENKS)

Charles Wesley (1707-1788)
Sts. 1-4, *Hymns for those that seek and those that have Redemption in the Blood of Jesus Christ,* 1747
St. 5, *The Brethren's Hymn Book,* 1867

Stephen Jenks (1772-1856)
The Brethren's Tune and Hymn Book, 1872

Titled "At Meeting of Friends," Wesley's hymn text was originally in three stanzas of eight lines each. The first four stanzas included here are derived from all of stanza 1 and the first half of stanzas 2 and 3 of the original. Stanza 4:3 originally read "A peace to sensual minds." The source of the fifth stanza has been traced to the *The Brethren's Hymn Book* (text only) of 1867. There the hymn appears with the scripture reference "Be perfectly joined together" (1 Cor. 1:10) under the heading "The salutation." Further searching may eventually produce an earlier source of this stanza, perhaps even among Wesley's 6,500 hymns. Even so, this Methodist hymn speaks to the heart of Brethren/Mennonite emphasis on Christian community.

The first documented appearance of this tune, RESIGNATION (JENKS), is in *The Brethren's Tune and Hymn Book,* the first Brethren hymnbook with musical notation, published by Benjamin Funk (1829-1909) and Henry Holsinger (1833-1905) at Singers Glen, Virginia. It contained musical settings of 809 of the 818 hymns of *The Brethren's Hymn Book* (1867), plus eight additional hymns. As was typical in songbooks of the time, the melody appeared in the tenor line; congregations today could try this for variety. When the tune was included with "In trouble and in grief, O God" in the *The Brethren Hymnal* (1901), the voicing was changed from three to four parts and the harmony altered considerably. In addition, the tune name was listed as COMMUNION and the composer as Stephen Jenks. Here the original tune name is retained, with the composer's name added to distinguish it from the tune for "My Shepherd will supply my need."

658

All praise to thee, my God

TALLIS' CANON

Thomas Ken (1637-1710 or 1711)
Pamphlet, 1694; Appendix to *A Manual of Prayers . . . ,* 1695

Thomas Tallis (ca. 1505-1585)
Parker's *The Whole Psalter Translated into English Metre,* ca. 1567

In Ken's 1695 edition of *A Manual of Prayers for Use of the Scholars of Winchester College* (1674), he included "Three Hymns for Morning, Evening and Midnight." This evening hymn, originally in twelve stanzas, was written for the devotional use of his students at Winchester College,

England. It is based on Psalm 91:4, the picture of God as a nurturing eagle, though there are many biblical images of communing with God at the close of day. Stanza 2 is a "sacrifice of repentence" to ready the soul for night and prepare for strength of spirit in the new day. The omitted stanzas further call on God's blessing and instruction even through the night, including a stanza for insomniacs:

When in the night I sleepless lie
my soul with heavenly thoughts supply;
let no ill dreams disturb my rest,
no powers of darkness me molest.

TALLIS' CANON has also used the names CANON, BRENTWOOD, BERWICK, SUFFOLK, MAGDALEN, and TALLIS' HYMN. This is the eighth of nine tunes Tallis composed for Archbishop Matthew Parker's *The Whole Psalter . . .*, in which it was a setting of Parker's paraphrase of Psalm 67. There the melody appears in the tenor part with the canon (round) entering four beats later at the octave in the soprano part. The canon may be sung in as many as eight parts, but it must be sung in unison. Each of Tallis's first eight tunes were written in one of the eight ecclesiastical modes (scales). This tune was thus in mode eight (mixolydian, plagal) described in the psalter as "the eighth goeth milde: in modest pace." TALLIS' CANON was first set to this evening hymn in Smith and Prelieur's *Harmonious Companion* (1732).

156
All things bright and beautiful

Cecil Frances Alexander (1818-1895)
Hymns for Little Children, 1848, alt.

ROYAL OAK

English melody, 17th c.
The Dancing Master, 1686
Adapt. by Martin Fallas Shaw (1875-1958), *Song Time*, 1915
Harm. for *The Hymnbook* (Presbyterian), 1955

Like most of Mrs. Alexander's hymns, this text was written especially for children and is a vivid and specific portrayal of creation. It is based on the line of the Apostles' Creed that describes God as "maker of heaven and earth," reflecting Genesis 1:31. Of the original seven four-line stanzas, stanzas 3 and 6 are commonly omitted. Stanza 3, below, is generally omitted because it reflects a predestined class system:

The rich man in his castle,
The poor man at his gate,
God made them high and lowly
And ordered their estate.

More than one hundred years after this text was written, James Herriot, the Yorkshire, England, veterinarian, used the four phrases of the refrain as the titles of his four autobiographical volumes (1972-1981).

ROYAL OAK was originally known as "The Twenty-Ninth of May" and was sung to words honoring Charles II's restoration to the throne on May 29, 1660.[1] It has also been used as a country dance tune. With such merriment in mind, a portion of the congregation could make a playful accompaniment by whistling the tune. The tune is named ROYAL OAK for a tree at Boscobel, Shropshire, England, in which King Charles II hid following the Battle of Worcester in 1651. FOREST GREEN may be used as an alternative to ROYAL OAK.

1. A version of the melody dating from 1667 is cited in *Guide to the Pilgrim Hymnal* (1966).

436
All who believe and are baptized

Enhver, som tror og bliver döbt
Thomas Hansen Kingo (1634-1703)
Vinterparten of *Hymnal Prepared for the Danish Church*, 1689
Tr. George Alfred Taylor Rygh (1860-1942), 1909
The Lutheran Hymnary, 1913

LOBT GOTT DEN HERREN

Melchior Vulpius (ca. 1560-1615)
Ein schön geistlich Gesangbuch, 1609
(Zahn No. 4533)

It may surprise some Brethren to know that the first stanza of this hymn appears in the *The Brethren Hymnal* (1951). It was included in the musical responses as a call to prayer ("He that believes and is baptized"), set to a different tune. It is a favorite hymn in Denmark and Norway where infant baptism predominates, yet the prominence of the word "believe" and the implication of the participant's promise (st. 2) make it highly relevant for believers baptism. At the same time, it is appropriate for occasions other than baptism, since it is both an affirmation of Christ's salvation and a prayer for the presence of the Holy Spirit throughout a believer's life.

This melody first appeared with an anonymous Epiphany text *Lobet den Herrn, ihr Heiden all'* and is sometimes known by that name. Although the tune does not appear in many hymnals, it has been preserved in anthems with various praise texts. It is a vigorous piece of music paired with a joyful proclamation of new life in Christ.

417

All who love and serve your city — CHARLESTOWN

Erik Reginald Routley (1917-1982), 1966
Dunblane Praises II, 1967

Pilsbury's *United States Sacred Harmony*, Boston, 1799

As a participant in a workshop exploring and creating new music for the church, Routley drafted this hymn text, his first, as he reflected on the 1960s riots in Watts (Los Angeles) and in Oakland, California. The poem echoes the message of the prophets, crying out for peace and justice. It combines our call to service in the name of Christ with concern for those who feel the stress of city life. The two scripture passages quoted (sts. 3,5) are from John 9:4 and Ezekiel 48:35b. The text was originally written for the tune BIRABUS by Peter Cutts.

This basically pentatonic melody is typical of the American folk tradition. Austin Lovelace traces this melody to Amos Pilsbury's collection listed above. There it was named CHARLESTON for Pilsbury's hometown in South Carolina. Stephen Jenks and Elijah Griswold included the tune in *The American Compiler of Sacred Harmony*, No. 1 (1803). In *The Christian Lyre* (1830), the tune was named BARTIMEUS for John Newton's text with which it often appeared (" 'Mercy, O thou Son of David,' Thus poor blind Bartimeus prayed").

101

Alleluia — (no tune name)

Jacques Berthier (1923-)

This *alleluia* from the Taizé community is a full, sonorous, and joyous acclamation that may be used in a variety of ways as a response.

Music from the Taizé community is one of the refreshingly new voices in our century, even though its patterns and ideas are drawn from very old sources. The Taizé community is centered at an old monastery southeast of Paris, France. It has become an ecumenical retreat center, and persons from all over the globe and from many different religious backgrounds come to spend time there. Taizé communities are active in many cities around the world. Because of differing backgrounds and experiences that people bring with them to the retreat center, and because of the importance of worshiping together as a body, it soon became apparent that new music would need to be created.

The Taizé music is characterized by melodic and harmonic simplicity, along with repetitive refrains, ostinatos, and canons. The use of refrains for the congregation and stanzas for soloists is common, much like the call-and-response pattern typical of folk music. The language was often Latin (because it was a neutral language for most retreatants), though many of the refrains and stanzas have been translated into numerous languages. There are also instrumental accompaniments for much of the music; one can use or not use them depending entirely on which instruments are available.

244

Alone thou goest forth

BANGOR

Solus ad victimam procedis, Domine
Peter Abelard (1079-1142)
Hymnarius Paraclitensis, ca. 1135
Tr. Francis Bland Tucker (1895-1984), 1938
The Hymnal 1940 (Episcopal)

William Tans'ur's *Compleat Melody or Harmony of Zion*, preface dated Sept. 29, 1734

The author, at the request of his wife, Heloise, wrote a cycle of hymns for the church year, including the canonical hours, Matins, and Vespers. They were published in a collection for the Convent of the Paraclete where Abelard's wife was prioress.

This text, which is for the third nocturnal office on Good Friday, is a meditation on human response to Christ's supreme sacrifice of love. Apparently only two of Abelard's approximately 130 hymns have been translated into English. This is a free translation from the original Latin.

BANGOR was a common-meter Scottish psalm tune in three-part harmony. Hymn references disagree whether it was set to Psalm 11 or 12. BANGOR was introduced without text in the U.S. as early as 1767 in the Boston, Massachusetts, edition of the *Royal Melody Compleat*. A folktale claims a prominent Maine town was named for this tune in 1781. The minister who brought the petition for incorporation of the town to the authorities stood idly humming the tune as papers were prepared. When the clerk asked, "What's the name?" the minister replied not with the town name, but with the name of the tune he was humming. Thus, the town was dubbed "Bangor" (*The Hymnal 1940 Companion*, 1951 ed.). Originally named for the ancient city of Bangor, Wales, the tune was mentioned by Robert Burns in his poem "The Ordination."

143

Amazing grace

NEW BRITAIN (AMAZING GRACE)

John Newton (1725-1807)
Sts. 1-5, *Olney Hymns*, 1779
St. 6, *A Collection of Sacred Ballads*, 1790

American folk melody
Virginia Harmony, 1831
Adapt. and harm. by Edwin Othello Excell (1851-1921), 1900
Make His Praise Glorious, 1900

This hymn is a musical autobiography of a former atheist and slave trader, but it has become the straightforward confession and faith affirmation of countless Christian converts. Because of its universal appeal, the text also appears in this hymnal in Spanish, Korean, Northern Ojibway, and Cheyenne—languages that represent some of the widening ethnicity of Mennonites and Brethren.

The text here includes five of the original six stanzas. Newton's fourth stanza is:

> The Lord has promised good to me,
> his word my hope secures;
> he will my shield and portion be
> as long as life endures.

Stanzas 4 and 5, omitted in many hymnals, attest to God's faithfulness even beyond human mortality and the existence of the earth.

What appears as the final stanza is not by Newton. Its origin has been traced by William J. Reynolds to numerous nineteenth-century American collections where it appears as the final stanza in other hymns (e.g., "Jerusalem, my happy home" and "When I can read my title clear"). Considered to be anonymous by some, this stanza has also been attributed to John P. Rees, who printed the lines as a separate text in the second appendix of the 1859 edition of *The Sacred Harp* (Gealy, Lovelace, Young 1970).

This popular tune first appeared in *Virginia Harmony,* compiled in 1831 by James P. Carrell and David S. Clayton. It also is identified by the tune names SOLON, HARMONY GROVE, SYMPHONY, and REDEMPTION. It was published in Funk's *Genuine Church Music* in 1832 and in many other oblong books of the nineteenth century.

381, 382, 643
Amens

In Hebrew, the word *Amen* means "so be it." As an expression of affirmation, the use of *Amen* in Christian worship was borrowed from Jewish practice. It is most appropriately used as a response to prayer.[1] The first two of the three settings included in this hymnal are familiar to Brethren and Mennonites. The "Dresden Amen" (**381**) is attributed to Johann Gottlieb Naumann (1741-1801), a composer of operas and church music. It derives its name from the fact that it was used at the Royal Chapel in Dresden, Germany. Both Felix Mendelssohn and Richard Wagner incorporated its few measures into their longer works—Mendelssohn in his *Reformation Symphony* and Wagner in the opera *Parsifal.*

The origin of the "Threefold Amen" (**382**) is unknown, but it may be Danish since it has been widely used in the churches of Denmark. The third "Amen" (**643**), composed by Richard Proulx, comes from "Eucharistic Prayer for Children II," published in 1986. The cue notes at the beginning refer to the accompaniment found in the *Accompaniment Handbook*. Written in canon (round), this "Amen" contrasts in style to the other two. All three were chosen because they may be sung by both congregations and choirs.

1. See also page 247 in the *Accompaniment Handbook* for an article on the use of *Amens*.

596
And I will raise you up — ON EAGLE'S WINGS

Based on Psalm 91
(Jan) Michael Joncas (1951-)
On Eagle's Wings, 1979, alt.

(Jan) Michael Joncas (1951-)
(same source as text)

This hymn seems destined to become a twentieth-century classic. The four stanzas found in the *Accompaniment Handbook* are well suited to a solo voice or small group. The congregation responds with the lyric refrain. The pronouns in the refrain, which originally began "And he will raise you up," have been changed to the first person so that the congregation sings as the voice of God. Professing God's promise in this way reflects a dramatic technique of the psalmists—to sing salvation history as if it were being retold in God's own words.

The tune name is the original title for this song and for the recording on which it was first released. An accompaniment book published with that recording is the first printed source.

406
And is the gospel peace and love — FARMINGTON

Anne Steele (1716-1778)
Poems on Subjects Chiefly Devotional, Vol. 1, 1760

Joseph Funk's *Genuine Church Music*, 1st ed., 1832, adapt.

This hymn, titled "Example of Christ," appeared first in seven stanzas of four lines each. It was introduced to congregational use in 1787 through John Rippon's *Selection of Hymns*. The poem seems admirably suited to Brethren and Mennonites, both of the historic peace church tradition. Yet it gently challenges the singer to a life of peace that may be even more demanding than refusing to participate in war: that of genuine peace among close neighbors.

FARMINGTON appeared in the first edition of *Genuine Church Music*, but it was not until the fifth edition (1851) that harmonizations were expanded from three to four parts. This hymn was used by Alice Parker in her folk opera *Singers Glen*. The opera, first performed in 1978 by the Lancaster and Franconia Choral Singers in Pennsylvania, is recreated on a regular basis in Singers Glen, Virginia, in the Shenandoah Valley where Joseph Funk lived.

197

Angels we have heard on high — GLORIA

Nouveau Recueil de Cantiques, 1855
Tr. anonymous; alt. version by Earl Bowman Marlatt (1892-1976)
New Church Hymnal, 1937

Traditional French carol
(same source as text)

The origin of this French *noel* is unknown and may date from the eighteenth century. Among the hymns appearing in Protestant hymnals, this is one of the few macaronic (using vernacular and Latin) texts. *Gloria in excelsis Deo* (Glory be to God on high) is one of only a handful of Latin phrases still in common use. The poem incorporates the entire cast of Luke's nativity story (angels, shepherds, Christ child, Mary, Joseph) and invites all Christians into the scene in the joyous refrain.

With just two exceptions in the refrain, the melody range of GLORIA stays within six notes of the scale, which is characteristic of many French carols. In the graceful refrain, the resonance of the *o* in "gloria" is both beautiful and easy to sing. GLORIA is found in many versions and harmonizations, with this setting coming originally from *Carols Old and New* (1916). The tune is also known as IRIS.

631

Anoint us, Lord — ANOINT US, LORD

John David Bowman (1945-), 1975
The Brethren Songbook, 1979

John David Bowman (1945-), 1975
(same source as text), adapt.

While serving as pastor of the Glade Valley Church of the Brethren in Maryland, John David Bowman prepared a sermon on anointing as part of a preaching series on ordinances. He writes: "I was excited about the implications of anointing not only for physical and emotional healing, but for consecration into service and for use as a metaphor alluding to the coming of the Spirit of God."

He stumbled, however, when it came to finding a sermon hymn. He wondered how it could be that Brethren, who cherish the anointing service along with congregational four-part singing, could have gotten along without a hymn to express their zeal for the ordinance of anointing. He decided to do something about it.

The three stanzas of the hymn mirror in verse the three-point sermon on which it was based. Written in first-person plural, the verses reflect the author's convictions about life in the covenant community.

While the music has been slightly adapted from the original to maintain flow, the tempo shouldn't feel rushed, allowing time for the music to convey the words. Bowman likes to give extra time to his "favorite chord," which occurs at the end of the phrase "Pour your cooling oils down."

386
As saints of old — REGWAL

Frank von Christierson (1900-), 1960
Ten New Stewardship Hymns, 1961, alt.

Leland Bernhard Sateren (1913-)
Published as an anthem, 1963
Sing! Hymnal for Youth and Adults, 1970

As pastor of two small churches with financial struggles, von Christierson was acutely concerned about stewardship and outreach. His text is reminiscent of exhortations of the ancients that offerings to God must not consist of what is left after meeting our own needs, but should be the first and the best of our blessings. Christians are to pattern their giving after that of God in Christ (st. 3), loving and laboring for the sake of the whole world. The hymn was one of ten chosen in a search conducted by the Hymn Society of America (now the Hymn Society of the United States and Canada) and the Department of Stewardship and Benevolence of the National Council of Churches of Christ in the U.S.A.

Leland Sateren's tune REGWAL was used with this text in an anthem published by Augsburg Publishing House in 1963. In 1970 the hymn was included in *Sing! Hymnal for Youth and Adults*, edited by R. Harold Terry.

568
As spring the winter doth succeed — PSALM 9

Anne Dudley Bradstreet (ca. 1612-1672), 1657, alt.

Henry Lawes (1595-1662)
George Sandys' *Paraphrase upon the Divine Poems*, 1638

Anne Bradstreet was one of the first poets in colonial America. In this text the change of seasons metamorphoses into the conversion of a flagging spirit. In stanza 1, the earth dresses up to express its joy at the return of the sun, and stanza 4 mirrors it; the soul praises the return of Christ, the Sun. The physical and metaphysical worlds are woven together, acknowledging the influence of flesh and spirit on one another. A few minor alterations have been made, including in stanza 1 "the earth, once dead," which was originally "the earth, all black." The last phrase of the hymn has been made more specific by changing "him that heard" to "God who heard."

This tune originally was set to "Thee will I praise with Heart and Voice" in George Sandys' collection. The first phrase of this tune is identical to the melody for "O God, our help in ages past" (ST. ANNE, 1708). The rising melodic contour of PSALM 9 matches the poetry of the rising of spring and the spirit.

500
As the hart with eager yearning

Based on Psalm 42
Christine Turner Curtis (1891-1961), 1939
The Hymnal (Evangelical and Reformed), 1941, alt.

GENEVA 42 (FREU DICH SEHR)

Louis Bourgeois (ca. 1510-ca. 1561)
Genevan Psalter, 1551
Harm. adapt. from Claude Goudimel (ca. 1505-1572)
Les Pseaumes . . . , 1565

This psalm has been cast in many metric versions, perhaps the best known being "As pants the hart for cooling streams"[1] from Tate and Brady's *New Version of the Psalms* (1696). In the earlier "Old Version," Sternhold and Hopkins (1562), the psalm did not fare as well. The first line there read "Like as the hart doth breathe and bray."

The present paraphrase is true to the psalmist's graphic portrayal of a deer in the midst of drought, which represents human yearning for God's presence. As water is basic to survival, so is God the source of life to the believer. The last two lines of the first stanza are somewhat convoluted from the original to make for easier singing:

> When shall I abide rejoicing
> In his presence, his praise voicing?

> When shall I, God's praises voicing,
> come before our God rejoicing?

This light, dancelike psalm tune suggests the skittishness of a deer. For comments on GENEVA 42, see "Comfort, comfort, O my people" (**176**).

1. A hart is a male deer.

218

As with gladness men of old — DIX

William Chatterdon Dix (1837-1898), ca. 1858
Hymns of Love and Joy, ca. 1860

Conrad Kocher (1786-1872)
Stimmen aus dem Reiche Gottes, 1838
Adapt. by William Henry Monk (1823-1889)
Hymns Ancient and Modern, 1861

Dix is said to have written these words during his recovery from an illness after reading the Gospel lesson for that day. It is an Epiphany text (the season immediately following Jesus' birth); the "men of old" are the wise men who visited the newborn Jesus. The words invite worshipers today to match the joy, reverence, and generosity of the magi in their own meeting with the Christ child.

It is uncertain in what year Dix wrote this hymn. It could have been as early as 1858, says Percy Dearmer, maintaining that the hymn appeared in the 1859 trial copy of *Hymns Ancient and Modern*. Others say it was written about 1860 and appeared in A. H. Ward's *Hymns for Public Worship and Private Devotion* that same year. After the hymn made the first edition of the seminal hymnbook *Hymns Ancient and Modern* (1861), it was included in the 1875 edition with two slight changes in the second stanza, approved by the author. The text has been restored to that form and includes the sometimes omitted fifth stanza.

Kocher's melody was written for the text *Treuer Heiland, wir sind hier*. In addition to its first printing in 1838, he also included it in his *Zionsharfe* (1855), a large collection of tunes "from all centuries and all confessions of the Christian Church." William H. Monk, one of the editors of *Hymns Ancient and Modern*, adapted the melody by deleting two measures from the original fourteen to fit this text. It was given the name DIX for the author. The hymn text "For the beauty of the earth" (**89**) is also set to this tune.

64

Asithi: Amen — (no tune name)

Sing amen
South African hymn

S. C. Molefe

This hymn was part of *In Spirit and in Truth*, the conference worship book for the 1991 Seventh Assembly of the World Council of Churches, held in Canberra, Australia. "Asithi" is pronounced "ah-see-tee," and the rest of the South African text is easier to sing than the English translation. As in many of the hymns from South Africa, the harmonies are quite tonal, frequently moving parallel to each other. Worshipers could be encouraged to sing this as a closing hymn as they leave worship.

337
Ask ye what great thing I know

Johann Christoph Schwedler (1672-1730)
Hirschberger Gesangbuch, 1741
Tr. Benjamin Hall Kennedy (l804-1889)
Hymnologia Christiana, 1863

HENDON

Henri Abraham César Malan (1787-1864), 1827
Carmina Sacra, 1841

This hymn was first published eleven years after Schwedler died. He wrote hundreds of hymns, but only this one has been translated into English. Its clear structure is a series of questions that funnel the reader to the center of faith: the crucified and risen Christ.

Malan's tune first appeared in France in a collection of his own texts and tunes. Lowell Mason is credited with bringing HENDON to America, including it in his *Carmina Sacra*. It is also associated with "Take my life" (**389**). These hymns could be used in combination for a Communion service, preceding the Communion with "Ask ye what great thing I know" as a dialogical confession of faith, and responding to the Communion with "Take my life."

628
At evening, when the sun had set

Henry Twells (1823-1900)
Hymns Ancient and Modern, Appendix, 1868
Rev. in *Hymns for Today's Church*, 1982, alt.

ANGELUS (WHITSUN HYMN)

Attrib. to Georg Joseph
Scheffler's *Heilige Seelenlust . . .* , 1657
Alt. version in *Cantica Spiritualia*, Munich, 1847

Twells, the headmaster of a large grammar school, wrote this hymn one afternoon while supervising boys who were taking an examination. Although, at first glance, this looks like an evening hymn, the text takes its cue from an incident out of Christ's healing ministry. It is based on Mark 1:32: "That evening, at sundown, they brought to him all who were sick . . . ." The specification of "when the sun had set" is not poetic redundancy, but deference to Jewish law, which dictated that such a gathering not occur until the sabbath ended at sundown. Minor changes have been made in this version to eliminate archaisms. Also, in stanzas 2 and 6, references to evening have been changed, making it appropriate for services of anointing and healing.

Two omitted stanzas are:

> And some are press'd with worldly care
> and some are tried with sinful doubt;

and some such grievous passions tare
that only thou canst cast them out.

And some have found the world is vain,
yet from the world they break not free;
and some have friends who give them pain,
yet have not sought a friend in thee.

ANGELUS derives from a melody attributed to Georg Joseph who provided the music for *Heilige Seelenlust . . .* , a collection of poems by Johann Scheffler. There it was set to the text *Du meiner Seelen güldne Ziehr*. When Scheffler became a Roman Catholic in 1653, he changed his name to Angelus Silesius—thus the tune name ANGELUS. The original form of the melody had no upbeat or "pick-up" notes at the beginning of the first two phrases. The revised melody, which appeared in 1847, altered the contours of the third and fourth phrases.[1] The present text was set to it a year later.

1. For a comparison, see page 136 of the *Historical Companion to Hymns Ancient and Modern.*

245
At the cross, her vigil keeping — STABAT MATER

Stabat Mater dolorosa
Attrib. to Jacopone da Todi (d. 1306), 13th c.
Tr. Edward Caswall (1814-1878) and others, alt.

Gesangbuch, Mainz and Frankfurt, 1661
Version from *The English Hymnal*, 1906

The original Latin text is a rhymed prayer for private devotions. Since it dwells on the suffering of Christ and his mother, it became popular with flagellants (those who ritually beat themselves as a method of self-denial) in the fourteenth century. By the fifteenth century, it could be found in several missals, and in 1727 it became part of the Roman liturgy.

The authorship of this text is uncertain, but the writer was apparently Italian and probably of the Franciscan order, since the text reflects the influence of the Franciscans in focusing on the sufferings of Christ as a human experience rather than as theological doctrine. It is most commonly attributed to Pope Innocent III (d. 1216) or Jacopone da Todi, also called Jacopone di Benedetti (d. 1306). The latter is more widely accepted as the possible author.

This hymn was subject to a popular practice of the Middle Ages called "troping," or adding to the authorized text and/or music of the Roman liturgy. The Council of Trent (1545-1563), in a fit of liturgical reform, banned all but five tropes (also called sequences), with *Stabat Mater* surviving (see also **271**, "Christ is arisen," another of these five). Change cannot be legislated or abolished, however; Edward Caswall's translation from his *Lyra Catholica* (1849) has been extensively altered and added to by Richard Mant (1776-1848) and others. The variety in translations is rivaled only by the number of music settings, often by the "great" composers.

This is indeed a mournful hymn in both melody and text, one that moves the singer to experience Christ's Passion not only from the viewpoint of a parent, but as any compassionate, faithful bystander at Jesus' execution. This hymn may be sung as an *a cappella* women's quartet or with some solo stanzas accompanied by parts singing on a hum or "ooo."

STABAT MATER, also known as MAINZ, is adapted from a setting of the *Stabat Mater* in the Roman Catholic *Gesangbuch* of the Mainz diocese (*Maintzisch Gesangbuch*). The changes in this adaptation involve differences in rhythmic values, a reduction in the length of the melody, and melodic alterations. The melody was published in England in the *Evening Office of the Church According to the Roman Breviary* (1748) and appeared first with an English translation in the *Bristol Tune Book* (1863). The version used here elongates the note values at the first two cadences.

262
At the Lamb's high feast

Ad coenam agni providi
Anonymous, ca. 6th c.
Ad regias agni dapes
Breviary, 1632
Tr. Robert Campbell (1814-1868)
Hymns and Anthems for use in the Holy Services of the Church within the United Diocese of St. Andrew's, Dunkeld, and Dunblane (a.k.a. "St. Andrew's Hymnal"), 1850, alt.

SONNE DER GERECHTIGKEIT

German folk melody, 15th c.
Bohemian Brethren's *Kirchengeseng*, 1566

The date of the original Latin text is placed anywhere between the fourth and ninth centuries. Under Pope Urban VIII, the text was revised and appeared in the Roman Breviary. It was this latter version, *Ad regias agni dapes*, that Robert Campbell translated in 1849. The second, third, and last of the eight quatrains have been omitted. The hymn is widely used in the Roman, Ambrosian, Mozarabic, and Anglican rites. It was sung as a vesper (sunset) hymn from Easter Eve until Ascension. It was also the custom of the early church to baptize catechumens (persons newly instructed in church membership) on Easter Eve in anticipation of their first Communion on Easter. Some translations relate specifically to these people, i.e., "The Lamb's high banquet we await."

The text combines images of deliverance in the Exodus story with those of our deliverance through Christ from sin and death. The paradox of Christ's victory through his life's sacrifice, a theme throughout, is intensified in stanza 3:1, "Mighty victim from the sky, hell's fierce pow'rs beneath you lie." In stanza 2 "Paschal" is another word for Passover. These words have been sung to a number of tunes, most frequently SALZBURG (ALLE MENSCHEN).

SONNE DER GERECHTIGKEIT originated as a fifteenth-century folk song, *Der reich Mann geritten aus*. It was first printed in 1556 by Georg Forster, a Nürnberg physician and musician. In 1566 it appeared with a sacred text, *Mensch, erheb dein Herz zu Gott*, in the *Kirchengeseng* of the Bohemian Brethren. This vigorous melody with its lilting, folk-dance rhythm exemplifies the rich musical heritage that the Bohemian Brethren, under the creative hymnic leadership of Michael Weisse (ca. 1480-1534), contributed to German hymnody. Edward W. Klammer first paired this text and tune for the *Worship Supplement to the Lutheran Hymnal* (1969).

342

At the name of Jesus — KING'S WESTON

Caroline Maria Noel (1817-1877)
The Name of Jesus and Other Verses . . . , Enlarged Ed., 1870, alt.

Ralph Vaughan Williams (1872-1958)
Songs of Praise, 1925
Arr. for *The Hymnbook* (Presbyterian), 1955

An invalid herself, the author titled her original edition of poems *The Name of Jesus and Other Verses for the Sick and Lonely* (1861). She wrote her finest hymns while she was ill and suffering. This text, based on Philippians 2:5-11, was written as a processional for Ascension Day. The fourth and fifth omitted stanzas are:

> 4. Bore it up triumphant with its human light,
> Through all ranks of creatures to the central height,
> To the throne of Godhead, to the Father's breast:
> Filled it with the glory of that perfect rest.
>
> 5. Name him, brothers, name him, with love as strong as death,
> But with awe and wonder, and with bated breath;
> He is God the Saviour, he is Christ the Lord,
> Ever to be worshipped, trusted, and adored.

In the words of Erik Routley, this is a hymn "full of heraldry and mysticism." It captures the ultimate splendor of Paul's "Christ hymn" in Philippians, describing Jesus' presence at creation, his humility and crucifixion, his example, and his triumphant return.

KING'S WESTON is named for the home of Philip Napier Miles, located in a park on the Avon River near Bristol, England, where Vaughan Williams enjoyed many weekends. This majestic tune moves gradually to an inevitable climax where the rhythm emphatically reverses its pattern from the previous phrases. This is the best-known hymn tune from the composer's later years, reflecting his concentrated study of the English folk song. It is the only accepted setting of the present text for which it was composed (Routley 1981). In the melody's earliest source, the composer intended the tune for unison singing and provided three-part harmony for keyboard. The present arrangement does not change the chords, but provides four-voice harmony.

467

Author of life divine

John Benjamin Wesley (1703-1791)
and Charles Wesley (1707-1788)
Hymns on the Lord's Supper, 1745
Rev. in *Hymns for Today's Church*, 1982

ST. JOHN

The Parish Choir, Vol. 3, 1851

There is no conclusive evidence to show which of the Wesley brothers is the author of this hymn text. It was not included in John Wesley's *Hymns and Spiritual Songs* (1753) or in his *Collection of Hymns for the Use of the People Called Methodists* (1780), which may be why it was not reprinted in any Methodist hymnal in England until 1933 and until 1966 in America. The unaltered original is in *The Methodist Hymnal* (1966).

The hymn spiritualizes the Lord's Supper, calling on Christ to transubstantiate his very life and strength to communicants through "fresh supplies of love."

ST. JOHN appeared unsigned in the source listed above, a monthly publication edited by W. H. Monk. The dynamic melodic contour moves the text along, particularly in the last two eight-syllable lines, which rise without pause to the final cadence.

56

Awake, arise, O sing a new song

Marna J. Leasure (1934-), 1974
Letters, Choristers Guild, March 1975

(no tune name)

Marna J. Leasure (1934-), 1974
(same source as text)

This delightful canon (round), written as an introit for Easter, was sung initially at the First Christian Church (Disciples of Christ), Ashland, Kentucky, where Marna Leasure was minister of music. The theme of praise for the new day plays on the words "sun" and "Son" by surprising the singer with the words "of God." An optional introduction is found in the *Accompaniment Handbook*.

448

Awake, awake, fling off the night

HILARY

Based on Ephesians 5:6-20
John Raphael Peacey (1896-1971)
100 Hymns for Today, 1969, alt.

Lawrence Francis Bartlett (1933-), 1974
The Australian Hymn Book, 1977

This hymn, suitable as either a morning or a baptismal hymn, is loosely based on Ephesians 5:6-20. Lawrence Bartlett felt that "a melody was required with a rhythm and energy that reflected the arresting quality of the words" (Milgate 1982) that appeared first in *Praise the Lord* (rev., 1972). The minor chords and challenging rhythms of the tune make for an unusual combination.

609

Awake, my soul

CHRISTMAS

Philip Doddridge (1702-1751)
Hymns, Founded on Various Texts in the Holy Scriptures, 1755

George Frederick Handel (1685-1759)
Siroe, 1728
Adapt. in Hewitt's *Harmonia Sacra*, 1812

This hymn was written after the author preached on Philippians 3:12-14. Its imagery is borrowed from early Greek athletic games, with which Paul would have been familiar. It was published posthumously by Job Orton (London 1755) under the subject heading of "Messengers, Embassadors" and titled "Pressing on in the Christian Race." Other scriptural allusions include 1 Corinthians 9:24; Hebrews 12:1; 2 Timothy 4:7; and Revelation 4:10. Stanza 4, frequently omitted, has been reinstated here to specify that the prize is not an earthly one.

CHRISTMAS is adapted from the soprano aria *Non vi piacque ingiusti Dei* in the second act of Handel's opera *Siroe*. The hymn adaptation first appeared in the 1812 source above and then in Weyman's *Melodia Sacra* (1815) as a setting of Psalm 132. Lowell Mason also included it in the *Boston Handel and Haydn Society Collection of Church Music* (1821). The present name, CHRISTMAS, comes from the tune's use with Nahum Tate's "While shepherds watched their flocks by night," for which it may be used as an alternate melody. The tune also is known as LUNENBERG, SANFORD, and HARLEIGH.

194

Away in a manger

CRADLE SONG

Anonymous
Sts. 1-2, *Little Children's Book for Schools and Family* (Lutheran), 1885
St. 3, Gabriel's *Vineyard Songs*, 1892

William James Kirkpatrick (1838-1921)
Around the World with Christmas . . ., 1895
Arr. by Joan Annette Fyock (1938-), 1989

When stanzas 1 and 2 were first published in 1885, they were listed as a "nursery" poem and did not appear in the Christmas section of the above source.

The words have been erroneously ascribed to Martin Luther by James R. Murray, who composed the familiar tune AWAY IN A MANGER used in *Dainty Songs for Little Lads and Lassies* (1887). There Murray labeled the song "Luther's Cradle Hymn, composed by Martin Luther for his children and still sung by German mothers to their little ones." Although research has proved that Luther is not connected to this hymn, the belief persists because the stanzas (without music) might have been used in a children's story about Martin Luther on the four hundredth anniversary of his birth (*The Hymnal 1940 Companion*, 1951 ed.).

Bert Polman describes it as "the musical equivalent of a child's Christmas card with its quaint nativity scene colored by crayons or markers" (*The Worshiping Church* 1990, 1991).

CRADLE SONG appeared in 1895 in a small pamphlet (seven songs), *Around the World with Christmas: A Christmas exercise.* This tune is the one that became known beyond the American continent, particularly in England, possibly due to the evangelistic meetings of Moody and Sankey. Other hymnals have set this tune either as an accompanied unison hymn or in four-part harmony. The three-voice setting created for this hymnal captures the simplicity and openness of both text and tune.

292

Away with our fears

ARDWICK

Charles Wesley (1707-1788)
Hymns of Petition and Thanksgiving for the Promise of the Father, 1746

Henry John Gauntlett (1805-1876)
Tunes New and Old, 1864

This hymn about the coming of the Holy Spirit is one of several by Wesley with similar first lines. The three short lines of text build up a verbal energy that is released in the long final line of this unusual 555. 11 meter.

The music of ARDWICK suits this text well. The strength of the opening phrase is enhanced with unison voicing, while the longer line of text is carried to its conclusion by the rising final phrase. To convey the joyous sense of this text and to sing the last phrase with ease, the tune should be sung with a feeling of one pulse per measure.

134

Babylon streams received our tears — LLEF

Based on Psalm 137
Versified by Calvin Seerveld (1930-), 1982
Psalter Hymnal, 1987

Griffith Hugh Jones (1849-1919)
Gemau Mawl, 1890

Seerveld put this psalm to verse in 1982, and it was introduced to the Fellowship Christian Reformed Church in Toronto, Ontario, "while liturgical dancers . . . proceeded down the aisles, portraying God's people captive in Babylon." We often shrink from the violence of this psalm, which calls down curses on Edom and Babylon. Seerveld's motivation was "to show how New Testament Christian believers may appropriate imprecatory psalms for a living testimony today in our worship services." The key to understanding the last verse of this psalm is "to realize that the Scripture is referring to God as the one who exercises retribution in holy anger at Evil" (*Psalter Hymnal Handbook*). Anger is appropriate, but retribution is God's.

Griffith Hugh Jones composed LLEF in memory of his brother, the Rev. D. H. Jones. Prior to its publication, the tune was sung at the *Cymanfa* (song festival) in Dolwyddelen, a village near Rhiwddolion, Wales, where the composer was schoolmaster. Its somber strength can support the anguish of the text.

457

Be present at our table, Lord — OLD HUNDREDTH

John Cennick (1718-1755)
Sacred Hymns for the Children of God in the Days of their Pilgrimage, 1741

Louis Bourgeois (ca. 1510-ca. 1561)
Genevan Psalter, 1551

This metrical text has been referred to as a "Wesley Grace," because tradition held that it was engraved on teapots crafted by Josiah Wedgewood and used by John Wesley (Young 1993). Misnamed by that unsubstantiated story, the text is really derived from the two graces Cennick wrote. The first stanza is from Cennick's "Before Meat," with a change in 1:3 from "Thy creatures" to "These mercies." Stanza 2 is taken from Edward Bickersteth's 1833 alteration of Cennick's "After Meat." Lines 2:1, 2:3, and 2:4 appeared in *Christian Psalmody* (1833), while 2:2, which originally read "But more for Jesu's Flesh and Blood," was further altered by Bickersteth in his 1874 edition of that collection. The first stanza, with its ethereal phrase "feast in paradise," is especially appropriate for Communion, while the second is a more "down-to-earth" table grace.

For comments on OLD HUNDREDTH, see "All people that on earth do dwell" (**42**).

545

Be thou my vision

Rob tu mo bhoile, a Comdi cride
Ancient Irish text
Tr. Mary Elizabeth Byrne (1880-1931), 1905
Byrne's *Erin*, Vol. II, 1905
Versified by Eleanor Henrietta Hull (1860-1935)

SLANE

Traditional Irish melody
Old Irish Folk Music and Songs, 1909
Harm. by Martin Fallas Shaw (1875-1958)
Enlarged Songs of Praise, 1931, alt.

This ancient poem from the eighth century has found increasing use in twentieth-century hymnals. The 1905 translation by Mary Elizabeth Byrne was versified by Eleanor H. Hull, Irish author and founder of the Irish Text Society.

The lilting Irish verse and music transport the listener's imagination to a restful green place to become absorbed in its message. The strong "visions" or images of each phrase peel away layers of distraction until only God is left to become our vision, our thought, our wisdom, our protection and dignity, our inheritance and treasure. God becomes our very heart.

This primarily pentatonic melody appeared in Patrick W. Joyce's *Old Irish Folk Music and Songs* (1909) with the ballad "With my love come on the road." It was used with "Be thou my vision" in the *Irish Church Hymnal* (1919) and the *Scottish Church Hymnary Revised* (1927).

The tune name refers to the hill where St. Patrick (ca. 389-461) lit the Paschal fire on Easter Eve in defiance of the pagan king Leoghaire, giving rise to the legend that St. Patrick established Christianity in Ireland. The harmonization used here is by Martin Shaw, prominent English conductor, organist, and composer who collaborated with Ralph Vaughan Williams and Percy Dearmer in editing *Songs of Praise* (1925). This harmonization also was included in *The Oxford Book of Carols* (1928).

345

Because he lives—see "God sent his Son"

475

Become to us the living Bread

Based on John 6:35-58
Miriam Drury (1900-1985), 1970
The Worshipbook: Services and Hymns, 1972

GELOBT SEI GOTT

Melchior Vulpius (ca. 1560-1615)
Vulpius's *Ein schön geistlich Gesangbuch*, Jena, 1609

"Become to us" is probably Miriam Drury's best-known hymn text. The intent of Communion is summed up in brief, packed statements:

The Christian life and community are renewed and imbued with joy to bear God's new covenant through the world. The words, though relatively new, echo a more universal and ancient Christian tradition well accommodated by an older tune. The third stanza, which points us to our unity in Christ, makes this hymn a suitable choice for Worldwide Communion Sunday.

For comments on GELOBT SEI GOTT, see "O sons and daughters, let us sing" (**274**).

18
Before Jehovah's aweful throne — WATTS

Based on Psalm 100
Isaac Watts (1674-1748)
The Psalms of David . . . , 1719

John David Brunk (1872-1926), 1910
Church and Sunday School Hymnal, Supplement, 1911

This metrical paraphrase of Psalm 100 consisted of six stanzas. Its original first stanza applied the psalm in a very specific way, which is actually reminiscent of the national centrism of Israelite worship:

> Sing to the Lord with joyful noise;
> let every land his name adore:
> the British Isles shall send the noise
> across the ocean to the shore.

Early North American editions further modified it to "America shall send the noise."

In Watts's day, the word *aweful* was used the way we today use *awesome* or *majestic.* The extra e, of course, differentiates it from the word that means terrible or bad. Other archaisms are also retained to preserve the text's contrast of divine and human functions. The psalm's call to praise in stanza 1 culminates in the spontaneous joy of the truly thankful heart.

WATTS is one of many hymn tunes by J. D. Brunk, a Mennonite composer. Mary Oyer writes that Brunk composed his tunes in various styles to suit the Mennonite manner of singing as he knew it. Listing six styles she sees in his music, Oyer names WATTS as an example of the chorale type, with its rich and varied four-voice harmony (Oyer 1980). In *The Mennonite Hymnal* (1969), the rhythm of WATTS is changed by adding quarter-note movement. *Hymnal: A Worship Book* returns to Brunk's original half-note rhythm.

243

Before the cock crew twice

Hallgrim Pjetursson (1614-1674)
Fimmtiu Passiusalmar, 1659
Tr. Charles Venn Pilcher (1879-1961), 1921
Icelandic Meditations on the Passion, 1923

HALLGRIM

Lawrence Francis Bartlett (1933-)
The Australian Hymn Book, 1977

This text by the Icelandic Lutheran pastor Hallgrim Pjetursson is the twelfth in a series of fifty Passion hymns he completed in 1659. Called "the remorse of Peter," this hymn follows the account of Peter's denial in Matthew 26. Stanza 4 turns from the narrative to a general prayer of confession and repentance, concluding with an assurance of pardon. The translation is "a free rendering of selected lines (with some rearrangement) of the hymn and admirably captures the movement and powerful terseness of Pjetursson's writing" (Milgate 1982).

Because the text is in an unusual meter, Australian pastor Lawrence Bartlett wrote HALLGRIM for these words. Since the hymn might be sung just once a year, he composed a simple melody congregations could learn quickly.

250

Beneath the cross of Jesus

Elizabeth Cecilia Clephane (1830-1869)
Family Treasury, 1872, alt.

ST. CHRISTOPHER

Frederick Charles Maker (1844-1927)
Bristol Tune Book, 1881

This hymn is one of eight poems that appeared in successive issues of the Scottish Presbyterian magazine *Family Treasury*. These poems, which bear the heading "Breathings on the Border," were written when the author was thirty-nine, near the end of her life. When they were published three years later, the magazine editor introduced them with this flowery preamble:

> These lines express the experiences, the hope and the longings of a young Christian lately released. Written on the very edge of this life, with the better land fully in view of faith, they seem to us footsteps printed on the sands of Time, where those sands touch the ocean of Eternity. These footprints of one whom the Good Shepherd led through the wilderness into rest, may, with God's blessing, contribute to comfort and direct succeeding pilgrims. (Loewen, Moyer, Oyer 1983)

Set against the background of Clephane's life of sacrifice and service to the poor, the third stanza is to be construed not as an escape from the world ("content to let the world go by"), but as a profound relinquishing of personal pain to the greater illumination of the cross. Hindsight allows one to discern healing and glory in the suffering of the crucifixion.

ST. CHRISTOPHER was written for these words when they were next published in the *Bristol Tune Book*. Its chromatic melody and harmony, along with the use of seventh chords, exemplifies the Victorian hymn style of the late nineteenth century.

Frederick Maker adopted for his tune the name of the patron saint of travelers. Legend depicts St. Christopher, a third-century Christian convert, as a giant who devoted his life to carrying people across a river. One of those travelers, a small child, weighed so much that Christopher staggered in the middle of the river and commented, "Child, you seem to weigh as much as the world." The child responded, "I created the world, bore the sins of the world, and redeemed the world." The image of the "Christ-bearer" (Christopher) with his burden is a popular one in Christian art.

323
Beyond a dying sun

Steve Engle (1943-), 1970
Church of the Brethren Annual Conference Booklet, 1970
Rev., 1984

ENGLE

Steve Engle (1943-), 1970
(same source as text)
Harm. by Donald R. Frederick (1917-) and Steve Engle

This song is more frequently referred to by the words of the refrain, "I see a new world coming." It was written in the late spring of 1970 when Steve Engle, a member of La Verne Church of the Brethren (Calif.), was invited by his pastor to write a song to reflect the sermon theme for a denomination-wide Annual Conference service. Since that time the song has become popular in Brethren circles as a hopeful peace and justice hymn. It lifts the singer above the hard, slogging pursuit of peace and justice to regain perspective and vision. Though not originally written with Revelation in mind, the text reflects the rich imagery of that book, with the second stanza reminiscent of Revelation 21:4: "And God shall wipe away all tears from their eyes . . . " (KJV).

After the third stanza, the refrain is often sung twice, the second time for emphasis.

40
Bless, O Lord, this church—see "Jesus Christ, God's only Son"

see "Jesus Christ, God's only Son"

174
Bless'd be the God of Israel — WEBB

Based on Luke 1:68-79
Michael Arnold Perry (1942-)
Psalm Praise, 1973

George James Webb (1803-1887), 1830
The Odeon, 1837

This text is based on Luke 1:68-79, the passage in which John the Baptist's father, Zechariah, regains his power of speech. Along with the Song of Mary (Magnificat) and Simeon's Song (*Nunc Dimittis*), this hymn is one of the first three Christian hymns recorded. Often referred to as the Canticle of Zechariah or Benedictus, it is a messianic hymn composed largely of Old Testament passages. In medieval times it was used as the canticle for Lauds, the service at dawn. Lauds was named for the Latin word *laudate* (praise ye), which occurs frequently in Psalms 148—150, sung during that hour of worship.

Perry's paraphrase, which originally began "O praise the God of Israel," has been revised a number of times. At the close of stanza 2 and the beginning of stanza 3, the stronger original words "harbinger" and "On prisoners of darkness" are retained. In these places some editions use "messengers" and "Where once were fear and darkness."

This contemporary version of the Benedictus is invigorated and supported by the tune WEBB. The melody, written while Webb was aboard a ship to North America, originally was the setting of the secular text "'Tis dawn, the lark is singing." In 1842 it was associated with the hymn "The morning light is breaking" in *The Wesleyan Psalmist*. It was not until 1861, thirty-one years after its writing, that William B. Bradbury paired the melody with the familiar hymn text "Stand up, stand up for Jesus."

421
Bless'd be the tie that binds — DENNIS

John Fawcett (1739 or 1740-1817)
Hymns Adapted to the Circumstances of Public Worship and Private Devotion, 1782, alt.

Arr. from Johann Georg Nägeli (1768 or 1773-1836) by Lowell Mason (1792-1872)
The Psaltery, 1845

This hymn of six stanzas was first published in Fawcett's *Hymns Adapted* . . . with the title "Brotherly Love." An unauthenticated story, first told in Josiah Miller's *Singers and Songs of the Church* (1869), says that Fawcett had decided to leave his small Baptist church in Wainsgate, Yorkshire, England, to become pastor of the more prestigious Carter's Lane Baptist Church in London. After his farewell sermon, when he and his family were ready to leave, the tears of his parishioners moved him to reverse his decision and stay despite financial disadvantage. Fawcett is said to have lined these words the next week. Though this text is commonly used for farewells, it was inspired by a decision to stay! The variety of versions and sentimental attachment to portions of this hymn made it difficult to finalize a text for this hymnal that would be recognizable for all its constituencies. The result itself points to the "tie that binds."

DENNIS was first published by Lowell Mason in *The Psaltery* as a setting for the text "How gentle God's commands!" Mason did not specify the exact source he used from Nägeli but marked his arrangement "Slow and soft, Cantabile." Some hymn handbook references cite Nägeli's *Christliches Gesangbuch* (1828) where a similar melody is set to *O selig, selig, wer vor dir*. This combination of text and tune has become, in the words of twentieth-century radio personality Garrison Keillor, "a Christian love song."

230
Blessed are the persecuted — (no tune name)

Balaacoolwe bapenzegwa
Based on Matthew 5
Tonga text adapt. by Esther Cathryn Klaassen Bergen (1921-)
Mennonite World Conference *International Songbook*, 1990

Tonga melody (Zambia)

This anonymous Tonga text from Zambia was first published for the 1990 Mennonite World Conference. The version submitted for that conference featured a three-part women's group from Zambia, singing primarily in parallel thirds and fifths. The printed harmonization is a transcription of that recording. Doreen Klassen, who assisted in editing the songbook, notes: "[A] Zambian ethnomusicologist . . . claims this type of harmony is indigenous, pre-dating Western harmonic influences and, furthermore, that it surprises Western listeners who expect to hear open fourths or fifths or pentatonic tonal systems." This song, which congregations will find musically appealing and accessible, is a dynamic expression of the Beatitudes.

332
Blessed assurance — BLESSED ASSURANCE

Fanny Jane Crosby (1820-1915)
Gems of Praise, Philadelphia, 1873

Phoebe Palmer Knapp (1839-1908)
(same source as text)

Of this beloved hymn, Fanny Crosby writes:

> Sometimes a tune is furnished me for which to write the words . . . . My dear friend, Mrs. Joseph F. Knapp, had composed the tune; and it seemed to me one of the sweetest I had heard for a long time. She asked me to write a hymn for it, and I felt while bringing the words and the tones together that the air and the hymn were meant for each other. (Crosby 1906)

The pairing has remained unaltered through the years.

Dubbed an "archetypal gospel song," the hymn has text phrases that bring to mind various scriptures. Rather than becoming a theological treatise, or even a "story however, the words constitute a flow of faith experiences.

179
Blessed be the Lord

(no tune name)

Luke 1:68-79
Tr. Ladies of the Grail

Abbey Notre Dame du Tamié, France

As with unison reading, a chant melody provides an opportunity for experiencing a scripture text in a unified manner. The musical setting further enhances the poetic qualities of this beautiful Song of Zechariah (Benedictus). The benediction ("Blessed be . . . ") pronounced by the leader is affirmed by the entire congregation, which responds in harmony, reiterating (and thus remembering) God's mighty acts. For additional comments on the scriptural passage from which this text is taken, see "Bless'd be the God of Israel" (**174**).

13
Blessed Jesus, at your word

LIEBSTER JESU, WIR SIND HIER

Liebster Jesu, wir sind hier
Tobias Clausnitzer (1619-1684)
Altdorffisches Gesang-büchlein, 1663
Tr. Catherine Winkworth (1827-1878)
Lyra Germanica, Series II
(Zahn No. 3498), 1858, alt.

Johann Rudolf Ahle (1625-1673)
Neue geistliche auf die Sonntage durchs gantze Jahr gerichtete Andachten, 1664

This three-stanza hymn first appeared with the designation "before the sermon." During the seventeenth century, the longer, "weightier" hymns were reserved for after the sermon. Thus, this three-stanza introit hymn was sung as a prayer between the readings that preceded the sermon. Stanza 3:2, "Light of light from God proceeding," reflects a portion of the Nicene Creed that would be spoken before the sermon hymn.

The alterations to the Winkworth translation consist primarily of substitutes for archaisms. In addition, the last phrase of stanza 1 once read:

> By thy teachings sweet and holy,
> drawn from earth to love you solely.

In the source listed above, LIEBSTER JESU, WIR SIND HIER was first coupled with Franz Burmeister's Advent hymn *Ja, er ist's, das Heil der Welt*. The original form of the melody was an example of the new style of sacred aria, influenced by Italian opera, which Ahle brought into the church.

The tune, also known as NUREMBERG and DESSAU, has undergone many changes. It was matched with this text as early as the 1671 edition of *Altdorffisches Gesang-büchlein*. This hymn has long been a favorite invocational hymn (calling on God's presence) among Russian Mennonites who came to North America. It boldly names the reason for gathering—to be instructed by the Light of God.

107
Blessed Savior, we adore thee

Baylus Benjamin McKinney (1886-1952), 1942
Teacher, July 1942
Look and Live Songs, 1945

GLORIOUS NAME

Baylus Benjamin McKinney (1886-1952), 1942
(same sources as text)

This hymn has strong musical similarities to "Angels we have heard on high," particularly in the concluding measures. While "Angels we have heard" is a joyous proclamation of a specific event (the birth of the Christ child), "Blessed Savior" is a hymn of pure praise. Whether McKinney, a Southern Baptist, was thinking about religious history, the hymn bursts with the answer to the first article of John Calvin's catechism (teaching): "What is a Christian's chief duty?" "To glorify God and enjoy him forever."

The tune was titled GLORIOUS NAME by the committee of the 1956 *Baptist Hymnal*. The rests in the refrain have been replaced by longer note values, as was done in the later *Baptist Hymnal*.

108
Blessing and honor and glory

Horatius N. Bonar (1808-1889), ca. 1866
Hymns of Faith and Hope, Third Series, 1866, alt.

AMERICAN HYMN

Matthias Keller (1813-1875), 1865
Common Service Book, 1917

This hymn erupts with the sevenfold ascription from John's Revelation (5:12). It is the "Song of the Lamb," written in eight stanzas for Ascension Day, 1866. The "weakness" of dying a criminal's death is obliterated as Christ is enveloped in his rightful glory. The exchange of joyful singing and heavenly love (st. 3) alerts the believer to the *immediate* presence of a divine realm that is also John's vision of the future.

This abridged version of Bonar's festal poem consists of stanzas 8, 4, 5, and 7. The original first stanza was:

> Into the heaven of the heavens hath he gone;
> sitteth he now in the joy of the throne;
> wealth he now of the Kingdom the crown;
> singeth he now the new song with his own.

The second stanza of the present hymn originally began:

> Soundeth the heaven of the heavens with his name;
> ringeth the earth with his glory and fame;

This shows the kind of minor alterations that have been made to this text.

AMERICAN HYMN was used for the first time with this text in the *Common Service Book*. The composer originally wrote this music for his own text as a contest piece: "Speed our republic, O Father on high." For this he won the advertised five-hundred-dollar prize. For many years this tune was played by bands on the Boston Common for July 4th celebrations. In 1869 the music was set to Oliver Wendell Holmes' "Ode to Peace" and used at the first Peace Jubilee in Boston.

Bonar's text also works well with O QUANTA QUALIA, or even as a dramatic antiphonal reading.

455
Bread of life — ROHRER

Kenneth I. Morse (1913-)
Gospel Messenger, Nov. 19, 1955, alt.

Wilbur E. Brumbaugh (1931-1977)
(same source as text)

This hymn was written originally as a "grace before meals" for the cover of *Gospel Messenger*, November 19, 1955. The hymn appeared again in *Gospel Messenger*, April 28, 1962, and the text was reprinted in *The Sabbath Recorder* (Seventh Day Baptists) of May 21 that same year. The entire hymn was included in *The Brethren Songbook* (1974). The original stanza 2 has been omitted and several changes made to make the language more contemporary.

The tune ROHRER was named by Wilbur Brumbaugh for his wife, Eula Rohrer Brumbaugh, who resides in Elgin, Illinois. This hymn could be used for Communion or as a table grace, and it sings well with a number of other familiar tunes, including STUTTGART.

469
Bread of the world — LES COMMANDEMENS DE DIEU

Reginald Heber (1783-1826)
Hymns written and adapted to the Weekly Service of the Church Year, 1827

La forme des prières . . . , Strasbourg, 1545
Harm. adapt. from Claude Goudimel (ca. 1505-1572)
Les Pseaumes . . . , 1565

In stanza 1:1-2, Heber's words directly address Christ as the "Bread of the world" and "Wine of the soul," designations Jesus himself used, according to John 6. The bread and cup thus take on meaning at many levels, not only pointing to Christ, but also signifying the communicant's participation in Christ's suffering and Jesus' willingness to be poured out for the sake of others. Stanza 2 is the appeal, or prayer, and expresses an underlying acceptance of the grace and sustenance by which souls and bodies are fed. This text has inspired numerous musical settings.

LES COMMANDEMENS DE DIEU (also named COMMANDMENTS, OLD 125th, and BAVA) was originally the setting for the metrical version of the Ten Commandments in the French psalter cited above. This melody is also set to an English metrical version of the Commandments in the *Psalter Hymnal* (1988). *The Hymnal 1940 Companion* claims that the first musical phrase came from a secular *chanson* (song) and that Bourgeois composed the rest. The irregular stress patterns, characteristic of French psalm tunes, have been indicated in some hymnals by placing bar lines at four- and six-beat intervals. Here bar lines are placed only at the close of each line, drawing the singer's attention to the musical phrases rather than the measures. The half note is the basic rhythmic pulse.

LES COMMANDEMENS DE DIEU, with its lighter Renaissance feel, lifts up the text's invocation of grace.

203
Break forth, O beauteous heavenly light — ERMUNTRE DICH

Ermuntre dich, mein schwacher Geist
Johann Rist (1607-1667)
Rist's *Himmlische Lieder,* Leipzig, 1641
St. 1, tr. John Troutbeck (ca. 1832-1889), ca. 1885
Sts. 2-3, tr. Fred Pratt Green (1903-), 1986

Johann Schop (ca. 1590- ca. 1665)
(same source as text)
(Zahn No. 5741a)
Harm. by Johann Sebastian Bach (1685-1750)
Christmas Oratorio, 1734

The original German hymn of twelve stanzas, based on Isaiah 9:2-7, was titled "A hymn of praise on the joyful Birth and Incarnation of our Lord and Savior Jesus Christ." Rist is yet another example of a prolific writer who somehow wrested moments of beauty from the suffering of the Thirty Years War. The first stanza, a translation of the original stanza 9, may be familiar to choral singers; it is the English text found in the Novello edition of Bach's *Christmas Oratorio.*

The second and third stanzas, translated by Fred Pratt Green, help contemporize the hymn. The text quickly moves from the birth story to ponder the paradox of a weak child destined to redeem the world.

This text/tune combination is a "proper" one, that is, the tune was composed for the text. It is a noble chorale created for a robust text full of action: breaking, ushering, shrinking, bidding, conquering. Schop originally set it in triple meter, but Bach later cast it in 4/4 for his *Christmas Oratorio.* Bach's two other harmonizations in Cantata Nos. 11 and 43 retain the triple meter.

360
Break thou the bread of life

BREAD OF LIFE

Mary Artemisia Lathbury (1841-1913)
Robinson and MacArthur's *Chautauqua Carols,* 1877

William Fiske Sherwin (1826-1888), 1877
The Calvary Selection of Spiritual Songs, 1878

Lathbury's hymn was written at the request of Bishop John H. Vincent for use at the Chautauqua Assembly in western New York, a favorite gathering place for Christian study and fellowship in the nineteenth century. This hymn, based on the account of Jesus feeding the multitude by the sea (Matt. 14:13-21), no doubt evoked a sense of unity for those at the Assembly on the shores of Chautauqua Lake. It is still a Chautauqua tradition to sing this hymn at Sunday evening vespers. Although it is sometimes used as a Communion hymn, the "bread of life" refers to the word of God.

Two other stanzas, drafted by Alexander Groves twenty-five years after Lathbury wrote the hymn, extend the "bread" imagery by picking up Jesus' words "I am the bread of life" (John 6:35).

> Thou art the bread of life, O Lord, to me,
> thy holy word the truth that saveth me.
> Give me to eat and live with thee above.
> Teach me to love thy truth, for thou art love.
>
> O send thy Spirit, Lord, now unto me,
> that he may touch my eyes and make me see:
> show me the truth concealed within thy word,
> and in thy book revealed I see thee, Lord.

Also in the summer of 1877, BREAD OF LIFE was composed for this text by William F. Sherwin. Although the meditative mood of the music reflects the prayer genre of the text, it should still be sung with some degree of urgency or "hunger."

356
Breathe on me, breath of God — TRENTHAM

Edwin Hatch (1835-1889)
Between Doubt and Prayer, 1878, alt.

Robert Jackson (1842-1914)
Fifty Sacred Leaflets, 1888

This petition to the Holy Spirit for renewal was originally intended as an ordination hymn, based on John 20:21-22 where Jesus breathed on the disciples as he consecrated them for a ministry of forgiveness. The hymn was written in a straightforward style that imitated the Christianity of its creator—"as simple and unaffected as that of a child" (*The Worshiping Church* 1990, 1991). "Breath of God" is a wonderful, nearly mystical image taken from the Hebrew and Greek word for spirit, which also means wind or air. When the hymn first appeared in Henry Allon and H. J. Gauntlett's *The Congregational Psalmist* (1886), stanza 3:1 was changed from the more colorful "Blend all my soul with thine" to "Till I am wholly thine." This has been the accepted text since that time; it conjures up the image of God breathing life into a human ember.

Jackson's tune was written for "O perfect life of love" and became associated with Hatch's text around 1900. TRENTHAM is named for a village in Staffordshire, England, the birthplace of the composer.

28
Breathe upon us, Holy Spirit — SHOWALTER

Elisha Albright Hoffman (1839-1929), 1899
The Brethren Hymnal, 1901

J. Henry Showalter (1864-1947),1899
(same source as text)

This hymn, well loved among the Brethren, has appeared in the Brethren hymnals dated 1901, 1925, and 1951. Elisha Hoffman, a Presbyterian pastor, was a prolific writer and composer; by 1914 he was credited with more than two thousand compositions in print. Among his more familiar hymns are "What a wonderful Savior," "Christ has for sin atonement made," and "I must tell Jesus."

The use of the words "altars" and "vow" in stanza 1, the notion of the church house as a "holy dwelling place" in stanza 1:5, and the appearance of "sacred incense" in stanza 4:1 are unexpected in Anabaptist worship; they are allusions to Old Testament worship blended with the post-Pentecost phenomenon of the Holy Spirit. Stanza 3:2 originally concluded with the words "Blot it from thy book on high." The change to "Lead us to thyself on high" was made in *The Brethren Hymnal* (1951).

J. Henry Showalter was a member of the committee for the 1901 hymnal where this tune appears unnamed. The name SHOWALTER was given to the tune by the 1951 hymnal committee.

8
Brethren, we have met to worship — HOLY MANNA

William Moore's *The Columbian Harmony*, 1825 — (same source as text)

The words to this hymn are attributed to George Atkins, and its first known publication was in William Moore's *The Columbian Harmony*. The text used here consists of stanzas 1, 3, 4, and 5 of the five stanzas in William Walker's *Southern Harmony* (1840).

The hymn is a call to believers to pray for and support new converts and alludes to biblical characters being brought to faith: Paul's jailer in Philippians 1:12-13 and Mary who anointed Jesus. Images of conversion were of more concern to this writer than accurate biblical chronology! References to the Old Testament stories of Moses and the wilderness experience are interwoven. The appeal for "manna" at the end of all four stanzas certainly ties in with the reference to Moses in stanza 2, but it is also a more extensive allusion to spiritual bread or nourishment. John 6:31-33,41 bridges Old and New Testament images of manna and bread. Thus, it is the very life of Christ that is being offered to all who come seeking him.

The "trembling mourners" of stanza 2 refers to those people "under conviction" who sat in prominent view of the audience during protracted revival meetings in vogue during the second Great Awakening of the early nineteenth century. The bench where they sat waiting for the Holy Spirit to fall upon them was known as the "anxious-bench" or "mourner's seat" (*The Brethren Encyclopedia* 1983).

The present popularity of this "namesake" hymn (though "brethren," in this case, is simply the old plural form for "brothers") belies its introduction into Brethren worship. Brethren were slow to accept the method of conversion induced by the "mourner's seat." In an 1878 polemic against such "new measures," Christian H. Balsbaugh writes: "Away with this miserable, soul-cheating machinery for inducting sinners into the Divine favor . . . . Conversion has no more to do with the anxious-bench than the doxology means the Yankee Doodle" (*The Brethren Encyclopedia*). Balsbaugh would not have appreciated the context of this hymn!

This pentatonic (five-note) melody was probably composed by William Moore and is representative of the early nineteenth-century American folk tradition. Little is known about Moore except that he lived in Wilson County in western Tennessee. HOLY MANNA has long been a popular melody in various southern denominations. For a variety of intriguing ways to use this melody, see the *Accompaniment Handbook*.

219
Bright and glorious is the sky

Nikolai Frederik Severin Grundtvig (1783-1872), 1810
Knud Lyhne Rahbek's *Sandsigeren*, Apr. 11, 1811
Tr. Jens Christian Aaberg (1877-1970)
Hymnal for Church and Home (Danish), Blair, Neb., 1927, 1938
Service Book and Hymnal, 1958

DEJLIG ER DEN HIMMEL BLAA

Danish melody, ca. 1840
Andreas Berggren's *Melodier til den af Roeskildes Praestreconvent udgivne Psalmebog*, Copenhagen, 1853

This hymn, one of the author's earliest, was written for Christmas 1810. After its first publication in 1811, it was included in Grundtvig's 1815 collection and later appeared in various hymnals. The present translation comes from both Aaberg and the commission that prepared the *Service Book and Hymnal* (Lutheran). The commission reworked the first half of the opening stanza and a second stanza, which is not used here. Aaberg's translation begins "Splendid are the heavens high."

The text begins with the story of the "sages from the East," which marks the beginning of the season of Epiphany (literally, manifestation or appearance, usually of a deity). Partway through stanza 4, the rest of Christendom is included in the search for the Lord with the Bible as our guiding "star."

DEJLIG ER DEN HIMMEL BLAA, also known as CELESTIA, is said to have been composed about 1840 by an elderly man who had "never before given himself to composition" (Stulken 1981).

221
Brightest and best—see "Hail the bless'd morn"

142
Brothers and sisters of mine

MINE ARE THE HUNGRY

Kenneth I. Morse (1913-)
The Brethren Songbook, 1974

Wilbur E. Brumbaugh (1931-1977)
(same source as text)

This text was written when Morse was book editor for Brethren Press and associate editor of the Brethren periodical *Messenger*. The straightforward, unison melody, written by Brumbaugh for this text, was originally named MORSE. It complements the text's unadorned admission of complacency. The song became familiar to Brethren as it was sung frequently at Annual Conferences, reminding participants of the denomination's history of compassion and service. Another musical setting by Emily R. Brink is in the Christian Reformed *Psalter Hymnal* under the title "God of all living."

309
Built on the Rock

KIRKEN DEN ER ET GAMMELT HUS

Kirken den er et gammelt hus
Nikolai Frederik Severin Grundtvig (1783-1872)
Grundtvig's *Sang-Värk til den Danske Kirke,* 1837
Tr. Carl Döving (1867-1937), 1909
The Lutheran Hymnary, 1913

Ludvig Mathias Lindeman (1812-1887)
Wexel's *Christelige Psalmer,* 1840

Kirken den er et gammelt hus literally means "The church, it is an old house." Grundtvig's poem, however, emphasizes that the church is not "made with hands," but is God's temple "high above earth" as well as in "our bodies," the dwelling of God's choice. The final stanza clearly identifies Jesus as the foundation of the church; it is the spirit and truth of Jesus that makes a holy temple, whether in the body of a believer or in the corporate body of believers.

This text, originally in seven stanzas, is one of the best-known hymns of Scandinavian origin. It appeared later in *Festsalmer* (1854), revised and abridged by the author. The present version consists of stanzas 1, 2, and 4 from *The Lutheran Hymnary*, with minor alterations.

KIRKEN DEN ER ET GAMMELT HUS was Lindeman's first hymn tune. He composed it for this text; it evokes the notion of "rock" in the solid feel of the music. This strong melody in the Dorian mode has been described as reflecting the style of Norse folk music, of which its composer was an active collector, scholar, and publisher. The hymn is equally effective whether sung in unison or in parts.

422

BWANA AWABARIKI

Swahili folk hymn
May God grant you a blessing

(no tune name)

Swahili melody

Sometimes the simplest words convey the most meaning and are the most memorable. The original text of this blessing is in Swahili, a language in widespread use in Kenya, Tanzania, Uganda, Zaire, and other parts of Africa. Although an English version of the text is provided, the original words of this parting hymn are a joy to sing and lead one naturally into the syncopated rhythms of the music. Some suggestions for pronunciation and the use of drumming instruments are included in the *Accompaniment Handbook.*

552

By gracious powers

Based on Ephesians 5:20
Dietrich Bonhöffer (1906-1945)
"New Year 1945," *The Cost of Discipleship*, 2nd ed., 1959
Tr. Fred Pratt Green (1903-), 1972
Cantate Domino, 1974

INTERCESSOR

Charles Hubert Hastings Parry (1848-1918)
Hymns Ancient and Modern, 1904 ed.

This hymn text is based on Dietrich Bonhöffer's 1945 New Year's message smuggled out of prison to his friends. It was the last New Year's Eve for Bonhöffer, the German theologian martyred April 9, 1945, twenty-eight days before the end of World War II. Hymnologist Erik Routley invited Fred Pratt Green to create a poetic translation of the text for *Cantate Domino,* an international, ecumenical hymnal prepared by the World Council of Churches. In this version, stanzas 1 and 5 of the original are omitted, and stanza 7 becomes stanza 1. The fifth stanza of the poem is:

> Now when your silence deeply spreads around us,
> O let us hear all your creation says:
> That world of sound which soundlessly invades us,
> And all your children's highest hymns of praise.

This strong expression of faith and hope in adversity is a marvelous addition to our contemporary hymnody. Stanza 3 especially is an astounding declaration of trust.

Parry composed the tune INTERCESSOR for the hymn text "O Word of pity, for our pardon pleading," by Ada R. Greenaway. Erik Routley praised the tune as "a new kind of melodic genius."

In some hymnals "By gracious powers" is set to the tune BONHÖFFER, also known as LE CENACLE, composed by Father Gelineau for the revision of *Cantate Domino.*

378

By Peter's house

HEALING HEM

Anne Metzler Albright (1925-), 1963
Messenger, 1963

Bradley P. Lehman (1964-), 1991
Hymnal: A Worship Book, 1992

The poem "By Peter's house" was first published in the Brethren magazine *Messenger*. It recalls specific incidences of Jesus' healing ministry in order to bolster the faith of contemporary sufferers. Albright writes: "My mother's . . . [critical] illness, in part, prompted me to re-examine my faith" and adds that the poem was written with a recurring refrain so that it might one day be a hymn. The poem resurfaced at a 1990 Church of the Brethren women's event that carried the theme "Wounds and Healing."

Bradley Lehman relates his response to the poem: "This text suggests two strongly contrasting types of music, as each time the imploring refrain breaks into the ongoing narrative. Therefore, I have written relatively gentle, objective music for the stanzas, but a sudden switch in the refrain to more passionate music in the minor mode."

148

By the waters

BY THE WATERS

Based on Psalm 137:1

Philip Hayes, *The Muses' Delight: Catches, Glees, Canzonets, and Canons*, 1786, adapt.

The minor mode of this hymn captures the lament expressed in the text, which comes from a psalm recalling the destruction of Jerusalem and the discouragement of the Exile. Each line descends from its beginning note, as if it were pulled down by the sorrow and yearning of a displaced people.

Psalms scholar Carroll Stuhlmueller notes that the author of this psalm could have belonged to a group of temple singers who gathered regularly for prayer and lamentation at the site of the ruined temple after the Exile and before reconstruction in 515 B.C. The key word "remember" prompted Jews to re-experience the heartbreak of the Exile, much as Christians, in the Eucharist, remember the death of Jesus. The vision of "waters" might have brought to mind the canals of Babylon, as well as having liturgical meaning in the "pouring out" of the spirit in times of mourning (Stuhlmueller 1983).

Only one stanza has been included in order to accommodate the traditional canon (round) style of the music. The tempo should reflect the mood of the words. A moderate, four-beat pattern or a slow two pulses per measure can achieve this.

249

Calvary

African American spiritual

(no tune name)

African American spiritual

This spiritual is made for moaning, both musically and emotionally. It is a reflection on the Gospel narratives of the crucifixion, as retold in the first four stanzas and refrain. The final two stanzas move beyond the events on Calvary to a realization of what that sacrifice means to us and other sinners. The refrain and stanzas use the same melody, with a harmonization of the "Calvary" section. Note how the shapes of the melodic phrases, each ending with a descending line, give a musical aura of mourning. The alternating B-naturals and B-flats add to this feeling. Sung in a slow and meditative manner, this song can help participants express the sorrow connected with Holy Week, especially Good Friday.

55

Cantemos al Señor

Let's sing unto the Lord
Carlos Rosas (1939-)
Diez Canciones para la Misa, 1976
Tr. Elise Eslinger (1942-), Roberto Escamilla (1931-) and George Frank Lockwood IV (1946-)
Celebremos, 1983

ROSAS

Carlos Rosas (1939-)
(same source as text)
Arr. by Raquel Mora Martínez
(same source as translation)

"Cantemos al Señor," one of the author's favorite songs, is also known by the name "Aleluya." Though loosely based on Psalm 19, the text reflects the optimistic wonder inherent in the ancient hymn. The first "aleluya" musically opens the doors of the hymn as it culminates the litany of praise.

586

Cast thy burden upon the Lord

Wirf dein Anliegen auf den Herrn
Julius Schubring (b. 1806)
Tr. William Bartholomew (1793-1867)
Elijah, 1846

BIRMINGHAM (MENDELSSOHN)

Neu-vermehrtes Gesangbuch, 1693
(Zahn No. 5148)
Adapt. by Felix Mendelssohn (1809-1847)
Elijah, 1846

Julius Schubring, pastor of a church at Dessau, Germany, and a friend of Mendelssohn, adapted the text of *Elijah* from Old Testament scripture passages. "Cast thy burden" picks up phrases from Psalms 55:22 and 16:8. In the oratorio the text is cast as the scriptural assurance Elijah receives after he has staked his life on the honor of God over the power of Baal in the confrontation on Mount Carmel. It also reminds us of support and priorities for life in a stressful modern era. It functions well as a call to worship or response to prayer and is useful for private meditation.

"Cast thy burden" is No. 15 in Mendelssohn's oratorio. Based on a seventeenth-century German hymn tune, Mendelssohn's version was later adapted as the hymn tune MUNICH ("I believe in you, Lord Jesus," **440**). The tune is named for Birmingham, England, where *Elijah* was first performed on August 26, 1846.

620
Child of blessing, child of promise

Ronald S. Cole-Turner (1948-)
Everflowing Streams, 1981, alt.

STUTTGART

Attrib. to Christian Friedrich Witt (ca. 1660-1716)
Psalmodia Sacra . . . , 1715
Adapt. by Henry John Gauntlett (1805-1876)
Hymns Ancient and Modern, 1861

This hymn was written when the United Church of Christ announced its intention to publish a collection of hymns to meet the need for inclusive-language resources. It was sung at the baptism of the author's second daughter, Rachel Elizabeth, in the spring of 1982. "Child of Blessing" first appeared in *Everflowing Streams* with two versions of the first stanza—one for infant baptism and an alternate text for child dedication.

In keeping with the Anabaptist emphasis on child dedication as opposed to infant baptism, this hymnal's committee created one stanza from Cole-Turner's first two, using the opening line of the first stanza and lines 2-4 of the second. The omitted stanza 2:1 was "Child of love, our love's expression." The words "blessing you in Jesus' name" replace "live as one who bears Christ's name" at the end of what is now the second stanza.

STUTTGART was either composed or arranged by Christian Friedrich Witt who, along with A. C. Ludwig, published the Lutheran hymnbook *Psalmodia Sacra, oder Andächtige und schöne Gesänge* at Gotha in 1715. Though the present form is somewhat different from the original, STUTTGART has been used with a variety of texts throughout the years, and it appears three times in this hymnal (also, **388** and **391**). With its regularity and familiarity, it is well paired with this tight text of strong phrases; there is no competition between text and tune.

207
Child so lovely—see "Niño lindo"

see "Niño lindo"

616
Children of the heavenly Father

SANDELL

Tryggare kan ingen vara
Caroline V. Sandell Berg (1832-1903)
Andeliga Daggdroppar, 1855
Tr. Ernst William Olson (1870-1958)
The Hymnal (Augustana Synod), 1925

Swedish melody
Song Book for Sunday School, 1871

This hymn has sometimes been confined to the context of children because of its unpretentious quality of text and music. It should be understood, however, that "children" in the text refers to heirs of God of any age. Furthermore, the text is about facing death and expresses utter trust in God despite life's confusing blend of sorrow and joy. Some sources claim that the author wrote this hymn while still in her teens; others say it was prompted a few years later when her pastor father drowned.

A prolific writer, Sandell Berg is sometimes known as the "Fanny Crosby of Sweden." Her collected works contain 650 poems, and some were made famous by Jenny Lind, the popular Swedish singer of that time.

The stanzas omitted from most hymnals are 4 and 5, as follows:

> 4. Lo, their very hairs he numbers,
> And no daily care encumbers
> Them that share his every blessing,
> And his help in woes distressing.
>
> 5. Praise the Lord in joyful numbers:
> Your protector never slumbers.
> At the will of your defender
> Every foeman must surrender.

Although the first known printing of SANDELL was in Stockholm in the *Song Book for Sunday School*, it is thought by some to be of English origin. Gerald Göransson, director of the Royal School of Music in Stockholm, speculates that it may have been brought to Sweden during the pietist movement that flourished during the latter part of the nineteenth century (Gealy, Lovelace, Young 1970). Marilyn Stulken cites the possibility of its Scandinavian or German origins: "It seems very possible that the tune has antecedents in the 1700s, which perhaps remain to be discovered" (Stulken 1981).

442
Christ be with me

Attrib. to St. Patrick (ca. 389-461)
Irish Liber Hymnorum, 1897
Tr. Cecil Frances Alexander (1818-1895), 1889
Leaflet, 1889
C. H. H. Wright's *Writings of St. Patrick,* Appendix, 1889

DEIRDRE

Traditional Irish melody
Supplement to Edward Bunting's *Ancient Music of Ireland,* 1840
Adapt. for *The English Hymnal,* 1906

This text, set to the tune DEIRDRE, is the fifth stanza of **441**, "I bind unto myself today" (see that article for more text information).

DEIRDRE is adapted from "The Lamentation of Deirdre for the sons of Usneach" (*Neaill ghubb a Dheirdre*) as it was published in the music supplement to Bunting's work cited above. Bunting relates the legend of Deirdre and her fatal romance and claims that this tune is the oldest known Irish melody. Here it is the setting for stanza 5 of Alexander's paraphrase. In the transition between the tunes, the quarter note of DEIRDRE should approximate the dotted-half-note pulse in ST. PATRICK. "Christ be with me" may be sung separately.

365
Christ, from whom all blessings

Charles Wesley (1707-1788)
Hymns and Sacred Poems, 1740, alt.

SONG 13

Orlando Gibbons (1583-1625)
Wither's *Hymnes and Songs of the Church,* 1623

This hymn text comes from "The Communion of Saints," Wesley's poem of thirty-nine stanzas, arranged in four parts. "Christ, from whom all blessings" is taken from the ten quatrains of Part IV. The quatrains used here are the first three and the last two.

This is a prayer of the church, Christ's "mystic body." Rather than admonishing members of the body to be unified, it calls on Christ to do the joining. Stanzas 4 and 5 contain allusions to Paul's letters to the Corinthians and Galatians. In stanza 5, the "great equalizer" (death) is matched in strength by love, which is also capable of destroying all distinctions that blur the focus of the church. Finally, we are reminded that heartache caused by cultural, religious, and political bickering ("names and sects and parties") is nothing new, but that it falls away under the mantle of Christ (st. 4).

SONG 13 is one of sixteen tunes written by Gibbons for Wither's collection above, one of the few sacred songbooks produced between 1551 and 1700 that were not psalters. Gibbons' melodies all appear at the end of the book, accompanied by the number of the text for which a tune was composed. This melody was for "Oh, my love, how comely now" from the Song of Solomon, the thirteenth text in that collection—thus its designation SONG 13. Other names for this tune are CANTERBURY (the place of Gibbons' death), GIBBONS, NORWICH, ST. IRENAEUS, and SIMPLICITY.

Though "Christ, from whom all blessings" originally was in six phrases, the repetition of phrases 3 and 4 has been omitted to fit a 77.77 text. The tunes for Wither's collection were written in only two voices: melody and bass. The alto and tenor parts for the present version are from the Yale *Hymnal for Colleges and Schools* (1956).[1] Discussing this beautifully shaped tune, Archibald Jacob concludes: "Orlando Gibbons has here produced a small but faultless work of art" (Dearmer 1933).

1. This tune appears in Ralph Vaughan Williams' piano composition "Hymn Tune Prelude on 'Song 13' (Orlando Gibbons)" and in a transcription by Christopher Morris of the same for organ, both published by Oxford University Press.

267
Christ has arisen — (no tune name)

Mfurahini, Halleluya
Bernard Kyamanywa, 20th c.
Tr. Howard S. Olson (1922-), 1969

Haya melody (Tanzania)

The Swahili text was created by Bernard Kyamanywa while he was a theology student. He is now a pastor in the Northwest Diocese of the Evangelical Lutheran Church in Tanzania. The translation is by Howard Olson, a minister in Tanzania for forty-two years. The opening line, which originally began "He has arisen," was strengthened and clarified with the change to "Christ has arisen" in *Lead Me, Guide Me* (1987). Several other minor alterations have been made for this hymnal, but the exuberant story line remains the same: It is Easter, and Christ has overcome death. The driving rhythms and the message itself propel singers out the doors of the meeting place and into the streets to tell the good news! The hymn has been translated into many languages and is used in both Protestant and Catholic churches. Egil Hovland, a leading hymnologist of the Lutheran Church in Norway, says it is the most popular hymn in his church.

The joyous melody comes from the Haya people of western Tanzania. Sung in one pulse per measure, it is enhanced with the rhythmic patterns found in the *Accompaniment Handbook*.

278
Christ is alive! Let Christians sing

TRURO

Brian Arthur Wren (1936-), 1968
New Church Praise, 1975

Anonymous
Williams' *Psalmodia Evangelica, Part II*, 1789

Written for an Easter season that followed on the heels of the assassination of Martin Luther King, Jr., this hymn "tries to see God's love winning over tragedy and suffering in the world. There is tension and tragedy in these words, not just a howl of Easter rejoicing" (*The Worshiping Church* 1990, 1991). The omitted stanzas 3 and 4 attempt to restore the concept of Christ's "reigning at the right hand of God" to connote Christ's universal sovereign presence with the believer, rather than the remoteness of Christ reigning "above."

This hymn should not be confined to the Easter season; it is appropriate whenever believers want to reaffirm Christ's presence and power in the midst of trouble.

First used with the words "Now to the Lord a noble song," TRURO has been associated with numerous texts, including another Easter hymn "I know that my Redeemer lives" (see **279**). The composer of TRURO is unknown. The tune is named for the ancient town in the southwestern part of Cornwall, England, noted for its cathedral and its pottery.

271
Christ is arisen

CHRIST IST ERSTANDEN

Christ ist erstanden, von der Marter alle
German hymn, ca. 1100
Klug's *Gesangbuch* (Wittenberg), 1529
Tr. William Gustave Polack (1890-1950), 1939
The Lutheran Hymnal, 1941

German melody, 12th c.
Version from Klug's *Gesangbuch*, Wittenberg, 1529
(Zahn No. 8584)

Christ ist erstanden is one of the earliest hymns in the German language; the author is lost in the mists of antiquity. The hymn is another testament to the way people of the Middle Ages insisted on adjusting the formal Mass to make it their own, much to the consternation of religious authorities. First came the Latin "sequence" on which this pre-Reformation chorale was built. Sequences (also called tropes) were additional words to complement the regular Mass. Like *Stabat Mater* (see "At the cross, her vigil keeping," **245**), this sequence, *Victimae paschali*, was one of only five to survive the purge by the Council of Trent of these popularized additions. From this particular sequence came the first liturgical dramas and miracle plays of the Middle Ages, because the lines lend themselves so well to dialogue.

About a century later, vernacular lines were interpolated between the Latin lines of this sequence. "Christ has arisen" comes from these German lines. It is one of the best-known chorales. Even Martin Luther once stated, "After a time one tires of singing all other hymns, but the *Christ ist erstanden* one can always sing again." Later, he used the sequence as a pattern for his chorale *Christ lag in Todesbanden* ("Christ Jesus lay in death's strong bands," **470**). By the fifteenth century, still more versions had appeared, some with as many as eleven stanzas. This is a translation of the three-stanza version from Klug's edition cited above. Each stanza concludes with the *Kyrie*, "Lord, have mercy."

The ancient hymn is presented in this hymnal in a melody-only version.

295
Christ is coming! Let creation

John Ross MacDuff (1818-1895)
Altar Stones, 1853, alt.

UNSER HERRSCHER (NEANDER)

Joachim Neander (1650-1680)
Alpha und Omega, Glaub-und Liebesübung, 1680

This text alternates between a yearning for (Rom. 8) and an assurance of (Rev. 22:20) Christ's second coming. That is the impetus of hope.

This text was in the *Hymnal: Church of the Brethren* (1925), the *Mennonite Hymnary* (1940), and *The Mennonite Hymnal* (1969), as well as Methodist, Moravian, and nondenominational hymnals.

UNSER HERRSCHER (NEANDER) was first set to Neander's text *Unser Herrscher, unser König*. For more information on the tune, see "Open now thy gates of beauty" (**19**). A setting in C major is in the *Accompaniment Handbook*.

43
Christ is our cornerstone

Angularis fundamentum lapis
Anonymous, 6th or 7th c.
Tr. John Chandler (1806-1876)
Chandler's *Hymns of the Primitive Church*, 1837, alt.

DARWALL'S 148th

John Darwall (1731-1789)
Aaron Williams' *New Universal Psalmodist*, 1770

The metaphor of Christ as a cornerstone or foundation hails from 1 Peter 2:4-8; Ephesians 2:20-22; and 1 Corinthians 3:11-14. This very ancient text comes from the longer Latin hymn *Urbs beata Hierusalem*, which was occasionally divided into two parts.

In medieval times this hymn was the proper office hymn for the dedication of a church building. As a hymn for gathering, Christ is the cornerstone upon whom the church, assembled as the people of God, rests in corporate worship.

This energetic tune was originally composed for Psalm 148, "Ye boundless realms of joy." The dramatic upward leaps reflect uncontained joy; then the melody descends more evenly in order to be able to leap again. Also known as DARWALL, the melody appears in the 1925 Brethren hymnal with "In loud exalted strains," and in *The Mennonite Hymnal* (1969), it is set to this text, as well as to Watts's "Lord of the worlds above."

1. The complete Latin text can be found in *The Hymnal 1940 Companion*.

272
Christ is risen! Shout hosanna

LADUE CHAPEL

Brian Arthur Wren (1936-), 1984
Praising a Mystery, 1986

Ronald Arnatt (1930-)
"Pentecost Anthem," 1968
More Hymns and Spiritual Songs, 1971

These words were inspired by a resurrection text in the same meter by Frank von Christierson and were written for William P. Rowan's tune JACKSON NEW. Wren comments that the tune's "rhythms and melody shaped the flow of the words." The final text, however, was not dependent on that tune.

LADUE CHAPEL first appeared in Arnatt's "Pentecost Anthem" for alto solo, SATB choir, two trumpets and trombone, percussion and organ—set to Elton Trueblood's poem "Baptism by fire." (See also "God, whose purpose is to kindle," **135**, based on that poem.) Arnatt's anthem was commissioned by Ladue Chapel, St. Louis, Missouri, in honor of its twenty-fifth anniversary. Wren's text also has been set to the Polish carol W ŻŁOBIE LEŻY, usually associated with *"Infant holy, Infant lowly"* (**206**).

334
Christ is the world's true light

ST. JOAN

George Wallace Briggs (1875-1959)
Enlarged Songs of Praise, 1931, alt.

Percy E. B. Coller (1895-), 1941
The Hymnal 1940

This text, extolling Christ as Light and Lord for all races, was categorized in its first printed source for the seasons of Advent and Epiphany, as well as for the theme of "Missions Oversea." It was written originally for the tune KOMMT SEELEN by J. S. Bach. A few archaisms have been eliminated. Especially in the context of missions, it is significant that the text invokes the *peace* of Christ in stanzas 2 and 3, the opposite of the more militant flavor of many missionary hymns of the same era.

ST. JOAN was composed for this text in 1941. Contributed anonymously by Coller for the *The Hymnal 1940* (Episcopal), the tune is named for the composer's wife.

470
Christ Jesus lay

CHRIST LAG IN TODESBANDEN

Christ lag in todesbanden
Martin Luther (1483-1546)
Eyn Enchiridion, Erfurt, 1524
Richard Massie (1800-1887)
Massie's *Martin Luther's Spiritual Songs,* 1854, alt.

Adapt. from CHRIST IST ERSTANDEN
Walther's *Geistliches Gesangbüchlein,* Wittenberg, 1524
(Zahn No. 7012)
Harm. by Johann Sebastian Bach (1685-1750)
Cantata No. 4, ca. 1708

In writing this hymn, Martin Luther thought he was simply "improving" on the beloved German hymn *Christ is erstanden.* In fact, he essentially wrote a new text. Patterned after the eleventh-century sequence *Victimae paschali,* it is considered one of Luther's finest hymnic achievements. (For more information on this sequence, see "Christ is arisen," **271**.)

Massie's translation of the German text, one of many, originally began "Christ lay awhile in Death's strong bands." Godfrey Thring's *Collection* (1882) was first to print the present opening line and reduced the seven stanzas to four. The few minor text alterations preserve the spirit of the original. The hymn can be made appropriate for Easter by singing "Easter day" in place of "holy day" in the last stanza.

The history of the melody CHRIST LAG IN TODESBANDEN is complex. Its opening phrase seems related to the Easter sequence *Victimae paschali,* which also resembles the twelfth-century German favorite CHRIST IST ERSTANDEN. Martin Luther and Johann Walther included two versions of the melody in their books cited above (both 1524). Walther's collection is also identified as *Geistliches Gesangbüchlein* or simply *Gesangbüchlein.* Bach used this melody in several works, making it the basis of all seven movements of his Cantata No. 4.

280
Christ the Lord is risen today

EASTER HYMN

Charles Wesley (1707-1788)
Hymns and Sacred Poems, Part II, 1739, alt.

Anonymous
Lyra Davidica, 1708

This magnificent, jubilant Easter hymn is taken from the eleven stanzas of Wesley's "Hymn for Easter Day." The "Alleluias" were added later and frame each of Wesley's phrases with praise. Such a form lends itself to antiphonal singing. The present text version consists of stanza 1, the first half of 2 combined with the second half of 3, 4, 5, and 11 of the original. In stanza 1:2, "Sons of men and angels say" has been changed to "All creation joins to say." The final stanza is not included in mosthymnals.

EASTER HYMN first came out in *Lyra Davidica* with a translation of a fourteenth-century carol "Jesus Christ is risen today." The only surviving copy of this collection is in the British Museum. The anonymous tune derives its present form from John Arnold's *Compleat Psalmodist* (1741), which was gradually altered through subsequent editions.

Although the tune is called WORGAN in some hymnals, its attribution to Dr. John Worgan is unfounded since he was not born until 1724. The tune also has been used with a Christmas carol. Thomas Butts, in his *Harmonia Sacra* (London ca. 1756), called the tune CHRISTMAS DAY and set it to an earlier version of "Hark, the herald angels sing."

232
Christ upon the mountain peak

MOUNTAIN PEAK

Brian Arthur Wren (1936-), 1962
English Praise, 1975, alt.

Bradley P. Lehman (1964-), 1984
Hymnal: A Worship Book, 1992

Based on the Gospel accounts of the transfiguration, this text places us as participants in the otherworldly scene and creates an atmosphere of worship and adoration. In the church year, this hymn rounds out the season of Epiphany, the period that focuses on the occasions in the Gospels when Jesus was revealed as the Son of God.

This text has appeared in a number of hymnals with Peter Cutts's tune SHILLINGTON, designed for unison singing. But Bradley Lehman writes: "Wanting to experience the text more closely and to share it with others, I decided to write a setting which is better suited to four-part unaccompanied congregational singing." The fourth-phrase transition from D major to E-flat major creates a feeling of expansiveness that leads us to "cry aloud in wonder! Alleluia!"

105
Christ, we do all adore thee

(no tune name)

Adoramus te Christe
English version by Theodore Baker (1851-1934)
The Seven Last Words of Christ, 1899 ed.

Théodore Dubois (1837-1924)
The Seven Last Words of Christ, 1867

This beautiful, chorale-like selection is the final portion of Dubois' Lenten cantata, *The Seven Last Words of Christ*. It appears here notated as it is in the cantata, minus its many dynamic markings. Originally intended as a choral composition, this hymn also is well known and loved by Mennonite and Brethren congregations. Although most useful during the Lenten season, it can be appropriate for Communion and other services.

333
Christ, who is in the form of God

SONG 34

Based on Philippians 2:5-11
David Theodore Koyzis (1955-), 1985
Psalter Hymnal, 1989

Orlando Gibbons (1583-1625)
Wither's *Hymnes and Songs of the Church,* 1623

This is Paul's "Christ hymn" from Philippians 2:5-11, a classic statement of adoptionist theology, in which Jesus is the second Adam who did not, like the first Adam, seek equality with God. That very separation (*not* alienation) from God allowed Jesus to be exalted with God later. Paul's concise and poetic statement of the incarnation helped his Philippian readers to focus on Christ, rather than on himself, as the instrument of their salvation and the object of their praise.

This versification was first published with the tune BISHOP. Another hymn based on this scripture passage is "At the name of Jesus" (**342**).

SONG 34, also known as ANGELS' SONG, was first associated with a one-stanza version of the nativity song of the angels:

> Thus angels sung, and thus sing we;
> to God on high all glory be;
> let him on earth his peace bestow,
> and unto men his favour show.

The version used here comes from *The Mennonite Hymnal* (1969). Although the meter is irregular and no time signature is indicated, the hymn is not difficult to sing if a constant half-note pulse is maintained throughout. Further details about Gibbons' tunes and Wither's collection are found with the hymn "Open are the gifts of God" (**255**).

283
Christ who left his home in glory — CHRIST IS RISEN

Abram Bowman Kolb (1862-1925), 1896
Church and Sunday School Hymnal, 1902

Abram Bowman Kolb (1862-1925), 1896
(same source as text)

This vigorous hymn in gospel-song style is based on the Easter story. Kolb heard the music in a dream and spent the rest of the night creating the hymn. Written and composed by a Mennonite, it is considered an important heritage piece. It comes to this hymnal by way of the *Church Hymnal* (1927) and *The Mennonite Hymnal* (1969).

216
Christ, whose glory fills the skies — LUX PRIMA

Charles Wesley (1707-1788)
Hymns and Sacred Poems, 1740

Charles François Gounod (1818-1893)
The Hymnary, 1872

The first stanza of this text draws on three vibrant scriptural images: Sun of righteousness (". . . the sun of righteousness shall rise, with healing in its wings" in Malachi 4:2), Dayspring (from the Song of Zechariah in Luke 1:78-79), and Daystar (2 Pet. 1:19).

Titled by Wesley as a "morning hymn," this hymn is packed with references to light and brightness, making it appropriate also for the season of Epiphany, the time when Christians celebrate the manifestations of God that were traditionally underscored by visions of blinding light. James Montgomery regards this text as "one of C. Wesley's loveliest progeny."

The energy of LUX PRIMA (Latin for "first light") further highlights the text. Although the source of LUX PRIMA among Gounod's works is not documented, it could have been extracted or adapted from the part-songs, sacred songs, or church music that he composed. Various hymnals give 1872 as the date of the tune, not indicating whether it is the year of composition or publication. The tune name GOUNOD is sometimes used because there is also a hymn tune by John Stainer named LUX PRIMA.

494
Christian, do you hear the Lord?

William Cowper (1731-1800)
New Appendix, 1768, to Maxwell's *Collection*, 1766
Olney Hymns, 1779
Rev. in *Hymns for Today's Church*, 1982

ORIENTIS PARTIBUS

Pierre de Corbeil (d. 1221 or 1222)
Harm. by Richard Redhead (1820-1901)
Church Hymn Tunes, Ancient and Modern, 1853

The first of six stanzas of Cowper's poem originally read:

> Hark, my soul, it is the Lord;
> 'tis thy Saviour, hear his word;
> Jesus speaks, and speaks to thee:
> "Say, poor sinner, lov'st thou me?"

In addition to the different first stanza and the change from "thy" to "your" throughout, major alterations of text occur in stanzas 3 and 5 where changes of the archaisms affect the rhyme scheme. Alluding to John 21:16, this text was written during a time of serenity in Cowper's troubled life. The hymn expresses in deeply personal terms Christ's call to Peter on the shores of Galilee and to each of us. Julian notes that the hymn "rapidly attained great popularity with hymn-book compilers and is found at the present time in most of the high-class hymnals in all English-speaking countries."

ORIENTIS PARTIBUS is a thirteenth-century *conductus*, a sacred, folklike melody set to rhythmic Latin verse, usually on a sacred subject. These songs, similar in character to the secular songs of the troubadours of the period, often were sung in procession as introductions to liturgical readings and were included in liturgical drama. Corbeil's thirteenth-century manuscript, which does not show a musical meter, is in the mixolydian mode (Tone VII). The sound of this mode can be achieved by playing the melody starting on G, using the white keys only.

402
Christian, let your burning light

E. G. Coleman (1872-?), 1898
Gospel Songs and Hymns No. 1, 1899

BURNING LIGHT

E. G. Coleman (1872-?), 1898
(same source as text)

This hymn, beloved among the Brethren, has appeared in all the hymnals of the denomination in this century. The author and composer may be Virginia native Emmett G. Coleman, who authored *The Temperance Bugle* (ca. 1934) and a temperance drama "At the last it biteth like a serpent . . . " (1912).

Though Brethren were admonished against the use of hard liquor, Annual Conference was reluctant to jump on the faddish temperance bandwagon that was gathering strength when this hymn was written. Still, given the author's special interests, it may be that the inclusion of this hymn in the 1901 hymnal reflected the new attitude of the Annual Conference of 1900 toward the involvement of Brethren in the temperance movement.

Even if the hymn was sung without the political baggage in mind, it picked up on familiar Brethren themes of living out one's faith both in word and in deed. On the other hand, it also represented its era, using a contemporary style that some Brethren may have considered a bit "flashy."

57
Come and give thanks to the Giver

Jean Wiebe Janzen (1933-), 1991
Hymnal: A Worship Book, 1992

BAY HALL

Michael William Dawney (1942-), 1973
Hymns for Celebration, 1974

This text was written specifically for the tune BAY HALL at the request of this hymnal's committee. Beginning with praise for the sanctity of life and all of God's creation, the last stanza of the hymn leads naturally to a call for the preservation of this gift. The text, echoing the literary tradition of the Psalms, lifts up a contemporary concern for the earth in vibrant imagery.

BAY HALL is a contemporary melody within the capabilities of the average congregation. The lilting movement of the verses gives way to a more energetic, insistent rhythm in the refrain. A strong accent on "All" at the opening of the refrain will keep the metric movement constant. The tune is named for an area of Huddersfield, England.

20
Come and see

Based on John 1
Marilyn Houser Hamm (1951-), 1974
Sing and Rejoice, 1979

(no tune name)

Marilyn Houser Hamm (1951-), 1974
(same source as text)

This is one of a cycle of seven songs written for the Festival of the Word, a weekend event focusing on the Gospel of John, held at Goshen College (Ind.) in 1974. It reiterates Jesus' invitation to "come and see" (John 1:39). Later these words were repeated by Philip (John 1:46) and by the Samaritan woman at the well (John 4:29). Like the invitation to "come as a child," the uncomplicated music reflects in a folk-contemporary idiom the simplicity of a childlike faith. The two-part refrain uses both Latin and Greek (the ancient text of the *Kyrie*). A phonetic pronunciation of these words is: Kyrie = Kee-ree-eh; eleison = eh-leh-ee-zohn; Christe = kree-steh; Adoramus te = ah-doh-rah-moos teh.

284
Come away to the skies — EXULTATION

Anonymous
Based on a hymn by Charles Wesley (1707-1788), 1755
Hymns for Families, 1767, alt.
Southern Harmony, 1835, alt.

Southern Harmony, 1835
Harm. by The Hymnal Project, 1991

According to Julian, Charles Wesley wrote this text on October 12, 1755, for his wife's birthday. Wesley wrote three texts on this theme; they appear in sequence in *A Collection of Hymns for the Use of the Methodist Episcopal Church* (1841). They are "Come away to the skies"; "Come, let us anew, our journey pursue"; and "Come, let us ascend, my companion and friend."

The first of these is apparently the source of this text, which appears without attribution in *Southern Harmony*. That collection contains the first seven of Wesley's original eight stanzas with some alterations and additions of syllables. The present hymn consists of stanzas 1, 3, 4, and 5 of the *Southern Harmony* text with some further changes. The second stanza has undergone the greatest transformation, as may be seen in the following comparison.

Wesley, as in *A Collection of Hymns . . . , 1841:*

With singing and praise, The original grace,
By our heavenly Father bestow'd;
Our being receive From his bounty and live
To the honor and glory of God.

Southern Harmony:

Now with singing and praise, *let us spend all the days,*
By our heavenly Father bestow'd,
While his grace we receive from his bounty, and live
To the honor and glory of God.

Present version:

Now with singing and praise, Let us spend all the days,
By our *gracious Creator* bestowed,
while in grace we receive from earth's bounty we live
To the honour and glory of God.

On one level, this hymn is a lyrical, joyful birthday poem that acknowledges a baptismal union with Jesus and with the faith community.

It could also be construed as a wedding hymn. In the context of Jesus' ascension, however, the text takes on a mystical quality: God calling to glory a beloved and worthy Son. Those who sing or hear the hymn anticipate eventual participation in that event, but while on earth, rejoice in God's "bounty" (st. 3) and in the community of Christ.

EXULTATION is a hexatonic tune (A, B, C#, D, E, F#) with a gapped melodic contour that is characteristic of folk melodies. Tunes related to it are SAMARANTHA and TRUE HAPPINESS, both of which are included in George Pullen Jackson's *Down-East Spirituals*. With the exception of three pitches, SAMARANTHA is identical to ZION'S PILGRIM, set in the present hymnal to "O thou, in whose presence my soul takes delight." EXULTATION appears in *Southern Harmony*, written in four voices with the melody in the tenor. All the voice parts are quite angular and sometimes move in parallel fifths, occasionally resulting in harmony of open fifths and octaves. Another tune, also called EXULTATION, appears with stanzas 1, 2, 5, and 7 of the text in Joseph Funk's *Harmonia Sacra*.

425
Come, come, ye saints — ALL IS WELL

William Clayton (1814-1879), 1846
Alt. by Joseph Franklin Green (1924-)
Broadman Songs for Men, No. 2, 1960

American folk melody
Adapt. from J. T. White's *Sacred Harp*, 1844

William Clayton, a Mormon pioneer, wrote this hymn in 1846 on the first westward trek with Brigham Young. During the journey, Clayton received word that his wife, who had remained in Illinois, had given birth to their son. She closed her message with the phrase "All is well." Eventually, Clayton's hymn became a favorite among the Mormons and is described by William J. Reynolds as a trademark of the Mormon Tabernacle Choir.

In 1960 Joseph Green, a Southern Baptist pastor and editor, rewrote the text, altering and replacing references to Mormon beliefs. Now Christians of various generations and traditions may project their own worries and assurances of God's presence onto the text, making it their own.

An early form of the tune ALL IS WELL appeared in 6/8 meter in *Revival Melodies, or Songs of Zion* (1842), which was attributed to C. Dingley, a New York City music teacher. The *Sacred Harp* version of 1844 was in 4/4. The tune version used here is found in *The Mennonite Hymnal* (1969). The meter alternates between 3/4 and 4/4 time. See the *Accompaniment Handbook* for conducting suggestions.

The original text to this melody began "What's this that steals, that steals upon my frame! Is it death? Is it death?" and ended with "All is well" (Reynolds 1976). It was written by an unknown author to ease the grief caused by his approaching death. With Clayton's text, prompted by a baby's birth, it is now also associated with new life.

302
Come, divine Interpreter

Charles Wesley (1707-1788)
Short Hymns on Select Passages of Holy Scripture, 1762

SPANISH CHANT

Arr. by Benjamin Carr (1768-1831)
Burgoyne's *Collection,* 1827

This text is especially suitable as a prelude to reading scripture, to encourage hearers to be receptive and responsive. To keep the focus on scripture, only the first stanza appears here as a musical worship resource.

Carr's piano variations on this parlor tune were published as *Spanish Hymn Arranged and Composed for the Concerts of the Musical Fund Society of Philadelphia by Benjamin Carr, The Air from an Ancient Spanish Melody* (1826). SPANISH CHANT, also known as MADRID and SPANISH HYMN, is familiar through its use with other texts in both Brethren and Mennonite hymnals. Despite its names, there is no reliable evidence connecting the tune with Spain.

501
Come down, O Love divine

Discendi, Amor santo
Bianco da Siena (d. 1434), ca. 1367
Laudi Spirituali del Bianco da Siena, 1851
Tr. Richard Frederick Littledale 1833-1890)
Littledale's *People's Hymnal,* 1867, alt.

DOWN AMPNEY

Ralph Vaughan Williams (1872-1958)
The English Hymnal, 1906

Acts 2 describes "tongues of fire" accompanying the arrival of the Holy Spirit. With that same image, this tightly constructed hymn weaves the metaphor of fire with the Spirit's gift of love and power. Each stanza of Littledale's English translation consists of six lines punctuated in two equal groups. The unity of each stanza is aided by the rhyme scheme (lines 1-2, 4-5, 3-6). The original translation of stanza 4:5-6 was "Till he become the place wherein the Holy Spirit makes his dwelling place." The alteration used here is found in several contemporary hymnals. It wonderfully describes the humility of heart necessary to accommodate God's Spirit. It also describes a paradox, for, as Jeannette F. Scholer puts it, "We really do not know our capacity for such a love until the Holy Spirit comes in fullness to dwell within us" (*The Worshiping Church* 1990, 1991).

The original hymn text from Bianco da Siena, a medieval Italian writer, is among a collection of "spiritual songs" that may date from around 1367. This hymn and the others of the collection were written in Italian rather than Latin to aid communication with the people.

DOWN AMPNEY, named after Vaughn Williams' birthplace, was composed for Littledale's translation, which has an unusual meter. The tune's rhythmic pace and melodic contour admirably match the meter and rhyme scheme of the text. Whole notes are used here at the ends of the two longer phrases to replace fermatas in the original.

303
Come, gracious Spirit — BACA

Simon Browne (1680-1732) and others
Hymns and Spiritual Songs, 1720, alt.

William Batchelder Bradbury (1816-1868)
Bradbury's *The Jubilee: An Extensive Collection of Church Music*, 1858

The original of this text, which consisted of seven stanzas of four lines each, has been extensively altered over the years, including changing the pronouns from singular to plural to make it a corporate rather than individual supplication.

BACA originally was set to a text beginning "We all, O Lord, have gone astray, and wandered from thy heavenly way." It first appeared in Bradbury's *The Jubilee . . .* , a volume of music intended for choirs, congregations, and singing schools. It sold in excess of a quarter of a million copies and was just one of more than fifty collections compiled and edited by Bradbury.

The tune HOLLEY, known to Brethren as the setting of Paul Robinson's Communion text, "Here in our upper room" (**450**), is an excellent alternate tune for this hymn.

298
Come, Holy Spirit—see "Veni Sancte Spiritus"

445
Come, Holy Spirit, Dove divine — MARYTON

Adoniram Judson (1788-1850), ca. 1829
Winchell's *Collection*, 1832, alt.

Henry Percy Smith (1825-1898)
Church Hymns with Tunes, 1874

Written during the time Judson was translating the Bible into the Burmese language, his original hymn began "Our Savior bowed beneath the wave." This text consists of selected stanzas from that baptism hymn, recalling images from the Gospel accounts of Jesus' own baptism.

MARYTON was composed for John Keble's text "Sun of my soul" and sometimes appears with that first line as its tune name. The melody is better known as the setting for "O Master, let me walk with thee" (**357**).

12
Come, let us all unite to sing

GOD IS LOVE

Anonymous
Attrib. to Howard Kingsbury
Complete Compendium of Revival Music, 1876

Edmund Simon Lorenz (1854-1942)
Notes of Triumph: for the Sunday School, Dayton, 1886

This energetic hymn inspires the whole congregation to assert that "God is love!" The unusual, lilting soprano/alto duet in the third phrase provides a springboard for the four-part run to the refrain. The rest of the text simply supplies the impetus and rationale for the hymn's repeated truth of God's love. Though the text has been attributed to Howard Kingsbury, it is usually listed as anonymous.

Lorenz's music was published in *Notes of Triumph*, a volume he co-edited with Isaiah Baltzell (1832-1893), a minister of the United Brethren. Among the pastorates Baltzell served were Baltimore and Hagerstown in Maryland and New Holland, Mountville, Harrisburg, and Reading in Pennsylvania.

587
Come, my Way, my Truth, my Life

THE CALL

George Herbert (1593-1633)
The Temple, 1633

Ralph Vaughan Williams (1872-1958)
Five Mystical Songs, No. 4, 1911
Adapt. in *Hymnal for Colleges and Schools*, 1956

This text, titled "The Call," is one of a large group of poems designated *The Temple*. This brief piece is distinctive not only in its beautiful, mystical imagery, but also for its construction; it invokes Christ by using nine striking metaphors in groups of three: Way, Truth, and Life; Light, Feast, and Strength; Joy, Love, and Heart. The first five images were used by Jesus in reference to himself (John 14:6; 8:12; 6:35). In stanza 2:2, the phrase "such a feast as mends in length" means that the feast improves as it continues. Another unusual feature is that the poem uses all one-syllable words, the only exception being "killeth" at the end of stanza 1.

An unidentified editor adjusted this tune from the fourth of Vaughan Williams' *Five Mystical Songs*. The melody and harmony of the hymn tune are taken from verse 1 of Vaughan Williams' original setting.

The author and composer also have a coincidental connection: both Herbert's and Vaughan Williams' fathers were clergymen in the Church of England and served the same parish of Bemerton, near Salisbury, some 230 years apart.

27
Come, O Creator Spirit, come — VENI CREATOR SPIRITUS

Veni Creator Spiritus
Anonymous, 9th c.
Tr. Robert Seymour Bridges (1844-1930)
Yattendon Hymnal, 1899

Plainsong, 4th c.

The origin of this Latin hymn, like most early, medieval poems, is uncertain. Possible authors are Charlemagne, Ambrose, Gregory the Great, and the most widely accepted—Rabanus Maurus—a German theologian and scholar. The hymn, which came into use during the latter part of the ninth century, was sung accompanied by special ringing of bells along with the use of incense and lights. Since the tenth century, it has been a devotional hymn for Pentecost, used for the service held at the third hour (9 a.m.) of that day to commemorate the outpouring of the Holy Spirit. For this reason it has been used at ordinations since the eleventh century. It was first translated into English in 1549 for the *Book of Common Prayer*, with more than fifty English versions by 1904 (Julian 1907).

This prayer hymn is intensely personal and emotional. When the "Comforter" (sts. 2-3) is introduced in stanza 2, however, it is not as one who comes to soothe, but as a power called in to aid and strengthen. That is the meaning of the original Greek word for Holy Spirit (Bailey 1950). The final stanza is a customary doxology that confirms the doctrine of the Trinity. But there also is a clue to religious politics of the time; "who art of both" was certain to stir up the dander of the Eastern Church, which maintained that the Spirit proceeded from the Father alone. The Western Church held that the Spirit was part of Father and Son equally, a theological argument that contributed to the great split in the church.

VENI CREATOR SPIRITUS has been associated with this Latin text since its first known manuscript. The melody, older than the text, was used earlier with the Ambrosian Easter hymn *Hic est dies verus Dei.* A simplified version of the melody was used by Luther for his German text *Komm, Gott Schöpfer, heiliger Geist.* J. S. Bach used Luther's version for his organ chorale of the same title in his *Orgelbüchlein* (Little Organ Book). The present plainsong is sung most authentically in unison and without keyboard accompaniment. Bells would make an appropriate accompaniment, however, since that is how the text was originally sung.

503

Come, O thou Traveler unknown

VERNON

Based on Genesis 32:24-32
Charles Wesley (1707-1788)
Hymns and Sacred Poems, 1742

American folk melody
J. Ingalls' *The Christian Harmony,* 1805

This narrative poem, based on Genesis 32:24-32, is Wesley's interpretation of the story of "wrestling Jacob." The first eleven of Wesley's fourteen stanzas are included here, and the other three are found in the *Accompaniment Handbook.* Most hymnals omit some stanzas. A selection of stanzas 1, 4, 9, and 10 provides the essence of the narrative clearly and concisely.

But more than mere narrative, this hymn is a "meditation on a mystery" and is regarded as Wesley's best work (Routley 1979). That "mystery" overwhelmed John Wesley when, a few weeks after his brother Charles' death, he gave out this hymn before the sermon and broke into tears when he came to the lines "My company before is gone, and I am left alone with thee." The congregation wept with him. The 1788 Methodist Conference minutes quoted Isaac Watts's tribute as part of Charles Wesley's obituary: "[The] single poem, *Wrestling Jacob,* was worth all the verses he himself [Watts] had written."

The *Companion to the Hymnal* describes the hymn's careful structure:

> The first eight stanzas set forth with mounting pathos the anguished cry of man—not "Who am I?" but "Who art *Thou?*" The last six with glad assurance provide the full answer, each ending with the line "*Thy nature and thy name is love.*" (Gealy, Lovelace, Young 1970)

This structure, however, has been subverted through an error in early printings of *The United Methodist Hymnal* (1989), a mistake that has been inadvertently perpetuated in *Hymnal: A Worship Book.* The stanza beginning "Contented now upon my thigh" was incorrectly printed as the seventh stanza and should be printed as the thirteenth stanza (Young 1993). The error has been corrected in the fifth printing (1996) of *Hymnal: A Worship Book.*

The haunting melody of VERNON is given here as a simple melodic line with chord markings, a form appropriate to the ballad style of the text. The tune was called WISDOM in Jeremiah Ingalls' collection. It was John Wyeth who named the tune VERNON and combined it with this text in his *Repository of Sacred Music, Part Second* (1813).

41
Come, thou Almighty King

ITALIAN HYMN

Anonymous
Whitefield's *Collection of Hymns for Social Worship*, 1757

Felice de Giardini (1716-1796)
Madan's *Collection of Psalm and Hymn Tunes*, 1769

This anonymous hymn text has sometimes been attributed to Charles Wesley, since it appeared in Whitefield's collection above with Wesley's "Jesus, let thy pitying eye." The hymn is in a meter Wesley did not use, however, and it never appeared in any of the Wesley collections. The original second stanza is omitted because of its militant flavor.

The text is rich in a variety of names for God: Almighty King, Father, Ancient of Days, Incarnate Word, Spirit of holiness, Holy Comforter, Spirit of power, One-in-Three. The hymn alludes in each of the first three stanzas to the persons of the Trinity and concludes with the Trinitarian doxology. Each of those entities enables worship—the Father helps us to praise, the Incarnate Word attends prayer, and the Comforter bears witness to the worship of the people of God.

At first this text was sung to the tune AMERICA, which in England is the melody of "God save the king." When British soldiers surprised colonial worshipers during a service in the middle of the Revolutionary War and ordered them to sing "God save the king," sing they did. But they substituted other words—"Come, thou, Almighty King" (Reynolds 1990).

ITALIAN HYMN is also known by a number of other names, the most familiar of which are TRINITY and MOSCOW, the city where the Italian composer Giardini died. The tune first appeared in Madan's collection above, set in three voices. In measure thirteen the tonic note was repeated throughout the measure.[1]

1. The original form of the melody may be found in *The Hymnal 1940*.

521
Come, thou fount

NETTLETON

Robert Robinson (1735-1790), 1758
A Collection of Hymns Used by the Church of Christ in Angel-Alley (Bishopsgate), 1759

American folk melody
John Wyeth's *Repository of Sacred Music, Part Second*, 1813

Robert Robinson was dramatically converted to Christianity after hearing the preaching of George Whitefield. "Come, thou fount" was written for Pentecost Sunday three years after that event. The text freely intersperses important Old and New Testament images: water (the thirsty land of the Middle East), "flaming tongues" (hosts of heaven and the Spirit), and shepherd's fold (parables and sayings of Jesus). The reference to "Ebenezer," which means "stone of help" in Hebrew, may be the most memorable. It comes from 1 Samuel 7:12: "Hitherto hath the Lord helped us." The stone raised there commemorated a miraculous Israelite victory over the Philistines, and Robinson raised this spiritual Ebenezer to mark his own conversion and progress on the pilgrim's way. Even more, he begs for "fetters" (chains) of grace to keep him from returning to his past life.

Robinson's text has been set to various hymn tunes, including NETTLETON and THE GOOD SHEPHERD. NETTLETON has been credited to Asahel Nettleton, a famous nineteenth-century evangelist, but there is no evidence that he wrote any tunes. The tune's earliest known appearance is in John Wyeth's book above, where it was known as HALLELUJAH. Not a musician himself, Wyeth saw this volume as an entrepreneurial venture catering to Methodists and Baptists who were influenced by the folk-style music used in camp meetings so popular at that time.

178
Come, thou long-expected Jesus

Charles Wesley (1707-1788)
Hymns for the Nativity of Our Lord, 1744

HYFRYDOL

Rowland Hugh Prichard (1811-1887), ca. 1830
Cyfaill y Cantorion (*The Singer's Friend*), 1844
Arr. by Ralph Vaughan Williams (1872-1958)
The English Hymnal, 1906 Adapt. in *BBC Hymn Book,* 1951

This Advent hymn is based on Haggai 2:7: ". . . the desire of all nations shall come" (KJV). The rhyme scheme of the text is *ababcdcd.* It appears here as it was written by Wesley, except for one word change dating from the mid-eighteenth century—"release" replaced "relieve" in stanza 1:3. Its earliest source, a small book of eighteen hymns, was the first collection of so-called "festival hymns."

The hymn begins with the messianic hopes of Israel, expanding them to encompass "all the earth." Jesus' role of deliverer, however, was both paradoxical ("born a child, and yet a king") and spiritual ("rule in all our hearts alone"). The "long-expected" came as the unexpected.

HYFRYDOL, a Welsh word meaning "good cheer," is pronounced "hu-fru-dul." This long-phrased melody with a simple but interesting contour was written when Prichard was twenty years old. Its range is only five notes, except for the climax, one step higher, near the end. This tune first appeared with English words in *The English Hymnal* to "Alleluya, sing to Jesus" by W. Chatterton Dix. STUTTGART may be used as an alternate tune by dividing the text into four stanzas of four lines each.

495
Come to the water—see "O let all who thirst"

14
Come, we that love the Lord

Isaac Watts (1674-1748)
Hymns and Spiritual Songs, 1707, alt.
Refrain added by Robert Lowry

WE'RE MARCHING TO ZION

Robert Lowry (1826-1899), 1867
Doane's *Silver Spray, A New and Choice Collection of Popular Sabbath-School Music*, 1868

This hymn says nothing about "counting the cost." It never reflects on the suffering of Jesus or his followers. It spurns any meditation on sin or evil. It contains no hints of historical theological controversies. It is a hymn dedicated solely to exuberance in the promises of God and in the assurance of salvation, even while we dwell on earth ("we're marching through Immanuel's ground to fairer worlds on high"). An omitted second stanza continues the theme even more pointedly:

> The sorrow of the mind
> be banished from this place;
> religion never was designed
> to make our pleasures less.

Watts's hymn was first published in ten stanzas under the title "Heavenly Joy on Earth." Among other alterations over the years, Watts changed the last line from "To a more joyful sky" to "To fairer worlds on high." The four stanzas used here are numbers 1, 3, 9, and 10 of the original.

The story is told of a disgruntled choir that decided to express its displeasure by going on strike the next Sunday. Warned of their recalcitrance, the pastor during the service announced this hymn and blithely invited the choir to lead in the second stanza:

> Let those refuse to sing
> who never knew our God,
> but children of the heavenly king
> may speak their joys abroad. (Reynolds 1990)

WE'RE MARCHING TO ZION is one of Robert Lowry's most popular melodies, along with "I need thee every hour" and "All the way my Savior leads me." The animated tune energizes the text even further. As the tune name implies, it should be sung as a march, not a waltz or a race (Hustad 1978). Lowry himself added the words of the refrain.

The text (minus refrain) has been set to ST. THOMAS in many hymnbooks. The Brethren hymnal committee in 1951 followed suit, opting for the more classical sound of ST. THOMAS and cutting back on the preponderance of gospel and victorian styles of music in the previous hymnal. A ground swell of popular sentiment for the "old tune" has prevailed, however, and WE'RE MARCHING TO ZION has been reinstated.

497
Come, ye disconsolate

CONSOLATOR (CONSOLATION)

Sts. 1-2, Thomas Moore (1779-1852)
Sacred Songs, Duets and Trios, 1816, alt.
St. 3, Thomas Hastings (1784-1872)
Spiritual Songs for Social Worship, 1831

Samuel Webbe, Sr. (1740-1816)
A Collection of Motetts and Antiphons, London, 1792

Moore's poem is a near-passionate, lyric invitation to all "wounded hearts." The invitation is to the "mercy seat" of God—Thomas Hastings' adaptation of the original "God's altar" or "shrine of God" (1816 and 1824 versions, respectively). The notion of the mercy seat comes from Exodus 25:17-22 where it is described as the elaborate gold covering of the ark of the covenant, which represents the place of atonement. Priests entered this high holy place once a year to sprinkle blood on it as atonement for the sins of Israel. Like the rending of the temple curtain during Jesus' crucifixion, Moore's poem presents this place of forgiveness to all who seek it.

Other text alterations occurred in stanza 2:2-3:

> Hope, when all others die, fadeless and pure,
> Here speaks the Comforter, in God's name saying . . .

Moore's original third stanza, replaced by Hastings, was:

> Go, ask the infidel, what boon he brings us
> What charm for aching hearts he can reveal,
> Sweet as that heavenly promise hope sings us,
> Earth has no sorrow, that God cannot heal.

The "feast of love" in stanza 3 is the communal meal of the Lord's Supper; Moore conveys that God's mercy is also revealed in the "Bread of life," Christ's presence in the company of believers. It should also be understood that "Heaven" in the last lines of the hymn refers to God, not to a traditional place of bliss. Thus, we are assured of God's presence now, and earthly sorrow is banished.

CONSOLATOR was originally published by Webbe, a Roman Catholic organist, as a solo song setting of the text *Alma redemptoris mater*. Moore wrote his poem to this music, which he called "a German air." It is unclear whether this music is a German air arranged by Webbe or if he actually is the composer. Thomas Hastings and Lowell Mason arranged this music for solo and duet in their *Spiritual Songs for Social Worship.*

265
Come, ye faithful, raise the strain

Greek hymn
St. John of Damascus (ca. 675-ca. 749)
First Ode of Canon for the Sunday after Easter, 8th c.
Tr. John Mason Neale (1818-1866)
Leisentritt and Neale's *Christian Remembrancer,* April 1859, alt.

AVE VIRGO VIRGINUM (GAUDEAMUS PARITER)

Johann Horn (ca. 1490-1547)
Horn's *Ein Gesangbuch der Brüder im Behemen und Merherrn,* Nürnberg, 1544
Rev. in *Catholicum Hymnologium Germanicum,* 1584

This hymn text was likely written about the middle of the eighth century and is based on the "Song of Moses" from Exodus 15. St. John of Damascus projected the Christian story onto this canticle so that the first-stanza references to Old Testament characters represent Christian entities. "Israel" and "Jacob's sons and daughters" are the church, "Pharaoh's bitter yoke" means hardships and persecutions, and "Red Sea waters" is death. As God marched Israel out of bondage, so was Jesus resurrected from death (st. 2, a compelling nature allegory), and the church is promised deliverance.

Neale's translation includes only the first half of the ode and is more literal than most translations of Greek hymnody. Its first appearance illustrated an article on "Greek Hymnology" at a time when poetry of the early Greek Orthodox Church was being rediscovered by nineteenth-century translators. In stanza 4, "the twelve" was originally "thy friends."

AVE VIRGO VIRGINUM originally had the title *Gaudeamus pariter omnes,* a Latin motto for a German Advent hymn that began *Nun lasst uns zu dieser Frist* (see Zahn No. 6285). *The English Hymnal* (1906) was the first to put this tune and text together.

264

Come, ye faithful, raise the strain

ST. KEVIN

Greek hymn
St. John of Damascus (ca. 675-ca. 749)
First Ode of Canon for the Sunday after Easter, 8th c.
Tr. John Mason Neale (1818-1866)
Leisentritt and Neale's *Christian Remembrancer*, April 1859, alt.

Arthur Seymour Sullivan (1842-1900)
The Hymnary, 1872

The text version with ST. KEVIN is derived from Neale's translation (see **265**). The first stanza is made up of the first half of the original stanza 1 and the second half of stanza 3. The doxological third stanza was added in 1868.

The tune ST. KEVIN, originally unnamed, was composed for this text when it appeared in *The Hymnary*. It got a dismal critique from prominent hymnologist Erik Routley, however, who said of Sullivan's tunes that "taken as a group [they] are by far the worst, the least sincere, the most pretentious and misconceived of any written by a major victorian composer . . . . " (Routley 1981). The tune was given its name in *Sullivan's Church Hymns with Tunes* (1903). St. Kevin was an Irish hermit who lived in the Vale of Glendalough (Valley of Two Lakes); it is said he established a monastery.

94

Come, ye thankful people

ST. GEORGE'S WINDSOR

Henry Alford (1810-1871)
Psalms and Hymns, 1844, alt.

George Job Elvey (1816-1893)
E. H. Thorne's *A Selection of Psalm and Hymn Tunes*, 1858

The English Harvest Festival, for which this poem was written, occurred on different dates and between villages according to the harvest season. This text has had a long history of revisions. The present version consists of stanzas 1-3 from an 1867 edition, with stanza 4 taken from Alford's original publication. One alteration in stanza 1:4 (from "want" to "need") reflects the conviction that God may not supply all our wants, but he does give what we need.

Based on Mark 4:26-29 and Matthew 13:24-30,36-43, this hymn is often selected for harvest festivals. With its reference to the parable of the Wheat and Tares (also translated "weeds"), it is not only a hymn of thanksgiving but also of admonition. Stanzas 2 through 4 direct our attention to the culmination of history and God's judgment.

ST. GEORGE'S WINDSOR derives its name from St. George's Chapel, Windsor, the home church of England's royal family. Elvey was organist there for forty-seven years, continuing in the church tradition of organists and choirmasters dating from 1362. This tune was written for James Montgomery's hymn "Hark! the song of jubilee" and put to the present text in 1861, the combination that has endured.

176
Comfort, comfort, O my people

Tröstet, tröstet, meine Lieben
Based on Isaiah 40:1-5
Johannes Olearius (1611-1684)
Geistliche Singe-kunst, 1671
Tr. Catherine Winkworth (1827-1878)
Chorale Book for England, 1863, alt.

GENEVA 42 (FREU DICH SEHR)

Louis Bourgeois (ca. 1510-ca. 1561)
Genevan Psalter, 1551
Harm. adapt. from Claude Goudimel (ca. 1505-1572)
Les Pseaumes . . . , 1565

Based on Isaiah 40:1-5, this hymn has become a significant text for Advent. Like the prophecies of Isaiah to the disheartened exiles in Babylon, the text speaks a long-awaited word of solace to those burdened by "their sorrows' load." It does not simply abolish grief, however. Stanzas 2 and 3 demand repentance and response, just as John the Baptist did when he called the people "to prepare the way." Advent not only anticipates the Savior, it calls for proper preparation.

The second of Winkworth's four stanzas is omitted, and stanza 3:1 originally read "For Elijah's voice is crying." Comparing the hymn stanzas with the Isaiah passage will show which ideas are expanded and which have been omitted. Olearius's hymnal, in which this hymn first appeared, was one of the most important German collections of the seventeenth century. Johannes Olearius was a preacher and church administrator in north Germany and is not to be confused with Johann Gottfried Olearius (1635-1711) who lived for some years in Halle and wrote hymn texts.

Louis Bourgeois was responsible for composing or arranging GENEVA 42. It was borrowed by the Germans for a number of texts, the first of which was *Freu dich sehr, O meine Seele* (1620). Thus, some hymnals refer to it as FREU DICH SEHR. It was also used in a "smoothed out" 2/4 meter by German Mennonite congregations for a variety of hymn texts. The *Gesangbuch der Mennonitengemeinschaft Nordamerikas* (1942) lists nine texts for the tune. J. S. Bach used this memorable tune in Cantata Nos. 13, 19, 25, 30, 32, 39, 70, and 194. Along with the welcoming words, the lightness and strength of the music lift the singer's spirit.

"As the hart with eager yearning" (**500**) is also set to this tune.

437

Count well the cost

Überschlag die Kost
Alexander Mack, Sr. (bapt.1679-1735)
Geistreiches Gesang-Buch vor alle Liebhabende Seelen der Warheit, 1720
Tr. Ora W. Garber (1903-1981)
European Origins of the Brethren, 1958, alt.

MACH'S MIT MIR

Johann Hermann Schein (1586-1630)
Published separately, 1628
(Zahn No. 2383)

It has been said (though not documented) that the first Brethren to be baptized prayed, then rose from their knees and sang "Count well the cost" before they proceeded to the Eder River. Because adult baptism was an act of treason, their leader Alexander Mack wanted to make the first Brethren fully aware of the risks involved, risks he lifts up in the first stanza of this hymn. It was through this hymn, mentioned in the *Chronicon Ephratense* (chronicle of the Ephrata Community), that the 1720 *Geistreiches Gesang-Buch* was positively identified as being of Brethren origin (H. Durnbaugh 1986). A close prose translation of the text appears in Hedwig Durnbaugh's study *The German Hymnody of the Brethren.* Ora Garber's metric translation of all thirteen stanzas appeared in 1958, while the cento (portion of the whole poem) used here is composed of stanzas 1, 2, 4, and 5. Those stanzas create a hymn that charges the new believer with explicit baptismal commitment, then hearkens back to the roots of Christian growth from childhood (st. 3), and forward into the communion of Christian fellowship (st. 4).

The opening phrase of Garber's translation has been reversed so that Jesus' potent words are emphasized. Among other minor alterations, several changes have been made in the third stanza, which may be compared with the original translation:

> Within the church's warm embrace
> the child of God is molded,
> God's Spirit lighting up his face
> and by his grace enfolded.
> His childlike steps trace out Christ's plan
> and he becomes a godly man.

MACH'S MIT MIR bears some resemblance to an earlier melody in Gesius's *Geistliche Deutsche Lieder*, published in Frankfurt (1607). As with many chorale tunes, it originally appeared with a varied rhythmic pattern characteristic of late Renaissance music. European Mennonites have used this popular chorale tune with a wide variety of texts for more than two hundred years. The tune, also called EISENACH and SCHEIN, is best known for its association with Johann Scheffler's *Mir nach, spricht Christus unser Held.* The 1720 Brethren collection listed above associated the tune with that text as well as with *Überschlag die Kost* (Count well the cost). The melody was used by J. S. Bach in two cantatas and his *Passion According to St. John.*

128
Create in me a clean heart — TONUS REGIUS

Psalm 51:10-12 (KJV)

The Common Service Book and Hymnal, 1917

These words of the psalmist David are a time-honored confessional prayer. This is one of two settings of the text used as the offertory in *The Common Service Book,* published by the United Lutheran Church in America in 1917.

In the tune name TONUS REGIUS, *tonus* means "tone." It refers to the practice, both in Gregorian chant and in psalmody, of reciting scripture and other liturgical texts on a particular tone related to one of the medieval modes. TONUS REGIUS would be translated "kingly" or "regal" tone.

3
Create my soul anew — MT. EPHRAIM

Isaac Watts (1674-1748)
Horae Lyricae, 1706

Benjamin Milgrove (1731-1810)
Sixteen Hymns as they are sung at the Right Honourable the Countess of Huntingdon's Chappell in Bath, 1769

This sensual text fairly sizzles with vibrant phrases and parts of speech: "wretched," "celestial Fire," "seize," "wrap me in flames of pure desire," "sweet perfumes of praise." Penned by an imaginative poet, they reflect his conviction that since our hymns are a "human offering of praise to God, . . . *plain* the words ought to be our own" (Bailey 1950). What a contrast to the Calvinist tenet of the day that held that the only suitable hymnody came directly from the Psalms. Still, the Psalms themselves can sometimes be an earthy read!

This hymn is a cento (portion of the whole poem) of three stanzas from Watts's text "Sincere Praise," which begins "Almighty Maker, God!" From this text of eleven stanzas, four lines each, come a number of centos differing in length and arrangement. This portion consists of the final three stanzas of No. 33 in the early American Collection of Psalms and Hymns (1737), also known as the *Charles-town* (Charleston) *Hymnal* from its place of publication.

MT. EPHRAIM is an expansive melody. It was used with the words:

O Patient, spotless Lamb,
my heart in Patience keep,

to bear the Cross so easy made,
by wounding Thee so deep.

The half note was the unit of beat in the original two-voice (melody and bass) setting. This melody could be used effectively as a vocal solo.

168
Creating God, your fingers trace — CHRISTOPHER DOCK

Jeffery William Rowthorn (1934-), 1974
The Hymn, 1979

Philip K. Clemens (1941-), 1982
Assembly Songs, 1983

As part of a workshop in contemporary worship at Yale Divinity School, New Haven, Connecticut, Rowthorn assigned his class psalms to paraphrase. Keeping pace with the class, he wrote his own paraphrase of Psalm 148 with the tune TRURO in mind. Later, unknown to him, the text was submitted to the Hymn Society of America's contest for "New Psalms for Today." Its first hymnal inclusion was in *Laudamus* (Yale Divinity School 1980), with the tune DE TAR.

Moving beyond the psalm's focus on the creative genius of God, the hymn also describes the sustaining, redeeming, and indwelling nature of God. Rowthorn's use of these "-ing" words conveys God's continuous action in all ways and through all time.

In Philip Clemens' setting, the text is expanded in a refrain that reiterates these four concepts. The composer writes, "The four-part setting is patterned after the style of gospel songs, including imitative, independent lines. The harmony purposely differs from that of familiar gospel songs, because I wanted to see if the gospel song style could transcend its time period." The tune name honors Christopher Dock, the eighteenth-century Pennsylvania schoolmaster, and Christopher Dock Mennonite High School, Lansdale, Pennsylvania, the composer's alma mater.

325
Creating God, your fingers trace — DEUS TUORUM MILITUM

Jeffery Rowthorn (1934-), 1974
The Hymn, 1979

French church melody
Grenoble Antiphoner, 1753

DEUS TUORUM MILITUM, with its wide intervals and range of melody, matches the expansive character of the text (see **168** above) while providing a more traditional musical setting. DEUS TUORUM MILITUM is designated a French church melody, one of a group of anonymous melodies developed in the sixteenth and seventeenth centuries in France. Their origins are unknown, but some were adapted from Gregorian chant and some from secular tunes. These melodies were a transition from Gregorian chant to metric tunes with bar lines, moving from the speech rhythm and ecclesiastical modes of the former to the measured rhythms and major or minor keys of the latter. Their meters were usually Sapphic (11.11.11.5) or long meter (8.8.8.8) in triple time. This melody was introduced to twentieth-century hymnody by Ralph Vaughan Williams in *The English Hymnal* (1906).

177
Creator of the stars of night — CONDITOR ALME SIDERUM

Conditor alme siderum
Anonymous, manuscript, 9th c., Bern (6 sts.)
Tr. *The Hymnal 1940*, alt.

Sarum plainsong, Mode IV

This hymn was originally intended to be sung at the monastic devotional service of Vespers (sunset) during the season of Advent. After its first appearance in a ninth-century manuscript, it was found in the tenth-century *Canterbury Hymnal*. This translation is an altered form of the version in *The Hymnal 1940*, which, in turn, was "after J. M. Neale."

This is the first text to include the Trinitarian form of praise known as the doxology (st. 6). Thomas Ken's seventeenth-century "Praise God from whom all blessings flow" is probably the most familiar to us. The early Hebrew doxologies contained two basic elements: a proclamation of praise to God, combined with an assertion of God's infinity in time. As Christianity evolved, the Son and the Holy Spirit were introduced into this form to combat certain theological doctrines considered by some to be anti-orthodox (*The Hymnal 1940 Companion*, 1951 ed.).

CONDITOR ALME SIDERUM, a traditional plainsong melody always coupled with this text, has a melodic contour that achieves "a touch of eloquence" (Routley 1981). Mode IV, called hypophrygian, is one of the eight church modes and can be played on the piano's white keys from B to B.

Plainsong melodies are part of an extensive body of Latin liturgical chant belonging to the Roman Catholic tradition. They may date as early as the fifth and sixth centuries. Plainsongs are unharmonized vocal melodies without meters or bar lines and should be sung in natural speech rhythm. Sarum plainsongs developed in England at the Cathedral of Salisbury between the thirteenth and sixteenth centuries and were adopted throughout much of the British Isles, exerting their influence elsewhere.[1]

1. Sarum is, "strictly speaking, an inaccurate rendering of the abbreviation used by medieval scribes when they wished to write the name of the place called Salisbury . . . . Sarum has been used in writing and probably in speech for seven hundred and fifty years,

to describe the town, the diocese, and the area of Salisbury" (Edward Rutherford, *Sarum, the Novel of England*, Ivy Books, 1987).

116
Crown him with many crowns — DIADEMATA

Matthew Bridges (1800-1894)
Sts. 1,3-5, *Hymns of the Heart*, 2nd. ed., 1851
Godfrey Thring (1823-1903)
St. 2, *Hymns and Sacred Lyrics*, 1874

George Job Elvey (1816-1893)
Hymns Ancient and Modern, Appendix, 1868

This hymn is an elaboration of Revelation 19:12: ". . . and on his head are many diadems" (NRSV). Bridges, and other authors following his poetic pattern, specified in various ways what these crowns represent. Other interpretations include "Crown him the Virgin's Son," "Crown him the Lord of heaven" (Bridges), "Crown him with crowns of gold" (Thring), and "Crown him upon the throne" (Dearmer). Many hymnals use a combination final stanza, consisting of 5a and 6b of Bridges' text. Percy Dearmer's (1867-1936) crowns, especially, represent some of the same attributes given by the other authors, but emphasize "the social reasons rather than the theological reasons why Christ should be crowned" (Bailey 1950).

DIADEMATA, the Greek word for "crowns," was composed for this text by Elvey expressly for the source listed above. This vigorous melody is supported by an expansive bass line that exceeds the range of an octave.

569
Day by day, dear Lord — (no tune name)

St. Richard of Chichester (1197-1253), 13th c.

Harold W. Friedell (1905-1958)
Eight Orisons, 1960

The text of this prayer was printed on a card published by Skeffington & Sons, Ltd., which was dated as received by the British Museum on March 18, 1915. The verse is described as being at least in part by St. Richard, bishop of Chichester from 1245 to 1253. The text has appeared as a hymn in numerous collections. These words could be a conversion description: First we "see" or understand God; we respond by loving; and so loving, we are compelled to follow. Prayed on a daily basis, these brief lines take on immense power. Imagine opening up the heart to conversion and commitment "day by day."

The musical setting presented in this hymnal comes from a set of orisons, or prayers, as used in St. Bartholomew's Church, New York City. These were published by H. W. Gray, Inc., after the composer's death. The arching phrases and parallel vocal lines underscore the three petitions of the prayer. Contemporary songwriter Stephen Schwartz also wrote a folk-rock setting for this text for the popular 1970s musical *Godspell*.

523

Dear Lord and Father of mankind — REST (WHITTIER)

John Greenleaf Whittier (1807-1892)
From "The Brewing of Soma," *The Atlantic Monthly*, 1872

Frederick Charles Maker (1844-1927)
Congregational Church Hymnal, London, 1887

Whittier's seventeen-stanza poem is essentially a prayer for the true worship of God and is a protest against pagan worship both outside of and within Christendom. His poem begins by describing a rite of the priests of Indra (the chief god of early Hinduism) during which "soma," an intoxicating beverage brewed from honey and milk, was drunk. Worshipers believed a joyous new life would come from this "high" of frenzied ecstasy:

> The fagots blazed, the caldron's smoke
> up through the green wood curled;
> "Bring honey from the hollow oak,
> bring milky sap," the brewers spoke,
> in the childhood of the world.

A later stanza parallels the early Hindu rite with the hysterical worship of Christian revivalist camp meetings:

> And yet the past comes round again,
> and new doth old fulfill;
> in sensual transports wild as vain
> we brew in many a Christian fane [temple or church]
> the heathen Soma still!

The final six stanzas of this poem comprise the hymn that expresses Whittier's idea of true worship, reflecting his Quaker beliefs. The words of quiet, calm, and rest are in sharp contrast to the wild religious orgies described at the beginning of the poem. "Reclothe" in the first stanza comes from the story of the Gerasene man from whom Jesus cast out a "legion" of unclean spirits.

This portion of the poem, which Whittier never intended as a hymn, first appeared in Harder's *Worship Song* (1884). Most current hymnals omit stanza 15. Although the opening phrase of this text is replete with masculine images, it has been retained because of its familiarity and ecumenical usage. The alternative, "Dear Lord, thou life of humankind," is provided as well.

REST, named for the emphasis of Whittier's words, was composed for this text to appear in Barrett and Hopkins' hymnal cited above.

346
Dona nobis pacem

Grant us peace

DONA NOBIS PACEM

Anonymous

The beauty of the harmonies created by this three-voice canon (round) reflects the peaceful mood of which the text speaks. Because of the simplicity of the text, congregations should have no difficulty with the Latin words, which are pronounced "Do-nah no-beess pah-tchem."

294
Dona nobis pacem Domine

Lord, grant us peace

(no tune name)

Jacques Berthier (1923-) and the Taizé community
Music from Taizé, Vol. II, 1982, 1983, 1984

While the Latin words for this congregational ostinato (a repetitive line of music) are a plea for peace, the verses provide scriptural assurances of God's peace. These verses, which are sung by a solo voice, are found in the *Accompaniment Handbook*. The Latin text is pronounced "Do-nah no-beess pah-tchem Do-mee-neh." For more discussion of Taizé, see "Alleluia" (**101**).

645
Each morning brings us

All Morgen ist ganz frisch und neu
Johannes Zwick (ca. 1496-1542), ca. 1536
Nüw Gesangbüchle, 3rd ed., 1545
Tr. Margaret Barclay (1932-), 1951
Cantate Domino, 1951

ALL MORGEN IST GANZ FRISCH

Wittenbergisch Gesangbüchli, 1537
Adapt. by Johann Walther (1496-1570)

Johannes Zwick, a leader of the Swiss Reformation, has been ranked "next to Blaurer as the most important of the early hymn writers of the Reformed Church" (Herzog's *Real-Encyclopädie*). This hymn first appeared in the 1545 (3rd) edition of the *Nüw Gesangbüchle,* which was the hymnal of the Reformed Church in Constanz, Zwick's birthplace.

The freshness and immediacy of Margaret Barclay's translation make one forget the age of the original. It is one of several she translated for *Cantate Domino,* the hymnal of the World Student Christian Federation.

The melody ALL MORGEN IST GANZ FRISCH was used with the text *Vom Himmel hoch* when it first appeared in the *Wittenbergische Gesangbüchli*. The open quality of the two-part setting used here complements the joyful anticipation in the text and provides a chance for congregations to experience musical textures other than traditional four-part harmonizations.

47

Earth and all stars

EARTH AND ALL STARS

Herbert Brokering (1926-), 1964
Twelve Folksongs and Spirituals, 1968, alt.

Jan Oskar Bender (1909-)
Contemporary Worship—1, 1969

This hymn of praise, which includes so many facets of life, was written for the ninetieth anniversary of St. Olaf College, Northfield, Minnesota. Imitating the psalmist's attention to descriptive detail, not only is all creation invited to "sing a new song," but participants are called to the concert by name. It is not a refined, quiet celebration. All those "loud" soundings make for a downright raucous praise chorus!

Two alterations to stanza 4 of Brokering's text are found in many current hymnals: the use of "engines" in place of "machines" and "workers" for "workmen." Two other changes have been made here. In stanza 1, "loud shouting army" was altered to "loud hosts of heaven" to avoid any confusion with the military entity. In the final stanza, "praising members" was changed to "praying members." Stanza 5 of the original 6, which included "classrooms and labs . . . athlete and band," has been omitted.

This hymn text first appeared with David N. Johnson's DEXTER, also called EARTH AND ALL STARS. The present melody by the Dutch composer Jan Bender was composed for Brokering's text when he was a member of the Lutheran hymnbook committee. A little later Bender was asked to write an accompaniment for Johnson's melody. Both settings were published in *Contemporary Worship—1*. Bender's melody complements the exuberance of the text and still contains words sufficient to maintain order.

471

Eat this bread

(no tune name)

Based on John 6:35 ff.
Paraphrased by Robert J. Batastini and the Taizé community, 1983

Jacques Berthier (1923-), 1983
Music from Taizé, Vol. II, 1982, 1983, 1984

One morning in 1983, during a week spent with Brother Robert, a musician at Taizé, and Jacques Berthier, Taizé composer, Batastini adapted this scripture passage. Berthier composed the music that same afternoon. The selection was designed so it could be memorized easily and sung while communicants came forward to partake of the elements of Communion. Solo stanzas and instrumental parts are found in the *Accompaniment Handbook*. Batastini is president of G. I. A. Publications,

Inc., the company primarily responsible for disseminating music of Taizé in North America. For more discussion of Taizé, see "Alleluia" (**101**).

78
Ehane he'ama
(no tune name)

Father God, you are holy
Harvey Whiteshield (ca. 1860-1941)
Tr. David Graber (1942-) and others
*Tsese-Ma'heone-Nemeotȯtse,*1982

Plains Indian melody

The text was inspired by the scripture "I am the Alpha and the Omega, the First and the Last," found in Isaiah 41:4 and Revelation 22:13. For many years Whiteshield used this hymn to introduce worship services he led. The repetitions of each of the three lines and the sensitive unity of small melodic details blend beautifully with the words of the prayer to an all-powerful yet deeply caring and merciful God. Note also the overall descent of the melody: When the words refer to God, the notes are higher, and when they refer to people or earth, they are lower. Since this is a sacred song, no drum would be used.

The melodic formulas in Plains Indian music differ from those in the European tradition. The non-Western sounding interval from "are" to "holy" near the beginning of the song may be missed. Lining out the song is an effective way to teach this hymn. The inflection or bending of notes is notated by a short diagonal line, as found at the word "Jesus." "HE-E" is a non-translatable exclamation that simply punctuates the words just sung. For further notes on the music of Native Americans, see the *Accompaniment Handbook*.

Traditionally, Cheyenne poets and musicians did not "own" their creations; rather, they considered their songs to be gifts from God. So the Cheyenne elders who sang and recorded their hymns were happy to have their songs put into print because they knew the tradition was being lost. The feeling existed, however, that printed words were not to be trusted because of the many broken treaties. For that reason, according to Dietrich Rempel, Faith and Life Press will not give anyone permission to reprint unless they contact the Mennonite Indian Leaders' Council, even though Faith and Life administers the copyright.

537
En medio de la vida
(no tune name)

You are the God within life
Mortimer Arias (1924-)
Celebremos, Segundo Parte, 1983
Tr. George Frank Lockwood IV (1946-)

Antonio Auza
(same source as text)
Arr. by Homero Perera

The author, who is from Uruguay, wrote this song for the opening of the new Methodist church offices in La Paz, Bolivia. The words of the text, originally in three stanzas, show that God is at work in the midst of urban life, as well as in the beauty of the rural areas.

The composer, a Methodist layman and music teacher in Sucre, Bolivia, was a friend of the author. The rhythm of the music is that of the Bolivian *cueca*, a dance of the Incas (today's Aymara and Quechua Indians) of the Andes. The rhythmic and melodic repetitions unify the melody while the ascending line of the refrain provides a contrasting and uplifting conclusion to the song. The music was arranged by Homero Perera, a prominent Argentine composer and professor of sacred music at the Instituto Superior de Educación Teológica, an ecumenical seminary in Buenos Aires.

518
Eternal light, shine in my heart — JACOB

Christopher Martin Idle (1938-), 1977
Published as an anthem
Hymns for Today's Church, 1982

Jane Manton Marshall (1924-)
The Hymnal 1982, 1985

This hymn text is based on a prayer by Alcuin (ca. 735-804), a medieval monk and scholar. An English translation of the prayer was included in *Daily Prayer* (Oxford, 1941, and Middlesex, England, 1959), which Idle used in leading worship. Moved by the prayer, Idle wrote this text at Limehouse Rectory, East London, with the tune HERONGATE in mind. Using a variety of names, the text petitions God to oversee the seeker's lifelong preparation for the ultimate meeting with the Divine. In the third stanza, "costly grace" is a phrase Dietrich Bonhöffer uses in the first chapter of *The Cost of Discipleship*. In contrast to "cheap grace," costly grace calls us to follow the sometimes difficult path of Christ, the way of discipleship (*The Hymnal 1982 Companion*).

This text was set to music by Jane Marshall for the confirmation of Sarah Jacob, hence the tune name. Although originally designed as an anthem, the rhythmic similarity of the phrases and the primarily stepwise movement of the melody make the tune quite usable for congregations.

117
Fairest Lord Jesus

Schönster Herr Jesu!
Sts. 1,3, *Gesangbuch,* Münster, 1677
St. 2, Heinrich August Hoffman von Fallersleben (1798-1874)
Schlesische Volkslieder, 1842
St. 4, anonymous
Sts. 1-3, tr. anonymous in R. S. Willis's *Church Chorals and Choir Studies,* New York, 1850, alt.
St. 4, tr. Joseph A. Seiss (1823-1904)
Sunday School Book for the Use of Evangelical Lutheran Congregations, 1873

CRUSADERS' HYMN

Schlesische Volkslieder, Leipzig, 1842
Harm. by Richard Storrs Willis (1819-1900)
Church Chorals and Choir Studies, New York, 1850

This hymn's complex and confusing history has resulted in some mythology about both text and tune. The original German text underwent considerable alterations by Fallersleben. Willis indicated he did not know the name of the translator when he included the English translation in his collection. The additional fourth stanza comes from a translation by Joseph A. Seiss, a Lutheran pastor in Philadelphia, Pennsylvania, where it was first published.

However scant, the histories of the text and tune are closely associated. CRUSADERS' HYMN is a folk song collected by Fallersleben on a visit to the region of Silesia (one hundred miles northeast of Prague). In the 1842 volume listed above, it appears as a melody harmonized in parallel thirds, in a style similar to SILENT NIGHT and SICILIAN MARINERS. Willis published it in traditional four-part harmony.

The tune name has fueled the unfounded tradition that this hymn dates back to the Crusades. An alternate tune name, ST. ELIZABETH, is better substantiated; it comes from Franz Liszt's use of this melody in his *Legend of St. Elizabeth,* an oratorio about the mother of John the Baptist. The tune is also known as ASCALON. Matching the uncomplicated words with a well-known folk tune has made for an enduringly popular hymn.

413
Faith of the martyrs

Frederick William Faber (1814-1863)
Jesus and Mary, 1849, alt.

ST. CATHERINE

Henri Frederic Hemy (1818-1888)
Crown of Jesus Music, 1864
Adapt. by James George Walton (1821-1905)
Plainsong Music for the Holy Communion Office, 1874

Soon after Faber converted to Roman Catholicism, he wrote this hymn to call the Church of England back to Catholicism. That Faber could be so bold is owed to new political freedoms for Catholics in mid-nineteenth-century England. The faithful martyrs in stanza 2 call to mind those who stayed true to the Roman Church during Protestant domination. Faber's religious and political agenda is evident in the two separate versions he wrote, one for the recalcitrant England:

> Faith of our Fathers! Mary's prayers
> Shall win our country back to thee;
> And through the truth that comes from God
> England shall then indeed be free.

and one for Catholic Ireland:

> (second half of st. 1): Oh! Ireland's hearts beat high with joy
> Whene'er they hear that glorious word.

However partisan its beginnings, this hymn has taken on new meanings about faith commitment that transcend nationality, sect, and gender. It also picks up themes from Hebrews 11. The current text consists of stanzas 1, 2, and 4 of the hymn edited from the English version.

With its references to persecution, this hymn has also become a historical watchword for Anabaptists, who suffered at the hands of Catholics and Protestants alike. To commemorate sufferings and commitment of both male and female believers, the word "martyrs" is used here. The illustration of the lamb in the midst of briars, found on the cover of this book and its hymnal, is a traditional Anabaptist symbol. Often associated with the martyrs, this symbol represents "the suffering lamb of God, who calls the faithful to obedient service." "Faith of our fathers" (the original wording) and "Faith of our mothers" are offered as options at the bottom of the hymn page.

ST. CATHERINE (PRINCE, TYNEMOUTH, ST. FINBAR) was originally composed for the Roman Catholic hymn "Sweet Saint Catherine, maid most pure." Walton's adaptation consists of the first sixteen measures of the original ten-line tune, plus his own addition of an eight-measure refrain. See also "God of the earth, the sky, the sea" (**53**).

139
Far, far away from my loving father

Anonymous
Philip P. Bliss's *Gospel Songs*, 1874

RESTORATION (I WILL ARISE)

American folk melody
W. Walker's *Southern Harmony*, 1835, alt.

This anonymous text reiterates the Luke 15:11-32 narrative from the perspective of the prodigal son. Notice how the use of alliteration in the words "wand'ring, wayward, wild" strengthens the pathos in stanza 1.

The "I will arise" refrain may be sung following the last stanza, all stanzas, or selected ones.

RESTORATION is a typical Southern folk tune, with elements of both major and minor modes. George Pullen Jackson, in his *Spiritual Folk-Songs of Early America*, points out several other tunes with similar musical phrases, including HUMBLE PENITENT and NEW ORLEANS. The influence of earlier secular melodies of the British Isles is reflected in the tune as well. The melody was first printed in *Southern Harmony* where it was the setting for John Newton's "Mercy, O Thou Son of David," which had no refrain.

Compare what two different folk traditions—American and Japanese—do to the same story by looking at "Ah, what shame I have to bear" (**531**).

78
Father God, you are holy—see "Ehane he'ama"

529
Father, I stretch my hands to thee

MARTYRDOM

Charles Wesley (1707-1788)
Psalms and Hymns, 1741

Hugh Wilson (1766-1824)
Lined by Judge Jefferson Cleveland (1937-1986) and Verolga Nix-Allen (1933-), 1979
Songs of Zion, 1981

Although some doubt has surrounded its authorship, this hymn is most likely by Charles Wesley. Originally in six stanzas, it was titled "A Prayer for Faith." This shortened version uses stanzas 1, 2, 5, and 4, in that order. The hymn text is included in earlier Mennonite and Brethren hymnals with a number of different tunes: AZMON, NAOMI, WEST MILTON, and MORNING SONG. The only text variation is in the last two words of stanza 2 where earlier Brethren hymnals used "second death" (1901) and "sin and death" (1951).

This hymn is representative of those that were lined out and sung by African American churches for much of the nineteenth century. Sung unaccompanied, they were passed from one generation to the next in this oral tradition. The notation here shows the vocal nuances of this style of singing. When it is sung slowly and with great feeling, it is scarcely recognizable as the same melody used in its metered form with "Alas! and did my Savior bleed?" (**253**). Just as the meter and phrasing are freely interpreted, so should it be freely harmonized.

650
Father, we praise thee

Nocte surgentes vigilemus omnes
6th c. or later
Attrib. to Gregory the Great (ca. 540-604)
Tr. Percy Dearmer (1867-1936)
The English Hymnal, 1906

CHRISTE SANCTORUM

French church melody
Paris Antiphoner, 1681

This is one of a number of Latin devotional hymns to come out of the Western monasteries beginning about the fourth century. Called "office hymns," they were each appropriate to a particular devotional time of day or night. This hymn of uncertain origin (Alcuin, ca. 735-804, is also a possible author) has survived in various eleventh-century manuscripts and in the Roman, Sarum, York, and Aberdeen breviaries, among others. It was used at predawn services as reflected by the initial words of the text *Nocte surgentes* (Rising by night). The night was not yet over, as the translation suggests!

This hymn is in Sapphic meter (11 11 11 5), named for Sappho, the Greek poetess of the seventh century. Because Carolingian Renaissance poets were using such meters in the ninth and tenth centuries, there is some supposition that this hymn might have originated around that time. Approximately twenty English translations have been made of this text, but the one most widely used is here. In a delightful poetic twist, "joy" in the last line of stanza 2 is used as a verb!

CHRISTE SANCTORUM is one of a number of anonymous French church melodies that developed during the sixteenth and seventeenth centuries in France. For further information on their origins and characteristics, see DEUS TUORUM MILITUM with "Creating God, your fingers trace" (**168**). CHRISTE SANCTORUM, in its earliest source cited above, was set to the hymn *Ceteri numquam nisi vagiendo*. This tune's most commonly used version comes from la Feillée's *Nouvelle Méthode du plain-chant*, 5th ed. (Paris 1782).

289
Filled with the Spirit's power

John Raphael Peacey (1896-1971), 1967
100 Hymns for Today, 1969

BIRMINGHAM (CUNNINGHAM)

Joseph Funk's *Genuine Church Music*, 1st ed., 1832

A saying on an old poster goes: "If you were arrested for being a Christian, would there be enough evidence to convict you?" This hymn text invokes the Holy Spirit, its unity and power, to just that end—"till we are known as Christ's and Christians prove" (st. 3).

J. R. Peacey, who was for many years a missionary in India, wrote these words after his retirement. They were first published in the collection listed above, which was a supplement to *Hymns Ancient and Modern*.

BIRMINGHAM is also known as CUNNINGHAM and BREWER. Birmingham is a large industrial city in England. The melody derived the name CUNNINGHAM from its appearance in Francis Cunningham's collection *A Selection of Psalm Tunes* (1834) where it was set to "Come, gracious Spirit, heavenly Dove." The tune is known as BREWER in several American collections, but neither the reason for that nor the name of the composer is known.

129
Fire of God, undying Flame

NUN KOMM, DER HEIDEN HEILAND

Albert Frederick Bayly (1901-1984), 1947
Rejoice, O God, 1950

9th c. melody
Geystliche Gesangk Buchleyn, 1524
Harm. by Melchior Vulpius (ca. 1560-1615)

This hymn was written in 1947 when Bayly was pastor of the Congregational church in Burnley, Lancashire, England. Each of the five stanzas begins with a different name for the Holy Spirit, while the second half of the stanza invites that aspect of the Spirit's dynamic power to work in our lives. This hymn is appropriate for any theme on the Holy Spirit, as well as supplicating the reconciling, rejuvenating Spirit when one is in the midst of trouble. Note that the word "bound" in the last stanza is "boundary," shortened to accommodate the rhyme scheme.

For comments on NUN KOMM, DER HEIDEN HEILAND, see "Savior of the nations, come" (**173**).

186
Fling wide the door, unbar the gate

MACHT HOCH DIE TÜR

Macht hoch die Tür, die Tor' macht weit
Georg Weissel (1590-1635)
Preussische Fest-Lieder, 1642
Tr. Gracia Grindal (1943-)
Lutheran Book of Worship, 1978

Freylinghausen's *Neues Geistreiches Gesangbuch*, 1704
(Zahn No. 5846)

This German hymn, written for the first Sunday in Advent, was not published until seven years after the author's death. Numerous hymnals use the 1855 translation by Catherine Winkworth, "Lift up your heads, ye mighty gates," sometimes set to the tune TRURO. Grindal's translation consists of stanzas 1, 2, 3, and 5 of the original five stanzas. It begins by alluding to Psalm 24, which suggests a literal interpretation for unbarring the great gates to Jerusalem. Subsequent stanzas, however, lead us inward; the King of Glory comes not only to bring salvation to the earth, but to enter every heart.

MACHT HOCH DIE TÜR is one of several tunes to which this text is set. The melody, spanning a range of only six notes, is sometimes attributed to Freylinghausen. With its lilting 6/8 rhythm, this tune is reminiscent of IN DULCI JUBILO ("Good Christian friends, rejoice," **210**). The late German hymnologist Wilhelm Nelle calls this "a festive hymn with compelling power. No other Advent hymn has attained such liturgical effectiveness" (Nelle 1918).

636

For all the saints — SINE NOMINE

William Walsham How (1823-1897)
Hymns for Saints' Days, and Other Hymns, 1864, alt.

Ralph Vaughan Williams (1872-1958)
The English Hymnal, 1906

With its majestic, driving tune, this has been considered one of the great hymns of the church. It recalls Hebrews 11 and the "cloud of witnesses" whose lives inspire us to commitment and emulation. The deleted stanzas of the original eleven laud three other groups of saints:

> 3. For the Apostles' glorious company
> Who, bearing forth the cross o'er land and sea,
> Shook all the mighty world, we sing to thee. Alleluia.
>
> 4. For the Evangelists, by whose blest word,
> Like fourfold streams, the garden of the Lord
> Is fair and fruitful, be thy name adored. Alleluia.
>
> 5. For Martyrs, who, with rapture-kindled eye,
> Saw the bright crown descending from the sky,
> And died to grasp it, thee we glorify. Alleluia.

Some of the metaphorical militancy of the original has been decreased by replacing certain words as follows: in stanza 3, "soldiers" ("people"), "victor's crown" ("glorious crown"); in stanza 5, "warfare" ("suffering"); and in stanza 6, "warriors" ("servants"). These changes also help expand our vision of Christian courage and faithfulness.

SINE NOMINE is unique in that the composer wrote two harmonizations, the first for unison singing and the second for four parts. Vaughan Williams must have had his tongue in his cheek when he assigned the name SINE NOMINE to his tune, for it means "without a name." *Sine nomine* was a designation assigned to masses in the fifteenth and sixteenth centuries if they had no identifying characteristics, or to a source, such as a secular melody, if the composer did not wish to reveal it (Grout 1980).

416

For Christ and the church

FOR CHRIST AND THE CHURCH

Eliza Edmunds Hewitt (1851-1920)
Living Hymns, 1890

William James Kirkpatrick (1838-1921)
(same source as text)

This hymn has had a longstanding place in the Brethren hymnals of 1901, 1925, and 1951. "For Christ and the church" makes it clear that Christianity is not just a Sunday proposition. All our heart, soul, mind, and strength are to be focused on Christ and making the church a visible sign of his life in the world.

William J. Kirkpatrick edited or co-edited approximately fifty songbooks between 1880 and 1897. Along with J. R. Sweney, he was one of the first to publish Eliza Hewitt's work. The collection in which this hymn first appeared was edited by Sweney and J. Wanamaker and published in Philadelphia, Pennsylvania, by J. J. Hood.

The refrain of this hymn originally had tenor and bass echoes on the first two phrases as well as on the third phrase. With its staccato rhythms, this rousing tune requires some of the same energy for singing that the text calls forth from servants of Christ. Kirkpatrick also wrote the tune for " 'Tis so sweet to trust in Jesus" (**340**).

167

For God so loved us

GOTT IST DIE LIEBE

Gott ist die Liebe
August Rische (1819-1906)
Paraphrase composite: sts. 1-3, Esther C. Bergen (1921-)
The Youth Hymnary, 1956
St. 4 and refrain, *The Hymn Book*, 1960

Thüringer melody, ca. 1840

This song, so enjoyed by both children and adults, is still sung in German as well as in this English translation. Little is known about the author except his birth and death dates. The composite paraphrase, or translation, comes from the two sources listed above via *The Mennonite Hymnal* (1969). The original German has been translated into numerous languages, including Hindi.

Early sources for this appealing folk melody, GOTT IST DIE LIEBE, are unknown. Erk and Boehme's *Deutscher Liederhort* (No. 860) lists a version of this melody as "old melody from Schönau." It has also been listed as a Thüringer folk song; the *Gesangbuch der Mennoniten* (1965) indicates Meiningen (1840), but the editors do not have further documentation (Loewen, Moyer, Oyer 1983).

89
For the beauty of the earth

DIX

Folliott Sandford Pierpoint (1835-1917)
Shipley's *Lyra Eucharistica*, 1864

Conrad Kocher (1786-1872)
Stimmen aus dem Reiche Gottes, 1838
Adapt. by William Henry Monk (1823-1889)
Hymns Ancient and Modern, 1861

This hymn of thanksgiving was written for Communion, inserting a note of joy into an otherwise solemn service. The allusion to Communion can be seen in the original refrain, which reads:

> Christ our God, to thee we raise
> This, our sacrifice of praise.

It was altered with approval of the author. This change, plus the deletion of the final three stanzas, which refer specifically to Communion, make the hymn an accolade suitable for many occasions. In stanza 3:2, "brain's delight" seemed a bit too cerebral and has been changed to "mind's delight." According to tradition Pierpoint wrote this hymn on a lovely day in late spring, inspired by the view from a hilltop near his home in Bath, England.

See "As with gladness men of old" (**218**) for information on the tune DIX.

477
For the bread

KINGDOM

Louis Fitzgerald Benson (1855-1930), 1924
Benson's *Hymns, Original and Translated*, 1925, alt.

Vicar Earle Copes (1921-), 1959
The Methodist Hymnal, 1966

Originally drafted in three stanzas, this hymn was intended by Benson to be sung after Communion. The first stanza was suggested by Horatius Bonar's "For the bread and for the wine" and focuses on the meaning of "Eucharist," which is thanksgiving. Stanza 2 rededicates the believer's life to Christ, a response to the gifts that Christ has given. At the suggestion of Henry Sloane Coffin, Benson added the present stanza 3, with its theme of service. The first, second, and fourth stanzas are used here in contemporary language as found in the *Lutheran Book of Worship* (1978).

KINGDOM was composed for this text for the National Conference of Methodist Youth (1960). The tune's varied rhythm uses both anapestic (two short-note values followed by a long one) and trochaic (a long-note value followed by two short ones) movement, giving the music a flowing quality. The tune name KINGDOM comes from the last line of the text.

90
For the fruit of all creation — FIRSTFRUITS

Fred Pratt Green (1903-)
Methodist Recorder, 1970, alt.

Bradley P. Lehman (1964-), 1991
Hymnal: A Worship Book, 1992

This text first appeared as a harvest hymn in the August 1970 issue of the *Methodist Recorder*. Meeting with almost immediate positive response, this text had been included in fourteen hymnals by 1982. The original first line, "For the fruits of his creation," was changed in subsequent publications. Although the text is appropriate for thanksgiving, it presses beyond a conventional harvest theme (st. 2), pointing to justice and mercy "in the harvests we are sharing." Stanza 3, in particular, extends the idea of harvest from pictures of cornstalks and pumpkins to non-material gifts bestowed by the Spirit.

Green's text was written for the tune EAST ACKLAM ("God that madest earth and heaven") and has also been sung with the Welsh folk song AR HYD Y NOS (see "Go, my children," **433**). Of this new setting, FIRSTFRUITS, composer Lehman writes:

> The meter of Fred Pratt Green's strong and congenial Thanksgiving text is striking and urgent. The alternation of long and short lines, with an unexpected triple group of long lines, led me to write music with similar parallels and surprises. Originally, my setting was metrically regular. . . . [T]he elimination of certain beats . . . added exuberance to the phrases "Thanks be to God" and "God's will is done."

367
For the healing of the nations — REGENT SQUARE

Fred (Frederik Herman) Kaan (1929-), 1965, alt.

Henry Thomas Smart (1813-1879)
Psalms and Hymns for Divine Worship, 1867

Of Fred Kaan's many texts, this is the one most widely used in current hymnals. It was first introduced to mark Human Rights Day in Plymouth, England. It has since been used for many other official occasions, including the twenty-fifth anniversary of the United Nations in Geneva, Switzerland.

This straightforward prayer acknowledges a variety of contemporary ills, yet avoids weighing us down with despair. The insistent movement and relatively high melody pitch of REGENT SQUARE also help turn us from discouragement about prevalent ills to active response and service. Perhaps the tune's association with "Angels from the realms of glory" also sends subliminal messages that we are not alone as God's workers on earth. In Europe Kaan's text is associated with Henry Purcell's tune WESTMINSTER ABBEY. It also has appeared with the tunes PICARDY and Carl Schalk's FORTUNATUS NEW.

The tune used here, REGENT SQUARE, was composed for Horatius Bonar's "Glory be to God the Father." That combination is included in *Psalms and Hymns for Divine Worship*, edited by James Hamilton, pastor of Regent Square Church, London, where Smart was organist.

322
For we are strangers no more — STRANGERS NO MORE

Kenneth I. Morse (1913-)
Published 1979, Daystar Associates

Dianne Huffman Morningstar (1944-)
(same source as text)

This hymn and its music were originally written to be used with a slide presentation for the World Ministries Commission of the Church of the Brethren. Kenneth Morse relates that the scope and content of the text were determined by the service and mission program of the church at that time. It is a very generalized, optimistic text, one that expresses the contemporary melding of cultures and shrinking of the global village.

Morningstar composed this musical setting at Morse's request. She writes: "It was our hope that this hymn would reflect and celebrate the joy of unity and oneness not only among our brothers and sisters in the Church of the Brethren, but throughout a far-reaching, singing community."

137
Forgive our sins as we forgive — DETROIT

Rosamond Eleanor Herklots (1905-1987)
100 Hymns for Today, 1969, and *Hymns and Songs*, 1969

Supplement to the Kentucky Harmony, 1820
Harm. by Alice Parker (1925-), 1991

"The idea of writing the 'Forgiveness' hymn," notes the author, "came to me . . . when I was digging up docks in a long-neglected garden. Realizing how these deeply rooted weeds were choking the life out of the flowers in the garden, I came to feel that deeply rooted resentments in our lives could destroy every Christian virtue and all joy and peace unless, by God's grace, we learned to forgive" (Stulken 1981). This is a compelling text, especially for those in the tradition of "historic peace churches" whose business clearly includes reconciliation.

In its first printing, DETROIT was not attributed to a composer. When it appeared in Walker's *Southern Harmony* (1835 ed.) and the *Virginia Harmony* (1831), it was credited to "Bradshaw," who remains unidentified.

415
Forth in thy name

KEBLE

Charles Wesley (1707-1788)
Hymns and Sacred Poems, Part II, 1749

John Bacchus Dykes (1823-1876)
Hymns Ancient and Modern, 1875

Subtitled "For Believers Before Work," this is a prayer for attentiveness to the presence of Christ in every facet of daily chores. The word "prove" in stanza 2 means discern. In his compact text, Wesley is calling Christians to let God permeate all of their lives, to make no distinction between secular and sacred in the application of their faith. The often-omitted third stanza uses colorful but archaic language to warn against "career satisfaction":

> Preserve me from my calling's snare,
> And hide my simple heart above,
> Above the thorns of choking care,
> The gilded baits of worldly love.

The tune KEBLE was composed for John Keble's text "Sun of my soul."

354
Fount of love, our Savior God

MAN-CHIANG-HUNG

Ernest Yin-Liu Yang (1899-1984), 1934
Hymns of Universal Praise, 1977
Tr. Frank W. Price (1895-1974), 1953
Hymns from the Four Winds, 1983, alt.

Chinese verse melody
Adapt. by Ernest Yin-Liu Yang (1899-1984), 1933
Chinese Hymns by Chinese Writers, 1953

The pilgrimage theme of this hymn is summarized in the final petition of each stanza: "Fount of love, our Savior God, be our guide." While some phrases of this text recall passages of scripture, many others bring fresh images to the mind's eye. Although the hymn is now more than fifty years old, its concepts seem both new and timeless.

Singing this hymn in unison will enable worshipers to focus on the expressive words and the beauty of the melodic line. The tune name MAN-CHIANG-HUNG means "All red the river." The tune, based on an ancient Chinese Tsu melody, was associated with a patriotic poem written by General Yueh-Fei (*Psalter Hymnal Handbook*). The melody was arranged by I-to Loh for the Asian American hymnal *Hymns from the Four Winds* (1983). That arrangement and further comments on the hymn may be found in the *Accompaniment Handbook.*

49

From all that dwell below the skies

DUKE STREET

Isaac Watts (1674-1748)
Sts. 1-2, *The Psalms of David . . . ,* 1719, alt.
Sts. 3-4, *A Pocket Hymn-Book. Designed as a Constant Companion for the Pious. Collected from Various Authors,* ca. 1781

Attrib. to John Hatton (ca. 1710-1793)
Henry Boyd's *Psalm and Hymn Tunes,* 1793

The first two stanzas of this hymn are Watts's long-meter paraphrase of the tidy, abrupt Psalm 117, titled "Praise to God from all nations." Watts wrote two other versions, one in common meter and one in short meter. Robert Spence, collector of the hymns in *A Pocket Hymn-Book . . . ,* may or may not be the author of stanzas 3 and 4. Sometimes these stanzas are ascribed to John or Charles Wesley, but there is no basis for this even though John Wesley included these verses in his *Pocket Hymn-Book for the Use of Christians of All Denominations* (1787).

At first glance it may seem that Watts has superimposed Christianity on a Hebrew psalm, since we usually think of God as Creator and Jesus as Redeemer. In Jewish theology, however, God is both Creator and Redeemer. Watts took his specific cues from verses in Colossians (1:14,16) and John's Gospel (1:1,3,12) where redemption and creation are linked. The unattributed stanzas 3 and 4 take up the same themes of praise and the magnitude of God's realm and introduce yet another Jewish name for God: Savior (Ps. 106; Isa. 43:3; 45:21).

DUKE STREET is believed to have been composed by John Hatton who lived on Duke Street in St. Helen's, in the township of Windle, England. At various times the tune has been called WINDLE or ST. HELEN'S. Published for the first time in Henry Boyd's 1793 collection, the melody was first credited to Hatton in William Dixon's *Euphonia* (1805) where it is given the name DUKE STREET and set to Addison's *Psalm 19.*

205
From heaven above to earth I come

VOM HIMMEL HOCH

Vom Himmel Hoch
Martin Luther (1483-1546)
Klug's *Geistliche Lieder*, Wittenberg, 1535
Tr. Catherine Winkworth (1827-1878)
Lyra Germanica, Series I, 1855, and composite translation by Inter-Lutheran Commission on Worship, 1978

V. Schumann's *Geistliche Lieder*, Leipzig, 1539
(Zahn No. 346)

Compare this gentle, narrative hymn with the pounding assertion of Luther's "Ein feste Burg" ("A mighty fortress is our God," **165, 329**). Martin Luther was capable of a wide range of styles and musical moods. He wrote this Christmas hymn of fifteen stanzas in 1534 for his son Hans. *Aus fremden Landen komm' ich her*, a garland song used in a popular singing game of his day, was the basis for his first stanza. In Klug's collection the hymn was paired with the tune of the garland song.

First used at the family Christmas Eve celebration in the Luther home, the opening five stanzas were sung by one person dressed as an angel, and the concluding stanzas were sung by the children in response. A variation on that practice is, as suggested by hymnwriter and collector Erik Routley, to begin the carol "with a solo voice, preferably that of a child; as it passes through stanzas 2-6 more voices should gradually be added, and then everybody present should join in the last stanza . . . fortissimo" (Routley 1985).

The present text is a selection of stanzas 1, 2, 3, 8, 14, and 15. The translation, prepared for the *Lutheran Book of Worship*, is based largely on Catherine Winkworth's translation.

The tune VOM HIMMEL HOCH, printed with this text four years after Luther wrote it, is believed to have been composed by Luther or arranged by him from a folk song. Today this melody is always associated with the text. J. S. Bach used VOM HIMMEL HOCH as the basis of a number of organ works, as well as at the conclusion of Part II of his *Christmas Oratorio.*

136
From the depths of sin

FROM THE DEPTHS

Willard F. Jabusch (1930-)
Hymnal for Young Christians, 1966, alt.

Russian folk melody
Harm. by Harris J. Loewen (1953-), 1988

This is a poignant, penitential psalm, based on Psalm 130, that affirms expectation of forgiveness even in the midst of admitting sin. The final two verses of the psalm are not included in the text; they confirm pardon and might have been spoken by a priest. The sense of alert expectancy in the final phrase would suggest that this hymn be followed by words of pardon or a hymn of assurance.

The text was written for use at St. Celestine Church in Elmwood Park, Illinois. In the third stanza, two minor alterations have been made: "for God's word" replaces "for his word," and "watchers" takes the place of "watchmen." In order to maintain the integrity of the psalm, a concluding fourth stanza, which uses New Testament imagery, has been omitted.

Though this melody is probably of secular origin, it is sung in Russia to a hymn text that begins "Joyful brothers, in spiritual songs, glorify Jesus' name." The seeming disparity between the character of the tune and those words reflects the oppression experienced by Christians in Russia. The somber mood of the melody is an appropriate setting for the words of Psalm 130.

97
From the hands — CLOVIS

Jean Wiebe Janzen (1933-), 1990
Hymnal: A Worship Book, 1992

Larry R. Warkentin (1940-), 1990
(same source as text)

Asked to come up with a table blessing suitable for all ages, Jean Janzen muses: "The metaphor of God's hands is not new, but maybe the sky being a lap of God will add freshness to our concept of the vastness of God's generosity."

The author had just returned to California from teaching poetry at Eastern Mennonite College, Harrisonburg, Virginia. She gave these words to Warkentin one Sunday after worship, challenging him to write a melody in canon (round) form. He did so and the collaborative effort was named for their mutual congregational home, Clovis Mennonite Brethren Church (Calif.).

484
From time beyond my memory — TRUSTING MERCY

Based on Psalm 71
Michael Arnold Perry (1942-)
A Selection of Hymns by Michael Perry, 1989, and *Psalms for Today*, 1990, alt.

John L. Horst (1938-), 1990
Hymnal: A Worship Book, 1992

This hymn is based on Psalm 71, a lament overlaid with confidence, likely written by an older person for the elderly. Still, it is a psalm of trust appropriate for all ages. The last line of the hymn is repeated to fit the musical form. The third stanza has been altered slightly and the doxological fourth stanza of the original omitted.

TRUSTING MERCY was originally composed for "The tree of life" (**509**). After much deliberation by the hymnal's music committee, Alice Parker's APPLE TREE was chosen for that text, and John Horst's music was adopted for these words. The lyric, folklike quality of the melody makes it easy to learn. Horst writes that "the tune was composed quickly (about an hour) during the fall of 1990." Once learned, the tune may also be sung with "The tree of life."

352

Gentle Shepherd, come and lead us — GENTLE SHEPHERD

Gloria Gaither (1942-), ca. 1974

William J. Gaither (1936-), ca. 1974

In this through-composed song (no repeated meter), the music captures well the spirit of the text, which is reminiscent of Isaiah 40:11 and the Psalms. When asked, "Which comes first, the music or the lyrics?" the Gaithers always answer, "The idea." This was the case, too, with "Gentle Shepherd." Gloria comments: "The idea came first, the musical 'feel' was created and the finished lyric followed. We have always enjoyed having this song sung with guitar and flute accompaniment. This treatment seems to reflect the simplicity of the message: an open admission of our need of a shepherd."

561

Give to the winds thy fears — HANTS

Befiehl du deine Wege
Paul Gerhardt (1607-1676)
Praxis Pietatis Melica, 1656
Tr. John Wesley (1703-1791)
Hymns and Sacred Poems, 1739, alt.

Joseph Funk's *Harmonia Sacra*, 5th ed., 1851
Harm. by Alice Parker (1925-), 1991

It is a difficult thing to give up control, to turn our lives over to God. Sometimes, however, it is the *only* thing left to do—and then breathe a sigh of relief. Paul Gerhardt knew this; thus, his hymns are more a reflection of his serene faith than of the tragedies of his life.

Gerhardt's German text is an acrostic on Luther's version of Psalm 37:5, in which each word of the psalm verse begins a stanza. Abandoning the acrostic, Wesley's translation freely paraphrases Gerhardt's twelve stanzas of eight lines into sixteen stanzas of four lines, dropping Gerhardt's stanzas 5, 9, 10, and 11. Because of the length of Wesley's paraphrase, two hymns were made by dividing the hymn at stanza 9: "Commit thou all thy griefs"[1] and "Give to the winds thy fears," respectively. Among the many English translations of Gerhardt's hymn, Wesley's is the most popular. He began learning German when he was captivated by the singing meetings of the Moravians who were fellow travelers on his 1735 voyage to Georgia (Young 1993).

HANTS appears in *Harmonia Sacra* in three-voice harmony (STB) with the melody in the tenor, set to the present text. In the 1851 edition, the third note of the melody is "sol" (do-mi-sol-do) while in the next edition (1854) the third note is the present "re" (do-mi-re-do). In both editions a reference is made after the tune name to "Hymn 72—Lutheran Collection," which is likely the source from which Funk took this tune. In the twelfth edition of *Harmonia Sacra* (1867), an alto part was added, retaining the same bass and tenor parts. The present harmonization, made for this hymnal, is a whole step lower and avoids some open-fifth harmony as well as some parallel fifths commonly found in *Harmonia Sacra* and similar collections. Alice Parker also used the melody as the finale in her folk opera *Singers Glen* where it is referred to as DIVINE GOODNESS.

Joseph Funk's popular collection went through four editions under the title *Genuine Church Music*. By the fifth edition, it became known as *Harmonia Sacra*. The full title of the collection is:

> *HARMONIA SACRA, being a compilation of GENUINE CHURCH MUSIC, comprising a great variety of metres, All Harmonized for Three Voices; together with a copious explication of THE PRINCIPLES OF VOCAL MUSIC, exemplified and illustrated by tables, in a plain and comprehensive manner.* By Joseph Funk and Sons from the fourth edition newly arranged, enlarged, and improved, WITH A NEW SYSTEM OF NOTATION OF SEVEN CHARACTER NOTES. Mountain Valley, near Harrisonburg, Va. Published by the authors. Solomon Funk, printer. 1851.[2]

1. The former hymn is in the *Hymnal of the Evangelical and Reformed Church*, 1941.

2. These editions of *Harmonia Sacra* were examined by John Barr at the Eastern Mennonite College Menno Simons Historical Library, Harrisonburg, Virginia, through the courtesy of Lois Bowman and Harold Huber.

204
Gloria

Traditional Latin

GLORIA III

Jacques Berthier (1923-)
Music from Taizé, Vol. I, 1978, 1980, 1981

This delightful "Gloria" is taken from the first phrase of the "Angel's Song" in Luke's nativity story. It may be sung as a canon (round) in as many as four parts. It is one of several settings of this text included in the music of Taizé, hence the tune designation GLORIA III. The second part of the text is pronounced "een ex-chel-sees deh-o." For further comments on the Taizé community, see "Alleluia" (**101**).

107
Glorious is thy name—see "Blessed Savior, we adore thee"

619
Glorious things of thee are spoken

AUSTRIAN HYMN

John Newton (1725-1807)
Olney Hymns, Book I, 1779, alt.

Franz Joseph Haydn (1732-1809), 1797
Edward Miller's *Sacred Music*, 1802

This hymn, said to be the "only joyful hymn in the Olney collection," was titled "Zion, or the City of God." Its opening phrase is based on Psalm 87:3, and the text as a whole makes reference to passages in Isaiah 33:20-21, Exodus 18:22, and Psalm 46:4. "Zion" is a metaphor for the church, founded on Jesus, the "Rock of ages." Confidence exudes from the entire text, which also reaches into the Hebrew Bible for illustrations of God's enduring presence and culminates in an idyllic future kingdom. The omitted fourth stanza is a picturesque vision of worship in this glorious future:

> Blest inhabitants of Zion
> Washed in the Redeemer's blood!
> Jesus, whom their souls rely on,
> Makes them kings and priests to God,
> 'Tis his love his people raises
> Over self to reign as kings,
> And as priests, his solemn praises
> Each for a thank-off'ring brings.

The tune, sometimes referred to as AUSTRIA or HAYDN, is one of the few hymn tunes written by a symphonic composer. It was composed by Haydn as a setting of Hauschka's Austrian national hymn, *Gott erhalte Franz den Kaiser*, to be sung for the emperor's birthday on February 12, 1797. The melody apparently was derived from a Croatian tune with the first three measures being identical. Later Haydn used his melody for a set of variations in the slow movement of his *String Quartet in C*, Opus 76, No. 3, called the "Emperor" quartet. It was first printed with this text in *Hymns Ancient and Modern* (1889). Brethren accustomed to repeating the final phrase may be surprised at the end!

127
Glory be to the Father

(no tune name)

Greek hymn
Anonymous
Gloria Patri, early Christian doxology

Christopher Meineke (1782-1850)
Music for the Church, 1844

The *Gloria Patri* (Glory to the Father) is an ancient Christian canticle (song) that may have been used as early as the second century. It is known as the Lesser Doxology to distinguish it from the longer *Gloria in excelsis Deo*. The Trinitarian doxology is based on Matthew 28:19, while the latter section, "As it was in the beginning . . . ," was added during the Arian controversy in the fourth century to affirm that the triune God of the New Testament is the same as the God of the Hebrew Bible and that the three persons of the Trinity are equal. This pattern of praise, similar in expression to Jude 25, finds its antecedents in passages in the Psalms, such as Psalm 106:48.

These words have been set by numerous composers. This one by Christopher Meineke (also called Christoph or Charles), a native of Germany who moved first to England and then to Baltimore, Maryland, was composed for St. Paul's Episcopal Church where Meineke was organist.

Christopher Smart's "To God, with the Lamb and the Dove" (**125**) is a less traditional *Gloria Patri,* with other names for the persons of the Trinity.

433
Go, my children — AR HYD Y NOS

Jaroslav J. Vajda (1919-), 1983 — Welsh folk melody

Vajda's words provide a whole new use for AR HYD Y NOS; no longer is the tune bound to nighttime lullabies with "All through the night." Even though the melody reminds one of children, the text does not refer to the under-twelve set; it is through baptism that believers are born into God's family, becoming "children" of God (st. 1).

The text was published in an anthem setting by Carl Schalk (1984) as an alternative to "God who made the earth and heaven." The hymn is based primarily on Numbers 6:24-26, which contains the familiar Aaronic benediction. Vajda writes: "To set it apart from other versifications of the benediction, I placed the words of the hymn into the mouth of the blessing triune God, dismissing the congregation after worship while drawing together a review of the events that transpired during the service" (Vajda 1987).

When asked for permission to make some alterations, Vajda said this about the use of the name "Lord" in the final stanza: "We must not confuse the sinful, arrogant, human distortions, caricatures, and abuses of human domination with the protective, supportive, and gracious Lordship of the God of love." The use of "Lord" reminds us that God is the One to whom all creation is subject. About the name "brother" in that stanza, he says: "Jesus . . . is our brother as he shares our humanity. What a comfort that is. . . . It was a name and relationship he himself cherished.

See Mark 3:35. I meant to have this name remind the singer . . . of the Incarnate Word to whom we are as close as children of the same Father."[1]

The Welsh melody AR HYD Y NOS is best known for its secular use. It is found in *Musical Relics of the Welsh Bards* (Edward Jones, Dublin, 1784). The folk song would have been sung by a soloist, often accompanied by harp, with the listeners joining in the refrain. In *The Christian Lyre* (1830), the tune was used for a sacred text, "There's a friend above all others."

1. Letter from Jaroslav J. Vajda to The Hymnal Project, 1991

429
Go now in peace — GO NOW IN PEACE

Natalie Allyn Wakeley Sleeth (1930-1992)
Sunday Songbook, 1976

Natalie Allyn Wakeley Sleeth (1930-1992)
(same source as text)

This delightful benediction may be sung in a canon (round) in as many as four parts, with each new part entering at the interval of two measures. Worshipers of all ages will learn this round easily, especially if "a little child shall lead them." Suggestions for instrumental accompaniment are in the *Accompaniment Handbook*.

240
Go to dark Gethsemane — REDHEAD NO. 76 (GETHSEMANE)

James Montgomery (1771-1854)
Christian Psalmist, 1825

Richard Redhead (1820-1901)
Church Hymn Tunes, Ancient and Modern, 1853

Montgomery's text presents the four final events in the life of Jesus and advises the reader to "learn of him . . . ." Though Christians are called to follow the difficult way of the cross, they have a guide.

The author's first version of this text appears in Thomas Cotterill's *A Selection of Psalms and Hymns for Public Worship* (9th ed., 1820). Montgomery later revised it to read the way it does now and headed it "Christ, our example in suffering." Both texts have come down through time in various hymnals. The fourth stanza, omitted in the hymnal because it changes the focus from Jesus' Passion to Easter, could be a worship resource for Easter:

> Early hasten to the tomb
> where they laid his breathless clay.
> All is solitude and gloom.
> Who hath taken him away?

Christ is risen! He meets our eyes.
Savior, teach us so to rise.

This tune was written by Richard Redhead for "Rock of ages, cleft for me." In Redhead's hymnal tunes were designated by number, not name; therefore, it is now called REDHEAD NO. 76. It also is known as PETRA (rock), from the text first used with it, and GETHSEMANE, by virtue of its association with the present text.

424
God, be merciful and gracious — TONUS PEREGRINUS

Based on Psalm 67

Psalm tone, pre-16th c.
Harm. by Johann Sebastian Bach (1685-1750)

These words of blessing from the psalmist are similar to the Aaronic benediction, "The Lord bless you and keep you," found in Numbers 6:24-26.

The melody is a psalm tone used by the early church in the singing of psalms. In addition to eight psalm tones based on each of the medieval modes or scales, there was a *tonus peregrinus*. Each psalm tone can be divided into two parts, each having a recitation note on which many words can be sung. Unlike the other tones, which use the same pitch for the two recitation notes, the *tonus peregrinus* has two differing pitches, making the second one the *peregrinus*, meaning "alien" or "foreign," tone. With the harmonization by J. S. Bach, this tone becomes more metric than its earlier form, in which the stresses of the words dictated the rhythmic flow.

430
God be with you — RANDOLPH

Jeremiah Eames Rankin (1828-1904)
Gospel Bells, Chicago, 1880, alt.

Ralph Vaughan Williams (1872-1958)
The English Hymnal, 1906

This hymn unfolds some of the meanings of the phrase "God be with you," which is the basis of the word *goodbye*. In its earliest source, this hymn is subtitled with Paul's blessing in Romans 16:20: "The grace of our Lord Jesus Christ be with you." Rankin wrote the hymn while he was pastor at First Congregational Church, Washington, D.C., and it was first sung there. The revival team of Moody and Sankey used it in their services, and it also became popular with Methodists at the Ocean Grove Campmeeting Association in New Jersey.

RANDOLPH, composed for this text, has an interesting melodic contour coupled with ample harmonic variety. Archibald Jacob comments: "In sentiment, as in build, the melody accords perfectly with the poem" (Dearmer 1933). Even though it is less than a century old, this tune is considered to be almost traditional.

As directed in *The English Hymnal* (1906), the first and last phrases are to be sung in unison while the middle two phrases are to be sung in harmony. The tune was probably named for the composer's cousin Ralph Wedgewood (1874-1956), known to his family as "Randolph." The friendship with this cousin was one of the most important ones in Vaughan Williams' life.

431
God be with you

Jeremiah Eames Rankin (1828-1904)
Gospel Bells, Chicago, 1880

The first two stanzas of Rankin's text are printed here in unaltered form. The tune GOD BE WITH YOU, by William Gould Tomer (1833-1896), is provided in the *Accompaniment Handbook*. Rankin chose this tune from two settings by composer-friends. It was revised by Rankin's church organist, J. W. Bischoff. The simple melody and harmony are well suited to *a cappella* singing. The combination of this tune and text has remained the standard one, particularly in the U.S. The music, readily learned and sung from memory, has not been printed in the hymnal because it is familiar to many.

160
God created heaven and earth

Traditional Taiwanese hymn
Tr. Boris and Clare Anderson
Hymns from the Four Winds, 1983

TOA-SIA

Taiwanese melody

This is a translation of a well-known Taiwanese hymn of creation. Stanza 3 reflects some of China's ancient and multi-religious culture, but different idols interfere with North American attentiveness to God's grace.

Other texts, similar in theme, appear with TOA-SIA in both *The Mennonite Hymnal* (1969) and the *International Songbook* of Mennonite World Conference (1990). In those two collections, the tune is designated as a Pepuhoan melody, which "indicates that it is a melody of the Plains aborigines of Taiwan who have been assimilated into the Chinese population and who do not exist as a distinct group anymore. Strains of this group are identifiable and always manifest a strong musical ability" (Oyer 1980). The melody is typically pentatonic, playable on the black keys of the piano if one begins on E-flat. Accompaniment and other musical suggestions are provided in the *Accompaniment Handbook.*

16
God is here among us — WUNDERBARER KÖNIG

Gott ist gegenwärtig
Gerhard Tersteegen (1697-1769)
Geistliches Blumengärtlein, 1729
Tr. from *The Hymnal 1940,* alt.

Alpha und Omega, Glaub- und Liebesübung, Bremen, 1680

Tersteegen may have derived his text from the work of French writer Labadie. However, his German paraphrase required as much creative skill as that of the original author. An introvert and ascetic, Tersteegen's "sense of the nearness of God is especially evident; he would have us think of God not merely as transcendent, but above all things as immanent . . . " (Haeussler 1952). In fact, the first adjective in the German, *gegenwärtig,* means present, actual, and current, and so the first-line alteration from "God himself is with us" is closer to the original German.

This is a good text for the Anabaptist/pietist mix that makes up the believers church tradition: Stanza 1 affirms God's presence in a corporate setting; then the second stanza becomes a personal prayer for transformation by the Holy Spirit. Stanza 3 reverts again to a community commitment, shunning all that deflects God's people from the course of "right" living.

WUNDERBARER KÖNIG was first used with Joachim Neander's "Wonderful King, ruler of us all." It is the first tune to which the present text was set; this combination continues to be the prevailing one. The tune is sometimes attributed to Neander and occasionally bears the name ARNSBERG. The original version of this tune, having undergone little alteration, is very similar to the one in use today.

638
God is working his purpose out — PURPOSE

Arthur Campbell Ainger (1841-1919), 1894
Church Missionary Hymn Book, 1899, alt.

Martin Fallas Shaw (1875-1958)
Enlarged Songs of Praise, 1931

God's kingdom is coming! It is expressed in this text with such confidence as to be a nearly inexorable fact. In their speaking and their serving, God's people will be its messengers, but God alone can "give life to the seed." The final line of each stanza comes from Habakkuk 2:14: "For the earth shall be filled with the knowledge of the glory of the Lord, as the waters cover the sea." A similar passage appears in Isaiah 11:9. These prophetic assurances came at times when oppression was at its heaviest and God's purpose seemed obscured.

Written while Ainger was a teacher at Eton College in England, this text was dedicated to Archbishop Edward White Benson. In stanza 2:1-2, "Where'er man's foot hath trod" is changed to "where human feet have trod." Stanza 3 of the original five has been omitted. It asks:

> What can we do to work God's work, to prosper and increase
> the brotherhood of all mankind, the reign of the Prince of peace?
> What can we do to hasten the time, the time that shall surely be,
> when the earth shall be filled with the glory of God as the waters
> cover the sea?

Composed for this text, the splendid melody of PURPOSE reflects the style of some English folk tunes. It is also one of the few hymn tunes composed as a canon (round). It should be sung "in moderate time. With breadth" (*Enlarged Songs of Praise*). When Ainger's text was first published in leaflet form, it appeared with the tune BENSON, by Millicent D. Kingham.

397
God loves all his many people — (no tune name)

Lubunda Mukungu
Tr. rev. by Anna Kreider Juhnke (1940-)
International Songbook (Mennonite World Conference), 1978, alt.

Tshiluba melody (Zaire)
(same source as text)

This hymn was in the songbook used at the 1978 and 1990 Mennonite World Conferences under the title "Come, receive his joy." The refrain especially is reminiscent of Jesus' admonition to store up treasures, like joy, that will last.

Anna Juhnke is a professor of English at Bethel College in North Newton, Kansas. A new literal translation of the Tshiluba text has been prepared by Leona Schrag, a former missionary to Zaire who serves on the staff of Africa Inter-Mennonite Mission.

Doreen Klassen, editor for the 1990 *International Songbook,* writes: "I suspect that Zairian soloists would improvise bridge passages between phrases, on the whole-note phrase endings. Of special interest is the additive drum rhythm (3+3+2) which may accompany the somewhat marchlike 4/4 meter."

492

God of Eve and God of Mary

PENHILL

Fred (Frederik Herman) Kaan (1929-), 1987
New Songs of Praise 4, 1988

Pamela Ward (1946-)
(same source as text)

This is an embrace in the form of a hymn. It radiates loving care, centering first on God's role as a gentle nurturer and then on the fostering that human parents provide. Long awaited is the acknowledgment in stanza 3 that parenting is provided even by those who have no birth children. The final stanza invokes the Three-in-One not in the usual powerful, majestic way, but as the divine caress that nourishes life.

British author Fred Kaan wrote this text for Penhill United Reformed Church, a small housing-estate congregation in North Swindon where he was part-time minister. The hymn was published by Oxford University Press after it received recognition in a competition sponsored by BBC television.

The tune, named PENHILL for Kaan's church, was composed by Pamela Ward, another United Reformed Church minister in Erdington, Birmingham.

366

God of grace and God of glory

CWM RHONDDA

Harry Emerson Fosdick (1878-1969), 1930
Smith's *Praise and Service*, New York, 1932

John Hughes (1873-1932), 1905 or 1907
The Voice of Thanksgiving, No. 4, Chicago, 1928
Fellowship Hymn Book, 1933

When Harry Emerson Fosdick changed pastorates in New York City, he was also promised a new church house. So in 1930 he wrote a hymn to open the services and dedicate the building—the eminent Riverside Church. Fosdick masterminded a poem as magnificent and robust as the church building for which it was written. Erik Routley calls this hymn text "the best known of all twentieth-century American hymns" (Routley 1979).

Originally the text was sung to REGENT SQUARE, a favorite of Fosdick's. It became associated with CWM RHONDDA, much to Fosdick's dismay, in the Methodist hymnal of 1935, and that combination has endured.

CWM RHONDDA was written for a Baptist *Cymanfu Ganu* (singing festival) and first used at Chapel Rhondda, Pontypridd, Wales. The tune (pronounced "coom rawnthuh") was at first named RHONDDA, with the CWM ("low valley") added later. Although the tune was first published in Great Britain in 1933, Donald Hustad states that it was "first copyrighted in the United States in 1927 in an arrangement by E. Edwin Young that appeared in *The Voice of Thanksgiving No. 4* (Chicago: The Bible Institute Colportage Association, 1928)" (Hustad 1978).

77

God of many names — MANY NAMES

Brian Arthur Wren (1936-), 1985
Praising a Mystery, 1986

William P. Rowan (1951-), 1985
(same source as text)

Moving from creation to the new creation, this hymn incorporates the sense (in the Hebrew of Exod. 4:13) of God as " 'moving, endlessly becoming.' [T]he 'many names' try to glimpse the glory of God, who cannot be defined and labelled" (Wren 1986). The stanzas are a prayer for an encounter with the holy mystery of God, while the refrain lifts up a variety of ways—hushed, shouting, singing—to approach and praise God. "The living God," Wren elaborates, "is a mystery, not a secret: secrets puzzle us, but lose their fascination when they are revealed. A mystery deepens the more it is pondered and known" (Wren 1986).

MANY NAMES was composed specifically for Wren's text. Originally written for unison voices with accompaniment, the composer developed this SATB version in 1988 at the request of Mary Oyer, a noted Mennonite hymnologist. Although set for congregational singing, the three stanzas could be sung effectively by a solo voice. Another suggestion is to "add tambourine, hand clapping, and circle dance in the style of bar mitzvah" (Young 1993).

486

God of our life — SANDON

Hugh Thompson Kerr (1872-1950), 1916
The Church School Hymnal (Presbyterian), 1928

Charles Henry Purday (1799-1885)
Church and Home Metrical Psalter and Hymnal, 1860

In a hymn so appropriate for the launching of any new venture, it is right that this text directs us first to the past. Stanza 1 invites singers to reflect on the ways God's hand has been present for them personally. On that foundation, then, we can have confidence in God's future faithfulness. The prayer in stanza 3:2 is especially noteworthy: "When we are strong, Lord, leave us not alone." In our tendency to turn to God primarily when we are in pain and trial, we are reminded that our strength still needs God; this is a "God of our life." This poem was written for the fiftieth anniversary of Shadyside Presbyterian Church, Pittsburgh, Pennsylvania, where Kerr was pastor.

SANDON was composed for John Henry Newman's "Lead, kindly light" and first appeared with that text in Purday's *Psalter*. Austin Lovelace writes that the original tune name was "LANDON, and the change from *L* to *S* may have been a typographical error, though there is an old English residence named Sandon" (Gealy, Lovelace, Young 1970).

36
God of our strength — GOD OF OUR STRENGTH

Fanny Jane Crosby (1820-1915), 1882
Baptist Hymnal, 1883

William Howard Doane (1832-1915)
(same source as text)

Fanny Crosby wrote many of her texts at the personal request of composers, including Doane, who was editor of the Baptist hymnal in which this hymn first appeared. This is another of the famous Crosby-Doane collaborations. Others include "Safe in the arms of Jesus"; "Rescue the perishing"; and "Jesus, keep me near the cross."

This is an atypical gospel song in its emphasis on a group, rather than on the individual. Blind from infancy, the author calls on inner sight in the beginning of stanza 2: "To thee we lift our joyful eyes." The song comes to this hymnal by way of the Mennonite *Life Songs No. 2* (1938) and *The Mennonite Hymnal* (1969).

53
God of the earth, the sky, the sea — ST. CATHERINE

Samuel Longfellow (1819-1892)
Longfellow and S. Johnson's *Hymns of the Spirit*, 1864, alt.

Henri Frederick Hemy (1818-1888)
Crown of Jesus Music, 1864
Adapt. by James George Walton (1821-1905)
Plainsong Music for the Holy Communion Office, 1874

This hymn vividly expresses the presence of God in the wonders of nature but affirms that God's clearest image can be seen in the human spirit. Stanza 2, usually omitted, is:

> Thee in the lonely woods we meet,
> On the bare hills or cultured plains,
> In every flower beneath our feet,
> And even the still rock's mossy stains.

The last line of the refrain is changed to "Almighty God, our praise we bring." This not only adds an extra dimension of praise, but also creates a parallel construction similar to the form used in numerous psalms.

For comments on ST. CATHERINE, see "Faith of the martyrs" (**413**).

390
God of the fertile fields — MILTON ABBAS

Georgia Elma Harkness (1891-1974)
Fourteen New Rural Hymns, 1955, alt.

Eric Harding Thiman (1900-1975)
Congregational Praise, 1951

Twentieth-century North America has experienced a dramatic movement from rural to urban and suburban communities. Though fewer of us spend the bulk of our time growing food, we dare not forget that God blossoms life out of the earth to provide our basic needs. This hymn echoes the assertion that the earth has enough for everyone's need, but not for everyone's greed.

Written for the Quadrennial National Methodist Town and Country Conference, held at Bloomington, Indiana, in June 1955, this text was the winner in one of the contests sponsored by the Hymn Society of America (now the Hymn Society of the United States and Canada).

MILTON ABBAS was originally written for the text "Christ for the world we sing." In many collections ITALIAN HYMN, the melody of "Come, thou Almighty King" (**41**), is an alternate tune for this text.

293
God sends us the Spirit — NATOMAH

Tom (Thomas Stevenson) Colvin (1925-), 1969, alt.

Gonja folk melody (Ghana)
Adapt. by Tom Colvin and C. J. Natomah

This is one of a collection of hymn texts that Tom Colvin wrote and set to traditional folk melodies recorded in Gonja, Dagomba, and other villages in Ghana where the traditional culture is still dynamic. He was aided in this work by C. J. Natomah, the first Gonja to become a minister of the Presbyterian Church of Ghana. These hymns were introduced to the Iona Community in Colvin's native Scotland and then shared with the wider church in two booklets, *Free to Serve* and *Leap, My Soul*. This tune was recorded at Damango and set to these words "written for those churches, particularly new ones, where the Spirit is experienced as a powerful presence" (Colvin 1983). The song should be sung fast and joyously, accompanied by drums and shakers. Add three claps to emphasize each "Spirit-Friend" in the refrain.

345
God sent his Son — BECAUSE HE LIVES

Gloria Gaither (1942-) and William J. Gaither (1936-), 1971

William J. Gaither (1936-), 1971

This gospel hymn, based on John 14:19, was written when news headlines were screaming drug trafficking, assassinations, and riots, and the world seemed poised on the abyss of nuclear destruction. The authors write:

> It was into . . . such a time that we were bringing our third little baby. . . . In the midst of this kind of uncertainty . . . the assurance of the Lordship of the risen Christ blew across our troubled minds like a cooling breeze in the parched desert. Holding our tiny son in our arms we were able to write. . . . (Reynolds 1976)

The Gaithers wrote three stanzas, the most familiar of which is included in this hymnal. To lengthen the hymn, the second half could be repeated as often as desired or sung before as well as after the stanza.

632
God the Spirit, Guide and Guardian

Carl Pickens Daw, Jr. (1944-), 1987
The United Methodist Hymnal, 1989

HYFRYDOL

Rowland Hugh Prichard (1811-1887), ca. 1830
Cyfaill y Cantorion (The Singer's Friend), 1844
Arr. by Ralph Vaughan Williams (1872-1958)
The English Hymnal, 1906
Adapt. in *BBC Hymn Book*, 1951

Daw wrote this hymn for the consecration of Jeffery Rowthorn as bishop of Connecticut. This meaty text begins with God the Spirit, the third person of the Trinity, who is the focus of the traditional prayers and hymns of the ordination rites (Daw 1990). The phrase "Guide and Guardian" is a paraphrase of the Greek term *paraclete* as found in John 14:26. Other phrases such as "wind-sped Flame," "hovering Dove," and "Breath of life" recall the work of the Spirit at Pentecost, at the baptism of Christ, and at creation.

In the second stanza, the central figure is Christ, whose metaphor as Shepherd is attached to those who minister. Stanzas 3 and 4, while valuable, are omitted because of nuances unbefitting believers church ministry understandings and because of the density of the text as a whole. The third stanza, directed to the first person of the Trinity, "attempts to recast traditional understandings in gender-free language. . . . 'Womb of mercy' reflects the fact that the Hebrew and Aramaic words for mercy are derived from a root meaning 'womb' " (Daw 1990). Stanza 4 voices the mystery of the Three-in-One.

For comments on HYFRYDOL, see "Come, thou long-expected Jesus" (**178**).

414
God, who stretched — HOLY MANNA

Catherine Cameron (1927-), 1967
Contemporary Worship I, 1969, alt.

The Columbian Harmony, 1825

This dynamic, contemporary hymn asks probing questions about creativity and scientific development. Do our labors reflect God's purposes? Do they bless life on earth?

The second stanza of the original text, which deals with the modern city, has been omitted, thus maintaining the focus on the infinite nature of our universe and its Creator. This version of the text comes from the *Lutheran Book of Worship* (1978) where extensive alterations were made in the final stanza.

Written originally to be sung with the tune AUSTRIAN HYMN (see "Glorious things of thee are spoken," **619**), the text has been set to HOLY MANNA in several recent hymnals. For more information on this tune, see "Brethren, we have met to worship" (**8**). An accompaniment by Marilyn Houser Hamm is found in the *Accompaniment Handbook*.

511
God, who touches earth with beauty — EARTHRISE

Mary Susanne Edgar (1889-1973), 1925, alt.

Alfred V. Fedak (1953-), 1988

This hymn text, written for campers in 1925, was awarded first place the following year in a contest held by the American Camping Association. It has been used around the world and translated into a number of languages. God's creation abounds with beautiful paradigms for healthy development and Edgar uses some of them in rhythmic simile here.

The tune EARTHRISE was written for the United Reformed Church in Somerville, New Jersey, to celebrate the twenty-fifth anniversary of its retreat center, an eighteenth-century farm situated on about one hundred acres near the Delaware River. The tune, named for the center, was composed for Edgar's text. Fedak writes: "The accompaniment is deliberately written for piano: it's meant to be used outside of church as well as inside and is especially appropriate for use at retreats, small group meetings, and other informal occasions." Fedak also arranged the hymn as a two-part children's choir anthem, published by Sacred Music Press.

391
God, whose farm is all creation

John Arlott (1914-), 1991
BBC Hymn Book, 1951

STUTTGART

Attrib. to Christian Friedrich Witt (ca. 1660-1716)
Psalmodia Sacra . . . , 1715
Adapt. by Henry J. Gauntlett (1805-1876)
Hymns Ancient and Modern, 1861

This hymn was written at the invitation of the compilers of the *BBC Hymn Book.* The opening line is based on Psalm 24:1 ("The earth is the Lord's and all that is in it . . ."). Whether directly involved in farming or not, all of us are dependent on the land and need to put our trust in God's providence. Stanza 3 is a kind of spiritual almanac, giving over to God all that occupies us, all our "calendar of care."

The straightforward quality of STUTTGART suits this text well. Comments on the tune may be found with "Child of blessing, child of promise" (**620**).

383
God, whose giving

Robert Lansing Edwards (1915-)
Ten New Stewardship Hymns, 1961

HYFRYDOL

Rowland Hugh Prichard (1811-1887), ca. 1830
Cyfaill y Cantorion (The Singer's Friend), 1844
Arr. by Ralph Vaughan Williams (1872-1958)
The English Hymnal, 1906
Adapt. in *BBC Hymn Book,* 1951

Edwards, minister of a Congregational church, wrote this text for a competition of stewardship hymns sponsored by the Hymn Society of America. The first stanza names some of the spiritual and physical gifts we have received from God and calls on us to respond in praise. The second and third stanzas make clear that we are given gifts in trust; our time, talent, and treasure are to be used in God's service.

This text was written to fit the tune HYFRYDOL. For comments on HYFRYDOL, see "Come, thou long-expected Jesus" (**178**). This text also has been set to NETTLETON ("Come, thou fount," **521**) and BEACH SPRING ("Holy Spirit, come with power," **26**).

135 God, whose purpose is to kindle

BAPTISM BY FIRE

Based on Luke 12:49
David Elton Trueblood (1900-1994)
The Incendiary Fellowship, 1967, alt.

Esther Wiebe (1932-)
General Conference Mennonite bulletin series, 1968

It has been said that the opposite of love is not hate, but apathy. This text attacks indifference, not merely inviting response, but demanding it. Based on Luke 12:49, it was first titled "Baptism by fire," and the first stanza burns with that metaphor. Stanza 2 alludes to some of Jesus' disturbing sayings about strife and division, and stanza 3 combines the worship elements of confession of sin, plea for forgiveness, and openness to transformation.

The poem originally began "Thou, whose purpose." Other minor alterations include the change of "brother's" to "neighbor's" at the end of stanza 2. The second and third stanzas have been reversed.

Trueblood's text was selected for the 1968 evangelism emphasis of the General Conference Mennonite Church. A new tune was commissioned, and the hymn was distributed for use on Evangelism Sunday. Wiebe originally composed the tune as a unison melody with keyboard accompaniment; she herself arranged it in four parts for this hymnal. The strong, modal melody makes a fitting vehicle for this challenging text.

210 Good Christian friends, rejoice

IN DULCI JUBILO

In dulci jubilo
Manuscript, 14th c.
Tr. John Mason Neale (1818-1866)
Carols for Christmastide, 1853, alt.

Joseph Klug's *Geistliche Lieder,* 1535
Harm. by Robert L. Pearsall (1795-1856)

The original macaronic text (bilingual), a combination of Latin and German phrases, has been traced to manuscript No. 1305, dated around 1400, at Leipzig University. This was the era when vernacular additions to Latin sacred song were just coming into vogue. The earliest mention of the carol is in the writings of a fourteenth-century author who reports that these words were first sung by angels to the mystic Heinrich Suso (d. 1366), a Dominican monk who joined his heavenly visitors in a dance (*The Hymnal 1940 Companion,* 1951 ed.). Here is the original first stanza and corresponding literal translation:

In dulce jubilo	In sweet jubilation
Nu singet und seyt wonne	Now sing and be joyful!
Unsers herzen wonne	The joy of our hearts
Leyt in praesepio	Lies in a manger
Und leuchtet als die sonne	And shines like the sun
Matris in gremio	In the lap of his mother
Alpha es et O!	Alpha and Omega! (Bailey 1950)

The English text by John Mason Neale is such a free rendering of the poem that some hymnals list him as author, rather than translator. Neale's translation originally began "Good Christian men, rejoice," and at the end of the third line of text, the words "News! News!" "Joy! Joy!" and "Peace! Peace!" appeared in each successive stanza. These exclamations have since been omitted, because additional melody notes had to be provided for them.

The text and tune appear together in the manuscript mentioned above. It is found in Joseph Klug's *Geistliche Lieder* in much the same form as it is sung today. Since it is a festive tune (the name means "in sweet jubilation"), possibly with origins in folk dance, it should be sung lightly.

24
Grace to you and peace

Based on Romans 1:7, KJV
Alice Parker (1925-), 1962
The Mennonite Hymnal, 1969

The words of this familiar salutation of Paul are found at the beginning of a number of the Epistles. Sung as a three-part canon (round), the first two voices may sustain the last tone of the "Amen" until the last voice has arrived at the final cadence.

507
Gracious Spirit, dwell with me

Thomas Toke Lynch (1818-1871)
The Rivulet: A Contribution to Sacred Song, 1855, alt.

REDHEAD NO. 76 (GETHSEMANE)

Richard Redhead (1820-1901)
Church Hymn Tunes, Ancient and Modern, 1853

Lynch, a teacher and Congregationalist minister, published *The Rivulet . . .* for his own church as a supplement to Isaac Watts's *Hymns and Spiritual Songs* (1707). Lynch says of his collection, "Christian poetry is indeed a river of the water of life, and to this river my rivulet brings its contribution" (Bailey 1950). *The Rivulet . . .* caused considerable unrest because some found Lynch's intense appreciation of God's world of nature to be "profane," even "negative," theology. For example,

"Gracious Spirit" does not clearly identify the third person of the Trinity, but is a prayer to the non-theological spirit of God that permeates the universe and inspires the human spirit (Bailey 1950). Today, however, Lynch's work is deemed significant among the body of sacred literature.

For comments on REDHEAD NO. 76 (GETHSEMANE), see "Go to dark Gethsemane" (**240**).

388
Grant us, Lord, the grace — STUTTGART

Anonymous

Attrib. to Christian Friedrich Witt (ca. 1660-1716)
Psalmodia Sacra . . . , 1715
Adapt. by Henry J. Gauntlett (1805-1876)
Hymns Ancient and Modern, 1861

This simple offertory stanza of unknown authorship is set to the familiar tune STUTTGART. For comments on the tune, see "Child of blessing, child of promise" (**620**).

82
Great God, how infinite art thou — WINDSOR

Isaac Watts (1674-1748)
Hymns and Spiritual Songs, 1707

The Second Booke of the Musicke of M. William Damon, 1591

In this text Watts seems to be peering into a yawning gulf separating God and humanity. His austere Calvinistic belief contrasts God's eternal dominion with the human condition *sans* God, as reflected in the original words of stanza 1: "What worthless worms are we!" Stanza 3, often omitted, is:

> Nature and Time quite naked lie
> To Thine immense Survey,
> From the Formation of the Sky,
> To the great Burning-Day.

While some question God's power and omnipotence, Watts did *not* err on the side of making his God too small.

WINDSOR, one of the earliest common meter (CM) tunes, is a setting for Psalm 116 in the above source. There the tune is the soprano part in a texture of four imitative voices (found also in Routley's *The Music of Christian Hymns*). The ancestor of this tune is likely Christopher Tye's setting of chapter 3 of *The Acts of the Apostles* (1553), where the first, third, and fourth phrases and a fragment of the second are found.[1]

WINDSOR appears with a variety of names in English and Scottish psalters dating from 1615: SUFFOLK TUNE, DUNDIE, and EATON. According to the Boston, Massachusetts, edition (1698) of *The Bay Psalm Book* (1640), WINDSOR was one of the tunes the Puritans sang with their psalms.[2] The rhythm of the present version is that used in *The English Hymnal* (1906) where it is cited as being from the *Scottish Psalter* of 1633.

1. For a discussion of Tye's settings of Acts, see Routley's *The Music of Christian Hymns*. This setting with the metrical text of Acts 3 can be seen in the article on WINDSOR in Grove's *Dictionary of Music and Musicians*, 5th ed.

2. The version in *The Bay Psalm Book*, 1698, can be seen in Christ-Janer, Hughes, and Smith's *American Hymns Old and New*, Columbia University Press, 1980.

149
Great God of wonders — SOVEREIGNTY

Samuel F. Davies (1723-1761)
Gibbons' *Hymns Adapted to Divine Worship*, 1769

John Newton (1802-1886)
Newton's *The Pilgrim*, 2nd ed., 1839

This text, originally in five stanzas, appeared in more than one hundred hymn books in England by the early 1900s, but it is found in relatively few sources today. It comes to this hymnal by way of the Mennonite *Life Songs No. 2* (1938). It is an ample assurance of pardon, based on Micah 7:18, but Christianized in successive stanzas. Stanza 3 is wonderment at how God could put aside offense in favor of a "miracle of love" (st. 4).

The text has appeared with a variety of tunes, but John Newton composed this tune, SOVEREIGNTY, for these words by Samuel Davies. This is not the same John Newton, however, who authored "Amazing grace." Written in a style that would lend itself to string quartet performance, the music seems well suited to the theme of God's grace. In *Life Songs No. 2* the tune is called HUDDERSFIELD.

458
Great God, the giver of all good — RETREAT

James Skinner (1818-1881)
Daily Service Hymnal, 1863, alt.

Thomas Hastings (1784-1872)
Juvenile Songs (Religious, Moral, and Sentimental), 1841

This is appropriate as a prayer before the fellowship meal of love feast or any time of eating together. No biographical information on the author has been found.

The tune RETREAT is better known for its association with the text for which it was written, "From every stormy wind that blows." In

Hastings' *Juvenile Songs . . .* , the third phrase is scored for the melody voices only. The music is easy to learn by rote, as befits a table grace.

639

Great God, we sing — WAREHAM

Philip Doddridge (1702-1751)
Orton's *Hymns Founded on Various Texts in Holy Scriptures,* 1755

William Knapp (ca. 1698-1768)
A Sett of New Psalm Tunes and Anthems, 1738

This hymn first came out under the heading "Help obtained from God. Acts 26:22. For the New Year." The scripture reference is part of Paul's defense before King Agrippa when Jewish authorities were complaining about Paul's preaching. Set against that backdrop, Doddridge's words take on meaning beyond that of a "changing times" or New Year's hymn. Like all of Doddridge's hymns, this text was first sung from a flyleaf by his congregation following one of his sermons. Doddridge's friend Job Orton published it in his *Hymns Founded on Various Texts . . . .*

The tune WAREHAM suits a variety of texts. It was the setting for a portion of Psalm 36 in Knapp's 1738 collection where it appears in a somewhat more florid form. By 1774 it had been altered to its present melodic form. The tune is named for the composer's birthplace in Dorset, England.

87

Great is the Lord — GREAT IS THE LORD

Michael W. Smith (1957-) and
Deborah D. Smith (1958-), 1982

Michael W. Smith (1957-) and
Deborah D. Smith (1958-), 1982

This spirited song of praise has proved to be a favorite since Michael W. Smith recorded it. Michael's wife, Deborah, is collaborator for many of his works. Reciting some of God's attributes (holy, just, faithful, true, merciful), "Great is the Lord" echoes Psalm 145. Like a good praise chorus, its repetition makes it easy to learn.

A variety of instrumentations are possible with this song, using the chord markings over the voice parts and Marilyn Houser Hamm's keyboard arrangement in the *Accompaniment Handbook.*

327

Great is thy faithfulness — FAITHFULNESS

Thomas Obediah Chisholm (1866-1960)
Runyan's *Songs of Salvation and Service,* Chicago, 1923

William Marion Runyan (1870-1957)
(same source as text)

Both author and composer claim that this hymn had "no special circumstance" connected with its composition. Its popularity, however, would indicate it has appealed to many special circumstances over the years. The hymn attests to the constancy of God ("there is no variation due to a shadow of tuning") as revealed in nature (st. 2) and in forgiveness (st. 3).

Over the years Runyan set some twenty of Chisholm's poems to music. Of this one Runyan writes: "This particular poem held such an appeal that I prayed most earnestly that my tune might carry over its message in a worthy way, and the subsequent history of its use indicates that God answered prayer" (Reynolds 1976).

Runyan did not write his first gospel hymn until 1915 when he was forty-five. This hymn was a most popular one at the Moody Bible Institute in Chicago, with which Runyan was associated during the latter part of his life. It was regarded by many as the unofficial school hymn of the institute.

582
Guide me, O thou great Jehovah

Arglwydd, arwain trwy'r anialwch
William Williams (1717-1791)
Williams' *Aleluia,* 1745
Tr. Peter Williams (1722-1796) and William Williams (1771-1772)
Hymns on Various Subjects, 1771

CWM RHONDDA

John Hughes (1873-1932), 1905 or 1907
The Voice of Thanksgiving, No. 4, 1928
Fellowship Hymn Book, 1933

The imagery of this hymn comes from the Israelite wanderings in the wilderness—the barren land, bread of heaven (manna), fiery pillar, the Jordan River, the land of Canaan. William Williams spiritualized this story into a hymn that recalls both Old and New Testament symbols. For Christians, Jordan is the river of death, hence the "anxious fears" until the believer arrives in heaven (Canaan).

Having written eight hundred hymns in Welsh (one hundred in English), Williams is said to have been more important as a hymnwriter to Wales than Isaac Watts was to England. In 1771 Peter Williams began the translation into the English of the original five stanzas of this hymn. His first stanza was retained, and another version was created by the original author or his son John. Stanzas 3 and 4 of the original were retranslated and a new fourth stanza was written. The first three stanzas of this second version comprise our text.

Numerous alterations have been made over the years. In the late eighteenth century, "Death of death's and hell's destruction" in stanza 3 was changed to "Bear me through the swelling current," a reference to crossing the Jordan. Here we return to the original form, but "death's" becomes "death."

For comments on CWM RHONDDA, see "God of grace and God of glory" (**366**).

583
Guide me, O thou great Jehovah—see "Ndikhokele, O Jehova"

546
Guide my feet

African American spiritual

GUIDE MY FEET

African American spiritual
Harm. by Wendell Phillips Whalum (1932-1987)

This spiritual unabashedly asks for God's guidance and support to "run this race" of life. The harmonization is by Wendell Whalum, a professor at Morehouse College, Atlanta, Georgia, who researched many older spirituals. This one, from the turn-of-the-century collection of Willis Laurence James, was printed in the AME (African Methodist Episcopal) hymnal (1984).

Music director/composer Leonardo Wilborn (Imperial Heights Church of the Brethren in California) distinguishes between African American spirituals and black gospel songs:

> [Spirituals] were sung by slaves and ex-slaves. . . . Sometimes used as social commentaries and secret communications, the [texts] . . . are based primarily on Old Testament teachings and the crucifixion and death of Christ. Spirituals are generally dark in nature, reflecting the mood and unrest of the Negro slave. . . . This song style is an historical account of a group of people striving to be reconciled to God.
>
> [By contrast], gospel songs . . . developed in the North . . . when [Negro] migrants took with them the tools that had helped them survive . . . slavery.
>
> Thus the northern "Negro experience" sprouted a modified approach to the "well of faith" and reflected the influences of their new urban environment. Traditional hymns of Watts and Wesley were "molded into a strictly 'Black American' idiom . . . characterized by modified harmonies, improvised lead lines, and . . . syncopated rhythm attacks." Eileen Southern, a noted writer on black music, writes, "Negro gospel music became essentially the sacred counterpart of the city blues . . . . "
>
> This idiom . . . achieved popularity in the . . . 20th century . . . through the . . . interpretation of such vocalists as Mahalia Jackson, Clara Ward, Shirley Caesar, and Aretha Franklin. This format uses lyrics drawn mainly from the four Gospels of the New Testament

and Paul's letters . . . [and] are largely positive, happy, even joyous in nature.

221
Hail the bless'd morn — STAR IN THE EAST

Reginald Heber (1783-1826)
Christian Observer, 1811, alt.

Southern Harmony, 1835
Harm. by Alice Parker (1925-), 1990

This Epiphany hymn, like many of Heber's poems, was first printed in the *Christian Observer* and later in Heber's *Hymns Written and Adapted to the Weekly Church Services of the Year*. The latter collection, completed posthumously, was apparently the earliest modern English hymnal arranged according to the church calendar. All of Heber's hymns were written before he became bishop of Calcutta, India, in 1823.

Epiphany (manifestation of a deity) traditionally begins about January 6 when the adoration of the magi is celebrated. Many hymnals begin with the second quatrain, "Brightest and best of the stars of the morning," a description of the star the magi followed to find the baby Jesus. It carries double meaning, however, when we remember that Jesus himself is described as the "bright morning star" (Rev. 22:16). Some hymnals even present the two parts as separate hymns.

The regular rhythm of STAR IN THE EAST makes it feel like a "journeying" song. Notice that in the harmony parts, as in the melody, the pitch E-flat appears only as a passing tone. This text appears in Joseph Funk's *Harmonia Sacra* with a different tune in C major, also called STAR IN THE EAST.

185
Hail to the Lord's anointed — FARMER

Based on Psalm 72
James Montgomery (1771-1854)
Evangelical Magazine, May 1822

John Farmer (1836-1901), 1892

The "Lord's anointed," in the psalmist's eyes, would have been the Messiah. This text is Montgomery's vibrant and detailed rendering of Psalm 72, a description of what this arrival of David's offspring will mean.

The hymn was written for Christmas 1821 at a Moravian settlement in England, possibly at Fulneck. A few weeks later the manuscript went with George Bennett on a mission tour in the South Seas. Beginning with Montgomery's *Songs of Zion*, this eight-stanza text is varied slightly in each of Montgomery's works, the authorized version being the one in *Original Hymns*. The first three stanzas used here are 1, 2, and 4 of the original, while the final stanza is composed of the first half of stanza 7 and the last half of stanza 8. Of the omitted stanzas, the fifth is especially interesting, asserting that non-Jews will also recognize the Messiah:

Arabia's desert ranger to him shall bow the knee,
the Ethiopian stranger his glory come to see:
with offerings of devotion, ships from the isles shall meet,
to pour the wealth of ocean in tribute at his feet.

In stanza 2:1, "justice surely" replaces "succor speedy."

FARMER is a marchlike tune reflecting the spirit of the text. It is similar in style to WEBB (see "Bless'd be the God of Israel," **174**), which would be a good alternative. The source and date of the tune are uncertain, but it may be Farmer's *Hymns and Chorales for Schools and Colleges* (1892) (*Psalter Hymnal Handbook*).

184
Hark! the glad sound

Philip Doddridge (1702-1751)
Translations and Paraphrases, 1745

COMMUNION

"Robinson" in John Wyeth's *Repository of Sacred Music, Part Second,* 1813
Harm. by J. Harold Moyer (1927-), 1965
The Mennonite Hymnal, 1969

In the manuscript dated December 28, 1735, the seven stanzas of this text appear under the caption "Christ's Message, from Luke IV, 18, 19." According to hymnologist Louis Benson, it is an embellished and lyric interpretation of that passage, almost "as if the poet had been present in the Nazareth synagogue when Jesus read the prophet's word . . . " (Loewen, Moyer, Oyer 1983). It is a hymn to inspire not only Advent preparation, but all prophetic work that reveals the dominion of God.

Published in the Church of Scotland's *Translations and Paraphrases* of 1745, 1751, and 1781, the hymn appears each time with alterations. Its first printing in England was in Doddridge's *Hymns,* published four years after his death by Job Orton. This text is taken from that basically unaltered version. Stanza 4, which has been omitted, reads:

He comes, from thickest films of vice
to clear the mental ray,
And on the eyeballs of the blind
to pour celestial day.

COMMUNION is typical of many American folk hymns of the early nineteenth century, with its unusual intervals and metrical groupings. In Moyer's harmonization, the unison beginnings of the first, second, and fourth lines strengthen the tune's rustic exuberance. Both text and tune are hardy, good for congregational singing.

201

Hark! the herald angels sing — MENDELSSOHN

Charles Wesley (1707-1788) and others
Hymns and Sacred Poems, 1739, alt.

Felix Mendelssohn (1809-1847), 1840
Adapt. by William Hayman Cummings (1831-1915), 1855
Chope's *Congregational Hymn and Tune Book*, 1857

Wesley's original hymn consisted of ten four-line stanzas, beginning "Hark! how all the welkin rings, Glory to the King of Kings." *Welkin* is an old English word for vault of heaven, or sky. The now-familiar opening lines first appeared in George Whitefield's *Collection of Hymns for Social Worship* (1753). Over the years other text alterations have been made; the recent change in stanza 2:4, from "pleased as man with men to dwell" to "pleased with us in flesh to dwell," was made without changing the theology of the incarnation expressed in the hymn. The hymn is packed with theological substance, and some stanzas were especially useful in teaching John Wesley's Methodism classes.

MENDELSSOHN was adapted from Chorus No. 2 of Mendelssohn's *Festgesang an die Künstler*, Opus 68, for male chorus and orchestra. This work was first performed in 1840 in Leipzig, Germany, to commemorate the four hundredth anniversary of the invention of printing. William Cummings set Wesley's text to the melody in 1855, a fortuitous combination of text and tune, though Mendelssohn himself thought this music inappropriate for sacred words. He writes, "There must be . . . something to which the soldier-like and buxom motion of the piece has some relation . . . " (*The Hymnal 1940 Companion*, 1951 ed.).

504

Have thine own way, Lord — ADELAIDE

Adelaide Addison Pollard (1862-1934)
Northfield Hymnal with Alexander's Supplement, 1907, alt.

George Coles Stebbins (1846-1945)
(same source as text)

The early twentieth century saw intense activity in the mission fields of Africa. Iowa-born Adelaide Pollard felt called there, but her plans were thwarted by poor health and insufficient funds. In her disappointment she attended a prayer meeting where she found peace of mind in submission to the will of God. Meditating on the story of the potter in Jeremiah 18:3-4, she wrote this well-loved hymn.

Debates have raged over the recently accepted change in stanza 2:3 from "whiter than snow" to "wash me just now." Though the cleansing can be construed as referring to the soul, it is one more example of how purity in North American Anglo culture has often been equated with whiteness, to the detriment of people of color.

Stebbins wrote ADELAIDE for this text and published it in the collection listed above. That same year it was released in two other Biglow and Main publications: Sankey's *Hallowed Hymns Old and New* and *Best Endeavor Hymns*, compiled by Sankey and Clement.

498

He comes to us as one unknown

REPTON

Timothy Dudley-Smith (1926-), 1982
On the Move, Australia, July 1983

Charles Hubert Hastings Parry (1848-1918)
Judith, 1888
Hymns Ancient and Modern, 1904 ed.

The author, who wrote this text in some moments of relaxation at the family summer home in Cornwall, tells about its genesis, development, and content:

> This hymn had its origin in [a] quotation . . . from the closing pages of Albert Schweitzer's *The Quest of the Historical Jesus,* which says of Christ: "He comes to us as One unknown, without a name, as of old, by the lakeside, He came to those first men who knew Him not." Taking as its theme our perception of God's approach to the soul, and the "sense of the divine" which is part of human experience, the first two verses were written at a sitting. The third is a reference to Revelation 1:15 and to 1 Kings 19; with the merest allusion to 1 Chronicles 14:15, when "a sound of going in the tops of the mulberry trees" is a sign or signal from the Lord himself: the NEB translation is "a rustling sound in the treetops." By verse 4 the text is explicitly Christian in its reference both to incarnation and to atonement; and by verse 5 there is the personal response of faith to the Lord Jesus Christ of the New Testament. (Dudley-Smith 1984)

REPTON, the tune suggested for this text by the author, originated in Parry's oratorio *Judith* (adapted from the Book of Judith in the Apocrypha), scene 2, where Mershallemeth sings it to the words "Long since in Egypt's plenteous land." This beautiful melody has also been used in British hymnals with John Greenleaf Whittier's familiar words "Dear Lord and Father of mankind" (**523**).

599

He leadeth me

HE LEADETH ME

Joseph Henry Gilmore (1834-1918)
Watchman and Reflector, Boston, Dec. 4, 1862, alt.

William Batchelder Bradbury (1816-1868)
Bradbury's *The Golden Censer,* New York, 1864

As a young minister briefly filling the pulpit of First Baptist Church of Philadelphia, Pennsylvania, Joseph Gilmore led a midweek service based on Psalm 23. He later wrote: "I did not get further than the words 'He leadeth me.' Those words took hold of me as they had never done before. I saw in them a significance and beauty of which I had never dreamed" (Reynolds 1976). Gilmore's conviction rings through the hymn: "[I]t makes no difference how we are led, (or) where we are led, so long as we are sure God is leading us" (*The Worshiping Church* 1990, 1991). Later that evening he "penciled the hymn, handed it to [his] wife and thought no more about it." Months later she sent it to the *Watchman and Reflector*, under the unexplained pseudonym "Contoocook."

William Bradbury, finding the poem in that publication, set it to music that first appeared in his *Golden Censer*. The third line of the refrain, "His faithful follower I would be," seems to have been added by Bradbury to fit the musical ideas of his setting. Gilmore did not know that his poem had been set to music until 1865 when he accidentally discovered it in the hymnal of Second Baptist Church, Rochester, New York, where he had gone to preach as a pastoral candidate.

375
Heal us, Immanuel, here we are — DUNFERMLINE

William Cowper (1731-1800)
Olney Hymns, Book I, 1779

Andro Hart's *The CL Psalmes of David* (Scottish Psalter), 1615

In *Olney Hymns* this text carries the heading "Jehovah Rophi—I am the Lord that healeth thee." It is a promise that tests our faith, much as it did the father of the child healed in Mark 9 and the woman healed of a flow of blood in Mark 5:34, both referred to in the hymn. We find comfort in the assurance that Christ takes "deep-wounded souls" to heart.

Cowper's opening line has also appeared as "Heal us, Emmanuel, here we stand," "Heal us, Immanuel, hear our prayer," and "Healer Divine, O hear our prayer."

DUNFERMLINE is one of the "common tunes" in Andro Hart's Scottish psalter, meaning that, instead of being assigned to a specific psalm, it could be used interchangeably with the rest of the group of "common tunes." Another form of the tune may be found with the hymn "How bless'd are they" (**525**).

377

Healer of our every ill — (no tune name)

Marty Haugen (1950-), 1986
Gather, 1988

Marty Haugen (1950-), 1986
(same source as text)

A natural choice for churches that offer ministries for healing, this song was composed for a service of healing at Holden Village, an ecumenical retreat center where Marty Haugen was composer-in-residence. Haugen relates: "Originally the refrain was intended to be sung by the congregation, while the verses were reserved for a choir or cantor as hands were laid on those who came forward. However, congregations typically began to sing the entire song, and today it is most often done that way."

The hymn moves from concern for physical healing to prayers for emotional and spiritual healing, as expressed in the requests in the last stanzas for "compassion" and "strength to love each other."

23

Hear thou our prayer, Lord

Nelson Thomas Huffman (1901-1992)
The Brethren Hymnal, 1951

Nelson Thomas Huffman (1901-1992)
(same source as text)

This was one of two calls to prayer written by Huffman for *The Brethren Hymnal* (1951). It was included in *The Mennonite Hymnal* (1969) as well. The author/composer served for many years as professor of voice and director of music at Bridgewater College, a Brethren-affiliated school in Virginia.

626

Hear us now, O God our Maker — HYFRYDOL

Harry Norman Huxhold (1922-), 1971
Lutheran Book of Worship, 1978, alt.

Rowland Hugh Prichard (1811-1887), ca. 1830
Cyfaill y Cantorion (The Singer's Friend), 1844
Arr. by Ralph Vaughan Williams (1872-1958)
The English Hymnal, 1906
Adapt. in *BBC Hymn Book*, 1951

This wedding hymn, designed for the congregation to sing to the bridal couple, was written for the marriage of the author's son, Timothy, to Pamela Jo on August 14, 1971. Huxhold's prayer of blessing will prove a welcome addition to the music available for Christian weddings.

For comments on HYFRYDOL, see "Come, thou long-expected Jesus" (**178**).

392

Heart and mind, possessions, Lord

TANA MANA DHANA

Krishnarao Rathnaji Sangle (1834-1908)
Tr. Alden H. Clark (1878-1960)
Pilgrim Hymnal, 1958 ed.

Ancient Indian melody
Adapt. by Marion Jean Chute (1901-) and others
Upasanasangit, *Marathi Christian Hymnal*
Pilgrim Hymnal, 1958

This is a favorite hymn in Marathi, a region of western India, near Bombay. The translator, Alden Clark, was a Congregational missionary to India for nearly thirty years. His daughter describes its use in India:

> This hymn is sung with many verses in all the Marathi churches and also with many variations. The hymn books have only the words in many places, and the Bhajan band, or instruments used in leading music, create variations, as in all folk music. . . . There might be six or seven players, all seated on the floor of course, with drums, cymbals, castanets, pipe, tabla, etc. (Ronander and Porter 1966)

As with many folk tunes, information on its earlier sources is incomplete.

The tune name TANA MANA DHANA comes from the language spoken in Marathi and means "Heart, mind, possessions." Missionary Marion Chute, along with the translator's wife and daughter, adapted the tune to the English words. The melody is pentatonic and may be played on the black keys of the piano by beginning on F-sharp.

420

Heart with loving heart united

O DU LIEBE MEINER LIEBE

Herz und Herz vereint zusammen
Nicolaus Ludwig von Zinzendorf (1700-1760), 1723
Zinzendorf's *Die letzten Reden unseres Herrn*, Frankfurt and Leipzig, 1725
Tr. Walter Klaassen (1926-), 1965, rev. 1983
The Mennonite Hymnal, 1969

Manuscript Chorale Book, Herrnhaag, 1735

These verses come from Zinzendorf's poetic setting of Jesus' farewell discourse to his disciples in John 14—17. Zinzendorf's work was a major treatise, 320 stanzas long. Three stanzas in this hymn focus on the important Anabaptist emphasis of the fellowship of believers. It is in this fellowship that the world visualizes the communion of the body of Christ. Long a favorite among Moravians, it has appeared in their hymnals in other translations as early as 1789, beginning "Flock of Jesus be united, covenant anew with Him" and "Christian hearts, in love united."

O DU LIEBE MEINER LIEBE was based on an earlier secular tune, popular around 1700. In the 1730s and 1740s, the Moravian Brethren used it with a hymn text at Herrnhut and Herrnhaag. The first published version was Johann Thommen's *Erbaulicher Musicalischer Christen-Schatz* (Basel 1745). The tune also is known as CASSEL.

75
Heilig, heilig, heilig

Holy, holy, holy
Johann Philipp Neumann (1774-1849)
Tr. John Donald Rempel (1944-), 1990
Hymnal: A Worship Book, 1992

(no tune name)

Franz Peter Schubert (1797-1828)
Gesänge zur Feier des heiligen Opfer der Messe, 1826

This composition is part of Schubert's Mass where it is marked *Zum Sanctus*. This part of the Mass comes from Isaiah 6, as well as from the song of the winged creatures in Revelation 4:8-9 who surround the throne of God to give unceasing praise. This was written initially as a vernacular of the Mass. The original orchestration calls for two each of oboes, clarinets, bassoons, and horns, three trombones, tympani, and organ. Throughout most of the score, the wind instruments double the organ part, which follows the vocal lines.

362
Help us to help each other

Charles Wesley (1707-1788)
Hymns and Sacred Poems, 1742
Rev. in *Hymns for Today's Church*, 1982

BALERMA

François Hippolyte Barthélémon (1741-1808)
Adapt. by Robert Simpson (1790-1832)
A Selection of Original Music . . . Intended to Form the Sixth Volume of Steven's Selection of Sacred Music, 1833

In this hymn Wesley offers yet another metaphor for Christ's love—a magnet (st. 4). This "magnetism" is not only in Christ's person, but is also a catalyst for loving fellowship among believers who allow Christ to transform their spirits.

Wesley's hymn, titled "A Prayer for Persons joined in Fellowship," is in four parts, originally beginning "Try us, O God, and search the ground." This hymn begins with stanza 3 of Part I. Appropriate scriptural allusions are: Acts 20:32; Galatians 6:2; Ephesians 4:1-16 and 5:25-27; and Revelation 21:2.

BALERMA (BALLERMA) is an adaptation of Barthélémon's melody that the composer set to "Belerma and Durandarte," a poem Matthew Gregory Lewis interpolated into his popular novel *The Monk* (1795). Lewis states in his preface "advertisement" that "Belerma and Durandarte" was translated from stanzas found in a collection of old Spanish poetry. James Boaden dramatized the novel in 1798 and titled it *Aurelio and Miranda*. Barthélémon may have written his music for that drama, though the poem is not included in published versions of the play (*Hymnal 1940 Companion*, 1951 ed.).

The manuscript of Simpson's adaptation was found among his papers after his death and subsequently published in the above-listed collection, which was edited by John Turnbull.

296
Here from all nations

Based on Revelation 7:9-17
Christopher Martin Idle (1938-), 1972
Psalm Praise, 1973

O QUANTA QUALIA

Paris Antiphoner, 1681
Adapt. by François de la Feillée (d. ca. 1780)
Méthode du plain-chant, 1808
Harm. by David Evans (1874-1948)
The Church Hymnary, 1927

During the preparation of *Psalm Praise*, the editorial group was invited to submit texts as "canticles" paraphrasing New Testament passages. This text based on Revelation was Idle's contribution. Drawing from "Then I saw a new heaven and earth" in chapter 21 and the song of the redeemed martyrs in chapter 7, Idle recasts a theme already used by Isaac Watts and William Cameron in "How bright those glorious spirits shine." Here is a rapturous scene from heaven where those who have suffered for Christ receive their recompense and are free to worship God with a fervor that makes earthly worship pale by comparison. Despite its futuristic theme taken from an apocalyptic vision, this, of all Idle's texts, is most frequently included in other hymnals, even ones as diverse as *Chinese Bilingual Hymn Book* (1989) and *Irish Church Praise* (1990).

O QUANTA QUALIA has become the accepted tune for these words. The name is derived from the opening words of a Latin text by Peter Abelard with which the melody has been associated: "Oh, what their joy and their glory must be." Abelard's text was set to this melody in *The Hymnal Noted* (1854) where the tune was first recast in metric form. The melody is also called REGNATOR ORBIS from the opening phrase of the Michaelmas hymn with which it is found in la Feillée's collection. The tune also may be used as an alternative to "Blessing and honor and glory" (**108**).

395

Here I am, Lord

Based on Isaiah 6
Daniel L. Schutte (1947-), 1980
Lord of Light, 1981

(no tune name)

Daniel L. Schutte (1947-)
(same source as text)
Arr. by Michael Pope, S.J., and
John Weissrock

Isaiah the visionary, dramatically cleansed by a burning coal upon his lips, offers himself as a prophet of the living God with these words: "Here am I; send me" (Isa. 6:8). It was a bold move, dangerous because of an unpopular message to a recalcitrant Israel. It required commitment that God still requests of believers by asking, "Whom shall I send, and who will go for us?"

Written for an ordination ceremony of some of Schutte's fellow Jesuits in Berkeley, California, the text was later slightly modified by the author at the suggestion of friends. He decided that the original refrain was "a bit too bold. Though we all would like to claim that our following the call of God is enthusiastic and wholehearted, I think our most human response is often much more timid and cautious. I wanted the lyrics of the hymn to reflect that humanness of our response to God. In my own mind, that does not make it any less courageous or holy."

The stanzas lift up the characteristics of God as described by the psalmists and prophets. The music for them is in the *Accompaniment Handbook*. The refrain is scored here in SATB harmony and may be sung as a response or benediction.

450

Here in our upper room

Paul Minnich Robinson (1914-), 1949
The Brethren Hymnal, 1951, rev. 1990

HOLLEY

George Hews (1806-1873)
Lowell Mason's *Boston Academy's Collection of Church Music*, 3rd ed., 1835

The text of this hymn takes us through all the experiences of love feast, from self-examination and footwashing to partaking of the bread and cup. Robinson wrote the words at the 1949 Church of the Brethren Annual Conference "out of the inspiration of the sessions which were endeavoring to set forth the unique ministry of the Church of the Brethren in the world. . . . While I was writing, . . . the tune HOLLEY kept going through my mind" (Statler, Fisher 1959). Robinson contemporized the language for this hymnal.

HOLLEY first appeared in Mason's . . . *Collection* . . . with two stanzas of the text "Softly now the light of day." The music was printed as a duet for treble (melody) and alto, with optional notes for the other two parts. The tune, credited to George Hews, was probably named for a village in

Orleans County, New York, which in turn had been named for one of the canal commissioners of that state.

6

Here in this place — GATHER US IN

Marty Haugen (1950-), 1981
Gather, 1988

Marty Haugen (1950-), 1981
(same source as text)

This hymn gathers in the spectrum of Christians, from the forsaken to the rich and haughty, from the lame to the strong. The images of the hymn are related to a number of biblical passages, especially from Jesus' Sermon on the Mount (Matt. 5:13-16). The "new light" that Jesus describes is no futuristic wish, but an indomitable beacon of God's presence among us (st. 4), palpable even in our "flesh and our bone." Worship leaders should be selective in choosing stanza 3, which deals with the Eucharist (Communion).

The simple melody, in A A' B A' form, has a driving, folklike character. Because the text is quite full of ideas, the long ends of the second and fourth phrases are important to give the singer time to absorb the words and prepare for the next section.

7

Here, O Lord, your servants gather — TOKYO

Tokuo Yamaguchi (1900-)
Christian Shimpō, 1958
Paraphrased by Everett M. Stowe (20th c.), 1958
Hymns of the Church, 1963, alt.

Gagku mode (Japan)
Isao Koizumi (1907-) (JASRAC), 1958
(same source as text)

This hymn, written in the era that saw both atomic devastation and the beginning of space exploration, is a prayer for international peace and unity in Christ. Both text and tune were written for the Fourteenth World Council of Christian Education Convention, held in Tokyo in 1958. The first three stanzas follow the theme of the convention, "Christ, the Way, the Truth, and the Life" (John 14:6), while the final stanza sums up the hymn.

After its appearance in the convention program booklet, the hymn was published in the hymnal of the United Church of Christ in Japan. Its first printing in the U.S. was in *The Mennonite Hymnal* (1969). The present English text, which changes the archaic forms of address, comes from the Asian American collection *Hymns from the Four Winds* (1983).

For the convention booklet, the text was set to two tunes: TOKYO, by Koizumi, and TOKYO CONVENTION, by Eisai Ikemiya. TOKYO is in the Gagku mode, which was used in the traditional music of the Japanese court. The composer's supporting keyboard score for this pentatonic melody may be found in the *Accompaniment Handbook*, along with other musical suggestions.

465

Here, O my Lord, I see thee — KINGSBORO

Horatius N. Bonar (1808-1889)
Leaflet, 1855
Hymns of Faith and Hope, 1857

M. Lee Suitor (1942-), 1975
Published in anthem form
Hymnal Supplement, 1984
Harm. by Marilyn Houser Hamm and M. Lee Suitor

Bonar's text is as tasteful and graceful as the Communion fellowship of which he writes. The mysticism of stanza 1 sets a tone of quiet and serenity in Christ's presence. At meal's end participants wistfully leave the table, but they anticipate refuge and refreshment at feasts to come—at the ultimate banquet of the Lamb.

Bonar wrote the hymn at the request of his brother, John J. Bonar, pastor of St. Andrew's Free Church, Greenock, Scotland. After Communion the newly composed hymn was distributed to the parishioners in a Communion leaflet in October 1855. Most hymnals do not include all ten original stanzas; five stanzas are included here and a sixth in the *Accompaniment Handbook* (1, 7, 2, 3, 4, and 10). Individual stanzas could be used effectively at different points in love feast or the Communion service.

The tune KINGSBORO was written for this text. The composer writes that when he "was first at St. Luke's Church, Atlanta, [Georgia], we lived on Kingsboro Road. . . . It was in that house, one morning, that I woke up with the seeds of the tune in my mind, and rather than get breakfast and go to church and prepare for rehearsal, I spent hours shaping and reshaping the notes in those sixteen measures." This musical exploration in a folk-music idiom provides a refreshing setting for a venerable text. The tune was first named FACE TO FACE and then renamed by Suitor to "bring joy to the eyes of my son Paul and his sister Jennifer" who grew up in that house on Kingsboro Road.

The familiar melody MORECAMBE, usually associated with "Spirit of God, descend" (**502**), is a good alternate tune.

121
Holy God, we praise thy name

Te Deum laudamus
Late 4th c.
Tr. Clarence Augustus Walworth (1820-1900), 1853, based on Ignaz Franz's German translation (ca. 1774) of *Te Deum laudamus,* alt.

GROSSER GOTT, WIR LOBEN DICH

Katholisches Gesangbuch, Vienna, 1774
(Zahn No. 3495)

The *Te Deum laudamus* is a familiar non-biblical canticle (song text); legend (disputed) has it that Ambrose and St. Augustine improvised it at Augustine's baptism in 385. In the *Book of Common Prayer*, it is arranged in three sections: a song of praise, a confession of faith, and a prayer for help. The fourth stanza used in the hymnal constitutes the first portion of the whole poem by Walworth. The three omitted stanzas paraphrase the rest of the *Te Deum*:

> 5. Thou art King of Glory, Christ!
> Son of God, yet born of Mary.
> For us sinners sacrificed,
> And to death a Tributary,
> First to break the bars of death,
> Thou hast opened Heaven to faith.
>
> 6. From Thy high, celestial Home,
> Judge of all, again returning,
> We believe that Thou shalt come,
> On the dreadful Doom's-day morning,
> When Thy Voice shall shake the earth,
> And the startled dead come forth.
>
> 7. Spare Thy people, Lord, we pray,
> By a thousand snares surrounded:
> Keep us without sin today,
> Never let us be confounded.
> Lo! I put my trust in Thee,
> Never, Lord, abandon me. (Oyer 1980)

A very important hymn historically, the *Te Deum* was given prominence by Martin Luther next to the Apostles' Creed and the Athanasian Creed (Oyer 1980). This is hymn No. 1 in *The Mennonite Hymnal* (1969), and it includes a German metrical translation by Ignaz Franz, written around 1774.

The melodic style of GROSSER GOTT is like that of a folk song.[1] The present form of the melody dates to J. G. Schicht's *Allgemeines Choralbuch* (Leipzig 1819). The tune also is related to HURSLEY (see **490** and **654**), which was published in North America in slightly different form with the name FRAMINGHAM.

1. The full history may be found in Wilhelm Bäumker's *Das Katholische Deutsche Kirchenlied in seinen Singweisen*, Vol. III.

120
Holy, holy, holy — NICAEA

Reginald Heber (1783-1826)
Heber's *A Selection of Psalms and Hymns for the Parish Church of Banbury*, 1826

John Bacchus Dykes (1823-1876)
Hymns Ancient and Modern, 1861

Reginald Heber had a special interest in collecting hymns appropriate for each Sunday of the church year. When he could not find one, he wrote one. This hymn, included in virtually all English-language hymnals, is a stately metrical paraphrase of Revelation 4:8-11. Often used as a morning hymn, it was penned by Heber for Trinity Sunday (eight weeks after Easter) while he was vicar at Hodnet, Shropshire (1807-1823). It was published posthumously in the third edition of the source above and was one of fifty-seven hymns by Heber in *Hymns, Written and Adapted to the Weekly Service of the Church Year* (1827).

NICAEA is named for the ancient city in Asia Minor where the first general council of the Christian church was convened by Constantine in 325. That council affirmed and clarified the doctrine of the Trinity in the Nicene Creed. Though NICAEA was written for this text, scholars have noted the resemblance of the opening and closing phrases to those of WACHET AUF. A similarity with John Hopkins' tune TRINITY, to which this text had been set in 1850, may be seen as well.[1] Whatever Dykes' inspiration, the melody and harmony have survived without alteration, a tribute to its quality.

1. An example is found in *Hymnal Companion to the Lutheran Book of Worship*, Fortress Press, 1981, page 256.

26
Holy Spirit, come with power — BEACH SPRING

Anne Neufeld Rupp (1932-), 1970, alt.

Attrib. to Benjamin Franklin White (1800-1879)
Sacred Harp, 1844
Harm. by Joan Annette Fyock (1938-), 1988

The Holy Spirit is often depicted as a dynamo, and no less so in this text. Breaking, burning, bursting, breathing upon a congregation, the Spirit has a way of upending our lives.

Anne Rupp wrote this text for a Pentecost service at First Mennonite Church in Beatrice, Nebraska, where her husband was pastor. It has been published several times, most recently in the adult Foundation Series Sunday school curriculum "Led by Word and Spirit." Stanza 3:6 has been changed from "Bare our arms . . ." to "Lend our hands to those who hurt."

BEACH SPRING is part of the shaped-note *Sacred Harp* collection that continues to be used for rousing music festivals. Fyock, director of music ministries at Lititz Church of the Brethren in Pennsylvania, harmonized BEACH SPRING as the setting of a text for the wedding of one of the congregation's adult choir members. NETTLETON (**521**) or EBENEZER (**410**) could also be used with these words.

542
Holy Spirit, gracious Guest — ANDERSON

Christopher Wordsworth (1807-1885)
The Holy Year . . . , 1862
Rev. in *Hymns for Today's Church,* 1982

Jane Manton Marshall (1924-), 1985
Hymnal Supplement II, 1987

This hymn is a paraphrase of 1 Corinthians 13, the Epistle reading for *Quinquagesima* (Latin for fiftieth), which corresponds to the Sunday before Ash Wednesday, fifty days before Easter. In the church calendar, this time frame balances the pre-Easter fast days with the post-Easter feast days. Along with other minor changes, the first stanza of this hymn has been greatly altered; the original was:

> Gracious Spirit, Holy Ghost,
> Taught by thee, we covet most
> Of thy gifts at Pentecost,
> Holy, heavenly love.

Of Wordsworth's eight stanzas, those used here are stanzas 1-5 and 7. The omitted stanzas 6 and 8, which do not adhere as closely to Paul's letter, follow:

> 6. Faith will vanish into sight;
> Hope be emptied in delight;
> Love in heaven will shine more bright;
> Therefore, give us love.

> 8. From the overshadowing
> Of thy gold and silver wing,
> Shed on us, who to thee sing,
> Holy heavenly love.

The tune ANDERSON, composed for this text, was originally in unison. Jane Marshall provided a new four-part harmonization for this hymnal.

132
Holy Spirit, Storm of love — STORM

Brian Arthur Wren (1936-), 1985
Praising a Mystery, 1986

Bradley P. Lehman (1964-), 1991
Hymnal: A Worship Book, 1992

Like many of Wren's poems, this mission text is compact, profuse with vibrant language and scriptural images. It explores the depths of Christ's sacrifice for us on the cross, which is the basis for our call to "witness unashamed, confident to give good news." Stanza 2 echoes Mark 14:33; stanzas 3 and 4 relate to 1 Peter 2:22-25 and 2 Corinthians 5:21 and Romans 6:5-11, respectively.

The text also functions as a confession of apathy, challenging us to face the agony of Jesus and to let it transform us to "meet the evils of our time." It had this impact on composer Bradley Lehman, who wrote the music of STORM during the U.S.'s military action in the Persian Gulf, Operation Desert Storm. The music was a vent for Lehman's anger and frustration that many civilians had been killed in bombings a few hours earlier. For Lehman the horror of that event led to "a twenty-minute tearful outburst one morning in February 1991. Wren's visceral text was a stark expression of my feelings that day. . . . All the frustration and its resolution came out as I composed this music. As soon as I read this text and chose the key signature of E minor . . . , everything fell into place."

508
Holy Spirit, Truth divine — MERCY

Samuel Longfellow (1819-1892)
Longfellow and Samuel Johnson's *Hymns of the Spirit*, 1864

Arr. from Louis Moreau Gottschalk (1829-1869)
"The Last Hope," 1854
Adapt. by Edwin Pond Parker (1836-1925)

Literary excellence in the Longfellow family was not the exclusive domain of Henry Wadsworth. His brother, Samuel, used each of these six stanzas like a catalogue entry to delineate one scriptural attribute of the Holy Spirit. "O come, O come, Immanuel" (**172**) treats the various names for the Messiah similarly. The version here comes from *Hymns for Today's Church* (1982). The original fourth stanza, omitted from earlier usage, is now the final stanza.

Early in its use, MERCY was associated with Charles Wesley's "Depth of mercy, can there be"—hence its tune name. The melody also is sometimes used with Andrew Reed's text "Holy Spirit, light divine," which has created some confusion between the two hymns. Parker's adaptation of the melody from Gottschalk's piano composition first appeared in a hymnal edited by Charles S. Robinson (Reynolds 1976).

238

Hosanna, loud hosanna — ELLACOMBE

Jeannette Threlfall (1821-1880)
Sunshine and Shadow, 1873, alt.

Adapt. from *Gesangbuch der Herzogl, Wirtembergischen katholischen Hofkapelle,* Württemberg, 1784
Harm. by William Henry Monk (1823-1889)
Hymns Ancient and Modern, Appendix, 1868

This is the best known of Threlfall's hymns, which she wrote in "idle moments." Despite the early death of her parents and an accident that left her with permanent disabilities, she was able to express in this text a victorious message of hope. The phrase "men and angels" in stanza 2:3 has been changed to "earth and heaven."

This hymn focuses on the children's role in Jesus' final entry into Jeruslem, as it is recorded in the Gospels. Though children sound the first praises, they invite all worshipers to join the joyous greeting.

The tune ELLACOMBE is an altered form of an anonymous tune that is traced to the *Gesangbuch . . . ,* a collection of German Catholic hymns used in the private chapel of the Duke of Württemberg.

By 1833, in Xavier Ludwig Hartig's Mainz collection, ELLACOMBE had evolved to something closer to the present form—a bright, cheerful tune appropriate for Palm Sunday.

525

How bless'd are they — DUNFERMLINE

Based on Psalm 1
Psalter, 1912, alt.

Andro Hart's *The CL Psalmes of David* (Scottish Psalter), 1615

Psalm 1 is an introduction to worship, as well as to the Book of Psalms. In God's eyes the acceptability of Israel's worship was based on its sincerity and impact on justice, not just on tasteful form. With instructions to shun evil and meditate on God's word, this psalmist writes as a person of integrity and conviction, combining common sense and the mysterious guidance of God (st. 5) (Stuhlmueller 1983). How shall we best worship? By following God's way daily.

For comments on DUNFERMLINE, see "Heal us, Immanuel, here we are" (**375**) where the tune appears in a different rhythmic form.

222

How brightly beams the morning

Wie schön leuchtet der Morgenstern
Philipp Nicolai (1556-1608)
Nicolai's *Appendix to Freuden-Spiegel des ewigen Lebens,* Frankfurt, 1599
Composite translation by Inter-Lutheran Commission on Worship, 1978, alt.
Text (German) from *Gesangbuch mit Noten,* ca. 1905

WIE SCHÖN LEUCHTET DER MORGENSTERN

Philipp Nicolai (1556-1608), 1599
(same source as text)
(Zahn No. 8359)

This "queen of chorales" has also been called the morning star of Philipp Nicolai. Regarding poetic form, text, tune, and content, it struck a totally new tone in German hymnody, expressing a personal love for Jesus never before found in serious German hymnwriting. The hymn became a favorite for weddings and was parodied in a popular love song during the seventeenth century. Its intimate language anticipates the best of the seventeenth- and eighteenth-century hymns of the pietist movement. Various terms of endearment, including the language of marriage, appear, for the most part, in the four stanzas that have been omitted. The hymn is delightfully full of poetic and musical intricacies.

Like Nicolai's "Sleepers, wake" (**188**), known as the "king of chorales," this hymn was also written during the horrors of plague. Nicolai chose verbs and adjectives that countered suffering in an almost flamboyant way. Even in the poetic structure, Nicolai adjusted the lengths of the musical phrases to give a graphic impression *(carmen figuratem)* of the chalice, itself a symbol of pain and healing.

How brightly beams the morning star
What sudden radiance from afar,
aglow with grace and mercy!
Of Jacob's race, King David's son,
our Lord and master, you have won
our hearts to serve you only!
Lowly,
holy!
great and glorious,
all victorious,
rich in blessing!
Rule in might, o'er all possessing!

The English seems to be a free translation and combination of several of Nicolai's original stanzas. The first line of the translation from the *Lutheran Book of Worship* (1978) has been altered so that it more closely follows William Mercer's 1859 paraphrase, "How bright appears the morning star, with mercy beaming from afar." The German text provided is from *Gesangbuch mit Noten* (1890).

The melody WIE SCHÖN LEUCHTET resembles an earlier tune for Psalm 100, *Jauchzet dem Herren, alle Lande,* as found in Wolff Köphel's *Psalter* (1538) (Stulken 1981). This older form of the chorale is more interesting rhythmically than later metric versions, which are set mostly in even quarter notes.

WIE SCHÖN LEUCHTET has been much loved by the Prussian-Russian Mennonites, who used it with fourteen texts in *Gesangbuch der Mennoniten* (1942), all of which were written after 1599. It indicates the strong appeal that this unusual poetic form held for future hymnwriters.

394
How buoyant and bold the stride — LIBERATION

Thomas Henry Troeger (1945-), 1983
New Hymns for the Lectionary, 1986

Carol Doran (1936-), 1983
(same source as text)

Thomas Troeger writes of this text:

> I am an avid walker and spend much of my summer vacation hiking in the mountains. I only go for day trips because I do not like to carry a lot on my back. Once I had quite a conversation with a man I met on a trail. He bore an overloaded pack and told me that I had the right idea in traveling light. That story came back to me as I read in Mark 6:8 that Jesus "charged them to take nothing for their journey." The alliteration of the *b*'s in the opening line and the loping gait of the dactylic meter reflect my own sense of exhilaration when walking, which is an outward expression of the spiritual joy of traveling light and unencumbered.

The tune LIBERATION was intended to give musical form to the words "buoyant" and "bold." Doran advises that it should have a sense of one beat to the measure, giving a slight emphasis to the first beat. There is also a sense of camaraderie in the tune and the texture of the music; the tempo should be marchlike rather than rushing. On the working copy of the hymn text given to the composer, the author writes: "The absence of commas in the last verse is deliberate. The sentence is one long exclamation. I'm depending on music to lift us through verses 3b and 4. They're part of the hardness of the task in the Bible text."

580
How can I keep from singing—see "My life flows on"

541
How clear is our vocation, Lord — REPTON

Fred Pratt Green (1903-), 1981
The Hymns and Ballads of Fred Pratt Green, 1982

Charles Hubert Hastings Parry (1848-1918)
Judith, 1888

This text was inspired by a request for a new hymn on vocation, preferably to the tune REPTON. The varied gifts for ministry brought to the church by its diverse members (1 Cor. 12:8-10) emerge in response to Christ's gift of life to us and seek the same goal—"to live according to [Christ's] word."

For comments on REPTON, see "He comes to us as one unknown" (**498**).

567
How firm a foundation — FOUNDATION (BELLEVUE)

"K" in John Rippon's *Selection of Hymns*, 1787

American folk melody
Joseph Funk's *Genuine Church Music*, 1st ed., 1832

This text has been attributed to various authors, including Keene, Keith, and Kirkham, but until more evidence is found, it is best labeled anonymous. Later reprints of Rippon's *Selections* credit "Kn" and "Keene," supporting Albert Bailey's contention that R. Keene composed the text and the melody first used with it.

Whoever the author, it was a person very familiar with the Bible. Introducing the hymn with a stanza declaring Jesus, God's Word, as our firm foundation, the writer carefully strings together a variety of scriptural words and references to compose an empowering speech by God (sts. 2-5). The original title was "Exceeding great and precious promises."

First printed in the U.S. in 1809 (*The Young Convert, a Collection of Divine Hymns or Spiritual Songs for the Use of Religious Families and Private Christians*), the text blossomed in popularity and scope; the 1840 edition of *Southern Harmony* provides seven stanzas of text, set to a tune named SINCERITY.

The tune FOUNDATION has appeared with various names. In Funk's collection it is PROTECTION; in Walker's *Southern Harmony* (1835), it is THE CHRISTIAN'S FAREWELL; and in White's *Sacred Harp* (1844), it is called BELLEVUE and is attributed to Chambless.

310

How good a thing it is — VENICE

Based on Psalm 133
James Edward Seddon (1915-1983)
Hymns for Today's Church, 1982

William Amps (1824-1910)
Thorne's *A Selection of Psalm and Hymn Tunes*, 1853

This psalm paraphrase commends unity and is a reminder of the blessings awaiting "those who live in peace." Though the psalm was written for pre-Christian pilgrimage festivals to Jerusalem, it serves as a lyric commentary on the long-held Anabaptist "gospel" of community life. In the Hebrew Bible, "dew" (st. 3:1) is often a symbol of God's mysterious, life-giving blessings.

The tune VENICE is associated with a number of texts. In *Hymns Ancient and Modern*, since the 1904 edition, it has been the setting of Watts's "How beauteous are their feet." Various sources list its first printing as both 1853 and 1858. The imitation of the treble voices in the first phrase by the lower voices in the second phrase is an interesting musical feature.

171

How lovely is your dwelling — (no tune name)

Based on Psalm 84
Jean Wiebe Janzen (1933-), 1991
Hymnal: A Worship Book, 1992

Heinrich Schütz (1585-1672)
Psalmen Davids . . ., 1628

In 1602 Cornelius Becker issued *Der Psalter Davids Gesangweis, auff die in Lutherischen Kirchen gewöhnliche Melodeyen zugerichtet* in Leipzig. This version of the Psalms was published to counteract Lobwasser's 1573 *Psalter*, which the Lutherans considered Calvinistic, believing it obscured the evangelical spirit of the Psalms.

Heinrich Schütz set the words of Becker's *Psalter* to four-part music, publishing his collection at Freiberg in Saxony in 1628. Revised and enlarged at the request of Elector Johann Georg II, Schütz's later edition of *Psalmen Davids, Hiebevor in Teutsche Reimen gebracht durch D. Cornelium Beckern*, was published in 1661 at Dresden.

Here we come full circle, with Schütz's music inspiring a new version of Psalm 84, written for this hymnal by Jean Janzen. She writes: "From the Becker texts and the psalms, I chose language and concepts which I believed would be nearest to the understanding and need of people today."

112
How majestic is your name—see "O Lord, our Lord, how majestic"

451
How pleasant is it

Attrib. to Wilhelm Knepper (1691-ca.1743)
Freylinghausen's *Geistreiches Gesang-Buch vor alle liebhabende Seelen der Warheit,* 1720
Tr. Ora W. Garber (1903-1981)
European Origins of the Brethren, 1958, alt.

KOMMT HER ZU MIR

Ain schöns newes Christlichs lyed, 1530
Freylinghausen's *Geistreiches Gesang-Buch . . . ,* 1741
(Zahn No. 2496a-c)
Harm. by Hedwig T. Durnbaugh (1929-)
"Hymns from the 1720 Hymnal," 1983

The original German text appeared in the first hymnal of the Schwarzenau Brethren as *Ach wie so lieblich und wie fein.* It appeared under the heading "Hymn [to be sung] During Foot-Washing." As with all the hymns in the early Brethren hymnals, the author's name was not given, but it may be assumed that he was Wilhelm Knepper, one of the six Solingen Brethren who were sentenced to hard labor in the fortress of Jülich, Germany. Knepper was reported to have written four hundred hymns during that time.

The German original consists of eleven stanzas, all of which were translated originally. Stanza 1 praises the state of unity among brothers and sisters in the faith, which allows them to wash one another's feet as faithful servants. Stanzas 2-4 recall the example of Jesus washing his disciples' feet; stanzas 5-8 expound on the significance of this rite for the community; and stanzas 9-11 are a prayer for true discipleship, the ability to proclaim Jesus' death and anguish, break his bread, and enter into communion with his true life. The eleventh stanza concludes with a plea for the power of Jesus' Spirit.

The translation follows the poetic meter and rhyme scheme of the German. The five stanzas in this hymnal correspond to stanzas 1, 2, 5, 7, and 11.

KOMMT HER ZU MIR is derived from a fifteenth-century German folk song associated with several different secular texts. The earliest form of the present melody, dated 1530 by Johannes Zahn, was published as a broadside, the title of which is translated "A fine new Christian song." German hymns do not have tune names; instead, the text incipit of the hymn to whose melody a given text is to be sung is printed above the first stanza. Thus, the tune name given here is the first line of the hymn text by Georg Grünwald to which it was set. The present form is taken from the 1741 edition of the chief pietist hymnal, which contains melodies with figured bass. That edition combined two earlier single volumes (1704, 1714), with which the Brethren undoubtedly were familiar.[1]

1. Sources: D. Durnbaugh, 1958; H. Durnbaugh, 1986; Stulken, 1981; Zahn, 1963

251
How shallow former shadows

Carl Pickens Daw, Jr. (1944-)
A Year of Grace, 1990

THE THIRD MELODY

Thomas Tallis (ca. 1505-1585)
Matthew Parker's *The Whole Psalter Translated into English Metre*, ca. 1567

Daw wrote this powerful Good Friday hymn to round out his collection of hymns for the church year. The first stanza envelops one in the darkness, earthquake, and rending of the veil of the temple at the time of Jesus' crucifixion, which Daw refers to as "the undoing of creation." Stanza 2 is a vivid meditation on the scene. "Chaos is come again" is borrowed from Shakespeare (Othello, III, iii, 92), and stanza 2:3 alludes to John Donne's "Good Friday, 1613, Riding Westward." The third stanza wonders at the power of sacrificial love and contemplates the "sublime irony of calling this day 'Good' Friday" (Daw 1990).

THE THIRD MELODY is the third of nine tunes composed for Archbishop Matthew Parker's *The Whole Psalter . . .* where it is a setting of Parker's metrical version of Psalm 2. Tallis's first eight tunes were metrical psalm settings while the ninth was composed for the *Veni Creator Spiritus*. This tune, frequently known as THIRD MODE MELODY and sometimes called THE THIRD TUNE or THE THIRD MODE, conforms to the third, or Phrygian, mode, which sounds when playing the white keys from E to E. In a section at the end of Parker's *The Whole Psalter . . .*, the nature of each of the eight psalm tunes was described, for example, "The third doth rage: and roughly brayeth" (Ellinwood 1948). Unlike present-day practice, Tallis placed the melody in the tenor voice so that the soprano would have a harmony part. Editor Ralph Vaughan Williams used most of Tallis's tunes in *The English Hymnal* (1906) and immortalizes THIRD MODE MELODY in his masterful "Fantasia on a Theme by Thomas Tallis" for double-string orchestra and string quartet (1910).

126

How wondrous great

Isaac Watts (1674-1748)
Hymns and Spiritual Songs, Book II, 1707-1709, alt.

AWEFUL MAJESTY

Joseph Funk's *Genuine Church Music*, 4th ed., 1847
Arr. by Alice Parker (1925-), 1967

This text displays Watts's gift for poetry, as well as his Calvinistic bent. It sometimes takes language as colorful as this to help our reason stretch "all its wings" to begin to fathom the wonder of God. Watts's original archaisms would sound still more unusual to our ears; the concluding stanza is a reworking of stanza 6, which originally read:

> In humble Notes our Faith adores
> The great mysterious King,
> While Angels strain their nobler Powers
> And sweep th' immortal String.

This text uses stanzas 1, 2, 3, and 6 of the original six stanzas. The final word of stanza 1 was "infinity," here changed to "eternity." In stanza 2:2, "the burning throne" was "the Celestial throne," and "There" replaces "Fain" at 2:3. In stanza 3:3, "mortal knowledge" was originally "groveling reason."

In the fourth edition of *Genuine Church Music*, this melody appears with the text "Sing to the Lord, ye heav'nly host." An alternate tune for this text is ARLINGTON, found with another Watts text "This is the day the Lord has made" (**642**).

532

I am leaning on the Lord

African American spiritual

TURNER

African American spiritual
Adapt. and arr. by William Farley Smith (1941-) 1986
The United Methodist Hymnal, 1989

Like the more familiar "When Israel was in Egypt's land," this spiritual's theme of coming out of the wilderness refers both to freedom found in the conversion experience and freedom from slavery. It would be especially appropriate to sing this when new members are received into the church body, either by baptism or reaffirmation of faith. Suggestions for singing are provided in the *Accompaniment Handbook.*

The tune is named for Nat Turner, leader of the 1831 slave rebellion in Southampton County, Virginia. Following the rebellion, Turner took refuge in the wilderness. After the militia torched the area, forcing him to flee, a reporter asked Turner, "How do you feel now that you have come out the wilderness?" Turner replied, "I am leaning on the Lord!" That newspaper story, reports William Farley Smith, became the basis of the spiritual's text.

472

I am the Bread of life

Yo soy el pan de vida
Suzanne Toolan (1927-)
Music for the Requiem Mass, 1966
Tr. Sara Claassen (1935-) (Spanish)

I AM THE BREAD OF LIFE

Suzanne Toolan (1927-)
(same source as text)

This text is very closely based on the words of Jesus in John 6:35,44,51, and 53. Translated into a number of languages, it appears here with the Spanish, *Yo soy el pan de vida.*

The Roman Catholic Archdiocese of San Francisco first published this song by Sister Suzanne Toolan in the source listed above. It has since been picked up in several contemporary hymnals and songbooks. The folklike character of the music and the chord markings for guitar make it usable in many settings. The words of the refrain, "And I will raise you up," are enhanced musically in the rising melodic line and the fullness of the four-part harmony. It is a stirring declaration of allegiance to Christ!

505

I am thine, O Lord

Fanny Jane Crosby (1820-1915)
Doane and Lowry's *Brightest and Best,* 1875

I AM THINE

William Howard Doane (1832-1915)
(same source as text)

One evening Fanny Crosby was visiting in the Cincinnati home of her musical collaborator, William H. Doane. They were discussing the nearness of God. Known for drawing on spontaneous moments for her poetry, Crosby wrote these words that same evening: "Let us draw near with a true heart . . ." (based on Heb. 10:22). The stanzas used here are 1, 3, and 2 of the original four.

Human beings long for intimacy; the experience of knowing and being known by God is a paradigm for personal relationships. In Crosby's text one finds not God the judge, but God the friend enthroned afar in the heavens (st. 2). The repetition of "nearer" in the refrain serves as a textual and musical means to help the singer actually feel the pull of being drawn to the Lord. This hymn would also be appropriate for the spiritual intimacy of love feast and Communion.

After his visit with Crosby, Doane wrote the melody I AM THINE, also known as DRAW ME NEARER, the original title of the text. The musical setting is like that in early editions; only the rests at the ends of phrases have been deleted.

564
I am trusting thee, Lord Jesus

(no tune name)

Adapt. from Frances Ridley Havergal (1836-1879), 1874
Loyal Responses, 1878

Julius Dietrich (19th c.)
Gemeinschaftsliederbuch, Offenbach, 1894

This text, written in Ormont-Dessous, Switzerland, was Havergal's favorite of the many poems she wrote. A copy was found in her pocket Bible after her death. The hymn has been included in all three Brethren hymnals published in this century, appearing with the tune HOLSINGER in 1901 and 1951 and with the tune BULLINGER in 1925. By adding or repeating certain words, the first four of the original six stanzas were adapted to fit the meter of this new melody. The refrain is a translation of the German text associated with that tune:

Ich vertraue dir, Herr Jesus,
Mein Erlöser und mein Hort,
Ich vertraue dir, Herr Jesus,
Ja, ich stütz mich auf dein Wort.

This very singable melody was found by David J. Rempel Smucker in the *Neues Gemeinschafts-Liederbuch* (Basel 1974). The German text of seven stanzas by Dora Rappard (1842-1923) in that hymnal paraphrases and expands upon Havergal's text.

553
I am weak and I need thy strength

LEAD ME, GUIDE ME

Doris Mae Akers (1922-), 1953

Doris Mae Akers (1922-), 1953

The stanzas of this black gospel hymn confess our need for God's strength and guidance in times of weakness and temptation, while the refrain affirms our faith that, with the Lord's leading, we "cannot stray." "Guide me, O thou great Jehovah" (**582**); "Lead me, Lord" (**538**); and "When we walk with the Lord" (**544**) are other hymns on the same theme in very different musical styles. Like them, this hymn is a strong and personal statement of faith.

The tune name LEAD ME, GUIDE ME is the title by which this hymn was originally known. In many hymnals the refrain is printed first, followed by the stanzas. This hymn typifies the first black gospel music, which is improvisational in nature. Thus, the printed score is just a guide to which the singers and accompanist may add their creativity. In the African American hymnals *Lift Every Voice and Sing* (1981) and *Lead Me, Guide Me* (1987), an arrangement by Richard Smallwood shows some of the improvisational possibilities, with added chords and triplet rhythms.

This hymn may be sung best at a slow gospel tempo, "swinging" the eighth notes.

330
I believe in God — NASADIKI

Based on the Nicene Creed, 4th c.
Composite translation

Samuel C. Ochieng' Okeyo (20th c., Kenya)
"Kariobangi Mass" in *Tumshangilie Bwana* (We Praise the Lord), 1988

The Nicene Creed is a statement that grew out of the meeting of a church council gathered to settle the great debate—was Christ the same as God, or was he subordinate as God's Son? In other words, what is the relationship of Christ's humanity and divinity?

While Brethren and Mennonites have historically rejected creeds as too confining to describe the complexities of faith, they have subscribed to the idea of faith affirmations, and the great creeds of the church can be used as such. Besides having weighty historical significance, these statements can help give verbal substance and form to faith. To say "I believe" is to express, with the wider Christian family, commitment and hope.

This setting of the Nicene Creed is very popular in the churches of Nairobi, Kenya. The Kariobangi Mass contains the Lord's Prayer in addition to the complete Ordinary of the Mass—*Kyrie, Gloria, Credo, Sanctus*, and *Agnus Dei.*

In the published edition listed above, the chords are quite complicated. This historic statement of faith is notated here as it is sung at St. Paul's Chapel where worshipers sing without printed music. The tune name NASADIKI comes from the Swahili word *Ninasadiki*, which means "I believe."

440
I believe in you, Lord Jesus — MUNICH

Mary Stoner Wine (1885-1959)
The Brethren Hymnal, 1951, alt.

Anonymous
Neu-vermehrtes und zu Übung Christl. Gottseligkeit ein gerichtetes Meiningisches Gesangbuch, Meiningen, 1693
Harm. by Felix Mendelssohn (1809-1847)
Elijah, 1846

This hymn was written at the request of the committee of *The Brethren Hymnal* (1951), who set it to the Welsh tune LLANGLOFFAN. Although originally intended as a hymn for baptism, the text is a solid statement of faith in Christ and makes an excellent hymn of discipleship and commitment.

It is believed that MUNICH, also called MEININGEN, may have been derived from phrases of various melodies by Hieronymous Gradenthaler in a Regensburg psalter of 1675. It was one of many tunes associated with *O Gott, du frommer Gott*, the text with which it appeared in the *Neu-vermehrtes . . . Gesangbuch* of 1693. The melody, which became known throughout Germany in the nineteenth century, was harmonized by Mendelssohn for "Cast thy burden upon the Lord" in his oratorio *Elijah*.

411
I bind my heart this tide — UNION

Lauchlan MacLean Watt (1867-1957)
The Tryst, A Book of the Soul, 1907, alt.

J. Randall Zercher (1940-), 1965
The Mennonite Hymnal, 1969

An act of voluntary bondage can be a powerful witness, especially when it involves personal suffering. Jesus did it by accepting the "cup" of suffering in the garden of Gethsemane just before his execution; Christians do it by aligning themselves with Christ's costly way of love.

Lauchlan Watt's text demonstrates that the "cords" of "thralldom" (servanthood) connect us not only to Christ, but to each other. In stanza 2, "brother" is replaced by "neighbor" and "stranger," which are paired with unusual modifiers in order to acknowledge a global neighborhood ("neighbor far away") and the way we sometimes turn a blind eye to those nearest us, making them next-door "strangers." This text has appeared in both *The Brethren Hymnal* (1951) and *The Mennonite Hymnal* (1969). In the former it was set to the tune FEALTY by Grace Wilbur Conant.

As a result of a tune search by the committee of *The Mennonite Hymnal* (1969), the text was paired with UNION. Mennonite composer J. Randall Zercher chose a contemporary musical style that could be sung without accompaniment. He writes:

> I kept the individual voices as simple as possible, and introduced dissonance by stepwise motion. The point of greatest tension in each stanza occurs in the third line, for example, on "wounds," so I let that be the high point of the melody, and used a wide spacing between men's and women's voices to help the singers feel that tension. The "funny" chord at the end serves two purposes: it makes the return to the tonic at the beginnings of verses 2, 3, and 4 fresher, and makes the "Amen" mandatory, if the congregation wants to resolve the tension created by the chord! The open chords at the beginning and end of the tune draw me back to an ancient musical style, just as the text draws me to my Anabaptist heritage. (Loewen, Moyer, Oyer 1983)

Zercher chose the name UNION to represent three things of importance to him: the joint effort of two Mennonite groups to make a hymnal, his then-recent marriage, and the seminary where he had just completed his master's degree.

441
I bind unto myself today

ST. PATRICK

Attrib. to St. Patrick (ca. 389-461)
Irish Liber Hymnorum, 1897
Tr. Cecil Frances Alexander (1818-1895)
Leaflet, 1889
C. H. H. Wright's *Writings of St. Patrick,* Appendix, 1889

Traditional Irish melody
Petrie's *Complete Collection of Irish Music,* 1902
Harm. adapt. from Charles Villiers Stanford, 1902

This text, part of which is set to a separate tune (see "Christ be with me," **442**), is known as the Lorica or Breastplate of St. Patrick. Legend says that Patrick, who is credited with bringing Christianity to Ireland, sang this at Tara when he was threatened by the Druid king Loegaire, who fumed at Patrick's religious impudence. By 690, according to the writings of Tirechan, it was being sung in all churches and monasteries throughout Ireland.

The earliest sources in existence are two eleventh-century manuscripts, edited by John H. Bernard and Robert Atkinson in the 1897 reference above. A manuscript preface to this hymn states that Patrick created this hymn to protect himself and his monks from the deadly enemies who lay in ambush for clerics. The daily recitation of this hymn, acting as a breastplate of faith, would protect the body and soul from demons, human enemies, vices, poison, envy, and sudden death. It would also arm the soul after death.

Mrs. Alexander's metrical paraphrase was written for St. Patrick's Day of 1889. Her initial line, "I bind unto myself today," is a "mistranslation of the Irish, 'Today I arise'; and the rest is a free rendering with expansions of her own . . . " (Dearmer 1933). Though the original was not written in meter, it may have been written in a particular shape, perhaps that of a breastplate. It also incorporated elements of Druid incantations and Christian creeds.

ST. PATRICK is No. 1048 in George Petrie's collection edited by C. V. Stanford. There it has the caption "The hymn by St. Bernard, *Jesu dulcis memoria* from Mr. Southwall." It is believed this tune was a setting for that Latin text.

45

I cannot dance, O Love — MAGDEBURG

Based on the writings of Mechthild of Magdeburg (1210-1297)
Jean Wiebe Janzen (1933-), 1991
Hymnal: A Worship Book, 1992

Alice Parker (1925-), 1991
(same source as text)

These words were submitted for this book in response to a request for texts based on the writings of three medieval mystics: Hildegard of Bingen, Julian of Norwich, and Mechthild of Magdeburg. Jean Janzen chose the poetry of Mechthild of Magdeburg and writes, "Her ecstasy of union with God as a dance partner and of Love as both music and God offered a frame for her swirling emotions and gives us a window into the . . . world of worship and prayer."

Alice Parker, who enjoys setting Jean Janzen's evocative poems, created the tune expressly for this text. She comments that this music "captures the essence of the 'dance,' the leading away from and then back to the center. The rhythm, in double triples, celebrates both the trinity and the circle."

459

I come with joy to meet my Lord — DOVE OF PEACE

Brian Arthur Wren (1936-), 1968, rev., 1977
The Hymn Book (United Church of Canada) 1971

American folk melody
Southern Harmony, 1854

This text was written for the author's congregation at Hockley, Essex, England, to "sum up a series of sermons on the meaning of communion" (Wren 1983). Wren explains in *Faith Looking Forward* that the hymn begins with the individual "I come" and progresses to the corporate ending, "together met, together bound." The revision that Wren made in 1977 was prompted by an American hymnal committee. The original wording in stanzas 2 and 3 include "man's true community of love" and "As Christ breaks bread for men to share." The author concludes that the present version "seems in every way an improvement" (Wren 1983).

In *Southern Harmony* the folk tune DOVE OF PEACE appears with the text "O tell me where the Dove has flown." Austin Lovelace, a noted composer and organist who also has arranged this folk melody, writes: "The tune is essentially pentatonic and probably is either English or Scottish in origin. It is possible that the tune appeared in some other earlier hymnal, but I have not found it." The lilting unison melody lends itself well to this text, which contemplates the significance of Communion.

493
I heard the voice of Jesus say

KINGSFOLD

Horatius N. Bonar (1808-1889)
Hymns Original and Selected, 1846, alt.

English folk melody
English County Songs, 1893
Adapt. and harm. by Ralph Vaughan Williams (1872-1958)
The English Hymnal, 1906, alt.

This hymn was one of several the Scottish pastor Bonar wrote for the children in his Sunday school in an attempt to alleviate the diet of "metrical psalms set to ponderous chorale tunes" (Bailey 1950). It was first titled "The Voice from Galilee." The text has been altered only slightly, eliminating archaic language. Another minor change was made in both text and music in the middle of line 3 to make the text syllables easier to sing.

In fact, with such songs based on scripture, Bonar himself was trying to make hymn-singing in the church of Scotland easier. According to hymn commentator Albert Bailey, "It is all so direct and simple: no theology; a transcript of Christian experience which the wayfaring man, though a fool, can understand and appropriate" (Bailey 1950).

In this text/tune combination, the hymn feels like a lullaby. The gentle KINGSFOLD, a folk song in A' B A' form, originated as early as the sixteenth century when it was mentioned in Fletcher's comedy *Monsieur Thomas.* KINGSFOLD was first published in Broadwood and Fuller Maitland's *English County Songs,* paired there with the tune name LAZARUS and a text about Dives and Lazarus that begins "As it fell out upon one day." In the *Oxford Book of Carols,* it is associated with another version of the Lazarus story, "Come all you worthy Christian men." The tune became known as KINGSFOLD in *The English Hymnal* where Vaughan Williams' arrangement provides the setting for Bonar's text. It is named for the village in Surrey where Vaughan Williams heard a variation of the tune. The tune is known in Ireland as THE STAR OF COUNTY DOWN.

474
I hunger and I thirst

IBSTONE

John Samuel Bewley Monsell (1811-1875)
Hymns of Love and Praise, 2nd ed., 1866, alt.

Maria Tiddeman (1837-ca. 1911)
Hymns Ancient and Modern, 1875, alt.

This prayer hymn is rich in both Old and New Testament imagery. Commenting on the nearly three hundred hymns Monsell wrote, Julian says they "are as a whole bright, joyous, and musical; but they lack massiveness, concentration of thought and strong emotion. A few only are of enduring excellence" (Julian 1907). Certainly, this must be one of those of enduring excellence. This version, from *Hymns for Today's Church* (1982), eliminates the archaic language of the author's Victorian era.

IBSTONE, named for one of two parishes where the composer's father was rector, was originally composed as a setting for Horatius Bonar's text "Thy way, not mine, O Lord" for use in *Hymns Ancient and Modern*. The last two phrases, originally symmetrical in cadence, have been changed to allow the rhythmic energy of the music to match that of this text.

338
I know not why God's wondrous grace — EL NATHAN

Daniel Webster Whittle (1840-1901)
Gospel Hymns No. 5, 1887, alt.

James McGranahan (1840-1907)
(same source as text)

This well-known hymn text takes its refrain directly from the King James Version of 2 Timothy 1:12. Whittle, converted in a Civil War prison camp, became an evangelist after his release, and this hymn reflects his experience of learning to trust God even when circumstances were bleak. The conversational structure of the hymn acknowledges that God's ways are not always obvious; the "but" at the beginning of the refrain counters that uncertainty with the confidence that faith gives.

Since no copyright date appears on the hymn itself, there is controversy as to its first printing. Numerous companions give the source as Sankey's *Gospel Hymns No. 4* (1883), but it was not listed in either the John Church or Biglow and Main editions of that collection (1881), nor was it in *Gospel Hymns Nos. 1-4 Consolidated* (1883). *Gospel Hymns No. 5* seems to be the first substantiated source.

McGranahan, who was music director for Whittle's revival meetings, composed music for a number of Whittle's texts. The tune name, added in later years, was Whittle's pseudonym, "El Nathan."

277
I know that my Redeemer lives — SHOUT ON, PRAY ON

Samuel Medley (1738-1799)
Whitefield's *Psalms and Hymns*, 21st ed., 1775, alt.

American folk melody
Sacred Harp, 2nd ed., 1850
Harm. by Alice Parker (1925-), 1988

In London, Samuel Medley often heard the preaching of George Whitefield, in whose twenty-first edition of *Psalms and Hymns* this text first appeared. The original consists of nine four-line stanzas, some of which pick up the trinity of Christ's roles reflected in the gifts of the magi (Matt. 2:11): Prophet, Priest, and King.

With the tune SHOUT ON, PRAY ON, the text is altered (at times back to the original) and the refrain and "hallelujahs" added. This melody was called ANTIOCH in *Sacred Harp* (1850) and attributed to F. C. Wood. It is still a favorite among *Sacred Harp* singers and has been retained in the 1971 edition of that book. The harmonization used in this hymnal was adapted from an earlier choral setting by Alice Parker. It has the leader/response structure of a working song; one music leader has instructed singers to "sing it like you're breaking rocks." That style can accommodate the resolute conviction of the text.

279

I know that my Redeemer lives — TRURO

Samuel Medley (1738-1799)
Whitefield's *Psalms and Hymns,* 21st ed., 1775, alt.

Anonymous
Williams' *Psalmodia Evangelica, Part II,* 1789

For comments on TRURO, see "Christ is alive! Let Christians sing" (**278**).

543

I long for your commandments — (no tune name)

Based on Psalm 119:131-135
Jean Wiebe Janzen (1933-)
Hymnal: A Worship Book, 1992

Heinrich Schütz (1585-1672)
Psalmen Davids . . . , rev. and enlarged ed., 1661

The thoughts of this hymn parallel several passages in Psalm 119, in particular verses 131-135. The first stanza is based on an earlier translation of the German paraphrase of this psalm found in the Becker *Psalter* of 1602. The second and third stanzas are entirely new, drawing their imagery from the words of the psalmist.

The spirit of the psalm is that of receiving the law directly from God, not from books or scrolls. Psalms scholar Carroll Stuhlmueller cautions: "When we realize that God is speaking in the silence of our heart, the only option to obedience is serious damage to our personality" (Stuhlmueller 1983).

This setting by Heinrich Schütz is quite easy to learn, with its repetition of the opening line and a very singable melody. This is the third of eight settings that appear with Psalm 119 in Schütz's revised *Psalter* of 1661. In his original edition of 1628, there was but a single setting of this lengthy psalm, which bears no resemblance to the present melody.

For another tune by Schütz and further comments on the Becker *Psalter*, see "How lovely is your dwelling" (**171**).

605
I love thee, Lord — AL LADO DE MI CABAÑA

No me mueve, mi Dios, para quererte
Spanish hymn, 17th c.
Tr. Edward Caswall (1814-1878)
Lyra Catholica, 1849
Adapt. by Percy Dearmer (1867-1936), alt.
Enlarged Songs of Praise, 1931

Spanish medieval folk melody
Harm. by The Hymnal Project, 1991

The fourteen lines of twelve syllables each in this Spanish text are rhymed in sonnet form—*abba cddc eee eee.* It spurns a Christianity based on fear, or greed for heaven, but values a commitment grown out of thanks for Christ's suffering love.

This hymn is traditionally ascribed to St. Francis Xavier who is believed to have written it about 1546. Although printed without attribution in *Epitome de la vida y muerte de San Ignacio de Loyola* (1662), another collection published the same year attributes it to Xavier. The text is older than these two Spanish collections, however, because it was translated into Latin by Johannes Nadasi in *Pretiosae Occupationes Morientium* (1657).

Numerous alterations of Caswall's translation from the Latin have been made over the years. Dearmer's adaptation has been used frequently since 1931. Jane Marshall set Caswall's text in her anthem "My Eternal King" (Carl Fischer 1954).

In searching for a Spanish tune similar in antiquity to the text, The Hymnal Project found this medieval melody in the anthology *Antológia Musical de Cantos Populares Españoles* (1930). The tune, harmonized for this hymnal, contains an interesting metrical shift from 3/2 to 3/4 time.

308
I love thy kingdom, Lord — BEALOTH

Timothy Dwight (1752-1817)
Psalms of David, 1801

Lowell Mason (1792-1872)
Sacred Hymns, 1842

Isaac Watts's *Psalms of David* (1719) did not come into widespread use in North America until the late 1700s. Timothy Dwight, at the request of the General Association of the Presbyterian Churches of Connecticut, revised Watts's *Psalms* in order to delete British references that the newly formed nation would find unacceptable. Dwight, president of Yale University, New Haven, Connecticut, and grandson of the fiery Puritan preacher Jonathan Edwards, wrote this text as a free paraphrase based on the latter part of Psalm 137. "Dear as the apple of thine eye and graven on thy hand" comes from Psalm 17:8 and Isaiah 49:16; the sentiment holds up the chosen people of God as the object of special care.

Today it is sung as an intense expression of love for the church, but in Dwight's day it also represented what Bailey calls "a tight little closed-corporation of the Calvinistic saints-elect" (Bailey 1950). Dwight was a Federalist opposed to the new U.S. Constitution that separated church and state, and his text unequivocally ranks the church supreme.

This is perhaps the oldest hymn written by a North American to remain in continuous use; it is the only one of thirty-three by Dwight that survives. Originally in eight four-line stanzas, it was titled "Love to the Church."

BEALOTH, from the Hebrew, means "citizens." Bealoth also is a city in the southeastern section of Judah mentioned in Joshua 15:24. Mason's tune is called PHILLPUT in the Disciples of Christ Church, but that name's origin is unknown. A fitting alternate tune for this text is ST. THOMAS (see "O bless the Lord, my soul," **600**), used in many hymnals with five four-line stanzas, omitting the first half of the final stanza as it appears with BEALOTH.

398

I love to tell the story — HANKEY

Catherine Hankey (1834-1911), 1866
Joyful Songs Nos. 1-3 Combined, 1869
Refrain by William Gustavus Fischer (1835-1912), 1869

William Gustavus Fischer (1835-1912)
(same source as text)

Arabella Catherine Hankey, known as "Kate," wrote these lines during a lengthy convalescence following a serious illness. They are taken from a long poem about the life of Jesus, written in two parts. The first section, titled "The Story Wanted" and dated January 29, 1866, is the source of another familiar gospel song "Tell me the old, old story." Part II, from which this text is taken, is dated November 18 of the same year and titled "The Story Told." Most of the actual "story" is in other parts of the poem, but Hankey's evangelical fervor leaps from these stanzas. The words of the refrain were added by the composer.

HANKEY, named for the author of the text, was composed for these words. First published with music in the Methodist pamphlet named above, it was one of twenty-four tunes by Fischer in the total of forty-one. The hymn became widely known through the evangelistic work of D. L. Moody and Ira D. Sankey and its publication in P. P. Bliss's *Gospel Songs* (1874) and Bliss and Sankey's *Gospel Hymns and Sacred Songs* (1875).

555

I need thee every hour — NEED

Annie Sherwood Hawks (1835-1918)
Convention Songbook, National Baptist Sunday School Convention, Cincinnati, 1872
Doane and Lowry's *Royal Diadem for the Sunday School*, 1873
Refrain by Robert Lowry (1826-1899)

Robert Lowry (1826-1899)
(same source as text)

Hawks wrote these words early in her life before times of grief had touched her. She comments:

> For myself the hymn was prophetic rather than expressive of my own experience at the time it was written . . . . It was not until long years after, when the shadow fell over my way—the shadow of a great loss—that I understood something of the comforting in the words I had been permitted to write and given out to others in my hours of sweet security and peace. (Haeussler 1952)

Following the hymn's introduction at the 1872 Baptist Sunday School Convention, it was published in Doane and Lowry's collection with a reference to John 15:5, "Without me ye can do nothing." Robert Lowry, who was Mrs. Hawks' pastor, also composed the music and the words of the refrain. The refrain could well stand alone as a call or response to prayer, or the stanzas could be sung antiphonally.

651

I owe the Lord a morning song — GRATITUDE

Amos Herr (1816-1897)
Hymns and Tunes, for Public and Private Worship and Sunday Schools, 1890

Amos Herr (1816-1897)
(same source as text)

The text was written by Lancaster County (Pa.) preacher Amos Herr on a snowy Sunday morning. Unable to get to church because of the storm, he created his own devotional time, including this hymn. An advocate of the use of English in worship, Herr even wrote his poem in English instead of in the standard Mennonite worship language of German. Even so, Mennonite hymnologist Mary K. Oyer characterizes this as a "typical (Old) Mennonite hymn": "Its language is simple, straightforward, and functional, presenting abstractions rather than concrete images. Like most pre-electricity morning songs, the text expresses relief that the night has passed and uses day and light as symbols for enlightenment and heaven" (Oyer 1980).

Hymns and Tunes . . . (1890), the first Mennonite Church hymnal to include texts with tunes, indicates that the music was written by a committee. At least no one claims sole credit for its creation. The 1927 *Church Hymnal* inserted Amos Herr's name for both text and tune, a practice continued here. GRATITUDE, like its text, is straightforward. The limited vocal ranges make it an excellent hymn for part-singing. Oyer describes it as a musical "journey," traveling through the accidental sharp in the middle, and coming home again through the naturals in the final phrase.

323
I see a new world coming—see "Beyond a dying sun"

46
I sing the mighty power of God — ELLACOMBE

Isaac Watts (1674-1748)
Divine Songs Attempted in Easy Language, for Children, 1715, alt.

Adapt. from *Gesangbuch der Herzogl* . . . , Württemberg, 1784
Harm. by William Henry Monk (1823-1889)
Hymns Ancient and Modern, Appendix, 1868

Watts's trademark reverence for God's wonders is evident in this hymn. This is not abstract pantheism, but a detailed proclamation that creation reveals its Creator. Even though verses from the "Moral Songs" section in *Divine Songs* . . . (1715) were once commonly used to teach children Christian values, this is the only surviving piece from Watts's collection. With this hymn, Wesley Milgate ascribes to Watts "a readiness rare in his time to credit children with some intelligence and imagination . . ." (Milgate 1982).

The hymn, which Watts titled "Praise for Creation and Providence," was written as eight four-line stanzas. The last two are usually deleted and the others combined into three eight-line stanzas. Watts's last two lines of our final stanza have been reinstated, echoing the psalmist's conviction of God's omnipresence.

A number of hymnals use the tune FOREST GREEN for this text. For comments on ELLACOMBE, see "Hosanna, loud hosanna" (**238**).

438
I sing with exultation

NUN WEND IHR HÖREN SAGEN

Mit Lust so will ich singen
Felix Manz (ca. 1498-1527), ca. 1526
Ausbund, 1564
Tr. Marion Wenger (1932-), 1966
The Mennonite Hymnal, 1969
Alt. by Harris J. Loewen (1953-) ,1990

Bentzenauer Ton, Nürnberg, 1540

Felix Manz was one of the founders and first martyrs of the Swiss Brethren congregation in Zürich, Switzerland. Originally a protégé of Ulrich Zwingli, Manz broke with him in 1524 on issues of adult baptism and Communion. After a series of disputations and imprisonments, he was drowned in Lake Zürich in January 1527, saying at the moment of his death, "Into thy hands I commend my spirit." Manz's text reveals the strong Anabaptist emphasis on following Christ in life and contains a veiled reference to adult baptism in the last two lines of this translation.

The translation in *The Mennonite Hymnal* (1969) was changed in some places for consistency of rhyme and the third-person voice and to coincide with the meaning of the original. One may compare the hymn with this literal translation of the German text:

> With delight, so will I sing; my heart is glad in God who brings me much art, that I may outrun death, which is eternally without end. I praise you, Christ from heaven, who turns away my anxiety, who is sent unto me by God as an example and light; who, before my end calls me to his realm, that I have eternal joy with him and love him, with all my heart, and all his righteousness.
>
> Christ—him I want to praise, who displays all patience, guides us with friendliness, shows love to everyone, bowing down with his grace, after the fashion of his Father, which no false one can.
>
> Christ coerces no one to his glory—and they will be successful who are willing to be ready, through right faith and true baptism to work penance with a pure heart; for them is heaven purchased.

Marion Wenger, translator and professor of German at Goshen College (Ind.), explains that "over the years, this song has literally been sung around the world, overcoming the narrow confines of the Passau dungeon, going beyond the treasured archaic language of the *Ausbund* and its cultural particularity, and in our time transcending the limits of Eurocentric culture and religion, as symbolized by the Japanese Mennonite poet, Yorifumi Yaguchi, who translated this same text for Japanese believers" (Oyer 1980).

The Mennonite Hymnal (1969) utilizes a sixteenth-century melody suggested for use with Jörg Wagner's text in *Ausbund* No. 34. The melody, *Im Bentzenhauer Ton,* a soldier tune, recalls a battle at Kufstein in 1540. The tune also appears in the church opera *Martyrs Mirror* (1971), composed by Alice Parker. This splendid tune should be sung at a fairly brisk tempo with joy and abandon, with the half note as the pulse.

506
I sought the Lord

FAITH

Anonymous
Robert Brothers' *Holy Songs, Carols and Sacred Ballads,* Boston, 1880

J. Harold Moyer (1927-), 1965
The Mennonite Hymnal, 1969

This text, along with the plaintive melody of FAITH, evokes the image of a lost child and the great feeling of relief of being found by the parent. Peter, too, would have known that relief (st. 2). Every lost wanderer has had the nagging anxiety that, even in a careful search, one could overlook something and miss the mark altogether. This text reminds us that we are not the only ones searching. When it is Christ who searches, the lost seekers are sure to be found.

Although some sources date this hymn as early as 1878, there seems to be no documentation prior to its appearance in the source above. It subsequently appeared in *The Pilgrim Hymnal* of 1904.

The text has been set to a variety of tunes, some of a folklike nature and others in the romantic, nineteenth-century style. The compilers of *The Mennonite Hymnal* (1969) invited Moyer to compose a new tune. He comments on the writing of FAITH:

> In the mid-twentieth century composers found some difficulty in choosing an authentic musical style for writing hymn tunes. The choices seemed to be an older nineteenth-century idiom, or a newer type of melody and harmony which would be difficult for congregational use. In this tune I have tried to combine freshness with practicality.

The tune, in natural minor, has "worn well" and has been picked up by other hymnals, including the *The Hymnal 1982* (Episcopalian) and *Worship,* 3rd ed. (Roman Catholic).

528
I stand amazed in the presence

HOW MARVELOUS

Sts. 1-3, Charles Hutchinson Gabriel (1856-1932)
St. 4, Anonymous
Excell's *Praises,* 1905

Charles Hutchinson Gabriel (1856-1932)
(same source as text)

Gabriel's hymn of wonderment at Christ's sacrifice has the ring of personal experience. Unless one has encountered such self-giving love, it is sometimes difficult to comprehend how Jesus' death centuries ago carried away the sin and grief of believers through the ages. An unknown author added a fourth stanza to Gabriel's rousing gospel song.

The tune HOW MARVELOUS also is known as MY SAVIOR'S LOVE, from the final phrase of the refrain.

395
I, the Lord of sea and sky—see "Here I am, Lord"

169
I to the hills will lift my eyes — DUNDEE

Based on Psalm 121
Psalter (United Presbyterian), 1912, alt.

Andro Hart's *The CL Psalmes of David* (Scottish Psalter), 1615

Both Psalm 121 and these versifications present paired images—heaven and earth, night and day, going out and coming in—all of which symbolize the completeness of God's care. It was probably a priestly blessing given to pilgrims departing Jerusalem on the dangerous, mountainous journey home. The church has traditionally used this psalm in the ancient office of the dead, to ease a lonely journey (Stuhlmueller 1983).

Two texts are provided. One (**169**) proclaims God's vigilant care, minus archaic and masculine language. The other (**563**) is the only remaining representation of the use of language in the Scottish Psalter. This text is placed in the "Doubt/Faith" section of the hymnal because it provides a different context for the hymn and highlights the assurance of God's care.

A characteristic of this and other metrical psalms is verbal inversion, as illustrated in the opening line ("I to the hills will lift my eyes" instead of "I will lift my eyes to the hills"). This device occurs only in the first phrase of the 1912 *Psalter* version.

DUNDEE first appeared with "gathering notes" (longer note values to start each phrase) as one of the twelve common meter tunes of the 1615 Scottish Psalter, where it was named FRENCH TUNE. No French source, however, has been identified. It was named DUNDY TUNE in Ravenscroft's 1621 *The Whole Booke of Psalmes,* used in England. Although Dundee is the name of a city in eastern Scotland on the Firth of Tey, the tune retained the name FRENCH TUNE in Scotland.

563
I to the hills will lift mine eyes

DUNDEE

Based on Psalm 121
The Psalms of David in Meeter (Scottish Psalter), 1650

Andro Hart's *The CL Psalmes of David* (Scottish Psalter), 1615

See "I to the hills will lift my eyes" (**169**) for discussion of this text and tune.

439
I want Jesus to walk with me

(no tune name)

African American spiritual

African American spiritual

This is a pilgrimage song, "very popular in the black church during prayer services and devotional services preceding the regular worship services" (McClain 1990). The possibility exists, however, that its roots may be among the English folk tunes sung in the Appalachian mountains for many generations. Whatever their origin, the stark plea of the text and the haunting tune combine to create a poignant spiritual experience.

109
I will praise the Lord

(no tune name)

Daniel Webster Whittle (1840-1901)
Winnowed Songs for Sunday Schools, 1890
Gospel Hymns, No. 6, 1891, alt.

James McGranahan (1840-1907)
(same sources as text)

In both *Gospel Hymns, No. 6* (1891) and *Winnowed Songs . . .* (1890), this text was attributed to El Nathan, the pen name used by Whittle. The author has packed the hymn with images of God; in general, stanzas 1 and 2 are Old Testament references, and stanzas 3 and 4 pull from the New Testament. While the images are plentiful, the point of the hymn is simply to praise God. Originally in five stanzas, the hymn's fourth has been omitted. Minor alterations were made to clarify names for God and to eliminate archaic language.

James McGranahan composed numerous settings for the publications he compiled with Ira D. Sankey and George C. Stebbins. McGranahan's music has a vitality and rhythmic energy not often found in gospel songs of the era.

344
I will sing of my Redeemer

MY REDEEEMER

Philip Paul Bliss (1838-1876)
Lowry, Doane, and Sankey's *Welcome Tidings, A New Collection for the Sunday School*, 1877

James McGranahan (1840-1907)
(same source as text)

Bliss's poem proclaims his vocation as an evangelistic singer/song-leader. The exact date of the writing of this hymn text is not known. When Bliss and his wife died in a tragic train wreck, the poem was found in his trunk, which had been aboard the train. The following year it was published in *Welcome Tidings* . . . (1877).

McGranahan's compositions helped pave the way for his succession to Bliss as the song leader for evangelist Daniel W. Whittle. Soon after Bliss's death in 1876, the new hymn was introduced by a men's quartet at Whittle's tabernacle services in Chicago. A few months later, George C. Stebbins, a member of that quartet, visited an exhibition of the early Edison phonograph in New York City. He sang this hymn for a demonstration recording, making it one of the first recorded songs. "Hearing my own voice," says Stebbins, "and every word with striking distinctness enunciated, and even my characteristic manner of singing, modulation of voice and phrasing, produced a unique sensation" (Reynolds 1990).

261
I will sing the Lord's high triumph

TYDDYN LLWYN

Based on Exodus 15, *The Easter Liturgy*
Christopher Martin Idle (1938-), 1975, rev., 1987
Psalms for Today, 1990

Evan Morgan (1846-1920)

The biblical passage upon which this hymn is based is known as the first "Song of Moses." This victory song, celebrating the crossing of the Red Sea, is traditionally read during the Easter season. The fourth stanza of the hymn symbolically equates the Exodus triumph with the death and resurrection of Christ.

Idle wrote the original version of this text while attending a conference for clergy and parish staff. After making his final revision more than a decade later, only eight of the twenty-four original lines match the original.

TYDDYN LLWYN has a stately rhythmic style and a dynamic melodic contour in the minor mode, traits characteristic of Welsh hymn tunes. Nothing more is known of the composer than his lifespan. Christopher Idle originally wrote this text for another Welsh tune, CWM RHONDDA.

512
If all you want, Lord — FIRST COMMAND

Thomas Henry Troeger (1945-)
The Hymn, October 1987
New Hymns for the Life of the Church, 1991

Carol Doran (1936-)
(same sources as text)

This text represents the spiritual process of coming to terms with the first and greatest commandment. It opens with an attempt to compromise with God but eventually ends in a gesture of humility and offering, an action dependent still on God's grace (st. 4). It is a text that early Anabaptists, with their emphasis on radical discipleship and obedience to God, would have liked to sing.

Thomas Troeger wrote this text "to give expression to a major theme . . . on the renewal of worship: all of us for all of God (a phrase I first learned from a former colleague, James B. Ashbrook)." The text first appeared in *The Hymn* in an article on "Personal, Cultural and Theological Influences on the Writing of Hymns."

Like the text for which it was written, the tune FIRST COMMAND was written at the request of Carlton R. Young, editor of *The United Methodist Hymnal* (1989), as the hymnal revision committee searched for hymns on the subject of "reconciliation of God with humanity." Doran explains how the tune's four brief phrases purposely reflect the form of the text. It is a mini-clinic in the technique of tune writing:

> (Phrase 1) a conditional statement expressed by seventh and ninth chords in inversion with suspensions, (phrase 2) a statement of agreement expressed in simple triads and singing thirds, (phrase 3) the qualifying prerequisite expressed in music which suddenly turns the corner by means of chromaticism back to the complex harmonic texture of the first line, leading to (phrase 4) the triumphant territorial claim of the last line, expressed in the melody's highest note above a second inversion chord (beat 2) which is eventually formed by the bass-line's stepping boldly upward. In the fourth stanza the complexity of lines 1 and 3 are appropriate for the attitude of submission; the more direct and uplifting music of lines 2 and 4 reflect the joy and the hope of these lines.

331
If Christ is mine

Lobt Gott, ihr Christen allzugleich
Benjamin Beddome (1717-1795), 1776
Hymns Adapted to Public Worship or Family Devotion . . ., 1817

LOBT GOTT, IHR CHRISTEN

Nicolaus Hermann (ca. 1485-1561)
Ein Christlicher Abentreien, 1554

This hymn text from the English Baptist minister Beddome comes by way of the *Hymnal of the Moravian Church* (1969), in which it is dated 1776. It is a derivation of his text "If God is mine, then present things," which was published posthumously in his collection above. Though more than one hundred of his hymns were in common use in Great Britain or North America at the turn of the century, few remain in general use today; however, his work paved the way for writers who followed him.

For comments on LOBT GOTT, IHR CHRISTEN, see "Let all together praise our God" (**213**) where the tune appears in another form with a harmonization by J. S. Bach. While the pulsing rhythm of LOBT GOTT punctuates the affirmation of this text, the light, early American sound of PRIMROSE is a good alternate tune.

608
If death my friend and me divide

Charles Wesley (1707-1788)
Short Hymns on Select Passages of Holy Scripture, 1762

CHAPEL

Joseph Funk's *Genuine Church Music*, 1st ed., 1832
Harm. by The Hymnal Project, 1992

This little-known text of Charles Wesley appears in his two-volume collection of *Short Hymns . . .* (1762), which contains 2,030 hymns. It is an intense text, especially in the context of its use. Death may deny us our loved ones, but our resurrection faith assures us that death is eventually restorative as well (st. 3). The hymn could also be read as a poem at a memorial service or funeral, rather than sung.

CHAPEL comes from the collection of the Virginia Mennonite Joseph Funk. The modal character of this early American tune matches the grief and loss expressed in the text. In *Genuine Church Music*, the melody is set to another Charles Wesley text on a similar theme, "And am I only born to die!" (*Hymns for Children* 1763).

576
If you but trust in God

Wer nur den lieben Gott lässt walten
Georg Neumark (1621-1681)
Neumark's *Fortgepflanzter musikalisch-poetischer Lustwald,* Jena, 1657
Sts. 1,3,4, tr. Catherine Winkworth (1827-1878)
Chorale Book for England, 1863, alt.
St. 2, tr. Jaroslav J. Vajda (1919-)
Lutheran Book of Worship, 1978

WER NUR DEN LIEBEN GOTT LÄSST WALTEN

Georg Neumark (1621-1681)
(same source as text)

As a young man, Neumark was on his way to Königsberg to study at the university when his caravan was attacked and robbed, leaving him only his prayer book and a few coins. Studies thwarted, Neumark wrote this hymn of trust and thanksgiving in 1641 when, after seeking employment in several cities, he finally secured a position as tutor to the family of Judge Stephen Henning at Kiel. Based on Psalm 55:22, the hymn was titled "A Song of Comfort: God will care for and help every one in His own time." It is a song of confidence that is still firmly grounded in the reality of the difficulties of life (sts. 2-4).

The *Lutheran Book of Worship* put its stamp on this text by altering stanzas 1, 3, and 7 of Winkworth's second translation of Neumark's text, "If thou but suffer God to guide thee," as well as including Vajda's work on stanza 2.

This is one of several outstanding chorales where both words and tune were written by the same person. Other examples are Luther's "A mighty fortress is our God" (**165** and **329**), Nicolai's "Sleepers, wake" (**188**), and Hermann's "Let all together praise our God" (**213**). This strong melody in triple meter alternates between harmonic and natural minor. Its musical style reflects the tradition of the solo aria, rather than a congregational or folk-song style. None other than J. S. Bach used this melody in numerous cantatas, preludes, and other organ works. The tune, sometimes found in duple meter, is also called NEUMARK, BREMEN, and AUGSBURG.

166
I'll praise my Maker

Based on Psalm 146
Isaac Watts (1674-1748)
The Psalms of David . . . , 1719, alt.

NASHVILLE

Lowell Mason (1792-1872)
The Choir, or Union Collection of Church Music, 1832

Samuel Duffield writes that John Wesley sang the opening lines of this hymn on the day of his death at age 88. Based on Psalm 146, the text extends beyond the scope of the psalm; even death cannot stifle the expression of praise. The words, like the psalm, reach majestically toward the One who made earth and heaven and extend introspectively into the loneliest of journeys, death (sts. 2-3). They also laud God's affinity for the helpless (Stuhlmueller 1983).

NASHVILLE, as reported in the *Boston Academy's Collection of Church Music*, 5th ed. (1837), was "arranged from a Gregorian Chant." Lowell Mason's grandson, Henry L. Mason, in his *Hymn Tunes of Lowell Mason*, cites "Gregorian Chant, Tone V " as the source.

70
Immortal, invisible, God only wise

ST. DENIO (JOANNA)

Walter Chalmers Smith (1824-1908)
Hymns of Christ and the Christian Life, 1867, alt.

Welsh melody
Caniadau y Cyssegr, 1839

Based on the doxology at 1 Timothy 1:17, this hymn uses the metaphor of the sun's unbearable radiance to convey God's glory. Even the sunlight we see is only a reflection of light from the hot gases surrounding the sun; we do not see the sun itself. Still, all life derives its existence from the sun, just as God is the source of life. God's eminence is underscored in the title "Ancient of Days" (st. 1:3), meaning that God is the one who precedes even the ages and outlives them. It is a term that occurs only once in scripture, in the apocalyptic book of Daniel (7:9).

After the text's first publication in 1867, Smith himself altered it for W. Garrett Horder's *Congregational Hymns* (1884).[1] The address in stanza 4:1 originally was "Great Father of glory, pure Father of light," but the change in this hymnal maintains the majestic tone established in the earlier stanzas.

The strength of ST. DENIO is underscored by the unison beginning of the first two phrases. Also known as JOANNA, it is based on the Welsh folk song *Can Mlynedd i 'nawr* (A Hundred Years from Now).

This tune first appeared as a hymn in John Roberts's *Caniadau y Cyssegr* (Sacred Songs) with the name PALESTRINA.

1. Five of the original six stanzas may be found in Erik Routley's *Panorama of Christian Hymnody*, No. 342.

629
Immortal Love, forever full

SERENITY

John Greenleaf Whittier (1807-1892)
From "Our Master," *The Independent*, Nov. 1, 1866
Whittier's *Tent on the Beach and Other Poems*, 1867
Rev. in *Hymns for Today's Church*, 1982

William Vincent Wallace (1814-1865)
Adapt. by Uzziah C. Burnap (1834-1900) from "Ye winds that waft . . . ," 1856

Whittier, a Quaker, never experienced hymn-singing in the silent meetings of the Society of Friends. He even denied that he could write hymns, yet his poetry has adapted admirably. This text is a cento (selected portions) from the author's poem of thirty-eight stanzas cited above. The first stanza of this text is also the first stanza of the complete poem. The second and last stanzas are the only ones altered in this revised version, in order to change archaic words like "comprehendeth." Another hymn taken from this poem begins "O Lord and Master of us all."

Whittier was convinced that Christ is not found and understood in heaven, in cathedrals, even in the Eucharist, without first being experienced and known as love. Here Whittier presents an intimate, loving, healer-God, recognized as a "warm, sweet, tender, . . . present help" (st. 4).

Since the text presents Jesus as the incarnation of Immortal Love, it is fitting that SERENITY is an arrangement of a love song, "Ye winds that waft my sighs to thee." The adaptation was made by Burnap for three hymns, one of which was "The Lord's my Shepherd, I'll not want." The present rhythmic version first appeared in the 1878 Methodist Episcopal hymnal.

306
In Christ there is no East or West

ST. PETER

John Oxenham (1852-1941), 1908
Bees in Amber, 1913, alt.

Alexander Robert Reinagle (1799-1877)
Psalm Tunes for the Voice and Pianoforte, ca. 1836

Oxenham's words, reminiscent of Paul's admonition in Galatians 3:28, "for you are all one in Christ Jesus," were written for the *Pageant of Darkness and Light*, a production about India that was the main attraction of the London Missionary Society's 1908 meeting.

This is a very optimistic text that has inspired reconciliation in a contemporary context. Because the hymn is about transcending barriers, it is appropriate to include Spanish and Korean texts, as well as the original English text. Alterations also have been made to eliminate gender boundaries.

ST. PETER originally was set to a version of Psalm 118 in Reinagle's collection. Some sources date publication as early as 1830. In Reinagle's *Collection of Psalm and Hymn Tunes* (1840), it is named ST. PETER after St. Peter's-in-the-East, Oxford, the church where Reinagle was organist.

As an alternate tune, McKEE is a good choice. It was derived from an African American spiritual and adapted by Harry T. Burleigh.

613

In heavenly love abiding — HEAVENLY LOVE

Anna Laetitia Waring (1823-1910)
Hymns and Meditations, 1850

Felix Mendelssohn (1809-1847)
"Abschied vom Wald" from *Sechs Lieder* (SATB), Opus 59, No. 3, 1843

This text turns the singer inward, to the hiding place of the soul, deep in the hand of God. Its allusions to Psalm 23 are reassuring to those in crisis. Waring's gentle, introverted nature is evident here, and so is her confidence in God's shelter and guidance.

HEAVENLY LOVE originated as Mendelssohn's part-song *Abschied vom Wald* (departure from the forest), which he finished in 1843.[1] Our version, from *Life Songs No. 2* (1938) preserves Mendelssohn's original setting. Various hymnals, including the Brethren hymnals since 1901, have used this music in abridged forms. The full score is included in the *Accompaniment Handbook*. Other tunes for this text are NYLAND, AURELIA, and WEBB.

1. This part-song can be seen in Felix Mendelssohn: *Lieder für gemischten Chor*, C. F. Peters, No. 1771.

560

In lonely mountain ways — GOLDEN HILL

Sugao Nishimura (1871-1964), 1903
Tr. Paul R. Gregory (1920-), 1981
Hymns from the Four Winds, 1983

Aaron Chapin (1753-1838), 1805
Kentucky Harmony, 1816

This hymn has been a great favorite of Japanese Christians since its publication in 1903. "Nishimura's glowing faith influenced countless young people," writes translator Paul Gregory, a nine-year veteran of missionary work in Japan. That faith shines through this hymn, which is based on the story of Jacob's dream at Bethel (Gen. 28:10-12). Though some have complained that stanza 1 seems "escapist" ("my heart knows naught of fear-scarred days"), some cultures see the ability to psychologically distance oneself from pain as a skill and an aid to successful living.

This pentatonic melody, despite its western origins, has been accepted in Asian hymnody "on the merit of its vivid expression of Japanese sentiment; it is almost regarded as a 'Japanese tune' " (*Hymns from the Four Winds* 1983). GOLDEN HILL has been used with a variety of texts in previous Brethren and Mennonite hymnals.

614
In the bulb there is a flower — PROMISE

Natalie Allyn Wakeley Sleeth (1930-1992)
"Hymn of Promise," 1985

Natalie Allyn Wakeley Sleeth (1930-1992)
(same source as text)

As winter gave way to spring in 1985, Natalie Sleeth was also pondering how "apparent opposites in life (death/resurrection, winter/spring, song/silence) suggested . . . that one opposite is inherent in the other . . ." (*The Worshiping Church* 1990, 1991). Simultaneously, a friend brought her a T. S. Eliot poem in which there was a phrase something like "In our end is our beginning." That became the catalyst for the form of the text (Sleeth 1987).

Soon after "Hymn of Promise" was written, the composer's husband, Ronald Sleeth, was diagnosed with a terminal malignancy. As death neared he requested that this anthem be used at his funeral service; the publication bears the dedication "for Ron." A few years later, the hymn was again used at a Sleeth memorial—this time that of the composer herself.

Though Sleeth acknowledges that the word "bulb" is very unsingable, it was the only word to convey the meaning she wished to express. To overcome this problem, singers should sustain the vowel as long as possible in the words "bulb" and "cocoons," as a footnote in the anthem suggests.

The symmetry of the text and the simplicity of the tune will have a special appeal for children. The unison setting may be augmented by one of two accompaniments in the *Accompaniment Handbook*.

566
In the cross of Christ I glory — RATHBUN

John Bowring (1792-1872)
Hymns, 1825

Ithamar Conkey (1815-1867), 1849
Greatorex's *Collection of Psalm and Hymn Tunes*, 1851

The story goes that Bowring wrote this text when he was inspired by the sight of a cross perched on a ruined cathedral near Hong Kong. However,

Bowring first visited Hong Kong twenty-four years *after* this text was published. His hymn is based on Galatians 6:14, "But God forbid that I should glory, save in the cross of our Lord Jesus Christ . . ." (KJV). The opening words of the hymn are inscribed on Bowring's tombstone.

This text should not be construed as veneration of the cross. When Paul "gloried" in the cross, he was pointing to the irony that this instrument of torture and death was also the vehicle for the world's redemption. Bowring could only have connected the cross with "peace" and "pleasure" *after* the experience of the resurrection.

The melody RATHBUN was composed for this text in 1849 while Conkey was organist and choirmaster of Central Baptist Church in Norwich, Connecticut. One rainy Sunday morning, discouraged because only one of his choir members, Mrs. Beriah S. Rathbun, had appeared for the service, Conkey abandoned the organ after the prelude. That afternoon, the words of Bowring's text kept running through his mind; they had been used that Lenten season with a sermon series on Christ's words on the cross. Newly inspired, Conkey composed the music and prepared the scores for his choir, who sang it the following Sunday (Haeussler 1952). He named the tune for his loyal soprano. Although RATHBUN is now firmly associated with this text, it was first published in 1851 with "Savior, who thy flock art feeding."

461
In the quiet consecration

STENKA RAZIN

Constance Headlam Coote (1844-1936), 1910
Coote's *At His Table*, 1913

Russian folk melody
Harm. by Esther Wiebe (1932-)
Hymnal: A Worship Book, 1992

This Communion hymn radiates quiet joy and vitality, complementing the solemn reverence of love feast and Communion. It is also a "blood and atonement" hymn (sts. 3 and 4), though the music is not what we usually associate with such hymns!

STENKA RAZIN is a simple, attractive melody that beautifully matches the communal spirit of the text. The tune is named for Stephan (diminutive, Stenka) Timofeyevich Razin, a popular hero of Russian folklore. He was a Cossack who led a peasant revolt in the southeastern portion of European Russia in 1670 but was finally defeated and broken on the wheel in Moscow. Razin died in 1671 (Utechin 1961).

526
In the rifted Rock I'm resting

RIFTED ROCK

Mary Dagworthy Yard James (1810-1883)
The Chautauqua Collection, 1875

W. Warren Bentley (late 19th c.)
(same source as text)

This gospel hymn is a classic example of a Canadian Mennonite "*Kernlied*" (core song), a term further described with "The Lord Is King" (**69**). These favorite chorales and gospel songs are characterized by lyrical, folklike, and tuneful melodies supported by beautiful harmonies. *Kernlieder* began with Lutheran hymnody in Prussia. As the Mennonites migrated to Russia, they also embraced German translations of eighteenth-century English hymns and nineteenth-century gospel songs. The Mennonites tended to select songs that best reflected their corporate experiences of "hurt and hope," along with a deep spirit of piety, devotion, and inner resolve. They brought this tradition to North America where it continues to flourish.

"In the rifted Rock" is known to Mennonites in Canada and parts of the U.S. by its German title, *Wehrlos und Verlassen*, which is more of a free re-creation than a faithful translation. Carl Rohl, who wrote the German version, exchanges the dominant imagery of the rifted Rock as a place of refuge for that of the comforting shelter of a mother bird's wings.

Here is the German, its literal translation, and the hymnal text:

Wehrlos und verlassen sehnt sich
Oft mein Herz in ach stiller Ruh,
doch Du dekkest mit dem Fittich
Deiner Liebe sanft mich zu.

Defenseless and forsaken
My heart longs for quiet rest;
But with the feathers (wings) of your love
You softly cover me.

In the rifted Rock I'm resting;
Safely sheltered I abide.
There no foes nor storms molest me,
While within the cleft I hide.

Hymnological sources reveal little information about the composer of RIFTED ROCK. Robert Perkins of Savage, Maryland, has verified that Bentley was senior editor for Kurzenknabe & Sons Publishing Company in Harrisburg, Pennsylvania, in 1891. From 1875 to 1902, when the hymn appeared in the Mennonite *Church and Sunday School Hymnal*, it was included in thirty-six hymnals indexed by the *Dictionary of American Hymnology*. In *The Brethren Hymnal* (1901), the hymn has the scripture reference "Isaiah 32:2," and the tune is listed as by "Warren W. Bentley, by per.," leading one to assume that Bentley was still living at that time.

RIFTED ROCK, a flowing, lyrical, and somewhat nostalgic tune, was selected by Toronto, Ontario, composer Victor Davies as the theme for a set of variations in the second movement of his popular *Mennonite Piano Concerto*. The work was premiered in Winnipeg, Manitoba, in 1974 at a *Sängerfest* to commemorate the 450th anniversary of the founding of the Anabaptist movement (in 1525).

551 In the stillness of the evening

I de sene timers stillhet
Svein Ellingsen (1929-), 1971
Det skjultk naervaer, Oslo, 1978
Tr. Hedwig T. Durnbaugh (1929-), 1990
Praises Resound!, Oslo, 1991

I DE SENE TIMERS STILLHET

Harald Herresthal (1944-), 1977
Noen må våke, Oslo, 1978

This evening hymn was written along with a morning hymn in an attempt to offer a new approach to this hymn genre. Both were published in the supplement to the official hymnal of the Norwegian Lutheran Church, *Salmer 1973*, with melodies by Ludvig Nielsen, composer and organist at the cathedral at Trondheim. Because these melodies were rather difficult to sing, the hymnal committee chose Harald Herresthal's melody for the new official hymnal in 1985, *Norsk Salmebok*.

The hymn opens with a simple statement of disquiet and continues in the second stanza with an honest assessment of the day. Having confessed the defeats of the day, the speaker is able to surrender all those troubling thoughts to an invisible Presence. That Presence, unnamed until the third stanza, is not an uninterested deity, but a personal God who loves and accepts even those who feel defeated. Stanza 4 identifies this God by naming Jesus Christ and his words of reassurance. The last stanza expresses resolve and transformation, brought about by the awareness of God's mercy, love, and acceptance.

Originally, the hymn consisted of nine three-line stanzas, without the present stanza 4. The hymn was reconstructed to fit Nielsen's tune, and the author added three introductory lines to create the present fourth stanza. It is written in the *ny enkel stil* (style of new simplicity), which avoids the use of rhyme and metaphors. Instead, tone, words, images, stanzaic form, and the development of the central thought are made to work together. Although its characteristics are intrinsic to all great hymns, this work represents a new genre in modern hymnody called the "identification-hymn." Swedish hymnwriter Anders Frostenson defines it as being "a hymn that aims at describing situations and difficulties of human life in such a way that one can recognize oneself in it, thus becoming better able to hear and understand the Christian message contained in the hymn" (Hauge 1986).

114

In thee is gladness

In dir ist Freude
Johann Lindemann (ca. 1550-ca. 1634)
Decades Amorum Filii Dei, Erfurt, 1594, 1596
Tr. Catherine Winkworth (1827-1878)
Lyra Germanica, Series II, 1858

IN DIR IST FREUDE

Adapt. from Giovanni Giacomo Gastoldi (ca. 1556-1622)
Gastoldi's *Balletti*, Venice, 1591

This German text is one of two significant poems written by Lindemann for melodies in Gastoldi's *Balletti*. The energy of this hymn is derived in part from the short phrases that propel the singer to the joyous "Hallelujahs." It is a sparkling piece in both text and music.

Gastoldi, an Italian priest and composer, was especially well known for his *balletti*. Many of these light, dancelike pieces use a fa-la-la refrain. Although this tune appears to be quite lengthy, the repetitions of entire lines, as well as sequential melodic development, make it more accessible than one might first presume. The tune name is taken from the first line of the German text.

316

In this world abound scrolls

Saichirō Yuya (1864-1941)
Tr. Esther Hibbard (1903-), 1962, alt.

MŌSŌ

Japanese melody of Chinese origin
Sambika, 1954

This text, written before 1903, creates the mysterious aura of the "depth of truth" found in scripture—depths we can never fully reach.

The ancient pentatonic melody adds the musical dimension of age to words already full of time: "scrolls," "sages," "wisdom." The oriental sounds, often associated with ancient wisdom, impart a sense of the timelessness of God's word.

2
In thy holy place we bow

Samuel Frederick Coffman (1872-1954), 1901
Church and Sunday School Hymnal, Supplement, 1911, alt.

(no tune name)

John David Brunk (1872-1926)
(same source as text)

When this hymn appeared in the Mennonite *Church Hymnal* (1927), "it became and remained one of the favorites of many congregations. Perhaps no other words reflect so precisely one dimension of S. F. [Samuel Frederick]: his sense of the presence of God and his ability to worship" (Bender 1982). For a Mennonite normally "unencumbered" by liturgical trappings, Coffman used many images from the "higher church" traditions: the notion of a specific "holy place" for God, "censers" (vessels for burning incense), the idea of saints. He also added worship elements of Communion (st. 3) reminiscent of traditions that celebrate the Eucharist every Sunday.

The music for this hymn was written in 1911 by J. D. Brunk for the supplement to the *Church and Sunday School Hymnal.* It's interesting to note that these two men, both of whom were known by their initials, were born in the same year.

585
In your sickness

Adapt. from the Twi language
Asempa Hymns

(no tune name)

Ghanaian melody
Ghana Praise

This song, originally written in the Twi language of southern Ghana, comes by way of the 1990 Mennonite World Conference *International Songbook.* Postal workers whistled this melody as they hand-canceled stamps. The background rhythm of their work falls on the "ands" after beats two, three, and four. The infectious pulse of the melody is sure to elicit a rhythmic response from the singer. Though it may at first seem unusual to North Americans to sing so buoyantly about sickness and suffering, the animation of the melody undergirds the positive message that we are not alone in the difficult times of life.

206

Infant holy, Infant lowly

Polish carol
Tr. Edith Margaret Gellibrand Reed (1885-1933)
Music and Youth, December 1925
Panpipes, December 1925

W ŻŁOBIE LEŻY

Polish folk melody
Adapt. by Arthur Ewart Rusbridge (1917-1969)
The Baptist Hymn Book, 1962

This translation combines the humble and the transcendent stations of the Christ child in a warm and personal manner. The text stacks up rhyming words in a way that sounds like bells adding on to each other.

The translator was an editor with both children's music magazines in which the text was first printed. Its first inclusion in a hymnal was in *School Worship* (Congregational Union of England and Wales 1926).

W ŻŁOBIE LEŻY (In a manger lying) traditionally has been associated with this text. The rhythms begin on the downbeat, as in the Polish dance (*mazurka*) from which they are derived. The verbal rhymes coincide beautifully with the tune's melodic sequences.

195

It came upon a midnight clear

Edmund Hamilton Sears (1810-1876)
Christian Register, Dec. 29, 1849, alt.

CAROL

Richard Storrs Willis (1819-1900)
Willis's *Church Chorals and Choir Studies*, 1850

This is one of the first carol-hymns written in North America and has the typically North American quality of incorporating the social implications of the Christmas message. Sears' 1849 text reveals the gathering storm of the U.S. Civil War, especially in stanza 3, which is frequently deleted from contemporary hymnals. It has been reinstated here but altered to be inclusive of both genders. Though this well-known carol makes no reference to Christ, the shepherds, or the wise men, its author, a Unitarian minister, proclaims the divinity of Christ.

The tune CAROL, which is an arrangement of "Study No. 23" in Willis's *Church Chorals . . .* (1850), was originally set to the text "See Israel's gentle Shepherd stand." Although the arrangement is sometimes attributed to Uzziah C. Burnap, an 1887 letter written by Willis verifies that he was responsible for the version in use today (*The Hymnal 1940 Companion*, 1951 ed.).

As pointed out in *The Worshiping Church* (worship leader's ed., 1991), the fit of this text and tune is excellent, especially in the "declamation" of the third line of each stanza: " 'the earth' drops an octave; 'above' is just that; 'over all the earth' spreads upward from the melody's lowest note."

76

Je louerai l'Eternel

(no tune name)

Praise, I will praise you Lord
Based on Psalm 9:1-2
Claude Frayssé (1941-), 1975
J'aime l'Eternel, Supplement, 1976
Tr. Kenneth I. Morse (1913-), 1988
Hymnal Sampler, 1989

Claude Frayssé (1941-), 1975
Harm. by Alain Bergèse, 1976
(same sources as text)

This simple yet moving song is already well loved through its use in the *Hymnal Sampler*. It was introduced to The Hymnal Project by members of the Plow Creek Mennonite Community, Tiskilwa, Illinois. Kenneth Morse, a member of the text committee for this hymnal, translated it.

The song was written in the high Alps during the last tour of the Troubadours of Hope in August 1975. The author gives this account in a letter dated October 29, 1991:

> Our eyes are again full of the magnificent scenery which the mountain offers us. Cow bells, the cry of the marmots, the falling water echo in our ears. Praise rises spontaneously from our hearts. However, I am preoccupied [because] Alain, our leader, has asked me to have the devotions tomorrow morning, and I have never done that before. I am a little distraught.

Searching for an appropriate passage, Frayssé came upon Psalm 9: *Je louerai l'Eternel de tout mon coeur, je raconterai toutes tes merveilles . . .* (I will praise you, O Lord, with all my heart; I will tell of all your wonders, NIV).

This song was Frayssé's creative devotional, and it became an expression of praise for all in the group. The following October, the song was on the program of the last public performance of the Troubadours of Hope "as a final offering to the universal church for the praise of her Lord." Very quickly many churches throughout Europe, then the whole world, adopted this song. It has been translated into the Scandinavian languages, English, German, Spanish, Dutch, Italian, Portuguese, and even Chinese.

A phonetic pronunciation of the French text is as follows:

> Djuh loo-ray lay tehr-nel duh too mohn kur,
> Djuh ray-kohn-tuh-ray too-tuh tay mehr-vay-yay.
> Djuh shahn-tuh-ray tohn nohm.
> Djuh loo-ray lay tehr-nel duh too mohn kur,
> Djuh feh-ray duh twah luh soo-djay duh ma djwah.
> Ah-lay-loo-yah!

604

Jesu, joy of man's desiring

Jesu, meiner Seelen Wonne
Martin Janus (Jahn) (ca. 1620-ca. 1682)
Christlich Herzens Andacht, Nürnberg, 1665
Tr. Robert Seymour Bridges (1844-1930)
Choral leaflet, edited by Hugh P. Allen, 1927

WERDE MUNTER

Johann Schop (ca. 1590-ca. 1665)
Das Dritte Zehn, Lüneberg, 1642
Harm. by J. S. Bach (1685-1750)
Cantata No. 147, *Herz und Mund und Tat und Leben,* 1716

The origin of this hymn text is the eighteen-stanza German hymn "Jesu, meiner Seelen Wonne." This is Janus's only hymn to have been translated into English. Bridges' "translation" may or may not be an original poem;[1] it at least is a free translation of stanzas 6 and 17 of the Janus hymn. Bridges' work was first published with Bach's chorale in a leaflet for the Church Music Society (Oxford University Press). Although the familiar version of the text is used here, an alternate first line, "Jesu, joy of our desiring," is provided.

The tune name WERDE MUNTER comes from Johann Rist's 1642 hymn text *Werde munter mein Gemüthe* (My heart becomes joyful), which was sung with this tune by Schop. J. S. Bach's harmonization of Schop's melody adds a flowing countermelody. It appears twice as an extended chorale in his Cantata No. 147, *Herz und Mund und Tat und Leben* (sections 6 and 10). These two sections use the sixth and sixteenth stanzas of the Janus hymn text. This original setting for choir, trumpet, strings, and continuo is the basis of numerous arrangements and transcriptions. This hymnal has included numbers to indicate the number of measures of rest to be observed between the hymn tune phrases if the Bach accompaniment is used.

1. *The Church Anthem Book, One Hundred Anthems* (edited by Davies and Ley, Oxford University Press, 1926) specifies Bridges as the translator, and a note in a piano arrangement by Myra Hess (Oxford University Press 1933) reads: " 'Jesu, Joy of Man's Desiring' is the first line of an original poem by the late Robert Bridges and is used by permission."

9

Jesus A, Nahetotaetanome

Jesus Lord, how joyful you have made
John Heap of Birds (1894-1966)
Tr. David Graber (1942-) and others
Tsese-Ma'heone-Nemeotȯtse, 1982

(no tune name)

Plains Indian melody

This hymn, often used to begin worship services when Cheyenne Christians gather, is one of the best known and loved of the hymns of John Heap of Birds. It is sung reverently and slowly as a processional, unaccompanied by any instruments. "In a few words we are drawn to focus deeply on Jesus. Our joy at gathering with him, because of his invitation, helps us pray with confidence, 'Lead us well in your way!' " (*Tsese-Ma'heone-Nemeotȯtse* [Cheyenne Spiritual Songs] 1982).

The first line is repeated at the end, an octave lower, a common melodic structure in Plains Indian music. The sweeping range of the melody, from high to very low, is also common and is sometimes called a terrace melodic profile. For further comments on Cheyenne hymns, see "Ehane he'ama" ("Father God, you are holy," **78**).

297

Jesus came—the heavens adoring

BENEDIC ANIMA

Godfrey Thring (1823-1903)
Chope's *Hymnal*, 1864
Rev. in *Hymns for Today's Church* (sts. 1-3,5), 1982

John Goss (1800-1880)
The Supplemental Hymn and Tune Book, 1869

This is one of Thring's earliest hymns. The five stanzas describe Jesus' advent and his spiritual arrival in the lives of believers, culminating in his physical second coming in stanza 5. While stanza 4 has remained relatively unaltered, stanzas 1,2,3, and 5 are from the version in *Hymns for Today's Church* (1982). The third stanza has undergone the most alteration. The original was:

> Jesus comes to hearts rejoicing,
> Bringing news of sins forgiven;
> Jesus comes in sounds of gladness,
> Leading souls redeemed to heav'n.
> Alleluia! Alleluia! Now the gate of death is riv'n.

Instead of the Latin "Alleluia," Thring's original version uses the Hebrew "Hallelujah," which means "Praise the Lord."

BENEDIC ANIMA, also known as LAUDA ANIMA or PRAISE MY SOUL, was composed for "Praise, my soul, the King of heaven" (**65**). It was originally published in two forms: in D major for unison voices, with a different organ accompaniment for each stanza, and in E major for four-part harmony.

40

Jesus Christ, God's only Son

PRAISE AND PRAYER

Alexander Mack, Jr. (1712-1803)
Etliche liebliche und erbauliche Lieder, 1788
Tr. Ora W. Garber (1903-1981)
The Brethren Hymnal, 1951

Nevin Wishard Fisher (1900-1984)
The Brethren Hymnal, 1951

Peter Leibert published his small volume of "beautiful and edifying songs" in 1788. The first selection was written by Alexander Mack, Jr., the son of one of the first Brethren. It was to be sung to the melody JESUS IST DER SCHÖNSTE NAM'. In *The Brethren Hymnal* (1951), the sequence of Mack's stanzas was reversed, beginning with "Bless, O Lord, this church of thine." The original order of praising God and then praying has been reinstated here. We begin our worship with praise and only then come to God with requests.

Nevin Fisher gave his musical setting the same name that Mack had titled his text. Fisher, aware that the Macks were contemporaries of J. S. Bach, made a "conscious attempt in this tune and harmony to revive a feeling for the solemnity, directness, and stolid character of the old chorale type of melody which our forefathers sang" (Statler, Fisher 1959).

621
Jesus, friend so kind and gentle — SICILIAN MARINERS

Philip E. Gregory (1886-1974), 1948
The Hymnbook (Presbyterian), 1955

The European Magazine and London Review, November 1792

This gentle hymn is tailored for services of dedication for children and parents. Even though it originated as a baptism poem, the lack of explicit reference to baptism of infants makes it suitable for believers church congregations. The author, a Congregational pastor, tells of the origin of the poem:

> On a particular Sunday I was to baptize a number of children and I wanted that part of the service to have a worship value with congregational participation. I looked in vain in the hymnbook for a children's hymn which might be used. . . . Failing to find such a hymn, I wrote this one. (Ronander, Porter 1966)

An omitted third stanza expands the hymn:

> Grant to us a deep compassion
> For thy children everywhere.
> May we see our human family
> Free from sorrow and despair,
> And behold thy kingdom glorious,
> In our world so bright and fair. (*Pilgrim Hymnal* 1958)

The origin of SICILIAN MARINERS (also known as O SANCTISSIMA) is unknown, but in its first known appearance, it was the setting for "The Sicilian Mariner's Hymn to the Virgin," which begins with the Latin words *O sanctissima.* Soon thereafter it appeared in various German, English, and North American hymnals with various texts. In Germany this tune is traditionally sung with the Christmas text

O du fröliche, O du Selige, a new English version of which appears on **209** ("Oh, how joyfully") in this hymnal. It also is used with "Lord, dismiss us with thy blessing."

617

Jesus, keep me near the cross — NEAR THE CROSS

Fanny Jane Crosby (1820-1915)
Bright Jewels for the Sunday School, 1869

William Howard Doane (1832-1915)
(same source as text)

This gospel song, one of a number of texts that Fanny Crosby wrote for an existing tune, is popular in African American churches. In the refrain "rest beyond the river" refers to the Jordan River, the traditional boundary between the "wilderness" (where the Israelites wandered with Moses) and the "promised land" of Canaan. Later the "river" became a Christian symbol of the boundary between earthly life and the eternal life of heaven. For slaves in North America, it was also the symbol of crossing into freedom. The way to making safe passage across that river was to "keep near the cross" in life.

9

Jesus Lord, how joyful you have made—see "Jesus A, Nahetotaetanome"

618

Jesus, lover of my soul — ABERYSTWYTH

Charles Wesley (1707-1788), 1738
Hymns and Sacred Poems, 1740

Joseph Parry (1841-1903)
Ail Llyfr Tonau ac Emynau, 1879

This widely known and beloved hymn, written in 1738 soon after Charles Wesley's conversion experience, was first published with the title "In Time of Prayer and Temptation." Charles' brother John felt that the intimate nature of this hymn made it unsuitable for corporate worship, so he omitted it from the 1780 *Collection of Hymns for the Use of the People Called Methodists.* It was not until the *Supplement* of 1797 that it was reinstated into Methodist hymnody.

Brushing aside the abundant legends surrounding the inspiration of this hymn, Albert Bailey speculates that it arose "spontaneously from the depths of [Wesley's] soul" in response to three formative experiences. Stanzas 1 and 2 correlate with a journal entry of 1736 reminiscent of a hurricane at sea:

> There was so prodigious a sea that it quickly washed away our sheep and half our hogs, and drowned most of our fowl. . . . I prayed for . . . faith in Jesus Christ, continually repeating his name, till I felt the virtue of it at last, and knew that I abode under the shadow of the Almighty.[1]

An omitted third stanza, along with the first part of the present stanza 3, may have been prompted by Wesley's being suddenly healed of a lingering fever on the day of his conversion in 1738. The last part of stanza 3 and the final stanza hearken back to another journal entry concerning Wesley's ministry with condemned criminals at Newgate prison, also in 1738. Bailey cautions that the text interpretation needs the background of "lower-class eighteenth-century conditions and of the passionate evangelistic temper of the Great Revival."[2]

ABERYSTWYTH (pronounced "a-bur-ust'-with" or "a-brust'-with") is named for the university town in Wales where Joseph Parry composed this tune. Originally the setting for the Welsh hymn *Beth sydd i mi yn y byd*, Parry combined it with these words in his cantata *Ceridwen*. The sturdy though haunting quality of this tune, with it final somber descent, makes it an appropriate choice for this text, which is frequently sung at funerals. This melody could be introduced to the congregation by way of an organ setting or an anthem based upon it. Congregations could also sing this hymn to the familiar tune MARTYN, available to accompanists in many hymnals.

1. More extensive excerpts from Wesley's journal are in Bailey (1950). Theron Brown and Hezekiah Butterworth also relate many of the legends regarding the inspiration of the origin of this text, as well as colorful "incidents of its heavenly service," in *The Story of the Hymns and Tunes*, George H. Doran Company, 1906.
2. Ibid.

341

Jesus loves me — JESUS LOVES ME

Anna Bartlett Warner (ca. 1822-1915), 1859

William Batchelder Bradbury (1816-1868)
The Golden Shower, 1862

Warner was a popular story writer, often collaborating with her older sister. In their novel *Say and Seal*, a sick little boy is comforted by his Sunday school teacher with words of this text. Warner's original song consisted of four stanzas, and William B. Bradbury composed his music specifically for this text. The *Baptist Hymnal* (1956) named the tune CHINA because of its popularity with the children in that country. In light of the song's universal appeal, it seems appropriate that "Jesus loves me" should be presented here in several languages.

There is also an apocryphal story about the German theologian Karl Barth, known for his rather intimidating, multi-volume work on church dogmatics. When Barth was asked to sum up his faith, however, he is said to have replied with the words of this song: "Jesus loves me, this I know, for the Bible tells me so."

533

Jesus, my Lord, my God, my all

Henry Collins (1827-1919)
Hymns for Missions, 1854

ADORO (ST. CHRYSOSTOM)

Joseph Barnby (1838-1896)
Musical Times, December 1871

These ardently devotional words are one of two original texts by Collins included in his collection cited above. They appear with the title "Love of Jesus desired." One hymnologist called this a hymn for closet devotionals, "almost too intimate" for public worship (Bailey 1950). It will appeal to Christians with pietist leanings.

ADORO, also called ST. CHRYSOSTOM after the great preacher (ca. 345-407) of the Greek church, is music of melodic and harmonic warmth. It has a hush that accents the intimacy of the words. Though composed for this text in the composer's collection *Hymnary* (1872), it first appeared the preceding year in the *Musical Times*.

595

Jesus, priceless treasure

Jesu, meine Freude
Johann Franck (1618-1677)
Crüger's *Praxis Pietatis Melica*, 5th ed., 1653
Tr. Catherine Winkworth (1827-1878)
Chorale Book for England, 1863
Christian Singers of Germany, 1869

JESU, MEINE FREUDE

Johann Crüger (1598-1662)
(same source as text)
(Zahn No. 8032)
Harm. by Johann Sebastian Bach (1685-1750)
Motet No. 3 in E minor, 1723

Johann Franck patterned his text after a secular love song, *Flora meine Freude*, by Heinrich Alberti (1641). Franck was heavily influenced by the German pietist movement, and his word choices reflect a very personal experience with Christ. In fact, some Lutherans considered this text too subjective to be used in corporate worship. Winkworth produced two translations as cited above. The three stanzas here are drawn from the latter version.

The threat of danger that pervades this hymn can be attributed to Franck's upbringing amid the horrors of the Thirty Years War. In this text the believer's walk with Christ is the surest protection and prompts courage in witnessing. "I will suffer naught to hide thee" in stanza 1:4-5 means "I will let nothing hide you."

The melody, which takes its name from the German text, was "either composed by Crüger or adapted by him from a traditional melody"

(Loewen, Moyer, Oyer 1983). In addition to the Bach motet from which this setting is taken, the melody was included in four of Bach's cantatas and several organ works. Canadian musician George Wiebe writes that this chorale was not favored by Canadian Mennonite congregations because in Russia Mennonites came to associate the minor mode of Russian folk songs with tragedy and sadness. Mennonite choirs, however, discovered the rich warmth and deep joy of Bach's harmonization of JESU, MEINE FREUDE and have inspired congregations to appreciate it anew. It is noteworthy that this hymn appeared in the earliest Brethren hymnal, *Geistreiches Gesang-Buch* (1720).

247
Jesus, remember me

Based on Luke 23:42
Jacques Berthier (1923-), 1981
Music from Taizé, Vol. I, 1978, 1980, 1981

These words of the thief on the cross (Luke 23:42) are presented here in a simple harmonic setting. There are many ways this brief response can be incorporated into worship, possibly between scripture, prayers, or litanies. It is especially effective during Lent. See "Alleluia" (**101**) for information about music from Taizé. The *Accompaniment Handbook* contains additional instrumental parts.

515
Jesus, Rock of ages

M. Gerald Derstine (1948-), 1973
Hymnal: A Worship Book, 1992

(no tune name)

M. Gerald Derstine (1948-), 1973
(same source as text)
Harm. by Marilyn Houser Hamm (1951-) and M. Gerald Derstine, 1991

Written in 1973, this song has been continuously revised until the present. It was first performed in 1973 at the Mennonite Youth Convention in Grand Rapids, Michigan. The hymn incorporates just two central biblical images, Jesus as Rock and Water. The composer, known professionally as J. D. Martin, incorporated this song into another, "Standing on the Rock," which was performed by his band, Tanglefoot. Marilyn Houser Hamm, who was living in Goshen, Indiana, when the song was written, has worked on a four-part harmonization and an accompaniment that are found in the *Accompaniment Handbook*. This hymn works well with a soloist singing the stanzas and the congregation responding with the refrain.

319

Jesus shall reign

Based on Psalm 72
Isaac Watts (1674-1748)
The Psalms of David . . ., 1719, alt.

DUKE STREET

Attrib. to John Hatton (ca. 1710-1793)
H. Boyd's *Psalm and Hymn Tunes*, 1793

Watts's paraphrase of the second part of Psalm 72 had the heading "Christ's Kingdom Among the Gentiles." Watts substituted Jesus for the king in the psalm, which calls on God to help the ruler govern in divine righteousness. Even when the Israelite royalty collapsed in 587 B.C., these royal psalms continued to evoke messianic hopes of *shalom*, life's fullest blessings for all (st. 4). Watts thus applied their vision to Christ.

This work has been called the first missionary hymn in the English language. Considered one of Watts's most popular texts, it has long been a favorite of various denominations and, in translation, of many cultures. Although minor alterations have been made in stanzas 1, 2, and 4, no suitable substitute was found for the word "peculiar" in stanza 5. In this context it should be defined as "particular" or "unique" rather than "odd."

For comments on DUKE STREET, see "From all that dwell below the skies" (**49**).

25

Jesus, stand among us

William Pennefather (1816-1873)
Original Hymns and Thoughts in Verse, 1873

WEM IN LEIDENSTAGEN

Friedrich Filitz (1804-1876)
Vierstimmiges Choralbuch, 1847

This invocation recalls John's report of Jesus' post-resurrection appearance to the disciples (John 20:19-22) and how he breathed the Holy Spirit upon them.

The text was first published in a leaflet, but the above source is the first to have the year of publication. It was written for the Barnet and Mildmay Conferences, meetings of a center of religious work in London, organized by the author in the 1850s. It is clearly appropriate for corporate worship. The third stanza, often omitted, is:

> Thus with quickened footsteps
> We pursue our way,
> Watching for the dawning
> Of eternal day.

WEM IN LEIDENSTAGEN, also known as BEMERTON, CASWELL, and FILITZ, was originally set to Heinrich Siegmund Oswald's hymn for mourners, *Wem in Leidenstagen* (O! let him whose sorrow). This tune appeared with Pennefather's text in *Worship Song* (1905). It has a simple, unassuming style, matching the directness of the words.

466

Jesus, sun and shield art thou

COLDREY

Horatius N. Bonar (1808-1889)
Hymns of Faith and Hope, Second Series, 1861

Henry Thomas Smart (1813-1879)
Psalms and Hymns for Divine Worship, 1867

This hymn, titled "Jesus the First and Last," was first published with five stanzas. Each stanza of Bonar's carefully structured text elaborates on a set of metaphors for Christ. Those used here are stanzas 1, 4, 5, and 2. The omitted third stanza began, "Jesus, love and life art thou." The final stanza makes this hymn particularly appropriate for Communion.

COLDREY's melodic curve and harmonic variety show a family likeness to the composer's REGENT SQUARE. Both tunes appear in the English Presbyterian collection listed above. Whether this was the earliest appearance of COLDREY is not documented.

588

Jesus, the very thought of thee

ST. AGNES

Jesu dulcis memoria
Attrib. to Bernard of Clairvaux (ca. 1091-1153)
Manuscript, 12th c. (42 sts.)
Tr. Edward Caswall (1814-1878)
Lyra Catholica, 1849, alt.

John Bacchus Dykes (1823-1876)
Grey's *Hymnal for Use in the English Church*, 1866

This ardent, personal devotional is considered "one of the most moving expressions of medieval piety" (*The Hymnal 1940 Companion*, 1951 ed.). It is a chaste love song focusing on Christ and the treasure of his love. The original Latin title sums up its purpose: *Jubilus rhythmicus de nomine Jesu* (Joyful rhythm on the name of Jesus).

The authorship of this Latin poem, forty-two stanzas long, can neither be conclusively established nor seriously challenged.[1] The mystic monk Bernard of Clairvaux has been credited with the poem because it is marked with his manner of passionate writing. Some of the best manuscripts, however, were found in England, indicating it could have originated there. It was probably written around 1150. Nine stanzas were added during the fifteenth century when the poem came into general use for Roman Catholic devotions. The five stanzas found here are those usually chosen from Caswall's fifty-stanza translation. "Jesus, thou joy of loving hearts," another well-known hymn, is also derived from *Jesu dulcis memoria*.

ST. AGNES was composed by Dykes for Caswall's translation and named for a thirteen-year-old Roman Christian girl martyred in 304. Already "trothed" to Christ, she declined to marry a nobleman and was put to death for her commitment. In England this tune sometimes is designated ST. AGNES DURHAM to distinguish it from a different tune also named ST. AGNES.

1. The full, original Latin text can be found in *Speculum*, III, 1928, and ten of the stanzas are in *The Hymnal 1940 Companion*, 1951 ed., pages 285 and 299.

115
Jesus, thou mighty Lord

DOANE

Fanny Jane Crosby (1820-1915)
Baptist Hymnal (American Baptist), 1883

William Howard Doane (1832-1915)
(same source as text)

The essence of this text is Christ's constancy. His power and mercy are the same—yesterday, today, and forever. The final phrase of each stanza functions as a refrain. This hymn comes from the Mennonite *Church Hymnal* (1927) and *The Mennonite Hymnal* (1969). Apparently no other current North American hymnals include it.

DOANE, unlike many of the composer's gospel songs, has the character of a traditional hymn tune.

449
Jesus took a towel

JESUS TOOK A TOWEL

Based on John 13
Chrysogonus Waddell (1930-), O.C.S.O., 1968
Worship III, 1986

Chrysogonus Waddell (1930-), O.C.S.O., 1968
(same source as text)

This text, based on John 13, was written for the Holy Thursday footwashing rite celebrated at Gethsemani Abbey in Kentucky. Waddell derived these words from the Byzantine Holy Thursday *kanon*. The composer writes that the song is "being widely used now in the Holy Week liturgy throughout the States; but, here at Gethsemani, I long ago replaced the rather folksy melody with something more in line with our chant tradition (based on Gregorian chant)."

The easily learned refrain makes this an ideal selection for singing during footwashing. It should be sung in a reflective style at a tempo that allows time for meditating on the text and on the experience of footwashing. Seven additional stanzas, found in the *Accompaniment Handbook*, convey and illuminate the scripture passage.

10

Jesus, we want to meet

Abraham Taiwo Olajide Olude 1908-1986), 1949
Tr. Biodun Adebesin (1928-), 1962
Versified by Austin Cole Lovelace (1919-), 1962
The Methodist Hymnal, 1966

(no tune name)

Nigerian melody adapted by Abraham Taiwo Olajide Olude (1908-1986)

This hymn was written for a monthly service at Abeokuta, Nigeria, to popularize the use of Yoruba music in Christian worship. The song was brought to the U.S. by the translator Adebesin, who was serving at the United Nations at the time the Methodist hymnal committee was meeting in New York City. Austin Lovelace, minister of music at Christ Methodist Church where the Adebesin family belonged, put the translation into verse (Gealy, Lovelace, Young 1970).

The text resembles an earlier one written by Elizabeth Parson (1812-1873) in the early 1840s in England. The first stanza in particular parallels the Parson text, which reads:

> Jesus, we love to meet, on this, Thy holy day;
> We worship round Thy seat, on this, Thy holy day.
> O tender, heavenly friend, to Thee our prayers ascend.
> Over our spirits bend, on this, Thy holy day.

British missionaries probably introduced Parson's hymn to Nigerian Christians in the late nineteenth or early twentieth century. However, "Olude's treatment . . . adds several new dimensions to the text. For example, in the first line it is not 'love to meet' but 'want to meet,' which is a more profound understanding of Sunday worship" (Young 1993). The text also is expanded from three to four stanzas and adds different imagery. The archaic forms of address, changed in some recent hymnals, are retained here for their aesthetic and rhythmic qualities.

In some hymnals the tune is named NIGERIA or JESU A FE PADE. Its call and response pattern, combined with the cross-rhythms of the drum patterns found in the *Accompaniment Handbook*, make this an exciting gathering hymn of praise.

318

Joy to the world

Based on Psalm 98
Isaac Watts (1674-1748)
The Psalms of David . . . , 1719, alt.

ANTIOCH

"Arranged from Handel"
Lowell Mason (1792-1872)
Mason's *Occasional Psalm and Hymn Tunes*, 1836

Rejoicing in the coming of Christ's kingdom, as proclaimed in this text, certainly should not be sequestered in the season of Christmastide. While this hymn certainly is appropriate for Christ's nativity, it also has a broader message, alluded to in Watts's original heading, "The Messiah's Coming and Kingdom." The text is based on Psalm 98:4-9; Watts merged his paraphrase with the gospel because he was convinced that the New Testament church should sing of prophecies accomplished.

There have been a few alterations to this text over the years, most notably in the first line; Watts originally wrote "Joy to the earth." In stanza 2, "Let men their songs employ" was unobtrusively changed to the inclusive "Let all their songs employ."

In Lowell Mason's collection above, ANTIOCH has the designation "Arranged from Handel." Although it cannot be traced with certainty, similarities can be found between the first four notes of ANTIOCH and the opening phrase of "Glory to God" and "Lift up your heads" from Handel's *Messiah*. Likewise, a parallel may be drawn between the tenor recitative "Comfort ye, my people" and the passage "And heaven and nature sing." Altered after its first appearance, it was published in its present form in *The National Psalmist* (1848). ANTIOCH is named for the ancient Syrian city where the disciples were first called Christians. Other tune names are COMFORT, HOLY TRIUMPH, MESSIAH, and JERUSALEM.

233

Joyful is the dark — JOYFUL DARK

Brian Arthur Wren (1936-), 1986
Bring Many Names, 1989

Philip K. Clemens (1941-), 1991
Hymnal: A Worship Book, 1992

In 1985 Tony Brown, chair of the text committee of this hymnal, expressed the concern that all too frequently "blackness" is associated with evil in our hymns. Hymnwriter Brian Wren read Brown's paper, and it coincided with Wren's work on the last stanza of a poem "Bring many names," in which the line "joyful darkness far beyond our seeing" inspired this text. Wren writes: "I'd also been helped by *Darkness*, a booklet by Philip Seddon (1983), which draws out the positive connotations of darkness in the Bible and Christian tradition. Finding the opening line gave the impetus needed . . . " (Wren 1989). Two scripture references for this text are Exodus 20:18-21 and Psalm 18:2-12.

Philip Clemens composed the music with the conviction that "the profound and refreshing text demands serious but joyful music, a blend of mystery and beauty." Even though we often expect the minor mode to express darkness, Clemens did not shy away from it, because the text itself challenges cliché understandings of the dark. He also avoided a major key, which would represent "too simple a joy." Clemens explains:

> As I worked with the text, a simple, undulating, pentatonic tune unaffectedly emerged. Suitably, this tune represents music from around the world, and is not tied to white North American and

European traditions. In accordance, the voice parts appear in unison, 2-part, 3-part, and 4-part relationships, and are neither major nor minor, but modal in nature. I hope congregations can sing this music unaccompanied, but imaginative use of a wide range of instruments can be added. Unison singing and the use of vocal or instrumental drones should not be overlooked.

71
Joyful, joyful, we adore thee

HYMN TO JOY

Henry van Dyke (1852-1933), 1907
Poems of Henry van Dyke, 1911, alt.

Adapted from Ludwig van Beethoven (1770-1827), 1823
Symphony No. 9
Based on adaptation by Edward Hodges (1796-1867)
Trinity Collection of Church Music, 1864

This hymn was written in 1907 when Henry van Dyke was a visiting preacher at Williams College, Williamstown, in the Berkshire Mountains of Massachusetts. He handed the manuscript to the college president at the breakfast table, saying: "Here is a hymn for you. Your mountains were my inspiration. It must be sung to the music of Beethoven's 'Hymn to Joy' " (*The Hymnal 1940 Companion*, 1951 ed.).

HYMN TO JOY is derived from the primary theme of the final movement of Beethoven's classic last symphony. The text he used for this unusual vocal movement was *Ode to Joy* by Friedrich Schiller. Hodges' arrangement is the one commonly used. However, the tune was in use in other versions and with other texts as early as 1846.

Van Dyke's new work transformed Schiller's ode *to* joy into a hymn *of* joy based on *agape* love (st. 3), "the enduring legacy given us by God" (*The Worshiping Church* 1990, 1991). Its first hymnal usage was in the *Presbyterian Hymnal* of 1911. In stanza 4:2 the problematic "Father-love is reigning o'er us, brother-love binds man to man" is changed to "Love divine is reigning o'er us, leading us with mercy's hand."

301
Joys are flowing like a river

(no tune name)

Manie Payne Ferguson (b. 1850-d. ?), alt.

W. S. Marshall
Adapt. by James M. Kirk (1854-1945)

This gospel song from the African American tradition is frequently known by the first words of its refrain, "Blessed quietness." The author, with her husband, founded the Peniel Missions, which later affiliated with the National Holiness Missionary Society. With the work of the Holy Spirit as its theme, the song has long been popular in the Holiness Movement in America. The hymn presents not the wild, flaming, rushing wind of the Spirit at Pentecost, but yet another side of God's Spirit—gentle rain, sustaining sunlight, and the "still, small voice" that Elijah experienced. The refrain recalls Jesus' command to the storm on Galilee, "Peace, be still."

"Blessed quietness" is known to Mennonites from its appearance in *Life Songs No. 2* (1938) and to the General Conference Mennonites from an arrangement for male choirs by Esther Wiebe recorded by the Faith and Life Choir, Winnipeg, Manitoba, in 1988. An alternate and faster rhythmic version, however, was written by Leonardo Wilborn, a Church of the Brethren member, choir conductor, and music arranger. See the *Accompaniment Handbook.*

103
Jubilate Deo omnis terra

(no tune name)

Rejoice in the Lord, all lands
Based on Psalm 100
Music from Taizé, Vol. I, 1978, 1980, 1981

Jacques Berthier (1923-),1980
(same source as text)

In this selection, as in many of those from the Taizé community (see "Alleluia," **101**), Latin is used, playing a role of neutrality and inclusiveness, because in this age the language belongs to no national or religious group. A phonetic pronunciation of the Latin text is as follows:

Yoo-bih-lah-teh Deh-oh, awm-nis teh-rah,
Sehr-vee-teh Daw-mee-noh een leh-tee-tzee-ah.
Ah-leh-loo-yah.

JUBILATE DEO OMNIS TERRA, titled "Jubilate, Servite," is a canon (round) in two voices, with the second voice imitating the first after one measure. However, as many voices as there are measures of music may be layered on, each joining at one-measure intervals. This piece presents a wealth of musical possibilities for vocal or instrumental improvisation. For accompaniment suggestions, see the *Accompaniment Handbook.*

516
Just as I am, without one plea

WOODWORTH

Charlotte Elliott (1789-1871), 1834
Invalid's Hymn Book, 1836

William Batchelder Bradbury (1816-1868)
The Mendelssohn Collection or Hastings and Bradbury's Third Book of Psalmody, 1849

This hymn, possibly the most famous of the author's 150 hymns, was written in 1834. As an invalid, Elliott was unable to help members of her family at a bazaar to raise money for St. Mary's Hall, a college to educate the daughters of the poorer clergy. She wrote this hymn in response to the disappointment and questioning of her life's purpose. It was first printed without her permission in a leaflet in 1835, but published the following year in her *Invalid's Hymn Book* headed by John 6:37: " . . . him that cometh to me, I will in no wise cast out." That same year this hymn also appeared in her *Hours of Sorrow Cheered and Comforted* with an additional stanza:

> Just as I am—of that free love,
> The breadth, length, depth, and height to prove,
> Here, for a reason, then above—
> O Lamb of God, I come!

Because the text is one of pure surrender and acceptance, the hymn is often used for services of commitment. When we come to Jesus for mercy, the implication is that we also dedicate ourselves to following him (st. 6).

This hymn has been translated into many different languages. The author's brother, Rev. H. V. Elliott, once said of this poem, "In the course of a long ministry, I hope I have been permitted to see some fruit of my labours; but I feel far more has been done by a single hymn of my sister's" (Julian 1907).

WOODWORTH first appeared in the key of C with the text "The God of love will sure indulge."

152
Kyrie

TAIZÉ KYRIE

Lord, have mercy
Greek litany

Jacques Berthier (1923-)
Music from Taizé, Vol. I, 1978, 1980, 1981

The *Kyrie eleison* is a response that was used in Christian litanies from the earliest days of the Eastern Church. The Greek words mean "Lord, have mercy." The writings of Pope Gregory I (ca. 540-604) describe the addition of the alternate words *Christe eleison* ("Christ, have mercy") and the way that it was sung antiphonally between clergy and congregation. By the eighth century, the number of repetitions had been established as nine, three of the *Kyrie*, three of the *Christe*, followed by three *Kyrie*. In this form, no longer associated with the litany petitions, the *Kyrie* became the first portion of the Ordinary of the Mass.

In his Strassburg liturgy of 1540, John Calvin introduced the singing of the *Kyrie* as a response after each of the Ten Commandments.

This simple setting from the Taizé community fulfills the earliest function of the *Kyrie* as a response to litany petitions or prayers. The text is pronounced: kee-ree-eh eh-leh-ee-sohn. For information about music from Taizé, see "Alleluia" (**101**).

144

Kyrie eleison

Lord, have mercy
Greek litany

ORTHODOX KYRIE

Russian Orthodox liturgy

This setting of the *Kyrie* exemplifies the triple statement of the text. The full chords are typical of the rich harmonic sounds found in the Russian Orthodox liturgy.

312

Lamp of our feet

Bernard Barton (1784-1849)
The Reliquary, 1836

GRÄFENBURG (NUN DANKET ALL')

Johann Crüger (1598-1662)
Praxis Pietatis Melica, 5th ed., 1653
(Zahn No. 207)

Along with Jews and Moslems, Christians are known as a "people of the book," that is, we are pointed to the way and meaning of life by an inspired volume of scripture. This hymn, which Barton titled "The Bible," directs us to that essential book, clothing it in rich metaphors, many from the Exodus story. Written in eleven stanzas, those selected here are stanzas 1, 2, 3, 9, and 11.

In Johann Crüger's volume, GRÄFENBURG was set to the text *Nun danket all und bringet Ehr*. Crüger's melodies tended to find their models in the Genevan psalm tunes of the previous century,[1] but he also pushed those limits to develop Lutheran hymnody. The name GRÄFENBURG comes from a small town in Silesia, a Prussian province in what is now southwestern Poland.

1. Note the resemblance of the first phrase of this melody with the opening phrase of GENEVA 118, a setting sometimes used for "Bread of the world in mercy broken" (*The Mennonite Hymnal*, No. 607, 1969).

553

Lead me, guide me—see "I am weak and I need thy strength"

538
Lead me, Lord

Based on Psalms 5:8 and 4:8

(no tune name)

Samuel Sebastian Wesley (1810-1876)
Anthem, 1861

This text is a paraphrase of the two Psalm verses cited above, with 5:8 leading out and 4:8 following.

In Samuel Wesley's anthem "Lead Me, Lord," from which this music is taken, each eight-measure musical statement is introduced by a solo voice and repeated by the choir. The four-part sections are presented here with only slight changes in voicing.

419
Lead on, O cloud of Presence

Ruth C. Duck (1947-)
Because We Are One People, 1974, alt.

LANCASHIRE

Henry Thomas Smart (1813-1879)
Leaflet, Blackburn, 1935
Smart's *Psalms and Hymns for Divine Worship*, 1867

When Ruth Duck encountered "Lead on, O King eternal" while editing *Because We Are One People*, she was convinced, she writes, that "the new wine did not fit the old wineskins." Thus, a new hymn emerged.

Like the original, it uses imagery based on the Exodus journey of the Israelites. Also as in the original, themes of light and mercy predominate. But where the old hymn used triumphalist military language, the new one grew out of movements for liberation. Duck continues: "The particular scripture passage I had in mind was Numbers 9:15-23, in which God's presence is symbolized or accompanied by a cloud which looks like fire at night. The cloud and fiery pillar are symbols of God's presence, guiding people in uncertain times as they journey toward freedom."

Several phrases other than the first line echo "Lead on, O King eternal." "The day of march has come" became "the Exodus has come," and the rhyme scheme of "the tents shall be our home" is copied with "our tribe shall make its home." Of the seemingly contradictory line "We follow, yet with fears," she says, "Of course, such a journey is fearful!" Just as the Hebrews sometimes balked on their way, so are we at times beset by uncertainty. Still, the "journey is our home," and we can rejoice in the light of God's leading.

Even the new hymn "Lead on, O cloud of Yahweh" came under criticism, since speaking the name "Yahweh" in worship is offensive to some Jews. Duck responded by changing the word to "Presence" in all future publications, with this hymnal being the first denominational volume to implement the change.

Smart wrote LANCASHIRE for the text "From Greenland's icy mountains" and used it at a missionary festival commemorating the three hundredth anniversary of the Reformation in England. It was printed in a leaflet for that occasion and later included with the same text in Smart's volume named above.

359
Lead us, O Father — ELLERS

William Henry Burleigh (1812-1871)
The New Congregational Hymn Book, 1859

Edward John Hopkins (1818-1901), 1866
Supplemental Tune and Hymn Book, 1869

Titled "A prayer for guidance" by its author, this text seeks divine guidance through the complexities of life. In 1868 it was included in C. D. Cleveland's *Lyra Sacra Americana*, a British publication often cited as its source. The popularity of that collection gave the hymn wide usage in England. The only change from the original is in stanza 3:3 where "mortal" has replaced "darksome." Alternate metaphors for "Father" in each stanza are provided at the bottom of the hymn page.

ELLERS was composed in 1866 for John Ellerton's hymn text "Savior, again to thy dear name." This tune originally was written for unison singing with an organ accompaniment, which varied with each stanza. In 1872 the composer created a four-part setting that came out in the *Appendix to the Bradford Tune Book*. This tune is an example of an "arch-form" melody, which rises gradually to a climax at midpoint, followed by a descent to the beginning pitch on the last word.

61
Let all creation bless the Lord — LOBT GOTT DEN HERREN

Carl Pickens Daw, Jr. (1944-)
A Year of Grace, 1990

Melchior Vulpius (ca. 1560-1615)
Ein schön geistlich Gesangbuch, 1609 (Zahn No. 4533)

This hymn is a paraphrase of the *Benedicite*, the canticle called "A Song of Creation," taken from verses 35-65 of the apocryphal book "The Song of the Three." This book, an addition in the Greek version of Daniel, was placed between verses 23 and 24 of the third chapter. The canticle falls into three sections paralleled by the stanzas of this hymn, which summon the universe, the earth and its creatures, and all people to praise God. The final phrase of each stanza, "Exalt the God who made you," is derived from the response "sing his praise and exalt him forever," which forms the second half of every verse in this passage of scripture.

For comments on LOBT GOTT DEN HERREN, see "All who believe and are baptized" (**436**).

463
Let all mortal flesh keep silence

Liturgy of St. James of Jerusalem, Greek hymn, 5th c.
Tr. Gerard Moultrie (1829-1885)
Shipley's *Lyra Eucharistica,* 2nd ed., 1864, alt.

PICARDY

French carol
Chansons populaires des provinces de France, IV, Paris, 1860

Attributed to St. James the Less, first bishop of Jerusalem, the text is derived from the "Prayer of the Cherubic Hymn." This part of the Eastern Orthodox liturgy is sung while the Communion elements are brought into the sanctuary. Though a eucharistic hymn, it is associated with Christmas Eve, since that is when the Eastern Church traditionally observes the Liturgy of St. James.

This text may have been used as early as the fifth century, but Moultrie's paraphrase in English meter did not come out until 1864. An English clergyman and noted linguist, Moultrie translated numerous works from German, Greek, and Latin texts.

PICARDY is named for the French province where this hymn was first sung.

213
Let all together praise our God

Lobt Gott, ihr Christen alle gleich
Nicolaus Hermann (ca. 1485-1561), ca. 1554
Die Sonntags Evangelia über das gantze Jahr, 1560
Tr. Arthur Tozer Russell (1806-1874)
Russell's *Psalms and Hymns,* 1851

LOBT GOTT, IHR CHRISTEN

Nicolaus Hermann (ca. 1485-1561)
Ein Christlicher Abentreien, 1554
(Zahn No. 198)
Harm. by Johann Sebastian Bach (1685-1750)
Cantata No. 151, 1725

This was the first of three Christmas songs Hermann included in his collection of hymns on the Gospels for the church year. It is a "joyous, charming Christmas hymn of eight original stanzas . . . characterized by a blend of dignity, simplicity, and mirth. The light and joy generated by these short stanzas is unique and has not been attained in other German Christmas hymns" (Bruppacher 1953). The hymn juxtaposes Christ's divinity and humanity in an unassuming way, so that one hardly notices the intensity of its theological implications.

The tune LOBT GOTT, IHR CHRISTEN appeared with this text in 1561, but it had been written earlier for Hermann's hymn for children on the life and work of John the Baptist, *Kommt her, ihr liebes Schwesterlein.* The melody is also known as HERMANN and JOACHIMSTHAL, the latter from St. Joachimsthal in Bohemia where Hermann had been a teacher, organist, and choirmaster.

It is a tune of jubilant energy, expressing great joy, as created in the four repeated notes at the beginning of the melody and in the deceptive cadence in measure 8, which leads to an additional fifth phrase. Confined to a range of a major 6th, Hermann has, by the simplest of means, created a radiant tune.

This is one of the most celebrated Christmas hymns among Canadian Mennonites who emigrated from Russia. It is also loved among the Hutterites who, after four hundred years of aural tradition, sing it with only minor deviations from the above version. This melodic form and harmonization come from Bach's Cantata No. 151, but another form of the melody is found in "If Christ is mine" (**331**).

138
Let God, who called the worlds

CHURCH TRIUMPHANT

Based on Psalm 50
David Mowbray (1938-)
Psalms for Today, 1990

James William Elliott (1833-1915)
Arthur Sullivan's *Church Hymns with Tunes*, 1874

Like the original psalm that was its inspiration, this paraphrase opens with a theophany (appearance of God)—"Let God . . . arise in all-consuming fire." Then a sort of prophetic lawsuit follows, in which heaven and earth are summoned as witnesses and the prosecutor (the writer) zeroes in on a proper and moral understanding of worship. Both psalm and paraphrase call for a communion of ritual and morality and caution that ritual not be made a cloak for religious shortcomings (Stuhlmueller 1983).

Although Mowbray intended these words to be sung to the tune SOLOTHURN, the text appeared in *Psalms for Today* with a traditional English melody in the minor mode. The strength of the text is complemented by CHURCH TRIUMPHANT, with its vigorous tune in a major key.

CHURCH TRIUMPHANT was composed originally for the text "Again the Lord's own day is here." However, in the collection listed above, it was set to three other texts. A line from one of those gave the tune its name.

634
Let hope and sorrow now unite

MIT FREUDEN ZART

Brian Arthur Wren (1936-), 1979
Faith Looking Forward, 1983, alt.

Adapt. from GENEVA 138, *Genevan Psalter*, Lyon, 1547
Bohemian Brethren's *Kirchengeseng . . .*, Berlin, 1566

This text was written for the funeral of the author's uncle William Wren. "Like many other such occasions," author Wren writes, "believers and non-believers came together to remember, mourn, and give thanks. I tried to frame words which both could sing with integrity: though my uncle loved 'justice, love and truth' he was not a Christian." It was for this reason that stanza 3:4 originally read "If faith comes true." The author later approved "as faith comes true" as the more assertive side of his original meaning. The text provides an expression of the grace that is available even in sorrow.

For comments on MIT FREUDEN ZART, see "Sing praise to God who reigns" (**59**).

198
Let our gladness have no end

NARODIL SE KRISTUS PÁN

T. Zavorke's *Kancional*, 1602
Tr. Anonymous

Bohemian carol, 15th c.
Harm. by Richard Walter Hillert (1923-)
The Lutheran Hymnal, 1941

This carol probably originated in the early fifteenth century. Two translations other than the one here are "Christ the Lord to us is born," by Vincent Pizek and John Bajus (*The Lutheran Hymnal* 1941), and "Be ye joyful, earth and sky," by Herman Brückner (*The Concordia Hymnal*, 1932).

NARODIL SE KRISTUS PÁN, an anonymous fifteenth-century tune, has the name SALVATOR NATUS in *The Lutheran Hymnal* (1941).

187
Let the heavens be glad

(no tune name)

Based on Psalm 96:11-13
John B. Foley, S.J. (1939-), 1975
Gentle Night, 1977

John B. Foley, S.J. (1939-)
(same source as text)

This song, titled "The Lord is come," was written for College Church at St. Louis University (Mo.). It was sung on Christmas Eve in the hour-long concert before midnight Mass, a tradition that continues to this day. In

1977 it was recorded on the album *Gentle Night*, and in 1979 the author revised the text to eliminate references to God as "he."

The tonal shift from major to minor, the use of canon (voices following one another), and the vigorous rhythms create an exciting musical experience well suited to the anticipation of the Advent season. Although the hymn is designed for unaccompanied singing, various instruments might be added to imitate the voices during the second stanza. The composer comments that almost every note should be accented as if the hymn were part of a march. The third phrase, beginning "Let fields and all they bear," should crescendo so the word "Lord" becomes the loudest point in the song. Each voice, as it arrives at the final word, may close to a hum, sustaining the sound until all three voices are humming.

464

Let the hungry come to me

Sts. 1-3, Delores Dufner, O.S.B. (1939-),1985
Order of Christian Funerals, 1989, alt.
Sts. 4-5, *Adoro te devote, latens Deitas*, 13th or 14th c.
Sts. 4-5, tr. Melvin L. Farrell, S.S. (1930-1987)
Praise the Lord, 1972

ADORO TE DEVOTE

Plainsong
Processionale, Paris, 1697

The first three stanzas come from a hymn text by Sister Delores Dufner, who wrote the original six stanzas as a Communion hymn for a large diocesan celebration in St. Mary's Cathedral, St. Cloud, Minnesota. A large choir sang the text with this well-known chant melody, joined by congregation and organ for the final stanzas. The hymn also is effective sung antiphonally. The unusual change from contemporary to archaic language corresponds with the final stanzas and the antiquity of the melody.

Stanzas 4 and 5, which express our response to Christ's invitation, are from Melvin Farrell's text "Humbly we adore thee." Listed as a translation from the Latin hymn *Adoro te devote, latens Deitas*, it is different enough from the original to be considered a new hymn.

In the *Roman Breviary* of 1570, the Latin text was added to the three hymns of the Eucharistic Cycle of Corpus Christi, written by Thomas Aquinas (ca. 1227-1274). Although the text has been attributed to Aquinas in many hymnals, recent scholarship has shown it was not his work. The earliest available manuscript containing the hymn dates to 1323.

In the Paris *Processionale*, the earliest source in which this tune has been found, ADORO TE DEVOTE was the setting for *Adoro te supplex*, a processional hymn for the feast of Corpus Christi. The tune, which postdates the text, appeared much later than most plainsongs, as indicated by the major triad outlined at the beginning of the melody.

51

Let the whole creation cry — LLANFAIR

Based on Psalm 148
Stopford Augustus Brooke (1832-1916), 1917
Christian Hymns, 1881, alt.

Robert Williams (ca. 1781-1821)
Joseph Parry's *Peroriaeth Hyfryd*, 1837

This hymn, based on Psalm 148, uses stanzas 1, 2, 7, and 9 of the original ten stanzas. The beginning phrase of stanza 7 is changed from "Warriors fighting for the Lord" to "Rulers bowing to the Lord," more closely paralleling verse 11 of the psalm.

The hymn's antiphonal style is conducive to a variety of uses. See the *Accompaniment Handbook for* instrumental and choir parts.

The Welsh melody LLANFAIR is dated July 14, 1817, in Robert Williams' manuscript book. However, several other composers have claimed it as well. The harmony by John Roberts, found in Joseph Parry's 1837 collection listed above, has been modified by the addition of a tenor passing tone in measures 4, 8, and 16. *Llan*, a Celtic word, means "saint" or "holy" and is the prefix used in the name of more than 450 places in Wales. LLANFAIR is a shortened form of the name of the village where Robert Williams was born.

371

Let there be light, Lord God — MISSIONARY CHANT

William Merrill Vories (1880-1964), 1908
American Peace Society's *Advocate of Peace*, February 1909, alt.

Charles Heinrich Christopher Zeuner (1795-1857)
Zeuner's *American Harp*, 1832

Three years after he went to Japan as a missionary/English teacher, Vories wrote this peace hymn in reaction to the pre-World War I buildup of military power in Europe. Its lines reflect his missionary vision of peace and unity. In his book *A Mustard Seed in Japan* (1911), which tells the story of the Omi Mission, he states:

> We believe that our central objective should be to demonstrate . . . that loyalty to the vision of the Kingdom of God can overcome all obstacles of race, social systems, and personal prejudices and make possible a community of brothers and sisters in Christ . . . since it was such unity that he prayed for, "in order that the World may believe." (Ronander, Porter 1966)

Only one text alteration has been made, which seems in keeping with Vories' philosophy: "Our brothers' good" becomes "each other's good."

In numerous Mennonite and Brethren predecessors of this hymnal, this hymn has appeared with MISSIONARY CHANT, deriving its tune name from its use with Draper's missionary text, "Ye Christian

Heralds." This text also has been set to a variety of other tunes, such as PENTECOST or ELTON. In 1910, Vories himself composed another tune that later appeared in a Japanese hymnal with the text translated into Japanese.

453

Let us break bread together — COMMUNION SPIRITUAL

African American spiritual — African American spiritual

Mark Fisher, author of *Negro Slave Songs in the United States* (1953), has suggested that this spiritual may have been a "gathering song" in Virginia, used as the signal to convene secret meetings of African slaves. As early as 1676 the colony prohibited slaves from using drums to call gatherings, so slaves adapted their signals. These meetings frequently took place before sunrise, which could explain the puzzling reference to facing "the rising sun." It also may refer to Christ as the "Sun of righteousness" (Mal. 4:2, KJV). After the Civil War, the first two stanzas were added and it developed into a song for Communion.

The history of the tune parallels that of the text. According to John W. Work, it was first published by William Lawrence in 1928. For J. Harold Moyer's arrangement, see the *Accompaniment Handbook.* This arrangement of the spiritual retains the simplicity and straightforward character of the text. Often sung as a solo or arranged for choirs, it is also appropriate for congregational singing.

380

Let us pray — PETITIONS LITANY

Byzantine chant

The second part of this text is a translation of the early Greek litany described in the article on the *Kyrie* (**152**). As the tune name indicates, this brief musical response is used with spoken prayers of petition. It can be sung any number of times.

55

Let's sing unto the Lord—see "Cantemos al Señor"

579
Lift every voice and sing — ANTHEM

John Rosamund Johnson (1873-1954), 1899
Printed as sheet music, 1921

John Rosamund Johnson (1873-1954), 1899
(same source as text)

This hymn by John Rosamund Johnson has become the official anthem of the National Association for the Advancement of Colored People (NAACP). It also represents this hymnal's effort to include significant hymns of major denominational and cultural groups in North America. It appears here in the four-part arrangement found in recent African American hymnals.

This hymn should be sung in an expansive style to allow the worshipers to experience the majesty of the melody.

321
Lift high the cross — CRUCIFER

George William Kitchin (1827-1912), 1887
Rev. by Michael Robert Newbolt (1874-1956)
Hymns Ancient and Modern, supplement, 1916, alt.

Sydney Hugo Nicholson (1875-1947)
(same source as text)

This mighty hymn proclaims the triumphal inauguration of Christ's resurrection kingdom. "Its images," writes hymnologist Stanley Osborne, "are biblical, its moods expectant, its promises courageous, and its demands costly" (*The Worshiping Church* 1990, 1991). It focuses on the cross, symbol of those costly demands and the incredible promise of the kingdom.

Newbolt's revision of Kitchin's processional hymn consists of stanzas 7, 6, 8, and 10 of the eleven stanzas in Newbolt's 1916 modification. The elimination of archaic language necessitated alteration from the original:

> O Lord, once lifted on the glorious Tree,
> As thou hast promised, draw men unto Thee.

The tune name CRUCIFER refers to the person who carries the cross in a liturgical procession, for which this hymn is ideally suited. The stirring refrain of CRUCIFER can be a prelude, interlude, and postlude to the verses.

602
Lift up your hearts — BOUNDING HEART

Henry Montagu Butler (1833-1918)
Harrow School Hymn Book, 1881, alt.

Alvin Franz Brightbill (1903-1976)
The Brethren Hymnal, 1951

The inspiration for this text is the liturgical summons and response called the *Sursum Corda,* "Lift up your hearts. We lift them up unto the Lord, our God. It is meet and right so to do." The *Sursum Corda* is an introduction to the prayer of consecration in the Roman Catholic Mass and the Anglican Service of Holy Communion. Butler's hymn, which develops and fulfills the *Sursum Corda,* originally had eight stanzas but was often abridged to four or five.

This text was written when the author was headmaster of Harrow School in England. Percy Dearmer, a British hymnal editor, concedes that it is a "little heavy for schoolboys, [but] its fine moral passion makes it too good a hymn to be missed by adults" (Dearmer 1933). The present altered version consists of stanzas 1, 4, and 5 from *Hymns for Today's Church* (1982). That hymnal's fourth stanza (st. 2 here) is unlike any stanza in older four- and five-stanza versions.

For more on *Sursum Corda,* see **660** in the worship resources section.

Brightbill composed BOUNDING HEART for Butler's text when it came into *The Brethren Hymnal* (1951) where the tune name originates in a stanza deleted from *Hymnal: A Worship Book.* This tune, dynamic in both melody and harmony, sensitively reflects the imagery of "lifted hearts" with its ascending melodic contours in the first two staves.

275
Lift your glad voices — RESURRECTION

Henry Ware, Jr. (1794-1843)
Christian Disciple, 1817, alt.

John Edgar Gould (1822-1875)
Methodist Hymnal with Tunes— Special Edition, New York City, ca. 1878

This joyous Easter hymn is one of the favorites in the Mennonite *Church Hymnal* (1927) and *The Mennonite Hymnal* (1969). It appeared earlier in the *Methodist Hymnal* of 1925 but seems absent from other current hymnals.

The exuberant melody RESURRECTION suits this text well. The rapidly rising first and last phrases create a musical sense of the resurrection. Although the eighth notes in phrase 3 are challenging to sing accurately, they contribute to the energy and forward motion of the hymn.

496

Like Noah's weary dove — (no tune name)

William Augustus Muhlenberg (1796-1877)
Prayer Book Collection, 1826

John Henry Hopkins, Jr. (1820-1891)
Carols, Hymns, and Songs, 3rd ed., 1882

Subtitled "The Ark of the Church," this delightful early American text envisions the church as a place of refuge for the seeking soul, much as Noah's ark was the resting place for the weary dove. Some collections begin the hymn with the second or third stanza. *The Brethren Hymnal* (1901) includes the first four stanzas under the heading "The Ark of God—1 Peter 3:21."

The sequential nature of the melodic line makes the music easy to learn. Hopkins, who composed music for his own poems as well as for those written by others, is best known for his Epiphany carol, "We three kings." Both the author and composer of "Like Noah's weary dove" were Episcopal clergymen.

29

Like the murmur of the dove's song — BRIDEGROOM

Carl Pickens Daw, Jr. (1944-)
The Hymnal 1982, 1985

Peter Warwick Cutts (1937-), 1969

Carl Daw claims that this hymn "got written backwards." With Cutts's tune BRIDEGROOM already in mind, Daw first heard the words of the refrain "Come, Holy Spirit, come." Once that hymn theme had come to him, he backtracked and wrote the stanzas, using biblical and traditional images for the Holy Spirit. "One of the things I wanted to emphasize," writes Daw, "was the extent to which the Holy Spirit is given to the church corporately; then that corporate gift goes to individual members . . . ."

This is one of some sixty hymn texts by Daw, and he says it was the easiest to write: "It essentially wrote itself once I knew what it was about" (Eskew 1989). Daw is noted for his psalm paraphrases as well as his hymn texts.

The tune BRIDEGROOM was written by Peter Cutts for the text "As the Bridegroom to his chosen," Emma Frances Bevan's paraphrase of work by fourteenth-century writer John Tauler. Introduced to the text by British hymnologist Eric Routley, Cutts claims Routley sat him down at the grand piano and retired to his room for a "siesta." The music Cutts wrote that day is considered by many to be his finest work.

The tempo selected for this hymn should create a flowing feeling without rushing the words sung with eighth notes. The composer also suggests singing the piece antiphonally, with the entire group participating in the invitation to the Spirit. Appropriate for Pentecost, the hymn is also an invocation of the Holy Spirit upon the body of believers gathered for worship.

550
Living and dying with Jesus — SMJET ZIVJET KRISTU

Croatian hymn
Duhovne Pjesme (Spiritual Songs), ca. 1950
Tr. Sara Wenger Shenk (1953-), 1990

Slavic melody
(same source as text)

This is one of the few hymns in *Duhovne Pjesme* that has a distinctly Slavic origin and is not simply a translation of Western hymnody. *Duhovne Pjesme*, a collection used by the Baptists throughout the former Yugoslavia, gives no original sources. However, the hymn also appears with this tune in *Christian Hymns in Russian*, published by First Russian Baptist Church of New York City, with the attribution "E. E. Vecherok."

A literal translation of the Croatian text reads:

> To be allowed to live to Christ, to die for him, is a greater treasure than the whole world. It is worthy to suffer for him, worthy to struggle, worthy also to leave this world.
>
> To be allowed to live to Christ, here to suffer shame, once to step into the heavenly temple, with a crown of glory to stand before God, be there forever, forever with him;
>
> To be allowed to live to Christ, while it is yet day, even when the sad darkness is lowering; always to serve him and never grow cold—this grace to believers is given by God.

Shenk learned the song by worshiping with the Baptists during her nearly nine years in Yugoslavia. Refering to its frequent use at funerals, she observes: "Its rich tones and fine text revealed to us, like no other song, the soul of a people who have suffered intensely but still remain steadfast."

Noting the repetitions in the form of this folk melody will make it easier to learn. Not only is the opening two-measure phrase repeated, but the closing figure of that phrase concludes each of the next four measures.

591
Lo, a gleam from yonder heaven — JUNIATA

Adaline Hohf Beery (1859-1929)
The Home Music Co., 1896
The Brethren Hymnal, 1901

William Beery (1852-1956)
(same source as text)

Adaline Hohf Beery, one of the more prolific Brethren poets, has painted a vivid word-picture of a wanderer seeking a way through the "starless night." The flamboyant imagery is typically nineteenth-century Victorian, and the upbeat music gives it added bounce.

Beery's husband, William, was even more prolific. He wrote this melody while he was head of the music department at Juniata College, Huntingdon, Pennsylvania. Though it appeared in the 1901 Brethren hymnal, the tune did not receive a name until *The Brethren Hymnal* (1951).

211
Lo, how a Rose e'er blooming

Es ist ein Ros' entsprungen
Sts. 1-2, anonymous
Alte Catholische Geistliche Kirchengeseng, Köln, 1599
St. 3, Friedrich Layritz (1808-1859)
Liederschatz, Berlin, 1832
Sts. 1-2, tr. Theodore Baker (1851-1934), 1894
St. 3, tr. Harriet K. Spaeth (1845-1925), 1875

ES IST EIN ROS'

(same source as text, sts. 1-2)
(Zahn No. 4296)
Harm. by Michael Praetorius (1571-1621)
Musae Sionae, VI, 1609

This song of unknown authorship may be derived from a German *Marienlied* (Song of Mary), songs popular in the fifteenth century. Mary herself was sometimes referred to as "the rose without thorns." The hymn was later rewritten for Protestant use, switching the emphasis from Mary to Jesus.

The reference to Isaiah's prophecy is from Isaiah 11:1-2. The birth of Christ is set against this backdrop of prophecy, with strands of folklore woven in. Or might the "cold of winter" heighten the irony of the presence of a "floweret bright"? Stanza 3 then introduces the theology of the birth story, explaining the significance of the prophecy fulfillment. Some isolated changes in wording have been made in the interest of modern usage and inclusive language.

The original form of ES IST EIN ROS' is in Johannes Zahn's *Die Melodien der deutschen evangelischen Kirchenlieder* (No. 4296), where it is in a regular 4/4 meter. The present barring helps reflect the verbal phrases. In this harmonization the alto occasionally crosses above the soprano. It is a delicate piece, wonderful for part-singing, and has the flavor and subtle rhythms of a Renaissance madrigal. Layritz (or Layriz), credited as the author of the third stanza, apparently was the one who introduced this melody into Lutheran usage.

286

Look, you saints

Based on Revelation 7:9-15
Thomas Kelly (1769-1855)
Hymns on Various Passages of Scripture, 3rd ed., 1809, alt.

BRYN CALFARIA

William Owen (1814-1893)
Y Perl Cerddorol (The Pearl of Music), Vol. II, 1886
Version from Alan Luff, *Welsh Hymns and Their Tunes*, 1990

This "majestic coronation paean for the second advent of Christ" (Hustad 1978) is considered one of the best of Kelly's 765 hymns. It is based on Revelation 7:9-15, with allusions to 11:15, the same text as Handel's "Hallelujah" chorus from *Messiah*. Original archaisms, such as "ye" in the opening phrase and "own his title" in stanza 3:4, have been altered, as per *Hymns for Today's Church* (1982). While mortal non-believers may scorn the suffering Christ, hosts of saints and angels more than compensate for the humiliation by raising a never-ending resurrection fanfare. Originally titled "The second Advent," the hymn also heralds Christ's second coming, both poetically and as an historical event.

BRYN CALFARIA, which means "Mount Calvary," was composed for an evangelistic hymn and became a prominent musical theme of the 1941 movie *How Green Was My Valley*, a story of Welsh coal miners. Hymnologist Routley calls it a "piece of real Celtic rock," and Archibald Jacob comments that the rhythmic pattern gives this tune a determined character that is intensified later in the repeated quickening of the same rhythm (Dearmer 1933). Its vitality also lies in the dynamic melodic contour, plus the imitation and rhythmic dialogue between the melody and the harmony parts.

93

Lord, bless the hands

M. Andrew Murray (1942-), 1974
The Brethren Songbook, 1974

(no tune name)

Teresa Robinson Murray (1943-), 1974
(same source as text)

This delightfully simple canon (round) was written for the 1974 National Youth Conference of the Church of the Brethren, held in Glorietta, New Mexico. The song was used in the opening service as young people from many states gathered for their conference on the theme "Everybody is a part of everything."

The song was published in *The Brethren Songbook* in 1974; this second stanza was added by the author at a later date:

> Lord, bless the dawning of this day,
> and bless the friends that come our way.
> Now hear your people as they pray.
> Amen, amen.

The first stanza functions as an offertory prayer or table grace, while the second would work well as an invocation.

514

Lord, I am fondly, earnestly — OPEN THE WELLS

Elisha Albright Hoffman (1839-1929)
Church and Sunday School Hymnal, 1902

Charles Edward Pollock (b. 1853- d. ?)
(same source as text)

In its source this hymn was captioned " 'Spring up, O well.' Num. 21:17." It may have come from an even earlier collection of gospel songs. It is a hymn of personal consecration, one that may rouse memories and invite spirited four-part singing. Hoffman, who also wrote "Breathe upon us, Holy Spirit," was a prodigious writer of gospel songs.

OPEN THE WELLS is a flowing tune with harmonic and melodic variety that rises to its zenith in the refrain. Little is known about the composer other than his date of birth and his name on a sizable number of gospel songs. The *Church and Sunday School Hymnal* (Mennonite Church 1902, 1911) contains many of the thirty-two hymn tunes with which Pollock is credited. Though eleven were used in *The Brethren Hymnal* (1901), only PAROUSIA, the setting for Wesley's "Lo, he comes with clouds descending," survived to the 1951 hymnal. Pollock published *The Beauty of Praise for Sunday Schools in Jefferson City, Missouri*, in 1884.

317

Lord, I have made thy word — IRISH

Based on Psalm 119
Isaac Watts (1674-1748)
The Psalms of David . . ., 1719

A Collection of Hymns and Sacred Poems, 1749

In this hymn Watts has paraphrased a portion of Psalm 119, a lengthy meditation upon the law that has none of the agony of the laments nor the community participation of other psalms. Primarily using verses 57-64, Watts has condensed the psalm to its central thrust: the law of God so ingrained in our living that it leads us gracefully to our ultimate destination—God. The hymn treats the Bible not just as a book but as a way of life.

IRISH, a typical eighteenth-century triple-time tune, appears unnamed in the source listed above, published by S. Powell in Dublin. There it is included among a few tunes at the end of the book as a setting of "Hymn CXCI: Time, what an empty vapour 'tis." In Scotland the tune was used with a political song called "The Cameronian Cat," a text which "sounds like the practice verses that developed in Scotland during the seventeenth and eighteenth centuries so that choirs would not profane the psalms when they were learning new tunes" (Osbourne 1976). This usage might indicate that the tune originated as a folk song rather than as a psalm tune. The tune received its present name from Caleb Ashworth when he included it in his *Collection of Tunes* (ca. 1760). Other names sometimes used are DUBLIN and IRISH TUNE. In Ireland this tune has commonly been sung with Watts's "O God, our help in ages past" (**328**).

444
Lord, I want to be a Christian

LORD, I WANT TO BE

African American spiritual
Work's *Folk Songs of the American Negro*, Nashville, 1907

African American spiritual
(same source as text)

The origin of this text is uncertain. According to eighteenth-century records, a Presbyterian named William Davis was preaching in Hanover, Virginia, around the middle 1700s. A slave came to him wanting to learn more about Jesus Christ and his duty to God and said, "Lord (sir), I want to be a Christian." This spiritual could have originated there about that time (Hustad 1978).

The stanza "I don't want to be like Judas," found in some traditional sources, is omitted here. Historian John Lovell, Jr., tells us that that stanza was a declaration that the slave would not be tempted by material goods to betray fellow slaves.

LORD, I WANT TO BE, like many Negro spirituals, is in the pentatonic mode and can be played on the black keys of the piano starting on G-flat. George Pullen Jackson notes that the refrain is similar to a setting of "Come to me, sweet Marie" that he heard sung in the 1880s in rural Maine. The antiphonal third line mirrors the call and response character of many spirituals. Like most folk songs, there are many versions of both text and music and, thus, much room for improvisation. See the *Accompaniment Handbook* for Donald R. Frederick's arrangement.

22
Lord Jesus Christ, be present now

HERR JESU CHRIST, DICH ZU UNS WEND

Herr Jesu Christ, dich zu uns wend
Sts. 1-3, *Pensum Sacrum*, 1648
St. 4, *Cantionale Sacrum*, 1651
Tr. Catherine Winkworth (1827-1878)
Chorale Book for England, 1863, alt.

Cantionale Germanicum, Gochsheim, 1628
(Zahn No. 624)

After the invocation of stanza 1, this hymn draws worshipers together around the center of all worship—praise. First concentrating on Christ, it then enfolds God and the Holy Spirit in a familiar triune doxology (st. 4), a slightly later addition.

Although this hymn is sometimes attributed to Wilhelm, Duke of Sachse-Weimar, his hand in it is doubtful. Until the publishing of *Gesangbuch der Mennoniten* (1965), German Mennonites in Canada consistently sang this as a "gathering hymn" to the isometric (smoothed out) version of OLD HUNDREDTH.

HERR JESU CHRIST, DICH ZU UNS WEND may be much older than the 1628 collection listed above. It was first associated with the present text in 1651. The *Hymnal of the Moravian Church* (1969) calls the tune HUS, implying that spiritual leader Jan Hus was possibly the author. Although the rhythmic organization may at first seem unusual, the repetition of the pattern for each of the four phrases makes it easy to learn.

527

Lord Jesus, think on me

Synesius of Cyrene (ca. 375-ca. 414)
Tenth Ode by Synesius, ca. 400
Tr. Allen William Chatfield (1808-1896)
Chatfield's *Songs and Hymns of the Earliest Greek Christian Poets*,1876

SOUTHWELL

William Damon's *The Psalmes of David . . .*, 1579

In the early fifth century, the Greek city of Cyrene, once a great center of culture and learning in North Africa, lay in ruins, invaded by Goths and violent desert peoples. Its bishop wrote this ode, the last in a series of ten, as an epilogue petitioning God to remember the one who wrote these hymns. Synesius, whose life and culture were both on the wane as he wrote these lines, faced a tottering future in which the only bulwark was his faith in Christ. Though written fifteen hundred years ago, the text embraces the human condition, unabashedly expressing loss and uncertainty, as well as confident dependence on God.

In the literal prose translation by Costley White, the author places no blame on circumstances but reveals himself as a believer preparing soul and body for meeting God:

> Be mindful, Christ Son of God who rules on high, of thy servant, sinful of heart, who wrote these words. And grant to me release from passions breeding death, which are inborn in my unclean soul. But give me to behold, Savior Jesus, thy divine brightness, wherein appearing I shall sing a song to the healer of souls, to the healer of limbs, with the great Father and the Holy Spirit. (Dearmer 1933)

Chatfield acknowledges that his translation was "a paraphrase of amplification rather than an exact translation of the original" (*The Hymnal 1940 Companion*, 1951 ed.). When he later revised it for his *Collected Psalms and Hymns*, he added four stanzas to the initial five. Those selected here are stanzas 2, 3, 5, 6, and 7. There have been several minor alterations of Chatfield's text; the most notable is in stanza 4:3—"When daunted by the enemy" replaces "When on doth rush the enemy."

SOUTHWELL is set to Psalm 45 in William Damon's psalter of 1579. The melody was in the Dorian mode, using D natural instead of D-flat. SOUTHWELL was named after the cathedral city in Nottinghamshire by Thomas Ravenscroft in his *Whole Book of Psalms* (1621).

428
Lord, let us now depart in peace — DISMISSAL

Anonymous

George Whelpton (1847-1930)

This text, drawn from a number of biblical passages, may be the work of the composer. The scriptural allusions call to account various promises of God and Jesus, beginning with the Song of Simeon in Luke 2 (*Nunc Dimittis*) and continuing with Matthew 18:20; 2 Corinthians 4:6; and Matthew 28:20.

Around 1900 Whelpton published a four-page leaflet of responses, and this tune may have been included among them. The problematic rhythm of measures 4 and 5, which originally involved fermatas and an eighth rest, has been altered here to simplify that passage.

353
Lord, listen to your children — CHILDREN PRAYING

Ken Medema (1943-), 1970

Ken Medema (1943-), 1970

Medema wrote this call for the presence of the Holy Spirit as part of a longer work, composed when he was with several youth praying for a hospitalized friend. Born of the inspiration and needs of that moment, the words and music have become well known and loved. It was first recorded on Medema's 1975 album *Son Shiny Day* (WORD). Easily learned by rote, the piece may be sung any number of times before and after prayer or as an invocation.

410
Lord of light, your name outshining — EBENEZER

Howell Elvet Lewis (1860-1953)
The Congregational Hymnary, 1916, alt.

Thomas John Williams (1869-1944), 1896
Baptist Book of Praise, 1901

Lewis wrote his text "to declare that in doing God's will active co-operation is as much needed as humble resignation" (Parry, Routley 1953). The determination and marchlike sound of the tune may, at first hearing, seem inappropriate for phrases in the text like "meekness," "suffering," "peace," and "healing" until one recalls the strength of those qualities in the person of the incarnate God, Jesus Christ.

In this version of the hymn, altered primarily to eliminate archaic forms of address, the most significant changes occur in the first four lines. The original text begins:

Lord of light whose name outshineth
All the stars and suns of space,
Deign to make us Thy co-workers
In the kingdom of Thy grace.

The concluding refrain, which originally began with the word "Father," is based on the Lord's Prayer.

The tune name, sometimes associated with the melody TON-Y-BOTL (or "tune-in-a-bottle") comes from the fanciful story that the tune had been found in a bottle washed ashore along the coast of Wales. The tune is named EBENEZER for the chapel where Williams was a member when he composed the music. The melody was included in an anthem *Golau yn y glyn* (Light in the valley), for which many hymnal companions give a date of 1890, citing *Llawlyfr Moliant* as the first source. However, Alan Luff, in his *Welsh Hymns and Their Tunes*, states that another source gives the date of its composition as 1896.

The melody may sound familiar to many through its association with two other texts: "Once to every man and nation," by James Russell Lowell, and "Oh, the deep, deep love of Jesus."

479

Lord of our growing years — NEWTON

David Mowbray (1938-)
Hymns for Today's Church, 1982

J. Harold Moyer (1927-), 1990
Hymnal: A Worship Book, 1992

In just a few lines of six syllables each, Mowbray has succeeded in capturing the essence of the stages of life. The refrain, like God, embraces each of those stages, concluding each stanza with confident assurance. The text, written about 1981 for the tune LITTLE CORNARD, has been used on the BBC television program "Songs of Praise" and for Girl Guide Thanksgivings in various locales, including Westminster Abbey.

Moyer, too, was attracted to the text because of its summary of the life cycle, and he crafted his melodic setting especially for these words. The rhythmic movement in measure 4 provides the musical equivalent of the "freshness and energy" of the text. The tune is named for Moyer's hometown—Newton, Kansas.

490
Lord of the home

Albert Frederick Bayly (1901-1984), 1947
Rejoice, O People, 1950, alt.

HURSLEY

Adapt. from GROSSER GOTT, WIR LOBEN DICH
Katholisches Gesangbuch, Vienna, ca. 1774

This hymn was written for the Young Wives' Fellowship of Hollingreave Congregational Church in Burnley, England, where the author was minister. It was published in the first of four collections of his hymns and poems with the tune WESTFIELDS, composed by another Congregational minister. The hymn has also appeared in the British Baptist *Hymn Book* (1962) and *The Mennonite Hymnal* (1969) with the tune PHILIPPINE, by Robert E. Roberts. The only alteration made here is from "thy" to "your."

For comments on HURSLEY (also known as PASCAL, HALLE, and FRAMINGHAM), see "Sun of my soul" (**654**).

39
Lord of the worlds above

Isaac Watts (1674-1748)
The Psalms of David . . . , 1719

LENOX

Lewis Edson, Sr. (1748-1820)
Simeon Joceyln and Amos Doolittle's *The Chorister's Companion*, 1782 or 1783

This is a psalm that pilgrims would have sung as they came within sight of the holy city of Jerusalem. The energy of the text is bolstered by the expanding exuberance of the fuguing section of the melody.

This paraphrase, one of Watts's best, is his third version of Psalm 84. Watts's paraphrase exists in several arrangements, of which an important one is found in the *Wesley Hymn Book* (1875). *Hymnal: A Worship Book* includes the first four of the original seven stanzas. Stanza 3 has been altered, replacing both "souls" in 3:1 and "men" in 3:3 with "those."

In its earliest source, LENOX appeared as a fuguing tune, so-called because of the succession of imitative voices in its last section. The bass leads and the other voices enter one at a time, one measure apart. Fuguing tunes set to psalm and hymn texts were very popular in North American singing schools, but they eventually fell out of practice. For this hymnal the melody, originally in the tenor, has been exchanged with the soprano and the arrangement has been placed a step lower in the key of B-flat. The variety and spunk of the fuguing section has been reinstated.

LENOX, named for a village in Massachusetts, is sometimes called TRUMPET since its most frequent setting is that of Wesley's "Blow ye the trumpet, blow."

157
Lord, our Lord, your glorious name — BINGHAM

Based on Psalm 8
Psalter (United Presbyterian), 1912, alt.

Dorothy Howell Sheets (1915-), 1983
The Hymnal 1982, 1985

This paraphrase of Psalm 8 is an expression of praise. The meditative quality of the music provides a sense of wonder at the contrast between the magnificence of creation and the insignificance of humanity. The intent is to influence the way humanity exerts "dominion" over the earth. There is no place for the notion that people are in some way entitled to their "exalted height." Rather, all the radiance of the earth points not to the caretakers, but to the glory of the Creator.

Most of the text changes replace "thy" with "your." In the present stanza 2:1-2, "Infant voices chant your praise, telling of your glorious ways" was originally "Infant lips Thou dost ordain Wrath and vengeance to restrain." This hymnal's final stanza is a composite of phrases from the last quatrain in the *Psalter,* coupled with two lines from stanza 1 (version from the *Psalter Hymnal,* 1987).

The tune BINGHAM was composed for the hymn text "Morning glory, starlit sky" by W. H. Vanstone. Since its appearance in *The Hymnal 1982,* the tune has been included in a number of contemporary hymnals. The composer writes, "The name BINGHAM was chosen . . . to honor Seth Bingham, my composition teacher in New York." This beautifully crafted melody creates an expansive feeling within the range of a seventh, well suited to the sweeping grandeur of the text theme.

92
Lord, should rising whirlwinds — ORIENTIS PARTIBUS

Based on Habakkuk 3:17-18
Anna Laetitia Barbauld (1743-1825)
William Enfield's *Hymns for Public Worship,* 1772, alt.

Pierre de Corbeil (d. 1221 or 1222)
Harm. by Richard Redhead (1820-1901)
Church Hymn Tunes, Ancient and Modern, 1853

This text is a four-stanza continuation (Part 2) of the author's poem beginning "Praise to God, immortal praise" (**91**). The full text was subtitled "Praise to God in Prosperity and Adversity," a theme that is retained by setting both parts of the nine-stanza poem side-by-side. In Barbauld's work, it appears with the text from Habakkuk 3:17-18 (KJV):

> Although the fig tree shall not blossom, neither shall fruit be in the vines; the labour of the olive shall fail, and the fields shall yield no

meat; the flock shall be cut off from the fold, and there shall be no herd in the stalls:

Yet I will rejoice in the Lord, I will joy in the God of my salvation.

Alterations over the past century may have leached some color from the original, especially in the second part of stanza 2, which reads "for the vine's exalted juice, for the generous olive's use." Even though meteorologically incorrect, the poetry of "clouds that drop their fattening dews" (original st. 3:1) is vibrant.

Since Part 1 and Part 2 are separate hymns, the first word of the present text was changed to "Lord" from "Yet," which began the sixth stanza of the combined text. The two hymns may be sung individually, in sequence, or with selected stanzas from each. They also may be sung to the same tune throughout or bridged with the music in the *Accompaniment Handbook*.

For comments on ORIENTIS PARTIBUS, see "Christian, do you hear the Lord?" (**494**).

499

Lord, speak to me — CANONBURY

Frances Ridley Havergal (1836-1879)
Parlane, music leaflets, 1872
Havergal's *Under the Surface*, 1874

Adapt. from Robert Alexander Schumann (1810-1856)
Nachtstücke, Opus 23, No. 4, 1839
Hymnal with Tunes, Old and New, 1872

This hymn was written in 1872 at Winterdyne, England. The text was headed "A Worker's Prayer. None of us liveth unto himself: Romans 14:7." Though the text calls for outreach, it is also a very personal prayer for one's own work to be an outgrowth of God's work in us. Stanza 5, usually omitted, reads:

O give Thine own sweet rest to me,
That I may speak with soothing power
A word in season, as from Thee,
To weary ones in needful hour.

CANONBURY is an adaptation of the principal theme of Schumann's piano piece cited above. That work could serve as a prelude or offertory when this hymn is chosen. Interested pianists can obtain it as edited by Clara Schumann from G. Schirmer, Vol. 1941 (see Addresses of Copyright Holders in *Hymnal: A Worship Book*). CANONBURY is also the name of a street and square in Islington, London.

350
Lord, teach us how to pray aright

James Montgomery (1771-1854)
Broadsheet, 1818
Thomas Cotterill's *Selection of Psalms and Hymns,* 1819

DAYTON

The Brethren's Tune and Hymn Book, 1872
Harm. by The Hymnal Project, 1991

Prayer is available to any who contritely "draw near" to God. The text invokes a promise, however, that God will meet us as we approach. Stanzas 3-6 go on to illuminate the spiritual graces necessary for prayer: truth, faith, patience, and courage.

This hymn first appeared on a broadsheet for Nonconformist (anything not Church of England) Sunday schools in Sheffield, England. It was included with "Prayer is the soul's sincere desire" (**572**) and two others by Montgomery. The poem has undergone text and format changes, some even by the author. Some American Unitarian hymnals begin this text with what appears as the third stanza here, with the text substantially altered from Montgomery's stanza 3:1-2, "God of all grace, we bring to thee a broken, contrite heart." The original stanza 5 reads:

> Patience to watch and wait and weep,
> Though mercy long delay;
> Courage our fainting souls to keep,
> And trust thee though thou slay.

DAYTON appears without any attribution in *The Brethren's Tune and Hymn Book* (1872) where it is set to a metrical paraphrase of Psalm 139, "In all my vast concerns with Thee." Since this collection was printed in Singers Glen, Virginia, the tune name may refer to the nearby town of Dayton. For further information on this Brethren hymnal, see "All praise to our redeeming Lord" (**21**).

DAYTON is purely pentatonic in both the melody and bass (C, D, E, G, A), as it is harmonized here primarily in three parts, the voicing in which it first appeared. Alice Parker arranged this tune with its original text for use in Donald F. Durnbaugh's pageant *That Bright Morning,* presented at the two hundredth recorded Church of the Brethren Annual Conference in 1986.

387
Lord, thou dost love

PLEADING SAVIOR

Robert Murray (1832-1909)
Scottish Church Hymnary, 1898

American folk melody
Christian Lyre, 1830
Version from *The Plymouth Collection of Hymns and Tunes*, 1855

This hymn, though suitable for emphasizing stewardship and service, is truly an offering hymn, a response to the great gift of Jesus' banishment of death, as well as God's blessings of "earthly store." The text contains many allusions to scripture, with the final stanza echoing the conclusion of the Lord's Prayer. The hymn comes by way of the *Canadian Book of Praise* (1918) and *The Mennonite Hymnal* (1969).

This pentatonic melody was first printed in Joshua Leavitt's *Christian Lyre*, although it may have been in use for some time before that. The tune name is derived from its use in that collection with John Leland's text "Now the Savior stands a-pleading." The tune was very popular in nineteenth-century Baptist congregations. The setting used here is from *The Plymouth Collection . . .*, a volume compiled for Henry Ward Beecher's church in Brooklyn, New York. Another setting of the tune may be found with "Thou true Vine, that heals" (**373**).

556
Lord, thou hast searched me

TENDER THOUGHT

Based on Psalm 139
The Psalter Hymnal (United Presbyterian), 1927

Ananias Davisson (1780-1857)
Kentucky Harmony, 1816
Harm. by The Hymnal Project, 1991

Psalm 139 probes the intensity of God's relationship with humans. Probably written by a faithful Jew lost in the dispersion of Jews throughout the known world, this hymn expresses both comfort and judgment in the fact that one cannot hide, or be hidden, from God.

The author of the psalm paraphrase is anonymous, but the index of Davisson's *Kentucky Harmony* attributes the melody TENDER THOUGHT to the compiler. Since it was common practice for compilers to use some of their own tunes and arrangements, it is possible that Davisson is the composer. With his music Davisson uses a text by Philip Doddridge beginning "Arise, my tender thoughts, arise," likely the source of the tune name.

369

Lord, whose love in humble service

Albert Frederick Bayly (1901-1984), 1961
Seven New Social Welfare Hymns, 1961, alt.

BEACH SPRING

Attrib. to Benjamin Franklin White (1800-1879)
Sacred Harp, 1844
Harm. by Joan Annette Fyock (1938-), 1988
Hymnal: A Worship Book, 1992

Just as students seek to emulate a beloved teacher, so Christians are to imitate the servanthood of Jesus Christ. Recognizing that serving is an act of worship, the Hymn Society of America put out a call in 1961 for new hymns on social welfare, and this hymn was written in response. It was selected that same year as the conference hymn for the second National Conference on the Churches and Social Welfare. The last lines of the hymn seem a blessed circle: By sharing with others the abundant life given us by Christ, we also share in that abundant life.

The first hymnal to include this hymn was *The Methodist Hymnal* (1966) where it was set to the tune BEECHER. Other appropriate tunes are HYFRYDOL and PLEADING SAVIOR. The hymn was updated by changing archaic forms of address, but the last lines of stanza 2 received the most alteration. The earlier version follows:

> Use the love Thy Spirit kindles
> Still to save and make men whole.

The final, fourth stanza has been omitted.

For comments on BEACH SPRING, see "Holy Spirit, come with power" (**26**).

79

Lord, with devotion we pray

Edyth Hillery Hay (1891-1943)
Hymnal: Church of the Brethren, 1925, alt.

HILLERY

Edyth Hillery Hay (1891-1943), alt.
Harm. by J. Henry Showalter (1864-1947)
(same source as text)

This text grew out of Hay's study of Psalm 71, an individual lament that was likely written by an elderly person for the elderly. The third stanza, in particular, uses the wording of the psalm (71:5 and 3b, KJV), while the refrain *does* the very thing that verses 8 and 23 command: "Let my mouth be filled with thy praise and with thy honour all the day . . . . My lips shall greatly rejoice when I sing unto Thee . . . " (KJV).

Ruth B. Statler writes: "[L]ike the Old Testament, this hymn reflects somewhat the conviction that the good will have extra smiles from above while here upon the earth. It is a hymn of faith and rejoicing in the goodness of God" (Statler, Fisher 1959). In keeping with the wording of the psalm, all of the references to God in the third person ("he," "his") have been changed to the more intimate second person ("thou," "thy").

It is not known whether the melody HILLERY was composed before or after the text was written. The tune flows naturally in a moderate two-beat tempo. Nevin Fisher suggests that singers "should give thought to the literary phrasing and treat the musical phrasing accordingly" (Statler, Fisher 1959). Showalter's harmonization should encourage part-singing, with or without accompaniment.

229
Lord, you have come to the lakeshore—see "Tú has venido a la orilla"

594
Lord, you sometimes speak — CLEVELAND

Christopher Martin Idle (1938-), 1966
Youth Praise 2, 1969

Christopher Johnson (1962-), 1987
New Songs of Praise 4, 1988

This text was one of Christopher Idle's first published hymns. He wrote it for the tune STUTTGART when he was curate of St. Mark's Church at Barrow-in-Furness, England. Though he has been "surprised" by the continuing demand for the hymn, Idle's work endures because of the gentle and persistent way he prompts singers to expand their awareness of God's work. At the beginning of stanza 4:1, Idle agreed to change "Lord, you often speak in scripture" to "Lord, you surely speak in scripture."

The tune CLEVELAND, written for this text, won a place for the hymn in the BBC/Oxford University Press series *New Songs of Praise.* Composer Johnson relates that "the tune was created a few months earlier for a service in All Souls Church, Langham Place, where I wanted to use Christopher Idle's inspiring text. . . . In the space of one summer's afternoon a new tune and harmony came into being, which also required the repetition of the last line of text." This repetition turns Idle's words into a chiasm, a strong poetic structure that inserts commentary text between statements of the author's main point.

The tune name CLEVELAND is the name of the street where Johnson lived at the time of its composition.

208
Love came down at Christmas

LOVE INCARNATE

Christina Georgina Rossetti (1830-1894), 1883
Time Flies: A Reading Diary, 1885
Rev. in *Hymns for Today's Church,* 1982

Charles Edgar Pettman (1866-1943)
University Carol Book, 1923

With the eloquence of a simple text, Rossetti has captured the essence of Christmas—love expressed most fully in Jesus' incarnation. That God chose to express love by becoming incarnate is itself a wonderful gift.

After this poem was first published in 1885, the author herself revised her original last line, changing "love, the universal sign" to "love for plea and gift and sign." Later alterations changed "plea" to "prayer" in stanza 3:3, "all men" to "neighbor" in stanza 3:2, and "But wherewith for sacred sign" to "what shall be our sacred sign" in stanza 2:3. Additionally, the "Sing noel" refrain was not part of Rossetti's original poem.

LOVE INCARNATE, written for these words, has appeared with and without the refrain. Several hymnals include this text with a traditional Irish melody GARTAN.

592
Love divine, all loves excelling

BEECHER

Charles Wesley (1707-1788)
Hymns for those that seek, and those that have Redemption in the Blood of Christ, 1747

John Zundel (1815-1882)
Zundel's *Christian Heart Songs,* 1870

This hymn reflects the Wesleys' belief that it is possible to live without sinning (the perfectionist doctrine). It is a prayer of imperatives, beginning with the first line "Joy of heaven, to earth come down" and ending with the plea that Christ's perfect "new creation" be accomplished. The text in between, like many hymns of the eighteenth century, is packed with further scriptural allusions. To craft this hymn, Wesley took a cue from the meter and poetry of the beginning of a John Dryden poem used in Purcell's opera *King Arthur*:

> Fairest Isle, all Isles excelling
> Seats of Pleasure and of Love;
> Venus here will choose her Dwelling
> And forsake her Cyprian Groves.

In its first publication, listed above, this hymn was titled "Jesus, show us thy salvation." It was published later in Madan's *Collection of Psalms and Hymns* (1760). In the 1780 printing of the *Wesley Hymn Book* and in some others, stanza 2 was omitted. The final line of this hymn is identical to the last line of stanza 1 in Joseph Addison's "When all thy mercies, O my God" (**72**), written in 1712.

The tune BEECHER was named for the great preacher Henry Ward Beecher, pastor of the church where Zundel was organist for thirty years. Composed for this text in 1870, the tune is sometimes called LOVE DIVINE and ZUNDEL. In the index to the collection cited above, Zundel indicates the tempo for each tune by providing the number of seconds needed to sing through one stanza. This one was to have taken sixty-five seconds (Reynolds 1976).

Because the hymn is so well known, the text might be refreshed by occasionally using a different tune. BLAENWERN (**573**) is a possibility.

273
Low in the grave he lay

Robert Lowry (1826-1899), 1874
Robert Lowry and William Doane's *Brightest and Best*, 1875

CHRIST AROSE

Robert Lowry (1826-1899), 1874
(same source as text)

Lowry wrote this hymn, both words and music, while he was pastor of a Baptist church in Lewisburg, Pennsylvania, and a professor at Bucknell University, Lewisburg. The brief stanzas of this hymn are often sung in a slow tempo while the refrain is sung faster to enhance the textual contrast between death and resurrection. In *Gospel Hymns Nos. 1 to 6 Complete* (1894), those designations appear on the page along with the scripture reference "He is not here, but is risen—Luke 24:5."

539
Make me a captive, Lord

George Matheson (1842-1906)
Sacred Songs, 1890

LEOMINSTER

George William Martin (1828-1881)
Martin's *The Journal of Part Music, Vol. II*, 1862
Harm. by Arthur Seymour Sullivan (1842-1900)
Church Hymns with Tunes, 1874

This hymn, based on Ephesians 3:1, was captioned "Christian Freedom" in its first source. By setting up many contradictory images, it conveys the powerful Christian paradox of finding life by losing it, accomplished not in any human subjugation but only when God's Spirit is given free rein.

The phrase "it varies with the wind" has nothing to do with the blowing of the wind, but refers to the tension of a wound spring. Therefore, "wind" will rhyme with "find" at the end of the previous line.

Despite poor eyesight, which left him virtually blind by age eighteen, Matheson was a brilliant scholar and preacher. His hymn "O Love that will not let me go" (**577**) is better known than this strong text.

LEOMINSTER was arranged from George Martin's "The Pilgrim Song," which he had published in *The Journal of Part Music, Vol. II.* Sullivan's arrangement was picked up in *The Wesleyan Tune-Book* two years after it appeared in *The Journal* . . . . This music has been used as the setting of numerous texts.

73

Make music to the Lord most high

Based on Psalm 92
Christopher Martin Idle (1938-), 1981
The Book of Praises, 1987

BISHOPTHORPE

Attrib. to Jeremiah Clarke (ca. 1669-1707)
Select Portions of the Psalms of David, ca. 1780

Psalm 92 is one that specifically encourages music in worship. Idle wrote this paraphrase while serving as rector at Limehouse, England. In order to fill one of the many gaps in a collection of contemporary versions of the psalms that a small group was then collecting, Idle made minor changes to the first and last stanzas in 1987 and 1988. This welcome addition to metrical psalmody was included in the Greenach Psalmody Festival in 1988. The author writes: "While the psalm begins with a recommendation to praise and closes with a testimony to personal experience, it also has some stern and clear words for the evildoer and the fool—God's 'enemies.' This is not the easiest of themes to develop in congregational worship, but is an integral part of this psalm as of others."

BISHOPTHORPE—also called ST. PAUL'S, REPENTANCE, or CHARMOUTH—appears in both the undated first edition of *Select Portions of the Psalms of David* and in the 1786 second edition. In Robert Bridges' *Yattendon Hymnal* (1920 ed.), this tune is given in three-part harmony. Archibald Jacob writes of this minuet-like melody: "It is a captivating tune, very characteristic of its century in the grace and suavity of the flexible melodic contour" (Dearmer 1933).

258

Man of sorrows

Philip Paul Bliss (1838-1876)
International Lessons Monthly, 1875

MAN OF SORROWS

Philip Paul Bliss (1838-1876)
(same source as text)

The opening phrase "Man of sorrows" is from Isaiah 53:3, part of the prophet's description of the "suffering servant." The hymn takes up this theme with Jesus' experience on the cross and moves over to exaltation in the final stanzas, just as Christ did.

Both words and music were published a year before Bliss died in a train accident. The hymn, with five stanzas, appears in the 1876 *Gospel Hymns No. 2*. The third stanza, omitted in *Hymnal: A Worship Book*, is:

Guilty, vile and helpless, we;
Spotless Lamb of God was He;
"Full atonement!" can it be?
Hallelujah, what a Savior!

About the music Methodist hymnal editor Carlton Young writes: "Bliss's setting is typical of the reflective, chordal, quasi-choral music of the Reconstruction era's revival that has been all but lost in the mounds of frivolous and repetitious dance tunes in the gospel hymn repertory" (Young 1993).

35

Many and great, O God — LACQUIPARLE

Joseph R. Renville
Dakota Dowanpi Kin (Odowan Wowapi), 1846
English paraphrase by Francis Philip Frazier (1892-1964), 1929, alt.

Plains Indian melody
Dakota Odowan, 1879

The seven original stanzas of text, based on Jeremiah 10:12-13, appeared with only the initials "J. R." Joseph Renville, a mid-eighteenth-century French Dakota fur trader and Bible translator, was later identified as the author. The hymn with the Dakota words caught on among YWCA groups, and Francis Philip Frazier, a full-blooded Sioux (Dakota) and Congregational minister, was requested to make an English version. His paraphrase of the first and last stanzas was presented at the national convention of the YWCA in 1930.

A contemporary translation of the full text into English by Sydney H. Byrd, a member of the Dakota tribe and a Presbyterian minister, reveals the great depth of faith expressed in this hymn, a faith that sustained its people through times of persecution (*The Hymnal 1982 Companion*). Byrd says the hymn was sung at the hanging of thirty-eight Dakota men following the Dakota uprising in 1862.

The full text, in its final three stanzas, also describes the sacrament of Communion, allusions that can be detected in the words "Grant unto us communion with you" and "with you are found the gifts of life." At the end of the first phrase, "works" replaces "things," and in the present version, archaic addresses have been contemporized.

The tune LACQUIPARLE, which in French means "lake that speaks," ends as it begins, creating an ABA form. The octave leap in the B section provides a tonal arch for the "heavens with stars," creating a musical description of God's expansive work.

151

Marvelous grace of our loving Lord

MARVELOUS GRACE

Julia Harriette Johnston (1849-1919)
Towner's *Hymns Tried and True*, 1911

Daniel Brink Towner (1850-1919), 1910
(same source as text)

In 1910 Towner wrote the music for these words by religious poet Julia Johnston. Several hymnals call the tune MOODY for Moody Bible Institute where Towner was head of the music department.

422

May God grant you a blessing—see "Bwana awabariki"

423

May the grace of Christ our Savior

FELLOWSHIP

John Newton (1725-1807)
Olney Hymns, Book III, 1779

Conrad Gillian Lint (1834-1918)

This short hymn for the close of a service is a paraphrase of 2 Corinthians 13:13: "The grace of the Lord Jesus Christ and the love of God and the fellowship of the Holy Spirit be with you all." This paraphrase first appeared as one stanza of eight lines in *Olney Hymns*. It has been translated into several languages.

With two slight text changes, this hymn can also be used as a wedding hymn. In stanza 1, one could change the last phrase to "rest upon *them* from above" and in stanza 2, the first phrase to "*So* may *they* abide in union . . . ."

The earliest source of FELLOWSHIP is apparently not documented. In Diehl's *Hymns and Tunes*, FELLOWSHIP is listed only with references to *Hymnal: Church of the Brethren* (1925) and *The Brethren Hymnal* (1951). A twofold "Amen," absent in the 1925 book, appears in the later version. The tune STUTTGART is a useful alternative for this text.

435
May the Lord, mighty God — WEN-TI

Based on Numbers 6:24-26

Chinese melody
Adapt. from Pao-chen Li's "Wen-Ti"

This lyric benediction is a paraphrase of the Aaronic blessing found in Numbers 6, which also forms the basis of Jaroslav Vajda's "Go, my children" (**433**). Because of its pentatonic nature, this song works well as a canon (round) at intervals of two beats, four beats, or two measures. This musical adaptation, with a countermelody to the second statement of the tune, was made for the Asian American hymnal *Hymns from the Four Winds* (1983). The hymn was included in the Mennonite World Conference *International Songbook* (1990), as well as in *New Songs of Peace* (1987), a hymnal used by the Taiwan Mennonite Church.

648
Morning has broken — BUNESSAN

Eleanor Farjeon (1881-1965)
Enlarged Songs of Praise, 1931, alt.

Gaelic melody
Songs and Hymns of the Gael, 1888
Harm. by Martin Fallas Shaw (1875-1958), alt.

British hymnal editor Percy Dearmer, searching for a thanksgiving hymn to fit the meter of BUNESSAN, prompted Farjeon to come up with a text to meet his criteria. Farjeon's radiant verse praises the Maker for each new day as if it were a re-creation of the perfection of God's very first morning.

BUNESSAN "was noted down by Alexander Fraser from the singing of a wandering Highland singer. Its bold movements are in keeping with the freedom shown in Gaelic song" (Hustad 1978). In addition to its earliest source, this tune was printed in the *Irish Church Hymnal* (1917) with the words "Child in the manger." This tune with "Morning has broken" was popularized in the U.S. by recording artist Cat Stevens in the early 1970s.

214
Morning Star, O cheering sight — HAGEN

Morgenstern auf finstre Nacht
Johann Angelus Silesius Scheffler (1624-1677)
Heilige Seelenlust, 1657
Tr. Bennet Harvey, Jr. (1829-1894), 1885

Francis Florentine Hagen (1815-1907), 1836

The references to the "Morning Star" throughout this entire text point to Jesus. In the first part of each of the first three stanzas, the words ponder in a general way the effect the "Morning Star" has upon the earth, the solar system, and the nations. But the brightness of the Star is not merely a heavenly phenomenon; it lights the human soul. In the second half of the stanzas, the text narrows to a personal prayer.

Scheffler's German text was originally in six stanzas of five lines each. Closely associated with the Moravians, this translation appears with two tunes in the 1891 American Moravian hymnal, *Offices of Worship and Hymns (with tunes)*. An earlier tune from Freylinghausen's *Gesangbuch* (1704) does not have any repetitions of text and consequently falls short of the way HAGEN creates a musical conversation between the solo voice and the congregation.

In 1836, when Hagen was twenty-one, he was teaching at the Moravian boys' school in Salem, North Carolina. That year he wrote this music for the "Christmas entertainment of Salem's little girls" (Lefevre 1978). Traditionally, the solo sections are sung by a child from the congregation at the Christmas Eve vigil services. Although Hagen died in July of 1907, this Christmas hymn was sung at his funeral (Adams 1984).

482
Mothering God, you gave me birth

MOTHERING GOD

Based on the writings of Julian of Norwich
Jean Wiebe Janzen (1933-), 1991
Hymnal: A Worship Book, 1992

Janet Peachey (1953-), 1991
(same source as text)

Janzen writes: "The English medieval mystic, St. Julian of Norwich, wrote of the mothering aspects of God. Her ideas moved me to address these characteristics in the Trinity." Little is known of Julian's life except from her writings. She received her revelations in the spring of 1373 at the age of thirty, which would place her date of birth late in 1342. Julian's *Showings*, completed in 1393, is a lengthy treatise of eighty-six chapters on the godly will of the soul and on the nature of God.

Peachey composed this tune in response to a request for settings of this new text. She explains her composition:

> The text expresses the concept of God as source and nurturer of all life, like "mother" earth. To me this is a mystical text, inspiring awe and reverence, which I tried to convey through the music. The pedal note E, which is present throughout the hymn, can be thought of as a solid ground, like the earth, embracing all of us.

418

Move in our midst

Kenneth I. Morse (1913-), sts. 1-2, 1942; sts. 3-4, 1949
The Brethren Hymnal, 1951

PINE GLEN

Perry Lee Huffaker (1902-1982), 1950
The Brethren Hymnal, 1951

This hymn has become the best loved of all those introduced in the *The Brethren Hymnal* (1951). Morse, who served on the hymnal committees of that hymnal and the present one, wrote the first two stanzas while at Camp Harmony in western Pennsylvania. The latter two stanzas were commissioned after the hymn was chosen for inclusion in the 1951 hymnal.

The tune was named PINE GLEN for the church where Perry Huffaker was pastor at the time he composed it. The hymn was first used in that church. Caleb W. Bucher, in his book *From Where I Stand*, tells this story of the creation of the hymn:

> One summer in the late 1940's, Kenneth Morse and Perry Huffaker accompanied me from Camp Harmony to an engagement in a church nearby. . . . I was the driver of the car. On the back seat, Ken's words were set to Perry's music to produce the hymn, "Move in our midst." It is as close as I ever came to being a musician.

Although its popularity can be traced in part to its frequent use at Brethren annual conferences, the hymn also stands on its own merit. Its marriage of music and text is especially effective in the rising unison passage that begins the third phrase.

547

My dear Redeemer and my Lord

Isaac Watts (1674-1748)
Hymns and Spiritual Songs, Book II, 1707-1709, alt.

SOCIAL BAND

American folk melody
Ingalls' *The Christian Harmony*, 1805
Harm. by J. Harold Moyer (1927-), 1965
The Mennonite Hymnal, 1969

This hymn, titled "The Example of Christ," appeared in four stanzas in Watts's collection cited above. While Brethren and Mennonites tend to see Christ's servanthood to others as the example for faithful living, this hymn lifts up Jesus' obedience to God as the paradigm. To drive home the model of obedience, stanza 2 alludes to Jesus' post-baptism temptations and his anguished, pre-crucifixion Gethsemane prayer.

The archaisms have been retained to fit the flavor of Watts's text and the old folk tune to which it is set. SOCIAL BAND, chosen for *The Mennonite Hymnal* (1969), is a vigorous tune also known as SHOUTING HYMN.

In his second edition of *Genuine Church Music* (1835), Joseph Funk called the tune SOCIAL BAND, from its use with another text that begins "Say now ye lovely social band, who walk the way to Canaan's land." The original four stanzas become two longer ones to fit this long-meter double-tune.

In Mennonite and Brethren traditions, the words of this hymn have been sung to a variety of tunes, including HAMBURG, ROCKINGHAM NEW, MISSIONARY CHANT, WARE, and ROCKINGHAM OLD.

565

My faith looks up to thee — OLIVET

Ray Palmer (1808-1887), 1830
Hastings and Mason's *Spiritual Songs for Social Worship*, Boston, 1832

Lowell Mason (1792-1872)
(same source as text)

Concerning this hymn, "there was not the slightest thought of writing for another eye," writes Ray Palmer, "least of all writing a hymn for Christian worship." Palmer penned his private poem at age twenty-one while teaching school in New York City. A year or two later, Lowell Mason chanced upon Palmer on a Boston street and mentioned the tunebook that he and Dr. Hastings were about to publish. He asked Palmer if he had any hymns to include. Palmer, who was still carrying the poem in a notebook, turned it over to Mason, who wrote the tune OLIVET for it. Inspired by the poem, Mason predicted Palmer would be best remembered for this hymn, and he is.

Mason's tune was arranged first for three voices and included the duet section (phrases 4 and 5), which has been reinstated here. The duet may be sung by any combination of high and low voices and the cue notes by basses or all men. In his subsequent publications, Mason himself altered the melody in several places. Most notable is the change of the first note in measure 3 from the lower "sol" to its present "re," as found in *The Modern Psalmist, A Collection of Church Music* (Boston 1839).

248

My God, my God, why — (no tune name)

Based on Psalm 22

Edward John Hopkins (1818-1901)
The Hymnal 1940

The opening words of this psalm, spoken by an agonized Jesus on the cross, are familiar to us because they are quoted so often in the New Testament. Without dwelling on the philosophical nature of suffering, without alluding to sin, and without showing bitterness, the psalmist asks only that God hear the cry of abandonment. Even in utter loneliness, the sufferer meets God's mystic presence and strength.

The text here continues with verses 1-5, 7-8, 17, and 19 of the psalm, with the intervening verses complete in the *Accompaniment Handbook.* This intense lament reveals an intimate relationship between the sufferer and God; the chant setting leaves ample room for rhythmic expression.

This double chant by the nineteenth-century composer Edward Hopkins is found in *The Hymnal 1940* in the key of F minor. There it is one of several settings of the *Benedictus*, or "Song of Zechariah."

"Why has God forsaken me?" (**246**) is another hymn that uses this heart-cry as its basis.

343
My hope is built on nothing less

SOLID ROCK

Edward Mote (1797-1874), ca. 1834
Spiritual Magazine, alt.

William Batchelder Bradbury (1816-1868), 1863
Devotional Hymn and Tune Book, 1864

Mote wrote the chorus of this hymn one morning as he walked up Holborn Street in London. Before the day was over, he had completed four stanzas on the "Gracious Experience of a Christian," drawing from the parable about building a house on rock rather than on sand (Matt. 7:24-27). The following Sunday, on a visit, he pulled out his poem when his host, Brother King, could not find his hymnbook for the customary devotions. Mrs. King, who was quite ill, enjoyed the verses so much that Mote went home and completed the last two stanzas and took them to Sister King.

The original six stanzas (printed below) have been redistributed in the hymnal's five-stanza version.

Nor earth, nor hell, my soul can move
I rest upon unchanging love;
I dare not trust the sweetest frame
But wholly lean on Jesus' name. (Refrain)

My hope is built on nothing less
Than Jesus' blood and righteousness;
'Midst all the hell I feel within,
On his completed work I lean.

When darkness veils his lovely face,
I rest upon unchanging grace;
In every high and stormy gale,
My anchor holds within the veil.

His oath, his covenant, his blood,
Support me in the sinking flood;

When all around my soul give way,
He then is all my hope and stay.

I trust his righteous character,
His council, promise, and his power;
His honor and his name's at stake
To save me from the burning lake.

When I shall launch in worlds unseen,
O may I then in Him be found,
Clad in his righteousness alone,
Faultless to stand before the throne.

Mote published the text in his book with the descriptive title *Hymns of Praise, A New Selection of Gospel Hymns, Combining All the Excellencies of our Spiritual Poets, with many Originals* (1836). This book contains what is believed to be the first use of the term "gospel hymn."

William Bradbury composed SOLID ROCK for this text in 1863 and published it the following year in his *Devotional Hymn and Tune Book*, the only Baptist hymnal published in the U.S. during the Civil War.

522
My Jesus, I love thee

William Ralph Featherstone (1846-1873), ca. 1862
Primitive Methodist Magazine, October 1862
The London Hymn Book, 1864

GORDON

Adoniram Judson Gordon (1836-1895), 1872
The Service of Song for Baptist Churches, 1876

The intimacy of this text hinges on a personal encounter with Jesus. The second stanza clarifies how this relationship came to be: "because [Jesus] first loved us" (1 John 4:19). Little is known about Featherstone (sometimes spelled Featherston) other than that he lived in Montréal, Québec, and was a member of Wesleyan Methodist Church. This poem, written when he was about sixteen, was sent to his aunt in Los Angeles who encouraged him to have it published. Some versions of the hymn begin "Lord Jesus, I love thee." Recent research by American hymnologist Leonard Ellinwood uncovered a letter that states the first published form of this hymn appeared in *Primitive Methodist Magazine*, London, October 1862 (Hooper, White 1988).

For a long time the text appeared anonymously. Browsing through his new *The London Hymn Book*, A. J. Gordon discovered it with another tune and "a beautiful new air sang itself" to him. Gordon's tune was printed in the 1876 collection above, edited by Gordon and S. L. Caldwell and published in Boston. *American Hymns Old and New* reports that the music was composed in 1872.

580
My life flows on

HOW CAN I KEEP FROM SINGING

Robert Lowry's *Bright Jewels for the Sunday School*, 1869, alt.

(same source as text)
Arr. by The Hymnal Project, 1989

Many hymnals credit Robert Lowry with this hymn, which appeared in his *Bright Jewels for the Sunday School* in 1869. Other hymnals list the melody as being a Quaker hymn. There is evidence, however, that both text and tune predate Lowry. According to one source, the text appears in an 1864 collection by Anne Warner, and the tune dates from at least 1864 as well.

Early versions of the hymn set the text as three full stanzas. Other versions have appeared over the years, many of which use the latter half of the second stanza for a refrain, as is done here. The arrangement used in this hymnal follows closely that which appeared in Lowry's *Bright Jewels* . . . . The most obvious departure is in the refrain where the use of all quarter notes in the first and fifth measures provides a contrast to the rhythmic repetition of the other phrases.

589
My Shepherd will supply my need

RESIGNATION

Based on Psalm 23
Isaac Watts (1674-1748)
The Psalms of David . . ., 1719

American folk melody
Freeman Lewis's *Beauties of Harmony*, 1828
Version from Joseph Funk's *Genuine Church Music*, 1st ed., 1832
Harm. by J. Harold Moyer (1927-), 1965

Watts's six-stanza paraphrase of Psalm 23 is arranged here to create three longer stanzas for the double-meter tune. As hymnologist Erik Routley notes, the psalm really ends in the middle of stanza 3. The last lines are an addition "and perhaps the most inspired such addition ever made" (Routley 1979).

The composer of RESIGNATION is unknown. The melody appears in Freeman Lewis's collection with the text "Come, humble sinner" and in Funk's publication with Charles Wesley's funeral hymn "And let this feeble body fail." Joseph Funk owned a copy of the 1818 edition of Lewis's *Beauties of Harmony* and may have owned or borrowed a copy of the 1828 version. Funk's setting of this pentatonic melody is in 3/2 meter; it is arranged for three voice parts with the melody in the middle (tenor) voice.

235

My song is love unknown

Samuel Crossman (ca. 1624-1683 or 1684)
Pamphlet, *The Young Man's Meditations . . . ,* 1664
Rev. in *Hymns for Today's Church,* 1982

LOVE UNKNOWN

John Nicholson Ireland (1879-1962)
Songs of Praise, 1925

This is one of nine sacred poems to come out of Crossman's short pamphlet with a long name, *The Young Man's Meditations, or some few Sacred Poems upon Select Subjects, and Scriptures.* In this remarkable piece, the poet has taken Christ's Passion personally and to heart. Though the stanzas begin with a tender but rather distanced tone concerning the person of Jesus, by the end there is a cry of intimacy: "This is my friend . . . ." Writes Percy Dearmer: "Crossman's work has a strong and naive directness and charm, which must have made his poetry sound a little old-world when it was published, and perhaps makes us appreciate it the more today" (Dearmer 1933). The meter of this poem is distinctive, with only four syllables in each of the last four lines of each stanza.

LOVE UNKNOWN, an inviting melody for unison singing, was composed for Crossman's text on the back of a lunch menu a few minutes after Ireland was given the poem. Its flexible rhythmic patterns, sometimes shifting between triple and duple pulses, provide a setting that fits the text in a most natural way. It treats the last four short lines as two. Erik Routley has said, "This tune requires intimate and free treatment," adding that it is especially notable for the "felicitous way in which it brings out the sense of the words," as in the phrases "But who am I" in stanza 1 and "Then 'crucify' " in stanza 3 (Parry, Routley 1953).

The reflective narrative in this hymn would make it suitable for use in smaller segments, interspersing hymn stanzas with scripture or commentary.

181

My soul proclaims with wonder

Based on Luke 1:46-55
Carl Pickens Daw, Jr. (1944-), 1986
Songs of Rejoicing, 1989

WALNUT

J. Harold Moyer (1927-), 1990
Hymnal: A Worship Book, 1992

Daw wrote this paraphrase of the Song of Mary (Luke 1:46-55) in order to have a metrical version of the Magnificat to use at evening prayer at St. Mark's Chapel, Storrs, Connecticut. Mary's Song, which echoes the Song of Hannah (1 Sam. 2:1-11), anticipates Paul's affirmation that God's strength "is made perfect in weakness" (2 Cor. 12:9). In stanza 2, the song remembers the defeat of the Egyptians at the Red Sea, and in stanza 3, it echoes Psalm 23 (Daw 1990).

The text was written for the tune ST. THEODULPH, traditionally associated with "All glory, laud, and honor" (**237**). As in that hymn, the refrain is designed to begin the hymn as well as follow each stanza, including the last. WALNUT is one of several tunes written by Moyer in response to the music committee's tune search for "orphan" texts. Moyer says the tune name has no special significance.

562
Nada te turbe

(no tune name)

Santa Teresa de Jesus (1515-1582)

Jacques Berthier (1923-)
Songs and Prayers from Taizé, 1991

These comforting words are by the sixteenth-century writer also known as St. Teresa of Spain and St. Teresa of Avila. An invalid for long periods in her life, Santa Teresa struggled in her prayer life to be close to God. This text testifies to her search for peace. The following is a pronunciation guide for the Spanish text:

> Nah-dah tay tur-bay, nah-dah tayes-pan-tay. Kyen ah Deeos tyen-ay nah-dah lay fahl-tah.

Berthier's musical setting was created for the Taizé community where many nationalities worship together. The text has been translated into French, German, Italian, English, and other languages. The English translation is: "Let nothing trouble you. Let nothing frighten you. Whoever has God lacks nothing. God alone is enough."

As with much Taizé music, the meditative quality of this piece is enhanced with repetition. For instrumental parts, see the *Accompaniment Handbook*; for comments on the Taizé community and its music, see "Allelluia" (**101**).

330
Nasadiki—see "I believe in God"

583
Ndikhokele, O Jehova

XHOSA HYMN

Guide me, O thou great Jehovah
William Williams (1717-1791)
Arglwydd arwain trwy'r anialwch, Williams' *Aleluia*, 1745
Xhosa transcription by Edith W. Ming (1932-)

Xhosa melody (Republic of South Africa)

The text of this hymn is discussed under its English title "Guide me, O thou great Jehovah." This version comes from the Fifteenth Episcopal District of the African Methodist Episcopal Church in South Africa.

XHOSA HYMN, though only four measures in length, has a strong, almost marchlike quality. Edith Ming, who transcribed the hymn, also provided the notation.

299

New earth, heavens new — ALEXANDRA

Harris J. Loewen (1953-), 1982
Assembly Songs, 1983

Harris J. Loewen (1953-), 1982
(same source as text)

Loewen wrote "All things new" while he was a student at Associated Mennonite Biblical Seminaries in Elkhart, Indiana. Of its origins he writes: "I did a fairly exhaustive search, with the help of a concordance, of all the uses of 'new' in the Bible. The idea of creation and re-creation was also in my mind." The four stanzas present these key concepts associated with the word "new": the Genesis creation (st. 1), the prophets (st. 2), the New Testament (new covenant, st. 3), and the Book of Revelation (st. 4).

Musically, this tune is simple and immediately singable. In the refrain Loewen uses the octave leap "to make the word 'behold' more arresting." The sharpest dissonance in the song also highlights the word "I," referring to God.

The tune is named ALEXANDRA for Loewen's daughter. The hymn was first published in *Assembly Songs*, a compilation prepared for the joint sessions in 1983 of the Mennonite Church and the General Conference Mennonite Church, in celebration of three hundred years of Mennonites living in North America.

207

Niño lindo — CARACAS

Child so lovely
Venezuelan hymn
Tr. George Frank Lockwood IV (1946-), 1987
The United Methodist Hymnal, 1989

Venezuelan melody

This delightful Christmas song has a Caribbean flavor, coming as it does from the coastal regions of Venezuela. It is an *aguinaldo*, a type of Christmas carol sung in that area of Latin America. The translator writes:

> "Aguinaldo" means a Christmas or New Year's present; the word is used for the Christmas bonus many employers give their workers at year's end in Latin America. In this case, it refers to the little gift

> of drink or candy given (like our North American carolers being invited in for hot chocolate and Christmas candy) to those who have shared the "aguinaldo" song.

The carol, with a four-part harmonization, is included in *Corazones Siempre Alegres* (1975).

657
Now all the woods are sleeping

Nun ruhen alle Wälder
Paul Gerhardt (1607-1676)
Crüger's *Praxis Pietatis Melica*, 1648
Composite translation from *Lutheran Book of Worship*, 1978, alt.

O WELT, ICH MUSS DICH LASSEN

Attrib. to Heinrich Isaac (ca. 1450-1517)
Forster's *Ein Auszug guter alter und neuer Teutschen Liedlein*, Nürnberg, 1539
(Zahn No. 2293)

Gerhardt's hymnody moved from the rather objective style of his predecessors to the more subjective mode of the Pietists, combining elements of both. In this beautiful evening prayer, the imagery is saturated with scriptural allusions. The first line of the hymn is a reflection of Isaiah 14:7: "All the lands are at peace; they break into singing." A characteristic feature of nearly all the stanzas is the way Gerhardt uses natural phenomena as metaphors for spiritual revelations (Kulp, Buchner, Fornacon 1958).

The hymn, widely known in Germany, was a favorite of the poet Schiller. The German version has been a beloved hymn of Russian Mennonites since the late 1800s and continues to be sung by those who immigrated to Canada in the 1920s and early 1950s. It appears with five of the original nine stanzas in the *Gesangbuch der Mennoniten* (1965), the most recent German Mennonite hymnal to be published in North America. The composite translation begins with the familiar opening phrase of Catherine Winkworth's translation published in her *Lyra Germanica*, Series I (1855). The third stanza is slightly revised from Robert Bridges' 1899 version of the text, "The duteous day now closeth."

In the sixteenth century, the use of secular songs and parodies of secular compositions for church purposes was common. This chorale melody, adapted from the song *Innsbruck, ich muss dich lassen*, is possibly the most famous and certainly one of the most beautiful examples of such a transformation. Whether the tune was composed by Isaac or was a folk melody has not been clearly established. The melody had been adapted to sacred use by 1505 when it appeared in a manuscript with a hymn to St. Anne and St. Joachim. In the Eisleben *Gesangbuch* (1598), it was associated with the text *O Welt, ich muss dich lassen*. The rhythmic version of the tune used here parallels Isaac's four-part polyphonic setting of the

Innsbruck text, which was printed in Forster's collection cited above. Bach used the melody in three of his cantatas and in two of his passions.

399

Now go forward — (no tune name)

Anonymous
Ancient Chinese hymn
Tr. Evelyn Sau-yee Chiu (1957-), 1986
Hymnal: A Worship Book, 1992

Traditional Chinese melody

From 1983 to 1989, David and Evelyn Sau-Yee Chiu worked to establish the Saskatoon Chinese Mennonite Church in Saskatchewan. Evelyn, who was born in Hong Kong, translated this ancient hymn in 1986 for the church building fund-raising program. It has since been used to challenge other churches in that conference to participate in outreach and evangelism. The translation, which originally began "Forward go ye," has been altered slightly in several other lines to better match syllables with music. This is its first appearance in print.

655

Now, on land and sea descending — VESPER HYMN

Samuel Longfellow (1819-1892)
Longfellow's *Vespers*, 1859

John Andrew Stevenson (1761-1833)
Stevenson's *A Selection of Popular National Airs*, London, 1818

This text belongs to a collection of evening hymns Longfellow wrote while he was pastor of Second Unitarian Church, Brooklyn, New York. *Jubilate*, a Latin word meaning "shout for joy," is pronounced yoo-bih-lah-teh.

Although VESPER HYMN is sometimes attributed to Dimitri Bortniansky, his published works do not include it. In Stevenson's collection, where the tune is called RUSSIAN AIR, there is a note indicating that the third line "is added to the original Air by Sir John Stevenson" (*The Hymnal 1940 Companion*, 1951 ed.), leading one to believe that Stevenson was the arranger and may have been the composer. The music first appeared as a glee (an unaccompanied song in three- or four-part harmony intended for entertainment) and soon became a popular glee club selection. The original words for the glee by Thomas Moore begins:

> Hark! the vesper hymn is stealing
> O'er the waters soft and clear;
> Nearer yet and nearer pealing,
> Now it bursts upon the ear.
> Jubilate, Jubilate, Jubilate, Amen.

The melody appears as a hymn tune in Leavitt's *Christian Lyre* (1830).

85, 86
Now thank we all our God

NUN DANKET ALLE GOTT

Nun danket alle Gott
Martin Rinckart (1586-1649)
Jesu Hertz-Büchlein, 1636
Tr. Catherine Winkworth (1827-1878)
Lyra Germanica, Series II, 1858, alt.

Johann Crüger (1598-1662)
Praxis Pietatis Melica, 4th ed., 1647
86 harm. by Felix Mendelssohn 1809-1847)
Symphony No. 2, Lobgesang (Hymn of Praise), Opus 52, 1840

This is the best known of those hymns coming from the second period of German hymnody (1570-1648). It appears in virtually all standard German and English hymnals. The first two stanzas are a *Tischlied* (table grace) based on the apocryphal book of Ecclesiasticus (50:22-24); the third is a doxology.

Often used for occasions of thanksgiving and celebration, this hymn that thanks God for "countless gifts of love" was written amid the violence and pestilence of the Thirty Years War. Rinckart, for a time the only pastor in the haven city of Eilenburg, sometimes conducted forty or fifty funerals a day. A fitting tribute, his hymn was sung at the conclusion of the Peace of Westphalia (1648), which ended the war.

Although no copies of Rinckart's 1636 edition of *Jesu Hertz-Büchlein* exist today, it is generally assumed to have included this hymn, since it is found in the 1663 edition. It also appears with its present tune in the 1647 volume by Crüger.

Winkworth's very familiar translation is used with little alteration. In stanza 1:3, "has" is used instead of "hath," and in stanza 2:4 "this world" is in place of "his world." Stanza 2:3 is changed to "and keep us safe in grace." Though Winkworth's rendition of the German *Mutterleib* in stanza 1:3 ("who, from our mother's *arms*") was probably the most socially acceptable at the time, the word actually means "womb," acknowledging God's care for us even before birth.

Crüger's *Praxis Pietatis Melica,* in which this tune first appeared, was issued in more than fifty editions over the century following its first publication. NUN DANKET ALLE GOTT appears in a number of melodic, rhythmic, and harmonic versions. The two settings presented here are a more rhythmic earlier one (**85**) and a metric version with richer harmonic movement (**86**). The latter, derived from Mendelssohn's six-part harmonization, is found in many hymnals, including Mennonite and Brethren hymnals of this century.

462
Now the silence

NOW

Jaroslav J. Vajda (1919-), 1968
Magazine, *This Day,* May, 1968

Carl Flentge Schalk (1929-)
Worship Supplement to the Lutheran Hymnal, 1969

This text, so tenacious about the immediacy of God's presence, took shape in the author's mind while he was shaving, "a time," he writes, "when I get a lot of original ideas . . . ." He continues:

> Somewhere in the back of my mind, during my previous 18 years in the full-time parish ministry, I was accumulating reasons and benefits in worship. I have felt that we often get so little out of worship because we anticipate so little, and we seldom come with a bucket large enough to catch all the shower of grace that comes to us in that setting.

The result was a hymn that lists the "awesome and exciting things that one should expect in worship." It is unusual in that repetition replaces rhyme as the unifying factor. At the conclusion the usual Trinitarian order is reversed, not only because it is the order in which the incarnation took place, but also to express the way "the Trinity approaches us in worship: The Spirit brings us the gospel, by which God's blessing is released in our lives" (Stulken 1981).

Vajda credits Carl Schalk for recognizing the potential of this unusual text as a hymn. "Its subsequent acceptance convinced me (and evidently many others) that hymns could take on new forms and yet perform their function in congregational worship" (Vajda 1987). In the last two decades, the hymn has been included in numerous hymnals in the United States, Canada, and England. See the *Accompaniment Handbook* for Schalk's accompaniment.

600
O bless the Lord, my soul

Based on Psalm 103
Isaac Watts (1674-1748)
The Psalms of David . . ., 1719

ST. THOMAS (WILLIAMS)

Aaron Williams (1731-1776)
The Universal Psalmodist, 1763

This version of Psalm 103 and "O bless the Lord, my soul" (**80**) are placed in different sections of the hymnal to highlight the different ways they may be used in worship. These words by Watts may be compared with James Montgomery's version that begins with the same six words. Watts's final stanza has been deleted:

> His wond'rous works and ways
> He made by Moses known;
> But sent the world his truth and grace
> By his beloved Son.

This melody is a portion of a sixteen-phrase tune called HOLBORN, which was published with four stanzas of Charles Wesley's text "Soldiers of Christ, arise." ST. THOMAS is the portion that was the setting for the second stanza. It acquired its present name in 1770 when it appeared in shortened form in both Isaac Smith's *A Collection of Psalm Tunes* and in

Williams' *New Universal Psalmodist*. The designation (WILLIAMS) is added to avoid confusion with a very different ST. THOMAS tune attributed to John Wade. The melody was erroneously attributed to Handel in some early nineteenth-century hymnals. Some hymnbooks have added passing tones in the melody of the third to last measure. The tune is frequently used with Timothy Dwight's "I love thy kingdom, Lord" (**308**) and Watts's "Come, we that love the Lord" (**14**).

80
O bless the Lord, my soul — VIGIL

Based on Psalm 103
James Montgomery (1771-1854)
Thomas Cotterill's *Selection of Psalms and Hymns*, 8th ed., 1819
Alt. by Jean Wiebe Janzen (1933-), 1991

St. Alban's Tune Book, 1865

This text is one of several in the hymnal based on Psalm 103. The psalm itself echoes the optimistic spirituality of the period during and after the Exile when prophets spoke to reassure people of God's presence and desire for reconciliation. The psalmist has returned to health, both physically and figuratively; even youthful vigor has returned "like the eagle." This phrase may refer to the "legend of the phoenix bird which, as it flew towards the sun, burned away its old feathers and acquired new ones" (Stuhlmueller 1983).

Janzen's version involves changes of archaic forms of address, as well as the use of "God" in place of a personal pronoun. Of Montgomery's six stanzas, the second has been deleted and the fifth is placed as the second. The third stanza is completely reworked. The original reads:

> He will not always chide;
> He will with patience wait;
> His wrath is ever slow to rise,
> And ready to abate.

Little is known about the origin of the tune VIGIL. It appears in both the 1925 and 1951 Brethren hymnals with this text. There, as well as in the Mennonite *Church Hymnal* (1927), it is designated as "Arr. from *St. Alban's Tune Book*, 1865." Hostetler's *Handbook to the Mennonite Hymnary*, however, claims that the tune is "by the Italian composer, Giovanni Paisiello, 1741-1816." Since Paisiello was a prolific composer of operas, masses, and motets, it is possible that the hymn tune was derived from one of his melodies.

468
O Bread of life, for sinners broken — SHENG EN

Timothy T'ing Fang Lew (1892-1947)
Hymns of Universal Praise, 1936
Tr. Frank W. Price (1895-1974), alt.

Su Yin-Lan (1915-1937), 1934
(same source as text)

This is a text with great theological strength and stately, haunting music. It connects us with the church universal, making it especially appropriate for Worldwide Communion Sunday observances. In stanza 3:2, "veils" refers to the tearing of the temple veil as Jesus died on the cross (Luke 23:45). Just as the Holy of Holies, where God was thought to dwell, was suddenly open to all, so the living presence of Christ shatters barriers between human and divine.

This translation of "O Bread of life for sinners broken" is used by the Taiwan Mennonite Church and was included in the *International Songbook* of the 1990 Mennonite World Conference where the author's name appears as Liu Ting Fong. Another translation by W. R. O. Taylor appears in differing versions in the more recent Methodist hymnals (1966 and 1989) and the ecumenical international hymnal *Cantate Domino III* (1974).

SHENG EN, which means "holy grace," was composed in 1934. The hymn first appeared in the Chinese Union hymnbook, also known as *Hymns of Universal Praise.*

510
O Christ, in thee my soul — NONE BUT CHRIST

Anonymous
Gospel Hymns No. 4, 1883

James McGranahan (1840-1907)
(same source as text)

This hymn text has only the designation "B. E. Arr." in *Gospel Hymns No. 4* where it is titled "None but Christ Can Satisfy." The scripture reference is Romans 5:11: "We also joy in God, through our Lord Jesus Christ, by whom we have now received the atonement." Beyond that, the text's authorship and background are unknown.

The collection that included this hymn was published by Sankey, McGranahan, and Stebbins in 1883. The margin of the hymn, however, is marked "Copyright, 1879, by James McGranahan." This hymn was a favorite of Professor Henry Drummond, who used it frequently at meetings for university students in Edinburgh in the late 1880s (L. Hostetler 1949).

379
O Christ, the healer — TYRANT HEROD

Fred Pratt Green (1903-), 1967
Hymns and Songs, 1969

David N. Johnson (1922-1987)
Hymnal for the Hours, 1989

When the British Methodist *Hymns and Songs* was being compiled, the author submitted this poem to fill a gap in the section on healing. This is a contemporary text that not only addresses physical ills, but also acknowledges the ill health that arises out of conflict—newly diagnosed, but not a new disease.

The final line of the hymn has changed from "Shall reach, and shall enrich mankind" to "Shall reach the whole of humankind" or "Shall reach and prosper humankind."

This text has appeared with a number of tunes, including WAREHAM. TYRANT HEROD was selected because its sweeping, chantlike phrases aptly fit the shape of the text.

153
O Christ, the Lamb of God — CHRISTE, DU LAMM GOTTES

Agnus Dei, based on John 1:29

Kirchenordnung, Braunschweig, 1528
Setting adapt. from Joachim Decker (ca. 1575-1611), 1604

The scripture text from which this portion of the ancient liturgy comes is the greeting of John the Baptist to Jesus; it is John's testimony that Jesus was God's Son. During the fifth century, this Latin text began to be repeated in the central portion of the *Gloria in excelsis*. It was in the seventh century that Pope Sergius I directed the people and the clergy to sing this together at the time of Communion. The ending of the third and final repetition was changed to *dona nobis pacem* (grant us your peace) during the eleventh century. Its first publication in Germany in 1528 was with a translation in Low German, *Christe, du lam Gades*. For more on the *Agnus Dei*, see "O Lamb of God all holy" (**146**).

CHRISTE, DU LAMM GOTTES, the tune name used here, is the High German version of the text (1531) with which the tune was first associated.

113
O Christe Domine Jesu — (no tune name)

O Christ, Lord Jesus
Jacques Berthier (1923-)
Music from Taizé, Vol. II, 1982, 1983, 1984

Jacques Berthier (1923-)
(same source as text)

This ostinato is the congregational accompaniment for stanzas that paraphrase Psalm 23 (stanzas in *Accompaniment Handbook*). *Ostinato* literally means "persistent"—it is the musical "groundwork," repeated again and again, over which other musical variation can occur.

The Latin text may be pronounced "oh kree-steh, daw-mee-neh yeh-soo." Instrumental parts for this worship resource are in the *Accompaniment Handbook*. For comments on music from Taizé, see "Alleluia" (**101**).

212
O come, all ye faithful — ADESTE FIDELES

Adeste fideles laeti triumphantes
John Francis Wade (ca. 1711-1786)
Manuscript, ca. 1743
Sts. 1,3-4, rev. form, *Office de St. Omer*, 1822
St. 2, Etienne J. F. Borderies (1764-1832), 1822
Sts. 1,3-4, tr. Frederick Oakeley (1802-1880)
Oakeley manuscript, 1841, alt.; Murray's *Hymnal*, 1852
St. 2, tr. William Mercer (1811-1873), 1854
Mercer's *Church Psalter and Hymn Book*, 1854

Attrib. to John Francis Wade (ca. 1711-1786)
Wade manuscript, ca. 1743
Samuel Webbe's *Essay on the Church Plain Chant*, 1st ed., 1782

Though the origins of this hymn were long a mystery, John Stephan (*Adeste Fideles: A Study on Its Origin and Development*, Buckfast Abbey, 1947) has provided extensive evidence that John Wade wrote both the text and tune of this very familiar carol. It has been found in several manuscripts bearing Wade's signature, including the earliest dated around 1743.

Wade was a musician and copyist in the Catholic center (Office de St. Omer) of Douay, France, where many English religious and political dissidents found refuge. There he provided calligraphy and music manuscripts for Catholic chapels and families, among them this "guided tour" of Jesus' birth.

The second stanza, part of the Nicene Creed that explains the nature of Christ, is a bit of teaching commentary along the way of the tour. It is from the later Office de St. Omer (1822), almost certainly by Abbé Etienne Jean François Borderies, who was consecrated bishop of Versailles in 1827.

Oakeley's translation of 1841 begins "Ye faithful, approach ye." In his *Hymnal* Murray revises the opening phrase to its present form.

The tune name ADESTE FIDELES is the same as the opening words of the original Latin hymn. It appears in triple meter in all the earliest manuscripts; then Webbe published the melody in duple meter in 1782, and ten years later it appeared in a four-part setting in his *Collection of Motetts or Antiphons*. The refrain is an example of a "fuguing tune," popular in the nineteenth-century singing schools, in which voices enter the tune in imitation of each other. For additional comments on fuguing tunes, see "Lord of the worlds above" (**39**).

68
O come, loud anthems let us sing — SALISBURY

Based on Psalm 95
Tate and Brady's *New Version of the Psalms of David,* 1696
Refrain added from Isaac Watts's Psalm 104

Anonymous
"Haydn" in Lowell Mason's *Boston Handel and Haydn Society Collection of Church Music,* 1822

This text is a metrical paraphrase of Psalm 95, one of many versions of the psalter. Thomas Sternhold (1500-1549) may have been the first to adapt the meter of popular ballads for use in psalter singing, in the hopes that the courtiers of Henry VIII "would sing them rather than their amorous and obscene songs" (Oyer 1980).

Because sixteenth- and seventeenth-century religious hymnwriters were restricted by custom and decree to the texts of the psalms, they exerted their creativity in producing different versions. By 1696 Nahum Tate and Nicholas Brady had come out with yet another psalter, the *New Version . . . ,* in which Psalm 95 had ten stanzas (eleven in the 1703 edition). This relegated the psalter produced by Sternhold and Hopkins to the status of "Old Version." The added refrain by Watts comes from his *The Psalms of David . . .* (1719).

The tune SALISBURY was spelled SALSBURY in the earliest known source where it is ascribed to the name "Haydn." In *Hymn-Tunes of Lowell Mason,* the tune is listed under "Hymn-tune arrangements" where it is dated 1819, with the *Boston . . . Collection of Church Music* (1822) as its printed source. In this volume the tune is the middle voice of three-part harmony. This harmony is provided with a figured bass (numbers to indicate chords for the keyboard player).

172

O come, O come, Immanuel VENI EMMANUEL

Veni, veni Emmanuel
Anonymous
Versification, 12th c., of antiphon, 6th-7th c.
Sts. 1-4, tr. John Mason Neale (1818-1866)
Neale's *Medieval Hymns and Sequences*, 1851
Rev. in *Hymns Ancient and Modern*, 1861
Sts. 5-6, tr. Henry Sloane Coffin (1877-1954)
Coffin's *Hymns of the Kingdom of God*,1916.

Trope melody, 15th c.
Manuscript 10581, Bibliotheque Nationale, Paris
The Hymnal Noted, Part II, 1854

This text is based on seven Latin texts known as the "Great Antiphons," or "Great O's," since each begins with the word "O." Each antiphon heralds the coming of the Messiah with an Old Testament name, and each one ends with a petition based on the greeting. These antiphons, possibly in use before the seventh century, were said before and after the Magnificat (Song of Mary) at Vespers, one each day from December 17 to 23. The order of their use is as follows:

O come, thou Wisdom (st. 5)
O come, O come, thou Lord of might, who to thy tribes, on Sinai's height, in ancient times didst give the law in cloud and majesty and awe. (here omitted)
O come, thou Rod of Jesse (st. 2)
O come, thou Key of David (st. 4)
O come, thou Dayspring (st. 3)
O come, Desire of nations (st. 6)
O come, O come, Immanuel (st. 1)

In the Middle Ages, the custom was for each of the principal officers in a monastery to "keep his O" by singing it and then providing some gift or feast for the monks. Such gifts might include providing for "figs and walnuts against Lent" or keeping a fire going in the common house hall (*The Hymnal 1940 Companion*, 1951 ed.).

The metrical version of the text, which dates to the twelfth century, is the basis for these translations. Its first known source is the 1710 appendix to *Psalteriolum Cantionum Catholicarum*. Neale's translation, which begins "Draw nigh, Draw nigh, Emmanuel," was altered by the compilers of *Hymns Ancient and Modern* (1861). Stanza 5 of that translation, which does not refer to Christ, has been omitted. Two stanzas of Henry Sloane Coffin's later translation, found in *The Brethren Hymnal* (1951) and others, are added. There is no Latin equivalent to the refrain.

Today's version of VENI EMMANUEL is taken from Thomas Helmore's tune adaptation in *The Hymnal Noted*, Part II, where it is marked

"From a French missal in the National Library, Lisbon"; however, no identical tune has been found there (*The Hymnal 1940 Companion*, 1951 ed.). The mystery of the melody's origin continued until the September 1966 *Musical Times* reported its discovery by Mother Thomas More in a manuscript used by a community of French Franciscan nuns. There it appears with a fifteenth-century trope, added to the funeral responsory *Libera me.*

370
O day of God, draw nigh — BELLWOODS

Robert Balgornie Young Scott (1899-1987)
Leaflet, Fellowship for a Christian Social Order, 1937
Hymns for Worship, 1939, alt.

James Hopkirk (1908-1972)
Book of Common Praise (Canadian), 1938

Though this hymn refers to the gathering fury of World War II, it is timeless in its call for peace and God's reign on earth. Echoing the description of the prophet Isaiah, it portrays the "day of God" as a day not only of judgment but also of salvation. After the text's first appearance, the last stanza was rewritten by the author. The original is:

O Day of God, bring nigh
Thy bright and shining light,
To rise resplendent on the world
And drive away the night.

BELLWOODS, with its varying lengths of measures, is "the most unusual tune" in the *Book of Common Praise* (Routley 1981). It was composed for the familiar text "Bless'd be the tie that binds" (**421**).

408
O day of peace — JERUSALEM

Carl Pickens Daw, Jr. (1944-)
The Hymnal 1982, 1985

Charles Hubert Hastings Parry (1848-1918), 1916
Harm. by Richard Proulx (1937-), 1986

Asked to create a peace text to fit the tune JERUSALEM, the author took his customary approach, playing the tune over and over on numerous instruments for several days. Still dry, he tried reading instead. Coming across a quotation of Isaiah 11:6-8 in Urban T. Holmes III's *Turning to Christ*, he found the heart of the hymn he was trying to write. Thus, the second stanza is a paraphrase of Isaiah 11:6-9, adapted to the rhythmic and melodic patterns of the Parry tune. The first stanza then evolved as a prayer for the peaceful existence described in stanza 2. Although the text "affirms that peace is always God's gift, it also recognizes the importance of human responsibility in preparing an environment in which peace can flourish" (Daw 1990).

JERUSALEM was composed for a poem of the same name by William Blake (1757-1827). The poem, referring to Christ, begins:

And did those feet in ancient time
Walk upon England's mountains green?

When Robert Bridges suggested that Parry compose "suitable simple music" for Blake's poem, Parry complied and presented his manuscript to Walford Davies with the remark, "Here's a tune for you, old chap. Do what you like with it" (Dearmer 1933).

JERUSALEM was first sung in Albert Hall, London, in 1916, at a great service of thanksgiving when women's suffrage became law. As a result, it achieved the status of a new national anthem and soon became the National Hymn of the Federation of Music Competition Festivals. *A Student's Hymnal* (1923) was the first hymnbook to include the tune.

641
O day of rest and gladness — MENDEBRAS

Christopher Wordsworth (1807-1885)
The Holy Year, or Hymns for Sundays and Holydays, 1862, alt.

German melody
Adapt. by Lowell Mason (1792-1872)
Modern Psalmist, 1839

This hymn, titled "Sunday," was hymn No. 1 in Wordsworth's *Holy Year* . . . . Three of the original six stanzas have been omitted. The last stanza, greatly altered over the years, originally read:

May we, new graces gaining
From this our day of rest,
Attain the rest remaining
To spirits of the blest;
And there our voice upraising
To Father and to Son,
And Holy Ghost, be praising
Ever the Three-in-One.

The author takes poetic license in stanza 2:1, implying that the "day of rest" was also the day that light was created, thus lumping the first and seventh days of creation together. Using the imagery of light, the conclusion of the stanza pulls together three great biblical events.

MENDEBRAS is one of a number of anonymous German melodies that made their way into North American hymnals. In Mason's *Modern Psalmist*, it is the setting for "I love thy kingdom, Lord" (**308**). When the tune appeared in Mason and Webb's *Psaltery* in 1845, it was changed to its 76.76D form and set to the text "The gloomy night of sadness." In a radical departure from that text theme, it eventually became associated with this text in Robinson's *Songs for the Sanctuary* (1865).

155
O God, great womb — BIXEL

Harris J. Loewen (1953-), 1982
Assembly Songs, 1983

James W. Bixel (1913-)
(same source as text)

As a student at Associated Mennonite Biblical Seminaries, Elkhart, Indiana, Loewen was providing instrumental accompaniment for another student's project in a church-music class. As she presented a series of readings about creation and images of God, Loewen was inspired to explore the feminine images linked with various biblical allusions to creation.

The resulting text loosely parallels the biblical order of creation, beginning with God's transformation of chaos, illumination with light, the seeds of plant and animal life, the conception of humanity, and the sabbath rest. In the last stanza, a play on words alludes to the continuing character of creation, the groaning labor of a world waiting for the fulfillment of Jesus Christ (Rom. 8:22-23).

Loewen's hymn, written in a standard meter, was first sung at the conclusion of the reading series with the plainsong melody SPLENDOR PATERNAE (see "O splendor of God's glory bright," **646**), an ancient tune style that parallels the primal nature of his text.

Mary K. Oyer, in preparing *Assembly Songs* for the Mennonite Bethlehem '83 General Assembly, sent this text to composer James Bixel. The pulsating rhythmic movement of his music captures a sense of the energy present both in creation and in Loewen's words: "pulsing, lighted world," "seething ferment's energy," "whirling waltz of life."

557
O God, in restless living — RUTHERFORD

Harry Emerson Fosdick (1878-1969), 1931

Edward Francis Rimbault (1816-1876)
Psalms and Hymns for Divine Worship, 1867

This text, found in relatively few hymnals, has become a favorite among Brethren since its inclusion in *The Brethren Hymnal* (1951). It applies the theme of peace to the personal dimension, the beginning point of true peace.

RUTHERFORD is more frequently associated with the hymn "The sands of time are sinking." It is named for Samuel Rutherford, whose writings form the basis of that text. Some sources say the melody comes from the earlier *Chants Cretien* (1834) and was only arranged by Rimbault, cited above. The gradually descending harmony in the tenor of the third line has the same quieting effect as the text.

368
O God of love, O Power of peace — TALLIS' CANON

Henry Williams Baker (1821-1877)
Hymns Ancient and Modern, 1861, alt.
St. 1 adapt. by Ruth C. Duck, 1980

Thomas Tallis (ca. 1505-1585)
Parker's *The Whole Psalter Translated into English Metre,* ca. 1567

This eloquent plea for peace first appeared in a hymnal section titled "In Times of Trouble" and a subsection called "War." The present stanza 1 is a 1980 adaptation by Ruth Duck; the original was:

> O God of love, O King of peace
> make wars throughout the world to cease.
> The wrath of sinful man restrain—
> give peace, O God, give peace again.

The concluding stanzas are the third and fourth of the original, with "Thy" changed to "your" and, in the final stanza, "knit" to "joined."

The tune TALLIS' CANON was chosen for the serenity of its melody and the interweaving of voices, befitting a peace hymn. These words were set to the tune ROCKINGHAM in *The Mennonite Hymnal* (1969) and to QUEBEC/HESPERUS in *The Brethren Hymnal* (1951).

For comments on TALLIS' CANON, see "All praise to thee, my God" (**658**).

130
O God of mystery and might — O GOD OF MYSTERY

Kenneth I. Morse (1913-), 1970
Messenger, Feb. 1, 1971, alt.

Wilbur E. Brumbaugh (1931-1977), 1970
(same source as text), alt.

This hymn was written when both the author and composer were on the editorial staff of *Messenger,* a denominational publication of the Church of the Brethren. Morse explains his intent:

> The text falls into the pattern of parallel concepts of God, made evident in the beginning phrases of stanzas 1 and 3, "mystery and might" and "tenderness and trust." In relation to the transcendence of God, a worshiper is overawed by the distance and feels the need to grasp and understand the "messages" God sends. In relation to the immanence of God, the worshiper senses nearness and the possibility of a close relationship. The hymn suggests appropriate responses to each aspect of God.

After its first printing in *Messenger,* the hymn was included in *The Brethren Songbook* (1974). In stanza 3:2, the original "our brother's pain" is now "each other's pain." Musically, the unison beginning creates a vastness and strength that undergirds the text.

328
O God, our help in ages past

ST. ANNE

Based on Psalm 90
Isaac Watts (1674-1748)
The Psalms of David Imitated in the Language of the New Testament, 1719, alt.

Attrib. to William Croft (1678-1727)
Supplement to the New Version of the Psalms by Dr. Brady and Mr. Tate, 6th ed., 1708

It is said that this hymn was written in 1714 when it was feared that the Protestant monarchy of England's Queen Anne would be followed by that of her Catholic brother, with ensuing religious persecution. It was in this tenuous political climate that Watts paraphrased Psalm 90, a prayer for deliverance in national adversity. About twenty-five years later, John Wesley took the liberty of changing Watts's original "Our God, our help" to "O God, our help." Most hymnals use only selected stanzas of the original nine.

ST. ANNE was first published as an anonymous tune set to Psalm 42. William Croft, believed to have been the musical editor for the *Supplement to the New Version . . . ,* likely took the tune name from the church St. Anne, in Soho, London, where he was organist at the time. The tune was first attributed to Croft by Philip Hart in 1719 and then by John Church in 1723 in their collections of psalmody. The authorship of this tune has been disputed, but the 1708 source presently prevails as the earliest.[1]

1. For a fuller discussion, see Grove's *Dictionary of Music and Musicians,* 5th ed., Vol. VII.

376
O God, thou faithful God

O GOTT, DU FROMMER GOTT (DARMSTADT)

O Gott, du frommer Gott
Johann Heermann (1585-1647)
Heermann's *Devoti Musica Cordis,* Breslau, 1630
Tr. Catherine Winkworth (1827-1878)
Lyra Germanica, Series II, 1858, alt.

A. Fritsch's *Himmels-Lust und Welt-Unlust,* Jena, 1679
Harm. by Johann Sebastian Bach (1685-1750)
Cantata No. 45, 1726

This hymn, considered by some a primer in practical Christianity, has been called Heermann's "master song." A. F. W. Fischer writes: "If it is somewhat 'home baked' yet it is excellent nourishing bread. It . . . especially strikes three notes—godly living, patient suffering, and happy dying" (Loewen, Moyer, Oyer 1983). Just as it was originally titled, it serves well as "a daily prayer."

The original hymn consists of eight stanzas of eight lines each. Over the years some alterations have been made to Winkworth's translation and may be compared to the present version: stanza 1:5-6 was "A pure and healthy frame O give me, and within," and the last part of stanza 2 was "with all my strength and bless the work I thus have wrought, for thou must give success." Stanza 3 now begins: "When dangers gather round" rather than "If dangers gather round."

O GOTT, DU FROMMER GOTT was originally set to the text *Die Wollust dieser Welt* by J. J. Schütz. *Himmels-Lust . . .*, the source of the tune, was edited by Ahasuerus Fritsch (1629-1701), an official at the court of Count Albert Anton von Schwarzburg-Rudolstadt. Whether Fritsch wrote the melody or whether it was the first melody to be used with this text is not known. The tune also is called DARMSTADT from its use in the 1698 Darmstadt *Geistreiches Gesangbuch* where it took on a musical form closer to the present one. The harmonization is from Bach's Cantata No. 45. Bach also uses the melody in his Cantata Nos. 64, 128, and 129, and it is similar to the final chorus of Cantata No. 94, *Was frag' ich nach der Welt*, the text to which it was set in the Darmstadt collection.

483
O God, who gives us life — GRACIOUS GIFT

Carl Pickens Daw, Jr. (1944-), 1989
A Year of Grace, 1990

Jonathan Adin Shively (1967-), 1991
Hymnal: A Worship Book, 1992

This text was written to provide a Lenten hymn based on images in Hebrew scripture. The first stanza refers both to creation and to the new creation, reflecting Jeremiah 31:31-34 and Isaiah 43:18-19. Then, in stanzas 2 and 3, as God called out Abraham and led the Israelites in the wilderness, so may we too be led and refreshed today. This is the first hymnal to include the text.

Rejecting existing tunes in favor of a new sound for a contemporary text, the music committee for this hymnal solicited tunes. This hymn appealed to the composer, then a theology student, as one which "speaks directly to God's love for us and graciousness toward us." Just as the text calls God's people "to venture and to dare" (st. 2:2-3), so the music contains a surprise element in the fifth measure from the end, where the melody holds C-sharp for a second beat, instead of moving immediately to the D.

The tune name GRACIOUS GIFT has several associations: God's gift of grace; the gift of music; and a free translation of the Hebrew meaning of the composer's name, Jonathan, "gift of God." Though this tune is eminently singable, Daw suggests KINGSFOLD as a more traditional alternative.

481
O God, your constant care
WAREHAM

H. Glen Lanier (1925-1978)
Pamphlet, *Ten New Hymns on Aging and the Later Years,* 1976

William Knapp (ca. 1698-1768)
A Sett of New Psalm Tunes and Anthems, 1738

This text was written for a hymn search by the Hymn Society of America (HSA) for hymns to "celebrate the later years of life and the meaning of aging." The search was conducted in cooperation with the National Retired Teachers Association and the American Association of Retired Persons. Among some twelve hundred submissions, this text was one of ten to be published in the HSA pamphlet cited above. Although it speaks to the topic of aging, this text rejoices in the care God gives us through "each day of life," making it an appropriate hymn for people of any age.

For comments on WAREHAM, see "Great God, we sing" (**639**).

33
O Gott Vater
AUS TIEFER NOT

Leenaerdt Clock, 16th-17th c.
Ausbund, early 17th c.

Kirchenampt, Strassburg, 1525
(Zahn No. 4438a)

"O Gott Vater" has been included in this hymnal because it is the longest continuously used hymn in the Protestant tradition from the longest continuously used hymnal in the Protestant tradition. The first of four stanzas of *O Gott Vater, wir loben dich* appears in this hymnal with notation representative of the very slow, embellished manner of singing of the Amish. The notation is based on those by J. W. Yoder in *Amische Lieder* (1940) and Olen F. Yoder in *Ausbund Songs with Notes* (1984). The German text of this Anabaptist hymn, called the *Lobg'sang* (song of praise) by the Amish, is the second hymn in every Amish service. Mennonite hymnologist Mary K. Oyer has adapted this hymn to the singing style of the Amish living a few miles east of Goshen, Indiana.

For other comments on this text, see the English version, "Our Father God, thy name we praise" (**32**).

Every pitch of the original chorale tune can be found within the ornamentation of each syllable. "To sing all four verses takes twenty minutes in some of the most conservative Amish communities, while in some places it is sung in eleven minutes. Amish music reflects culture, and the speed of singing can be positively correlated with a degree of assimilation" (J. Hostetler 1963).

This melody, used in *The Mennonite Hymnal* (1969) with the text "Out of the depths," is different from the AUS TIEFER NOT associated with "Out of the depths I cry to you" (**133**) in this hymnal.

372

O healing river

(no tune name)

Anonymous

Traditional North American hymn melody

This hymn readily lends itself to services of baptism, anointing, and healing. It is very effective when sung antiphonally, with a single voice leading and the congregation responding with the same music and text. This hymn is referred to as a "traditional Baptist hymn" in the Catholic publication *Gather* (1988), despite the fact that it has not been found in any Baptist hymnals. A keyboard arrangement and instrumental part are found in the *Accompaniment Handbook.*

291

O Holy Spirit, by whose breath

ST. BARTHOLOMEW

Veni Creator Spiritus
Attrib. to Rabanus Maurus, 9th c.
Tr. John Webster Grant (1919-)
Hymn Book (Canada), 1971, alt.

Henry Duncalf (18th c.)
Parochial Harmony, 1762

The origins of *Veni Creator Spiritus* are discussed with "Come, O Creator Spirit, come" (**27**), the translation by Robert Bridges that is paired with the plainsong melody. This Latin text has been the subject of numerous translations; this one was written by Grant, a member of the editorial committee of the Canadian *Hymn Book.* Only the first two lines of the final doxological stanza have been altered.

Nothing is known of the composer of ST. BARTHOLOMEW except that he was organist of St. Bartholomew's, a famous church in London.

300

O Holy Spirit, making whole

MELITA

Henry Hallam Tweedy (1868-1953)
Christian Worship and Praise, 1939, alt.

John Bacchus Dykes (1823-1876)
Hymns Ancient and Modern, 1861

This text appears in only two of the seventy-eight hymnals surveyed in Diehl's *Hymns and Tunes—an Index.* Those two are *The Brethren Hymnal* (1951) and Tweedy's own compilation, *Christian Worship and Praise* (1939), published under the auspices of the Reformed Church in America. In Tweedy's volume the text, dated 1932, is set to this same tune. The closing phrase of each stanza "Christ shall rule the hearts of men, And Pentecost shall come again!" has been changed to "Christ shall rule in every heart, and Pentecost its power impart." The fifth stanza, which has been omitted, reads:

> So shall youth's visions be fulfilled,
> As here on earth thy heaven we build!
> So shall there come that shining peace,
> When wrath and war and woe shall cease,
> And Christ shall rule . . . .

MELITA was written by John B. Dykes for the text "Eternal Father, Strong to Save," with which it appears in the original music edition of *Hymns Ancient and Modern*. The tune name is derived from the ancient name of the island of Malta where Paul was shipwrecked (Acts 28:1-2).

123
O Holy Spirit, Root of life — HEALER

Based on the writings of Hildegard of Bingen
Jean Wiebe Janzen (1933-), 1991
Hymnal: A Worship Book, 1992

Leonard Jacob Enns (1948-), 1989
(same source as text)

Janzen's text is based on writings of the spiritual leader Hildegard of Bingen (1098-1179). Hildegard was a woman ahead of her time, whose accomplishments included painting; the composition of more than seventy songs; an opera, which first appeared around 1600; and writings on science, theology, and healing. Like the biblical story of Samuel, Hildegard's parents offered her as a gift to God. From the age of eight, she was tutored by Jutta of Spanheim, leader of the women's cloister, which was part of the Benedictine monastic community in the diocese of Mainz (Germany). In 1136, when Jutta died, Hildegard became the leader of her community. In 1151, four years after leaving the famous Disibode monastery, she and her sisters moved into a new cloister near the present-day town of Bingen (Fox 1987).

It has only been in recent years that Hildegard's works have been translated into English. Inspired by those writings, poet Jean Janzen has expanded the way she imagines the Holy Spirit. "With these metaphors," writes Janzen, "the Spirit intertwines actively within the Trinity, celebrating union with all life and our longings."

Leonard Enns composed this tune for "O Christ, the healer" (**379**), one of several texts sent to composers in a call for new hymn tunes. Although HEALER was not written for this text, its rhythmic structure and gentle mood are well suited to these words.

404
O Jesus Christ, may grateful hymns — CITY OF GOD

Bradford Gray Webster (1898-1991)
Five New Hymns of the City, 1954, alt.

Daniel Moe (1926-), 1956
Published as an anthem, 1957

This text was the first choice from hymns submitted to the Hymn Society of America for the Convocation on Urban Life in America, called by the Council of Bishops of the Methodist Church. Five were chosen and published in a folder for a convocation held in Columbus, Ohio, in February of 1964.

Webster's first stanza acknowledges the role of worship in preparing hearts for the service described in stanza 2. Stanza 3 is replete with scriptural imagery: the brooding, haunting life-force of God's Spirit; Jesus' "love and pity" for individuals reaching for healing (Matt. 9:20-22), as well as for the woes of an entire city (Matt. 23:37).

For the convocation mentioned above, this text was set to a familiar tune O PERFECT LOVE (SANDRINGHAM). Daniel Moe, not convinced that the gentle character of that tune was suitable for the demands of Webster's text, composed CITY OF GOD. This strong, contemporary setting was arranged as an anthem, and the tune has since been included in *Contemporary Worship—I* (1969), *The Mennonite Hymnal* (1969), and the *Lutheran Book of Worship* (1978).

447
O Jesus, I have promised — ANGEL'S STORY

John Ernest Bode (1816-1874)
Leaflet, 1868
Psalms and Hymns, Appendix, 1869

Arthur Henry Mann (1850-1929)
The Methodist Sunday School Hymn Book, 1881

As he prepared for the confirmation of his daughter and two sons, John Bode, pastor of the parish, composed a six-stanza prayer of commitment that begins "O Jesus, we have promised." The English Society for Promoting Christian Knowledge (SPCK) published it first in *Psalms and Hymns, Appendix,* connecting it with the scripture "Lord, I will follow thee whithersoever thou goest" (Luke 9:57). Stanzas 4 and 6, usually omitted, pick up the sense of sight while the others dwell on feeling and hearing:

> O let me see thy features,
> The look that once could make
> So many a true disciple
> Leave all things for thy sake:
> The look that beamed on Peter
> When he thy name denied;

The look that draws thy lovers
Close to thy pierced side.

O let me see thy foot-marks
And in them plant mine own;
My hope to follow duly
Is in thy strength alone.
O guide me, call me, draw me,
Uphold me to the end;
And then in heaven receive me,
My Saviour and my friend.

ANGEL'S STORY, also called WATERMOUTH and SUPPLICATION, was composed for the hymn "I love to hear the story which angel voices tell," by Emily H. Miller. The tune NYLAND (in the *Accompaniment Handbook*) is a good alternative, fitting the challenge of Bode's call to service and stewardship.

146
O Lamb of God all holy

O Lamm Gottes unschuldig
Based on Agnus Dei
Nicolaus Decius (ca. 1485-ca. 1546), ca. 1522
Geystlyke Leder, Rostock, 1531
Tr. Arthur Tozer Russell (1806-1874)
Sts. 1-2, *German Hospital Collection*, 1848
St. 3, Russell's *Psalms and Hymns*, 1851

O LAMM GOTTES

Based on a Gregorian melody
Nicolaus Decius (ca. 1485-ca. 1546)
Christliche Kirchen-Ordnung, Erfurt, 1542

The *Agnus Dei* is based on the words of John the Baptist, "Behold the Lamb of God, who takes away the sin of the world" (John 1:29). It was introduced into the liturgy of the Mass in the time of Pope Sergius I (687-701). Its three repetitions, fully written out here so as to discourage "shortcuts," allow time and space for introspection. During the eleventh century, the ending of the third repetition was changed to *dona nobis pacem*, here translated "Thy peace be with us." The third line, which reads "Our sins by thee were taken, or hope had us forsaken," may be better understood as "You took on our sins; otherwise we would be without hope." For more on the *Agnus Dei*, see "O Christ, the Lamb of God" (**153**).

The melody O LAMM GOTTES is based on an earlier plainsong associated with the *Agnus Dei* text. The arrangement in this form is generally attributed to Decius. The collection in which it appeared was prepared for use in Calenberg and Göttingen, principalities over which Elisabeth, Duchess of Brunswick-Lüneburg, was regent. J. S. Bach used the melody in a number of works, including his *Passion According to St. Matthew*.

495

O let all who thirst

Based on Isaiah 55:1-2 and Matthew 11:28-30
John B. Foley, S.J. (1939-), 1974
Wood Hath Hope, 1978

COME TO THE WATER

John B. Foley, S.J. (1939-)
(same source as text)
Harm. rev., 1991

In the summer of 1974, five Jesuit composers gathered in Berkeley, California, to write and critique each other's work. This piece was one of the happy results of that event. Later, at a national convention in 1983, a speaker charting the history of Roman Catholic music since the liturgical movement commented that "Come to the Water" was squarely within the early American Protestant style. "Imagine the response of some Protestant historian in the future," he said, "discovering that this (by then) traditional hymn was written not only by a Catholic, but by a Jesuit!"

The song was released in 1978 on the composer's recording *Wood Hath Hope* and was later printed in a collection of the same name. Originally published as a unison song in the key of F major, it has been arranged here for four-part singing. Other instrumental accompaniments are in the *Accompaniment Handbook*.

489

O little children, gather

Ach Kinder, wollt ihr lieben
Christopher Dock (d. 1771)
Geistliches Magazien, after 1764
Tr. Alice Parker (1925-), 1962
Come, Let Us Join, 1966, alt.

BEAUTIFUL FLOWER

The Philharmonia, 1875
Arr. by Alice Parker (1925-)
(same source as translation)

This text is one of several Christopher Dock hymns that Alice Parker translated and arranged under a commission by Hiram Hershey for the Franconia Chorus, Souderton, Pennsylvania. This text is dated "after 1764," since the years of publication for Christopher Sauer's *Geistliches Magazien* in which it appeared were 1764-1773. *Assembly Songs*, which includes S. W. Pennypacker's translation of the text "O children, may you cherish," places it around 1770.

Although the English version is not a strict translation of the German, it retains the spirit of the original words in an inviting way. Parker updated her work for this hymnal. The text, reminiscent of Jesus' words in Luke 18:16-17, is appropriate for children of all ages and reveals the philosophy and piety of this important early American educator.

To set Christopher Dock's texts, Parker chose tunes from *The Philharmonia*, a Mennonite collection published in Elkhart, Indiana, by Lancaster County (Pa.) native Martin D. Wenger. This lilting melody is arranged for four-part *a cappella* singing. First published in a small collection, these hymns were later incorporated into Parker's 1967 cantata *Christopher Dock.*

191
O little town of Bethlehem

ST. LOUIS

Phillips Brooks (1835-1893)
Brooks manuscript, 1868
Huntingdon's *The Church Porch . . . ,* 1874

Lewis Henry Redner (1830 or 1831-1908)
Redner manuscript, 1868
(same source as text)

The text of this carol is believed to have been inspired by a trip to the Holy Land. Thinking back to his Christmas trip two years earlier, Brooks wrote these verses for a children's hymn, using as his setting the fields around Bethlehem, the traditional site of the angels' appearance to the shepherds the night Jesus was born. Long before Brooks became a famous preacher, this Christmas program collaboration with his organist, Lewis Redner, resulted in a widely loved hymn.

Originally in five stanzas, the hymn's fourth is usually omitted:

> Where children pure and happy pray to the blessed Child;
> Where misery cries out to thee, Son of the mother mild;
> Where charity stands watching and faith holds wide the door
> The dark night wakes, and glory breaks,
> And Christmas comes once more.

"In great haste" Redner set the text to music on Christmas Eve of 1868. Six years later the text and tune were published in *The Church Porch, a Service Book and Hymnal for Sunday Schools,* which was prepared by William R. Huntingdon. He named the tune ST. LOUIS, possibly as a homonym for the composer's first name (Young 1993). This text is sometimes sung to the tune FOREST GREEN.

348
O Lord, hear my prayer

(no tune name)

Based on Psalm 102:1-2
Music from Taizé, Vol. II, 1982, 1983, 1984

Jacques Berthier (1923-)
(same source as text)

This eight-measure call to prayer can also function as a response following prayer. Without the repeat it also would work well as a refrain in a litany. Typical of the Taizé musical resources, the text, melody, and harmony parts are all readily committed to memory. For further comments on the Taizé community, see "Allelluia" (**101**).

635
O Lord of life, wherever they be

Frederick Lucian Hosmer (1840-1929), 1888
"Chicago Unity"
The Thoughts of God in Hymns and Poems, 2nd series, 1894

VICTORY

Giovanni Pierluigi da Palestrina (ca. 1525-1594)
"Gloria Patri" from *Magnificat in the Third Mode,* 1591
Adapt. by William Henry Monk (1823-1889)
Hymns Ancient and Modern, 1861

This hymn text was written for an Easter service conducted in the author's Church of Unity, Cleveland, Ohio. It was intended for the stirring tune VICTORY and includes one "Alleluia" at the end of each stanza. "Requiem," in stanza 3:2, is the first word of the Mass of the Dead (thus known as Requiem Mass) and is Latin for "rest."

VICTORY is adapted from the choral work specified above, which can be seen in Breitkopf and Härtel's edition of Palestrina's *Werke, XXVII,* 14.

Monk took two phrases from Palestrina, repeated the first, and composed music for the "alleluia" sections at the beginning and the end. For Hosmer's text the beginning "alleluias" are omitted.

112
O Lord, our Lord, how majestic

Based on Psalm 8
Michael W. Smith (1957-), 1981

HOW MAJESTIC IS YOUR NAME

Michael W. Smith (1957-), 1981
Arr. by Martha Buckwalter Hershberger (1927-), 1990

A newly committed Christian, Smith got inspiration from the Psalms to express his enthusiastic love for God. This acclamation of praise takes its cue from the opening and closing words of Psalm 8. It was Smith's first attempt at this kind of songwriting. The contemporary Christian song is known by the title "How Majestic Is Your Name," which is used here as the tune name. The four-part arrangement of Smith's melody was made by Hershberger for this hymnal, and a separate keyboard part may be found in the *Accompaniment Handbook.*

236

O love, how deep, how broad

DEO GRACIAS

Apparuit benignitas
Attrib. To Thomas à Kempis (ca. 1380-1471)
Karlsruhe manuscript 368, 15th c.
Tr. Benjamin Webb (1819-1885)
The Hymnal Noted, 1851, alt.

English melody, 15th c.
"The Agincourt Song"

This hymn originated in an anonymous Latin hymn of twenty-three rhymed stanzas,[1] though it is sometimes attributed to Thomas à Kempis. Such conjecture is based on its affinity with the *moderna devotio* movement with which he was associated.

Webb promoted his English translation as a hymn for Sundays after Epiphany, the season celebrating the earthly ministry of Christ. The most widely used stanzas of this translation include Christ's incarnation, baptism, fasting and temptation, teaching and daily works, intercession and suffering. Some hymnals include a stanza on Christ's resurrection and ascension, as well as the descent of the Holy Spirit:

> For us he rose from death again;
> for us he went on high to reign;
> for us he sent his Spirit here
> to guide, to comfort, and to cheer.

Thus, we have a hymn for all seasons, and stanzas appropriate to specific celebrations could also be used individually.

DEO GRACIAS was the melody sung to a ballad celebrating the victory of King Henry V of England over the French at Agincourt in 1415. The king, however, insisted that credit be given to God instead; hence the words *Deo gratias* (thanks be to God). Following the Latin refrain *Deo gratias, Anglia, redde pro victoria*, the first stanza is:

> Our king went forth to Normandy,
> With grace and might and chivalry:
> There God for him wrought marv'lously
> Wherefore England may call and cry: Deo gracias.
> (Loewen, Moyer, Oyer 1983)

Like the boisterous event for which it was first sung, DEO GRACIAS is a vigorous tune in the Dorian mode (the scale on the white keys of the piano from D to D). The present hymn tune does not include the music of the refrain since there is no text refrain. The complete tune has been published in vocal arrangements[2] as "The Agincourt Song," and an organ version is ascribed to John Dunstable (ca. 1370-1453). It is believed that Dunstable was in the service of the Chapel Royal and could have authored "The Agincourt Song." The music of this song was adapted as a hymn for *The English Hymnal* (1906).

Early English sources for DEO GRACIAS include a parchment roll "dating from the first half of the fifteenth century and a manuscript in the Bodleian Library at Oxford, coming probably from the mid-fifteenth century"[3] (Stulken 1981).

1. The complete Latin text is found in *The Hymnal 1940 Companion.*

2. Oxford University Press: one by Arthur S. Warrell in *Oxford Choral Songs* for male voices, 1928; and another by Healey Willan for mixed voices, 1929

3. The first manuscript is transcribed with a quotation of the full ballad text in J. A. Fuller-Maitland's *English Carols of the Fifteenth Century*, 1891, and the second is given with extensive notes in John Stainer's *Early Bodleian Music*, 1901. Noted in *Hymnal Companion to the Lutheran Book of Worship*

326
O Love of God — ALFRETON

Horatius N. Bonar (1808-1889)
Hymns of Faith and Hope, Second Series, 1861, alt.

William Beastall
Allen's *New York Selection of Sacred Music*, 1818

This beautiful text uses a wealth of adjectives to describe the love of God, which is evident not only in the natural world, but also in the life and death of Christ. The first two stanzas and part of the third are one long address to this Love, which *is* God. In the final two stanzas, Bonar certifies the power of God's love to overcome the "darkness of the grave" with "resurrection light" and to serve as "our shield and stay." Of Bonar's complete text of ten stanzas, those used here are stanzas 1, 3, 4, 5, 9, and 10. The archaic forms of address have been changed, and stanza 4:2, "sent by the Father from on high," is now "sent from the Fount of love on high."

ALFRETON appeared in Allen's *New York Selection . . .* in the key of F with the melody in the tenor. Each line was extended by two additional beats. The tune in its original key is in Joseph Funk's *Harmonia Sacra*, 13th ed. (1869), with "O thou to whose all-searching sight."

577
O Love that will not let me go — ST. MARGARET

George Matheson (1842-1906), 1882
Life and Work: Record of the Church of Scotland, January 1883

Albert Lister Peace (1844-1912), 1884
Scottish Hymnal, 1885

Matheson was alone in the parsonage of Innellan, Argyllshire, the evening of June 6, 1882. He writes:

> It was the day of my sister's marriage, and the rest of the family were staying overnight in Glasgow. Something had happened to me, which was known only to myself, and which caused me the

> most severe mental suffering. The hymn was the fruit of that suffering. It was the quickest bit of work I ever did in my life. I had the impression rather of having it dictated to me by some inward voice than of working it out myself. I am quite sure that the whole work was completed in five minutes, and equally sure that it never received at my hands any retouching or correction. (Haeussler 1952)

The hymnal committee of the Church of Scotland, however, *did* ask for a retouching on "I *climb* the rainbow in the rain." Matheson obliged them by changing the word to "trace."

Though Matheson never elaborated on the nature of the suffering that birthed this hymn, it may have been either his increasing blindness or the breakup with his fiancée over his impairment. At any rate, he considered it his masterwork of hymnwriting. "I have no natural gift of rhythm," he complained. "All the other verses I have written are manufactured articles; this came like a dayspring from on high. I have never been able to gain once more the same fervor in verse" (Bailey 1950).

Albert Peace, musical editor of that 1855 *Scottish Hymnal,* composed ST. MARGARET at the request of the same hymnal committee. The music came to him with much the same speed as the text had come to Matheson, for "the ink of the first note was hardly dry when [he] had finished the tune" (Haeussler 1952).

357
O Master, let me walk with thee — MARYTON

Washington Gladden (1836-1918)
Magazine, *Sunday Afternoon,* 1879
C. H. Richards' *Christian Praise,* 1880

Henry Percy Smith (1825-1898)
Arthur Sullivan's *Church Hymns with Tunes,* 1874

Washington Gladden, editor of the magazine *Sunday Afternoon,* included this poem in the devotional column "The Still Hour." Titled "Walking with God," his poem originally consisted of three eight-line stanzas. The following year, when Charles H. Richards included the hymn in his collection (later editions were titled *Songs of Christian Praise*), the second stanza was omitted and the remaining two divided into four four-line stanzas. While the present hymn is a gentle, patient meditation, the omitted stanza reveals more of the controversy surrounding Gladden's assertive, outspoken ministry:

> O Master, let me walk with thee
> Before the taunting Pharisee;
> Help me to bear the sting of spite,
> The hate of men who hide thy light,
> The sore distrust of souls sincere
> Who cannot read thy judgments clear,

The dullness of the multitude
Who dimly guess that thou art good.

MARYTON was composed for John Keble's text "Sun of my soul" and sometimes appears with that first line as its tune name. MARYTON was Gladden's choice for his hymn.

624
O perfect Love

Dorothy Frances Blomfield Gurney (1858-1932), 1883
Supplement to Hymns Ancient and Modern, 1889

SANDRINGHAM

Joseph Barnby (1838-1896), 1889
Church Hymnary, 1898

Mrs. Gurney gives the following account of how she came to write this wedding hymn for her sister:

> We were all singing hymns one Sunday evening and had just finished "O strength and stay," the tune to which was an especial favorite of my sister's, when someone remarked what a pity it was that the words should be unsuitable for a wedding. My sister, turning suddenly to me said: "What is the use of a sister who composes poetry if she cannot write me new words to this tune?" I picked up a hymn-book and said: "Well, if no one will disturb me I will go into the library and see what I can do." (Haeussler 1952)

Fifteen minutes later there was a hymn, "O perfect Love." Convinced that God helped her write it, Gurney emphasizes in her text what she considered the twofold aspect of perfect union: love and life. Stanza 2 also alludes to Paul's words on love in 1 Corinthians 13.

SANDRINGHAM, known sometimes as PERFECT LOVE, is the first section from an anthem setting[1] of Mrs. Gurney's text, which Barnby composed in 1889 for the wedding of the duke and duchess of Fife. It is with this tune that the text has become more widely known. SANDRINGHAM is named for the royal family residence in Norfolk, England.

1. A solo version of Barnby's anthem is available from Larrabee Publications, 39 W. 60th St., New York, NY 10023.

593

O Power of love — ST. PETERSBURG

Ich bete an die Macht der Liebe
Gerhard Tersteegen (1697-1769)
Geistliches Blumengärtlein, 6th ed., 1757
Later form, Gossner's *Sammlung*, 1825
Tr. Herman Brückner (1866-1942)
Wartburg Hymnal for Church, School, and Home, 1918, alt.

Dimitri Stepanovich Bortniansky (1751-1825)
Tscherlitzky's *Choralbuch*, 1825
(Zahn No. 2964)

This text is a translation drawn from Tersteegen's longer poem *Für dich sei ganz mein Herz und Leben.* When Gossner, a pastor, and Tscherlitzky, his organist, included this poem in their hymnal, they rearranged the order of the stanzas. Two lines of the translation have been altered over the years. In stanza 1:3, "thy name to honor and adore" was originally "And sing of thy celestial lore"; and in stanza 2:4, "so possessing" was the revision of "and caressing." "So possessing" contrasts more strongly with "love, so tender" immediately preceding.

The power of God's love not only prompts adoration and devotion from the believer, but is all-encompassing, even inexorable, as implied by the image of the ocean in stanza 1:4 and "so possessing" in stanza 2:4. This same powerful love was also the impetus for Jesus' sacrifice on the cross (st. 3:2).

ST. PETERSBURG is included in the sacred works of Bortniansky compiled by Peter Tchaikovsky in 1884. It is the setting of a Russian hymn in that volume; no evidence has been found to substantiate earlier suppositions that the tune was adapted from a larger work. Possibly written around 1822, it first appeared in the *Choralbuch* edited by Tscherlitzky and published in Moscow in 1825.

The original version of the melody (Zahn No. 2964) presented here shows that measures 7 and 15 are different from each other. In some hymnals they are identical. The hymn has long been a favorite among Mennonites of Russian heritage.

111

O praise the gracious power — CHRISTPRAISE RAY

Based on Ephesians 2:11-14
Thomas H. Troeger (1945-), 1984
New Hymns for the Lectionary, 1986

Carol Doran (1936-), 1984
(same source as text)

Troeger and Doran have collaborated on a large number of hymns for the lectionary, which lists cycles of scripture readings for each Sunday. This hymn is based on Ephesians 2:11-14, which is the scripture designated for the ninth Sunday after Pentecost. The author writes:

> The opening image, "that tumbles walls of fear," was inspired by a Sunday school class which I led with third and fourth graders. We made a wall of cardboard cartons, talking about how walls get built between people and how they are taken down.

The hymn continues its litany of praise for five great gifts that disclose Christ's living presence in the world. The hymn was written for the ordination of Judith Ray as a teaching elder in the Presbyterian Church.

15
O Prince of peace

Duh Pangeran ingkang
Saptayaadi (ca. 1950-)
Mennonite World Conference
International Songbook, 1978
Tr. Lawrence McCulloh Yoder (1943-)
(same source as text)

(no tune name)

Saptayaadi (ca. 1950-)
(same source as text)

In preparation for the 1978 world gathering, the compilers of the Mennonite World Conference *International Songbook* invited Mennonite churches around the world to submit songs indigenous to the various countries. This song was written in response to that invitation during a period of fruitful ministry and relative political and economic calm. The Reverend Saptayaadi, author of the original Javanese language text and composer of the tune, was pastor of Tanjungrejo Congregation of the Gereja Injili di Tanah Jawa (Evangelical [Mennonite] Church of Java) at the time. He still serves that Indonesian congregation on the shores of the Java Sea.

Titled "The Lord of nations" in the *International Songbook*, this hymn was translated into English, German, Spanish, and Dutch. Lawrence M. Yoder, who had been Saptayaadi's teacher at Wiyata Wacana School of Theology in Java in the early 1970s, provided the English translation. The only alteration is a change of the personal pronouns from archaic to contemporary usage.

Yoder writes: "While the tune of 'O Prince of peace' is original with Saptayaadi, one of his goals in writing it was to communicate some of the musical flavor of traditional Javanese melodies, not many of which had yet found their way into the hymnody of Javanese churches." He obviously achieved his objective, for the tune was listed in the *International Songbook* as a "Javanese melody."

252

O sacred Head, now wounded

Based on *Salve caput cruentatum*
Anonymous, 13th c.
O Haupt voll Blut und Wunden
Paul Gerhardt (1607-1676)
Crüger's *Praxis Pietatis Melica*, Berlin, 1656
Tr. James Waddell Alexander (1804-1859)
The New York Observer, Apr. 24, 1830, and Leavitt's *Christian Lyre*, 1830
Rev. in Alexander's *The Breaking Crucible*, 1861

HERZLICH TUT MICH VERLANGEN

Hans Leo Hassler (1564-1612)
Hassler's *Lustgarten neuer Deutscher Gesäng*, Nürnberg, 1601
Harmoniae Sacrae, 3rd ed., 1613
Harm. by Johann Sebastian Bach (1685-1750)
Passion According to St. Matthew, 1729

The Latin text has been ascribed to St. Bernard of Clairvaux (ca. 1091-1153) or to Arnulf von Loewen (Louvain, 1200-1251). Written in an era when crucifixes were crafted to graphically display Christ's sufferings, the hymn is a kind of literary crucifix. Each of its seven parts addresses some portion of Christ's body on the cross (feet, knees, hands, side, breast, heart, and face), and each part was intended to be sung on a different day of the week. Paul Gerhardt's free translation of the final section, *O Haupt voll Blut und Wunden*, has become one of the best-loved chorales. Of the several English translations of Gerhardt's poem, this one by Alexander is the most universally used, attesting to the hymn's "imperishable vitality" by its use in three languages. Of Alexander's ten stanzas, those included here are numbers 1, 2, 4, 8, and 10.

This is a hymn of intense personal devotion, well suited to meditation. Though it is traditionally used on Good Friday, it is appropriate for other occasions or services that dwell on Christ's atoning death.

Early Protestant hymnody drew its music from many sources, including secular songs. Hassler's melody was first set to a German love song *Mein G'muth ist mir verwirret von einer Jungfrau zart* (My heart is distracted by a gentle maid). Twelve years later it was used as a hymn tune with the text *Herzlich thut mich verlangen*; then in 1656 it became the setting for Gerhardt's text, an association maintained in German and English hymnals ever since. The harmonization is one of five settings of the chorale melody by J. S. Bach in his *Passion According to St. Matthew*. Bach also used the melody in two cantatas and in his *Christmas Oratorio* with the text *Wie soll ich dich empfangen*.

175

O Savior, rend the heavens

O HEILAND, REISS DIE HIMMEL AUF

O Heiland, reiss die Himmel auf
Friedrich von Spee (1591-1635)
Gesangbuch, Köln, 1623
Tr. Martin Louis Seltz (1909-1967), 1965
The Mennonite Hymnal, 1969, alt.

Gesangbuch, Augsburg, 1666
Harm. by Esther Wiebe (1932-), 1964
Gesangbuch der Mennoniten (Canadian Mennonite), 1965

The text and tune of this powerful Advent hymn are of Catholic origin. The text is saturated with biblical images of nature from Isaiah 11:1; 21:6; 45:8; and 64:1. Until 1920 this hymn was virtually unknown in Protestant German churches, and it was not until 1965 that it was first published by Mennonites (*Gesangbuch der Mennoniten*). Today, after two world wars and the Vietnam and Gulf Wars, it speaks with urgency for Jesus Christ to tangibly manifest himself.

Seltz, a Lutheran pastor in Minnesota, prepared this translation for possible use in a revised *Lutheran Hymnal* (Missouri Synod). It appeared in *The Mennonite Hymnal* (1969) and the *Worship Supplement to The Lutheran Hymnal* the same year. Only two alterations have been made. Stanza 2 now begins "O Dayspring" instead of "O Father," and stanza 4 concludes with "promised land" rather than "fatherland."

O HEILAND, REISS DIE HIMMEL AUF appeared anonymously in the Augsburg collection *Rheinfelsisches Deutsches Catholisches Gesangbuch* (1666). The irregular triple rhythm and the harmonic shift from D minor to F major in the middle phrases are essential elements in the musical and dramatic strength of this tune. "The hymn should be sung," suggests George Wiebe, "in a vigorous, declamatory manner while maintaining the sense of a forward-moving linear flow." Many choral works have been written based on this tune, including chorale motets by Johannes Brahms and Hugo Distler.

274

O sons and daughters, let us sing

GELOBT SEI GOTT

O Filii et Filiae
Jean Tisserand (d. 1494)
Untitled booklet, printed between 1518 and 1536
Tr. John Mason Neale (1818-1866)
Neale's *Medieval Hymns and Sequences*, 1851, alt.
Hymns Ancient and Modern, 1861

Melchior Vulpius (ca. 1560-1615)
Vulpius's *Ein schön geistlich Gesangbuch*, Jena, 1609

The narrative style of this hymn, while common for the Christmas season, is rather unusual for Easter. After the author sets the general scene of the resurrection, the details follow in the rest of the stanzas. The "sons and daughters" are the women and men to whom the resurrected Jesus first appeared, but all Christians are called to witness to this great event.

L'aleluya du jour de Pasques, probably written by the Franciscan friar Jean Tisserand, was originally in nine stanzas of Latin. Three more were added soon thereafter. Neale translated all twelve, but by the time his 1856 *The Hymnal Noted* came out, he omitted stanzas 3 and 5 and made some alterations in others. *Hymns Ancient and Modern* (1861) radically alters the translation, leaving only one stanza unchanged.[1] The three omitted stanzas of Neale's translation are the story of Thomas's questioning of the risen Lord:

When Didymus had after heard
That Jesus had fulfilled His Word,
He doubted if it were the Lord. Alleluia!

"Thomas, behold My Side," saith He;
"My Hands, My Feet, My Body see:
And doubt not, but believe in Me." Alleluia!

No longer Didymus denied;
He saw the Hands, the Feet, the Side;
"Thou art my Lord and God," he cried. Alleluia!

In its first printing, this melody, also known by the tune name VULPIUS, was the setting of *Gelobt sei Gott in höchsten Thron*, a hymn text by Michael Weisse. The original text was given an Italian balletto rhythm, "and in doing so [Vulpius] introduced a new type of Protestant hymn of great originality . . . " (Sadie 1980). The harmonization used here retains that madrigal-like quality.

1. Nine stanzas of the Latin text may be found in the *Historical Companion* to *Hymns Ancient and Modern*.

361
O Spirit of the living God — PLAINFIELD

Henry Hallam Tweedy (1868-1953), 1933
The Methodist Hymnal, 1935, alt.

Jacob Kimball (1761-1826)
Essex Harmony, 1800

Jesus' disciples, disoriented by the extraordinary events and contrasting emotions of Jesus' arrest, death, resurrection, and ascension, probably took comfort in the steadying celebration of tradition—Pentecost. This was the feast of firstfruits—a dedication of the new harvest of barley—observed seven weeks after Passover. But God was not finished "doing a new thing." It was at this celebratory gathering that the Spirit of God descended with light and fire to empower the disciples of Christ.

Tweedy wrote this hymn to interpret the story of Pentecost in Acts 2, fashioning it especially for present-day Christians. Tweedy's text is not to be confused with another hymn (not in this hymnal) with the same first line, by James Montgomery (1771-1854), or with "Spirit of the living God" (**349**), by Daniel Iverson (1890-1977).

For those who are used to ST. LEONARD or FOREST GREEN, the tune PLAINFIELD gives this strong text a spirited new flavor. It comes first from *Essex Harmony,* edited by Kimball and Samuel Holyoke in Exeter, New Hampshire. In *American Hymns Old and New,* it is coupled with a free paraphrase of Psalm 24 by Martha Brewster, an eighteenth-century poet. The melody, originally in the tenor voice, is now in the soprano. The tunes mentioned above make good alternatives.

646
O Splendor of God's glory bright — SPLENDOR PATERNAE

Splendor paternae gloriae
Ambrose of Milan (ca. 340-397), 4th c.
Composite translation

Sarum plainsong, Mode I
Sarum Antiphonal

This beautiful morning hymn invokes the Holy Trinity, especially Christ as the Light of the world, as help and guidance for the day. The hymn has always been intended for the monastic devotional services of Lauds (sunrise) on Monday.[1] The lovely poetry of "very Sun of heaven's love" is reminiscent of Hebrews 1:3 where Jesus is called the "reflection" of God's glory, sometimes "the radiance."

Out of at least twenty-five different translations, the present rendition is a composite; the first three stanzas were compiled by Louis Benson (1855-1930) for *The Hymnal* (Presbyterian, 1911), and stanzas 4 and 5 come from *Rejoice in the Lord* (1985).

SPLENDOR PATERNAE is the Sarum form[2] of the traditional melody for this text. It is used with other texts for Lauds as well."This is one of the great plainsong melodies," writes Archibald Jacob. "The mere curve of the notes on paper is beautiful and perfectly proportional. When well sung in exact accordance with the rhythm of the Latin words, it produces an impression of unsurpassed sublimity" (Dearmer, Jacob 1933).

The tune PUER NATUS NASCITUR ("That Easter day with joy was bright") may be used as an alternate tune for this text. Notice that both tunes begin with the same melodic intervals and have a similar arch form.

1. The full eight stanzas of Latin text are given in *The Hymnal 1940 Companion*.
2. For more on "Sarum," see "Sing, my tongue, the song" (**256**).

559
O thou, in whose presence — ZION'S PILGRIM

Joseph Swain (1762-1796)
Redemption, a Poem in Five Books, 1791

Joshua Leavitt's *Christian Lyre,* 1830
Harm. by J. Harold Moyer (1927-), 1965
The Mennonite Hymnal, 1969

The author writes as a seeker bent on recovering his source of joy and comfort, singing out all his lonely misery in the search until, at the end of stanza 2, the Shepherd is found.

This text, originally titled "A Description of Christ by his Graces and Power," paraphrases portions of the Song of Solomon. Various early American hymnbooks contain a version of this text with ten stanzas. In Joseph Funk's *Harmonia Sacra,* the text is divided between this tune and NEW SALEM (sts. 1-4). The present text consists of stanzas 1, 2, 3, and 10.

ZION'S PILGRIM, a shaped-note tune, is of unknown origin. Erik Routley writes that this tune has "a very strong Welsh flavour, especially in its metre (which it shares with the Welsh carol tune 'All poor men and humble,' called OLWEN in Wales)" (Routley 1981). In Leavitt's collection this tune appears in two voices. When Moyer made the present harmonization in 1965, he left many of the chords open (without a third), in "keeping with the expressive but melancholic flavor of the melody" (Loewen, Moyer, Oyer 1983).

66
O worship the King — LYONS

Based on Psalm 104
Robert H. Grant (1779-1838)
E. Bickersteth's *Christian Psalmody,* 1833

W. Gardiner's *Sacred Melodies,* Vol. 2, 1815

Psalm 104 has been called the "pearl of the psalter," because of its shimmering poetry and passionate detail in describing creation. When Grant did this paraphrase of the psalm, he was hard put to improve on its creativity, but, as Albert Bailey writes, "It is no small accomplishment to combine . . . the majestic, the tender, and a smooth-flowing poetical rendering" (Bailey 1950).

The "Ancient of Days," one of the hymn's names for God, does not appear in the psalm. It comes from Daniel 7:9 and conveys the idea that God is the one who precedes the ages and outlives them. Set in the apocalyptic context of Daniel, the term means that God, not the apocalypse, is ultimate. This notion is compatible with the sweeping nature of both the psalm and the hymn text.

Grant based his work on an earlier paraphrase by William Kethe. Retaining Kethe's meter, he reset the psalm in a more ornate style, actually more akin to the psalm itself. This can be seen by comparing it with Kethe's first stanza:

My soule praise the Lord,
speake good of his Name
O Lord our great God
how doest thou appeare,
So passing in glorie, that great is thy fame,
Honour and majestie, in thee shine most cleare. (Julian 1907)

Grant's third and sixth stanzas, which are omitted in the hymnal, are:

The earth, with its store of wonders untold
Almighty, thy power hath founded of old,
Hath 'stablished it fast by a changeless decree,
And round it hath cast, like a mantle, the sea.

O Lord of all might, how boundless thy love!
While angels delight to hymn thee above,
The humbler creation, though feeble their lays,
With true adoration shall lisp to thy praise.

Grant wrote just twelve hymns, and this is the only one in common use, but it can be found in more than eighty hymnals of the twentieth century.

Although the tune LYONS has been attributed to Haydn, its source has not been found in the works of either Franz Joseph or Johann Michael Haydn. In Gardiner's publication the tune was set for mixed voices and orchestra to the text "O praise ye the Lord, prepare a new song."

124
O worship the Lord — BEAUTY OF HOLINESS

Robert Lowry (1826-1899)
Royal Diadem for the Sunday School, 1873, alt.

Robert Lowry (1826-1899)
(same source as text)

The appearances of this hymn seem to be quite rare; it is in the 1925 and 1951 Church of the Brethren hymnals and the Mennonite *Life Songs No. 2.* The hymn is a three-section call to worship. The first comes from 1 Chronicles 16:29b: "Worship the Lord in holy splendor." The second section, in each of its three stanzas, focuses on a member of the Trinity. The third section is a refrain, which closes with part of Psalm 95:2. The only alterations of the original words occur in stanza 1:2 where the original "Jehovah" was changed to "the Lord God" and in stanza 3:2 where a masculine reference to the Spirit is deleted by rephrasing the expression of the Trinity. The Bible does not say that the Spirit is specifically masculine; the Hebrew word for Spirit is feminine in gender; the Greek is neuter.

The tune name BEAUTY OF HOLINESS appears for the first time in *The Brethren Hymnal* (1951). The tune is organized into three contrasting melodies that correspond to the three sections of text. Originally, the musical setting provided a contrasting texture in the second section by using only the two treble voices, with the first and third sections voiced in four parts. The 1951 publication filled in the harmonies and changed a few chord structures in other places. The original 1873 publication also had a fermata placed over the first chord of the hymn and the expressive direction "Earnestly" placed at the beginning.

374
O young and fearless Prophet
BLAIRGOWRIE

Samuel Ralph Harlow (1885-1972), 1930 or 1931
The Methodist Hymnal, 1935, alt.

John Bacchus Dykes (1823-1876), 1872

During the days of the Depression in the U.S., as Harlow and his wife were driving from Pittsfield to Northampton, Massachusetts, the words of this hymn kept ringing through his head. When they stopped along the road, he related them to his wife who wrote them down. Continuing their trip, they passed a poorly dressed man who looked quite tired and discouraged. Harlow relates:

> My wife suggested that if we lived up to the words of the hymn we ought to pick him up, which we did. He was most grateful and told us that he had walked from Boston to Albany and out to Rochester looking for work and finding none. He said: "Just as you passed I felt that I was at the end of my rope. . . . Somehow when you think you are utterly forgotten, God shows you that you are not as forgotten as you think you are." (McCutchan 1937)[1]

Unfortunately, the Methodist hymnal in which the hymn was first published did not include the stanza related to this incident that reads:

> Stir up in us a protest against unearned wealth,
> While men go starved and hungry, who plead for work and health;
> Whose wives and little children cry out for lack of bread,
> And spend their years o'erweighted, beneath a gloomy dread.
> (McCutchan 1937)

When the above stanza was rejected, the chairman of the Methodist hymnal committee told the author, "The church is not ready to sing that yet." The author replied, "It was not as radical as the Magnificat in Luke 1:46-55" (Gealey, Lovelace, Young 1970). Harlow later changed "unearned wealth" to "the greed of wealth."

Harlow may have mellowed over the years, becoming more reluctant to go against the grain. He later rejected his original stanza 3, which appeared in previous Brethren and Mennonite hymnals (and appears in this one), preferring the following version that came out in *The Methodist Hymnal* in 1966:

> O help us walk unflinching in paths that lead to peace,
> Where justice conquers violence and wars at last shall cease;
> O grant that love of country may help us hear his call,
> Who would unite the nations in brotherhood for all.

Minor alterations from the original were made for this hymnal, including changing the word "brotherhood" in stanza 3:4 to "unity," as well as shifting from archaic to contemporary language for this hymn that is so contemporary in its prophetic voice.

BLAIRGOWRIE was composed for a friend's wedding as a setting of John Keble's wedding hymn, "The Voice That Breathed o'er Eden." This tune name is Gaelic and means "plain of the wild goats"; it is also the name of a small inland town northwest of Dundee, Scotland. Its first printed source is obscure, being described as among the "stray tunes found in print," as listed by the composer's biographer, Rev. J. T. Fowler (McCutchan 1937). Harlow's text is set to this tune in *The Methodist Hymnal* (1935).

1. Later accounts of how this text came to be written vary slightly from that quoted above. See Haeussler, 1952, and Gealy, Lovelace, Young, 1970.

163
Obey my voice

Based on Jeremiah 7:23 (KJV)

OBEY MY VOICE

Sheilagh Porto Nowacki (1947-), 1970
Festival of the Holy Spirit Song Book, Goshen College (Ind.), 1972

Most of the songs Nowacki has written take their texts directly from scripture. Although she has no training in music theory, she says, "As I am reading Scripture there are times when I can just hear the tune for a verse or for several verses in my mind."

"Obey my voice" was Sheilagh Nowacki's first song. It was written while she was attending Goshen College and worshiping at Zion Chapel near Goshen. She relates:

> On a Sunday morning . . . my pastor, Vic Hildebrand, asked if I would sing the following week. I said "yes," but I said to the Lord, "only if I receive my prayer language before then." It isn't wise to give the Lord an ultimatum, but I suppose He honored my sincerity and overlooked my immaturity. That evening I received my prayer language and a couple days later as I was reading in Jeremiah, the song was just there.

See the *Accompaniment Handbook* for Marilyn Houser Hamm's arrangement of this hymn.

104
Of the Father's love begotten

DIVINUM MYSTERIUM

Corde natus ex Parentis
Marcus Aurelius Clemens Prudentius (348-ca. 410)
Cathemerinon, 5th c.
Tr. John Mason Neale (1818-1866)
The Hymnal Noted, 1851
Rev. by Henry William Baker (1821-1877)
Hymns Ancient and Modern, 1861

Plainsong, 13th c.
Petri's *Piae Cantiones . . .*, 1582

"This is a fighting hymn," writes commentator Albert Bailey. The original Latin text is part of the ninth poem of twelve by Prudentius and was written at a time when Christianity in Spain was threatened by paganism and heresy. Stanza 1 counters the doctrine that Christ was a sort of "secondary God," a creature related to but apart from God. The argument is bolstered with evidence from nature (st. 2) and prophecy (st. 3) and ends with an outburst of praise for these mysteries.

The refrain *saeculorum saeculis* (evermore and evermore) was not a part of the original text but was added through liturgical usage. John Neale published a translation in his *The Hymnal Noted* in 1851. Neale himself altered his original opening line, "Of the Father, sole-begotten," to its present wording. Neale's version was revised by Henry W. Baker for the first edition of *Hymns Ancient and Modern* (1861).

This melody, with the Latin text *Divinum mysterium*, has been located in various chant collections of the twelfth to fifteenth centuries. It was a trope (a musical interpolation into the medieval liturgy) of a Gregorian *Sanctus* (meaning "holy"). Later the melody appeared in *Piae Cantiones Ecclesiasticae et Scholasticae*, published by Theodoricis Petri of Finland in 1582. It was first associated with Neale's text in *The Hymnal Noted* nearly three hundred years later, transcribed by Thomas Helmore. The lack of stems on the notes takes the eye to the text, allowing a free-sung style appropriate for plainsong.

231
Oh, blessed are the poor in spirit — KONTAKION

Based on Matthew 5:3-12

Russian Orthodox liturgy
Adapt. by Richard Proulx (1937-), 1985
Worship III, 1986

This concise setting of the Beatitudes comes from the liturgy of the Russian Orthodox Church. The name KONTAKION means a verse or hymn for the day. Note that the melody, which begins in the soprano, moves to the bass part in the second half, where the alto voices join the tenors and the sopranos take the alto part. Participation in this kind of singing requires careful listening to other voices, thus uniting the body of believers in the singing of a significant passage of scripture.

520
Oh, for a closer walk with God — CAITHNESS

William Cowper (1731-1800)
Conyers' *A Collection of Psalms and Hymns*, 2nd ed., 1772

The Psalmes of David in Prose and Meeter, 1635
Harm. from *The English Hymnal*, 1906

Cowper wrote this hymn in December of 1769 during the serious illness of his friend Mrs. Unwin who had cared for him during his own illness. He began to compose the verses one morning before daybreak but fell asleep at the end of the first two lines. "When I waked again," he writes, "the third and fourth were whispered to my heart in a way which I have often experienced" (Bailey 1950).

Titled "Walking with God," the hymn bore a reference to Genesis 5:24, "Enoch walked with God." All six stanzas of this deeply devotional hymn appear here as they did in Book 1 of *Olney Hymns* (1779). They are the testament that faith cannot be taken for granted—they are the cry of a soul that was first found, then lost, and yearns to be found again.

CAITHNESS is one of thirty-one common tunes in the 1635 *Scottish Psalter*, all written to fit any of the psalms in common meter. This psalter was the first to print its tunes in four voices with the melody in the tenor part. It also was the first psalter to print names to the tunes. CAITHNESS is named for the extreme northeasterly county of Scotland. Described as "a smooth tune with an elegant contour," the melody also appears with a slight rhythmic variation with the text "Shepherd of souls, refresh" (**456**).

110

Oh, for a thousand tongues to sing — AZMON

Charles Wesley (1707-1788), 1739
Hymns and Sacred Poems, 1740

Carl Gotthelf Gläser (1784-1829)
Arr. by Lowell Mason (1792-1872)
Mason's *Modern Psalmist,* 1839

We set great store in the celebration of birthdays; should the Christian not also celebrate the day of *re*-birth? This hymn was written "for the anniversary day of one's conversion," and since Charles Wesley's conversion happened on May 21, 1738, this radiant text was probably written in 1739. The first line, which began Wesley's seventh stanza, was derived from a statement made to him by Peter Böhler, a Moravian missionary: "Had I a thousand tongues I would praise him with them all."

The original first stanza has become the concluding stanza in both settings. R. Conyers' *A Collection of Psalms and Hymns,* 1st ed. (1767), was the first to use "O for a thousand tongues" to open the hymn. John Wesley followed suit in 1780 and also changed "dear Redeemer" in stanza 1:2 to "great Redeemer."

For the tune AZMON, the sequence of stanzas from the original is 7, 8, 9, 11, and 1. Lowell Mason chose the name *azmon,* the Hebrew word for "fortress" (Num. 34:4-5), for his *Modern Psalmist.* There the tune appears in 4/4 meter with Watts's text "Come, let us lift our joyful eyes" and two years later in 3/2 meter in his *Carmina Sacra.*

81

Oh, for a thousand tongues to sing — LYNGHAM

Charles Wesley (1707-1788), 1739
Hymns and Sacred Poems, 1740

Thomas Jarman (1776-1861)
Thomas Jarman's *Sacred Music,* 1803

See the preceding article on **110** for commentary on this text by Charles Wesley.

LYNGHAM, an example of the more flamboyant Methodist style, was in fact written by a Baptist, Thomas Jarman. Since this setting is rather repetitive, only stanzas 7, 8, and 1 of the original eighteen were selected.

606
Oh, have you not heard — THE BEAUTIFUL RIVER

R. Torry, Jr.
Sabbath School Gems, 1864
Tr. to German by Ernst Heinrich Gebhardt (1832-1899)
Frohe Botschaft, 1875, alt.

Asa Hull (1828-ca. 1908)
(same source as text), alt.

Written around 1862, this text is based on Revelation 22:1-2 and 17. This well-traveled North American hymn was published in England in 1870 and translated into German in 1875. Sung by German-speaking Mennonites in Russia, the song returned to North America with those believers. That German version appears in the Mennonite *Gesangbuch mit Noten* (1890). The Mennonite Brethren liked the German version so much that it was retranslated back to English, treating the German translation as the original text. The original English version is among the hymns more frequently sung by General Conference Mennonites. One text change, using "the promised land" in place of "our Father's land," appears in stanza 1:2.

THE BEAUTIFUL RIVER is a simple and tuneful melody in triple meter that invites part-singing. Originally in 6/4 meter, the melody was changed into quadruple meter through oral transmission in the Mennonite Brethren Church, resulting from Gebhardt's German translation. The form of the melody has been altered by adding three beats to the final note of phrase 2 and phrase 4. Comparable changes occur in the refrain. *The Mennonite Hymnal* (1969) and earlier Mennonite hymnals had the cadence notes as half notes. These changes restore the balanced phrase lengths of the earliest versions of this melody and conform to a common singing practice of holding these notes longer than indicated by the notation.

320
Oh, holy city seen of John — MORNING SONG (CONSOLATION)

Walter Russell Bowie (1882-1969), 1909
Henry Sloane Coffin and A. W. Vernon, editors, *Hymns of the Kingdom of God,* 1910

Anonymous
Pamphlet, 1811 or 1812
John Wyeth's *Repository of Sacred Music, Part Second,* 1813

In the Book of Revelation shines a vision of the Holy City (chapters 21-22)—a bright contrast to the cities of our world. This text was written at the request of Henry Sloane Coffin who wanted "some new hymns that would express the conviction that our hope of the Kingdom of God is not alone some far-off eschatological possibility but in its beginnings, at least, may be prepared for here on our actual earth" (*The Hymnal 1940 Companion*, 1951 ed.).

CONSOLATION is attributed to Amzi Chapin,[1] a singing-school teacher active in Virginia, North Carolina, and Kentucky in the late eighteenth and early nineteenth centuries. Andrew Law was the first to print the tune, based on a manuscript of Southern folk tunes submitted by John Logan, a singing-school teacher who lived near Greenville, Virginia. The tune subsequently appeared in other collections, including Wyeth and Davisson's *Kentucky Harmony*. Only two copies of the first printing are known to exist, one owned by Carl N. Shull and the other donated by him to the University of Michigan Clements Library.

1. Carl N. Shull makes this attribution, according to research published in the Augustana County (Va.) Historical Society Bulletin, Vol. 16, No. 1, Spring 1980.

597
Oh, how happy are they

Charles Wesley (1707-1788)
Hymns and Sacred Poems, 1749, 16 sts., alt.

NEW CONCORD

American folk melody
Joseph Funk's *Genuine Church Music*, 1st ed., 1832
Harm. by J. Harold Moyer (1927-), 1965
The Mennonite Hymnal, 1969

This text, which originally began "How happy are they," was divided into two parts, one of seven stanzas and the other of nine. In the source listed above, it appeared under the topic "Hymns for one fallen from grace"; in the *American Methodist Pocket Hymn Book* (Philadelphia 1802), it was included under the topic "Convinced of backsliding." By 1849 the number of stanzas was reduced and the hymn given yet another title, this one more positive—"Joy of the young convert." *The Brethren Hymnal* (1901) picked up seven stanzas, and the present text consists of the first four stanzas of Part I, with only minor alterations.

This is a joyous text, deserving of the buoyancy of NEW CONCORD, called TRUE HAPPINESS in *Southern Harmony* (1835). It is a vital pentatonic melody, the scale of which conforms to the five black keys of the piano. This melodic structure is characteristic of many folk tunes. The present harmonization retains the flavor of the harmony found in such early tunebooks as *Genuine Church Music*.

209

Oh, how joyfully

O du fröhliche
St. 1, Johannes Daniel Falk (1768-1826), 1816
Auserlesene Werke, 1819
Sts. 2-3, Heinrich Holzschuher
Tr. Harris J. Loewen (1953-) and re-envisioned by Brian Arthur Wren (1936-), 1990

O SANCTISSIMA

The European Magazine and London Review, November 1792
Arr. by Robert Lawson Shaw (1916-) and Alice Parker (1925-), 1953

This delightful hymn appears here in both the original German and in a new English version. Though it is specifically a Christmas text, each stanza foreshadows the salvation brought by Christ's life (st. 1:2, "love comes healing, God revealing"), death (st. 2:2, "sins are covered, grace discovered"), and resurrection (st. 3:2, "God has spoken, death is broken").

The first stanza of the German text is from Falk's three-stanza "Hymn for All the Three Festivals," which encompasses the three seasons of Christmas, Easter, and Whitsuntide. (Whitsuntide, the day of Pentecost, or the fiftieth day of Easter, is so named because of the tradition of baptizing converts in white robes.) The additional stanzas are sometimes listed as anonymous.

O SANCTISSIMA, also called O DU FRÖHLICHE, is a rhythmic variant of the tune known as SICILIAN MARINERS. For comments on that tune, see "Jesus, friend so kind and gentle" (**621**). The arrangement used here is from an octavo setting published by G. Schirmer, Inc.

182

Oh, how shall I receive thee

Wie soll ich dich empfangen
Based on Matthew 21:9
Paul Gerhardt (1607-1676)
Crüger's *Praxis Pietatis Melica*, 5th ed., 1653 (10 sts.)
Tr. Arthur Tozer Russell (1806-1874)
Psalms and Hymns, 1851, alt.

ST. THEODULPH (VALET WILL ICH DIR GEBEN)

Melchior Teschner (1584-1635), 1613
Herberger's *Ein andächtiges Gebet . . .*, Leipzig, 1615
(Zahn No. 5404)

This hymn is based on Matthew 21:9, the Gospel lesson for the first Sunday in Advent. Though the scripture verses detail Christ's triumphal entry into Jerusalem, the hymn text focuses on a personal encounter with Christ, an event that could be acclaimed anytime.

Allusions in stanzas 6-9 of the German text suggest that this hymn was written during the Thirty Years War. It may be one of Gerhardt's finest texts and "probably the best German Advent hymn" (Julian 1907). Austin Lovelace comments:

> How do we prepare to meet Christ? We . . . can bring our love which reflects Christ's love that led him to be born, to serve humanity and to give his life for us. What a fitting hymn to sing during the Advent season! (Lovelace 1987)

For comments on ST. THEODULPH (VALET WILL ICH DIR GEBEN), see "All glory, laud, and honor" (**237**).

147
Oh, how wondrous the grace — RICHES OF GRACE

Mrs. W. J. Kennedy
The Brethren Hymnal, 1901

J. Henry Showalter (1864-1947)
(same source as text)

Little is known about the origins of this gospel song, and nothing is known about the author except her (husband's) name. Copyrighted by J. Henry Showalter in 1899, it appears in *The Brethren Hymnal* (1901) and bears the scriptural allusion "By grace ye are saved—Eph. 2:5." *The Brethren Hymnal* (1951) exchanged the original first stanza ("We are saved by the grace of our God") with the third stanza. The omitted fourth stanza reads:

> Ye poor souls, who are wand'ring astray,
> So far, far away from your God,
> If ye come to the Savior today,
> He'll cleanse all your sins in his blood.

The tune name RICHES OF GRACE is taken from the title under which the melody first appeared. Changes introduced with *The Brethren Hymnal* (1951) include the chromaticism in the alto of the refrain, even eighth notes, and the use of A-flat instead of A major. Coupled with the music by a Brethren composer, this hymn continues to be a favorite.

84
Oh, that I had a thousand voices — O DASS ICH TAUSEND ZUNGEN HÄTTE

O dass ich tausend Zungen hätte
Johann Mentzer (1658-1734)
Freylinghausen's *Neues Geistreiches Gesangbuch*, 1704 (15 sts.)
Tr. *The Lutheran Hymnal*, 1941 (5 sts.), alt.

Johann Balthasar König (1691-1758)
König's *Harmonischer Liederschatz*, Frankfurt, 1738

An unconfirmed story claims that Mentzer wrote this text after losing his house to fire. Considered by some to be Mentzer's best hymn, it encourages the praise of God in spite of adversity.

The composite translation, used here with some alterations, is based on translations in Henry Mills' *Horae Germanicae* (1845) and Catherine Winkworth's *Lyra Germanica*, Series I (1855).

O DASS ICH TAUSEND ZUNGEN HÄTTE, probably by König, first appeared as a setting of the text *Ach, sagt mir nichts von Gold und Schätzen*, by Angelus Silesius. Having no meter signature, the tune's measures alternate between four and six beats. The hymn leader can, however, beat a steady half-note pulse throughout the hymn.

596
On eagle's wings—see "And I will raise you up"

183
On Jordan's banks the Baptist's cry — WINCHESTER NEW

Jordanis oras praevia
Charles Coffin (1676-1749)
Hymni Sacri and *Paris Breviary*, 1736
Sts. 1-3, tr. John Chandler (1806-1876)
Chandler's *Hymns of the Primitive Church*, 1837, alt.
St. 4, *Hymns Ancient and Modern*, 1861, alt.

Musicalisch Handbuch der Geistlichen Melodien, published by George Rebelein's widow, 1690
Arr. by William Henry Havergal (1793-1870)
Old Church Psalmody, 1847

John the Baptist's announcement of Christ's coming necessitated a call to repentance—preparation for the Messiah. Even though the Baptist heralded the ministry of the adult Jesus, Advent, the traditional period of preparation for Christ's nativity, is an appropriate season for this hymn. In fact, the Latin of this text[1] was intended as a hymn for the service of Lauds (sunrise) during Advent. It was designated a ferial hymn, meaning that it could be used for any day on which no feast falls (*The New Harvard Dictionary of Music* 1986).

Chandler, thinking he was translating a medieval hymn, included it in *Hymns of the Primitive Church*. The present version is based on Chandler's stanzas 1, 3, and 5, plus the doxology written for the original edition of *Hymns Ancient and Modern*. Chandler's work has been altered over the years so that only his first stanza appears to remain intact.

WINCHESTER NEW was first set to the hymn *Wer nur den lieben Gott lässt walten* in 98.98.88 meter in the source listed above. Later, because many hymns by Watts and Wesley were in long meter, the tune was adapted to triple time by Thomas Moore for the *Psalm-Singers Delightful Pocket-Companion* (Glasgow 1762). The final and present long-meter version in common time was made by Havergal for the *Old Church Psalmody*. WINCHESTER NEW is named for the city of Winchester in Hampshire, England; other names are SWIFT, GERMAN

TUNE (from Wesley's *Foundery Collection*, 1742), FRANKFORT, BARRE, and CRASSELIUS.

1. The full Latin text of six stanzas is in *The Hymnal 1940 Companion*.

610

On Jordan's stormy banks I stand

Samuel Stennett (1727-1795)
Rippon's *A Selection of Hymns from the Best Authors*, 1787

BOUND FOR THE PROMISED LAND

American folk melody
W. Walker's *Southern Harmony*, 1835
Harm. by J. Harold Moyer (1927-), 1965

Though this hymn borrows its imagery from the Israelites crossing the Jordan into Canaan (Josh. 3), for Christians the Jordan represents the boundary between life and death. The "promised land" is, as the hymn was originally headed, "Heaven anticipated." The author seems confident that he has followed the admonition of Jesus in Matthew 6:20 and has laid up his treasures in heaven (st. 1:2, "where my possessions lie").

Originally, the hymn consisted of eight four-line stanzas, and the refrain was not part of it. Rather, it was a "mother hymn," meaning that refrains could be tacked on, or could even interrupt the text. Another refrain, by Edmund Dumas, is:

We'll stem the storm, it won't be long;
The heav'nly port is nigh;
We'll stem the storm, it won't be long;
We'll anchor by and by.

The tune, called PROMISED LAND in W. Walker's *Southern Harmony*, is found in many of the oblong tunebooks of the nineteenth century. It was attributed to "Miss M. Durham," but "we do not know whether she collected, supplied, or arranged it" (Oyer 1980). The tune likely was sung for a number of years before the music was notated, and it would have spread through the revival meetings orally. Thus, it would have been subject to continuous variations of text and music.[1]

Though the tune was originally in a minor key, over the years a version of it in the major has come into use. It is found in numerous current denominational hymnals. A completely different tune by T. C. O' Kane was used in both *Life Songs* (1916) and *The Brethren Hymnal* (1901).

1. Details concerning tunes in the shaped note tradition are on pages 79-84 of Oyer's book *Exploring the Mennonite Hymnal: Essays*, 1980.

649

On the radiant threshold — BE THOU OUR GUIDE

Albert Cassel Wieand (1871-1954)
Holsinger's *Gospel Songs and Hymns, No. 1*, 1898, alt.

George B. Holsinger (1857-1908)
(same source as text)

A. C. Wieand was a founder of Bethany Bible School (now Bethany Theological Seminary, Richmond, Indiana) and served as its president. Author of various publications, he is believed to have written this text in the late 1890s, perhaps for Holsinger's collection. In stanza 2:1, "the Savior" replaces Wieand's original "the Father" in order to keep the text consistently focused on Christ.

Titled "Morning Hymn," the tune was in the key of B-flat and differs slightly from the setting as it appears here and in *The Brethren Hymnal* (1951). Holsinger composed a number of hymn settings; this particular tune has remained one of his most popular.

192

On this day earth shall ring — PERSONENT HODIE

Petri's *Piae Cantiones* . . . , 1582
Tr. Jane Marion Joseph (1894-1929)

German melody, 1360
Petri's *Piae Cantiones* . . . , 1582

Theodoric Petri, a young Finn studying at the University of Rostock near Lübeck, Germany, compiled the pre-Reformation songs and carols current in his day.[1] He named his collection *Piae Cantiones Ecclesiasticae et Scholasticae*, and the songs he preserved made their mark on the Protestant Reformation in Scandinavia. They were still being used in Swedish schools in 1700 and survived in Finland until late in the nineteenth century. The single existing copy of *Piae Cantiones* . . . was brought to England about 1852 by the British Minister to Sweden and is now in the British Museum. John Mason Neale and Thomas Helmore used some of the texts in their carol books for Easter and Christmas (1853, 1854). DIVINUM MYSTERIUM ("Of the Father's love begotten," **104**) is another melody perpetuated in this important collection.

"On this day earth shall ring" is a pulsing, joyful rendition of Christ's birth story. The refrain, *Ideo gloria in excelsis Deo*, is the last line of the original Latin text.[2] *Ideo* (pronounced ee-deh-oh) means "therefore." Combined with the rest of the familiar phrase, we have "Therefore, glory to God in the highest."

A vigorous harmonization of PERSONENT HODIE by Gustav T. Holst (1874-1934) is found in the *Accompaniment Handbook*.

1. *The Presbyterian Hymnal Companion* claims Jacob Finno was the compiler and Petri the publisher.
2. The Latin text is in *The Oxford Book of Carols* as PERSONENT HODIE.

255

Open are the gifts of God — SONG 13

William Hubert Vanstone (1923-)
The Risk of Love, 1978
More Hymns for Today, 1980

Orlando Gibbons (1583-1625)
Wither's *Hymnes and Songs of the Church*, 1623

When Jesus poured out his life on the cross to give us life, it was a supreme paradox. This hymn makes poetry of that paradox, building in each stanza until, in the end, it is the very weariness of spent love that enables Christ to sustain the world.

This text, called "Hymn to the Creator," was the conclusion of the author's book *The Risk of Love*. Its first publication in a hymnal was in *More Hymns for Today*, a supplement to *Hymns Ancient and Modern*. The original first two stanzas, omitted here, are a prelude of praise for God's creation, the "gifts of love to mind and sense".

Dorothy Sheets was inspired by this text to compose BINGHAM, used in this hymnal with "Lord, our Lord, your glorious name" (**157**). *Hymnal Supplement II* (1987) was the first to include Vanstone's text with Gibbons' melody.

For comments on SONG 13, see "Christ, from whom all blessings" (**365**).

140

Open, Lord, my inward ear — WHISPER

Charles Wesley (1707-1788)
Hymns and Spiritual Songs, 1742

Bradley P. Lehman (1964-), 1991
Hymnal: A Worship Book, 1992

This text begins with stanza 2 of Wesley's six-stanza hymn "Christ, my hidden life, appear." The hymn opens by alluding to Elijah's encounter with God (1 Kings 19:11-12), then centers on the sacrifice of Christ (st. 3), and ends with a humble commitment to turn from pride (st. 4) and put on the ways of Christ (st. 5).

The composer writes of being introduced to Wesley's "powerfully intimate but little-known poem":

> Immediately, the text suggested to me music with an easygoing, chant-like rhythm, and gentle harmonies. A few weeks after I wrote WHISPER, the choir of University Reformed Church (Ann Arbor, Mich.) sang it to unify a Sunday morning service: the first three stanzas as an introit, the fourth as a call to confession, and the fifth as a benediction.

Although the hymn has no time signature, the music is well crafted to the text. Note the similarity of the first, second, and last phrases, as well as the rhythmic repetition in the third phrase.

517

Open my eyes, that I may see

Clara H. Scott (1841-1897)
Hoffman and Sayles' *Best Hymns, No. 2*, 1895

OPEN MY EYES

Clara H. Scott (1841-1897)
(same source as text)

In the Eastern Orthodox tradition, worshipers stand for the entire service so that they might be always in an "attitude of readiness," alert to receive the word and Spirit of God. Though we often sing this hymn sitting down, preparing for prayer, its words "stand us up," calling us to be ready to hear, see, understand, and tell of God's Spirit.

Both tune and text were written by Clara H. Scott and first appeared in the above collection just before her death. The tune was named SCOTT by the hymnal committee of the 1956 *Baptist Hymnal* (Southern Baptist Convention).

19

Open now thy gates of beauty

Tut mir auf die schöne Pforte
Benjamin Schmolck (1672-1737)
Kirchen-Gefährte, 1732
Tr. Catherine Winkworth (1827-1878)
Chorale Book for England, 1863, alt.

UNSER HERRSCHER (NEANDER)

Joachim Neander (1650-1680)
Alpha und Omega, Glaub- und Liebesübung, 1680

Schmolck, a prolific and beloved poet in his day, placed his original German text of seven six-line stanzas under the heading "Appearing before God." Like the psalms in the Bible, Schmolck's text is at once confident and intimate in meeting the great Creator of the universe; God, though wreathed in mysterious beauty and might, is also the One who answers prayer and feeds and heals people.

Winkworth translated five of the stanzas, of which stanzas 1, 2, and 5 are used here. Stanza 2 originally began:

> Yes, my God, I come before Thee,
> Come thou also down to me.

The tune UNSER HERRSCHER is also known as NEANDER, having first appeared with Neander's text *Unser Herrscher, unser König*. In its original form, the last two lines of the melody were in triple meter. Later in the seventeenth century, they were changed to a rhythmic pattern closer to the one in use today. The key of D major used here creates a bright and vigorous setting for this hymn. As an alternative, the *Accompaniment Handbook* has it in the original key of C major.

32

Our Father God, thy name we praise

NUN FREUT EUCH

O Gott Vater, wir loben dich
Leenaerdt Clock, 16th-17th c.
Ausbund, early 17th c.
Tr. Ernest Alexander Payne (1902-1980), 1956
British Baptist Hymn Book, 1962, alt.

J. Klug's *Geistliche Lieder,* 1535

The German text of this Anabaptist hymn, called the *Lobg'sang* (song of praise) by the Amish, is the second hymn in every Amish service. In addition to the *Ausbund* (the hymnal of the Amish), the hymn appears in German in the first "Free Church" hymnal and in *The Mennonite Hymnal* (1969). Ernest Payne, a Baptist, found a copy of the *Ausbund* in a bookstore in Goshen, Indiana, in 1950. Six years later he made the present translation for a lecture he delivered to the Congregational Historical Society in England.

A remnant of the German text, "O Gott Vater" (**33**), which consists of four stanzas of seven lines each, appears in this hymnal with the tune AUS TIEFER NOT.

NUN FREUT EUCH is an anonymous tune originating in the early Reformation. Reflecting the influence of the German medieval songs of the *Minnesingers* (poet-musicians), its melody follows a phrase pattern of A A B, which is called bar form.

228

Our Father who art in heaven

(no tune name)

Matthew 6:9-13

Anonymous chant

The hymnal presents three settings of the Lord's Prayer in varied musical styles. This first setting is sometimes described as an "Anglican chant" and was included in *The Brethren Hymnal* (1951) and *The Mennonite Hymnal* (1969). It is accessible because of its limited range and simplicity of melodic and harmonic lines. For an article on singing the Anglican chant, see page 179 in the *Accompaniment Handbook.*

351

Our Father who art in heaven

(no tune name)

Matthew 6:9-13

Jabani P. Mambula (1935-), 1962
The Brethren Songbook, 1974

This second setting of the Lord's Prayer is by a Nigerian Brethren and was written for use in the primary schools there, probably at Waka. Mambula testifies that the tune was revealed to him during a church service. "This particular song revealed the effectiveness of God as a Mighty Father feeding his children from heaven," he writes. "When his children become naughty he forgives them. He is seen as a protector shielding us from the destructive Satan." This setting is similar in style to tunes heard at funeral services in Margi. The call-and-response style, indicated by the repeat signs, will be facilitated by using the percussion parts provided in the *Accompaniment Handbook.*

554
Our Father who art in heaven

Based on Matthew 6:9-13
Music from Taizé, Vol. I, 1978, 1980, 1981

(no tune name)

Jacques Berthier (1923-), 1980
(same source as text)

The third setting here of the Lord's Prayer comes from the Taizé community and includes the Latin words for the opening of the Lord's Prayer, *Pater noster qui es in coelis*, pronounced "Pah-tehr noh-stehr kwee es een cheh-lees." The solo verses are in the *Accompaniment Handbook*, along with instrumental parts. This congregational ostinato, which acts as a baseline for the verses, may begin with the soprano line, gradually adding the bass, tenor, and alto parts, in that order.

133
Out of the depths I cry to you

Based on Psalm 130
Aus tiefer Not schrei ich zu dir
Martin Luther (1483-1546), 1523-1524
Etlich Christlich Lieder, 1524
Tr. Gracia Grindal (1943-)
Lutheran Book of Worship, 1978, alt.

AUS TIEFER NOT (DE PROFUNDIS)

Attrib. to Martin Luther (1483-1546)
Johann Walther's *Geystliche Gesangk Buchleyn*, 1524
(Zahn No. 4437)
Harm. by The Hymnal Project, 1990

The inimitable Martin Luther, who was instrumental in bringing vernacular hymn singing to worship, not only made his own translation of the Bible, but also wrote his own hymns, including psalm paraphrases. In 1523 he wrote this one in four stanzas from Psalm 130. It was published in that form in a broadside and in his *Eyn Enchiridion* (Erfurt 1524). That same year, in Wittenberg, Johann Walther published a five-stanza version created by the rewriting of stanza 2 for his *Geystliche Gesangk Buchleyn*. The translation in *Hymnal: A Worship Book* uses the first four stanzas of the latter text. Although this hymn takes its cue from Psalm 130, it interweaves distinctly Christian concepts, notably the Pauline teaching of salvation by grace alone, which dominates the middle stanzas. In stanza 3:4, "the holy signature" is probably an allusion to Ephesians 1:13-14 where Paul describes the mark of the seal of the promised Holy Spirit on the believer, the sign of the hope of redemption.

Though Luther was a thorn in the side of the Roman Catholic hierarchy, his hymn found wide acceptance among the people. In Lübeck a blind beggar took to singing it continually until the city council banned the beggar from the city because of his association with the work of the troublesome Luther. In spite of that, the song was taken up soon after in congregational worship, and the council was forced to reverse its position (Eltz-Hoffmann 1980).

Like Isaac Watts's "O God, our help in ages past," this hymn is appropriate for Christian funerals. It was sung in 1525 at the funeral of Luther's patron, Frederick the Wise; and in 1546 it was sung as Luther's body was being brought to Wittenberg for burial.

The tune is possibly by Luther himself. It opens with a musical descent into and coming "out of the depths." The eighth-note upbeats help to convey the urgency of supplication. The plaintive quality of the Phrygian mode is especially appropriate for the melancholy first stanza. The Phrygian, or third, mode is equivalent to the white keys of the piano from E to E. The tune has been called DE PROFUNDIS, from the Latin version of the text, and COBURG. Cantata No. 38 by J. S. Bach is based on this chorale tune. The harmonization was prepared especially for this hymnal.

358

Oyenos, mi Dios

(no tune name)

Owen Alstott (20th c.)
Tr. (Spanish) Mary F. Reza (20th c.)
Everlasting Your Love, 1988

Bob Hurd (20th c.) and Owen Alstott (20th c.)
(same source as text)

Although first published in the collection cited above, this song later became part of *Misa de las Americas.* The Spanish portion of the text is pronounced "Oh-yay-nos me Deeos" ("Hear us, my God"). Because it is bilingual, this song has been used by several liturgical conventions. In the full score, the prayers of the people are spoken or sung by a solo voice as a countermelody, beginning at the second measure of the refrain (see *Accompaniment Handbook*).

554

Pater noster qui es in coelis—see "Our Father who art in heaven"

647
Pero queda Cristo—see "Por la mañana"

229
Pescador de hombres—see "Tú has venido a la orilla"

647
Por la mañana

At break of day
Alfredo Colom M.
Himnos de Fey y Alabanza, 1954
Tr. Mary B. Valencia
International Songbook, 1978

(no tune name)

Alfredo Colom M.
(same source as text)

This song, originally titled "Pero Queda Cristo," was included in the *International Songbook* for both the 1978 and 1990 Mennonite World Conferences. The earlier collection was the first to publish this English translation of the text, as well as one in German by Esther C. Bergen. Only one change has been made: "Christ's merit" replaces "God's merit" in stanza 1:3. The two stanzas take us from "break of day" until "the sun goes down," reminding us that God's love and mercy are indeed "everlasting."

The harmony, with the warm sound of sixths and thirds, creates a sense of the comfort described in the text. The use of only two chords makes this an easy song for guitarists to play.

118, 119
Praise God from whom

Thomas Ken (1637-1710 or 1711)
Manual of Prayers for Use of the Scholars of Winchester College, 1695
Alt. in 1709

DEDICATION ANTHEM (606)

Lowell Mason's *Boston Handel and Haydn Society Collection . . . ,* 9th ed., 1830

OLD HUNDREDTH

Louis Bourgeois (ca. 1510-ca. 1561)
Genevan Psalter, 1551

The basic elements of a doxology are "the proclamation of God's praise, coupled with an affirmation of his infinity in time" (*The Hymnal 1940 Companion,* 1951 ed.). Both the Hebrew and early Christian writings contain doxologies, and when a movement arose that questioned the pre-existence of Jesus as God's Son (Arian controversy), the *Gloria Patri,* or Lesser Doxology, evolved. About the year 400, it became a nearly mandated tradition to conclude all psalms and antiphons with this doxology. Often doxologies were appended to previously existing works; this practice continued with Reformation metrical psalmody and even into recent centuries. The Greater Doxology (*Gloria in excelsis Deo*) is an expansion of Luke 2:14 and came into use at the beginning of the sixth century.

This doxology concludes a morning hymn ("Awake, my soul, and with the sun") and an evening hymn ("All praise to thee"), written by Thomas Ken for the students of Winchester College. It is likely that it was written some time prior to its appearance in the 1695 edition of the *Manual of Prayers . . .* , for in a 1674 edition Ken directs the scholars to "be sure to sing the Morning and Evening Hymn in your Chamber devoutly." The form in present use is Ken's revision of 1709.[1]

While Ken's words have been sung perhaps more frequently than any others ever written, the music of DEDICATION ANTHEM is not as universally well known. It has, however, become a very popular piece among the Mennonites. Its usage has been so widespread in the time since the publication of *The Mennonite Hymnal* (1969) that it is known simply as "606," its number designation in that hymnal. Appropriate for nearly every occasion, the anthem uses a basic text, then meditates upon it musically, repeating the text in order to give varied facets of the words (Oyer 1980).

The ninth edition (1830) of Lowell Mason's *Boston Handel and Haydn Society Collection of Church Music* is the earliest appearance in print found to date, but 1830 may be a bit late for an anthem of this sort (Oyer 1980). The tune designation there is DOXOLOGY, while the title DEDICATION ANTHEM is used in *Harmonia Sacra,* in which it first appeared in the fifteenth edition, 1876.

No composer's name is given, though a footnote in the eleventh edition (1831) of *Boston Handel and Haydn Society Collection . . .* reads "For this very popular piece the editor acknowledges his obligations to Mr. James Sharp." The attribution to Samuel Stanley (d. 1822), which appears in *The Mennonite Hymnal* (1969), is taken from a copy of *Harmonia Sacra* (1876) (Oyer 1980).

For information on OLD HUNDREDTH, see "All people that on earth do dwell" (**42**) where the melody appears in an alternate rhythmic form. The text is presented in English in both traditional and contemporary versions, as well as in various translations representing current Brethren and Mennonite ethnic constituencies.

1. In the 1695 version, the third line reads "Praise him above y'Angelic Host." The text before and after revision is in Julian's *Dictionary of Hymnology,* pages 618-619.

95

Praise God, the Source of life

DEUS TUORUM MILITUM

Ruth C. Duck (1947-), ca. 1986
Touch Holiness, 1990

French church melody
Grenoble Antiphoner, 1753

This ascription of praise grew out of a project of the Massachusetts Conference of the United Church of Christ, searching for alternatives to traditional worship texts. It was initially sung to the tune AZMON, usually associated with the hymn "Oh, for a thousand tongues to sing" (**110**). The text was subsequently published in the conference newsletter and later in the collection of worship resources cited above, edited by Ruth Duck and Tira Bassi.

For comments on DEUS TUORUM MILITUM, see "Creating God, your fingers trace" (**325**).

100

Praise him, praise him

ALLEN

Fanny Jane Crosby (1820-1915)
Bright Jewels for the Sunday School, 1869

Chester G. Allen (1838-1878)
(same source as text)

This exuberant hymn praises Jesus Christ in his many guises. Names like Prophet, Priest, King, and Shepherd are reminiscent of the attributes of God in the Old Testament, yet when appended to Jesus, they convey a new intimacy with God's people, because we have seen them embodied.

Though originating with Fanny Crosby, this text has undergone various changes by unidentified editors. In the original D.S. section, there was no refrain, but rather a new text for each stanza. The last half of stanzas 2 and 3 have been completely changed. *Gospel Hymns Nos. 1 to 6 Complete* (1894) contain the hymn in the form we sing today.

The tune ALLEN, also known as JOYFUL SONG, has abundant energy. ALLEN was written for this text for *Bright Jewels . . .*, edited by Bradbury, Doane, Sherwin, and Allen for the publishers Biglow and Main.

76

Praise, I will praise you, Lord—see "Je louerai l'Eternel"

63
Praise, my soul, the God of heaven

Based on Psalm 103
Henry Francis Lyte (1793-1847)
Lyte's *The Spirit of the Psalms*, 1834, alt.

LAUDA ANIMA (ANDREWS)

Mark Andrews (1875-1939)
Published as an anthem, 1931
Arr. by Nevin Wishard Fisher (1900-1984)
The Brethren Hymnal, 1951

This hymn, based on Psalm 103, is one of more than 280 Psalm paraphrases by Lyte included in his *The Spirit of the Psalms*. This collection was made for his congregation in Lower Brixham, Devonshire, England, a small fishing village where he was pastor for twenty-four years until his death. There are more alterations in this version than in "Praise, my soul, the King of heaven" (**65**), which contains only two changes from the original. One stanza, the fourth, has been omitted in both hymns:

> Frail as summer's flower we flourish;
> Blows the wind, and it is gone,
> But while mortals rise and perish,
> God endures unchanging on.
> Praise him! Praise him!
> Praise the high eternal One!

LAUDA ANIMA (ANDREWS) includes the name of the composer as part of the tune name to avoid confusion with the Goss tune sometimes known by the same name. Andrews' anthem on the original Lyte text, published by G. Schirmer, was arranged by Fisher for *The Brethren Hymnal* (1951). The two tunes and text versions (**63, 65**) are interchangeable.

65
Praise, my soul, the King of heaven

Based on Psalm 103
Henry Francis Lyte (1793-1847)
Lyte's *The Spirit of the Psalms*, 1834, alt.

BENEDIC ANIMA

John Goss (1800-1880)
The Supplemental Hymn and Tune Book, 1869

The origins of this hymn text are described under "Praise, my soul, the God of heaven" (**63**).

Britain's Queen Elizabeth II requested this hymn as the processional for her wedding, which took place in 1947 on the hundredth anniversary of Lyte's death. This was quite a posthumous honor for the author, whom Erik Routley describes in *Hymns and Human Life* as "an obscure country curate who [had] no claim to fame beyond his saintly character and a handful of hymns." In Canadian churches the hymn with Goss's tune is still widely used for wedding processionals. For additional comments on BENEDIC ANIMA, see "Jesus came—the heavens adoring" (**297**).

52

Praise the Lord — SAKURA

Nobuaki Hanaoka(1944-), 1980
Hymns from the Four Winds, 1983

Traditional Japanese melody
Transcribed by AAH, 1981

As Hanaoka traveled from San Francisco to San Jose, California, one beautiful day, he "was struck by the majesty of the ocean to the west and the beauty of the hills to the east. Soon I began to praise God for all the things that surrounded me with such grace and beauty." By the time he reached his destination, the text was completed in his mind and later published with very little revision.

This hymn makes an engaging companion to the familiar "For the beauty of the earth" (**89**), with its similar emphasis on the gifts of God in nature, friends, and the church.

This traditional melody is the setting for the "Cherry Blossom Song," known in Japan as *Sakura, sakura*. The movement of the melody in two pulses per measure may be felt by singing this bit of Japanese text. Though the tune's gentle sounds require little or no accompaniment, instrumentation options include windchimes, handbells, recorder, or flute.

50

Praise the Lord, sing hallelujah — PRAISE JEHOVAH

Based on Psalm 148
Adapt. by William James Kirkpatrick (1838-1921)
The Book of Psalms, 1871, alt.

William James Kirkpatrick (1838-1921), ca. 1893

The versification from which Kirkpatrick made his adaptation originally had eight four-line stanzas. In Kirkpatrick's adaptation, which begins "Hallelujah, praise Jehovah," each of the three stanzas corresponds to four verses of the psalm. The refrain, which was in the original stanza 7, is derived from the last two verses of the psalm. In addition to a change in the first line found in other sources, here the form of address has been changed to make it the same as in the psalm itself, calling both the heavenly world and all the earthly realm to praise the Lord. In stanza 3:4, "princes" is now "rulers," and in stanza 3:5 "maidens, aged men" becomes "women, aged ones."

The buoyant music of PRAISE JEHOVAH, so well suited to this text, has been dated 1893 in *Great Songs of the Church* (1986) and 1899 in *Life Songs* (1916).

54
Praise the Lord who reigns above — AMSTERDAM

Based on Psalm 150
Charles Wesley (1707-1788)
A Collection of Psalms and Hymns, 1743, alt.

Freylinghausen's *Geistreiches Gesangbuch,* Halle, 1704
Adapt. by John Benjamin Wesley (1703-1791), *Foundery Collection,* London, 1742

Psalm 150 is the majestic, musical curtain call of the Book of Psalms. Having run dry of verbal expressions in the previous finale of five praise psalms, the psalmist turns to musical instruments of all shapes, sounds, and sizes. Wesley adds his own note: the music of the heart. The entire cast of characters is assembled in the final shout of praise of the whole book: "Praise the Lord" or "Hallelujah!"

Originally consisting of four eight-line stanzas, the hymn's stanzas 1, 2, and 4 were used in other collections, including Augustus Toplady's *Psalms and Hymns* (1776). After this, the hymn was mistakenly credited to Toplady in some subsequent nineteenth-century collections. John Wesley included three stanzas in his collection *Sunday Services* (1788), prepared for the American colonies. However, this hymn did not appear in any American Methodist hymnal until 1966 when stanzas 1, 3, and 4 of the original hymn were used. Those same stanzas, in somewhat altered form, are the ones included here.

AMSTERDAM is one of six tunes that John Wesley adapted from the *Geistreiches Gesangbuch,* to which he was probably introduced by his Moravian shipmates on his journey to Georgia. Wesley included the tune in his *Foundery Collection,* the first Methodist hymnal. There it is erroneously ascribed to James Nares, an eighteenth-century composer. The harmonization used here comes from Joseph Funk's nineteenth-century collection, *Harmonia Sacra,* where it appears with the text "Rise, my soul, and stretch thy wings."

91
Praise to God, immortal praise — PRAYER

Anna Laetitia Barbauld (1743-1825)
William Enfield's *Hymns for Public Worship,* 1772, alt.

Asahel Abbot (19th c.)
The Devotional Harmonist, 1850

"Praise to God, immortal praise" is Part 1 of a nine-stanza poem titled "Praise to God in Prosperity and Adversity." This portion (cento) of five stanzas is much like the original[1] except for a reversal of the couplets in stanza 3 and the revision of the last couplet of stanza 2. The original is: "For the vine's exalted juice, For the generous olive's use . . . ."

Many hymnals reduce this initial portion of the poem to four stanzas by combining the original first couplets of stanzas 2 and 3 into one stanza. Both the *Pilgrim Hymnal* (1904) and *The Brethren Hymnal* (1951) combine some of the lines of this text with those of "Come, ye thankful people, come," an alternative which Routley describes as "most intelligent" (Routley 1979).

Part 2 of the poem appears in the hymn "Lord, should rising whirlwinds" (**92**). Further information on these hymns and their use may be found under that listing.

The simple vocal lines of PRAYER lend themselves to resonant, four-part *a cappella* singing. The music originally appeared with the text "Gracious Spirit—Love Divine" in Charles Dingley's *The Devotional Harmonist: A Collection of Sacred Music*, a teaching book published for a group of Methodist Episcopal churches near New York City (Oyer 1980). Composer Abbot's tunes appear in North American books of the 1840s and 1850s, but further information on his life is not readily accessible.

1. The complete, original text may be found in *The Hymnal 1940 Companion*, pages 100-101.

37

Praise to the Lord, the Almighty

LOBE DEN HERREN

Lobe den Herren, den mächtigen König der Ehren
Joachim Neander (1650-1680)
Alpha und Omega, Glaub- und Liebesübung, 1680
Tr. Catherine Winkworth (1827-1878)
Chorale Book for England, 1863, alt.

Erneuerten Gesangbuch, Stralsund, 1665

This widely known hymn is freely adapted from portions of Psalms 103 and 150. It is one of about sixty hymns (and one of his last) written by Joachim Neander during his short lifetime. This is the best-known hymn by Neander, who posthumously has been regarded as the principal poet of the Reformed Church in Germany.

The translation by Catherine Winkworth has been altered only slightly. In stanza 3:4, the theologically problematic "if" turns out to be a mistranslation of Neander's *wer*, which means "who." "As" seemed to be the least disruptive alternative, though *The United Methodist Hymnal* (1989) has the felicitous "who with his love doth befriend thee." In the concluding line of the hymn, the word "aye," which often presented problems of pronunciation and understanding, has been changed to "ever." Stanza 2:2, which in some hymnals reads "Shieldeth thee gently from harm, or when fainting sustaineth," returns to Winkworth's original "Shelters thee under his wings, yea, so gently sustaineth."

LOBE DEN HERREN is a variation of a melody that appeared in the Stralsund *Ander thiel des erneuerten Gesangbuch*. Neander chose this tune for the first printing of his text, but it had quite a different form by 1680. The way we use this tune today incorporates further alterations made with the hymnals of 1692, 1701, and 1708. The melody is believed to be based on an older secular tune and took its name, LOBE DEN HERREN, from the first words of Neander's German text.

572

Prayer is the soul's sincere desire — DORKING

James Montgomery (1771-1854)
Pamphlet, 1818, alt.

Stephanie Martin (1962-), 1990
Hymnal: A Worship Book, 1992

When Edward Bickersteth was preparing his *Treatise on Prayer* (1819), he asked Montgomery to come up with a text to answer the question, What is prayer? Montgomery complied with eight stanzas,[1] a set of concise, powerful metaphors that became one of his most requested hymns. He first published it on a broadsheet for use in the Sunday schools of Sheffield, England, along with two other hymns on prayer. Bickersteth made some alterations of the original, as did the author in later reprints. A few additional changes have been made for this hymnal, including changing two archaisms in the final stanza. One of Montgomery's other hymns, "Lord, teach us how to pray aright" (**350**), picks up where this one leaves off.

In previous Mennonite and Brethren hymnals, this text was sung to NEWCASTLE or SHADDICK. DORKING, however, is the result of a special tune search and was written for this hymnal. Mennonite Stephanie Martin writes that the name "is derived from a small town in southwestern Ontario (known for its general store) near my parents' farm in the country, where this tune and others were written." One change in text was made to accommodate the new music. In stanza 1:2, "uttered or unexpressed" has been transposed to read "unuttered or expressed."

The gentle lyricism of Martin's music is a welcome companion to this text, and the rising final pitch of the melody lends an air of expectation at its conclusion.

1. The three omitted stanzas are in *The Hymnal 1940 Companion*, 1951 ed.

575

Precious Lord, take my hand

Thomas Andrew Dorsey (1899-1993), 1932

PRECIOUS LORD

George Nelson Allen (1812-1877)
The Oberlin Social and Sabbath School Hymn Book, 1844
Adapt. by Thomas Andrew Dorsey, 1932

Gospel songwriter Thomas A. Dorsey was out of town when his wife, Nettie, who was expecting their first baby, died in childbirth. "I buried Nettie and our little boy together, in the same casket," Dorsey writes. "Then I fell apart. For days I closeted myself. I felt that God had done me an injustice. I didn't want to serve Him anymore or write gospel songs" (Dorsey 1987).

Wracked with grief, Dorsey finally let a friend Theodore Frye take him to a neighborhood music school the following Saturday evening. Dorsey continues:

> He left me there, alone in a room with a piano. It was quiet; the late evening sun crept through the curtained windows. I sat down at the piano, and my hands began to browse over the keys. Something happened to me then. I felt at peace. I felt as though I could reach out and touch God. I found myself playing a melody, one I'd never heard or played before, and words came into my head—they just seemed to fall into place. (Dorsey 1987)

The melody was, in reality, an adaptation of the tune MAITLAND, composed by George Allen for the text "Must Jesus bear the cross alone." This hymn, which healed Dorsey's spirit, has been a balm for many. Dorsey concludes: "I learned that when we are in our deepest grief, when we feel farthest from God, this is when He is closest, and when we are most open to His restoring power" (Dorsey 1987).

534

Prince of peace, control my will

Mary Ann Serrett Barber (1801-1864), ca. 1838
Hymns for the Use of the Methodist Episcopal Church, Revised Edition, 1853

OYER

Bradley P. Lehman (1964-), 1984
Oregon '91 conference booklet, July 1991

Listed as anonymous until the 1881 *Methodist Hymnal* included the author's name, this gentle text points to the beginning of peace: being one with God in will and intent.

The hymn has been set to Bradbury's ALETTA, but Lehman thought the music seemed "too easygoing and generic for this intimate text." He composed OYER for a church-music class taught by Mary K. Oyer at Goshen College (Ind.). He named the tune for his professor "because of her contagious enthusiasm for deeply expressive church music."

282
Proclaim the tidings near and far — SING GLORY, HALLELUJAH

Fronia Savage Smith
Gems and Jewels, 1890

James Henry Fillmore (1849-1936)
(same source as text)

This hymn proclaims "The Lord is risen!" and is based on verses in two Gospels: Matthew 28:6-7 and Mark 16:6-7. The first stanza is identical with that in *Gems and Jewels*, but the second and third stanzas differ greatly. Whether these are portions of other stanzas from the same poem or alterations of the original is not known. The 1890 version is as follows:

The Lord is risen, Oh, rejoice
Ye hearts grown sad and weary;
Let songs of gladness swell each voice
That bears the wondrous story.

Death has no sting for those who love
This risen Lord to follow;
Across their hearts the gloomy grave
Throws not its gloomy shadow.

In the 1925 Brethren hymnal, the tune was erroneously attributed to Sam Mason. For *The Brethren Hymnal* (1951), the hymn was titled "Sing Glory, Hallelujah" at the request of Fillmore Brothers Co., the copyright holder. The purposeful stepping of the three lower voices in the chorus reminds one of striding out to "proclaim the tidings." This chorus has a vitality that intensifies the joy of the Easter message.

313
Rejoice, rejoice in God — REJOICE IN GOD

Freut euch, Freut euch in dieser Zeit
Balthasar Hubmaier (ca. 1480-1528), ca. 1520
Tr. Ruth Eileen Bundy Naylor (1934-)
Assembly Songs, 1983, alt.

James W. Bixel (1913-)
(same source as text)

At the time of Hubmaier's martyrdom, the *Hutterian Chronicle* reported that "two hymns are still in our brotherhood which this Balthasar Hubmaier composed" (*Mennonite Encyclopedia* 1957). Of those two, only this one of eighteen eight-line stanzas has been found thus far. Titled "A Song in Praise of God's Word," the poem is a compendium of the heroes of the

Bible, from Adam and Noah to Jesus Christ and the writers of the Gospels and Epistles. The unifying thought of the poem is found in the last couplet of each of Hubmaier's stanzas, *Dann Gottes Wort bleibt ewig b'stan*. "God's word will stand eternally" captures this faith statement in the final stanza of Ruth Naylor's text, which is drawn primarily from stanzas 1, 7, and 18 of the original.[1]

James Bixel chose Hubmaier's text out of several he was sent just prior to "Bethlehem '83," a gathering of seven thousand Mennonites in eastern Pennsylvania. He wanted to set it to music, but it needed revision in order to work as a hymn. "I showed it to Ruth Naylor, assistant pastor of the First Mennonite Church, Bluffton, Ohio, and asked if she could distill the essential thoughts of the piece. . . . She wrote a beautiful poetic version which I then set to music."

1. A complete copy of the original text is in *Balthasar Hubmaier, Theologian of Anabaptism*, translated and edited by H. Wayne Pipkin and John H. Yoder, Herald Press, 1989.

288
Rejoice, the Lord is King — DARWALL'S 148th

Charles Wesley (1707-1788)
J. Wesley's *Moral and Sacred Poems*, 1744

John Darwall (1731-1789)
Aaron Williams' *New Universal Psalmodist*, 1770

Charles and John Wesley, often the target of Anglican animosity and disdain, had more than one occasion to sing a song to bolster their spirits. Exhorted by Paul's writings to rejoice in adversity as well as in blessing, Charles likely based the last part of this text on Philippians 4:4: "Rejoice in the Lord always; again I will say, rejoice." The form, however, with "Lift up your heart" is reminiscent of part of the Great Thanksgiving that begins the service of the Eucharist.

The hymn's rather unusual rhyme scheme of *ababcc* creates the feeling of a refrain at the close of each stanza. The rest of the text proclaims Christ's lordship. In the manuscript the hymn was labeled "for Easter and Ascension" when Christ showed himself to be the the Lord of life. Wesley's original had six stanzas; stanzas 4 and 5 have been omitted.

For comments on DARWALL'S 148th, also called DARWALL, see "Christ is our cornerstone" (**43**).

363

Renew your church — ALL IS WELL

Kenneth Lorne Cober (1902-)
American Baptist Convention, May 1960, alt.

American folk melody
Adapt. from J. T. White's *Sacred Harp,* 1844

Church and spiritual renewal is ever an imperative, and it cannot be done without the vigor of God working in us. Cober's hymn sums up the ministry of the church in just three words: "serve and adore." It echoes Matthew 5:13-14 in calling on the church for "saltiness" and "light" in stanza 1:2-3. This is a densely packed prayer for both the times when the church is ministering strongly and when it is turned in upon itself.

Cober wrote this hymn text while traveling across the country on trains and planes for denominational work. It appeared as part of the Baptist Jubilee Advance, a five-year denominational program. Written specifically for the second year's emphasis on "The Renewal of the Church: Imperative to Evangelism," the hymn was first sung at the American Baptist Convention in May of 1960.

Brethren became acquainted with "Renew your church" when it was included in *The Brethren Songbook* (1974); it appeared in a number of other nondenominational hymnals in the 1970s. Originally beginning "Renew thy church," the text is altered here to eliminate archaic forms of speech.

For comments on ALL IS WELL, see "Come, come, ye saints" (**425**).

239

Ride on, ride on in majesty — WINCHESTER NEW

Henry Hart Milman (1791-1868)
Heber's *Hymns Written and Adapted to the Weekly Service of the Church Year,* 1827
Rev. in *Hymns for Today's Church,* 1982

Musicalisch Handbuch der Geistlichen Melodien, published by George Rebelein's widow, 1690
Arr. by William Henry Havergal (1793-1870)
Old Church Psalmody, 1847

Milman wrote this hymn in 1821, the same year he became professor of poetry at Oxford University. This poem is a dramatic presentation of the Palm Sunday dichotomies of meekness and majesty, sacrifice and victory, suffering and glory.

Already altered in earlier editions, the contemporary version used here includes several further changes. The most notable comes in the last lines of stanza 1, which originally read:

> Thine humble beast pursues thy road
> With palms and scattered garments strowed.

The original third stanza, often omitted, is included here, because it heightens the sense of approaching tragedy to have even the "the angel armies of the sky" (originally "The winged squadrons of the sky") witness the incongruity of Jesus' ride through an adoring crowd to a waiting cross.

For comments on WINCHESTER NEW, see "On Jordan's banks the Baptist's cry" (**183**).

400

Santo, santo, santo — SANTO

Holy, holy, holy
Guillermo Cuellar (1955-), 1980
Misa Popular Salvadoreña, 1978-1980
Tr. Linda McCrae

Guillermo Cuellar (1955-), 1980
(same source as text)

The Mass from which this song comes was "born in the communities of San Salvador in the years 1978-1980, especially in the 'Parroquia (Parish) Zacamil' and the 'Parroquia Resurreccion.' It was supported by Monseñor [Oscar] Romero, Father Placido Erdozain, and Father Rutilio Grande. These songs were born like a 'hope' for us in the most difficult (times) of our country" (Ramirez 1992). This song of praise has enjoyed wide usage not only in Latin America, but also in Europe and Scandinavia. It has been published in paperback collections of songs produced by the World Council of Churches. The song may be sung using Spanish for the opening section and English for the verses, or a single language throughout.

The composer, who was born in El Salvador, does not know how to write or read music, but his creative work has nonetheless inspired his people. The lilting music moves between 3/4 and 6/8 meters. A keyboard part and further performance suggestions are in the *Accompaniment Handbook.*

656

Savior, again to your dear name — ELLERS

John Ellerton (1826-1893), 1866
Hymns Ancient and Modern, Appendix, 1868, alt.

Edward John Hopkins (1818-1901), 1866
Supplemental Tune and Hymn Book, 1869

This hymn was written for the 1866 Festival of the Malpas, Middlewich, England, and Nantwick Choral Association, closing the final session with a benediction of peace and sending the singers to their various homes (st. 2:1). Titled "The Lord shall give His people the blessing of peace," the hymn was written by John Ellerton on the back of his preceding Sunday's sermon. It has been noted that it superbly blends the corporate nature of worship with the spirituality of the individual.

The textual variants of this hymn are rather complex,[1] and there is some question as to whether it was originally five or six stanzas. References do agree that the author shortened his hymn to four stanzas and revised it for *Hymns Ancient and Modern, Appendix*, the most popular of the versions. This is also Ellerton's most successful and extensively used hymn. In the more contemporary version selected for this hymnal, the words "you" and "your" have replaced "thee" and "thy." By omitting stanza 3, the hymn may be used for occasions other than evening services.

Ellerton wrote his text for J. Langran's tune ST. AGNES. John B. Dykes composed the tune PAX DEI for Ellerton's text, and more recently Ralph Vaughan Williams composed his tune MAGDA for it. Comments on ELLERS are given with the hymn text "Lead us, O Father" (**359**).

1. For a description, see Julian's *Dictionary of Hymnology*, page 995.

355
Savior, like a shepherd lead us — BRADBURY

Anonymous
D. Thrupp's *Hymns for the Young*, 4th ed., 1836

William Batchelder Bradbury (1816-1868)
Oriola, 1859

This childlike hymn, which often alludes to Psalm 23, was used frequently by Dwight L. Moody and Ira D. Sankey when they preached or wrote about the Good Shepherd. It is unknown who wrote it, however. Both Dorothy Ann Thrupp and H. F. Lyte have been suggested as possible authors, but neither with conclusive evidence.[1] In *Hymns for the Young*, its earliest source, all the hymns appear anonymously.

BRADBURY was composed particularly for these words. It was first published in the key of E major with three-part harmony, SAB. The musical version used here is the one found in E. O. Excell's *Hymns and Sacred Songs* (1918), the same as the one used in the 1925 Brethren hymnal and the *The Mennonite Hymnal* (1969).

1. This uncertainty of authorship is discussed fully by Haeussler in *The Story of Our Hymns*, 1952.

549
Savior of my soul — JOHN NAAS

Heiland meiner Seel'
John (Johannes) Naas (1669-1741)
Die Kleine Harfe, 1792
Tr. Lillian E. Grisso (1889-1974)

William Beery (1852-1956), 1944
The Brethren Hymnal, 1951

John Naas, an early Brethren leader, was on a preaching mission when he was conscripted by force by agents of the king of Prussia, Frederick William I. Because of his height, Naas was considered an ideal recruit for the king's personal guards, all of whom were more than six feet tall. When he refused to enlist, he was tortured. When he was later taken before the king to explain his noncompliance, he stated, "I have already long ago enlisted.... My captain is the great Prince Emmanuel, our Lord, Jesus Christ" (D. Durnbaugh 1958). The story has become a favorite children's book, *The Tall Man*, published by Brethren Press.

Though Naas's poem first appeared in *Die Kleine Harfe* in 1792 (published by Samuel Sauer), it was not until the second edition in 1797 that his name was added. This hymn later made its way into only one other German hymnal of the Brethren, *Neue Sammlung* (1870).

The translation by Lillian Grisso is a "very free paraphrase utilizing only stanzas 1, 3, and 8 of the original 17 stanzas. . . . This poem is . . . a typical Pietist hymn. It deals with the individual's troubles in this world and life and with the state of one's soul" (H. Durnbaugh 1991).

The tune JOHN NAAS, composed by Beery when he was ninety-two, "was inspired by the sentiments expressed, and it came about as rapidly as I could write it down. Of course a knowledge of the life of the author may have had something to do with it" (Statler, Fisher 1959).

173
Savior of the nations, come

Veni, Redemptor gentium
Attrib. to Ambrose of Milan (ca. 340-397)
Nun komm, der Heiden Heiland
Tr. Martin Luther (1483-1546), 1523
Luther's *Eyn Enchiridion*, Erfurt, 1524
Sts. 1-2, tr. William Morton Reynolds (1812-1876)
Hymns Original and Selected, 1851
Sts. 3-4, tr. Martin Louis Seltz (1909-1967)
Worship Supplement to *The Lutheran Hymnal*, 1969, alt.

NUN KOMM, DER HEIDEN HEILAND

Plainsong, 9th c.
Johann Walther's *Geystliche Gesangk Buchleyn*, 1524
Harm. by Melchior Vulpius (ca. 1560-1615)
(Zahn No. 1174)

The original Latin version of "Savior of the nations" was ascribed to Ambrose of Milan by his great contemporary St. Augustine in 372. *Veni, Redemptor gentium*, written in lilting iambic dimeter, appears in eighth- and ninth-century manuscripts. The eight eight-line stanzas blend the nativity story with powerful theological teaching on the incarnation. Ambrose preferred to express the deepest affection of the heart with simplicity and economy (Trench 1864), but he was also passionate about doctrine. Like Luther, Ambrose wrote his hymns for congregational rather than for private devotional use in an effort to strengthen faith for the trials ahead.

Martin Luther's excellent, but somewhat literal, translation of the text into German has become the oldest and one of the most celebrated Advent hymns of the Reformation. By 1524 it was already associated with this melody in both Walther's and Luther's publications mentioned above. The English translation, taken from the two sources cited above, parallels stanzas 1, 2, 3, and 7 of the earlier Latin and German hymns. The play of the "night" and "light" words in stanza 4 is especially striking.

The oldest known source for the original plainsong melody is an early twelfth-century manuscript from the Benedictine monastery at Einsiedeln, Switzerland. This adaptation of the ancient plainsong is new to twentieth-century Brethren and Mennonites; however, this chorale tune appeared with three other texts in the early Brethren *Das Kleine Davidische Psalter-Spiel* (1744) (H. Durnbaugh 1991). J. S. Bach used this melody in four organ settings and two cantatas, Nos. 36 and 62. Also see "Fire of God, undying Flame" (**129**).

268

See the splendor of the morning — TINMINAGO

Francisco F. Feliciano (1941-), 1977
Hymns from the Four Winds, 1983

Francisco F. Feliciano (1941-), 1977
(same source as text)

Feliciano wrote this hymn while studying in the 1970s at the Akademie der Künste in Berlin, West Germany. The joyous text lifts up the resurrection theme of Easter. A fifth stanza, a doxology, has been omitted.

The music for this hymn, with its air of subtle excitement, was inspired by the style found in the rural northern Philippines. The rhythmic pattern is native to the gong-music tradition of the mountain province. This type of music puts weight on every beat of the melody, dictating that the rhythm should be steady but not fast. Percussion parts and additional comments are in the *Accompaniment Handbook.* Another hymn by Feliciano, in a very different style, is "Still, I search for my God" (**88**).

454

Seed, scattered and sown — EKKLESIA

Based on Didache 9, ca. 110;
1 Corinthians 10; and Mark 4:3-6
Dan Feiten (1953-), 1987
Gather, 1988

Dan Feiten (1953-), 1987
(same source as text)
Harm. by Marilyn Houser Hamm (1951-), 1990

A passage from the Didache entreats the church to become one, just as grain is scattered when it is sown, then gathered together when it is harvested. "I was struck with the fact that the Bread of God comes from the work of our hands," notes Feiten, who was inspired by this ancient writing. "We must rely on one another for our spiritual and physical nourishment." Allusions to 1 Corinthians 10 and Mark 4:3-6 are also interwoven in the text.

The Didache, also known as the Teaching of the Twelve Apostles, was discovered in Constantinople (Turkey) in 1875 and published in 1883. It is made up of fifteen readings in two sections: the first (1-5) is a moral catechism and the second (6-15) is a sort of manual of church order, giving rules for baptism, fasting, the Lord's Supper, and numerous prayers. It sheds light on the practices of the churches of Syria near the end of the first century (Gealey, Lovelace, Young 1970).

Feiten's song became the title cut for the album of the same name made by the musical group Ekklesia (Greek for "church"). A four-part harmonization was prepared for this hymnal by Marilyn Houser Hamm, but the melody may also be sung in unison, using the keyboard part in the *Accompaniment Handbook.*

324
Seek ye first the kingdom of God — SEEK YE FIRST

Based on Matthew 6:33 and 7:7
Adapt. by Karen Lafferty (1948-), 1972

Karen Lafferty (1948-), 1972

In the fall of 1971, Karen Lafferty felt God was calling her to leave her job as an entertainer to concentrate her efforts on Christian training and ministry. When she quit her job, she struggled to pay her monthly bills and began to wonder if she had missed the Lord's guidance when she quit her job. Then, moved by a Bible study on "Seek ye first . . . " (Matt. 6:33), she composed music and adapted the words as the first stanza of this scripture song.

Lafferty's faith risk was later confirmed. She won scholarship money in a contest, but the rules stipulated that it be used at an accredited university. Lafferty nevertheless requested it for Bible training. "The scholarship committee called me just a few days after I wrote 'Seek ye first,' " she writes. "They had decided to make an exception to the rule. . . . Truly, as we seek Him first all the things we need will be added to us."

Easily memorized, the song was passed along orally, and as it was picked up in songbooks, a second stanza was added anonymously, based on another portion of Jesus' Sermon on the Mount. Other anonymous stanzas based on Matthew 4:4 and 11:28 have been created as well:

We do not live by bread alone,
but by every word
that proceeds from the mouth of God.
Allelu, Alleluia.

Come unto me, all ye that labor
and are heavy laden,
and I will give rest for your souls.
Allelu, Alleluia.

The tune, now appearing in denominational hymnals, is sometimes called LAFFERTY. The "Alleluia," which provides a lovely counterpoint to the melody, can be used both vocally and instrumentally. The simplicity of the original material allows for many possibilities in the re-creation of this song.

434
Send me, Jesus—see "Thuma mina"

478
Sent forth by God's blessing ASH GROVE

Omer Westendorf (1916-)
People's Mass Book, 1964, alt.

Welsh folk melody
Harm. by Gerald Hocken Knight (1908-1979)

This joyous conclusion to the Lord's Supper celebration was first published under one of Westendorf's pseudonyms, J. Clifford Evers. Westendorf's text was altered for inclusion in *Contemporary Worship—4* (1972) and again for the *Lutheran Book of Worship* (1978). Several other alterations have been made here, most notably at the beginning of the harmonized section where "The fruit of Christ's teaching" replaces "The seed of his teaching."

ASH GROVE is a beautiful melody that lends itself to contrasting moods. The secular words are a lament for a "sweet maiden . . . who sleeps 'neath the green turf down by the Ash-grove."[1] Katherine K. Davis combined this melody with her original text "Let all things now living" in choral arrangements for a variety of voicings. In the setting used here, the bass line of the harmonized section makes an interesting descant when sung in the treble range.

1. *Benjamin Britten: Folk Songs of the British Isles,* Vol. 1, Voice and Piano; Boosey and Hawkes, 1943

615
Shall we gather at the river — BEAUTIFUL RIVER

Robert Lowry (1826-1899), 1864
Lowry and Doane's *Happy Voices*, 1865

Robert Lowry (1826-1899)
(same source as text)

A sultry July day in Brooklyn, New York, would do nothing to stem the tide of an epidemic disease that swept the area in the summer of 1864. Lowry's hymn, written while he was pastor of Hanson Place Baptist Church in Brooklyn, answers the questions raised by many people as their loved ones were dying: "Shall we meet again? We are parting at the river of death, shall we meet at the river of life?" (Hughes 1980). In his home at Elliott Place, Lowry wrote down the words as quickly as they came to him, words about a crystal river of life (Rev. 22:1), composed in the midst of heat and death. Lowry answered his own question with a resounding "Yes" in the chorus—"we'll gather with the saints at the river." He then composed the tune at his parlor organ.

Lowry describes his tune as "brass band music [which] has a march movement, and for that reason has become popular, though . . . , I do not think much of it." Nevertheless, Lowry's hymn has nearly reached the status of a folk song. The tune has been given creative settings by Charles Ives (1874-1954) as a solo song "At the River," and as the finale of *Violin Sonata No. 4* (1916). Aaron Copland's solo setting in his collection of *Old American Songs, Set 2* (1952) has been published in a choral arrangement by R. Wilding Whitey.

460
Sheaves of summer—see "una espiga"

519
Shepherd me, O God — (no tune name)

Based on Psalm 23
Marty Haugen (1950-), 1985
Shepherd Me, O God (recording), 1986
Gather, 1988

Marty Haugen (1950-)
(same sources as text)

This setting of Psalm 23 was commissioned by Ken Mervine for St. Ann's Church in Raritan, New Jersey. The congregation there had requested a setting in responsorial form, for cantor, choir, and congregation. About its composition Marty Haugen writes:

> For me, [this] psalm is the most difficult to set. Its familiarity means that it will be associated with other musical settings . . . , and the im-

> ages of shepherd, staff and rod are firmly fixed in popular consciousness, even while they are distant from everyday experience. After numerous attempts I decided to make the word "shepherd" a verb rather than a noun. In the rest of the setting, I sought to make the language inclusive both in terms of humanity and images of God.

The words of the refrain distill the essence of the psalm. And the simplicity of the music of the refrain, following the diatonic scale, makes it easily accessible for a congregation on the first hearing, even without music. The *Accompaniment Handbook* provides music for stanzas and for other instruments.

456
Shepherd of souls, refresh — CAITHNESS

Sts. 1-2, anonymous
A Collection of Hymns for the use of the . . . United Brethren (Moravian), Philadelphia, 1832, alt.
Sts. 3-4, James Montgomery (1771-1854)
Montgomery's *Christian Psalmist,*1825

The Psalmes of David in Prose and Meeter, 1635
Harm. from *The English Hymnal,* 1906

Since this anonymous text does not appear in the 1819 edition of the above source, it was likely written between 1819 and 1832. The last two stanzas by Montgomery, a Moravian poet-journalist, were titled "The Family Table." They are based on the story in which the disciples recognized Christ in the breaking of bread after speaking with him on the road to Emmaus (Luke 24:30-31). Since both sets of stanzas share the theme of spiritual refreshment (manna and water in the desert; bread and cup at the table), their combination seems appropriate. This combined hymn first appeared in the *The Hymnal* (Episcopal) in 1874.

For comments on CAITHNESS, see "Oh, for a closer walk with God" (**520**).

480
Shepherd of tender youth — HUMMEL STREET

Clement of Alexandria (ca. 170-ca. 220) 2nd or 3rd c.
Tr. Henry Martyn Dexter (1821-1890)
The Congregationalist, Dec. 21, 1849

Richard David Brode (1963-), 1990
Hymnal: A Worship Book, 1992

This hymn is a paraphrase of a passage appended to Clement's treatise *The Tutor.* A prayer for the curbing and directing influence of Christ, Clement's text is certainly one of the earliest Christian hymns and is considered by many to be the oldest known. Written in the context of wild Alexandria, Clement was addressing young Christian converts (not children!) who had to change their lives radically to fit the Christian life. It is a potent text calling on the church to "break-in these rambunctious colts and harness them to its wagon so that their energies may advance the Kingdom of God. Christ had the same idea when He said, 'Take my yoke upon you' (Matt. 11:29)" (Bailey 1950). A literal translation of the Greek captures Clement's raw poetry:

> Bridle of colts untamed,
> Wing of unwandering birds,
> Sure helm of ships,
> Shepherd of royal lambs,
> Assemble thy simple children to raise holily, to hymn guilelessly with innocent mouths, Christ the guide of children.
>
> O King of Saints, all-subduing Word of the most high Father, Ruler of Wisdom, Support of sorrows, rejoicing in eternity, Jesus, Saviour of the human race, Shepherd, Husbandman, Helm, Bridle, Heavenly Wing of the all-holy flock, Fisher of men who are saved, catching the chaste fishes with sweet life from the hateful wave of the sea of vices—
>
> Guide us, Shepherd of rational sheep; guide, O holy King, thy children safely along the footsteps of Christ; O heavenly Way, perennial Word, immeasurable Age, eternal Light, Fount of mercy, Performer of virtue.
>
> Noble is the life of those who hymn God, O Christ Jesus, heavenly milk of the sweet breasts of the graces of the Bride, pressed out of thy wisdom. Babes nourished with tender mouths, filled with the dewy spirit of the rational pap, let us sing together simple praises, true hymns to Christ our King, holy fee for the teaching of life; let us sing in simplicity the powerful Child.
>
> O choir of peace, the Christ-begotten,
> O chaste people, let us sing together the God of peace. (Bailey 1950)

Dexter developed his paraphrase in preparation for a sermon about early Christians, first translating the Greek literally into prose. He then developed the poetic hymn, retaining some of the spirit and concepts of the original. Dexter's hymn was first printed in the periodical *The Congregationalist*, then in *Hymns for the Church of Christ* (1853). The word "eager," sometimes substituted for "tender," is taken from another paraphrase "Master of eager youth," by F. Bland Tucker.

Brode's tune was written for the text "Lord of our growing years." Although another tune was chosen for that hymn, the mood of this text is similar to that of "growing years." Thus, Brode was asked to adapt his melody for these words. The music also contains a surprise element: Just when one expects to hold a note for two beats at the end of some of the phrases, the music gives a gentle push onward, much like growing up.

The tune is named HUMMEL STREET for the location of Brode's home church in Harrisburg, Pennsylvania, First Church of the Brethren.

He writes: "Harrisburg First Church is where I spent many days of my 'tender youth'; I hold fond memories of being lovingly shepherded and nurtured by many, many wonderful people at that church."

630
Silence! frenzied, unclean spirit — AUTHORITY

Based on Mark 1:21-28 and Luke 4:31-37
Thomas Henry Troeger (1945-), 1984
New Hymns for the Lectionary, 1986

Carol Doran (1936-), 1984
(same source as text)

This hymn text is based on the miracle described in Mark 1:21-28 and Luke 4:31-37. Troeger writes of his hymn:

> I was eager to interpret the meaning of demons for people who live in a post-Freudian, psychological, scientific culture. While writing the text, I recalled when I was a pastor and a popular movie, "The Exorcist," touched off a wave of questions about the meaning of demons and exorcism in the New Testament. I wished at the time I had had an appropriate hymn. . . . So this hymn fills that gap. It has been used by some groups in very creative ways to develop liturgies for the exorcism of social as well as personal demons.

The composer Carol Doran, who has collaborated with Troeger on numerous hymns, wrote AUTHORITY specifically for this text "in an effort to express the drama of the moment of this extraordinary healing and to allow the congregation, through their singing of this music, to participate in a strong retelling of the story." Though not included here, the accompaniment is provided in the *Accompaniment Handbook.*

Of all their hymns, this one most vividly exemplifies Troeger and Doran's goal of creating "a fusion of poetic and musical idioms" with the character of "corporate art song." With that aim, the first part of the stanzas benefits from an angry, nearly unmusical "singing," stressing each note and syllable. As the text mellows in the second half of each stanza, so can the singing be more lyrical and calm.

193
Silent night, holy night — STILLE NACHT

Stille Nacht, Heilige Nacht
Joseph Mohr (1792-1848), 1818
Mohr manuscript, 1833
Leipziger Gesangbuch, 1838
Tr. John Freeman Young (1820-1885)
Hollister's *The Sunday School Service and Tune Book,* 1863

Franz Xaver Gruber (1787-1863), 1818
(same source as text)

When the organ stopped working just before the 1818 Christmas Eve service in Oberndorf, Austria, assistant priest Joseph Mohr decided a new hymn was in order, one that did not depend on the organ. He took his text to Franz Gruber, his organist, and asked for a tune. The pair sang the fledgling piece that night with guitar.

From there the hymn was picked up by the organ repairman Karl Mauracher, who spread it as a "Tyrolian carol." Such carols and those who sang them were popular music hall acts in the mid-nineteenth century, so the song was sung for many years without attribution in many languages and countries. In 1854, amid erroneous credit to Mozart and Haydn, Gruber told the now-familiar story of the carol's birth.

Though the English translation was first published in 1863, it was not credited to Young until 1887 in *Great Hymns of the Church*. The translator of the fourth stanza is unknown.

Gruber set Mohr's text for two solo voices and guitar accompaniment, providing four parts for a choir in the final phrase. The original melody has been changed slightly and the entire carol arranged in four parts. While the vocal range of the melody is challenging, the simple harmony uses only three basic chords.

158
Since o'er thy footstool

William Augustus Muhlenberg (1796-1877)
A Collection of Psalms and Hymns . . ., 2nd ed., 1837

MAGNIFICENCE

Asa Brooks Everett (1828-1875)
(same source as text)

If the earth, God's footstool, is so magnificent, how much more wonderful heaven must be! Muhlenberg's poem is like a canvas splattered with brilliant color, a melodrama of metaphor. His text was first published in North America in *A Collection of Psalms and Hymns for the Use of Universalist Societies and Families*.[1] Although the 1925 Brethren hymnal gives a date of 1824, this has not been substantiated. In *The Brethren Hymnal* (1901), the hymn appears with the scripture verse, " 'The Unspeakable Glory of God,' Rev. 1:17." Muhlenberg composed a number of hymns including "Shout the glad tidings"; "Like Noah's weary dove"; and perhaps his best known, "Savior, who thy flock art feeding."

Asa Brooks Everett was one of the leading music educators in the southern and mid-Atlantic states during the mid-nineteenth century. He composed a considerable number of hymn settings, of which sixteen were included in *The Brethren Hymnal* (1901). His settings of the texts "Footsteps of Jesus" and "Who at my door still standing" are considered his most popular.

1. This volume, edited by H. Ballou, was printed in Boston by Benjamin Mussey in 1837.

64
Sing amen—see "Asithi: Amen"

67
Sing hallelujah, praise the Lord

BECHLER

John Swertner (1746-1813)
English Moravian Hymnbook, 1789

John (Johann) Christian Bechler (1784-1857), before 1822

John Swertner was responsible for compiling the *English Moravian Hymnbook* of 1789. Finding almost a half page of space remaining before the index, he wrote two stanzas of eight lines to fill the page. An exuberant hymn was born! Reminiscent of Revelation 1:6 and 5:10 ("You have made them to be a kingdom and priests serving our God"), the text resonates with praise because of the sacrifice of the Lamb. The second stanza, which originally began "There we to all eternity shall join th'angelic lays, and sing . . . ," now reads "There we to all eternity for never-ending days shall sing . . . ."

John C. Bechler, Moravian pastor and teacher, composed the music for Swertner's text sometime prior to 1822, the year he became pastor at Lititz, Pennsylvania, and "inspector of the girls' boarding school there" (now Linden Hall). Thor Johnson, director of many American Moravian Music Festivals, humorously refers to this hymn as the "Moravian National Anthem" because of the enthusiastic way it has been sung at the close of those festivals (Adams 1984).

256
Sing, my tongue, the song

PANGE LINGUA

Pange lingua gloriosi praelium certaminis
Venatius Honorius Fortunatus (ca. 530-609), 569
Sts. 2,4-5, composite translation
The Hymnal 1982 (sts. 2, 4-5), 1985

Sarum plainsong

W. A. Shoults considers this "one of the finest of the mediaeval Latin hymns; a wonderful union of sweetness of melody with clear-cut dogmatic teaching" (Julian 1907). This hymn was considered so strong that the early Anabaptists did not give it up even when they broke with the established church. It was written for the service of the Festival of Corpus Christi, at the request of Pope Urban IV. The meter and opening line of a text by Thomas Aquinas, *Pange lingua gloriosi corporis mysterium*, imitate this earlier processional hymn by Fortunatus. The Aquinas text is "a response to the mystery of the incarnation and belief in the atonement"

(Loewen, Moyer, Oyer 1983). Even the horrors of the crucifixion—the broken body, the cross itself (st. 4)—are seen as foreordained and necessary elements in the "scheme of our salvation." The ultimate paradox upon which the hymn hinges is revealed in one short phrase at the end of stanza 1: In dying the "victim" overthrew death itself.

The original hymn was ten stanzas long and was often divided into two groups of five stanzas, with a doxology following each group. In this way it was used at the post-midnight service (Matins) and again at sunrise (Lauds) each day from Palm Sunday to Maundy Thursday. A similar division using the present six stanzas could be used at various points in a single service or for devotions during Passion Week.

This translation comes from various sources, including *The Three Days*, 1981 (st. 1,); Percy Dearmer's 1931 translation (sts. 4a,6); and *Rejoice in the Lord* (sts. 4b,5).

PANGE LINGUA is a beautiful plainsong melody in the Phrygian mode, a scale that can be played on the white keys of the piano from E to E. Plainsong melodies are part of an extensive body of Latin liturgical chant, belonging to the Roman Catholic tradition and may date as early as the fifth and sixth centuries. See "Creator of the stars of night" (**177**) for a discussion of Sarum plainsong.

This melody is quoted and developed in Gustav Holst's great choral work *The Hymn of Jesus*, Opus 37, composed 1917-1919.

59
Sing praise to God who reigns

MIT FREUDEN ZART

Sei Lob und Ehr dem höchsten Gut
Johann Jacob Schütz (1640-1690)
Christliches Gedenckbüchlein, 1675
Tr. Frances Elizabeth Cox (1812-1897)
Cox's *Hymns from the German*, 1864, alt.

Adapt. from GENEVA 138, *Genevan Psalter*, Lyon, 1547
Bohemian Brethren's *Kirchengeseng*, Berlin, 1566

Deuteronomy 32:3 forms the basis of this hymn of praise by the pietist lawyer Jacob Schütz. The German text was first published in the author's own collection, *Christliches Gedenckbüchlein*, in 1675. Methodist hymn commentator Fred Gealy praises this hymn, saying it "is a hymn to aspire to: it both demands and releases power" (Young 1993).

MIT FREUDEN ZART ("with gentle joy") is also known as BOHEMIAN BRETHREN, from the collection in which it was first found in print. The tune may be traced to the earlier *Genevan Psalter* tune for Psalm 138, which in turn has similarities to the French *chanson* "Une pastourelle Gentille," published 1529-1530 by Pierre Attaignant. The hymn is equally effective sung in four parts or in unison with accompaniment.

98

Sing to the Lord of harvest

John Samuel Bewley Monsell (1811-1875)
Hymns of Love and Praise, 2nd ed., 1866, alt.

WIE LIEBLICH IST DER MAIEN

Johann Steurlein (1546-1613)
Adapt. by Healey Willan (1880-1968), 1958

This text first appeared in the second edition of the source listed above, one of eleven volumes of poetry published by the author. In his *Parish Hymnal* (1873), Monsell altered the text to "Sing to the Lord of bounty" and designated it for Rogation Day. This holiday, adapted from a Roman agricultural ritual and celebrated around April 25, is a special time for asking God's blessing on the newly planted fields and grass. *Rogation* comes from the Latin meaning "to ask." Thus, this hymn could be as appropriate for the time of planting as for autumn harvest; in fact, the tune name indicates the music was written with the spirit of May in mind. Stanza 2 opens with a colorful idiom—clouds not laden with oil and cholesterol, but with rain, the promise of "fat" bounty. Stanzas 3 and 4 widen the concept of harvest to include the "gathering in" of souls given to Christ.

WIE LIEBLICH IST DER MAIEN ("How lovely is May") is thought to have been composed in Nürnberg, Germany, in 1581. It was first used with Monsell's text in *Worship Song* (1905), edited by Garrett Horder. Healey Willan harmonized Steurlein's tune for a hymn anthem he composed in 1958. The present setting is derived from that anthem (Concordia Publishing House).

287

Sing we triumphant hymns

Hymnum canamus gloriae
The Venerable Bede (673-735)
Manuscript, 11th c., British Museum
Tr. Benjamin Webb (1819-1885)
The Hymnal Noted, 1851

DEO GRACIAS

English melody, 15th c.
"The Agincourt Song"

This Latin ascension hymn, written by an English monk when Christianity was still new to his northern islands, first appeared in an eleventh-century manuscript. Three other manuscripts from the same century, two at the British Museum and one at Durham, contain a variant of this text beginning *Hymnum canamus Domino.* Four of Webb's seven stanzas are used here. Another hymn translated from this Latin text is "A hymn of glory let us sing!" by Elizabeth Rundle Charles.

For comments on DEO GRACIAS, see "O love, how deep, how broad" (**236**).

188
Sleepers, wake

Wachet auf, ruft uns die Stimme
Philipp Nicolai (1556-1608)
Nicolai's *Appendix to Freuden-Spiegel des ewigen Lebens,* Frankfurt, 1599
Tr. Carl Pickens Daw, Jr. (1944-) and others, alt.
The Hymnal 1982, 1985

WACHET AUF

Philipp Nicolai (1556-1608)
(same source as text)
(Zahn No. 8405)

Bubonic plague ravaged Unna, Westphalia, from July 1597 to January 1598, resulting in the deaths of about thirteen hundred members of the local Lutheran congregation. Nicolai, their pastor, sometimes buried thirty people a day. In his preface to *Freuden-Spiegel . . . ,* the book that includes this hymn, he wrote: "Day by day I wrote out my meditations . . . to leave behind me [if God should call me from this world] as the token of my peaceful, joyful, Christian departure, or [if God should spare me in health] to comfort other sufferers whom he should also visit with the pestilence . . . " (*The Hymnal 1940 Companion,* 1951 ed.).

This hymn text draws its aura of expectancy from several passages of scripture: Isaiah 52:8, with reference to the watchmen announcing the return of the Lord to Zion; Matthew 25:1-13, the parable of the wise and foolish virgins; and Revelation 19:6-9, the victorious hymn of praise to the Lamb in heaven. The opening letters of each German stanza[1] reveal a reversed acrostic, "W. Z. G.," for Graf zu Waldeck, a former pupil of Nicolai.

Numerous earlier translations exist, perhaps the best known being Catherine Winkworth's, which begins "Wake, awake, for night is flying." Carl Daw's translation in contemporary English appears here as it was altered for *Rejoice in the Lord* (1985). In stanza 2:1, "nightwatch" replaces "watchman"; and the conclusion of the stanza, "We follow all into the hall to join the wedding festival," was earlier "We follow all and heed your call to come into the banquet hall."

The melody WACHET AUF appeared with Nicolai's text, so it was probably composed by the author, though it may have been prompted by other tunes. Its stately character has earned it the designation "king of chorales." Later composers have made notable use of fragments of WACHET AUF: John B. Dyke's tune NICEA and Handel's setting of "The kingdoms of this world . . . " in the "Hallelujah Chorus" from *Messiah* (Routley 1981). J. S. Bach has enshrined the melody of WACHET AUF in his Cantata No. 140 and in his Schübler organ chorale of the same name. The version of the melody used here is quite close to the original, and the harmonization, as found in several hymnals, is similar to that by J. Praetorius (1586-1651).

1. The German text is in *The Hymnal 1940 Companion* and the *Handbook to the Mennonite Hymnary.*

69
So lange Jesus bleibt—see "The Lord is King"

581
So nimm denn meine Hände—see "Take thou my hand, O Father"

491
Softly and tenderly Jesus is calling — THOMPSON

Will Lamartine Thompson (1847-1909)
Bushey's *Sparkling Gems Nos. 1 & 2 Combined*, 1880[1]

Will Lamartine Thompson (1847-1909)
(same source as text)

When the great evangelist Dwight L. Moody lay dying, gospel song writer Will Thompson was present to receive a unique tribute to his (Thompson's) work:

> Moody was quite ill. Visitors had been forbidden, but when Moody heard that Thompson was there, he insisted that he be admitted to the room. Moody greeted him most cordially and said, "Will, I would rather have written 'Softly and tenderly Jesus is calling' than anything I have been able to do in my whole life." (Reynolds 1976)

This popular hymn has another stanza that is usually omitted:

> Time is now fleeting, the moments are passing,
> passing from you and from me;
> shadows are gathering, deathbeds are coming, coming for you and for me.

This hymn gained renewed recognition in recent years when it was used in the musical score of the film *Trip to Bountiful* (1985). The tender, flowing arrangement in the *Accompaniment Handbook* is derived from that score by its creator, J. A. C. Redford, who has a number of film and television credits to his name.

The tune name THOMPSON was given to this music by the editors of *Baptist Hymnal* (1956) to honor the creator of the hymn.

1. Earlier hymnal companions list J. S. Inskip's *Songs of Triumph*, 1882, as the source. This citation comes from Reynolds, *Companion to Baptist Hymnal*, 1976.

603
Sometimes a light surprises — SURPRISE

William Cowper (1731-1800)
Olney Hymns, Book III, 1779, alt.

Jane Manton Marshall (1924-), 1974

Scriptural allusions in this text are drawn from Malachi 4:2 and 2 Samuel 23:4 in stanza 1 and from Matthew 6:34 and 28 in stanzas 2 and 3, respectively. Stanza 4 comes from the solid faith assertion in Habakkuk 3:17-18, rounding out a text that acknowledges sorrow in life, but finds still more trust and hope. Headed "Joy and Peace in Believing" when it first came out in *Olney Hymns, Book III*, the text belies Cowper's lifetime struggle with severe depression.

Jane Marshall's SURPRISE provides a fresh and lilting setting for this text, capturing its aura of childlike trust and hope. The rhythms, which may at first seem difficult to read, are very singable. See the *Accompaniment Handbook* for Marshall's setting.

60
Songs of praise the angels sang — MONKLAND

James Montgomery (1771-1854)
Thomas Cotterill's *Selection of Psalms and Hymns*, 1819, alt.

John Antes (1740-1811)
Hymn Tunes of the United Brethren (Moravian), 1824
Adapt. by John B. Wilkes (d. 1882)
Hymns Ancient and Modern, 1861

The original six stanzas are inundated with musical praise to God, using the phrase "songs of praise" a total of ten times. The stanzas used here are 1, 2, 3, and 5. In stanza 1, the original closing couplet was:[1]

> When Jehovah's work begun
> When He spake and it was done.

This resounding praise is an umbrella over all of time, beginning with creation (st. 1) and continuing into eternity (st. 4).

The earliest published source for MONKLAND is an English Moravian collection, edited by John Lees at Manchester. In that hymnbook the melody was set to the text "What good news the angels bring." The tune was found in an earlier unpublished manuscript book (ca. 1790), titled *A Collection of Hymn Tunes chiefly composed for Private Amusement* by John Antes.[2] The present adaptation of MONKLAND is credited to John Wilkes, but the form of the tune differs little from the version in the Moravian collection. Confusion also exists over the identity of Wilkes, who is sometimes identified incorrectly as John Bernard Wilkes (1785-1869), organist at Henry Baker's church. It is easy to see why this confusion exists, since MONKLAND was a setting for one of

Baker's texts, "Praise, O praise our God and King," in *Hymns Ancient and Modern* (1861). Also, MONKLAND is named for the village in Herefordshire where Henry Baker was vicar.

1. This hymn appears unaltered and unabridged in *The Hymnal 1940* (Episcopal).
2. The tune as it appeared in Antes' manuscript and its first printing may be seen in *Guide to the Pilgrim Hymnal*, 1966, page 353.

611
Soon and very soon

Based on Revelation 21:4
Andraé Crouch (1945-)

(no tune name)

Andraé Crouch (1945-)

The syncopated music and positive message of this song make it a vibrant addition to the collection of hymns on death and eternal life. The music is already familiar to many, and the text repetitions help congregations learn the song quickly. Its author and composer, one of the most prolific gospel musicians in the 1970s and 1980s, toured and recorded with The Disciples from 1969 to 1980.

473
Soul, adorn thyself with gladness

Schmücke dich, O liebe Seele
Johann Franck (1618-1677)
Crüger's *Geistliche Kirchen-Melodien*, 1649 (1 st.)
Crüger-Runge's *Gesangbuch*, 1653 (9 sts.)
Tr. Catherine Winkworth (1827-1878)
Chorale Book for England, 1863, alt.

SCHMÜCKE DICH, O LIEBE SEELE

Johann Crüger (1598-1662)
Crüger's *Geistliche Kirchen-Melodien*, 1649
(Zahn No. 6923)
Harm. by Johann Sebastian Bach (1685-1750), from Cantata No. 180, ca. 1724

Franck designated this as a "hymn of preparation for Holy Communion." Adds James Mearns: "It is an exhortation to the soul to arise and draw near to partake of the Heavenly Food and to meditate on the wonders of Heavenly Love; ending with a prayer for final reception at the Eternal Feast" (Julian 1907). The two-syllable feminine rhymes of all the lines, found in both the English and German texts, is a unique feature of the poetic structure. These are matched perfectly by the strong/weak accentuation of the musical cadences. The translation represents stanzas 1, 7, and 9 of the German text.

SCHMÜCKE DICH, O LIEBE SEELE has been associated with this text from the beginning, a strong combination. It is presented here in the harmonization by J. S. Bach from his Cantata No. 180. The *Gesangbuch der Mennoniten-Gemeinden Russlands* (1904) lists nine other texts that were sung with this tune, attesting to its considerable popularity in Russia at the turn of the century.

290

Spirit, come, dispel our sadness

O du allersüsste Freude
Paul Gerhardt (1607-1676)
Praxis Pietatis Melica, 1648
Tr. John Christian Jacobi (1670-1750)
Psalmodia Germanica, Part II, ca. 1725
Rev. by Augustus M. Toplady (1740-1778)
Gospel Magazine, 1776, alt.

O MEIN JESU, ICH MUSS STERBEN

Geistliche Volkslieder, Paderborn, ca. 1858

The original German text by Gerhardt consists of ten eight-line stanzas. Jacobi's full translation begins "O Thou sweetest Source of gladness." When the two parts of his *Psalmodia Germanica* were published in a combined edition in 1732, this text was altered greatly. In 1776 Toplady again altered the text, printing it as "Holy Ghost, dispel our sadness." In *The Presbyterian Hymnal* (1990), the phrases "Come with unction and with power" and "On our souls thy graces shower" in the second stanza were made more contemporary. Here again the text has been altered, changing "Holy Ghost" to "Spirit, come."

The tune O MEIN JESU, ICH MUSS STERBEN ("O my Jesus, I must die") is the setting of a Thomas Kelly text, "Stricken, smitten, and afflicted," in the 1927 Mennonite *Church Hymnal*. The simplicity of the folk quality of this tune of substance suits the forthright text. In other hymnals the text has been set to GENEVA, by George Henry Day, and to the familiar tune HYFRYDOL.

30

Spirit divine, inspire our prayers

Andrew Reed (1787-1862)
Evangelical Magazine, June 1829
Rev. in *Hymns for Today's Church,* 1982

GRÄFENBURG (NUN DANKET ALL')

Johann Crüger (1598-1662)
Praxis Pietatis Melica, 5th ed., 1653
(Zahn No. 207)

This hymn was written for Good Friday of 1829, which the London Board of Congregational Ministers had designated as a day of intercession for the revival of religion in British churches. The hymn originally began "Spirit Divine, attend our prayers" and was included in Reed's *Hymn Book* (1842). The opening line, as well as numerous others, has been changed in this version from *Hymns for Today's Church* (1982). The original stanza 4 is an earthy one, and the reason for its revision may be evident:

> Come as the dew, and sweetly bless this consecrated hour;
> May barrenness rejoice to own thy fertilizing power.

The new version allows us to sing in contemporary language while retaining all the wonderful metaphors for the Holy Spirit.

For comments on GRÄFENBURG, see "Lamp of our feet" (**312**).

502
Spirit of God! descend — MORECAMBE

George Croly (1780-1860)
Charles Rogers' *Lyra Britannica*, 1867

Frederick Cook Atkinson (1841-1896)
Leaflet, 1870
Barrett and Hopkins' *Congregational Church Hymnal*, 1887

This is an intensely personal, meditative hymn; sung by the congregation, it has the possibility of uniting believers in a very intimate way. The last line, "My heart an altar, and thy love the flame," is a metaphor of exceptional beauty and clarity. "There is no science, no sociology, no biblical criticism. The poet has entered into his closet and shut the door" (Bailey 1950).

We have only Rogers' attribution, most likely accurate, that this hymn is by Croly, but more conclusive evidence would be desirable.[1] Rogers coupled it, aptly, with the scripture from Galatians 5:25, "If we live by the Spirit, let us also walk in the Spirit."

MORECAMBE, originally called HELLESPONT, was composed for "Abide with me" when Atkinson was organist at Manningham. We don't know when it was combined with the present text. The name MORECAMBE is taken from a well-known town on Morecambe Bay in West England.

1. For a detailed account of research on this hymn's authorship, see Haeussler, *The Story of Our Hymns*, 1952.

364
Spirit of God, unleashed on earth — LLEDROD (LLANGOLLEN)

John W. Arthur (1922-1980)
Contemporary Worship—4, 1972, alt.

Welsh melody
Llyfr Tonau Cynulleidfaol, 1859

With a striking economy of words, this text describes the event of Pentecost. It links the historic event of Acts 2 with petitions for continual renewal from the Holy Spirit. The phrases "from living waters raise new saints" and "revive in us baptismal grace" make it an appropriate hymn for the conclusion of a baptismal service. For Anabaptists, these phrases need not connote infant baptism but can strengthen the connection of believers' baptism with God's grace.

LLEDROD is a tune with a dynamic melodic contour, complemented by surprising rhythmic patterns. It should be sung in a half-note pulse, and hymn leaders should be prepared to direct measures 9 and 10 in four beats and three beats, respectively.

349
Spirit of the living God — (no tune name)

Daniel Iverson (1890-1977), 1926
Revival Songs, 1929

Daniel Iverson (1890-1977), 1926
(same source as text)
Arr. by Herbert G. Tovey

When Daniel Iverson, a Presbyterian minister from North Carolina, met up with the George Stephans evangelistic team in Orlando, Florida, he expected to renew acquaintance with some Christian friends, but he also heard an inspiring sermon on the Holy Spirit as part of the series of revival meetings. Iverson was so moved that he wrote down his hymn that day. The team's song leader E. Powell Lee was so impressed that he taught it through the rest of the crusade (Reynolds 1976).

In 1929 the song appeared in Robert H. Coleman's *Revival Songs* without Iverson's name or knowledge. Alterations in the music were made by E. L. Wolslagel in that first publication and later by B. B. McKinney in *Songs of Victory* (1937). Finally, in the 1960s, E. Powell Lee contacted Iverson and the hymn was rightly attributed, though the changes had already become ingrained in people's minds. The present version, similar to that in *The Brethren Hymnal* (1951), is the one used in several other current hymnals.

242
Stay with me — (no tune name)

Based on Matthew 26:36-46
Music from Taizé, Vol. II, 1982, 1983, 1984

Jacques Berthier (1923-)
(same source as text)

This brief musical resource recalls the words of Christ in the garden of Gethsemane. It is especially appropriate during Holy Week, but the wording is such that it may be used anytime when a note of solidarity is desired.

The music, which ends on the dominant chord, creates a sense of anticipation for prayers or readings that may follow the singing. For more information on Taizé, see "Alleluia" (**101**).

612
Steal away — STEAL AWAY TO JESUS

African American spiritual

African American spiritual

John Wesley Work tells the story of a group of slaves who were allowed by their master to cross the Red River to worship with the Native Americans at the mission there. Fearing that the missionary, who was a northerner, might give the slaves ideas of freedom, the master denied his slaves permission to continue worshiping with the Native Americans. The slaves, undaunted by their master's change of heart, continued to "steal away to Jesus" (McClain 1990).

As with a number of spirituals, this one has a dual meaning. From its use as a call to secret meetings, it has become a call to believers to join in worship. Like "Swing low, sweet chariot," it expresses a desire for "release in death [which] sometimes became the ultimate hope and goal" (Cleveland, McClain 1981).

The original melody probably was composed by the slave-turned-insurrectionist Nat Turner, then developed further over a period of time. Its melodic line is based on the pentatonic scale, which omits the fourth and seventh tones of a major scale. The melody may be played on the black keys of the piano beginning on F-sharp. Note also the trumpet-call pattern of pitches and rhythms with the words "the trumpet sounds." The verses are frequently sung by a solo voice, with the congregation responding "I ain't got long to stay here."

A version in four-part harmony is provided in the *Accompaniment Handbook.*

88
Still, I search for my God — WASDIN PANG IPAAD

Francisco F. Feliciano (1941-), 1977
Hymns from the Four Winds, 1983

Francisco F. Feliciano (1941-), 1977
(same source as text)

Feliciano wrote this hymn in the 1970s while he was a student at the Akademie der Künste in Berlin, West Germany. It has a tone of tender, quiet, alert praise. Its meditative mood is in stark contrast to "See the splendor of the morning" (**268**), one of Feliciano's other hymns.

Feliciano writes that his musical style is "very much influenced by Buddhist philosophy—a singular note in the course of time becomes the cosmos." Consequently, a note in *Hymns from the Four Winds* indicates that it should be sung "with utmost simplicity." Feliciano himself says the melody should be sung freely; there can be pauses of different lengths at the punctuation marks of the first and last lines. The light, arpeggiated accompaniment (in the *Accompaniment Handbook*) allows the freedom to sing in this manner and "as near to the edge of silence as possible."

540
Strong, righteous man of Galilee

MELITA

Harry Webb Farrington (1879-1931), 1921

John Bacchus Dykes (1823-1876)
Hymns Ancient and Modern, 1861

The core of Christ's character is strength and peace; each of the first three stanzas of this hymn views this core from a different angle. The first makes reference to the cleansing of the temple (Matt. 21:12); the second reminds us of the way of peace and reconciliation; the third alludes to the woman at the well (John 4), Martha's loss (John 11), and Christ's forgiveness from the cross (Luke 23:34). Then, robed with Christ's peace, strength, and grace, we are challenged in the last stanza to follow Jesus, who is "Love's triumph."

This hymn, a favorite of Brethren, has seen relatively little use elsewhere; it is included in only three of the seventy-eight hymnals catalogued in Diehl's *Hymns and Tunes—an Index* (1966).

MELITA is often associated with the U.S. Navy hymn, which makes for rich irony when it is used with this text about the peaceful Christ. The striding, authoritative feel of MELITA augments the text's intimation that peacefulness is a quality of true strength. For comments on MELITA, see "O Holy Spirit, making whole" (**300**).

488
Strong Son of God, immortal Love

ST. CRISPIN

Alfred Tennyson (1809-1892)
Prologue to *In Memoriam,* 1850 (11 sts.), alt.

George J. Elvey (1816-1893), 1862
E. H. Thorne's *A Selection of Psalm and Hymn Tunes,* 1863 ed.

Tennyson wrote *In Memoriam,* a series of elegiac poems, in memory of Arthur Henry Hallam, a close friend who died suddenly at the age of twenty-two. While the poems were written between 1833 and 1850 when the collection was first published, the prologue is dated 1849. Though not intended to be sung, a cento (portion) of the prologue, usually four to seven stanzas, is used in many hymnals. Hymnals generally omit the second stanza and the last three, which are quite personal and unsuited to congregational singing. Stanzas 1, 4, 5, 6, and 7 are used here.

Tennyson's writing represents the mature judgment of a thinker, the fruit of sixteen years of meditation. In his prologue he was reacting to the effects of the then-new sciences and philosophy. Assuming that rational thought necessarily excluded faith, professing Christians were turning agnostic (Bailey 1950). This text brings perspective (especially st. 3) on the advances of science and politics and on daily stresses, adjusting our sight to the center of Christian life, which is faith. It pulls us around to the biblical proverb (paraphrased): The beginning of wisdom is to stand in awe of God.

ST. CRISPIN was originally composed for the hymn "Just as I am, without one plea." It is a well-constructed melody supported by appropriately varied harmony.

654

Sun of my soul — HURSLEY

John Keble (1792-1866), 1820
Christian Year, 1827

Adapt. from GROSSER GOTT, WIR LOBEN DICH
Katholisches Gesangbuch, Vienna, ca. 1774

This evening hymn, written in late November 1820, had Luke 24:29 as its heading: "Abide with us, for it is towards evening and the day is far spent." Combined with HURSLEY, it sings like a lullaby. The third stanza here is specific and almost medicinal: the intercessory prayer asks for companionship for the sick, bounty for the destitute, and restful sleep for those who are sad.

Many hymnals use six stanzas selected from Keble's complete text of fourteen stanzas. Those used here are stanzas 3, 8, 13, and 14. The first quatrain paints the evening setting:

> 'Tis gone, that bright and orbed blaze
> Fast fading from our wistful gaze;
> Yon mantling cloud has hid from sight
> The last faint pulse of quivering light.

The original melody of HURSLEY was a setting for the German *Te Deum*, GROSSER GOTT, WIR LOBEN DICH. (See "Holy God, we praise thy name," **121**.) The present version was chosen by John Keble and his wife as a setting for this text. The text and tune have been combined since the publication of the *Metrical Psalter* (1855). The tune has also been known as PASCAL, HALLE, and FRAMINGHAM, but the editors of *Hymns Ancient and Modern* (1861) named it HURSLEY after the village near Westchester, England, where Keble was vicar for thirty years.

11

Sweet hour of prayer — SWEET HOUR

Anonymous
The New York Observer, Sept. 13, 1845

William Batchelder Bradbury (1816-1868)
Cottage Melodies, 1859

This text was contributed to *The New York Observer* by Thomas Salmon, who had recently returned from England. He said that the poem was written by W. W. Walford, a blind clergyman in Warwickshire who was known for his memorization of the Bible. However, no such person has been found in the records of the area from that time. William J. Reynolds, in *Companion to the Baptist Hymnal* (1976), links this text with a William Walford of Homerton, who was not blind and did write a book on prayer but not on poetry. Sufficient doubt and confusion exist to label the authorship unknown. The text's first appearance in a hymnal was in the Baptist edition of *Cottage Melodies* (1859), compiled by Thomas Hastings and Robert Turnbull.

Bradbury wrote SWEET HOUR for this text; two years after it first appeared in *Cottage Melodies*, he included it in his own *Golden Chain* (1861). This hymn has had fermatas added at many places in its numerous publications. In the 1861 edition, they were placed at the ends of the first, third, fourth, and sixth phrases.

601
Take my hand and lead me, Father — HUNTINGDON

Gertrude A. Flory (1862-1930)
J. H. Kurzenknabe's *Sowing and Reaping*, 1889

William Beery (1852-1956)
(same source as text)

This is one of the early hymns by prolific Brethren composer William Beery. When it was first published, it was set for a solo voice with piano accompaniment. The original refrain, deleted from the 1925 and 1951 Brethren hymnals, has been reinstated. Although no credit was given to any author until *The Brethren Hymnal* (1951), this was a "mistake, which though corrected by the composer, was unknown to the general public" (Statler, Fisher 1959).

The hymn had no tune name until 1951 when it was dubbed HUNTINGDON for the town where William Beery lived and taught at Juniata College in Pennsylvania. That tune name had been used earlier by J. C. Ewing for his text "Christian, the morn breaks sweetly o'er thee." At that time Ewing was William Beery's music teacher.

A fermata has been added and the original, even, eighth-note patterns changed to dotted eighth and sixteenth notes in some places to conform to what has become common practice in singing this hymn. These dotted rhythms should be sung in a relaxed manner with the feeling of triplets. The refrain may be sung after each stanza or at the conclusion of all three stanzas.

389

Take my life

Frances Ridley Havergal (1836-1879)
Appendix to Shepp's *Songs of Grace and Glory*, 1874

HENDON

Henri Abraham César Malan (1787-1864), 1827
Carmina Sacra, 1841

This hymn, the basis of a book also written by Havergal (*Kept for the Master's Work*), was born out of a prayer meeting she attended at Areley House, Worcestershire, England, in February of 1874. Havergal writes exuberantly about its history:

> There were ten persons in the house, some unconverted and long prayed-for, some converted but not rejoicing Christians. He gave me the prayer, "Lord, give me all in this house!" And He just did! Before I left the house everyone had got a blessing. The night of my visit I was too happy to sleep, and passed most of the night in praise and renewal of my own consecration, and these little couplets formed themselves and chimed in my heart one after another, till they finished with "Ever, only, *all* for Thee!" (Havergal 1880)

Interpreting stanza 4, she writes:

> "Take my silver and my gold" now means shipping off all my ornaments, including a jewell cabinet which is really fit for a countess, to the Church Missionary Society where they will be accepted and disposed of for me. I retain only a brooch for daily wear, which is a memorial of my dear parents; also a locket with the only portrait I have of my niece in heaven, Evelyn. I had no idea I had such a jewellers shop; nearly fifty articles are being packed off. I don't think I need tell you I never packed a box with such pleasure. (Loewen, Moyer, Oyer 1983)

This hymn, which has been translated into languages of Europe, Africa, and Asia, is sometimes printed with the accompanying scripture verse "Present your bodies as a living sacrifice" (Rom. 12:1).

The hymn's first tune PATMOS was composed by Havergal's father, himself a pastor and composer; this tune is in the *Lutheran Book of Worship* (1978). For information about HENDON, see "Ask ye what great thing I know" (**337**).

581

Take thou my hand, O Father

So nimm denn meine Hände und führe mich
Julie Katharina Hausmann (1825 or 1826-1901)
Maiblumen, Lieder einer Stillen im Lande, Vol. 1, 1862
Tr. Herman M. Brückner (1866-1942)
Wartburg Hymnal for Church, School, and Home, Chicago, 1918

SO NIMM DENN MEINE HÄNDE

Friedrich Silcher (1789-1860)
Kinderlieder, Vol. III, 1842

Since the original German text of this hymn did not use the words "God" or "Christ," some couples used it as a wedding song, misinterpreting the "thou" to mean the bride or groom. The English translations by both Brückner and Rudolph A. John have clarified that misunderstanding.

In the late nineteenth century, the hymn was widely used in German-language churches, especially for confirmation services. North American Mennonites from the Russian tradition also sang it frequently in both German and English. The words, however, are universal in scope, a prayer that reaches like a child's hand for God's leading.

The tune SO NIMM DENN MEINE HÄNDE (Take my hands) first appeared with the text *Wie könnt ich ruhig schlafen* (How could I sleep peacefully?). Its first publication with this text, in German, was in 1883 in *Grosse Missionharfe*.

536

Take up your cross

Charles William Everest (1814-1877)
Visions of Death and Other Poems, 1833, alt.

KEDRON

American folk melody
Version from Joseph Funk's *Genuine Church Music*, 1st ed., 1832
Harm. by The Hymnal Project

Everest was just nineteen when he published his *Visions of Death and Other Poems;* and this text from that collection was one of only two American hymns[1] to be included in the first edition of the eminent English hymnal, *Hymns Ancient and Modern* (1861). In that volume the text underwent a good deal of alteration, some by Earl Nelson, from *The Salisbury Hymn-Book* (1857). The present text is a contemporary version close to the original. Stanza 3:3 changes "The Lord refused not ev'n to die" to "the Lord for you accepted death," and stanza 4:2 replaces "sin's wild deluge brave" with "sin's temptations brave."

With its discipleship theme, this hymn is appropriate for Lent and the week of Jesus' Passion. The worship leader's edition of *The Worshiping Church* (1990, 1991) outlines a devotional service built around this hymn using scripture before each of the stanzas: Philippians 2:5-8 (st. 1);

2 Corinthians 12:7-10 (st. 2); 1 Corinthians 1:22-30 (st. 3); 1 Corinthians 15:56-58 (st. 4); and Galatians 6:14 (st. 5).

The haunting, angular melody of KEDRON makes a dramatic musical setting for a text that contemplates the sacrifice of Christ and the cost of discipleship. The tune was first set to Charles Wesley's text "Thou man of grief, remember me." Amos Pilsbury, a singing-school teacher in Charleston, South Carolina, may have been the composer. The tune is named for the river, usually spelled Kidron, that flows through the valley between Jerusalem and the Mount of Olives.

1. The other is "Thou art the way" (**339**).

487

Teach me, O Lord — BISHOP

Based on Psalm 119:33-40
Psalter, 1912 (U.S. Presbyterian)

Joseph Perry Holbrook (1822-1888)
Duryea's *The Presbyterian Hymnal*, 1874

The psalm on which this hymn is based is a long meditation on the law. It is settled firmly in personal, individual piety and does not exude either the excitement of community psalms or the agony of lament. It looks to God's word, the Bible, as a steadying force and the mold for a satisfying life. As a hymn, this metrical psalm may have been written earlier than 1912, the date of the earliest known source given above.

This straightforward melody, similar in character to earlier psalm tunes, should be sung at a walking half-note pulse.

485

Teach me the measure of my days — MORTALITY

Based on Psalm 39
Isaac Watts (1674-1748)
The Psalms of David . . ., 1719, alt.

The Brethren's Tune and Hymn Book, 1872

Isaac Watts, though a strong-willed soul among mortals, was ever mindful of his frailty (he suffered recurring illness) as a human being, especially compared with the great, high majesty of God. In this text his tightly written, vivid poetry reins in our daily struggles and gives perspective to scattered lives—"I give my mortal interest up, and make my God my all."

Though the words, originally titled "The vanity of man as mortal," are based on Psalm 39:4-7, this hymn has had a scripture citation of Psalm 90:12 in *The Brethren's Hymn Book* (1867). The fourth stanza has been omitted and slight alterations made in the first two stanzas.

MORTALITY is a haunting, natural, minor tune with an unusually wide melodic range. In its original source, the music was pitched a major third higher. As was typical for *The Brethren's Tune and Hymn Book*, the melody in the middle voice was harmonized by a soprano and bass part. The harmony, with its open fifths and occasional dissonances, supports the melody's austere folk style.

548
Teach me thy truth — GOSHEN

Edith M. Witmer (1902-1982), 1937
Life Songs No. 2, 1938

Walter E. Yoder (1889-1964)
(same source as text)

While teaching at Goshen College in Indiana, Witmer was convinced that a Christian college should have, in addition to its alma mater, a special college hymn for worship services. So she wrote one. The consistent theme of service that rounds out each stanza was inspired by the college's motto, "Culture for Service."[1]

GOSHEN was composed for this text and was one of four tunes by Yoder to appear in *Life Songs No. 2*. Yoder composed hymn tunes in varying styles, this one reflecting the rhythmic form of English psalm tunes with gathering notes (notes in longer values) at the beginning of each phrase. The dynamic harmony and the range of the voice parts are well suited to *a cappella* singing.

1. *Gospel Herald*, Dec. 4, 1956

281
That Easter day with joy was bright — PUER NOBIS NASCITUR

Aurora lucis rutilat
Anonymous
Part III from *Claro Paschali gaudio*, 4th or 5th c.
Tr. John Mason Neale (1818-1866)
The Hymnal Noted, 1851, alt.

Spangenberg's *Christliches Gesangbüchlein*, Eisleben, 1568

This text is a translation of Part III from *Claro Paschali gaudio*, the final portion of the very old Latin hymn cited above, which occasionally has been ascribed to Ambrose. This Latin hymn was one of the earliest to be adopted for a special season. Parts I and II include elements of the Easter story while Part III tells of Jesus' post-resurrection appearance to the disciples, after which it concludes with a doxology. Part III was traditionally sung at Lauds (sunrise) from the Sunday after Easter to Ascension.

Neale's original translation begins:

In this our bright and Paschal day
The sun shines out in purer ray;
When Christ, to earthly sight made plain,
The glad Apostles see again.

His translation was altered extensively for *Hymns Ancient and Modern* (1861).

PUER NOBIS NASCITUR appeared in print (as early as 1568) where its rhythm is a mixture of duple and triple patterns.[1] This version is one of many variants of the original tune that was set to the words *Puer nobis nascitur*, a fifteenth-century Trier manuscript. A duple version of this melody is in *Piae Cantiones*... (1582), and the present triple-meter version is from Michael Praetorius's *Musae Sioniae*, Part VI (1609), where it is set to *Geborn ist Gottes Söhnelein*.

1. Illustrated in Dearmer and Jacob's *Songs of Praise Discussed*, 1933

180
The angel Gabriel — GABRIEL'S MESSAGE

Sabine Baring-Gould (1834-1924)
University Carol Book, 1923

Basque carol
Arr. by Charles Edgar Pettman (1866-1943), *University Carol Book*, 1961 ed.

This text retells and gently embellishes the encounter between Gabriel and Mary as found in Luke 1. The author wrote these words for the present tune, which Erik Routley considers one of the finest melodies set to Baring-Gould's texts. The fourth stanza, which changes the focus from the annunciation to the birth of Christ, has been omitted.

Basque carol tunes have been a rich source of melodies for English use. They became known in England through the *University Carol Books* (small books, each having about six carols) that began to be published in 1923. By about 1958 the collection totaled twenty-four books. Those who transmitted these Basque melodies to England did not preserve any information regarding their original versions. The present text and tune were used at the King's College Festival of Nine Lessons and Carols, Christmas Eve (1937). The carol may be familiar to those who have heard the recording (London 5523) of the King's College 1958 Christmas Eve service.

590
The care the eagle gives her young

Based on Deuteronomy 32:11
R. Deane Postlethwaite (1925-1980)

CRIMOND

Jessie Seymour Irvine (1836-1887)
Harm. and adapt. by David Grant (1833-1893)
The Northern Psalter, 1872

This contemporary text describes God's love with rich imagery drawn from Deuteronomy 32:11. This verse is one of the most tender portions of the Song of Moses, which is otherwise a poetic harangue against a rebellious Israel. The hymn, however, paints a picture of God's strong and compassionate care, which young and old alike can understand. Another hymn that likens God to an eagle is Michael Joncas's "And I will raise you up" (**596**).

The pastoral quality of CRIMOND makes it an especially fitting companion to this text. For comments on the tune, see "The Lord's my shepherd" (**578**).

403
The church of Christ, in every age

Fred Pratt Green (1903-), 1969
26 Hymns, 1971

DICKINSON COLLEGE

Lee Hastings Bristol, Jr. (1923-1979)
Published in anthem form, 1962
More Hymns and Spiritual Songs, 1971

When the committee preparing the *Lutheran Book of Worship* (1978) requested some changes in this hymn, the author not only approved them, but decided he preferred the revised version. A stanza was omitted from the original and the second verse became the last, leaving a strong justice hymn. Though the followers of Christ sometimes find themselves subject to the vagaries of time and human foibles, this text pushes the church to the edges of discipleship and service. With the sacrificial love of Christ as the example, "feeding the multitude" becomes a tangible sign of obedience (st. 4).

Bristol adapted the tune DICKINSON COLLEGE from his anthem "Lord of all being throned afar." It first appeared as a hymn tune with a text by Rosamond Herklots, "Lord God, by whose creative might." The tune is named for Dickinson College, Carlisle, Pennsylvania, from which Bristol received an honorary degree. This well-crafted tune will make the irregular 5/4 meter seem natural because it fits the text so well.

311

The church's one foundation AURELIA

Samuel John Stone (1839-1900)
Lyra Fidelium, 1866, alt.

Samuel Sebastian Wesley (1810-1876)
Charles Kemble's *Selection of Psalms and Hymns*, 1864

This hymn comes from the heart of a controversy in the Church of England. In 1866 Samuel Stone, then a pastor at Windsor, wrote a series of twelve hymns based on the twelve articles of the Apostles' Creed. A staunch literalist where the Bible was concerned, Stone in his work was prompted in part by Bishop Colenso's introduction of historical criticism as a tool for reading the Pentateuch (the first five books of the Bible). This hymn is based on and headed by the ninth article of the creed. The references to schisms and heresies in stanza 3:2 were, for Stone, not generalizations, but pointed responses to the "liberals."

The original number of stanzas was seven,[1] but in 1868 the number was reduced to the five most familiar and published in the appendix to the first edition of *Hymns Ancient and Modern*. In stanza 3:1, the phrase "Men see her sore oppressed" has been changed to "The world sees her oppressed." This stanza does not appear in the last three Brethren hymnals.

Wesley's AURELIA was first used with the text "Jerusalem the Golden" (*Urbs Syon aurea*) from Bernard of Cluny's long poem *Hora novissima*. The tune name AURELIA, which means "golden," was suggested by the composer's wife because of its association with Cluny's text. AURELIA was not widely used, however, until it was set to the present text in 1868. This combination of text and tune has remained the standard one ever since.

1. An expanded version of ten stanzas, undertaken in 1885 for processional use in Salisbury Cathedral, can be found in Julian's *Dictionary of Hymnology*, 1907.

652

The day you gave us, Lord ST. CLEMENT

John Ellerton (1826-1893), 1870
Church Hymns, 1871, alt.

Clement C. Scholefield (1839-1904)
Arthur Sullivan's *Church Hymns with Tunes*, 1874

This hymn, which originally began "The day thou gavest, Lord," was a missionary hymn, written for "A Liturgy for Missionary Meetings." It was revised for the English Society for Promoting Christian Knowledge (SPCK) *Church Hymns* (1871), of which Ellerton was a chief compiler. For greater clarity the archaic language is altered in this version. Most notable are the changes from "behest" to "request" in stanza 1:2 and "nor do the praises die away" in place of "nor die the strains of praise away" in stanza 3:3. What begins simply as an evening hymn of praise expands in later stanzas to a description of the church universal and its unceasing prayer and praise around the world—most fitting for its use as a missions hymn.

ST. CLEMENT was composed for this text in the SPCK *Church Hymns with Tunes* (1874), edited by Arthur Sullivan. While preparing the music for this hymnal, Sullivan was organist at St. Peter's Church in South Kensington where the composer, Clement Scholefield, was curate.

199
The first Noel, the angel did say — THE FIRST NOEL

English carol
Gilbert's *Some Ancient Christmas Carols*, 2nd ed., 1823

English carol
W. Sandys' *Christmas Carols, Ancient and Modern*, 1833
Harm. by John Stainer (1840-1901), 1871

The old English *nowell* is related to the French *noel*, which is derived from the Latin *natalis*, meaning birth. It has long been a term "shouted or sung as an expression of joy, originally to commemorate the birth of Christ . . . " (*The Hymnal 1940 Companion*, 1951 ed.). Also, the shepherds get credit in this hymn for seeing the star. The preponderance of stanzas about Jesus' natal *star* would indicate, however, that this hymn is more for Epiphany than for Christmas. Biblically, the wise men from the East saw the star, and the season of Epiphany traditionally begins on January 6 with the visit of the magi.

The following omitted stanzas could be used in a processional for Epiphany. They are given in their original order, picking up where stanza 4 in the hymnal leaves off:

5. Then did they know assuredly
Within that house the King did lie:
One entered in then for to see,
And found the babe in poverty:
Noel . . .

6. Then entered in those wise men three . . . (see hymnal).

7. Between an ox-stall and an ass
This child truly there born he was;
For want of clothing they did him lay
All in the manger, among the hay:
Noel . . .

8. Then let us all with one accord
sing praises to our heavenly Lord,
who hath made heaven and earth of naught,
and with his blood our life hath bought.
Noel . . .

9. If we in our time shall do well,
We shall be free from death and hell;
For God hath preparèd for us all
A resting place in general:
Noel . . .

The origins of the tune, as well as the text, are unknown. Some scholars believe the tune derives from another carol, from either the melody or another voice part. The unusual character of this melody, with its many repetitions of the upper tones of the scale, often goes unnoticed because of its familiarity. The sweep of the "Noels" gives a feel of joyfully broadcasting the good news. With the exception of a few passing tones added in the tenor, the harmonization is by John Stainer from Bramley and Stainer's *Christmas Carols Old and New* (1871). William Sandys, a London lawyer, included both text and tune in his 1833 collection cited above.

225

The glory of these forty days

Clarum decus jejunii
Attrib. to Gregory the Great (ca. 540-604)
Manuscript, 11th c.
Tr. Maurice Frederick Bell (1862-1931)
The English Hymnal, 1906, alt.

ERHALT UNS, HERR

Attrib. to Martin Luther (1483-1546)
Klug's *Geistliche Lieder*, 1543
(Zahn No. 350)

The "forty days" in this hymn are the forty days of Lent, during which some Christians adhere to Christ's example of fasting and prayer (st. 1:3) to prepare themselves for the spiritual turmoil of Passion and Easter. This hymn is unusual, however, in that it draws on the experience of other paragons who practiced these religious disciplines—Moses and Elijah (st. 2) and Daniel and John (st. 3).

This Latin hymn, sometimes attributed to Gregory the Great, appears in three manuscripts of the eleventh century, two at the British Museum and one at Durham. The hymn was used extensively in England, as shown by its inclusion in the breviaries (books of prayers, hymns, psalms, and readings) of Sarum, York, Canterbury, and others.

Bell's translation of this Lenten hymn has been altered to eliminate the use of "thy" and "thee," and the final stanza, a doxology, has been omitted. The fourth stanza originally read:

Then grant us, Lord, like them to be
Full oft in fast and prayer with thee;

ERHALT UNS, HERR—also known as SPIRES, READING, or PRESERVE US LORD—is believed by some scholars to be the work of Martin Luther. It was first published in Wittenberg with Luther's text that began *Erhalt uns, Herr* (Preserve us, Lord). The tune is a variant of the twelfth-century plainsong *Veni redemptor genitum (Nun komm der Heiden Heiland).* Note the logical melodic structure; although no phrase is repeated, each flows naturally from the preceding one. "Everything is healthy, clear, natural and therefore musical art at its best" (Bruppacher 1953).

162
The God of Abraham praise — LEONI

Yigdal 'elohim hay we yistabba
Jewish doxology, 14th c.
Translated and paraphrased jointly, ca. 1885, by Max Landsberg (1845-1928) and Newton M. Mann (1836-1926), alt.

Hebrew melody
Transcribed by Meyer Leoni (1751-1797), ca. 1770

The Hebrew *Yigdal* is a metrical version of the thirteen articles of the Hebrew creed. These thirteen articles were formed by Moses Maimonides (1130-1205), followed by the *Yigdal*, probably written by Daniel ben Judah Dayyan between 1396 and 1404.[1]

When Thomas Olivers, a Methodist minister, visited the Great Synagogue in London, he was so taken with a melody he heard the cantor sing that he asked for a transcription. The tune was later named for Meyer Leoni (Lyon), the cantor and transcriber. Olivers also paraphrased the text, which was part of the *Yigdal*, but he imbued it "with Christian character." He published both the traditional tune and his text around 1770.

The paraphrase used here, which is closer to the Hebrew text, was done jointly around 1885 by a rabbi, Max Landsberg, and a Unitarian clergyman, Newton Mann. In 1889 Rabbi Landsberg asked William Channing Gannett to recast the text into the meter of the tune LEONI. The familiar first line of the earlier paraphrase by Thomas Olivers has been retained, replacing Landsberg and Mann's "Praise to the living God." Among the alterations made to the text, the phrase "the Name" is used in stanzas 1 and 3 to convey the traditional Hebrew respect for the sacredness of the name of God.

LEONI is one of seven traditional *Yigdal* tunes. Though Leoni's synagogue version was unwritten, it was probably sung in unison with an improvised accompaniment provided by singers who supported the *Hazan*, or song leader.

1. A literal translation to English of the *Yigdal* is in Julian's *Dictionary of Hymnology*, 1907, pages 1149-1150, along with the earliest paraphrase, 1770, by Thomas Olivers (1725-1799).

170

The King of love my shepherd is

ST. COLUMBA

Based on Psalm 23
Henry Williams Baker (1821-1877)
Hymns Ancient and Modern, Appendix, 1868

Ancient Irish melody
Irish Church Hymnal, 1873 or 1874

This text, considered to be one of the finest English metrical paraphrases of Psalm 23, includes New Testament expressions. Stanza 3 is reminiscent of the parable of the lost sheep in Luke 15:3-6, and "Thy cross before to guide me" in stanza 4:3 supplements "thy rod and staff. . . ." Reportedly, the author breathed the third stanza as he lay dying.

ST. COLUMBA is named for the Irish saint who brought Irish Christianity to Scotland and was the first to report a sighting of the Loch Ness monster in 546. This tune is in Charles V. Stanford's *Complete Collection of Irish Music, as noted by George Petrie* (1902), even though it did not appear in Petrie's 1855 compilation (*The Hymnal 1940 Companion*, 1951 ed.). Stanford's caption is "Irish hymn sung on the dedication of a chapel—County of Londonderry." He also cites the similarity of the opening phrase with that of "Soggarth Shamus O'Finn. A lament," which is also in his *Complete Collection* . . . . The melody, in a simpler form, appeared in the *Irish Church Hymnal* in the mid-1870s, but "this masterpiece of Irish folk song" was likely from the 1700s (Douglas 1936). The present combination of text and tune with its harmonization is from *The English Hymnal* (1906).

224

The kingdom of God

MUSTARD SEED

Based on Mark 4:30-34
Gracia Grindal (1943-)
Singing the Story, 1983

Austin Cole Lovelace (1919-), 1987
Hymnal Supplement II, 1987

Grindal's text is based on the parable of the sower found in Mark 4:30-34. She wrote her own paraphrase in order to explore the passage more fully. She also was interested in the use of a refrain that reverses the comparison of the kingdom and the mustard seed. The third stanza originally concluded with "away from any evil prey," but it was changed to "away from evil things that prey" to distinguish the prey from the predator. The text appears with another tune in *Singing the Story*.

In 1986 Gracia Grindal sent composer Austin Lovelace a batch of her scripture-based texts, all set in a wide variety of meters. Attracted by the simplicity and charm of "The kingdom of God ," he composed a setting that "tries to keep the same freedom and ease in the meter found in the words." A four-part harmonization can be found in the *Accompaniment Handbook*.

The United Methodist Hymnal (1989) was the first denominational hymnal to include "The kingdom of God."

187
The Lord is come—see "Let the heavens be glad"

38
The Lord is in his holy temple

(no tune name)

Habakkuk 2:20 (KJV)

Edwin Othello Excell (1851-1921)
International Praise, 1902

This now-familiar call to worship is the conclusion of a passage in Habakkuk that scorns the worship of idols, because in them "there is no breath at all." While idols have no life, by contrast the Lord is a living God of action, worthy of the awe of all on earth.

This simple musical setting enhances the text as the rhythmic patterns follow the natural accents of the words. Following its printing in the source listed above, it appeared in Excell's collection *Joy to the World* (1915). It has been included in several Brethren and Mennonite hymnals.

69
The Lord is King

SO LANGE JESUS BLEIBT

So lange Jesus bleibt der Herr
Nicolaus Ludwig von Zinzendorf (1700-1760), 1742
Tr. Esther Cathryn Klaassen Bergen (1921-)
The Hymn Book (Canadian Mennonite Brethren), 1960

Russian Mennonite oral tradition
Written form from *Gesangbuch* (Canadian Mennonite Brethren), 1955

Nicolaus Ludwig von Zinzendorf was a Saxon nobleman and Lutheran Pietist who offered asylum to the Moravian Brethren in 1722. On one of his estates in Dresden, the persecuted members of the Unitas Fratrum established the community known as Herrnhut. Five years later Zinzendorf joined them, being consecrated as a Moravian bishop in 1737. His output of hymn texts was prolific, numbering about two thousand.

Esther Bergen's translation was made for the 1960 English version of the Canadian Mennonite Brethren Gesangbuch, which contains 122 of her translations.

This hymn came to Canada via Mennonite Brethren who emigrated from Russia in the 1920s. They brought with them a wealth of German-language hymnody with folklike tunes, a reservoir of several hundred songs that form the heart of the Mennonite Brethren hymn heritage.

Called *Kernlieder* (core songs), they are "a part of the oral history of [their] congregational song that was characterized by rote singing in the congregations, improvisation and an almost intuitive disregard for any consideration regarding authenticity" (Oyer 1980).

The musical form preserved here is taken from the oral tradition of the immigrants, as it was notated by the Mennonite Brethren in their *Gesangbuch* of 1955. The compilers of that book took pains to print harmonies as they had been adjusted through oral practice.

SO LANGE JESUS BLEIBT appears in *The Mennonite Hymnary* (1940) with the text "Come, Father, Son and Holy Ghost," by Charles Wesley.

578
The Lord's my shepherd

Based on Psalm 23
The Psalms of David in Meeter (Scottish Psalter), Edinburgh, 1650

CRIMOND

Jessie Seymour Irvine (1836-1887)
Harm. and adapt. by David Grant (1833-1893)
The Northern Psalter, 1872

This anonymous paraphrase of Psalm 23 is a composite of at least seven different versions in existence prior to 1650;[1] it parallels most closely the 1646 edition of Francis Rous. In fact, the second stanza changes only one word and the final stanza is exactly as it was in 1646. The Scottish Psalter of 1650, considered a classic of English-language psalmody and the only psalter authorized by the Church of Scotland, is still in use. In stanza 3:2, "I fear none ill" is not a misprint, but an archaic expression true to the language of this very old psalter.

The tune CRIMOND is named for the village in Scotland where Jessie S. Irvine's father was a pastor for thirty years and where Irvine died. The earliest source of this tune ascribes it to David Grant. Anna Irvine claimed, however, that her sister Jessie composed the melody in 1871 and then sent it to Grant to harmonize. Though there is no conclusive proof, the ascription of the tune to Jessie Irvine in the 1929 Scottish Psalter has been widely accepted. This truly Scottish hymn gained great popularity, especially among English Christians, after it was used at the wedding of Queen Elizabeth II and Prince Philip in 1947 in Westminster Abbey.

1. Its development and relationship to the various psalters that preceded it are traced in Julian's *Dictionary of Hymnology*, 1907.

141
The sacrifice you accept, O God

Based on Psalm 51
Tr. Ladies of the Grail, 1985

(no tune name)

David Clark Isele (1946-), 1979

The music for this responsorial psalm was written for a worship service at the University of Notre Dame Chapel, South Bend, Indiana. During the years Isele taught at Notre Dame (1973-1979), he was frequently called upon by the director of the chapel choir to create a setting of a liturgical text "for rehearsal tomorrow." His guidelines were to make a piece of music suited to text that was easily learned and could be sung over and over without wearing out. The simplicity of this melodic line makes it very singable, while the harmonic accompaniment (in the *Accompaniment Handbook*) keeps the music fresh, giving it a durability akin to the lasting quality of this ancient psalm.

Many congregations may be unaccustomed to musical chant. Chant requires careful listening to one's neighbor, so that voices move to new pitches at the same time. Although the text is in the first-person singular, singing this confessional psalm together makes it a meaningful corporate worship event. Two recordings of David Isele's service music, *Song of Sunday* and *Song of David*, have been produced by G.I.A. Publications.

263
The strife is o'er

Finita jam sunt praelia
Anonymous
Symphonia Sirenum Selectarum, 1695
Tr. Francis Pott (1832-1909)
Pott's *Hymns Fitted to the Order of Common Prayer*, 1861

VICTORY

Giovanni Pierluigi da Palestrina (ca. 1525-1594)
"Gloria Patri" from *Magnificat in the Third Mode*, 1591
Adapt. by William Henry Monk (1823-1889)
Hymns Ancient and Modern, 1861

The authorship of this Latin hymn is uncertain, though it has been traced to the Jesuit *Symphonia Sirenum* . . . . The date is equally indefinite; it has been placed as early as the twelfth century and as late as the seventeenth. This text is a forceful rendering of Paul's affirmation—Christ's resurrection is the victory cry in the battle with death (1 Cor. 15:55-56).

Comments on the tune VICTORY may be found with "O Lord of life, wherever they be" (**635**). With "The strife is o'er," however, the opening "Alleluias" are added as an introduction to the hymn. They are usually sung only before the first stanza. GELOBT SEI GOTT could be an alternate tune, with "alleluias" increased to three.

For a completely different experience, the *Accompaniment Handbook* offers an arrangement that uses stanza 1 as a refrain for a chanted version of the resurrection story. This arrangement comes to us via a Polish Dominican priest/musician, Jacek Gałuszka.

509
The tree of life — APPLE TREE

Anonymous
Joshua Smith's *Divine Hymns*, 1784

Alice Parker (1925-), 1989
Hymnal: A Worship Book, 1992

There is a long tradition of speaking of Christ as a tree. Paul refers to Christ as the "firstfruits" (1 Cor. 15). Bonaventure (13th c.) envisioned a tree with twelve branches adorned with leaves, flowers, and fruit. "This is the fruit," he wrote, "that took its origin from the Virgin's womb and reached its savory maturity on the tree of the cross under the midday heat of the Eternal Sun, that is the love of Christ. In the garden of the heavenly paradise—God's table—this fruit is served to those who desire it."

Ambrose, the fourteenth-century Christian bishop, writes: "The church rejoices in the redemption of many . . . and so she says, 'Let my beloved come into his garden and eat the fruits of his apple trees.' What are these apple trees? You were made dry wood in Adam, but now through the grace of Christ you flower as apple trees" (Huck, Ramshaw, Lathrop 1987).

A spiritualized reading of the Song of Solomon may also have contributed to the tender beauty of this metaphor: "As an apple tree among the trees of the wood, so is my beloved among young men. With great delight I sat in his shadow, and his fruit was sweet to my taste" (2:3).

This early American text extends the apple tree analogy to the fruit, the shade, and the everlasting quality of the tree of life, which is "always green."

Alice Parker's melody, written for this text, has a simple, folklike quality. Although the meter is irregular, it is closely wedded to the text rhythms, making the melody easier to sing than it first appears.

Another tune that was originally written for this text is TRUSTING MERCY (**484**), which gives the hymn a gentle, lyrical sound, like trees blowing in a breeze. See the *Accompaniment Handbook* for a keyboard accompaniment.

202
The virgin Mary had a baby boy — (no tune name)

West Indian carol
Edric Conner Collection of West Indian Spirituals, 1945

West Indian carol
(same source as text)

This carol from the West Indies provides a charming stylistic contrast to traditional European Christmas carols. It may be familiar to some through its inclusion in the Mennonite publication *Sing and Rejoice* or through its choral settings and recordings. Note that in the third stanza the pattern of exact repetition is broken. The wise men saw "when" and "where" the baby was born and then "went." The refrain emphasizes the incarnation, "He come from the glory." An effort may be made to sing the song with calypso-like syncopation. This carol can give an international flavor to the celebration of Christ's birth.

314
The word of God is solid ground

THE WORD OF GOD

Anonymous, ca. 1550
Ausbund, 1564
Adapt. by Harris J. Loewen (1953-)
Assembly Songs, 1983

J. Harold Moyer (1927-)
Assembly Songs, 1983

This text is an adaptation of stanzas 2, 10, and 12 of No. 15 in the *Ausbund,* the earliest collection of hymn texts for Anabaptists. The *Ausbund* is also important because it is the oldest Protestant hymnal in continuous publication still in use today (Oyer 1980).[1] At its core are fifty-one hymns written by Anabaptists who were imprisoned in the dungeons of Passau between 1537 and 1540. The hymns, therefore, have the distinct flavor of martyrdom; commitment and reliance on God are the watchwords of these texts. Other *Ausbund* texts in this hymnal are "I sing with exultation" (**438**), "Who now would follow Christ" (**535**), and "Our Father God, thy name we praise" (**32, 33**).

Moyer's melody was originally written as it appears in the hymnal—with chord symbols only. He added a full harmonization[2] for *Assembly Songs,* the songbook for Bethlehem '83, the joint conference of the Mennonite Church and the General Conference Mennonite Church. In writing a tune for this text, he says he was trying to complement the sturdy, forthright character of this Anabaptist text, the legacy of "a courageous and persecuted group."

1. Herald Press's *Four Hundred Years with the Ausbund* (1964) is a source for in-depth information (Mennonite Publishing House, Scottdale, Pennsylvania).

2. This harmonization is in the *Accompaniment Handbook.*

396
The work is thine, O Christ

DIE SACH' IST DEIN

Die Sach' ist dein
Sts. 1-2, Samuel Preiswerk (1799-1871), 1829
St. 3, Felician Martin von Kalinowa Zaremba (1794-1874)
Tr. Julius Henry Horstmann (1869-1954)
Christian Hymns (Evangelical Synod), 1908

Johann Michael Haydn (1737-1806)
Hier liegt vor deiner Majestät, Salzburg, late 18th c.

Preiswerk's German words were written for this melody at the request of students at the Basel Mission House (Switzerland), and his two stanzas were sung at their annual missionary festival in June of 1829. Count Zaremba's third stanza adds a more global emphasis. The change of "warriors" to "workers" in stanza 3:6 is true to the original German.

This melody, DIE SACH' IST DEIN, was written originally for the opening text, *Hier liegt vor deiner Majestät,* in a *Singmesse* by Johann Michael Haydn. The *Singmesse* (sung-mass) consisted of German-language responses to the sections of the Latin mass spoken or sung by the priest. Johann Michael Haydn, younger brother of Franz Joseph, wrote eight of these works, a form popular in eighteenth-century Austria.

The vigorous character of the melody, criticized as inappropriate for use in a Catholic service, is well suited for this sturdy text. This hymn, used frequently by Prussian Mennonites and their descendants, was sung at the cornerstone-laying at Bethel College, North Newton, Kansas, in 1888.

304
There are many gifts

MANY GIFTS

Based on 1 Corinthians 12
Patricia Joyce Shelly (1951-), 1976
Many Gifts, 1977

Patricia Joyce Shelly (1951-), 1976
(same source as text)

Shelly developed this scripture hymn in connection with Laity Sunday at a local Methodist church where some friends were members. "This song itself was a fusion of many gifts," she writes. "Such diversity can sometimes be a painful challenge for the church—as Paul found out with the church at Corinth—but it is surely a cause of celebration as well. Many tasks, many talents, many gifts—but the church looks for unity in the Spirit."

Shelly says "the text and tune for the chorus came together at the same time; and the cadence of the words influenced the shape of the melody" with its alternating meters. This song, with an accompaniment by Dennis Friesen-Carper, was published in *Sing and Rejoice* in

1979. It has been widely used in Mennonite circles since that time. An accompaniment by Marilyn Houser Hamm is found in the *Accompaniment Handbook.*

627
There is a balm in Gilead — BALM IN GILEAD

African American spiritual — African American spiritual

The refrain of this spiritual answers Jeremiah's question, "Is there no balm in Gilead?" (Jer. 8:22). Gilead, the mountainous country east of the Jordan, was known in biblical times for medicinal ointments made from the gum of a tree found only in that area. Here, however, the "balm" refers to Christ. The creator of this spiritual may have experienced hymns by Charles Wesley and John Newton, both of whom used the phrase "sin-sick soul." The two most familiar stanzas have been included here, the first reminding us of the encouragement of the Holy Spirit and the second calling us to witness.

The refrain of the spiritual was published in the *Revivalist,* printed in upstate New York in 1868. The entire spiritual was included in *Folk Songs of the American Negro* (1907), compiled by Frederick Jerome Work and John Wesley Work, Jr. A harmonized version can be found in the *Accompaniment Handbook.*

5
There is a place of quiet rest — McAFEE

Cleland Boyd McAfee (1866-1944), 1901
The Choir Leader, 1903

Cleland Boyd McAfee (1866-1944), 1901
(same source as text)

McAfee, preacher and choir director at Park College Church in Parkville, Missouri, had the custom of writing a hymn for each Communion service. This hymn, though it was used at Communion, had a special poignancy: McAfee wrote it in 1901 shortly after his two young nieces had died of diphtheria within twenty-four hours of each other. After the choir members had learned this hymn at their Saturday night rehearsal, "they went to Howard McAfee's home and sang it as they stood . . . outside the darkened, quarantined house"[1] (Reynolds 1976).

The hymn first appeared in the October 1903 issue of *The Choir Leader,* a periodical published by Lorenz Publishing Company in Dayton, Ohio. The restful mood of this hymn can set the stage for meditative worship.

1. Recounted by the author's daughter, Katharine McAfee Parker, in her book *Near to the Heart of God*

145

There's a wideness in God's mercy — WELLESLEY

Frederick William Faber (1814-1863)
Oratory Hymns, 1854 (8 sts.)
Hymns, 1862 (13 sts.), alt.

Lizzie Shove Tourjée (1858-1913)
Hymnal of the Methodist Church with Tunes, 1878

This hymn consists of selected verses from the complete thirteen-stanza version. The first eight stanzas, headed "Come to Jesus," were published in 1854; Faber added five more stanzas in 1862. Faber's first stanza, omitted in *Hymnal: A Worship Book,* begins:

Souls of men, why will ye scatter
Like a crowd of frightened sheep?
Foolish hearts, why will ye wander
From a love so true and deep?

Thankfully, God's love is wide, deep, broad, and high enough to surround even "foolish hearts," as Faber's hymn asserts.

This tune is named for Wellesley College, in Massachusetts, which Tourjée attended for one year. She wrote it as a high school senior when she was asked to compose a tune for the graduation hymn used at her commencement ceremony in Newton, Massachusetts.

Various tunes are used with this text, some of which combine two stanzas into a single eight-line verse.

266

They crucified my Savior — ASCENSIUS

African American spiritual

African American spiritual

Frequently called "He arose" or "He 'rose," this spiritual remains a standard one for Easter. It is more than just a retelling of the events of the crucifixion and resurrection. The words "The Lord will bear my spirit home" express the hope of eternal life, which is a central legacy of Christ's resurrection.

The name ASCENSIUS comes from the word *ascensus,* which means "to climb." This spiritual should be sung at a tempo slow enough to allow the music to say the same thing as the text. Too fast a tempo will trivialize both the music and the text. The musical material of the refrain is much like the stanzas, with variations created by antiphonal passages and a moving bass line in the final phrase.

584
They that wait upon the Lord

(no tune name)

Based on Isaiah 40:31
Stuart Hamblen (1908-1989), 1953

Stuart Hamblen (1908-1989), 1953

This song, also called "Teach me, Lord, to wait," draws from the heartening promise of Isaiah. The song has been sung around the world and is a favorite of congregations and choirs. Because it is so often sung by rote, it is known in many different musical variations. Stuart Hamblen, for many years the host of the "Cowboy Church of the Air" radio program, also wrote "It is no secret what God can do."

269
Thine is the glory

JUDAS MACCABEUS

A toi la gloire, O Ressuscité
Edmond L. Budry (1854-1932), 1884
Chants Evangéliques, Lausanne, 1885
Tr. Richard Birch Hoyle (1875-1939)
Cantate Domino, 1925

George Frederick Handel (1685-1759)
Joshua, 1748

First written in French by a Swiss pastor, this hymn makes a fine Easter processional. Paul Laufer, however, has suggested that the text is based on an Advent hymn by Friedrich-Heinrich Ranke (1798-1876), found with this tune by Handel in the *Evangelisches Gesangbuch für Elsass-Lothringern* (Stulken 1981).

JUDAS MACCABEUS is taken from Handel's chorus "See, the conquering hero comes" in the oratorio *Judas Maccabeus.* This chorus, however, was not in the oratorio's first performance in 1747 but was transferred to it in 1751 from the oratorio *Joshua.* Thomas Butts was the first to use it as a hymn tune in his *Harmonia Sacra* (ca. 1760), where it was set to Charles Wesley's text "Christ the Lord is risen today."

640
This is a day of new beginnings

NEW BEGINNINGS

Brian Arthur Wren (1936-), 1978
Faith Looking Forward, 1983
Rev. in *Hymnal Supplement II,* 1987, alt.

Richard David Brode (1963-), 1991
Hymnal: A Worship Book, 1992

Wren's text originally began as a question, "Is this a day of new beginnings?" He revised it in 1987 after being challenged to frame it as a positive statement. First written for a New Year's Day service at Holy Family Church in Blackbird Leys, Oxford, England, the hymn was published in *Faith Looking Forward* under the heading "The new year (and other new beginnings)." Wren writes:

> In itself, the new year is an arbitrary convention . . . .The recurrent awakening of life in nature is not a strong enough foundation for hope of real change. Yet by faith in the *really* new events of the Christian story, a day, or a month, or an hour can become charged with promise, and be a springboard to a changed life. (Wren 1983)

The present stanzas 2 and 3, which relate to 2 Corinthians 5:16-17, summon us to seize and act on the hope we find in Christ. The final stanza is similar to the original stanza 5, which began "In faith we'll gather 'round the table to taste and share what love can do."

The tune NEW BEGINNINGS was inspired by the text itself. In the spring of 1991, Brode, grieving the end of an important relationship, was searching for a text that would inspire a new melody. He writes: "Suddenly, the text 'This is a day of new beginnings' sprang to my attention; [its] message of new beginnings, that God is making all things new, touched the pain I was feeling . . . and gave me a sense of hope. The tune quickly emerged from that emotional encounter with the text." The tune was written originally in C major with guitar accompaniment. The hymn was first used at the 1991 commencement service of Bethany Theological Seminary, Oak Brook, Illinois, where Brode was a student.

315
This is a story full of love

Brian Arthur Wren (1936-), 1985
Praising a Mystery, 1986

PRIMROSE

Amzi Chapin (1768-1835) or
Lucius Chapin (1760-1842)
Pamphlet, 1811 or 1812
John Wyeth's *Repository of Sacred Music, Part Second,* 1813

Wren's text is a capsulized story of the Bible, sandwiched between an introduction (st. 1) and a doxology (st. 7). He features significant biblical events: creation (st. 2), covenant and the Exodus (st. 3), the incarnation (st. 4), the crucifixion (st. 5), and the resurrection (st. 6). Using images of "the Wisdom and the Word" to unify the poem, Wren has created an alliteration that is strong in theology and is also gracious to sing. Scriptural allusions include Proverbs 8:22-30; John 1:1-16; and Ephesians 1.

Wren originally wrote this text for TIMOTHY, the tune William Rowan had written for one of his earlier texts, "I come with joy."

The lightness of the melody PRIMROSE and its rhythmic energy, especially in the second phrase, make the chronological sweep of this text both manageable and appealing. The tune appears in a number of early American hymnbooks, with a variety of names: TWENTY-FOURTH, ORANGE, MELODY, CHELMSFORD, and MEMPHIS. It was first printed by Andrew Law in his shaped-note staffless notation in a supplement he printed for John Logan.[1] John Wyeth's claim of first publication is probably true in the sense that it was the first in conventional shaped notes. The tune also appeared that same year in Robert Patterson's *Church Music*, published in Cincinnati, Ohio.

Of the seven musical Chapins known to be active in the first part of the nineteenth century, several have been credited with this tune. William Hauser's *Olive Leaf* (1878) lists Aaron Chapin as the composer, while Charles Hamm attributes the tune to Lucius Chapin (Hamm 1960). Carl N. Shull, however, in his research on John Logan, lists Amzi Chapin as the probable composer.

To give this hymn a different feel, the tune RESIGNATION (**589**) can be used, combining two stanzas of text to complete the tune. Because of the odd number of stanzas, selected ones may be chosen or the final stanza omitted.

1. See "Oh, holy city seen of John" (**320**) for more information on this supplement.

154

This is my Father's world — TERRA BEATA

Maltbie Davenport Babcock (1858-1901)
Babcock's *Thoughts for Every-Day Living*, 1901

Franklin Lawrence Sheppard (1852-1930)
Franklin Sheppard's *Alleluia*, 1915

This much-loved hymn is made up of six of the original sixteen four-line stanzas. Babcock, a Presbyterian minister, wrote the hymn during his first pastorate at Lockport, New York. An outstanding athlete, he often took early morning walks near Lake Ontario, saying, "I am going out to see my Father's world" (Ronander, Porter 1966). His declaration opens each quatrain.

The tune name TERRA BEATA means "blessed earth." The music, written for this text by Franklin Sheppard, a friend of the author, bears some resemblance to an English folk song he recalled from his childhood. The folk song, which appeared as RUSPER in *The English Hymnal* (1906), is in triple meter and shows the strongest melodic relationship to TERRA BEATA in its closing phrase. The tune is also known as TERRA PATRIS, which means "Father's world."

58
This is the day

OTO JEST DZIEŃ

Based on Psalm 118
Liturgia Godzin, Vol. 3, Poznań, 1982

André Gouzes, O.P., 1989
Arr. by Jacek Gałuszka, O.P. (1965-)

This familiar scriptural passage was set to music by Gouzes, a French member of the Order of Preachers (Dominicans). The Polish arranger also composed the tune OTO SĄ BARANKI for "Who are these" (**270**). The refrain of "This is the day," which sings the words of Psalm 118:24, is included in the hymnal. As with Gałuszka's other composition, the stanzas are in the *Accompaniment Handbook.*

642
This is the day the Lord has made

ARLINGTON

Based on Psalm 118:24-26
Isaac Watts (1674-1748)
The Psalms of David . . ., 1719

Thomas Augustine Arne (1710-1778), 1762
Adapt. by Ralph Harrison (1748-1810)
Sacred Harmony, Vol. I, 1784

Based on Psalm 118:24-26, the broader content of this hymn is revealed in the title given in Watts's *The Psalms of David . . .* (1719): "Hosanna: the Lord's Day; or Christ's Resurrection and our Salvation." As was typical for his work, Watts's interpretation of this Psalm renders the Lord's Day as distinctly Christian, despite its Jewish origins. The omitted third stanza is:

> Hosanna to the anointed King,
> To David's holy Son!
> Make haste to help us, Lord and bring
> Salvation from thy throne.

ARLINGTON was adapted from the minuet in the overture to Arne's opera *Artaxerxes*, produced in 1762 in London. Its other tune names include ARTAXERXES, PRINCE'S STREET, and TRIUMPH. There are other interesting alternatives for both the tune and text: ARLINGTON, also associated with "Am I a soldier of the cross," by George Doane, would work with another Watts text "Thou art the way" (**339**). Or this text may be used with PRIMROSE (**315**).

476
This is the feast of victory — FESTIVAL CANTICLE

Based on Revelation 5:12-13
John W. Arthur (1922-1980), 1970
Lutheran Book of Worship, 1978

Richard Walter Hillert (1923-), 1975
(same source as text)

Scholars believe that the songs in Revelation 4 and 5 may be early Christian hymns that were incorporated into the writing. Arthur's paraphrase of Revelation 5:12-13 is surrounded by the big, joyful antiphon "This is the feast of victory for our God. Alleluia!" The antiphon is sung at the beginning of the hymn and after each verse.

FESTIVAL CANTICLE is a tuneful unison melody in a comfortable vocal range. Hillert adapted it for the *Lutheran Book of Worship* (1978) from his choir setting "Festival Canticle: Worthy Is Christ." He went on to develop a new format in hymn style for its use in *The Hymnal 1982* (1985) and *The United Methodist Hymnal* (1989). The music should have a moderate tempo with a half-note pulse. Most measures will have two beats, while the two longer measures contain three beats.

335
This is the threefold truth — ACCLAMATIONS

Fred Pratt Green (1903-), 1979
Hymns of Faith, 1980

Jack (John Albert) Schrader (1942-)
(same source as text)

The refrain of this hymn, taken from ancient sources, is reclaimed in many recent liturgies. It declares that Christ's action on our behalf is valid in the past, present, and future. Acknowledged as "a most necessary truth" to the Christian faith, it means that "Christ's death and resurrection are the very sum and substance of evangelical truth" (*The Worshiping Church*, worship leader's ed., 1991). The rest of the hymn is a commentary on the relevance of the affirmation in the refrain.

The refrain could be used alone as a litany response. By omitting the third stanza, which deals with Communion in a form unfamiliar to Mennonites and Brethren, the hymn has been made useful for general worship.

Jack Schrader wrote the music of this hymn shortly after he joined the staff at Hope Publishing Company in 1978. Hope's president, George Shorney, presented Schrader with a number of texts by Fred Pratt Green, with the assignment to create musical settings for them.[1] In the refrain, note how the descending interval at "died" and the succeeding rising melodic line give a feeling of soaring hope after the presumed finality of Christ's death.

1. An anthem setting is in Hope Publishing Company's *Hymnal Supplement*, 1984, and *The Worshiping Church*, 1990, 1991, as well as in the *Baptist Hymnal*, Southern Baptist, 1991.

276
This joyful Eastertide — VRUECHTEN

George Ratcliffe Woodward (1848-1934)
Carols for Easter and Ascension, 1894

David's Psalmen, 1685
Harm. by Alice Parker (1925-), 1966
The Mennonite Hymnal, 1969

Woodward was responsible for collecting and editing numerous texts, including making translations that intentionally retained the original meters of foreign-language texts. He wrote this exuberant hymn specifically for the tune VRUECHTEN, which leaps and dances along with the words in the middle of the stanza phrases. The music of the refrain, however, accommodates the weight of "what might have been" if Christ had not been resurrected. But neither the music nor the words can long contain the reality, and both build to bursting with the news: "Now hath Christ arisen!"

This playful tune originated as the melody of a popular seventeenth-century Dutch text *De Liefde Voortgebracht*. In *David's Psalmen*, edited by Joachim Oudaen, it was set to *Hoe groot de Vruechten zijn*, from which the tune name is derived.

401
This little light of mine — LATTIMER

African American spiritual

African American spiritual
Adapt. by William Farley Smith (1941-), 1987
The United Methodist Hymnal, 1989

This spiritual is based on the familiar words of Matthew 5:14-16, but it is also about shining like the stars. "One reason for shining," writes John Lovell, Jr., "is that you worship a Deity who created light and who deals in it" (Lovell 1972). An additional stanza, found in some collections, begins "Jesus gave it to me."

A musician and historian, Smith named his adaptation for Louis Lattimer, an African American who was born into slavery and became a college-trained electrical engineer. While employed by Thomas Edison at Menlo Park, Lattimer invented the tungsten filament and inserted it into a vacuum tube. While Edison's incandescent lamp failed to burn more than three hours, Lattimer's invention burned more than twelve hundred hours.

Several forms of this melody are found in various collections. The arrangement of the spiritual in *Songs of Zion* is marked "Slow, with feeling," though the version of this song that is frequently used in camps and Sunday schools is more lively. The music in this hymnal should be sung in a more meditative fashion, like a solemn march but not a dirge. Both Lydia Parrish and John Lovell, Jr., historians of African American music, state that slaves used this song as a candlelight procession throughout Advent, Christmas, and Epiphany.

339
Thou art the way

George Washington Doane (1799-1859)
Songs by the Way, Chiefly Devotional, 1824, alt.

RICHMOND

Thomas Haweis (ca. 1734-1820)
Carmina Christo, ca. 1792

Jesus' declaration in John 14:6, "I am the way, and the truth, and the life," provides the basis for this hymn. The final stanza is a prayer that summarizes the first three. The final line of stanza 3, "*nor* death *nor* hell," can be understood as "neither death nor hell can harm those who put their trust in the risen Christ."

This hymn gained wide usage in England and was one of only two American hymns[1] to be included in the original edition of the eminent *Hymns Ancient and Modern* (1861). All later editions of that hymnal retained this text.

RICHMOND was named for Leigh Richmond, the rector at Turvey, Bedfordshire, and a friend of the composer. The tune is also known as CHESTERFIELD, HAWEIS, and SPA FIELDS CHAPEL. In Samuel Webbe's *Psalmody* (1853), a melodic extension that required repetition of the last line of text was omitted from the original tune. The *Hymnal 1940* (Episcopal) coupled this melody with the carol "Joy to the world." ARLINGTON, the tune found with "This is the day the Lord has made" (**642**), is often associated with this text and makes a good alternative.

1. The other is "Take up your cross" (**536**).

373
Thou true Vine, that heals

Percy Dearmer (1867-1936)
Songs of Praise, 1925

PLEADING SAVIOR

American folk hymn
Christian Lyre, 1830
Harm. by Ralph Vaughan Williams (1872-1958)
The English Hymnal, 1906

The Vine, Tree, branches, fruit, Vintage—the image of a tree is as thorough and dense in this hymn as it is in the scripture upon which it is based—John 15:1-5. Nowhere does Jesus' name appear, but the referent is very clear; after all, the "branches" know the Tree from which they spring. Dearmer also has crafted a beautiful alliterative prayer that seems tailored for Brethren and Mennonites: "Cleanse us, make us sane and simple, till we merge our lives in thine."

This text was written for *Songs of Praise* by a writer identified only as "T. S. N." The mystery author was, according to Oxford Univerity Press, London, none other than Percy Dearmer, editor of that collection, as well as the *Oxford Book of Carols* (1928).

The original composer of PLEADING SAVIOR is unknown, but this musical setting by Vaughan Williams is found in numerous hymnals. The melody and alto voices are very similar to William Hauser's arrangement in his 1878 collection *The Olive Leaf* where it is set to "Now behold the Savior pleading." For information about PLEADING SAVIOR in another setting from the *Plymouth Collection of Hymns*, see "Lord, thou dost love" (**387**).

347
Through our fragmentary prayers — WORDLESS

Thomas Henry Troeger (1945-), 1985
New Hymns for the Life of the Church, 1991

Carol Doran (1936-), 1985
(same source as text)

In this text Troeger expresses one of his deepest understandings of prayer and the creative process. He writes:

> People frequently ask me where I keep getting so many ideas. I travel to a place in the soul that is on the borderline of music, language, and silence, and from that region there arise hummings within me, unheard sounds that eventually become aural and condense into the syllables and meters of poetry. Sometimes they are instead simply the yearnings of the heart, . . . yearnings which I believe are the Spirit praying for us "in sighs too deep for words" (Rom. 8).

The word "fragmentary," comments Troeger, comes from Robert Frost's poem "Fragmentary Blue," which "deals in that poet's peculiar way with issues of transcendence and immanence":

> Why make so much of fragmentary blue
> In here and there a bird, or butterfly,
> Or flower, or wearing-stone, or open eye,
> When heaven presents in sheets the solid hue?

Troeger goes on to say: "For me our fragmentary prayers are a way of tasting heaven's blue, a 'whet' of the Spirit that brings us 'Strength to do the work of love.' "

It is appropriate that the refrain should be, as the tune name indicates, "wordless." The author and composer intended to have singers experience these "sighs too deep for words" during the second two lines, humming or singing "Alleluia" in free rhythm while the accompaniment goes solo around their voices. The beautiful chords all include the sustained pitch "A," the one being sung. (See the *Accompaniment Handbook.*) Troeger praises Doran's music, declaring that it "comes about as close as actual music can to the spiritual music" described in the prose above.

434
Thuma mina

Send me, Jesus
South African text

THUMA MINA

South African melody

The first words of this hymn, which are also the tune name, are pronounced "Too-mah mee-nah." Over the ending of each stanza, the solo voice of the leader introduces the next words to be sung. In this way other stanzas, such as "Heal me, Jesus," may easily be added, going beyond the printed text. The rich harmonies, heard so well in *a cappella* singing, ring away wonderfully if this is used as a congregational recessional.

241
'Tis midnight, and on Olive's brow

William Bingham Tappan (1794-1849)
Poems, 1822

OLIVE'S BROW

William Batchelder Bradbury (1816-1868)
The Shawm, 1853

Praying alone on the Mount of Olives, Jesus poignantly revealed his humanity as he "wrestled lone with fears" (st. 2:2). Tappan's hymn, based on scripture passages found in Mark 14 and Luke 22, transports us to Gethsemane to witness the dimming of Jesus' earthly ministry. Consistently setting the stage at the darkest hour of night, the text escorts us through the agony of the moment. Even Jesus' natal star wanes, for the ancients a sign of impending death (st. 1:2). The only note of hope in this pre-Easter scene is in the last few words: The anguished Jesus is not forsaken by God.

Bradbury's setting of this text first appeared in *The Shawm,* an oblong singing-school/church collection he edited jointly with George F. Root. There Bradbury's tune is in four parts, with the melody in the tenor voice and having three stanzas of text.

571
'Tis not with eyes of flesh we see — ST. PETERSBURG

Ora W. Garber (1903-1981)
The Brethren Hymnal, 1951, alt.

Dimitri Stepanovich Bortniansky (1751-1825)
Tscherlitzky's *Choralbuch*, 1825, alt.

Ora Garber, one of the editors of *The Brethren Hymnal* (1951), studied a multitude of texts as that book was being prepared. While reviewing the hymns chosen for inclusion, Garber balked when he came to "We saw thee not." Feeling that the hymn needed a further expression of Christian commitment, he wrote a fifth stanza. Then he added two more. When the other editors saw Garber's three stanzas, they decided the new material could stand without the first hymn text. Garber had created a new hymn (Statler, Fisher 1959).

The tune ST. PETERSBURG, which had been chosen for the first hymn, was retained. Among the scriptural allusions used in Garber's text are John 20:29 in stanza 1, Simon Peter's words in John 6:68 at the beginning of stanza 2, and Hebrews 4:15 and John 10:9 in stanza 2:3-4.

Kenneth I. Morse, who helped prepare both the 1951 and 1992 hymnals, altered the text to eliminate the archaisms in Garber's hymn. The most significant changes are in stanza 1:2 where "That thou art" is changed to "That Christ is"; and in 1:3, "we look to thee" becomes "we know that he . . . ." Stanza 2 begins "O Christ, you have," replacing "Thou only hast . . . ."

For comments on ST. PETERSBURG, see "O power of love" (**593**) where the tune appears in the key of D major.

340
'Tis so sweet to trust in Jesus — TRUST IN JESUS

Louisa M. R. Stead (ca. 1850-1917)
Songs of Triumph, 1882, alt.

William James Kirkpatrick (1838-1921)
(same source as text)

The story behind the creation of this hymn text is not known, but many have conjectured that Stead wrote it following the death of her husband who drowned trying to rescue a child (Reynolds 1990). This was prior to 1880 when she went to South Africa as a missionary. She died there in 1917 in Southern Rhodesia (now Zimbabwe). A fellow missionary writes, "We miss her very much, but her influence goes on as our five thousand native Christians continually sing [' 'Tis so sweet' in their native language]" (Reynolds 1976).

TRUST IN JESUS was written by Kirkpatrick for this text. Both words and music first appeared together in *Songs of Triumph*, compiled by the composer and J. R. Sweney.

513

To go to heaven

Ndilivako Ndelwa (20th c.)
Tr. Howard S. Olson (1922-)
Lead Us, Lord, 1977

(no tune name)

Kinga melody (Tanzania)

Ndilivako Ndelwa wrote this Swahili text while studying at the Lutheran Theological Seminary, Makumira, in Tanzania. After seminary study Ndelwa, also a gifted musician and skilled ebony carver, returned to his vocation as a teacher in Tanzanian elementary schools. When Olson translated the hymn into English, he condensed the Swahili text of eight stanzas to four.

This tune comes from the traditional music of the Kinga people of southern Tanzania. The three-part harmony is traditional as well. Although the melody of this hymn is in an irregular seven beats per measure, the regularity of the rhythmic pattern makes it easy to learn.

102

To God be the glory

Fanny Jane Crosby (1820-1915)
Doane and Lowry's *Brightest and Best*, 1875

TO GOD BE THE GLORY

William Howard Doane (1832-1915)
(same source as text)

Gospel song collaborators Doane and Crosby wrote this hymn for inclusion in *Brightest and Best*, but it was not included in later North American collections. Ira D. Sankey, however, picked it up for his *Sacred Songs and Solos*, published in England where the hymn became better known during the Moody and Sankey revivals.

Finally, almost eighty years later, the hymn was "rediscovered" for the 1954 Billy Graham Greater London Crusade. It was taken back to Nashville, Tennessee, that same year for the crusade there, and that launched its popularity in North America.

This vigorous tune was written specifically for Crosby's hymn text. She and Doane began their collaboration in 1868, producing more than a thousand hymns.

125
To God, with the Lamb

Christopher Smart (1722-1771)
A Translation of the Psalms of David, Attempted in the Spirit of Christianity, and Adapted to the Divine Service, 1765

EDGEFIELD

Sacred Harp, 1844

In Christopher Smart's book cited above, this text is a part of the *Gloria Patri* that follows Psalm 150. Smart has used other biblical names for the persons of the Trinity to form his rendition of a traditional part of worship that we know better as "Glory be to the Father, and to the Son, and to the Holy Ghost."

In the *Sacred Harp* collection, where it was used with John Newton's text "How tedious and tasteless the hours," this tune was pitched a major third higher, beginning on F-sharp. As is true with many early American hymn tunes, EDGEFIELD works well when sung in imitation (fuguing) or as a round. The singers may be divided into as many as five parts. This can be a majestic praise chorus or take on the reverberating, mystic sound of plainsong, depending on the number and variety of instruments used. Parts in the *Accompaniment Handbook* are by Marilyn Houser Hamm.

189
To us a Child of hope is born

Based on Isaiah 9:6-7
John Morison (1749-1798)
Scottish Paraphrases, 1781

ZERAH

Lowell Mason (1792-1872)
Occasional Psalm and Hymn Tunes, 1836

With its emphasis on Christ as the Prince of Peace, this hymn has been a favorite among both Brethren and Mennonites; however, it has not found wide usage outside Anabaptist, Presbyterian, and Reformed hymn traditions. The present text comes from John Morison's stanzas 4, 5, and 6 of a paraphrase of Isaiah 9:6-7 that begins "The race that long in darkness pin'd" (Loewen, Moyer, Oyer 1983).

ZERAH, one of 1,210 tunes composed by Lowell Mason, is among those that were given biblical or ancient Hebrew names. With the grandeur of his tune, Mason matched the high anticipation expressed by Isaiah; it sings like a coronation march for a beloved king. In its first printing there were many interpretive markings that may aid song leaders today: " 'mf' for the first phrase, 'p' and 'rit' for the second, then 'f' and 'a tempo,' and 'ff' at the unison in the fourth phrase" (Loewen, Moyer, Oyer 1983). The last three notes were lengthened to fill four full measures.

607

Today I live — HEARTBEAT

Fred (Frederik Herman) Kaan (1929-)
Break Not the Circle, 1975

Jane Manton Marshall (1924-), 1980
Hymnal Supplement, 1984

"The subject of this hymn," notes author Fred Kaan, "was suggested by my wife, Elly, who once commented how few hymns there are about death and dying. I called it 'A hymn in the first person singular,' as it is a rather personal statement on this issue, but also because dying is an experience through which everyone has to pass individually" (Kaan 1985). In the opening lines of stanza 2, Kaan alludes to his extensive travel as a staff person for the World Alliance of Reformed Churches. The final lines of the poem are an especially artistic prayer for an attitude of love to accompany daily discipleship.

The hymn first appeared in *Break Not the Circle,* a collection of Kaan's texts set to music by Doreen Potter. HEARTBEAT, the tune selected here, was composed by Jane Marshall.

229

Tú has venido a la orilla — PESCADOR DE HOMBRES

Lord, you have come to the lakeshore
Cesáreo Gabaraín (1936-1991)
Dios con Nosotros, 1979
Tr. Gertrude C. Suppe (1911-),
George Frank Lockwood IV (1946-),
and Raquel Gutiérrez-Achon
(1927-), 1987
The United Methodist Hymnal, 1989

Cesáreo Gabaraín (1936-1991)
(same source as text)

This song, gentle as waves lapping on the beach, places our feet in the sandals of the first disciples when Jesus invited them to an unexplored life of love (Matt. 4:19). Written by a Spanish parish priest, the directness and folk-music style of this hymn reflect his involvement with young people throughout his ministry.

This song was included in four languages in the *International Songbook* of the 1990 Mennonite World Conference. Its tune name PESCADOR DE HOMBRES (Fisher of Men) was the original title of the song. It is appropriate for commissioning services, reception of members, and services of commitment.

190
'Twas in the moon of wintertime

JESOUS AHATONHIA

Estennial de tsonue Jesous ahatonhia
Jean de Brébeuf (1593-1649), ca. 1643
Myrand's *Noels Anciens de la Nouvelle France,* 1899
Tr. Jesse Edgar Middleton (1872-1960)
Pamphlet, 1926

French folk melody, 16th c.

Jean de Brébeuf, a French Jesuit priest who began a mission among the Hurons, is credited with the authorship of this earliest of all Canadian carols. In 1625 he traveled from Québec to Georgian Bay in what is now the province of Ontario, where he served four years before going back to France to take his final vows. Returning to Canada in 1633, Brébeuf ministered to the Huron people until his slaying on March 16, 1649, during the wars between the Iroquois and the Hurons.

The evolution of the text from Brébeuf to today's version involves more than 350 years and many people. An early manuscript of Huron music collected by Father Chaumonot, a contemporary of Brébeuf, has been lost. Etienne de Villeneuve, S.J., a later missionary to the Hurons near Québec, provided a French paraphrase along with the original language in his 1794 manuscript. Ernest Myrand's 1899 source cited above was the first to print the French text. It was this volume that Middleton used as the basis for his free English version.

This interpretation of Jesus' nativity replaces the Middle Eastern setting of the birth with cultural symbols of the Hurons: "lodge of broken bark"; "robe of rabbit skin"; even using their name for God "Gitchi Manitou." Continuing in that vein, Hugh McKellar comments that Brébeuf "mentions the wise men rather than the shepherds because . . . converted Indians made a point of reaching a church at Christmas even if they had to travel for days" (Young 1993).

It is not known if the tune JESOUS AHATONHIA was originally associated with this text. Because it was used with the French noel *Une jeune pucelle* (a young maiden), however, the melody was undoubtedly known by the missionaries before they came to Canada. A keyboard arrangement is in the *Accompaniment Handbook.*

227
Two fishermen

LEAVE ALL THINGS BEHIND

Suzanne Toolan (1927-)
Worship III, 1986

Suzanne Toolan (1927-)
Living Spirit, 1970

This folklike melody was written for another of Suzanne Toolan's texts, "How brightly deep, how glory sprung," published in 1970. For the third edition of *Worship* in 1986, she created this new text for her earlier melody. The gently undulating melodic patterns create a seaside mood for the narrative, which recounts the calling of the disciples. The refrain and final stanza, moving us beyond the biblical account, call us to leave "the trappings of our day"—and, even more difficult, to "leave all things [we] have." But we are assured that in leaving everything we are not left dangling, or with nothing. Jesus offers the alternative to follow him.

452
Ubi caritas et amor

Ubi caritas et amor, 9th c.

UBI CARITAS

Jacques Berthier (1923-)
Music from Taizé, Vol. I, 1978, 1980, 1981

In the Roman Catholic Church, before the extensive liturgical reforms of Vatican II, this Latin antiphon was always associated with the washing of feet in the Maundy Thursday Communion service. The message of the text, however, does not limit its use to this occasion. Neither the author nor the exact date of this antiphon is known. The Latin words are pronounced "oo-bee kah-ree-tahs eht ah-mawr . . . Deh-oos ee-bee ehst."

Note that the melody of the congregational part is found in the tenor voice. Solo stanzas and instrumental accompaniments are in the *Accompaniment Handbook*. For more information on the Taizé community from which the music of this antiphon comes, see "Alleluia" (**101**).

460
Una espiga

Sheaves of summer
Cesáreo Gabaraín (1936-1991), 1973
Tr. George Frank Lockwood IV 1946-)
The United Methodist Hymnal, 1989

UNA ESPIGA

Cesáreo Gabaraín (1936-1991), 1973
(same source as text)

This text points to the sea, to song, and to the bread of Communion for analogies relating to Christian unity. The hymn, written by a Spanish priest, has been translated into more than forty languages and is used in ecumenical Communion celebrations. It is appropriate that the hymn is printed in both the original Spanish and in English, illustrating our unity in diversity.

The lilting simplicity of UNA ESPIGA makes the melody easy to learn. The song has been included in the recent United Methodist and Presbyterian hymnals. The accompaniment is provided in the *Accompaniment Handbook*.

4
Unto thy temple, Lord, we come

ROCKINGHAM OLD

Robert Collyer (1823-1912), 1866
The River of Life, 1873

Aaron Williams' *Supplement to Psalmody*, ca. 1780
Arr. by Edward Miller (1735-1807)
Psalms of David, 1790

Although Anabaptists do not use the word "temple" to describe their place of worship, it conveys the biblical significance of a place where the community of faith gathers in the presence of God.

This was the first text that Collyer, a Unitarian minister, ever wrote. He composed it for the dedication of a church that had been destroyed by fire (Putnam 1875). The hymn originally began:

> With thankful hearts, O God, we come
> To a new temple built for thee;

Collyer became minister of Church of the Messiah in Chicago in 1866. But just five years later, he and his congregation were again victims of fire—this time the great Chicago fire of 1871 (Ronander, Porter 1966). A new church, Second Church of the Messiah, was built late in 1873. For that dedication Collyer wrote another hymn that began "O Lord, our God, when storm and flame."

ROCKINGHAM OLD is an anonymous tune adapted from a melody called TUNBRIDGE in Aaron Williams' collection. Miller used the tune seven times in his *Psalms of David* and headed it "Part of the melody taken from a hymn tune" (Loewen, Moyer, Oyer 1983). The name ROCKINGHAM was chosen by Miller to honor the marquis of Rockingham, who was twice prime minister of Great Britain. The designation "old" is used to distinguish it from a later tune of the same name by Lowell Mason. The tune is a very applicable one; it appears four times in *The Brethren Hymnal* (1951) and five times in *The Mennonite Hymnal* (1969).

298
Veni Sancte Spiritus

VENI SANCTE SPIRITUS

Come, Holy Spirit
Based on Latin sequence, 13th c.
Taizé Community

Jacques Berthier (1923-), 1978
Music from Taizé, Vol. I, 1978, 1980, 1981

The Latin text of this hymn, called the "Golden Sequence," is one of only a few medieval sequences to remain in the liturgy following the reforms of the sixteenth century. A "sequence" was made up of additional words to complement the regular Mass. Called "one of the masterpieces of Latin sacred poetry" by Julian, it must have been written prior to 1200, the date of the earliest manuscripts. The hymn has been attributed to a number of authors, the most likely of whom is Pope Innocent III (1161-1216) (Julian 1907).

This congregational response is to be sung "in a quiet, interior fashion." Its meditative value grows with increased pause between the verses, leaving only the melodic drone of the repeated response. Detailed information on the music of the Taizé community may be found in the article on "Alleluia" (**101**).

446

Wade in the water

African American spiritual

(no tune name)

African American spiritual

This spiritual blends stories from both the Old and New Testaments. In both, water symbolizes deliverance and salvation. The first four stanzas recall Moses and the Exodus from Egypt, while the final stanza echoes 1 Corinthans 1:10-12. The refrain is taken from the story of the healing at the pool of Bethesda where an angel "troubled the water" (John 5:4).

407

We are people of God's peace

Menno Simons (1496-1561)
"Reply to False Accusations," 1552
Tr. Esther Cathryn Klaassen Bergen (1921-)
International Songbook, Mennonite World Conference, 1990

AVE VIRGO VIRGINUM (GAUDEAMUS PARITER)

Johann Horn (ca. 1490-1547)
Ein Gesangbuch der Brüder im Behemen und Merherrn, 1544
Rev. version: Leisentritt's *Catholicum Hymnologium Germanicum,* 1584

After his renunciation of the Catholic Church in favor of an Anabaptist understanding of faithfulness to Christ, Menno Simons was hunted as a religious criminal. Still, he survived to become leader of a group of believers later known as Mennonites. Simons was an articulate man who carefully defined his positions in writing and countered the arguments of his detractors. This hymn is derived from a passage of his prose that declared that Christ is the Prince of peace and his people are those called "to be such a glorious people of God, a church, kingdom, inheritance, body, and possession of peace" (Wenger 1956).

An earlier English metric version by David Augsburger, found in the 1978 Mennonite World Conference songbook and *The Brethren Songbook* (1974), adds an extra syllable to each line of text, requiring a rearrangement of the musical rhythm. This translation was prepared by Esther Bergen in 1989 to conform to the original 76. 76D. meter of the melody.

For comments on AVE VIRGO VIRGINUM, also known as GAUDEAMUS PARITER, see "Come, ye faithful, raise the strain" (**265**).

17

We gather together — KREMSER

Adrian Valerius's *Nederlandtsche Gedenckclanck*, 1626
Tr. Theodore Baker (1851-1934)
Bos's *Dutch Folk Songs*, 1917

(same source as text)
Adapt. by Edward Kremser (1838-1914)
Sechs altniederländische Volkslieder, 1877

This nationalistic hymn of praise and thanksgiving, born out of political and religious turmoil at the end of the sixteenth century, was written to celebrate the freedom of the Netherlands from Spanish rule. Protestant Holland had chafed under persecution by Spanish Catholics ("the wicked oppressing now cease from distressing"), but by the time this hymn was written, the country had recovered sufficiently to assert that God had sided with them all the while (st. 2:4). The anonymous text first appeared in the 1626 edition of Valerius's *Nederlandtsche Gedenckclanck*.

As with many folk melodies, KREMSER originally was sung with secular words. Edward Kremser discovered this tune in Valerius's collection of Dutch folk songs, rescuing it from 250 years of neglect. It is the best known of his six arrangements from that collection.

161

We give thanks unto you — (no tune name)

Based on Psalm 136
Marty Haugen (1950-)
Shepherd Me, O God, 1986

Marty Haugen (1950-)
(same source as text)

This setting of Psalm 136 was titled "Your love is never ending." Haugen composed it while he was composer-in-residence for a year at Holden Village, a Lutheran retreat center in Washington's Cascade Mountains. Psalm 136 is central to the celebration of the Jewish Passover. Haugen recounts:

> The week before Easter we celebrated a *seder* meal. I set the psalm in a call-and-response form, much as it is found in the scriptures (and in the form it was almost certainly first sung). I tried to make the language contemporary and inclusive, while remaining true to the original meaning.

The music is simple and straightforward, with the flavor of a Jewish folk melody. According to Haugen, at that *seder* meal "when we first sang the setting, a number of people memorized verses, all memorized the response, and we danced in a circle, singing *a cappella*."

First recorded on the album *Shepherd Me, O God*, the song has subsequently appeared in the hymnal supplement *Gather* (1988).

384

We give thee but thine own — SCHUMANN

William Walsham How (1823-1897), 1858
Morrell and How's *Psalms and Hymns*, 1864

Mason and Webb's *Cantica Laudis*, 1850

Written by a clergyman known as "the poor man's bishop," this hymn "sounds the real humanitarian note to the fatherless and widows," comments George Matheson (Haeussler 1952). This is particularly true of the present stanzas 3 and 4, which seem to reflect the words of Isaiah 61:1-3, a portion of which Jesus quotes in Luke 4:18-19. This is a stewardship hymn in the largest sense in that it acknowledges that all we have is a gift from God (1 Chron. 29:14), and thus, all we have is to be returned to God in acts of mercy and justice. The original third stanza, usually omitted, implies that to be a steward also means to have an eye toward those of wavering faith:

> Oh, hearts are bruised and dead
> and homes are bare and cold,
> and lambs for whom the Shepherd bled
> are straying from the fold.

SCHUMANN is called WHITE in its earliest printed source where its attribution says "arranged from Schumann." No one, including Schumann's wife, has been able to identify a musical source from his compositions, so the source of the tune remains unclear. The tune's original setting in *Cantica Laudis* was to the text "Thou shalt, O Lord, descend." *Cantica Laudis* was made up of tunes of the great composers, adapted for congregational singing in order to increase appreciation for classical music. The tune has also been called HEATH, not to be confused with a different tune of the same name in Mason's *Carmina Sacra* (1841).

443

We know that Christ is raised — ENGELBERG

Based on Romans 6
John Brownlow Geyer (1932-), 1967
Hymns and Songs, 1969, alt.

Charles Villiers Stanford (1852-1924)
Hymns Ancient and Modern, 1904 ed.

This hymn, so popular for Easter, appears under the baptism heading because that is the sacrament, or ordinance, for which it was first intended. Geyer, a tutor at Cheshunt College, Cambridge, England, when he wrote this, recalls that "at that time a good deal of work was going on around the corner (involving a number of American research students) producing living cells ('the baby in the test tube')." The hymn attempts to illustrate the Christian doctrine of baptism in relation to those experiments (Stulken 1981).

The text makes vivid poetic use of the language of twentieth-century scientific experimentation in the Trinitarian stanza 3: "The Spirit's fission shakes the church of God." And the words in stanza 4 provide an incarnational view of the church. The Easter/baptism connection makes for a hymn that is very strong theologically for either context.

Written for the tune ENGLEBERG, the hymn first appeared in *Hymns and Songs,* a supplement to *The Methodist Hymnal* (1966). It has subsequently appeared in other supplements and hymnals, including *Cantate Domino* (1974) and the *Lutheran Book of Worship* (1978). For a keyboard accompaniment and additional information on ENGELBERG, see "When in our music God is glorified" (**44**).

96
We plow the fields and scatter

WIR PFLÜGEN

Wir pflügen und wir streuen
Matthias Claudius (1740-1815)
Claudius's *Paul Erdmann's Fest,* 1782
Tr. Jane Montgomery Campbell (1817-1878)
Charles S. Bere's *Garland of Song,* 1861, alt.

Attrib. to Johann Abraham Peter Schulz (1747-1800)
Lieder für Volksschulen mit Musik, 1800

Matthias Claudius was for a time a commissioner of agriculture in Darmstadt, Germany. A newspaperman and editor as well, he wrote out his love for the land in a poem he called *Paul Erdmann's Fest*, a delightful picture of the harvest celebration in a German farmhouse. Jane M. Campbell's translation is an adaptation of selected stanzas of the "Peasant's Song" from that sketch. It has been altered in favor of contemporary language. Campbell assisted Charles S. Bere in the compilation of the collection in which this text first appeared, as well as his *Children's Choral Book* of 1869.

WIR PFLÜGEN matches the rural folk character of the text. The tune first appeared in A. L. Hoppenstadt's collection as an anonymous melody. Later, in Lindner's *Jugendfreund* of 1812, it was attributed to Johann A. P. Schulz. The tune, also known as CLAUDIUS or DRESDEN, was introduced to the U.S. in the January 1840 issue of *The Seraph*, a monthly church music publication edited by Lowell Mason (Ronander, Porter 1966).

99

We praise thee, O God

William Paton Mackay (1839-1885), 1863
Rev. in Biglow and Main's *New Praises of Jesus,* ca. 1867

REVIVE US AGAIN

Attrib. to John Jenkins Husband (1760-1825), ca. 1815
(same source as text)

This text is probably Scottish pastor William Mackay's most familiar hymn. The chorus is based on Habakkuk 3:2 ("In our own time revive [your renown]") and Psalm 85:6 ("Will you not revive us again, so that your people may rejoice in you?"), but stanzas 1-4 all have a distinctly New Testament flavor. The energetic "hallelujahs" in the chorus, so well suited to large-group singing, foreordained the hymn's popularity in the mass revival meetings of the late 1800s.

The tune REVIVE US AGAIN was initially used with a different text, possibly a secular one. It appears with the hymn "Rejoice and be glad" by Horatius Bonar in *Gospel Hymns and Sacred Songs* (1875) where "We praise thee, O God!" follows as an alternate text. It appears with the same texts in *Gospel Hymns, Nos. 1 to 6* (1894) where it is attributed to John J. Husband. In later hymnals Mackay's text has become firmly wedded to this tune.

412

We shall walk through the valley

African American spiritual

(no tune name)

African American spiritual
Adapt. by W. Appling, 1970

This gentle "peace piece" is a mood unto itself. It has none of the friction or inferences of confrontation sometimes inherent in other peace and justice hymns. It is simply a reassurance of Jesus' presence in the valley of the shadow.

It was adapted from a male chorus (TTBB) arrangement written for the Case Institute of Technology and the Western Reserve Academy Glee Club. The hymn arrangement follows Appling's musical setting of the first stanza, including the movement of the melody through various voices. It has been transposed a major third higher to accommodate the treble voices.

570

We walk by faith

Henry Alford (1810-1871)
Psalms and Hymns, 1844

SHANTI

Marty Haugen (1950-), 1983
Mass of Creation, 1984

This text is based on John 20:25-29, which records the statement of Thomas, dubbed through history as the "doubter": "Unless I see the mark of the nails in his hands . . . I will not believe." Christ replied, "Blessed are those who have not seen and yet have come to believe." This text by Henry Alford, who also wrote the better-known "Come, ye thankful people, come," was among those sent to composers by the planning committee for the Episcopal *Hymnal 1982* (1985). Composer Marty Haugen states: "The text is an excellent example of connecting historical Gospel events with the life of Christians today. I was also impressed with the way in which each succeeding verse builds upon the one before it."

The musical setting Haugen created is simple and supportive of the key words of the text ("faith," "sight," etc.). The flow of each verse is enhanced by shortening the second full measure by one beat, thus keeping the text better connected. The tune name SHANTI is an ancient Sanscrit word meaning "shalom" or "peace." It also is the middle name of the composer's daughter. The hymn was recorded by G.I.A. on *Mass of Creation* and later included in the hymnal supplement *Gather* (1988).

74

We would extol thee

Based on Psalm 145
The Psalms of David in Meeter (Scottish Psalter), 1650
Alt. by Nichol James Grieve (1868-1954)
Grieve's *The Scottish Metrical Psalter of 1650: A Revision*, 1940

GENEVA 124 (OLD 124th)

Louis Bourgeois (ca. 1510-ca. 1561)
Genevan Psalter, 1551
Harm. adapt. from Claude Goudimel (ca. 1505-1572)
Les Pseaumes . . ., 1565

In the Babylonian Talmud (commentary on the Hebrew Bible), it was said that anyone who recited Psalm 145 three times daily would be assured of a place in the world to come (Stuhlmueller 1983). This text is a paraphrase of that psalm, which originally was written as an acrostic in which each line began with a succeeding letter of the alphabet. Though the style constrained poetic flow, portions of this inspirational psalm have had major influence on Jewish and Christian worship.

Hundreds of years after the psalm was written down, Nichol Grieve revised the Scottish Psalter, intent on modifying "flaws." These included defective rhymes, broken lines (incomplete statements carried into the next line), inverted word order, and confusion of personal pronouns (Loewen,

Moyer, Oyer 1983). Undaunted by Jewish authorship of the original psalm, he also repaired "unchristian statements" and "Judaisms."

GENEVA 124 was composed or adapted by Louis Bourgeois for Psalm 124 in the *Genevan Psalter* (1551). By 1551 Goudimel was composing harmonies for the Genevan psalm melodies. He finished all 125 tunes of the *Genevan Psalter* in simple note-for-note, four-part harmony in which the melody was usually in the tenor voice, but occasionally in the soprano. These four-part harmonizations, plus additional elaborate polyphonic settings for twenty-seven of the melodies, were published in a single volume in 1565.

257

Were you there

African American spiritual
Barton's *Old Plantation Hymns*, 1899

WERE YOU THERE

African American spiritual
(same source as text)
Rev. form in F. J. Work's *Folk Songs of the American Negro*, Nashville, 1907

This beloved spiritual has the ability to erase the span of time between Jesus' crucifixion and the present. The extended melodic passage on the word "Oh!" gives voice to otherwise inexpressible feelings of grief and wonder. Rising to the highest point of the melody, it is a musical moan befitting Jesus' Passion, but not the resurrection. That stanza is not part of the early versions of the spiritual.

It is not surprising that this spiritual places the singer at the scene of tragedy, since black slaves identified so closely with Jesus' suffering. His death, says James Cone, was a "symbol of their suffering, trials, and tribulations in an unfriendly world. They knew the agony of rejection and the pain of hanging from a tree" (Cone 1972).

WERE YOU THERE is, with one exception, a pentatonic melody (without the fourth and seventh steps of the scale). The melody is similar to the white spiritual "Have you heard how they crucified our Lord?" sung in the mainly white, upper Cumberland area of Tennessee. The sources listed above indicate the earliest known printed sources of this spiritual. See the *Accompaniment Handbook* for a four-part setting of this hymn.

573, 574
What a friend we have in Jesus

Joseph Medlicott Scriven (1819-1886), ca. 1855
Packard's *Spirit Minstrel: A Collection of Hymns and Music*, Boston, 1857, alt.

BLAENWERN

William Penfro Rowlands (1860-1937)
Can a moliant, 1916

ERIE (CONVERSE)

Charles Crozat Converse (1832-1918), 1868
Silver Wings, 1870

Scriven did not receive credit for this hymn in its earliest appearances, probably because he never intended it for public use. He later explained that he wrote it around 1855 and sent it to his mother in Ireland to comfort her in a time of sorrow. One story has it that he was also writing out of his own grief, after his second fiancée died before they could be married (Reynolds 1990).

It is not clear how the hymn reached its first publication, but Philip P. Bliss and Ira D. Sankey, who included it in their *Gospel Hymns and Sacred Songs* (1875), were largely responsible for its dissemination. The hymn reflects the assurance of the familiar words "Cast your burden upon the Lord, and he will sustain you" (Ps. 55).

Although BLAENWERN(**573**) appeared in Welsh hymnody in 1916, it did not become popular in England until the time of World War II. It was introduced to many other countries by way of the Billy Graham Crusades as the setting for "Love divine, all loves excelling."

ERIE (**574**), also known as CONVERSE or WHAT A FRIEND, has been applauded as a "masterpiece of simplicity . . . composed for ease of learning . . . and . . . further strengthened by the quasi antiphon 'Take it to the Lord in prayer' " (Young 1993). It was composed for this text in 1868. The composer listed in *Silver Wings* is Karl Reden, a pseudonym for Converse who also compiled the collection. The tune name ERIE is likely taken from the city in Pennsylvania where Converse lived. This melody is set with the text in a wide variety of languages, representative of the universal appeal of this hymn.

See the *Accompaniment Handbook* for a four-part setting.

215
What Child is this

William Chatterton Dix (1837-1898)
The Manger Throne, ca. 1865

GREENSLEEVES

Traditional English melody

Dix wrote these words after reading the Gospel for Epiphany Day, Matthew 2:1-12. Marked by the coming of the wise men, Epiphany is celebrated beginning January 6. Though the carol has the rocking motion of a lullaby, Dix's text foreshadows the terror of the crucifixion (st. 2:3-4), making the poetic portrait of the sleeping baby that much more poignant. These three stanzas are believed to have been taken from a longer Christmas poem titled *The Manger Throne*[1] and were included in *Christmas Carols New and Old*, published by Bramley and Stainer in 1871.

The folk melody GREENSLEEVES, of unknown origin, dates from 1580 when Richard Jones received his license for "A new Northern Dittye of the Lady Greene Sleeves" (*The Hymnal 1940 Companion*, 1951 ed.). Evidently it was already a popular ballad, as several other licenses were issued for it within a short time. It was known well enough that Shakespeare mentioned it twice in his *Merry Wives of Windsor*. Twelve days after the first license, the ballad of "Greensleeves" was adapted to sacred use, "moralised to the Scripture, declaring the manifold benefites and blessings of God bestowed on sinful man" (*The Hymnal 1940 Companion*, 1951 ed.). In *New Christmas Carols* (1642), the tune was used with the words "The old year now away is fled" and is reprinted in the *Oxford Book of Carols* (1928).

1. Young, 1993, cites Routley, 1979, in refuting the text's appearance as part of *The Manger Throne*, contending that it first appeared in *Christmas Carols New and Old* (1871).

409

What does the Lord require — MICAH

Based on Micah 6:6-8
Albert Frederick Bayly (1901-1984), 1949
Rejoice, O People, 1950

Larry R. Warkentin (1940-), 1990
Hymnal: A Worship Book, 1992

This text, based on the stern words of the prophet Micah (6:6-8), is one of a series of hymns by Bayly on the minor prophets. Originally in five stanzas, the omitted stanza calls for economic justice.

While Micah's writing reproves believers for abetting injustice, he does not neglect to offer the alternative that God desires—justice, humility, and mercy. In addition to other slight alterations to contemporize the language, the beginning of stanza 2, "Rulers of men," now reads "People of earth."

Larry Warkentin was on a break from teaching when he received Bayley's text from the committee preparing this hymnal. Though he was energized by a pause in his schedule, the tune also "seemed to 'spring from the text' and in a few short hours it was complete." Although there is no time signature, the music is basically in triple meter, with two extended measures. A repetition of the opening phrase sets off the last four measures as a sort of refrain. This conclusion, with its expanded harmonies and shift to a major tonality, contrasts with the more contemplative sound of the earlier part of the hymn.

385

What gift can we bring — ANNIVERSARY SONG

Jane Manton Marshall (1924-), 1980
Hymnal Supplement II, 1987, alt.

Jane Manton Marshall (1924-)
(same source as text)

Marshall wrote the words and music of this hymn for the twenty-fifth anniversary of her home church, Northaven United Methodist Church in Dallas, Texas. The hymn begins with a question akin to the psalmist's: "What shall I render to the Lord . . . ?" (Ps. 116:12). In succeeding stanzas the text explores the gifts of the church in the past, present, and future, making it an appropriate expression of gratitude for any anniversary occasion, including the beginning of a new year. The final stanza provides a dynamic answer to the opening question, and the hymn itself becomes a part of our offering "in honor and praise."

1

What is this place — KOMT NU MET ZANG

Zomaar een dak boven wat hoofden
Huub Oosterhuis (1933-), 1968
Tr. David Smith (1933-), ca. 1970

Adrian Valerius's *Nederlandtsche Gedenckclanck*, 1626
Harm. by Bernard Huijbers (1922-), 1968

Though written by a Roman Catholic, this text so clearly expresses Anabaptist concepts of the church and worship that it leads off the entire hymnal. "This text celebrates the essence of the community," says Anthony Barr of Salem, Oregon. "The song *is* the gathering, not something which happens while the people are gathering." Bernard Huijbers, a co-worker of the author and the musician who harmonized this hymn, says the original ("Zomaar") was made for the Students Ekklesia Amsterdam. During that time Oosterhuis, a Jesuit and a student of linguistics, was called upon to create texts that were closer to scripture than traditional Roman Catholic song. His first work on a collection of fifty psalms led to hymns and eucharistic table prayers. These texts were written for St. Ignatius College in Amsterdam where Huijbers, also a Jesuit, was working in campus ministries.

The first stanza clearly differentiates the concepts of meetinghouse and church. Stanza 2 is a lyrical treatise on receiving, remembering, and speaking the word of God. The concluding stanza is built around the focal point of Christianity: the Eucharist, or Communion. It contains an intensely powerful incarnation statement: "Here in this world, dying and living, we are each other's bread and wine."

The Dutch language contains many words that have several meanings. This translation works for the English imagination but is not entirely true to the original. For example, what is translated "windows for light" in the Dutch refers to the "windows of the eyes."

The old Dutch melody comes from the same source as the familiar Thanksgiving hymn "We gather together" and its tune KREMSER. The use of familiar tunes was important in introducing these new texts, and any new tunes required were composed in an easily learned folk style.

524
What mercy and divine compassion

MIR IST ERBARMUNG

Mir ist Erbarmung widerfahren
Philipp Friedrich Hiller (1699-1769)
Geistliches Liederkästlein, Part II, 1767
Tr. Frieda Kaufman (1883-1944), 1938
The Mennonite Hymnary, 1940, alt.

J. G. Schicht's *Allgemeines Choral-Buch*, 1819
(Zahn No. 2907)

The following note by the author accompanied the first publication of this text: "An unconverted person is much too proud to say these words sincerely from the heart; but the converted person confesses them freely before God and man" (Loewen, Moyer, Oyer 1983). Based in part on 1 Timothy 1:12-17, the hymn was frequently sung with great fervor by Mennonites in Russia and Canada, especially when accompanied by strong evangelistic preaching!

A number of Hiller's 1,075 hymns have been translated into English, but this translation by Frieda Kaufman, a Mennonite deaconess, is apparently the first English version of this text. It consists of stanzas 1, 2, 4, and 5 of the original five in German.

The origin of MIR IST ERBARMUNG is uncertain. Zahn considers it a Swiss melody but gives no date (Loewen, Moyer, Oyer 1983). Hostetler, in *Handbook to the Mennonite Hymnary*, credits the tune to Schicht, the editor of the 1819 source listed above. The 1956 Canadian Mennonite *Gesangbuch*, however, gives Leipzig (1813) as an earlier source. Outside of Mennonite hymnody, the tune is not in common use. The lilting triple meter, phrase repetitions, and sequences make this a most singable melody.

530
What wondrous love is this

American folk text
Jesse Mercer's *Cluster of Spiritual Songs . . .*, 3rd ed., 1823

WONDROUS LOVE

American folk hymn
William Walker's *Southern Harmony,* 1840
Harm. by Alice Parker (1925-), 1966
The Mennonite Hymnal, 1969

This beautiful, introspective hymn is like a musical letter addressed to the soul. One of its sources, *Cluster of Spiritual Songs, Divine Hymns, and Sacred Poems,* was originally published in pamphlet form for congregational use, but it became so popular that it was reissued a number of times. The third edition, printed in 1823, includes seven stanzas of "Wondrous love," though there is some evidence that the text may have been in print as early as 1811. Mercer's collection, which includes some of his own poems, was widely used in Baptist circles in the nineteenth century. Jesse Mercer, pastor and editor of a religious paper, was president of the Georgia Baptist Convention for eighteen years.

The tune associated with "Wondrous love" was first published more than fifteen years after the text; however, "it looks as though tune and words were born together, so beautifully they fit" (Jackson 1964). In the 1840 edition of William Walker's *Southern Harmony,* it is attributed to "Christopher." According to Harry Eskew, an authority on the *Southern Harmony* editions, the 1840 printing is the second edition of this popular collection. In this book the tune is part of an "Appendix, containing several tunes entirely new." But Walker later identified WONDROUS LOVE in his *Christian Harmony* (1866 and 1867 editions) as "a very popular old southern tune," one arranged by James Christopher of Spartansburg, South Carolina; he has not been further identified.

The tune's structure is taken from a ballad about the seventeenth-century pirate Captain Kidd. The melody of WONDROUS LOVE fits these words:

> My name was Robert Kidd, when I sailed, when I sailed,
> My name was Robert Kidd, when I sailed;
> My name was Robert Kidd, God's laws I did forbid,
> So wickedly I did when I sailed, when I sailed,
> So wickedly I did when I sailed. (Gealey, Lovelace, Young 1970)

72
When all thy mercies, O my God

GENEVA

Joseph Addison (1672-1719)
The Spectator, Aug. 9, 1712

John Cole (1774-1855)
Ecclesiastical Harmony, 1805
Version from the Funk brothers' *Harmonia Sacra,* 12th ed., 1867

In 1711 Joseph Addison and Richard Steele began publishing *The Spectator,* a London daily, "to enliven morality with wit, and to temper wit with morality" (Oyer 1980). When they published the thirteen stanzas of "When all thy mercies" about a year later, it must have been part of the morality portion of the paper, though Addison contends that the "duty" of gratitude is "attended with so much pleasure, that were there no . . . recompense laid up for it hereafter, a generous mind would indulge in it, for the natural gratification that accompanies it" (Gealey, Lovelace, Young 1970).

That statement was part of Addison's essay titled "Gratitude," which ended with the stanzas of "When all thy mercies." Although Addison's authorship has been questioned, Julian disputes other claimants (Julian 1907). Brown and Butterworth, in their book *The Story of Hymns and Tunes,* say Addison wrote the text to express his thankfulness for having been saved from a shipwreck off Genoa, Italy.

Stanzas 1, 10, 11, and 13 are those used in this hymnal. The text must have been quite popular, because even though it was not a psalm, it was included in the 1718 printing of Tate and Brady's *New Version of the Psalms of David* (Oyer 1980).

The tune GENEVA was first printed with John Cole's name in his *Ecclesiastical Harmony* (1805). There it appeared in a three-voice setting with the text "Unite, my roving thoughts, unite." Later that same year, it was included in Cole's *The Beauties of Harmony* in four voices with the full thirteen stanzas of "When all thy mercies." The unusual three-step entrance of the parts creates a rich, canonlike blending of voices; it's easy to understand why Cole included this hymn in *The Beauties of Harmony.* The musical version here is taken from the 1867 edition of *Harmonia Sacra.* The tenor line of the original, which contained the melody, has been exchanged with the soprano.

217
When Christ's appearing

Hostis Herodes impie
Coelius Sedulius, 5th c.
Composite translation: sts. 2-5,
John Mason Neale (1818-1866)
The Hymnal Noted, 1851

ERHALT UNS, HERR

Attrib. to Martin Luther (1483-1546)
Klug's *Geistliche Lieder,* 1543
(Zahn No. 350)

This Epiphany text walks us through three incidents in Jesus' early life that "manifest the presence of a deity," which is the meaning of Epiphany: the arrival of the wise men, the baptism of Jesus in the Jordan, and the first miracle at Cana. It is based on stanzas 8, 9, 11, and 13 of the Latin hymn *Paean Alphabeticus de Christo,* an acrostic which begins each of its twenty-three stanzas with a different letter of the alphabet. The final-stanza doxology was a later addition. The composite translation includes stanza 1 from *The Hymn Book* (1971) of the United Church of Canada and the Anglican Church of Canada and stanzas 2-5 by John Mason Neale from *The Hymnal Noted* (1851). Neale's first stanza begins "The star proclaims the King is here."

For comments on ERHALT UNS, HERR, see "The glory of these forty days" (**225**).

637
When grief is raw

Brian Arthur Wren (1936-), 1976
Faith Looking Forward, 1983

RYAN

Larry R. Warkentin (1940-), 1989
Hymnal: A Worship Book, 1992

Wren tells how he came to write this text:

> Two close friends [of mine] were about to be married when the bridegroom's father died suddenly, a week before the wedding day. Believing it would have reflected his wishes, they carried on with the ceremony, which was a deep occasion, shot through with grief and joy. (Wren 1983)

Composer Warkentin, also no stranger to the death of loved ones, suffered the loss of two children who died shortly after birth. He was attracted to this text "because of the way it acknowledges the difficulties of life . . . yet it ends with a testimony to God's faithfulness." He wrote RYAN especially for these words and named the tune for the middle name of Richard, his older child.

Like the moments of transfixed meditation in the midst of grief, the music holds awhile on a single note at the beginning of the second and third staves. The unison passage and the brightness of the final chords are a musical affirmation of the text "I am the resurrection."

259, 260
When I survey the wondrous cross

Isaac Watts (1674-1748)
Hymns and Spiritual Songs, 1707

HAMBURG

Lowell Mason (1792-1872), 1824
Boston Handel and Haydn Society Collection . . ., 3rd ed., 1825

(no tune name)

African hymn melody

This text is one of twenty-five hymns written by Isaac Watts for use at Communion. Hymnwriter Kenneth I. Morse notes "how Watts's familiar hymn, though it begins on a personal note using the personal pronoun, immediately directs attention to Jesus Christ. . . . Therefore we can say that this hymn is essentially objective; the crucified Christ is constantly the center of attention. Yet we cannot contemplate the cross for long without wanting to make some response of our own" (Morse 1982).

A poetry prodigy, Watts wrote this text (and 109 others) before he turned twenty-three. It was headed "Crucifixion to the World by the Cross of Christ" and took its cue from Galatians 6:14: "May I never boast of anything except the cross of our Lord Jesus Christ, by which the world has been crucified to me, and I to the world."

In his 1709 edition, Watts offers this stanza as an option, which graphically zeroes in on the last part of the scripture verse:

> His dying crimson like a robe
> spread o'er his body on the tree,
> then am I dead to all the globe,
> and all the globe is dead to me.

HAMBURG (**259**), which may or may not have been named after the German city, has become one of Lowell Mason's most beloved melodies. It was written in 1824 while Mason was living in Savannah, Georgia. Mason indicates in the 1841 edition of *Carmina Sacra* that the melody, which encompasses a range of only five tones, was derived from a Gregorian chant.

The second setting of this text (**260**) comes from Africa. The warm sounds of the full chords provide rich tones for this significant Watts poem. As with another African piece "In your sickness" (**585**), the music may at first seem too buoyant to sing with a text about suffering and loss. Yet this style can teach us to sing with energy, even through heartache and pain.

Curiously, this second setting bears a striking resemblance to the chant melody for "Abide with me," found in the twelfth edition of Joseph Funk's *Harmonia Sacra* (1867). In the 1917 *Common Service Book* of the Lutheran Church, it is identified as TROYTE NO. 1 by Arthur H. D. Troyte and dated 1848, prompting speculation that the tune may have gone to Africa with a missionary and has now returned to North America (Mary Oyer).

44

When in our music God is glorified

ENGELBERG

Fred Pratt Green (1903-), 1972
The Hymn, July 1973

Charles Villiers Stanford (1852-1924)
Hymns Ancient and Modern, 1904 ed.

John Wilson, a musician who once taught at the Royal College of Music, London, prompted retired Methodist minister/hymnist Fred Pratt Green to write this text. Supplied with the tune ENGELBERG, Green responded with this resounding hymn, which was used at a 1972 festival of praise, or choir anniversary. Although it is especially appropriate for musical occasions, it is useful as well for general worship and praise. "No finer hymn has been written about the reasons for the use of music in worship," contends hymn commentator Austin Lovelace. "It is reassuring to know that a new hymn can become immensely popular world-wide in a few short years while the author is still living" (Lovelace 1987).

ENGELBERG was composed originally for the text "For all the saints" for the "new" (1904) edition of *Hymns Ancient and Modern*. The accompaniment used here is the one that was with the first three stanzas in that 1904 edition. The fourth stanza was written in four-part harmony with the melody moving from voice to voice. Other tunes that have been used with this text are MIRIAM, by Ida Prins-Buttle, and FREDERICK-TOWN, by Charles Richard Anders, Jr.

131

When in the hour of deepest need

WENN WIR IN HÖCHSTEN NÖTEN SEIN

Wenn wir in höchsten Nöten sein
Paul Eber (1511-1569)
Broadsheet, Nürnberg, 1560
Naw Betbüchlein, Dresden, 1566
Tr. Catherine Winkworth (1827-1878)
Lyra Germanica, Series II, 1858, alt.

Adapt. from LES COMMANDEMENS DE DIEU
La forme des prières . . ., Strasbourg, 1545
Das Gebet Josaphat, Wittenberg, 1567
(Zahn No. 750)

This text grew out of the Latin hymn *In tenebris nostrae* by Joachim Camerarius, a teacher of Eber's. Based on the prayer of King Jehoshaphat (2 Chron. 20:6-12), it may have been written much earlier than the first printing listed above, possibly during the time of rival factions following Martin Luther's death, since Eber was a close friend of Luther and Philipp Melanchthon.

One of the original seven stanzas has been omitted. With words of penitence, confession, assurance, and thanks, this text is wonderful for private as well as corporate devotions. A judicious selection of stanzas can shape the hymn to meet the need. Though it originally had a first line of "When in the hour of utmost need," several alterations have been made to the Winkworth translation to effect a more contemporarywordorder.

The tune, the name of which is taken from the first line of Eber's German text, originated in Geneva, Switzerland, and could have been composed by Louis Bourgeois. In the 1545 edition of the Genevan Psalter, the tune was used for Clement Marot's metrical version of the Ten Commandments. From this it received its French name, LES COMMANDEMENS DE DIEU (see "Bread of the world," **469**). In 1567 the German text and tune appeared together in the source listed above. It is said that on the day Bach died, he dictated his famous final organ chorale based on this tune: *Vor deinem Thron tret ich hiemit* (Before thy throne I step, O Lord).

One story about this hymn occurred nearly one hundred years after it was written. In 1644, during the Thirty Years War, Swedes attacked the Saxon city of Pegau and burned it, leaving the entire population homeless. Hungry and in dire need, the pastor and twelve boys dressed in white sang this hymn in front of the quarters of the Swedish general, who was moved enough by the song and the sight of the people that he provided the captives with food and spared their lives. The pastor then gathered the townspeople on the market square and admonished them to fulfill the final stanza of the hymn as a token of their thanks to God. For two hundred years following that dramatic incident, this hymn was sung every Sunday in that town in remembrance (Eltz-Hoffmann 1980).

164
When Israel was in Egypt's land — (no tune name)

African American spiritual — African American spiritual

This popular spiritual, which recounts Israelite slaves' flight from Egypt (the biblical Exodus), gave black slaves hope that freedom was coming for them, too. In a call-and-response style, it remains a standard in modern-day collections such as *Songs of Zion* (1981), which contains eighteen stanzas.

The plaintive sound of the melody, sometimes called GO DOWN MOSES, is typical of this type of spiritual. A question regarding its origin was raised, however, by a social worker who heard two different women's groups, African American and Jewish, recognize the tune as "one of their own songs, 'Cain and Abel.' Whether of Hebrew or Negro origin, there seems to be no way of determining, but it bears all the evidences of Negro music" (Work 1940).

An obscure YMCA missionary Lewis C. Lockwood was responsible for the publication of this spiritual. He heard it sung in 1861 at his post at Fort Monroe, Chesapeake Bay, Virginia, where refugee slaves found haven. They were called "contraband of war" by officers who refused to return them to their owners; thus, the song was known as the "song of the contrabands." Lockwood reported "there is evidence in this hymn that the slaves in a considerable part of Virginia . . . have had a superstitious faith in being freed sometime in the future" (Epstein 1977).

234
When Jesus wept, the falling tear — WHEN JESUS WEPT

William Billings (1746-1800)
The New England Psalm Singer, 1770

William Billings (1746-1800)
(same source as text)

"When Jesus wept" can be sung as a four-part round and is often used in choral and instrumental arrangements in that way. The text, a musical comment on Jesus' lament over Jerusalem (Matt. 23:37-39), is also attributed to Billings.

Additional stanzas, an elaboration on Billings' words, written by Frank A. Brooks, Jr., are found in *The Brethren Songbook* (1974) and *The Worshipbook—Services and Hymns* (Presbyterian 1972).

623
When love is found — O WALY WALY

Brian Arthur Wren (1936-), 1978
Faith Looking Forward, 1983

Traditional English melody
Harm. by Alice Parker (1925-), 1989

This tender hymn, originally titled "Love song," is a welcome addition to the relatively small number of wedding hymns. It is an eloquent Christian statement that addresses both the joys and sorrows of married life. Wren writes: "It is important that verse 2 . . . asks that love may reach out *beyond* the nuclear family, rather than the more cozy and familiar theme of inviting others *into* 'home's warmth and light' " (Wren 1983). With this intent in mind, stanzas 2-4, in particular, have merit for use in services of Communion or reconciliation.

O WALY WALY was traditionally sung with the words (*O*) *Waly, Waly, gin Love be Bony.* That text's earliest source is Allan Ramsay's *Tea Table Miscellany* (1724-1732). The prominent English folk song collector Cecil Sharp noted down three versions of the melody in *Somerset* (1904-1906) where they were sung to many lines of text given in Ramsay's collection. This tune is also associated with the ballad of Jamie Douglas and another folk song "The water is wide." The arrangement prepared for this hymnal is specifically suited to *a cappella* singing and provides each voice with a tuneful part.

644
When morning gilds the skies

LAUDES DOMINI

Beim frühen Morgenlicht
Katholisches Gesangbuch, Würzburg, 1828
Tr. Edward Caswall (1814-1878)
Sts. 1-6, Formby's *Catholic Hymns*, 1854
Sts. 7-16, Caswall's *Masque of Mary*, 1858
Rev., 1873, alt.

Joseph Barnby (1838-1896)
Hymns Ancient and Modern, Appendix, 1868

Though it first appeared in the 1828 *Katholisches Gesangbuch*, this anonymous German hymn emerged in other German Roman Catholic hymnals in variant forms over the next thirty years. This could mean it was written earlier than 1828. The couplet form with the recurring response "May Jesus Christ be praised" parallels the German with its *Gelobt sei Jesus Christus*. Caswall translated a total of sixteen stanzas, revising them in 1873 to twenty-eight couplets. Those used here are Nos. 1-2, 11-12, 20-21, and 27-28. Among the couplets omitted are:

> My tongue shall never tire
> of chanting in the choir
>
> Be this at meals your grace,
> in every time and place
>
> When sleep her balm denies
> my silent spirit sighs
>
> Though break my heart in twain,
> still this shall be my strain

The joyous melody and dynamic harmony of LAUDES DOMINI were composed especially for eight of Caswall's stanzas, which appeared slightly altered in the appendix to *Hymns Ancient and Modern*. The tune name is Latin for "Praises of the Lord."

336
When peace, like a river

VILLE DU HAVRE

Horatio Gates Spafford (1828-1888)
Sankey and Bliss's *Gospel Hymns, No. 2*, 1876, alt.

Philip Paul Bliss (1838-1876)
(same source as text)

In 1873 Spafford's wife and four daughters sailed on the steamship *Ville du Havre* for France while Spafford finished up some business details in Chicago before joining them. In mid-ocean the vessel struck a large sailing ship and sank within half an hour. Many perished, including the four girls, but Mrs. Spafford was rescued. She cabled the message "saved alone" to her husband who then sailed for Liverpool to accompany his wife back to Chicago. Some say he wrote this hymn when their ship passed the place where their daughters died.

The evangelist D. L. Moody, a friend of the Spaffords, left his meetings in Edinburgh and went to Liverpool to comfort them. He was glad to hear them say, "It is well; the will of God be done."

Ira D. Sankey claims that Spafford wrote this hymn three years after the tragedy:

> In 1876, when we returned to Chicago to work, I was entertained at the home of Mr. and Mrs. Spafford for a number of weeks. During that time Mr. Spafford wrote the hymn, "It is well with my soul," in commemoration of the death of his children. (Sankey 1906)

In Sankey's *Sacred Songs and Solos* (enlarged, 1877), two additional verses appear, one based on Philippians 1:21 ("For me to live is Christ . . .") and the other on the second coming of Christ. Stanza 3, which once began "My sin, oh, the bliss of this glorious thought!" now reads "Redeemed! O the bliss of this glorious thought," thereby removing any possible ambiguity in that line. One other alteration was made in stanza 4:2 where "trumpet shall sound" replaces the archaic "trump shall resound."

The tune, written for Spafford's text, is named VILLE DU HAVRE after the steamship. It is also frequently known by the tune name IT IS WELL. The composer "sang it for the first time at a meeting in Farwell Hall [Chicago]" (Sankey 1906).

34
When the morning stars together

WEISSE FLÄGGEN

Albert Frederick Bayly (1901-1984), ca. 1966
Again I Say Rejoice, 1967

Anonymous
Tochter Sion, Köln, 1741

This text was written at the joint invitation of Lee H. Bristol, Jr., then president of Westminster Choir College and the school's senior class. Bayly himself altered stanza 2, the present version of which comes from Routley's *Rejoice in the Lord* where it is dated 1969. The alterations occur in the last three lines of the stanza, which originally read:

> . . . with the trumpets praised, thee, Lord.
> Glory filled the house of worship
> and thy people's souls were awed.

Through the entire text, the archaic personal pronouns have been replaced, which is in keeping with Bayly's concession in his supplement to *Again I Say Rejoice*: "In several hymns I have adopted the 'you' mode of address to God which seems to be gaining ground." As with "When in our music God is glorified" (**44**), this hymn dedicates our music to God's service.

The exhilarating WEISSE FLÄGGEN bears some resemblance to a tune called ALL SAINTS from the Darmstadt *Geistreiches Gesang-buch* (1698), and in its first three phrases, it also seems related to an anonymous melody from a 1732 Catholic hymnal printed in Bamberg with the text *Grosse Sorgen, Grosse Schmerzen*. In *Tochter Sion* (1741), a variant of the melody was set to *Lasst die weissen Fläggen wehen*, from which the present tune name is taken. Hymn analyst Bäumker believes the melody likely originated in a popular folk song (Ronander, Porter 1966).

558
When the storms of life are raging

STAND BY ME

Charles Albert Tindley (1851-1933)
Songs of Paradise, ca. 1906

Charles Albert Tindley (1851-1933)
(same source as text)
Arr. by William Farley Smith (1941-)
The United Methodist Hymnal, 1989

The gospel songs composed by Tindley were greatly influenced by the spirituals of his African American heritage. Tindley, a Methodist preacher, poet, and songwriter, often focused on "transforming the evil world for Christ through love, personal holiness, the apocalyptic hope, and . . . the suffering of this world" (Young 1993). Such transformation was only possible if the protector Jesus was "standing by."

Tindley included all of the "storms of life" in this hymn, using "proverbs, folk images, biblical allusions well-known to black Christians . . ." (McClain 1990). The emphasis on aging found in the last stanza is a theme often omitted by other hymnwriters.

The hymn was included in the 1966 and 1989 Methodist hymnals. In the latter collection, the opening phrase, "When the storms of life are raging, stand by me," is also used as a response with Psalm 124. This hymn should be sung at a moderate tempo befitting the "troubles" in the text.

544
When we walk with the Lord — TRUST AND OBEY

John H. Sammis (1846-1919)
Hymns Old and New, 1887

Daniel Brink Towner (1850-1919)
(same source as text)

The composer reports on the origin of this hymn:

> Mr. Moody was conducting a series of meetings in Brockton, Massachusetts, and I had the pleasure of singing for him there. One night a young man rose in a testimony meeting and said, "I am not quite sure—but I am going to trust, and I am going to obey." I just jotted that sentence down, and sent it with the little story to the Rev. J. H. Sammis, a Presbyterian minister. He wrote the hymn, and the tune was born. The chorus . . . was written before the hymn was. (Sankey 1906)

One stanza of the original five is omitted in the hymnal, but it is familiar to Brethren from their 1951 hymnal:

> Not a shadow can rise,
> not a cloud in the skies
> but his smile quickly drives it away;
> not a doubt or a fear,
> not a sigh nor a tear,
> can abide while we trust and obey.

In the refrain of the tune, the fermata on the word "Jesus," omitted in some hymnals, is printed here because of strong traditional usage.

305
Where charity and love prevail — CHESHIRE

Ubi caritas et amor
Anonymous, 9th c.
Tr. Omer Westendorf (1916-)
The People's Mass Book, 1964, alt.

Thomas Est's *The Whole Booke of Psalmes . . .*, 1592

The Latin text for this hymn is discussed with the Taizé antiphon "Ubi caritas et amor" (**452**). Omer Westendorf's translation of the Latin text presents a hope for the church well worth striving for—its dramatic counterpart would be the service of footwashing in the love feast. This text first came out in *The People's Mass Book*, the first hymn and service book published in English following the decree of Vatican Council II. Originally in six stanzas, the fourth is omitted here.

Several alterations, as found in *The United Methodist Hymnal* (1989), are used. These occur primarily in the final stanza where the word order of the first line is reversed and "Our family" and "Father" are replaced by "Our common life" and "Maker" (st. 5:2-3).

The more complete title of Thomas Est's collection, published in London, is *The Whole Booke of Psalmes with their wonted Tunes, as they are sung in the Churches, composed into foure parts . . . Compiled by sondry authors.* In that volume CHESHIRE, spelled CHESSHIRE, was harmonized by John Farmer as the setting of Psalm 146 and by John Dowland with a "Prayer for the Queen's Majesty." Est's collection contains the earliest examples of tunes with names. The melody, originally in the tenor voice, is now in the soprano.

ST. FLAVIAN makes a good alternate tune.

405
Where cross the crowded ways

GERMANY

Frank Mason North (1850-1935)
Christian City, XV, No. 4, June 1903, alt.

William Gardiner's *Sacred Melodies*, Vol. 2, 1815

This eloquent urban hymn, one of the first of the social gospel genre, was written for the *The Methodist Hymnal* (1905) at the request of Caleb T. Winchester of the editorial committee. North replied that he was no hymnwriter, but he promised to try. Shortly before writing the hymn, North, a longtime minister in the slums of New York City, had preached a sermon from Matthew 22:9 using the translation "Go ye therefore into the parting of the highways." This phrase prompted the imagery of the first two lines of the hymn. North's words synthesize urban need with the grace of Christ.

As urbanization increases worldwide, this hymn is finding broad acceptance and has been translated into various languages, including some of the Far East. Although the words of the final stanza " 'Til sons of men" have been changed to " 'Til all the world," this hymnal's editors felt that the phrase "O Son of Man" in stanza 1:3 had a theological punch stronger than any substitute and should be retained.

The tune GERMANY is also known by the names BEETHOVEN, BONN, FULDA, GARDINER, MELCHIZEDEC, and WALTON. Gardiner attributes the theme of the melody to Beethoven but could not identify the specific composition to which it belonged. *The Hymnal 1940 Companion* points out a musical example from Beethoven's Piano Trio, Opus 70, No. 2 (1809), the *Allegretto ma non troppo* movement that has a noticeable resemblance to the beginning and end of this hymn tune.

200
Where is this stupendous Stranger? — McRAE

Christopher Smart (1722-1771)
Hymns and Spiritual Songs for the Fasts and Festivals of the Church of England, 1765, alt.

Joan Annette Fyock (1938-), 1989

This is a hymn rich with the paradox of the incarnation, expressed in archaisms that require some study if they are to be fully appreciated. Notice the phrases: "magnitude of meekness," "the strength of infant weakness," "if eternal is so young." The circle of God Incarnate meeting God Creator is wonderfully tight in Smart's final phrase: "[God] is incarnate and a native of the very world he made."

Smart's complete poem "The Nativity of Our Lord" consists of nine stanzas. The original text of stanza 1:2 is "Swains of Solyma, advise." It is believed that the poem was not used as a hymn until F. Bland Tucker selected stanzas 2, 3, and 9 for the *The Hymnal 1940* (Episcopal). There it was set to a melody by the Swiss composer Johann Ludwig Steiner, a contemporary of Christopher Smart. The omitted stanzas that come between the present third and fourth stanzas are:

If so young and thus eternal,
Michael tune the shepherd's reed,
where the scenes are ever vernal,
and the loves be love indeed!

See the God blasphemed and doubted
in the schools of Greece and Rome;
See the powers of darkness routed,
taken at their utmost gloom.

Nature's decorations glisten
far above their usual trim;
birds on box and laurel listen,
as so near the cherubs hymn.

Boreas now no longer winters
on the desolated coast;
oaks no more are riven in splinters
By the whirlwind and his host.

Spinks and ousels sing sublimely,
"We too have a Saviour born";
whiter blossoms burst untimely
on the blest Mosaic thorn.

Following a call for new music by the preparers of this hymnal, Joan Fyock, a member of the music committee, composed the tune McRAE and submitted it under the pseudonym of David McRae, chosen for her great-grandfather David Fyock and her father, Ray L. Fyock. "In reading through the text," writes Fyock, "the rhythmic shape of the melody revealed itself immediately. The shift of the rhythmic pattern in the next to last measure was created by the word stresses of the text." The tune rises to the midpoint of the melody, creating one long, arching melodiccontour.

196
While shepherds watched — WINCHESTER OLD

Based on Luke 2:8-14
Nahum Tate (1652-1715)
Tate and Brady's *A Supplement to the New Version of the Psalms*, 1700, alt.

Thomas Est's *The Whole Booke of Psalmes . . .*, 1592
Arr. by George Kirbye (ca. 1565-1634)

Sternhold and Hopkins' "Old Version" of the Psalms (1562) enjoyed ecclesiastical sanction by the "established church" in England for more than one hundred years before being replaced by Nahum Tate and Nicholas Brady's "New Version," published in 1696.[1] A few years later they published a supplement, and this paraphrase of Luke 2:8-14 was one of only six hymns other than biblical canticles and Psalms permitted to be used in English churches at the time. Tate's paraphrase is his only surviving hymn and has been translated into Latin and many other languages.

WINCHESTER OLD at first had no name and was a setting of the metrical version of Psalm 84, "How pleasant is thy dwelling place," in Est's *The Whole Booke of Psalmes . . . .* In this volume the melody was in the tenor, and gathering notes (longer notes to aid in breathing) were used at the beginning and end of phrases. The three other voice parts were added by George Kirbye (or Kirby). There is a strong resemblance of phrases 2, 3, and 4 of this melody to those of Christopher Tye's chapter 8 of *The Acts of the Apostles* (1553).[2]

The reason for the name WINCHESTER is not known, but it first appeared in Ravenscroft's *Psalter* of 1621. OLD was added later to indicate that the tune was used in Sternhold and Hopkins' "Old Version" of the Psalms and to distinguish it from the tune WINCHESTER NEW (1690).

CHRISTMAS (**609**) is a familiar alternative for this hymn.

1. For a concise discussion of psalm-singing and the development of these psalters, see Oyer's *Exploring the Mennonite Hymnal: Essays*, 1980, pages 55-56.
2. Examples of the two are in *The Hymnal 1940 Companion*, page 203, and *Songs of Praise Discussed*, page 57, respectively.

270
Who are these

Ad coenam agni providi
Anonymous, ca. 6th c.
Tr. The Hymnal Project
Hymnal: A Worship Book, 1992

OTO SĄ BARANKI

Jacek Gałuszka, O.P. (1965-), 1989

This is one of two Polish hymns included in this hymnal. The refrain "Who are these" is in the hymnal, while the stanzas and instrumental parts are in the *Accompaniment Handbook*. The words of the refrain are reminiscent of Revelation 7:13-14: "Who are these, robed in white, and where have they come from?" Translated from the Latin to Polish by F. Malaczynski, O.S.B., the text appears in *Kyriale dla wiernych* (1960).

The tune name represents the first three words of the Polish text. Music editor, Kenneth Nafziger, first heard this hymn sung at an Easter vigil in Krakow, Poland.

62
Who is so great a God

From Russian Orthodox liturgy

THE GREAT PROKEIMENON

Dimitri Stepanovich Bortniansky (1751-1825)

In the liturgy of the Russian Orthodox Church, a *prokeimenon* (Greek, "to set forth") is a responsorial psalm verse sung before the reading of the Epistle lesson. A "Great Prokeimenon" is one sung on major festival days; this one is used especially on Easter and Pentecost. Sung at a slow pulse, it serves as a time of preparation for hearing God's word.

The expansive range and rich harmonies of the music, coupled with the repetitions of the text, create a sense of awe and majesty. Bortniansky's music is much loved in both the Orthodox and Protestant traditions in Russia.

535
Who now would follow Christ

Wer Christo jetzt will folgen nach
Ausbund, 1564
Tr. David W. Augsburger (1938-), 1962
The Mennonite Hymnal, 1969
Rev. in *Assembly Songs*, 1983

WARUM BETRÜBST DU DICH, MEIN HERZ

Bartholomeus Monoetius
Manuscript, Crailsheim, 1565
(Zahn No. 1689a)
Harm. by J. Harold Moyer (1927-), 1965
The Mennonite Hymnal, 1969

This hymn, originally in twenty-seven five-line stanzas, is an anonymous hymn commemorating Jörg (Georg) Wagner, a spiritual leader of the

Anabaptists who died a martyr's death in Munich, Germany, in 1527. David Augsburger, the translator, distills this text from stanzas 1-5 of the German. An example of his literal translation of stanza 2 follows:

Also thät Jörg der Wagner auch,
Gen Himmel Fuhr er in dem Rauch,
Durchs Creutz ward er bewähret
Gleich wie man thut dem klaren Gold,
Von Herzen ers begehret.

Accordingly Jörg Wagner also
towards heaven rose in smoke.
Through the cross he was preserved
just as gold is purified,
from his heart he this desired.

The third stanza refers to the Falkenturm (in Bavaria) where Wagner was tortured. Details of his life recur through the twenty-seven stanzas, but Augsburger paraphrases the poem so that it represents martyrs in general rather than Wagner in particular (Oyer 1980).

WARUM BETRÜBST DU DICH, MEIN HERZ comes from the time of the first edition of the *Ausbund* (1564). The tune appeared in two secular songs in the major mode in 1560 (Zahn 1689a), and Zahn claims that it must have had earlier secular uses (Oyer 1980). The melody was included in one of the earliest Brethren hymnals, *Geistliche und andächtige Lieder*, published in Germantown (Philadelphia), Pennsylvania, by Christopher Sauer in 1753. There it appeared with the text *Wie ein Blum', O Mensch*, by Johannes Preiss (1702-1724), a Brethren poet from Pennsylvania (H. Durnbaugh 1986). This hymn was an obvious choice for Alice Parker to include in her church opera *Martyrs Mirror*. It is most effective sung in a rugged unison, reflecting the trials and martyrdom described in the text. Hymnologist Mary Oyer notes, however, that caution must be taken in choosing the tempo: "It is easy to begin too rapidly for the quick notes and chord changes of the last half" (Oyer 1980).

633
Whom shall I send?

Fred Pratt Green (1903-)
26 Hymns, 1971

DEUS TUORUM MILITUM

French church melody
Grenoble Antiphoner, 1753

Green wrote this text in response to a request from the Presbyterian Church in Canada for a hymn that would challenge young people to consider the vocation of Christian ministry. It is based on Isaiah 6:8, the prophet's autobiographical account of his own calling as a servant of God. The hymn was sung to DEUS TUORUM MILITUM in Norwich Cathedral in December of 1970.

DEUS TUORUM MILITUM, also known as GRENOBLE, is a stirring melody for eliciting action and thus helps overcome the hesitancy in the words of the first three stanzas. For comments on the tune, see "Creating God, your fingers trace" (**325**).

246
Why has God forsaken me? SHIMPI

Bill Wallace (20th c.)
Something to Sing About, 1981

Taihei Sato (20th c.), 1981
Hymns from the Four Winds, 1983

Wallace, a New Zealand minister, based this text on several scriptural passages surrounding the last week of Jesus' life. Matthew recorded in his Gospel (27:46) that the dying Jesus repeated the words of Psalm 22; Wallace takes these for his first stanza. Stanza 2 reflects on the story of Lazarus (John 11:35), while the third returns to the scene of the crucifixion (Luke 23:46). This hymn contemplates the mystery of life and death that Jesus experienced so that we, too, might dare to look into "the mystery's heart" for "the love which conquers fear."

Sato composed SHIMPI for Wallace's text after they participated together in the Asian Consultation on Liturgy and Music conducted in Manila in the Philippines in 1980. The collection in which this hymn first appeared was put out by the Joint Board of Christian Education of Australia and New Zealand, and it was included in the funeral resource packet of the New Zealand Methodist Church (McKim 1993). Sung in a slow tempo, the melody undergirds the meditative nature of the text.

307
Will you let me be your servant THE SERVANT SONG

Richard Gillard (1953-), 1976, alt.

Richard Gillard (1953-), 1976
Adapt. by Betty Carr Pulkingham (1928-)

This hymn of servanthood was included in the 1989 sampler of this hymnal with the first stanza beginning "Sister, let me be your servant" and the last beginning with "Brother." Here an altered form of the text, adopted by a number of contemporary hymnals, combines the two into one request, "Will you let me be your servant." The change accomplishes two things: It is a more universal address, and it retains the dignity of the recipient by *asking* permission before service is rendered.

Gillard is a self-taught guitarist whose songs are inspired by the Bible and the lives of Christians around him. He also finds that his own experience of God in prayer and worship is the best of all sources of inspiration. What became the "Servant's Song" percolated in him for nearly a year, and "what subsequently became the third verse lived on a scrap of paper in the bottom of my guitar case in my brother-in-law's home" during a 1976 tour of England, Scotland, Europe and Israel.

Through the ministry of "Scripture in Song," based in Australia, this song has become known around the world.

31
Wind who makes all winds

FALCONE

Thomas Henry Troeger (1945-)
The Christian Ministry, May 1983

Carol Doran (1936-), 1985
New Hymns for the Lectionary, 1986
Harm. in four parts by Carol Doran, 1988

This hymn, so animated by metaphor and vibrant imagery, is an eye-catching example of Troeger's careful crafting of texts. He wrote it for Father Sebastian Falcone, director of St. Bernard's Institute, for a Mass celebrating the gift of the Holy Spirit. St. Bernard's is a Roman Catholic affiliate school with Colgate Rochester Divinity School/Bexley Hall/Crozer Theological Seminary in Hamilton, New York. The text is based on the famous Acts 2 scripture for Pentecost Sunday in the lectionary. Notice how the use of the word "who" imitates the sound for the wind.

Accustomed to writing unison tunes with instrumental accompaniment, Doran made this four-part setting of FALCONE especially for this hymnal in deference to Brethren and Mennonites who so love part-singing. She says that "the musical setting is intended to reflect the contrasting halves of each stanza: a gentle address followed by a spirited petition."

The keyboard accompaniment is found in the *Accompaniment Handbook.*

432
With all my heart I offer

BENEDICTION

Carol Ann Weaver (1948-)
Jericho, 1979

Carol Ann Weaver (1948-)
(same source as text)

Weaver composed the children's music drama Jericho[1] for the children's choir of Maryann Bergen in Hepburn, Saskatchewan. It was premiered in late summer 1979 by that choir, with subsequent performances by the adult choir at Associated Mennonite Biblical Seminaries, Elkhart, Indiana, and by the children at Rockway Mennonite Church, Kitchener, Ontario. Weaver says the "Benediction," which is the portion found in this hymnal, "came of its own accord as a sort of tribute to Gregorian chant music, as I went walking one day in Winnipeg . . . ." As the final work in *Jericho*, it was meant to be sung with great reverence and gratitude to God.

1. Written for voices and piano, the work has been published by Runningbrook Music, Ontario, and is available from the composer.

83

With happy voices singing

William George Tarrant (1853-1928), 1888
Supplement to Essex Hall Hymnal, 1892

FAITHFUL

Adapt. from Johann Sebastian Bach (1685-1750)
Cantata No. 68, *Also hat Gott die Welt geliebt*, 1735

This hymn text, suitable for children of all ages, involves the worshiper in an awareness of God through nature, home, and loved ones. It prompts us to enter into praise through music and to consecrate our lives to God.

FAITHFUL is an adaptation of Bach's aria *Mein gläubiges Herze* (from Cantata No. 68) for soprano, cello, violin, oboe, and continuo. The German text of the aria has been translated:

> My believing heart, should for joy, sing, frolic,
> your Jesus is there; away, terror, away complaining,
> I will merely say to you: my Jesus is near.[1]

The lively tempo of the aria suggests that this arrangement is best sung in two beats per measure, which is in keeping with the joyful spirit of the cantata and the hymn text. A setting suitable for unison singing is in the *Accompaniment Handbook*. For those desiring a lower key, the hymn is printed in C major in *The Brethren Hymnal* (1951).

1. German text and translation: *Bach: Arias for Voices and Instruments*, Bach Aria Group, William H. Scheide, Director; Decca DL 9405

223

Woman in the night

Brian Arthur Wren (1936-), 1982
Faith Looking Forward, 1983

CANDLE

Marilyn Houser Hamm (1951-), 1990
Hymnal: A Worship Book, 1992

The last stanza of this text began as part of a Christmas carol that Wren initially "abandoned because it was stale and secondhand." That final stanza, however, took on a life of its own when it prompted his thinking about the "women around Jesus," and from there it became a song (Wren 1983). The stanzas name eight places where the lives of women converged with Jesus' life. These glimpses are all from the Gospels, beginning with the mother, Mary: Luke 2:6-7; Mark 5:24-34; John 4:7-30; Luke 7:36-50; Luke 10:38-42; John 19:25; and Luke 23:55—24:10.

Several recent tunes have been written for this text—including NEW DISCIPLES by Peter Cutts, NOEL NEW by Jane Marshall, and WICKLUND, by William Rowan—that appeared in the sampler for this hymnal in 1989. Ultimately, CANDLE was chosen "to reflect the element of struggle that so many feel, particularly women, in their journey for faith and wholeness."

Although there is no meter, CANDLE is not difficult to sing because the music follows the natural rhythms of the text. The refrain, rather than standing as a separate musical element, is an extension and conclusion of each stanza. The rising lines, expanding by whole steps in many places, represent a "sense of hope that emerges from great pain," says composer Hamm. It is "not a sudden event that 'makes it all better,' but a strong hope that one can find life again." The name CANDLE was chosen as a symbol of that hope expressed in the refrain "Jesus makes us free to live again."

622
Wonder of wonders — LOVELLE

Brian Arthur Wren (1936-), 1974
Faith Looking Forward, 1983

Larry R. Warkentin (1940-), 1988
Hymnal: A Worship Book, 1992

Wren wrote this text for friends whose six-week-old child was soon to be dedicated in the Baptist Church. The parents suggested the concepts they wished to include and chose the tune of "Morning has broken." The words and phrases fell into place so quickly that Wren was able to give them the completed hymn the next morning (Wren 1983). Notice that in the last line of the first stanza the pronoun ("his," "her," "their") should be changed to fit the child or children being dedicated.

Since the tune BUNESSAN ("Morning has broken") was already so well used, the compilers of this hymnal were glad to have Warkentin's setting of the text. Warkentin, who represented the Mennonite Brethren denomination as an observer during the preparation of this hymnal, used the first four lines of text as a refrain to conclude each stanza. The rocking character of LOVELLE's 9/8 meter and the folklike singability of the melody create a nurserylike ambiance for the text. LOVELLE is the middle name of the composer's daughter.

150
Wonderful grace of Jesus — WONDERFUL GRACE

Haldor Lillenas (1885-1959)
Tabernacle Choir, 1922

Haldor Lillenas (1885-1959)
(same source as text)

From 1916 to 1919, Haldor Lillenas was pastor of Church of the Nazarene in Auburn, Illinois. During those years he wrote a great deal of music, including this choir selection, for Charles M. Alexander, a noted evangelistic singer. This song was first introduced by Homer Hammontree in 1918 at the Northfield Bible Conference (Mass.), founded by evangelist D. L. Moody.

Lillenas felt that most people sing this hymn too fast, racing into the exuberant music without savoring the text. "A song should be performed in such a fashion that the words can be comfortably pronounced without undue haste," he writes (Hustad 1978). During his hymnwriting before the era of careful copyrighting and remuneration, Lillenas received only five dollars for this composition that has become popular around the world.

220

Worship the Lord in the beauty

John Samuel Bewley Monsell (1811-1875)
Hymns of Love and Praise, 1st ed., 1863, alt.

WAS LEBET, WAS SCHWEBET

Manuscript Chorale Book, 1754 (Zahn No. 1457)

Monsell originally launched this Epiphany hymn with "O" but changed the opening line when he revised the text for the *Parish Hymnal* (1873). Repeating the first stanza as the last, however, is part of Monsell's original design. The text alterations made here are slight, adapting "thee" and "thy" language to contemporary usage. Stanza 2:4 is adjusted for the rhyme scheme and the last word of stanza 3 is changed from "shrine" to "throne."

Although the text mentions the gold and incense associated with the magi, which marks this as an Epiphany hymn, the gifts of obedience, lowliness, truth, and love are appropriate at any season. Monsell has taken great care in the structure of this hymn, ending each first and third phrase of the stanzas with a three-syllable rhyme. The "burden of carefulness" of stanza 2:1 has more to do with laying aside anxiety than renouncing caution.

This melody comes from the manuscript chorale book of Johann Heinrich Reinhardt, written at Üttingen in 1754. The tune, which also appears in another form in Zahn, is probably from an earlier source. *Songs of Praise Discussed* suggests that the triple meter and repeated notes beginning each measure are typical of traditional popular songs, leading to the supposition that this may be an adaptation of one of them (Dearmer 1933).

472
Yo soy el pan de vida—see "I am the Bread of life"

226
You are salt for the earth — BRING FORTH THE KINGDOM

Marty Haugen (1950-), 1985
Gather, 1988

Marty Haugen (1950-), 1985
(same source as text)

In *Gather*, a collection of contemporary folk-style hymns, songs, and psalms, this song appears under the title "Bring forth the kingdom," from which its tune name comes. It was composed for a catechetical conference in 1985. The challenges in the stanzas come from the familiar passages in Matthew 5 and 13. If enthusiastic singing of such "kingdom" intentions could help usher in God's reign, this song would be the one to sing.

Haugen chose the musical form of call and response with a refrain, because of its simplicity and because it fosters a strong sense of dialog between music ministers and the congregation.

537
You are the God within life—see "En medio de la vida"

427
You shall go out with joy — THE TREES OF THE FIELD

Based on Isaiah 55:12
Adapt. by Steffi Geiser Rubin

Stuart Dauermann (1944-), 1975

This is part of the promise of the prophet Isaiah to the Jewish exiles, whose greatest desire was to return home—to "go out" from Babylon. With triumphant and delightful poetry, Isaiah's mountains sing out and the trees applaud God's salvation. No longer confined to displaced Jews, the prophecy has been set as a contemporary scripture song, full of the energy and excitement of a homecoming.

Set in the minor mode, THE TREES OF THE FIELD has many of the qualities of an Israeli folk song. Stuart Dauermann, music director for Jews for Jesus, says he has been "writing Christ-honoring music in a Jewish idiom since the mid-1960s. We wanted to produce Jewish-sounding music which would so express the sentiments and faith of Christian people as to find a place in their hearts and in their hymnals."

The repetitions in the song make it easy to learn, while the handclapping is fun and also captures the character of Jewish music. It is important to note that in the second part of the song the "trees of the field" is in a straightforward rhythm and does not repeat the syncopation that appears with that text in the first part of the melody.

596
You who dwell in the shelter (On eagle's wings)—see "And I will raise you up"

625
Your love, O God, has called us — CORNISH

Russell E. Schulz-Widmar (1944-), 1981
The Hymnal 1982, 1985

M. Lee Suitor (1942-), ca. 1975
(same source as text)

This text, written in response to a call for marriage hymns for *The Hymnal 1982* (Episcopal), was submitted anonymously to the editors of that hymnal. The hymn first declares that all love springs from God's love and then asks God's blessing not only on those being married but on all married couples. Thus, the hymn is appropriate both for weddings and for the renewal of marriage vows, as well as for other services focusing on the family. Originally intended to be sung to the tune GARDINER (GERMANY), the text appears in *The Baptist Hymnal* (Southern Baptist 1991) set to CANONBURY.

The tune CORNISH was composed for Frederick J. Gillman's text "God, send us men whose aim 'twill be, not to defend some ancient creed . . . ." Suitor wrote it for his high school choir in about 1975 as the choir prepared for a youth service at St. Luke's Episcopal Church, Atlanta, Georgia, where he was organist and choirmaster. CORNISH appears with the present text in both *The Hymnal 1982* and *The United Methodist Hymnal* (1989).

WORSHIP RESOURCE ARTICLES

659
Grace unto you and peace

Ruth C. Duck (1947-)
Bread for the Journey, 1981, alt.

This call to worship is a paraphrase of Revelation 1:4-6. It comes from Duck's collection *Bread for the Journey*, which, along with its companion, *Flames of the Spirit*, contains resources that use names for God and language about God that are not limited by masculine representation. They use metaphors and images found in the scripture readings of the *Ecumenical Lectionary* (1974).

For other resources from the Duck collections, see **661, 664, 669, 696, 745, 747,** and **758**.

What is the lectionary?

"Lectionary" is based on the Latin word *lectio*, which means a reading. A lectionary is a set of prescribed readings for each Sunday of the year and may also include readings suggested for each day of the year. Current lectionaries are generally organized on a three-year cycle, designated Years A, B, or C. If the lectionary is followed daily, most of the Bible will be read in three years; if it is followed for Sunday worship only, the significant events and teachings of the Bible will be heard.

Daily patterns of reading were a prominent part of synagogue worship and study and included readings for Jewish holidays. Isaiah 61 was the prescribed scripture for the synagogue on the day Jesus read in Nazareth (Luke 4:16-21). By the fourth century, various churches had developed patterns of reading scripture. As believers remembered Jesus' life and ministry in their celebrations of Easter, Pentecost, and Epiphany, they read passages of the Gospels and Hebrew scriptures appropriate for the day. As other celebrations and seasons were added to the church year (e.g., Lent, Christmas, Advent, and much later the season of Pentecost), more lectionary readings developed.

Each set of Sunday lections has a Hebrew scripture, a Psalm (intended as a response to the Hebrew scripture), an Epistle, and a Gospel reading. Particularly during the time from Advent to Pentecost, these readings center around an important theme in the life of Jesus, one that reveals God's purpose and nature more fully.

Throughout the centuries various lectionaries have developed, usually under the supervision of church and denominational governing bodies. Since 1970 denominations and churches have tried to integrate their lectionaries to achieve a greater sense of unity among Christians as they share common passages from God's word. *The Ecumenical Lectionary* (1974) is based on the revised Roman Catholic lectionary and harmonized with those of other denominations; it is commonly called the COCU lectionary, or lectionary of the Consultation on Church Union. *The Common Lectionary* (1987) brought further integration and is widely used in most North American and English-speaking churches. A revision of this lectionary was introduced during Advent of 1992. Work on the *The Common Lectionary* was sponsored by the Consultation on Common Texts (CCT).

660
The Lord be with you

Sursum Corda in *The Apostolic Tradition of Hippolytus*, 215
Tr. English Language Liturgical Consultation, 1988

This greeting and response form a text usually called the *Sursum Corda* (Latin for "let us lift up our hearts"). See also "Lift up your heads" (**602**).The first evidence of its use comes from Rome in a document called *The Apostolic Tradition of Hippolytus* (215). In that source the text begins the service of Communion. There is evidence that Cyprian also used the dialogue (ca. 252) and that Cyril, bishop of Jerusalem (ca. 350), also opened Communion celebrations with this text. Holy Communion, or Eucharist, in the more formal liturgical traditions still begins with this dialogue.

Eucharist means "thanksgiving" in Greek and was the most prominent theme of the Communion in the early church. The *Sursum Corda* introduces the moods of thanksgiving and praise immediately into the celebration. This resource can also be used with **786, 788,** and **789** in the Lord's Supper section of the hymnal.

This form of the *Sursum Corda* is from *Prayers We Have in Common* (1972), a collection of worship texts translated and edited by the International Consultation on English Texts (ICET). This ecumenical organization included scholars and liturgists from Australia, Canada, Great Britain, and the United States. ICET disbanded in 1975, and little was done ecumenically with common worship texts for the next eight years. Concerned about updating the 1972 text editions, the English Language Liturgical Consultation (ELLC) began functioning in 1983 and consists of associates working regionally in Australia, Canada, England, Ireland, New Zealand, South Africa, and the U.S. *Praying Together* is the ELLC's updated collection of prayers.

Other ELLC/ICET prayers in this worship book are **702, 712, 731,** and **840**.

662
Come, let us worship, for we are the people

Based on Psalm 95:6-7a
Earle W. Fike, Jr. (1930-)
We Gather Together, 1979

Verses 1-7a of Psalm 95 have a "liturgical" setting; they bring people into the presence of an awesome God. Psalm 95 might have been used by the Jews in the autumn festival where God is revealed as Creator and Lord of the universe (Weiser 1962). Psalm 95 has had a significant place in the Christian tradition since the sixth century when St. Benedict prescribed it as the opening psalm in the daily service of morning prayer for his monastic communities (Melloh, Storey 1979). The psalm's structure, imagery, and imperative mood provide an excellent model for crafting other calls to worship.

664
Watch! Wait! The day of God is at hand

Sandra E. Graham (1954-)
Ruth Duck's *Flames of the Spirit*, 1985, alt.

The primary themes of Advent reverberate through this call to worship: waiting, the reign of God, judgment on the day of God, justice, and hope.

> ***What is Advent?***
>
> The four Sundays of Advent (which means "coming") anticipate the fullness of God's reign on earth, promising peace, justice, and wholeness. Advent is not so much about waiting one more time for Jesus' birth in Bethlehem as it is about Jesus being reborn in each Christian believer, bringing God's presence and God's reign near. The themes of the lectionary readings for these Sundays move from judgment to justice, hope for

peace and wholeness, the anticipation of God's saving presence on earth through Jesus, and Christ's second coming.

Since its beginning in the fifth century, Advent has been a season of preparation and penitence, possibly because January 6 (Epiphany) was often a time for baptism. The themes for each Sunday elicit reflection on our readiness to receive God's gift in Jesus. This reflective or penitential mood clearly distinguishes the observance of Advent from the celebration of Christmas. Observing Advent keeps the church from focusing solely on the sweetness of the baby and from blurring the fact that, beyond the manger, Jesus' birth inaugurated a new reign of judgment, forgiveness, justice, suffering, peace, and love.

665
Glory to God in the highest

The Hymnal Project, 1991
Hymnal: A Worship Book, 1992

This is a Christmas call to worship based on Luke 2:11,14, sometimes called the angel's song. It is one of the Gospel canticles that became the basis for a fourth-century hymn of praise (*Gloria in excelsis Deo*). It is the first praise hymn sung in Sunday worship in Roman Catholic, Lutheran, and Episcopal churches.

What is a canticle?

Canticles ("little songs") are portions of biblical poetry found outside of the Psalms; often these passages had a history of being sung before they were written down. Some examples of canticles are the songs of Moses (Exod. 15:1-27), Miriam (Exod. 15:21), Deborah (Judg. 5:2-31), and Hannah (1 Sam. 2:1-10); the servant songs of Isaiah; the songs of Zechariah (Luke 1:68-79), Mary (Luke 1:46-55), and Simeon (Luke 2:29-32); the Christ hymn of Philippians; and the songs of Revelation.

Other canticles in *Hymnal: A Worship Book* are **61, 179, 181, 715, 771, 831, 840, 855, 860,** and **861**.

What is the Season of Christmas?

The Season of Christmas (twelve days) begins on December 25 and continues until Epiphany (January 6). The mood is a joyful contrast to the season of Advent (see "What is Advent," article **664**). Gift giving and celebrating are extensions of God's great gift in Jesus. Before December 25 was established to celebrate Christmas in the Western Church, January 6 (Epiphany) was the date on which Jesus' incarnation was observed. The Amish continue to commemorate Jesus' birth on January 6. The Eastern Church recognizes December 25 as the date for celebrating Jesus' birth but gives priority to Epiphany in commemorating Jesus' baptism and the miracles performed at Cana. Epiphany means "manifestations of a god"; thus, these events are observed as significant manifestations (epiphanies) of God's power and authority present in Jesus.

Celebrating the entire season of Christmas expands our awareness of how the greatness of God's gift in Jesus and God's purpose for the world through him are inextricably linked.

666
Call a solemn assembly

Lavon Bayler (1933-)
Refreshing Rains of the Living Word, 1988, alt.

Bayler uses lectionary readings for Ash Wednesday (the first day of Lent) as bases for this call to worship. The source, *Refreshing Rains of the Living Word,* is a collection of resources for each Sunday and holiday of the Christian year. This book, along with *Fresh Winds of the Spirit* and *Whispers of God,* comprises a set of resources for the three-year lectionary cycle (see article **659,** "What is the lectionary?").

What is Lent?

In the first centuries of the Christian church, new believers were baptized on Easter Sunday. Symbolically and theologically, this was the day of choice since Jesus' resurrection was the ultimate example of the believer's new life. The days prior to Easter were for preparation and instruction of new believers or catechumens. They studied scripture, fasted, prayed, and learned the essential disciplines of Christian life. By the fourth century, when infant baptism became the standard practice, instruction during this period lessened in importance, and penance became a dominant theme of preparation. This was also a time when those who had fallen into error could participate in instruction and confession and be reunited with the church.

Already in the second century, many believers prepared for Easter by fasting for two days; by the third century, the fast was extended from Palm/Passion Sunday until the Easter celebration. By the fourth century, a forty-day period of preparation and fasting was a common practice (Adam 1981). Fasting did not require total abstinence from food but rather permitted eating a single meal a day, usually in the evening.

The season of Lent, then, was formed as a result of early church practices of instruction and devotion. Forty days became the significant number since it paralleled Jesus' forty days of temptation and his preparation for ministry. Lent originally spanned the period of six Sundays before Easter until Maundy Thursday (or Holy Thursday), but eventually it included Good Friday and Holy Saturday. By the fifth century, Ash Wednesday and the following days were added to the six-week period. The actual number of calendar days from Ash Wednesday until Easter Sunday is more than forty; however, Sunday is never recognized as a fast day in the Christian church and is not part of the forty-day count.

The lectionary readings for the season of Lent focus on Jesus' teachings and his invitations to follow in his way. It is a time to reflect on the meaning of discipleship and to make a recommitment to follow Christ.

667
He's coming, he's coming

Linea Reimer Geiser (1936-), 1990
Adapt. from "He's Coming," 1990

This call to worship is appropriate for Palm Sunday, but it also points to Jesus' upcoming Passion.

What do the palm branches mean?

Palms were symbols of life, hope, and victory in Greek and Roman cultures; they were believed to hold mysterious and magical powers. Strewing a path with garments or fronds was a sign of honor or oblation. Thus, the political implications of Jesus' ride into Jerusalem cannot be overlooked.

Only the Gospel of John mentions palms as part of the procession. In the fifth century, Christians in and around Jerusalem would go to the Mount of Olives and re-enact Jesus' pilgrimage into the city with palm or olive branches waving. This practice soon spread to other churches in the East and eventually made its way into the church in the West (Adam 1981).

Passion Sunday, another name for Palm Sunday, characterizes the events of the week before Easter. Jesus' festive ride into Jerusalem ended in confrontation with the religious and civil authorities, betrayal by the disciples, suffering, humiliation, and death. The lectionary readings for this Sunday and this call to worship sound themes of both victory and suffering.

668
This is the day that the Lord has made

Diane Karay Tripp (1954-)
All the Seasons of Mercy, 1987, alt.

Psalm 118:24, the source for the opening two lines, is the conclusion of the lectionary psalm appointed for Easter Sunday. The *Alleluias* will speak with particular force, since these acclamations of praise are not usually sung or spoken during Lent. This resource provides a strong opening for Easter Sunday worship. The affirmations apply, though, to every Sunday, because Sunday celebrates Jesus' resurrection.

Why Sunday?

The first Christians gathered on Sunday to celebrate the Lord's Supper, even while continuing to practice Jewish customs, because Jesus' presence with them in Spirit through a common meal was linked with their experience of the resurrection. Over the course of three centuries, Sunday, for Christians, became the primary day of worship and celebration of the Lord's Supper. While Jewish symbolism, practices, and interpretations for sabbath were transferred to Christian practices on Sunday, the cornerstone of Christian understanding is that Sunday is the day of Jesus' resurrection. It is the day of salvation.

669
A mighty wind has blown

Wheadon United Methodist Church Worship Commission (Evanston, Ill.)
Ruth Duck's *Bread for the Journey*, 1981, alt.

What is Pentecost?

Pentecost originally was a Jewish holiday known as the feast of weeks (*Shavuoth*). It marked the end of the barley harvest and the beginning of the wheat harvest fifty days after Passover. Gradually, the themes of the feast changed, and the celebration became a memorial for God giving the Torah (the first five books of the Hebrew scriptures). God's revelation was the significant theme. It was for this celebration that many people were in Jerusalem on the day the Holy Spirit came to the early Christians with mighty winds and in tongues of flame.

Pentecost in the Christian church year comes fifty days after Easter. It marks the fulfillment of Joel's prophecy about God's restoration of Israel and the fulfillment of Jesus' promise to send the Spirit of truth (John 16:7-15). The Pentecost celebration is often associated with the beginning of the Christian church, since its preaching and evangelizing work began with the outpouring of the Spirit.

The season of Pentecost fills the remaining weeks of the church year, lasting until the Sunday before Advent. The season has also been called Ordinary Time and Kingdomtide.

670
Our God, we gather to worship you

Ruth A.Yoder (1949-), 1988

When this resource appeared in the *Hymnal Sampler*, several people expressed concern over the last line, suggesting that it may border on trinitarian heresy. Presently, there is a good deal of experimentation with trinitarian language, stimulated in part by concerns about the exclusively masculine imagery of God. This resource is a reminder that one God is present with us through three persons; we recognize God's action in our lives through the Creator, the Redeemer, and the Sustainer. These attributes are stated with different metaphors that can help us name more fully our daily experiences of God, Jesus Christ, and the Holy Spirit.

Certainly, the last line of the resource does not show the familial relationship between God, Jesus, and the Spirit that traditional trinitarian language shows; it is, therefore, not intended as a replacement for the Father-Son metaphor. This worship book includes different ways of naming the threefold-but-unified nature of God; however, the classical form "Father, Son, and Holy Spirit" is still recognized as the formula of choice for the church.

672
With all your saints across the generations

Lavon Bayler (1933-)
Refreshing Rains of the Living Word, 1988, alt.

Mystery is making a comeback in common religious language; its use is a sign of different winds blowing in our spiritual lives.

Mystery is translated as "secrets" in the Gospels, a usage that reflects its common definition: something that is known only to the initiated. Other New Testament passages associate it with wisdom, insight, or knowledge. We know God in various ways through our daily lives, yet often what we know about God transcends our rational understanding. The mystery of God does not baffle us as much as it awes us; with God we always stand on the edge of the unknown (Robinson 1990).

This prayer could be used for the celebration of Memorial Day, Eternity Sunday, or All Saints Day.

673
O God, author of eternal light

Sarum missal, 11th c.

This prayer is in collect (pronounced "caw'-lect") form, which has been used since the fifth century in the Western Church. It opens with an address to God ("O God"), expresses one of God's attributes ("author of eternal light"), petitions God for a particular need ("lead us in our worshiping this day"), then closes in Jesus' name.

What is a collect?

Although a collect prayer may include more than one attribute or act of God and additional petitions, the essential form distinguishes it from other prayer forms (e.g., litany, free prayer). In the more formal liturgical traditions, collects are used each Sunday to announce the congregation's purpose in gathering and the day's theme of God's saving acts. The body of collect prayers, composed over hundreds of years, represents a wealth of Christian experience, theology, and piety.

What is a missal?

Missals contain all the directions, prayers, and readings for Sunday worship. The organization and contents of the *Sarum missal* were influenced by early Christian sources of Britain, the Roman liturgy, and the liturgy of Rouen, France. It was named for the fortress of Old Sarum, England, which became the principal center of the dioceses of Salisbury in 1075. A new cathedral in the valley below the fortress was completed at the beginning of the fourteenth century and is considered one of the most beautiful buildings and surroundings in the world.

674
Dear God, our friend

The Hymnal Project, 1992
Hymnal: A Worship Book, 1992

This prayer is one of several resources included specifically for children to read. It also teaches that the nature of worship is communication: speaking and listening. The prayer is simple in form and language, yet its sentiments are also entirely appropriate for adults to express.

Other worship resources especially suitable for children are **667, 682, 714, 719, 748,** and **759.**

675
Come, Lord, work upon us

St. Augustine of Hippo (354-430), ca. 400
Confessions

Book 8, Chapter 4 of St. Augustine's *Confessions* is the source for this prayer. Following his dramatic conversion, Augustine became bishop of Hippo, North Africa, in 395. The source of this translation, Tony Castle's *The New Book of Christian Prayers* (1986), does not cite the original translator. Several English translations have phrases that are similar to this rendering, but none is a perfect match.

No resource in the worship book matches this one in its appeal to the senses; rarely do we pray to be so physically confronted and held by God's presence.

676
O God, you withdraw from our sight

Janet Morley (1951-)
All Desires Known, 1988

Morley wrote this prayer for Ascension Day, the fortieth day after Easter, when the church remembers Jesus' departure from earthly life. Jesus promised to send the Holy Spirit, the Advocate, when he had gone (John 16:7-11). Since Ascension Day always falls on Thursday, it is rarely celebrated by contemporary Brethren and Mennonite congregations. However, earlier generations of Brethren and Mennonites observed the day. The Amish continue to observe Ascension Day by closing schools, resting from work, and gathering for worship.

The title of Morley's book, *All Desires Known*, reflects her fundamental beliefs:

> I have chosen it because I understand the Christian life to be about the integration of desire: our personal desires, our political vision, and our longing for God. So far from being separate or in competition with one another, I believe that our deepest desires ultimately spring from the same source; and worship is the place where this can be acknowledged.

In this prayer Morley avoids focusing on the feminine attributes of God, instead using addresses and biblical images that startle worshipers with freshness and vitality.

678
Come, Child of Bethlehem

Rebecca J. Slough (1952-)
Edward Ziegler's *Prayers for Public Worship*, 1986, alt.

This resource was written to be used as a call to worship during Advent season in the mid-1980s at First Mennonite Church of San Francisco, California. The images of Jesus as a child, servant King, and brother were chosen to span the immanent and cosmic dimensions of the incarnation. In the original version, the third name of Christ was "Child of God." The Hymnal Project altered it to read "Brother of All."

679
Holy Spirit, Creating Presence

Jesus Christ—The Life of the World, World Council of Churches, 1983

This litany was written originally for worship at the Taizé community in France. Taizé is an ecumenical community of brothers that has set worship at the center of its life. Every year thousands of visitors from around the world visit the community to worship, study scripture, and share in its religious life.

See the article on "Alleluia" (**101**) for more information on Taizé. Article **691** provides information about the litany form.

As an alternative, the congregation could sing the ostinato "Veni Sancte Spiritus" (**298**) as the worship leader reads the petitions, instead of using the spoken response. If this alternative is used, the worship leader would do well to observe some moments of silence between the petitions.

683
Praise the One who hears the cry

Based on Psalm 146:7-9
Pat Kozak (1947-) and Janet Schaffran (1945-)
More Than Words, 1988, adapt.

While the themes of this reading echo Isaiah 61:1-2, they are not based on that passage. These themes are found in several places in scripture: Song of Hannah (1 Sam. 2:1-10); Psalm 146; Mary's Song (Magnificat in Luke 1:46-55); and, indirectly, in Isaiah 61:1-2 and Luke 4:18-19. This would be an appropriate reading for Advent.

688
Praise the Holy One

The Hymnal Project, 1992
Hymnal: A Worship Book, 1992

Several worship resources in this collection address God as One (see **670, 683, 780**). Deuteronomy 6:4 is the source for the allusion. "One" was preferred over *Yahweh* as a Hebrew scripture reference for God. *Yahweh,* the transliteration of the Hebrew consonants *YHWH,* was incorrectly translated as "Jehovah" in early English Bible translations. It is the word Jews never speak in naming God. When the word appears in a Hebrew text, Jewish readers substitute *Adonai* (meaning "familiar spirit"). Out of respect to the Jewish tradition and to honor the power of that holy name, many Christians working on worship texts have discontinued using the word *Yahweh.*

690
Have mercy on us, O God

Based on Psalm 51
Ruth Yoder (1949-), 1988

This two-part reading presents the complete action of confession and reconciliation. Confession without assurance of pardon creates a distorted sense of God's purpose and promise. (See article **705** for comments about words of assurance.)

This resource is one of three in *Hymnal: A Worship Book* that specify a period of silence (the others are **722** and **799**). In earlier Anabaptist and pietist history, public prayer was silent prayer, though Hans de Ries introduced written and spoken prayer into worship among Dutch Anabaptists in the late sixteenth century. Achieving and maintaining silence in worship has been difficult for many people in recent generations. In the fast pace of daily life, silence can be frightening, even threatening, as one is confronted with oneself. Silence can also signal the onset of boredom, the bane of life in the late twentieth century.

As the Friends have discovered, worship needs periods of silence so God can speak to the soul or so the Spirit can move in the congregation. Silence is a gesture of openness. Congregations that are now comfortable with silence usually began with periods of a minute or less, then gradually lengthened the time for dwelling wordlessly together in God's presence.

691
Almighty God, Spirit of purity and grace

Edward K. Ziegler (1903-1989)
Paul Bowman's *The Adventurous Future*, 1959, alt.

This litany of repentance was included in *The Adventurous Future*, a book of sermons, worship resources, and readings compiled in honor of the 250th anniversary of the Church of the Brethren. Ziegler composed this prayer as part of a larger celebration in Germantown (Philadelphia), Pennsylvania, on January 1, 1958.

What is a litany?

Contrary to much of the popular practice in Brethren and Mennonite worship, a litany is a responsive *prayer* addressed to God or to Jesus and made up of blessings, petitions, or intercessions. Frequently, so-called "litanies" are only responsive readings, not prayers in the truest sense.

The litany style of prayer has not been widely used in Brethren and Mennonite circles in recent generations. The repetition of the congregation's response often has been deemed "uninteresting," "not creative," or "too ritualistic." Nevertheless, the "monotony" of the response allows the petitions spoken by the leader to sink into the congregation's consciousness. Without having to worry about what the next response will be, worshipers are encouraged to listen. An example of this prayer style is Psalm 136, which clearly shaped early Christian use of the form.

The congregation could sing "Kyrie eleison" (**152**) in place of the response "Forgive us, O God."

When to use Amen

The *Amen* of this prayer is left to the congregation and illustrates the purpose of the word. *Amen* loosely means "so be it." It was added to prayers spoken by the priest, minister, or worship leader on behalf of the congregation. *Amen* is the congregation's assent to what has been publicly prayed. Nearly all the *Amens* found in the worship resource section are unnecessary because the congregation already has voiced its own prayer. The practice of speaking *Amen* at the end of every prayer, however, is so deeply ingrained that it would have been neither gracious nor sensitive for The Hymnal Project's worship committee to have omitted them without warning or proper teaching. Perhaps in the next worship book written *Amens* will be unnecessary.

693
Father, I have sinned against heaven

Based on Luke 15:18-19,21 and 18:13
Balthasar Hubmaier (1480-1528)
A Form of the Supper of Christ (1527)
Tr. John D. Rempel (1944-), 1991
Hymnal: A Worship Book, 1992

Hubmaier, an Anabaptist theologian and martyr, included this prayer in his book as part of the preparation for Communion. It is spoken by the "priest," but it is intended to be the prayer of confession for all who are participating in the supper.The first three lines are an allusion to the story of the prodigal son (Luke 15:21). The third line comes from the Roman Mass, but in an entirely different context. In the Mass, the priest speaks the prayer as he is receiving the bread (host). Hubmaier's usage in confession sounds a different note of grace.

In *A Form of the Supper of Christ,* Hubmaier ends the prayer with these words of assurance:

> May the almighty, eternal, and gracious God have mercy on all our sins and forgive us graciously, and when he has forgiven us, lead us into eternal life without blemish or impurity, through Jesus Christ our Lord and Savior. (Pipkin, Yoder 1989)

694
Forgiving God, you do not deal with us

Based on Psalm 103:10-12

In Psalm 103 God is described in the third person; in this prayer God is addressed directly in the second person. This change illustrates a way to adapt scriptures that use exclusively masculine imagery for God so that they can be made inclusive in prayer.

The prayer is neither a petition nor an intercession; it is a reminder that forgiveness is part of God's nature. The psalmists prayed this way frequently, reciting God's past actions of faithfulness to elicit faith that God will act that way again. The prayer is as much an affirmation of faith as a prayer for forgiveness.

695
Our lives are cluttered, Lord Jesus . . .

Marlene Kropf (1943-), 1990
Hymnal: A Worship Book, 1992

At the request of the worship committee of The Hymnal Project, this prayer of confession was written to address our tendency at the end of the twentieth century to crowd our lives too full—even with good things. Often inspired and convicted by the story of Jesus' visit to Mary and Martha at their home in Bethany (Luke 10:38-42), the author turned to this story to shape the concluding petition of the prayer.

697
O Prince of peace

Peace litany, 20th c.
Source unknown

An Argentine student at Associated Mennonite Biblical Seminaries, Elkhart, Indiana, obtained this litany at an international conference in the former Yugoslavia in 1990. The opening address and the closing, "Grant us peace," have been added to transform it from a reading to a prayer.

The repetitions of "from" and "by" in the leader's part soon dictate a rhythm that can create a sense of urgency in the first half of the prayer and a sense of calm in the second half. The form of the prayer and the repetitions allow worshipers to absorb more fully the troubling, even shocking, petitions.

698
Forgive me my sins, O Lord

Lancelot Andrewes (1555-1626)

Andrewes, an Anglican theologian and court preacher, is credited with this prayer of confession in Tony Castle's *The New Book of Christian Prayers* (1986). Other expanded versions of the prayer are also ascribed to John Wesley and to Thomas Wilson.

699
Lord, our God, great, eternal, wonderful

St. Basil of Caesarea (ca. 329-379), adapt.

This prayer of confession—adapted from an ancient source, The Liturgy of St. Basil of Caesarea—was taken from *Contemporary Prayers for Public Worship* (1967), edited by Caryl Micklem. This collection of original prayers for worship was written by a group of seven writers for Congregationalist churches in England. The goal of the collection was to use modern language and thought-forms in public worship.

The Liturgy of St. Basil is still in use in the Eastern Church today.

700
Lord Jesus, blind I am

Menno Simons (1496-1561)
"Meditation on the 25th Psalm," ca. 1537

Apparently, Psalm 25 was Simons' favorite. This prayer was part of his seventh meditation included in writings that resemble St. Augustine's *Confessions* in form and, to a certain degree, in content. Twenty-two meditations, one for each verse of the psalm, comprise the work.

702
Jesus, Lamb of God, have mercy on us

Agnus Dei
Tr. English Language Liturgical Consultation, 1988

The hymn "Jesus, Lamb of God, have mercy on us" (*Agnus Dei*) is based on John 1:29 and is an allusion to Isaiah 53:7. Scholars believe it is of Eastern origin because of the prevalent imagery of the Lamb in Eastern writings. By the seventh century, the hymn was sung in the Roman Catholic Communion liturgy at the point where the bread was broken by the priest. Originally, the first line was sung numerous times; around the ninth century, the limit was set on three repetitions. Sometime during the late tenth and early eleventh centuries the hymn was sung during the kiss of peace. That practice prompted the church ministers to change the last phrase to "give [or grant] us peace."

See article **660** for information on ELLC/ICET. See also **146** and **153** for sung versions of the *Agnus Dei.*

703
Gracious God, hear our confession

Harris J. Loewen (1953-)
Prayer Phrases, 1986, adapt.

Loewen was commissioned to write *Prayer Phrases* for the General Conference Mennonite Church delegate meetings in Saskatoon, Saskatchewan (1986). The composition requires two youth choirs, readers, and the congregation. Readings alternate with songs or hymns and elaborate each phrase of the Lord's Prayer. "Gracious God . . . " is an adaptation of Litany No. 6. Loewen's composition remains unpublished, but parts of the work have been performed in various settings.

This prayer alludes to Psalm 146, the Song of Hannah, and Mary's Song (Magnificat).

704
Seek God who may be found

Based on Isaiah 55:6-7
An Inclusive Language Lectionary, Year A, 1982

The lectionary source for this version of Isaiah 55:6-7 was a project sponsored by the National Council of Churches (NCC). The texts of the *Revised Standard Version* were used except where male-biased and other exclusive language were found. The readings follow those prescribed by the *Ecumenical Lectionary*, also known as the *COCU Lectionary*. See article **659** for more information on lectionaries.

705
Christ has set us free

Based on Galatians 5:1,13
The Hymnal Project, 1992
Hymnal: A Worship Book, 1992

Words of assurance were once called "absolution." They were pronounced by a priest at the end of a service of reconciliation. The practice is rooted in Matthew 16:19 and 18:18. In the first centuries of the church, reconciliation was a public event; slow, public services gave way to private ones.

Martin Bucer's liturgy in Strassburg (1539) and John Calvin's *Form of Church Prayers, Strassburg* (1545) were the first Reformation services of worship to pronounce the "words of comfort" or "absolution" following the general confession of worshipers. This practice has continued in the Reformed Church traditions and in those denominations influenced by the Reformed churches.

Anabaptists and pietists have been hesitant to include this "priestly" practice because some have feared that pronouncing absolution or words of assurance would place pastors and ministers in a place of authority that does not match our beliefs about leadership. But because the church is a "priesthood of believers," words of assurance may be spoken often. The words of this resource, based on Galatians 5:1, show an important understanding of how reconciliation in our traditions is practiced. The congregation and the worship leader/pastor proclaim their freedom and joy.

706
Because of God's great love for you

Marlene Kropf (1943-)
Church bulletin service of Mennonite Publishing House, 1988

This responsive reading of words of assurance was inspired by Ephesians 2:4-9 and was originally part of a Lenten series of prayers of confession and words of assurance based on the lectionary texts for Lent, 1988.

Because some Christians find it difficult to claim forgiveness for sin, it is important for worshipers both to hear God's words of forgiveness and to affirm them by speaking them aloud. This resource offers the congregation an opportunity to declare their acceptance of God's grace and their intention to live as forgiven people.

708
May God, who is almighty and merciful

From Mass of the Roman Rite

The Mass of the Roman Rite is the service of Communion (Eucharist) practiced by Roman Catholics around the world. While the word *Mass* properly refers exclusively to the service of the Eucharist, it is commonly understood as the entire service, including the opening rite, the liturgy of the Word, the Eucharist, and the closing rite. The structure of this complete service remains fixed, but prayers, songs, and scripture readings vary in each celebration. Four eucharistic prayers—which include a variety of musical settings for the Sanctus/Benedictus, Memorial Acclamation, and Amen—may be used in alternating patterns. The only fixed spoken elements of the Mass at present are the Nicene Creed, the Lord's Prayer, and the dismissal. Local adaptations of specific elements of the service abound, and numerous differences in cultural and social emphases may be found within any given region. One way for Free Church people to understand the current liturgical practice of the Roman Mass is to think of it as variations on a theme within a set structure of action.

The Roman Rite is one of seven enduring liturgical rites that evolved during the first four centuries of Christian history. Early eucharistic prayers in Rome were spoken in Greek; by the third century, the developing liturgy was in Latin. Many of the set features of the rite can be seen by the fifth century. It became the dominant rite of Roman Catholics in Europe by the ninth century. The basic pattern has undergone periods of great elaboration and extravagance—and periods of reform—to reestablish simplicity. In the early stages of the Mass's development, the congregation was actively involved in the worship action. During the medieval period, priests and the choir were the central participants. The reforms of Vatican II restored the congregation to "full and active participation" in the Roman Rite.

710
We affirm that the God of Abraham

Liturgy of baptism
Assembly Mennonite Church (Goshen, Ind.)
James Waltner's *Baptism and Church Membership*, 1979, adapt.

How do creeds and affirmations of faith differ?

Affirmations of faith are similar in purpose to confessions of faith and creeds. They express common points of belief or agreement among Christian believers. Affirmations often begin with the phrase "I believe" or "we believe" and frequently echo the vows a Christian makes at the time of baptism.

Creeds are those claims recognized by the universal church as being foundational for Christian life. Confessions of faith are usually drafted by denominations; they state beliefs and understandings of Christian faith that may not be shared by all Christians. Their purpose is to outline the "essential" elements of Christian belief as revealed in scripture and in the denomination's tradition. They help guide the church's interpretation and practice. Affirmations of faith in this worship book are not complete summaries of essential claims. They do, however, highlight important truths about the Christian tradition with an Anabaptist and pietist slant.

Brethren and Mennonites approach affirmations, confessions of faith, and creeds differently. Brethren claim the New Testament as their only creed; thus they have not drafted confessions of faith during their history. A believer's response to the three questions asked at the time of baptism constitutes a confession of faith. In 1969 the "Statement of Faith," containing positions on doctrinal matters, was adopted by the Church of the Brethren Annual Conference; in 1980 it was included in the constitution. Reading affirmations of faith in a worship setting is an accepted practice. However, many Brethren are uneasy about using creeds.

On the other hand, Mennonites have a long history of making confessions of faith to reflect their biblical beliefs and understandings, their tradition, and their current practice. The Schleitheim Confession (1527) and the Dordrecht Confession (1632) were two influential summaries of early Anabaptist faith and practice. While Anabaptist/Mennonite confessions of faith have been used rarely in worship due to their length, other creeds, confessions of faith, and affirmations have been used frequently.

711
Jesus taught us to speak of hope

South African creed, 20th c.

Third World Solidarity Day, Share Lent '87 (Canadian Catholic Organization for Development and Peace, 1987) cites this affirmation as a creed from South Africa. Whether this resource has been recognized officially as a creed by a church in South Africa is unknown.

The affirmation demonstrates the relationships between faith and power, worship and justice. It takes on added power when read in the context of the violent oppression in South Africa in the twentieth century.

712
I believe in God, the Father almighty

Affirmation of faith, 2nd c.
Tr. English Language Liturgical Consultation, 1988

This creed, commonly called the Apostles' Creed, is used only in the Western Church. Its development began in the second century, and it appeared in various forms until the late sixth or early seventh centuries. It is found in its present form in French liturgical sources.

The questions asked of baptismal candidates of the early church provided the basic framework of the creed. In current practice, the questions asked of candidates for baptism are still based on the Apostles' Creed, as are the questions asked of ordination candidates. This translation is from the English Language Liturgical Consulation (ELLC). For more information on ELLC/ICET, see article **660**.

713
We believe in Jesus Christ

Affirmation of faith, 20th c.
The Mennonite Hymnal, 1969, adapt.

This affirmation is an adaptation of the one created especially for *The Mennonite Hymnal* (1969). Its structure is different from most affirmations in that it begins with Jesus, then moves to statements about God, the Holy Spirit, and the church. Worthy of note is that statements about Jesus and the church are more numerous than statements about God and the Holy Spirit. The reading uses the literary technique of beginning every new thought with "who," which was a style commonly used by the

Anabaptists. This affirmation outlines the ethical imperative that being God's people entails, which is an uncommon feature in creeds, confessions of faith, and affirmations.

This resource was edited greatly from its original form. See article **765** for a description of the worship committee's principles for editing.

714
He was the Son of God

Kenneth I. Morse (1913-)
We Gather Together, 1979, adapt.

This affirmation by Morse, a former editor of the Church of the Brethren magazine, *Messenger*, has been adapted for use by children. Naming Jesus' human and divine qualities antiphonally helps create the rhythm and tension of this resource. The words of Jesus announce the ethical response that belief in Jesus calls forth.

715
My soul proclaims your greatness, O my God

Based on Luke 1:46-55
Mother Thunder Mission
A Daily Office, 1976

This Gospel canticle is often called Mary's Song or Magnificat (after the first word of the Latin text). Since the third century, it has been sung at evening prayer (Vespers) as a response to the scripture reading. The counterpart to Mary's Song is the Song of Zechariah (Luke 1:68-79), which is sung in response to the scripture reading at morning prayer (Lauds or Matins). (See **179** for a musical setting of the Song of Zechariah.) The imagery of the Song of Hannah (1 Sam. 2:1-10) and Psalm 146 is also echoed in the canticle. (See **181** in *Hymnal: A Worship Book* for a musical setting and **179** in the *Accompaniment Handbook* for a chant setting of Mary's Song.)

Mary's Song is appropriate for the Advent season. In Luke's Gospel, God is described in the third person, but in this resource God is addressed directly in the second person, solving the difficulties of exclusively masculine references to God. This shift technically changes the resource from an affirmation of faith into a prayer. It was assigned to this section because of its historical usage as a response of faith and willingness to serve.

See article **665** for a description of canticles.

717
I believe in God, the giver of grain

Alvin F. Brightbill (1903-1976)
"Affirmations of Faith" paper
We Gather Together, 1979, adapt.

Alvin Brightbill, church musician and professor at Bethany Theological Seminary, Oak Brook, Illinois, collected affirmations of faith from various sources and included them in a paper titled "Affirmations of Faith." He used the paper with seminarians preparing for worship leading. The editors of *We Gather Together* (1979) were uncertain whether Brightbill actually wrote the original form of this affirmation or whether this is the paraphrase of a poem he encountered in his research. The original has been edited to bring out more clearly the double meanings of various images. This affirmation is particularly appropriate for celebrations of Communion and love feast.

720
Listening God, you hear our prayers

The Hymnal Project, 1992
Hymnal: A Worship Book, 1992

See article **691** for a description of litany and use of *Amen*. "Let us pray" (**380**), with the alternate phrase "Lord, hear our prayer" could be used as the congregational response. The worship leader or music leader would sing the "leader" part of the musical response. "O Lord, hear my prayer" (**348**) is another alternative for a musical response.

721
Almighty God, from whom comes each good gift

The Hymnal of the United Church of Christ, 1974

The refrain "Lord of all, to thee we raise this our hymn of grateful praise" (**89**) could be used as the congregational response in this litany of thanksgiving. See article **691** for information on the litany form.

724
Lord God, in whom I find life

Rueben P. Job (1928-) and Norman Shawchuck (1935-)
A Guide to Prayer for Ministers and Other Servants, 1983

A Guide to Prayer . . . grew out of the daily prayer life of two ministers, Rueben Job and Norman Shawchuck, who shared the discipline of devotion, meditation, and prayer. In the book's preface they state:

> This book was prepared out of our own desperation and search: desperation to find forgiveness for sin, release from guilt, the living God as a companion in our lives and ministries; and a search for resources and disciplines to help keep our relationship with God alive and vital every day. This book, therefore, is not a treatise written by experts; rather, it is a collection of resources by two pilgrims.

This prayer is in collect form. See article **673** for a description of a collect.

725
God of guidance, quicken your Holy Spirit

William Barclay (1907-1978)
Prayers for the Christian Year, 1964, adapt.

This prayer for guidance makes use of the rhetorical device known as parallelism, a poetic technique often used in Hebrew poetry. The antithetical phrases "which way to choose and which to refuse; which course to claim and which to reject, which action to take and which to avoid" underscore the desires of those who pray to make good choices in difficult circumstances.

727
Merciful and loving Father, we ask you

Elizabethan prayer, 16th c.
Anonymous
Greene and Gollancz's *God of a Hundred Names*, 1962, adapt.

God of a Hundred Names indicates that this prayer for one's enemies comes from the Elizabethan era, although the original source of this prayer is not presently known. Tony Castle's *The New Book of Christian Prayers* (1986) calls it an "Old English Prayer." The prayer in *God of a Hundred Names* is much longer than the adaptation in this worship book.

728
Almighty God, you have given us grace

Attrib. to St. John Chrysostom, 4th c., adapt.

The 1637 *Scottish Prayer Book* and the 1662 *Prayer Book* of the Church of England cite John Chrysostom, the fourth-century bishop of Constantinople, as the writer of this prayer. It is claimed in *Commentary on the American Prayer Book* (1980) only that the prayer is found in medieval manuscripts of the Eastern liturgies of St. Chrysostom and St. Basil. Prayers from a later period, which were inserted into an earlier liturgical form, often have been attributed to the church's original leader or to the source of the liturgical form. The final phrase, "through Jesus Christ our Lord," is a modification of the text found in the *Book of Common Prayer* (1978); the last phrase in both *Book of Common Prayer* and *Hymnal: A Worship Book* is an addition to the original.

This collect is often used to "gather up" the petitions of various collects spoken during a period of prayer. Among Mennonites and Brethren, it could be used to close a period of free prayer.

729
Spirit of peace, quiet our hearts

Marlene Kropf (1943-), 1990
Hymnal: A Worship Book, 1992

One of only three prayers in the worship resources addressed to the Spirit (the other two are **679** and **762**), this prayer is a plea for quietness and calm in the midst of noise and confusion. It expresses sentiments similar to those in the hymn "Dear Lord and Father of mankind" (**523**). The prayer affirms that radical trust is the antidote to fear and anxiety.

730
Most gracious God, protect us from worry

Thomas à Kempis (ca. 1379-1471)
The Imitation of Christ, 15th c., alt.

Versions of this prayer in *Hymnal: A Worship Book* and the Church of the Brethren *Manual of Worship and Polity* (1955) have been heavily edited so that the spirit of the original is recognizable, but wording and form have been altered. Unlike the first-person plural in these books, the words in Book 3, Chapter 26, of *The Imitation of Christ* are in the first-person singular.

Thomas à Kempis was a fifteenth-century monk whose writings took a variety of forms: ascetical, homiletical, poetical, biographical, and devotional.

731
Our Father in heaven

The Lord's Prayer
Tr. English Language Liturgical Consultation, 1988

This prayer, common to the experience of so many Christians, is an excellent choice for diverse gatherings. But when the group comes to the phrases "Forgive us our . . . " and "as we forgive those who . . . ," there likely will be so many combinations of "debts," "trespasses," and "sins" and "those who sin against us" that an observer might think the gift of tongues had been manifested. This ELLC version of the prayer was included for those occasions when the prayer is used in ecumenical gatherings or when the worship leader believes that differences in practice exist.

For musical settings of the Lord's Prayer, see **228, 351,** and **554**.

733
Lord, make me an instrument

Attrib. to St. Francis of Assisi, 13th c.

The custom of attributing this prayer to St. Francis of Assisi prevails. It appears in none of Francis's works, however, and has not been found in texts earlier than the twentieth century. The original source for this prayer and its author are unknown (Hatchett 1981).

735
Transforming God, you come to us

Rebecca J. Slough (1952-)
Mennonite Publishing House bulletin series, 1986, adapt.

This prayer is a partial version of a longer prayer written for a church bulletin series. It was inspired by Genesis 32:22-30, the story of Jacob wrestling with a stranger during the night while he camped at Peniel. The prayer is written in the form of a collect (see article **673**).

737
Almighty God, in whom we live and move

St. Augustine of Hippo (354-430)
Confessions, ca. 400

The first half of this prayer was taken from St. Augustine's *Confessions,* Book 1, Chapter 1, which is based on Acts 17:28 and is a quotation from a Greek poet. The second half of the prayer is likely not from St.

Augustine, but is a more recent addition. This section may have a history in liturgical practice, possibly having been added at some point in the monastic prayer tradition.

738
God be in my head

Sarum primer, ca. 11th c.

The literalness of this prayer is shocking; we are not accustomed to asking God to permeate us so completely. It shows influences of Celtic and pre-Saxon spiritualities that express concretely the experience of God's presence in bodily and spatial terms. "Christ be with me" (**442**) is another prayer showing similar Celtic influence.

This *Sarum primer* (not the *Sarum missal*) was one of numerous primers available from the eleventh to the eighteenth centuries in England. They contained parts of the liturgy and various scripture translations in the vernacular and were used by lay people for study and devotion. The specific source for this prayer is unknown.

See article **673** for information about Sarum.

739
Almighty God, to you all hearts are open

Leonine missal, 7th c.

The *Leonine missal* is one of earliest repositories of the Roman Catholic rite and originates in Rome. Notes in the *Sarum missal,* a later missal that came out of the British Isles, prescribed for the priest to speak the prayer privately after the choir sang the *Veni Creator Spiritus* ("Come, Creator Spirit").

This prayer opens the *Cloud of Unknowing,* a fourteenth-century manuscript on the spiritual life, which was composed by an anonymous monk. Thomas Cranmer assigned the prayer to the opening of the Communion service in the 1549 *Prayer Book,* and it has remained in constant use in the Anglican and Episcopal traditions since the sixteenth century.

The third line of the prayer alludes to the name of Janet Morley's collection of resources from which a number of prayers were taken for this worship book.

Using this piece in combination with **27** or **291** could approximate a contemporary compliance with the *Sarum missal* instructions.

See article **673** for information on Sarum and Salisbury.

741
Almighty God, to those chosen to see

The Hymnal Project, 1992
Hymnal: A Worship Book, 1992

This reading tells of Jesus' transfiguration, when the disciples saw him meeting with Moses and Elijah. From the cloud that overtook them, God's voice announced Jesus as the Son. Peter, James, and John were no longer in doubt about Jesus' identity and purpose. Traditionally, the church remembers God's announcement on the last Sunday before Lent so that it can hear the authority of Jesus' teaching in the lectionary readings leading up to the Passion.

Since the fifteenth century, August 6 has been commemorated as the Feast of the Transfiguration in some Christian traditions. This celebration coincides with the international memorial of the bombing of Hiroshima, resulting in interesting interpretations of the cloud(s) of darkness.

743
Merciful and everlasting God, you have not spared

Saxon Order of Duke Henry, 1539

In *Prayers of the Reformers* (1958), Clyde Manschreck cites the Saxon Order of Duke Henry (1539) as the source for this prayer. As part of the German Lutheran Reformation, schools and churches drafted orders of organization that included worship and business practices. In the area of Saxony, Duke Henry, Justus Jonas, and George Spalatin (the latter two on the faculty at Wittenberg University) wrote the church orders. The document was formally accepted by the political and religious authorities in 1540. This order influenced Thomas Cranmer and other reformers in England. "Merciful and everlasting God . . ." is the prayer for Good Friday (Reed 1947).

What is Good Friday?

Good Friday has been observed by the Christian church from a very early date. Due to the mournful character of the day, fasting became an essential part of the observance. Records show that by the second century Christians fasted for forty hours before the Easter vigil celebration. According to Adolf Adam,the words of Jesus about the coming time when the disciples would fast because the bridegroom was taken from them (Matt. 9:15; Mark 2:20; Luke 5:34-35) were applied to the days of his death and repose in the tomb (Adam 1981).

By the fourth century, Good Friday services were organized in Jerusalem at Golgotha where the Passion story was read. The commemoration of Holy Week in fourth-century

Jerusalem became the pattern for Holy Week celebrations throughout the Western Church and into the present.

747
God of resurrection and life

Robert H. Midgley (1921-)
Ruth Duck's *Flames of the Spirit*, 1985, alt.

The Christian theology of Sunday as the day of resurrection permits us to use this prayer throughout the entire season of Easter (the forty-nine days following Easter Sunday).

See article **668** for information about the relationship between Sunday and Easter and article **659** for information about *Flames of the Spirit.*

749
O God, our offerings proclaim

Anne Neufeld Rupp (1932-)
Prayers for Corporate Worship, 1981

Rupp's *Prayers . . .* was part of a series on topics related to worship, published jointly by Mennonite Publishing House, Scottdale, Pennsylvania, and Faith and Life Press, Newton, Kansas. While Brethren and Mennonites have placed much value on service as a form of worship, this piece is an urgent reminder that work and worship are different types of activities, yet part of our complete response to God.

The act of offering is probably one of the most underrated practices in worship. When the concept of offering is as narrow as the collection of money for church expenses, we fail to see that offering and service spring from the same desire to minister to people. This prayer, along with **750** and **751**, expands our awareness of how offering extends God's love and grace beyond ourselves and into the world.

755
Speak to all the world of the Child

John D. Rempel (1944-)
Hymnal: A Worship Book, 1992

Rempel arranged this reading in a way that moves from exhortation to prayer, to praise, to commitment. He intended for worshipers to catch a broader vision of the church's evangelistic mission and, at the same time, to realize that it is the Spirit working in us that leads us to witness for Christ. The scriptural allusions in the reading are Isaiah 6:8; John 14:25; Philippians 2:6-7; and Acts 10:37-42.

This reading could be used during the Christmas season, but it is most fitting for Pentecost Sunday.

756
O God, for too long the world

Linea Reimer Geiser (1936-), 1988

During the weeks of the 1991 Persian Gulf War, Geiser's poem was used in a classroom at Associated Mennonite Biblical Seminaries, Elkhart, Indiana, with the original ending line of ". . . into blossoms of shalom." Though the Hebrew *shalom*—meaning peace, health, harmony, and success—has become a well-known and loved concept even beyond Jewish circles, it was pointed out that the word had become offensive to some Arab Christians, who connect Israelis with war rather than shalom. Even though the line was aesthetically pleasing, Geiser agreed to change it as a gesture of reconciliation. The new ending became " . . . into blossoms of hope."

757
Savior God, through your grace we hold

Marlene Kropf (1943-), 1990
Hymnal: A Worship Book, 1992

This prayer for the church's ministries of witness and evangelism was written at the request of the worship committee of The Hymnal Project. Inspired by 2 Corinthians 4:6-7, the prayer alludes to the mystery of God entrusting the treasure of Christ's glory to the church, a fragile and earthen vessel. It is both a humble recognition of God's grace and a confident statement of our intention to join with God's redeeming, liberating work in the world.

762
Come, Holy Spirit. Come as Holy Fire

Ancient prayer
Source unknown
Adapt. by Charles Francis Whiston (1900-1992), *Prayer Companion,* 1959
Last paragraph revised by The Hymnal Project

The first seven lines of this prayer are from an ancient, but unknown source. *The Mennonite Hymnal* (1969) credits these lines and two additional paragraphs to Charles F. Whiston and *Prayer Companion* (1959). *The New Book of Christian Prayers* (1986) cites the seven lines as an ancient prayer adapted by Whiston; the original source is not given. The last

"All" section was added by the worship committee of *Hymnal: A Worship Book.*

765
Gentle God, you have come near to us

The Hymnal Project, 1992
Hymnal: A Worship Book, 1992

This piece appears in *The Mennonite Hymnal* (1969) and is based on a prayer from a collection by Caryl Micklem titled *Contemporary Prayers for Public Worship* (1967). Even though most of the prayers in that collection were intended for a minister or worship leader to read, a number of them were included in this worship book.

This prayer was reworked so thoroughly that it became a new piece. A comparison of the two prayers reveals much about the editing principles that guided the worship committee:

- Use simple language, at points bordering on sparseness.
- Use concise units of thought.
- Use bold and assertive verbs.
- Focus on congregational use and accessibility.
- Structure prayers and readings so congregations can read easily in unison.

766
Now may the Lord Jesus bless your soul

Alexander Mack, Sr. (ca. 1679-1735)
Rights and Ordinances, 1713
Tr. in *European Origins of the Brethren*, 1958, alt.

In 1713 Alexander Mack, Sr., wrote *Rights and Ordinances: A brief and simple exposition of the outward but yet sacred rights and ordinances of the house of God as the true householder commanded and bequeathed in writing in his testament; Presented in a conversation between father and son in question and answer.* This "testimony" presents Mack's responses on forty topics submitted in the form of questions by friends and believers (baptism, Lord's Supper, separation, the ban, scriptures, love and faith, worship, rewards and punishments). The document concludes with the benediction "Now may the Lord Jesus bless your soul . . . " and a hymn.

The original translation reads: "Let this simple instruction grow within you"; the worship book adaptation reads: "Let this hour of worship grow within you."

770
The blessing of the God of Sarah

Lois M. Wilson (1927-)
Jesus Christ—The Life of the World: A Worship Book, 1983

The source for this benediction was compiled for the 1983 World Council of Churches (WCC) meeting in Vancouver, British Columbia. Hymns, resources, and liturgies from around the world were included. Several years after the conference, the WCC published the music in one collection and the worship resources in a second collection, both using the original title. These books have been superseded by the collection used at Canberra, Australia, *In Spirit and in Truth* (1991).

The names of Sarah and Mary and reference to feminine nurturing qualities in this benediction offer biblical models for how inclusive language may be used in worship.

771
Master, now you are dismissing your servant

Luke 2:29-32

This canticle is known as Song of Simeon or *Nunc Dimittis* (the first two words of the Latin text). Fourth-century documents called the *Apostolic Constitutions*, which outline various practices in the Syrian Church, indicate the canticle was sung as an evening hymn. In the Western Church, it is used most frequently at Compline (community night prayer before bed), though it also has been used at Vespers.

Brethren and Mennonites will find the resource useful in a retreat setting, which represents one of the few times groups are gathered late at night. The other appropriate use is during Christmas.

See article **665** for information about canticles. A chant form of the Song of Simeon is "Lord, bid your servant," **179** in the *Accompaniment Handbook*.

772
May God bless and keep you

Numbers 6:24-26
Adapt. by The Hymnal Project, 1992
Hymnal: A Worship Book, 1992

This passage from Numbers is also known as the Aaronic or threefold blessing. It is associated with worship in the first Jewish temple where it followed the daily sacrifices. Those gathered for the ritual were blessed with outstretched hands, a variation on the gesture of laying on hands. During the period of the second temple, it was also used in the synagogues. In Jewish daily prayer, it is the last benediction of the *Amidah*, or prayer of eighteen benedictions (Posner, Kaploun, Cohen 1975). The sixteenth-century reformers placed the blessing after the Communion.

One way of using this blessing is for one part of the congregation to face the other part: the worship leader then speaks the entire blessing to the whole congregation; the first group speaks the entire blessing to the other; the second group speaks the entire blessing to the first group. Many variations are possible.

What is a blessing?

A blessing is a "declaration of divine favor" or "a formula for sanctification" (*The Westminster Dictionary of Worship*). Since a blessing often has been performed by priests or appointed ministers, some Mennonite and Brethren congregations are reluctant to use blessings. They fear that this priestly function is not consistent with denominational understandings of ministry and leadership. As a priesthood of believers, however, every member should be able to exercise this role. Any person serving a leadership function, regardless of whether he or she is ordained, is free to bless others, and congregational members also are free to bless each other.

775
We declare anew our covenant

Covenants: From liturgy of baptism, Assembly Mennonite Church (Goshen, Ind.)
James H. Waltner's *Baptism and Church Membership*, 1979, adapt.
Congregational prayer: John D. Rempel (1944-), 1991
Hymnal: A Worship Book, 1992

The form of this "order" for baptism demonstrates a principle that is fundamental to Brethren and Mennonites: New believers are baptized into new life in Christ and into Christ's body. The congregation's covenant echoes the promises that members took at their own baptism; new believers then make their own promises publicly for the first time. The church speaks as a body ready to receive its new members; the new believers pledge themselves to a common path of discipleship.

The congregational prayer by John Rempel is based on writings from a collection by Reinhard Rahusen, an eighteenth-century German Mennonite pastor. The outer washing of water complemented by the inner washing of the Spirit is a strong Anabaptist theme. The prayer demonstrates the complete baptismal action: washing with water and confirmation of the Spirit.

The covenants of this resource are intended to be made before the water rite; placement of the prayer, however, should be determined by the worship leader or pastor. It might be spoken after the covenants and before the water rite, as suggested by the page layout in the hymnal. Or it might be spoken by the entire group of candidates after the water baptisms are completed. Placing the prayer after the water rite makes the action of confirmation clearer.

> ***How do baptism and confirmation differ?***
>
> Well before the sixteenth century the water rite of baptism, which could be done by the priest, and the rite of confirmation, which could be done only by the bishop, were separated due to political, cultural, and church-polity quirks, as well as the rise of infant baptism in Europe. In the believers church traditions, the prayer of confirmation following the water administration of baptism has always been part and parcel of the baptismal ceremony. Among Anabaptists and pietists, the confirmation prayer is not understood as giving new believers the Holy Spirit; the Spirit has already begun working in them. The confirmation prayer asks God to keep the Spirit's work alive as believers grow deeper in faith.

776
God our deliverer, we remember

F. Russell Mitman (1940-)
Worship Vessels: Resources for Renewal, 1987, adapt.

This prayer and response recite what the church has come to understand about the act of baptism. The images and metaphors of salvation, particularly that of water, appear repeatedly in scripture and in the church's practice. The liberation/Passover theme of Exodus announces our freedom. Jesus' baptism and death opened the way for our new life. By water and the Spirit, we are brought into God's life-giving covenant, which is filled with grace and responsibility. Through these acts we are made into God's people. Baptism is a personal event for every new believer, but it is also a shared event with communal memory. Its meaning goes beyond an individual's personal experience.

777
As we now receive you

Based on Anabaptist baptismal vows, 16th c.
The Mennonite Hymnal, 1969, adapt.

This covenant spells out clearly what discipleship involves for members of the body. It could be used with **775** in place of the congregation's covenant, though the symmetry with the candidate's covenant would be lost.

In *The Mennonite Hymnal* (1969), this resource is for baptism. The reading was patterned after baptismal vows taken in an Anabaptist congregation in or near Strasbourg, France, around 1557.

778
Through baptism we are united

Anonymous
Book of Worship of the United Church of Christ, 1986, adapt.

The leader's part of this resource forms a succinct teaching on the nature of baptism and confirmation. The statement "Baptism is the visible sign of an invisible event" reflects St. Augustine's teaching on the nature of divine signs in *De Catechizandis Rudibus*, Chapter 26, Section 50.

Baptism, like other actions, has tangible aspects such as gestures, water, declarations, presiding minister, and a congregation. But there are also invisible aspects that give the declarations, water, and gestures special character. God works through the visible and invisible aspects of baptism to complete the work of forgiveness and regeneration.

779
O God, you brooded over the water

John D. Rempel (1944-), 1991
Hymnal: A Worship Book, 1992

John Rempel took images used in Pilgram Marpeck's *Confession of 1542* and constructed this baptismal prayer for the candidates. The image of God brooding over the water is common to most Christian rites of baptism.

780
All-powerful God, grant __________ the fullness

John D. Rempel (1944-), 1991
Hymnal: A Worship Book, 1992

> ***What does the laying on of hands mean?***
>
> Laying on of hands is a common practice found in the Hebrew scriptures and the New Testament. The gesture is typically an action of blessing, consecrating, commissioning, granting absolution, anointing, confirming, and ordaining. Laying on of hands may signify a transfer of spiritual power, but it also may mean that both minister and believer(s) share in a common spiritual power. Frequently, laying on of hands

is accompanied by an anointing of oil, a traditional symbol of the Holy Spirit's gifts. Raising hands while speaking benedictions is a larger form of this gesture.

Laying on of hands is a powerful form of touching that communicates power and grace. Local customs and circumstances will guide the appropriate use of this prayer and blessing, but options include:

- the congregation speaking the prayer as the presiding minister lays on hands,
- a few members of the congregation laying on hands while the prayer is read,
- all people present laying on hands while the prayer is read.

781
How can we discern our errors, O God?

Johann (John) Wichert (1897-1983), Wichert's prayer book
Tr. and adapt. by John D. Rempel (1944-), 1991
Hymnal: A Worship Book, 1992

Both Mennonites and Brethren have had traditions of Communion preparation: visits from the bishops or deacons; a preparation sermon given the previous Sunday; a period of self-examination, confession, and/or reconciliation. The purpose was to be in a spiritual state worthy of receiving the bread and cup, both individually and collectively.

Confession before receiving Communion has been ingrained in Christian tradition since Paul's admonition to the Corinthians (1 Cor. 11:27-29). During the Reformation Ulrich Zwingli and John Calvin emphasized the importance of "worthy participation," particularly since many believers were receiving the bread and cup more often than they had in earlier generations.

The first paragraph of this resource provides a period for confession. Though not indicated, a time of silence could be observed between the two paragraphs. The second paragraph anticipates the gifts and responsibilities of Communion.

Johann (John) Wichert, a minister in Ontario, recorded this prayer, which circulated in oral tradition in his region. This resource is likely based on a prayer by Wichert's mentor, Jacob Janzen. John Rempel received the prayer from Wichert.

782
O Eternal Wisdom, O Vulnerable God

Janet Morley (1951-)
All Desires Known, 1988

Each of the three sections of this reading has a different "voice" or mood.

The first "Leader/People/All" section praises God, who became vulnerable by becoming human. The second "Leader/People" part declares the story of how and why Jesus washed the disciples' feet. The last "All" section prays for the Spirit's presence to make the act of footwashing an expression of love and liberation.

Since this reading is long and changes "voices," care should be taken to read at a pace that allows worshipers to absorb the meaning of each section. "Jesus took a towel" (**449**) could be used in place of the second section.

What is footwashing?

Brethren have practiced footwashing since the founding of their church. They understand the rite to be a covenantal act resulting from a desire to follow the New Testament in obedience to the command and example of the Lord ("Feetwashing," *The Brethren Encyclopedia* 1983).

Footwashing is part of love feast, which Alexander Mack outlined in *Rechte und Ordnungen* (1715). It included a fellowship meal, washing of feet, breaking bread, drinking the cup, proclaiming the death and suffering of Jesus, praise and adoration, and exhortation to moral Christian life. Usually after washing feet, members offer each other a holy kiss.

Most Mennonite Church congregations have practiced footwashing in various forms over the years. General Conference Mennonites, however, generally have not observed the practice.

785
Blessed are you, O God. You made bread

Reinhard Rahusen (1735-1793)
Prediten und Reden (18th c.)
Tr. John D. Rempel (1944-)
Hymnal: A Worship Book, 1992

Reinhard Rahusen, a German Mennonite pastor, wrote and compiled several volumes of prayers, orders of service, and sermons in the eighteenth century, titled *Prediten und Reden*. This prayer, composed of two parts, is in one of his collections.

Most Brethren and Mennonites celebrate Communion by speaking Jesus' words of institution for the bread, offering prayer for the bread, then distributing it. The same pattern is used for the cup. These prayers by Rahusen could be spoken by the congregation after the words of institution in each case.

The first phrases of each prayer echo the prayers for opening and closing of Jewish meals. The first prayer (*berakah*) was a blessing for the bread: "Blessed are you, O Lord our God, ruler of the universe who brings forth bread from the earth." The second prayer is over the wine: "Blessed are you, O Lord our God, ruler of the universe, creator of the fruit of the vine."

Thanksgiving, fellowship, forgiveness, memorial, Jesus' sacrifice, and the feast of the Lamb are themes associated with Communion (or the Lord's Supper) in the New Testament. These themes resound throughout this worship book, and Rahusen's prayers consolidate a majority of these important convictions.

787
Almighty, merciful, and loving Father

Leenaerdt Clock, ca. 1600
Tr. and adapt. by John D. Rempel (1944-), 1991
Hymnal: A Worship Book, 1992

This Communion prayer was widely used by European Mennonites from 1625 to 1925. Leenaerdt Clock, a second-generation Dutch Anabaptist, included it as one of three prayers in *Forma eenigher christelijker ghebeden* (Christian Formulary). This book was circulated in Swiss and Russian Mennonite circles. It became the first part of *Ernsthafte Christenpflict*, a devotional and prayer book still used among the Amish.

The themes of both memorial and fellowship are eminently evident in this prayer.

788
Blessed are you, God of heaven and earth

Author unknown
From *Lutheran Book of Worship*, 1978

This Comunion prayer is one section of a longer eucharistic prayer; Eucharist means "thanksgiving." Eucharistic prayers have been part of Communion liturgies since the third century. They generally have these parts: opening prayer, thanksgiving for what God has done, *Sanctus* (Holy, holy, holy), words of institution and acclamation, prayer for the Holy Spirit's *epiclesis* (presence), petitions for the church, and the final doxology.

The prominent themes of this prayer are thanksgiving and fellowship.

791
You have offered your child

John H. Mosemann (1907-1989)
The Mennonite Hymnal, 1969, adapt.

This congregational response does not so much bless the child as it commits the congregation to the responsibilities of Christian nurture.

792
Maker of galaxies and planets

John D. Rempel (1944-), 1991
Hymnal: A Worship Book, 1992

Rempel borrowed images and themes found in several of Pilgram Marpeck's writings, particularly his *Confession of 1542*, for this child blessing.

Marpeck and Balthasar Hubmaier wrote in opposition to the practice of infant baptism. They based their arguments on the New Testament accounts of Jesus blessing the children (Matt. 19:13; Mark 10:13; and Luke 18:15). Hubmaier, a former parish priest who had performed many baptisms, developed a service of child dedication that paralleled the structure of the Roman Catholic rite. In a letter to Johannes Oecolampadius (1525), a Zwinglian reformer, Hubmaier outlined his service:

> I like to assemble the congregation in the place of baptism [likely, the baptistry], bringing in the child. I exposit in the native tongue the gospel text: "Children were brought . . . " (Matt. 19:13). As soon as his name has been given to him, the whole congregation on bended knee prays for the child, entrusting him to the hands of Christ, that he may be ever closer to the child and pray on his behalf. (Pipkin, Yoder 1989)

In those cases where a child was ill and the parents were afraid for its safety, Hubmaier would baptize the child.

Marpeck writes:

> The infants shall be named before a congregation and God shall duly be praised for them; thanks and blessing shall be given to his fatherly goodness that, through Christ Jesus our Lord and Savior, he has also had mercy on innocent creatures. . . . We admonish the parents to cleanse their conscience, as much as lies in them, with respect to the child, to do whatever is needed to raise the child up to the praise and glory of God, and to commit the child to God until it

is clearly seen that God is working in him for faith or unfaith. (Klassen, Klassen 1978)

These passages show four dimensions of child dedication among the early Anabaptists: naming the child, consecrating the child, praising God, and parents confessing and committing themselves to nurture the child.

Child dedication, child consecration, and child blessing are names used among Brethren and Mennonites for the congregational acknowledgment of a child's birth and presence in the community. Pastorally, the most common practice includes a child blessing and parental and congregational dedications. This worship book uses child blessing over other terms, primarily because it is more in keeping with the New Testament accounts.

793
We commit ourselves to follow Jesus Christ

Mennonite Church of the Servant (Wichita, Kan.), 1977

This covenant, written by members of Church of the Servant, could be used as part of a baptismal service or as a replacement for the congregational covenant of **775**.

What is a covenant?

Covenants create bonds of faith and trust. God's covenant with Abraham is the earliest example in the Judeo-Christian tradition of this type of relationship. Some commentators on the Psalms believe that Israel participated yearly in a service of covenant renewal between God and the people.

Early Christians celebrated the new relationship between God and humanity by sharing the cup of the new covenant in Communion.

Balthasar Hubmaier was one of the first anabaptist reformers to include a "pledge of love" in *A Form of the Supper of Christ* (1527). In this pledge the congregation commits itself to love God; to love and serve the neighbor; to practice fraternal admonition, reconciliation, and love toward other believers and neighbors; and to exclude people from fellowship only according to the rule of Christ (Matt. 18). The pledge was confirmed by sharing in the Lord's Supper. This covenant emphasizes relationships within the community, as well as the community's relationship with God.

Many congregations use covenants for documenting membership, often renewing covenants on a regular basis. Presently, covenants are made most frequently by congregational members with each other for mutual support and accountability and are not made as frequently between members of the congregation and God. Except in unusual circumstances (that involve renouncing the faith), those commitments have been sealed at baptism and, because of Christian assurance, need not be called into question at every turn.

794
These persons now presented to you

John H. Mosemann (1907-1989)
The Mennonite Hymnal, 1969, adapt.

The original first paragraph, in which the congregation renews its covenant with Christ, is eliminated in this worship book. And "We pledge our willingness to give and receive counsel . . . " originally read "We commit ourselves to watch over you and one another with a heart of concern and caring."

The response in this worship book could be used in baptismal services. In the Brethren service the congregation could give this response after the candidates have made their vows and before the water rite and confirmation. In the Mennonite service the congregation could give the response following the right hand of fellowship.

795
In company with your faithful people

The Hymnal Project, 1992
Hymnal: A Worship Book, 1992
Last three lines by Gail Anderson Ricciuti (1948-)
"Litany of Praise and Hope," Gjerding and Kinnamon's *Women's Prayer Services*, 1983, adapt.

Based on such scriptures as Jesus' story of the sheep and the goats (Matt. 25:31-46), service in Christ's name is a long tradition in Mennonite and Brethren churches. Although not always fully practiced, the priesthood of believers—the concept that each person in the church has gifts to be used in ministry to others—has been a cardinal principle in our churches since their beginnings in the Radical Reformation (e.g., see 1 Cor. 12). It is through commissioning services that we offer a sign of our support to those who minister to others.

Serving with joy probably has not been a strong emphasis in many of our churches. On the contrary, how often do we serve out of a dreary sense of duty? Yet a forced, superficial cheerfulness surely is not indicated. The Psalms express both joy and despair, the joy flowing from the psalmist's remembrances of God's benevolence to him. Motivated by God's love for us ("we love because [God] first loved us," 1 John 4:19) and empowered by God's Spirit (one of those fruits is joy, Gal. 5:22), we will be able to love our neighbors as ourselves (Matt. 19:19) and serve them gladly.

Note the birthing imagery in the last three lines of the prayer, suggesting that gifts of ministry are not always obvious, but they can be developed and may require the midwifery of the church.

796
As God's Spirit calls and the church commissions

John H. Mosemann (1907-1989)
The Mennonite Hymnal, 1969, adapt.

These resources are appropriate for commissioning workers to a variety of tasks. Even though **795** is intended for church workers (deacons, elders, teachers, committee members, church leaders), it is also suitable for commissioning ministries performed outside the congregation. Together with the laying on of hands, the statement signifies a sharing in ministry, congregational support, and spiritual empowerment.

The congregation commissions its members for specific tasks of ministry that last for a limited period of time. The congregation and its regional denominational body ordain men and women who have a vocation of ministry. While the language of these two rites is similar, there are significant differences in the types of commitment, accountability, and vocation that each entails.

See article **780** for more information on the laying on of hands.

797
As _________'s and __________'s community(ies) of faith

Nadine Pence Frantz (1953-)
Hymnal: A Worship Book, 1992, adapt.

Christian weddings usually have focused on the needs and desires of the couple getting married; the community of witnesses is rarely acknowledged in the ceremony. This response commits family and friends to remain faithful in their relationships with the couple. By speaking this covenant, the congregation and the couple acknowledge that marriage requires the support and persistent love provided by a network of relationships.

This response could substitute for comparable portions of the wedding services outlined in pastors/ministers manuals.

798
God of all life, in you we live

Author unknown
Esther and Bruggink's *Worship the Lord*, 1987, adapt.

In *Worship the Lord*, a book of liturgical services for the Reformed Church in America, this wedding blessing is spoken by the minister; the congregation affirms with "Amen." The use of the prayer as a congregational piece presumes that all present are carrying out their priestly functions and responsibilities as members of Christ's body. The blessing could be said after the vows and pronouncement of marriage as a closing prayer before the recessional or at the conclusion of the service.

The congregation acknowledges the joys and difficulties that wedded life involves; yet it calls forth God's grace, love, mercy, peace, and presence to sustain the couple in their unfolding life together.

799
O God, we come to you at this moment

Pastor's Manual, 1978, adapt.
Revised by The Hymnal Project, 1992

What does anointing mean?

Anointings of kings, priests, and sacred objects are recorded in the Hebrew scriptures. The title of Anointed One, given to the Messiah, reveals the political and spiritual significance of the rite prior to New Testament times. Mark 6:13 and James 5:14 broaden the meaning of the practice to include healing. Anointing has been practiced at baptisms, ordinations, commissionings, and healings throughout Christian history. All of these rites rely on the power of the Spirit to accomplish God's purpose. Thus, anointing for healing is connected with baptism, ordination, and commissioning in ways that are often unrecognized.

Although this prayer appears in the Mennonite *Minister's Manual* (1983) as well as the Brethren *Pastor's Manual* (1978), the Church of the Brethren has a longer and more frequent practice of anointing than Mennonites—at least as part of public worship services. Mennonites generally practice anointing in homes or hospital rooms. Anointing is considered one of the ordinances. The basic pattern among Brethren was established at the 1827 Annual Meeting: A few verses are sung; the congregation unites in prayer; one minister receives oil from another minister and places the hand on the head of the sick person saying, "You are anointed in the name of the

Lord"; two more times the minister receives oil and anoints the head but does not speak the words. Both ministers then lay hands on the person and pray ("Anointing," A *The Brethren Encyclopedia* 1983).

As the above suggests, this prayer of anointing should be part of a complete service of worship. Congregational hymns like "Healer of our every ill" (**377**) or "At evening, when the sun had set" (**628**) are appropriate. During the designated leader's part, members of the congregation or the leader might lay hands on the person requesting anointing. Using olive oil or scented balm and laying on of hands are tangible substances and gestures associated with the presence of the Spirit.

800
We accept your confession of failure

John H. Mosemann (1907-1989)
The Mennonite Hymnal, 1969, adapt.

Public confessions often became traumatic and spiritually damaging events. Rather than achieving reconciliation, they frequently drove away members who had sinned or failed spiritually. The tone of this response is free of self-righteousness and pride. The congregation acknowledges its failure to provide support and counsel, but it also speaks the word of forgiveness and assurance.

Both the Brethren *For All Who Minister* (1993) and the Mennonite *Minister's Manual* (1983) provide services of reconciliation. Both allow the congregation also to acknowledge its failure, making this an appropriate response in those services.

See article **705** for information about words of assurance.

801
Everlasting God, you are our refuge

Anonymous
Micklem's *Contemporary Prayers for Public Worship*, 1967, adapt.

This prayer of comfort, from Caryl Micklem's collection, was edited by Heinz and Dorothea Janzen for inclusion in the 1983 Mennonite *Minister's Manual*. The Janzens altered the original address of the prayer, "God, our Father," to "O God." The Hymnal Project changed the address to "Everlasting God" in order to emphasize the trustworthy, reliable character of the One on whom Christians depend in times of sorrow.

Another change in the prayer reflects current psychological wisdom about the necessity of walking through grief rather than avoiding it. The last sentence of the prayer originally began: "May the Holy Spirit lift us above our natural sorrow." In The Hymnal Project version, the line reads: "May your Holy Spirit carry us through our sorrow."

802
Eternal Light, shine into our hearts

Based on a prayer by Alcuin (732-804), 8th c.

Like the hymn "Eternal Light, shine in my heart" (**518**), this text is based on a prayer by Alcuin, a medieval monk and scholar.

Using this resource as a funeral prayer may seem odd, since it makes no direct reference to death or grief. It does, however, voice the hope of a person who is confused and uncertain, common feelings for survivors. The eternal attributes of light, goodness, power, wisdom, and pity can be great comfort to those who mourn.

803
O God, Sovereign of the universe

John D. Rempel (1944-), 1991
Hymnal: A Worship Book, 1992

Since national celebrations are often associated with displays of military power and aggrandizement, particularly in the U.S., they have caused difficulty for many Mennonites and Brethren. Rempel's litany sets God's reign as the supreme goal and the model against which all human regimes are measured.

See article **691** for information on litanies.

804
Lord of all creation, provider of every good

The Hymnal Project
Hymnal: A Worship Book, 1992

This litany is based on John Eby's litany of thanksgiving and dedication written on behalf of the Mennonite Economic Development Association. The hope of this group has been to combat a growing perception that only certain kinds of work qualify as being worthwhile and faithful to God's purpose. This prayer is radically altered from the original and does not highlight particular jobs, but rather the qualities of various dimensions of work. Of particular interest is the petition for those who are "retired" and those unable to work.

805
Eternal God, before you the generations

Since the fourth century, the church has observed some form of All Saints Day (sometimes called All Souls Day), either on November 1 or 2. The observances of these days to honor those who died confessing faith in Christ became more elaborate in subsequent centuries. The sixteenth-century Anabaptists, and later the pietists, rejected observance of these days and, as a result, many Brethren and Mennonites have not experienced their Christian lives as a part of the "communion of saints."

Congregations that observe All Saints Day on the Sunday closest to November 1 commonly understand saints in the New Testament sense—that is, all who believe and die in Christ.

What is Eternity Sunday?

In the early nineteenth century, German Protestant churches agreed that the last Sunday of the church year (the Sunday before the beginning of Advent) should be observed as Eternity Sunday. Mennonites in Russia adopted the practice.

Since the church year focuses on the life and mission of Jesus Christ, the last Sunday is called Christ the King Sunday and celebrates Christ's reign over all creation. Marking that day as Eternity Sunday unites the deaths of our ancestors with Christ's victory over all principalities and powers, including death. John Rempel writes:

> Eternity Sunday . . . filled a gap in Protestant church life. It did not make a distinction between "saints" and other Christians; its prayers for the dead were of thanks rather than intercession; it was held on a Sunday rather than a weekday, bringing the memorial day into the center of worship life. (*Mennonite Reporter* 18:19, 26 Sept. 1988)

806-861
Scripture Readings

The goal for these passages, which might otherwise be provided in pew Bibles, is that they be especially appropriate for congregational reading. They are also formatted to make unison reading easier.

Selecting readings was a formidable task since none of the participating denominations has had a consistent practice of congregational reading. The worship committee considered five questions in the sorting process:

1. Was the reading currently in *The Brethren Hymnal* (1951) and *The Mennonite Hymnal* (1969)?

2. Was the passage significant historically in the development of Brethren or Anabaptist/Mennonite thought and practice?

3. Was the passage significant in the cycle of lectionary readings or important for seasonal celebrations of the church year?

4. Did the passage raise themes for congregational life and personal devotion that were significant but neglected in the past?

5. Which translation of scripture should be used?
   After much debate, the worship committee of The Hymnal Project determined that the New Revised Standard Version (NRSV) would be the primary translation. Occasionally, substitutions in the NRSV were made to give passages a tone more in keeping with Brethren and Mennonite theological concerns or to create a sense of familiarity for worshipers where they were more accustomed to another reading, as with Psalm 23. In a few cases substitutions were made for the sake of smoother congregational reading.

818
Have mercy on me, O God

Psalm 51:1-12, 15-17
Verses 5,7, tr. Eugene Roop (1942-)

Verses 5 and 7 of this psalm were retranslated by Eugene Roop, Brethren Hebrew Bible scholar and president of Bethany Theological Seminary (Church of the Brethren), Richmond, Indiana, and substituted in the NRSV text. The concern with verse 5 centered around the possible misunderstanding of "indeed, I was born guilty, a sinner when my mother conceived me." Rather than suggesting that humans are sinful because of the act of physical love, Roop's translation recognizes that humans are born into sinfulness. Roop writes:

> The verse starts out, "Indeed I was born in iniquity." I think it means " 'in the midst of ' iniquity I was born." That certainly is a possible translation of the Hebrew preposition. The phrase then goes on to say again, "in" or "with" or "in the midst" of sin my mother conceived me. Again, the sense is that the world in which the poet [psalmist] was born was a world distorted, and the poet understands that she or he participated in that distortion. That is as dramatically as the poets of ancient Israel can talk about sin: the complete disruption, distortion, and destruction that make up the human drama.

The phrase in verse 7 traditionally translated "wash me and I shall be whiter than snow" is problematic because of the associations of whiteness with purity. In the North American context, where being "white" has meant greater power, opportunity, wealth, and an assumed purity of virtue and being "black" has often been read as "shiftless," "inferior," or "evil," the use of black or white adjectives is a sensitive issue. Roop notes that Hebrew lexicons usually include "clean" or "pure" as possible meanings for the word usually translated "white." His preference was "clean" since it did not carry "a one-sided moral connotation" as "pure" frequently does.

840

My soul proclaims the greatness of the Lord

Magnificat, Luke 1:47-55
International Consultation on English Texts, 1975

This rendering of Mary's Song (Magnificat) is from the collection *Prayers We Have in Common*, but it is revised to agree with the text in *Praying Together*. These collections were published by the International Consultation on English Texts, later renamed the English Language Liturgical Consultation. See article **660** for information on ELLC/ICET.

The worship book includes this version of the Magnificat instead of the NRSV translation because it can be read in unison more easily, and the translation has more vitality, using the active voice instead of the passive voice.

849

For we know that in all things God works

Romans 8:28-39
Tr. Virginia Wiles (1954-), 1991

Translations of this passage render verses 29-30 in various ways. Those renderings represent a particular theological orientation. The NRSV rendering tended toward predestinarian thought:

> For those whom he [God] foreknew he also predestined to be conformed to the image of his Son, in order that he might be the firstborn within a large family.

Virginia Wiles, a Brethren biblical scholar, provided a new translation with language more compatible with believers church understandings. It also eliminated several masculine references for God. Where the translation provided different textual possibilities, words were chosen that had appeared in earlier translations and were thus familiar to worshipers' ears.

BIOGRAPHIES

AABERG, JENS CHRISTIAN (b. Nov. 8, 1877, Moberg, Denmark; d. June 22, 1970, Minneapolis, Minn.) moved to the United States in 1901 and attended St. Ansgar's College and Grand View College and Seminary in Des Moines, Iowa. He married in 1908 and was ordained in the Danish Evangelical Lutheran Church in America. He served pastorates in Wisconsin and Illinois, as well as a twenty-year tenure in Minneapolis, before retiring in 1946. He served on committees for various Lutheran hymnals, translated approximately eighty hymns and songs from Danish, edited *Favored Hymns and Songs* (1961), and authored *Hymns and Hymnwriters of Denmark* (1945).

Translator: *Bright and glorious is the sky,* **219**

ABELARD, PETER (b. 1079, Le Pallet, France; d. Apr. 21, 1142, St. Martel, near Chalon, France) was the oldest son of a noble Breton family. A brilliant man, he became a lecturer and canon at Notre Dame Cathedral, Paris, by age twenty-two. The ease with which he conveyed his keen scholarship drew many students, but his critical approach to the scriptures and church writings caused conflict with his colleagues.

While he was at Notre Dame, a mutual love developed between Abelard and Heloise, niece of Canon Fulbert. When Heloise became pregnant, they fled to Brittany (western France) where they married privately, and eventually Heloise gave birth to a son. On their return to Paris, Canon Fulbert retaliated by hiring thugs to castrate Abelard.

Tumbled from his intellectual pinnacle, Abelard sent Heloise to a convent, and he became a monk and resumed his teaching. His *Theologia,* however, sparked a heresy trial set up by St. Bernard of Clairvaux. Abelard was found guilty and barred from teaching. Disgraced and broken, he died on the way to Rome to appeal his case.

Abelard and Heloise are buried together in the Cemetery of Père-Lachaise, Paris. Their correspondence is widely published, and their relationship has been recounted in various novels and plays. Abelard wrote a hymnal for his wife's convent, *Hymnarius Paraclitensis* (ca. 1135), from which his hymns were collected and re-edited in Dreves' *Hymnarius Paraclitensis* (1891).

Author: *Alone thou goest forth,* **244**

ADDISON, JOSEPH (b. May 1, 1672, Milston, Wiltshire, England; d. June 17, 1719, London, England), the son of an Anglican clergyman, was educated at the Charterhouse in London and studied law and politics at Magdalen College, Oxford University, England. He later was appointed to several governmental posts, including Chief Secretary for Ireland. While a student, Addison displayed outstanding literary talent for writing Latin verse. He also wrote for the stage but was noted primarily for his contributions to the *Tatler*, the *Guardian*, the *Freeholder*, and the *Spectator*. He published several of his hymns in the *Spectator*, a daily paper he established in 1711.

Author: *When all thy mercies, O my God,* **72**

ADEBESIN, BIODUN AKINREMI OLVSOJI (b. Jan. 1, 1928, Lagos, Nigeria) learned to play the piano at the age of nine and continued to study music throughout his school and college years. He received a certificate from Cambridge University, England, and is an associate of the Royal College of Music, London. As a jazz musician, he formed his own group in 1952 and has also played with and led other bands and orchestras in jazz, theater, and club settings, including the African Cultural Group Band in New York City (1962-1965). He has been a teacher, banker, and member of the Nigerian diplomatic service. His writings include *Okanlawon* and *Ale Wa Adara*.

Translator: *Jesus, we want to meet,* **10**

AHLE, JOHANN RUDOLF (b. Dec. 24, 1625, Mühlhausen, Thüringen, Germany; d. July 9, 1673, Mühlhausen) was a leading organist, composer, author on musical topics, and poet. He studied theology at Erfurt University, but nothing is known of his musical study. He became cantor of St. Andreas's Church, Erfurt, and taught at its elementary school in 1646 while studying at the university. After Ahle returned to Mühlhausen to marry in 1650, it appears he became organist at St. Blasius in 1654, holding the position for the rest of his life. He was succeeded by his son, who in turn was followed by J. S. Bach. Ahle held several municipal offices, served on the town council, and was elected mayor.

Ahle's work reflects the influence of the sixteenth-century German chorale and the seventeenth-century Italian vocal solo style. He is remembered mainly for his large group of sacred songs for one to four voices set to texts from the Bible and from works by local poets, including himself. These songs, though not intended for congregational singing, were included in the eighteenth-century Mühlhausen hymnbook. Besides his well-known LIEBSTER JESU, WIR SIND HIER, at least MORGENGLANZ DER EWIGKEIT and ES IST GENUG survive in present-day Protestant services and instrumental works.

Composer: LIEBSTER JESU, WIR SIND HIER (*Blessed Jesus, at your word*), **13**

AINGER, ARTHUR CAMPBELL (b. July 4, 1841, Blackheath, England; d. Oct. 26, 1919, Eton, England) was educated at Eton College and at Trinity College, Cambridge, receiving his B.A. in 1864. He returned to Eton as an assistant master until his retirement in 1901. In 1899 Ainger edited, with H. G. Wintle, an English-Latin *gradus*, or verse dictionary. In 1901 his *Carmen Etonese* was published. He is remembered as a fine scholar and teacher—and a man with a sense of humor—who won the respect and admiration of his students.

Author: *God is working his purpose out*, **638**

AKERS, DORIS MAE (b. 1922, Brookfield, Mo.), who wrote her first song at the age of ten, has since had more than four hundred hymns and songs published, most of them by Manna Music. In addition to her songwriting, Akers is also a singer and choir director. She is a member of St. James Pentecostal Church in Columbus, Ohio.

Author/Composer: *I am weak and I need thy strength* (LEAD ME, GUIDE ME), **553**

ALBRIGHT, ANNE METZLER (b. Jan. 22, 1925, Louisville, Ky.), daughter of Burton Metzler, a respected Bible teacher at the Brethren-affiliated McPherson College (Kan.), graduated from McPherson College. There she met her husband, W. David Albright. She writes: "Seven children later, I got my master's in guidance and counseling." She taught English and reading and was a guidance counselor in secondary schools. She and her husband recently retired in McPherson where they find themselves "busier than ever."

Author: *By Peter's house*, **378**

ALCUIN (b. ca. 732, York, England; d. May 19, 804, Tours, France) was educated at the renowned cathedral school of York; he later taught there and became headmaster. On a trip to Italy, he met Charlemagne and accepted the emperor's invitation to head the palace school he was establishing at the royal seat of Aachen. Under Alcuin's influence, the school developed into a center of knowledge and culture. In 796 Alcuin was appointed by Charlemagne to become abbot of the monastery of St. Martin at Tours where he remained until his death. He is especially noted for his introduction of Anglo-Saxon humanism into Western Europe; for inspiring the revival of learning known as the Carolingian Renaissance; for leaving, among other writings, many letters that have proved to be a valuable historical resource; and for making important reforms in the Roman Catholic liturgy.

Author: Eternal Light, shine into our hearts, **802**

ALEXANDER, CECIL FRANCES (HUMPHREYS) (b. 1818,[1] County Tyrone, Ireland; d. Oct. 12, 1895, Londonderry, Ireland) was a strong advocate of religious education for children and eventually wrote *Verses for Holy Seasons* (1846) to introduce children to the substance of creeds and the church year. In 1850 she married William Alexander, who later became bishop of Derry and Raphoe, archbishop of Armagh, and primate of Ireland. Though in the public eye because of her husband's position, she maintained her customary "errands of charity and helpfulness" and was said to be as much at home with the poor and ill as she was in the archbishop's palace.

Alexander began writing hymns early in life but wrote most of her four hundred hymns between 1846 and 1866. Most of these were written for children and considered the finest of their kind; however, some are used regularly by adults. Her best-known collection, *Hymns for Little Children* (1848), went through more than one hundred editions, and many of her hymns were included in the *Irish Church Hymnal* (1917).

Author: *All things bright and beautiful*, **156**. Translator: *Christ be with me*, **442**; *I bind unto myself today*, **441**

1. Although some sources give Alexander's date of birth as 1823, the earlier date is documented in the *Dictionary of English Literature* and other authoritative sources.

ALEXANDER, JAMES WADDELL (b. Mar. 13, 1804, Hopewell, Va.; d. July 31, 1859, Sweetsprings, Va.) graduated in 1820 from the College of New Jersey, which later became Princeton University. Licensed to preach by the presbytery of New Brunswick in 1825, he attended Princeton Theological Seminary and was ordained in 1827. In later years he taught at both of his alma maters, as professor of rhetoric at the college (1832-1844) and as professor of church history at the seminary (1849-1851). He served in several pastorates, including First Presbyterian Church, Trenton, New Jersey (1829-1832); Duane Street Presbyterian Church, New York City (1844-1849); and Fifth Avenue Presbyterian Church, New York City (1851-1859). A prolific writer, Alexander authored more than thirty books for the American Sunday School Union, as well as articles for *The Princeton Quarterly Review*. His interest in Latin and German hymnody led to his writings and translations being published in various journals and in *The Breaking Crucible, and Other Translations*, published posthumously in 1861.

Translator: *O sacred Head, now wounded*, **252**

ALFORD, HENRY (b. Oct. 7, 1810, London, England; d. Jan. 12, 1871, Canterbury, England) was born into a family that had five consecutive generations of clergymen. He was educated at Ilminster Grammar School and Trinity College, Cambridge (B.A., 1832). In 1833 he was ordained in the Church of England; he served as curate, assisting his father at Winkfield, Wiltshire, then at Ampton. In 1835 he became vicar of Wymeswold, Leicestershire, and finally was appointed dean of Canterbury Cathedral. Alford was also an eminent Greek scholar and is known for his four-volume commentary on the Greek New Testament (1844-1861), which became a standard reference work. In addition, he wrote many original hymns and translations that are included in *Psalms and Hymns* (1844), *Poetical Works* (1853), and *Year of Praise* (1867).

Author: *Come, ye thankful people*, **94**; *We walk by faith*, **570**

ALLEN, CHESTER G. (b. 1838; d. 1878) was one of the editors, along with Robert Lowry, of the song collection *Bright Jewels for the Sunday School*, published in 1869 by Biglow and Main. No additional biographical information is available.

Composer: ALLEN (*Praise him, praise him*), **100**

ALLEN, GEORGE NELSON (b. Sept. 7, 1812, Mansfield, Mass.; d. Dec. 9, 1877, Cincinnati, Ohio) graduated from Oberlin College (Ohio) in 1838. He remained on the faculty of his alma mater where he taught music and geology until his retirement in 1864. The choral and instrumental music education departments he built provided the foundation upon which the Oberlin Conservatory of Music was later established. He compiled the *Oberlin Social and Sabbath Hymn Book* (1844).

Composer: PRECIOUS LORD (*Precious Lord, take my hand*), **575**

ALSTOTT, OWEN (20th c.) has composed music for the liturgy since the early 1970s. He studied organ at Willamette University, Salem, Oregon, and composition at Marylhurst College for Lifelong Learning, Portland, Oregon. Alstott is currently publisher at Oregon Catholic Press.

Author/Composer: *Oyenos, mi Dios*, **358**

AMBROSE OF MILAN (b. ca. 340, Treves, Gaul; d. Apr. 4, 397, Milan, Italy) was the son of a Roman nobleman, prefect of the Gauls (the area that later became Germany). Upon his father's death, he moved to Rome with his mother, brother, and sister. There he learned Greek, studied law, and became governor of northern Italy, living in Milan.

With the Roman Empire tottering and the new church split into factions, Ambrose found himself in the midst of political upheaval when the Arian Bishop of Milan died. When Ambrose eloquently pleaded for tolerance in an effort to stem rioting, he was elected to the position by acclamation, though he was still a catechumen (in training before baptism). He was baptized and consecrated bishop on December 7, 374. Ambrose, who gave his wealth to the poor as well as to the church, was a vigorous defender of the Trinitarian faith. The theological controversies of his time are reflected in his hymns.

Known as a scholar, statesman, and theologian, he has been called "the father of church song." It was Ambrose who introduced the practice of antiphonal chanting and completed the work begun by Gregory I of systematizing the music of the church. As many as ninety-two hymns have been attributed to Ambrose, but only a few of these are likely from his pen. His died on Easter eve, 397.

Author: *O Splendor of God's glory bright*, **646**; *Savior of the nations, come*, **173**

AMPS, WILLIAM (b. Dec. 18, 1824, Cambridge, England; d. May 20, 1910, Cambridge) was organist of King's College (1855-1876) and of St. Peter's Church, both in Cambridge. He was also conductor of the Cambridge University Musical Society.

Composer: VENICE (*How good a thing it is*), **310**

ANDREWES, LANCELOT (b. 1555, London, England; d. Sept. 26, 1626, London) was a bishop in the Church of England. He studied at Pembroke College, Cambridge, where in 1575 he was elected a fellow. In 1580 he was ordained a deacon. After service in several parishes, he was consecrated as bishop of Chichester in 1605; he was subsequently transferred to Ely and then to Winchester. Known for his eloquent and learned sermons, Bishop Andrewes was called upon to preach periodically at court. Under James I, he was selected as one of the translators of the Authorized Version of the Bible. As a theologian he defended Anglican doctrines—in a time of strife in the English Church—against both Calvinism and Roman Catholicism. Some of the prayers he wrote in Greek and Latin have been translated and published in the *Manual of Private Devotions* (1903).

Author: Forgive me my sins, O Lord, **698**

ANDREWS, MARK (b. Mar. 21, 1875, Gainsborough, Lincolnshire, England; d. Dec. 10, 1939, Montclair, N.J.) studied music at Westminster Abbey, London, with John Thomas Ruck before moving to the U.S. in 1902. He was a member of the American Guild of Organists and served as organist and choirmaster in a number of churches in

Montclair. His compositions include songs, anthems, cantatas, organ works, and string quartets.

Composer: LAUDA ANIMA (ANDREWS) (*Praise, my soul, the God of heaven*), **63**

ANTES, JOHN (b. Mar. 24, 1740, Frederick, near Bethlehem, Pa.; d. Dec. 17, 1811, Bristol, England), one of eleven children, was educated in Bethlehem at the Moravian boys' school. As a young man, he made at least seven stringed instruments (five violins, a viola, and a cello), some of which are in museums in Nazareth and Lititz, Pennsylvania. A watchmaker by profession, he also invented an apparatus that would automatically turn pages as a musician was playing.

In 1769 Antes was ordained to the Moravian ministry and served as a missionary to Egypt from 1770 to 1781. After living in Germany for a few years, he moved to the Fulneck Moravian community in England in 1785 where he served as warder (business manager), a position he held for most of his remaining days.

Antes' surviving music includes three trios for two violins and cello, Opus 3 (ca. 1790), considered the earliest chamber music by a U.S.-born composer (Young 1993). Manuscripts of his thirty-one anthems are in the Moravian archives in the U.S., as well as in the Archiv der Brüder-Unität at Herrnhut, Germany. Two manuscript books of his fifty-nine hymn tunes are in the London Moravian Archives. His music "is close to Haydn's in technique and spirit" (Hitchcock, Sadie 1986).

Composer: MONKLAND (*Songs of praise the angels sang*), **60**

ARIAS, MORTIMER (b. Jan. 7, 1924, Durazno, Uruguay) received his education at Montevideo University (B.Pre-medicine, 1948) and Union Theological Seminary in Buenos Aires (B.Th., 1946; M.Th., 1957). In 1977 he earned a D.Min. from Perkins School of Theology, Dallas, Texas, and received an honorary doctorate from DePauw University, Greencastle, Indiana, in 1985. Ordained to the Methodist ministry in 1947, Arias has served a variety of positions in the United Methodist Church: executive pastor of the Methodist Church of Uruguay (1947-1956, 1958-1961); pastor and district superintendent of the United Methodist Church in Bolivia (1962-1967); Bolivian national executive secretary (1968-1969); and bishop of Bolivia (1969-1976).

In more recent years, Arias has taught at Perkins School of Theology; Boston University (Mass.; 1970-1976); Claremont School of Theology (Calif.; 1981-1985); and Iliff School of Theology in Denver, Colorado. In 1986 he was named president of the Latin American seminary in San José, Costa Rica. He has served on a number of international committees, including the World Council of Churches Commission on World Mission (1973-1983). Among his writings, which have been published in English, Spanish, and Portuguese, are *Salvation Is Liberation* (1973), *Your Kingdom*

Come (1980), and *Announcing the Reign of God* (1983). In 1989 the United Methodist Foundation for Evangelism cited Arias as one of forty outstanding evangelists, a list that includes such names as E. Stanley Jones and Emilio Castro (general secretary of the World Council of Churches).

Author: *En medio de la vida* (*You are the God within life*), **537**

ARLOTT, JOHN (b. Feb. 25, 1914, Basingstoke, Hampshire, England; d. 1991) was educated at Queen Mary's School in Basingstoke. A man of eclectic interests, Arlott worked from 1930 to 1934 as a clerk in a mental hospital, then as a police detective until 1945 when he joined the British Broadcasting Corporation as a producer. Five years later he became general instructor in the BBC Training School. In 1953 he began concentrating on his writing, living at Alresford. In 1973 Southampton University made him an honorary M.A. An aficionado of cricket, Arlott wrote some thirty books on the sport. His poetry has been published in *Of Period and Place* (1944), *Clausentum* (1945), and two anthologies, *Landmarks* (1943) and *First in America* (1949).

Author: *God, whose farm is all creation*, **391**

ARNATT, RONALD (b. Jan. 16, 1930, London, England) attended the choir schools of Westminster Abbey and King's College, Cambridge; studied at Trent College, Derbyshire; and received the B.Mus. from Durham University, England. In 1947 he came to the U.S., becoming a citizen in 1953. He was a church organist in Washington, D.C., and also served on the faculty of American University, Washington, D.C. (1949-1954), during which he was founder and conductor of the Washington Cantata Chorus and organist/choirmaster of the Congregation Adas Israel.

In 1954 Arnatt was named director of music and organist at Christ Church Cathedral, St. Louis, Missouri, a position he held until 1980. During these years he was also director of music at Mary Institute, director of music and organist at Congregation Shaare Emeth, on the faculty of the University of Missouri, founder/conductor of the St. Louis Chamber Chorus and Orchestra, conductor of the Kirkwood Symphony Orchestra (Mo.), and music director/conductor of the Bach Society.

In 1970 Arnatt received an honorary D.Mus. from Westminster Choir College, Princeton, New Jersey, and later was professor there (1987-1991). He was president of the Association of Anglican Musicians in 1972 and vice-president of the American Guild of Organists in 1979. His compositions include numerous anthems, sacred solos, and organ works.

Composer: LADUE CHAPEL (*Christ is risen! Shout hosanna*), **272**

ARNE, THOMAS AUGUSTINE (b. Mar. 12, 1710, London, England; d. Mar. 5, 1778, London) studied law at prestigious Eton College, but a love for music prompted him to prepare for and sustain a career as a composer. He became a skilled violinist and orchestra leader. Through his sister, an actress/singer, he applied his musical abilities as a composer and producer of theatrical music. His best-known work today, the renowned patriotic song "Rule Britannia," is the finale of James Thomson and David Mallet's masque *Alfred* (1740).

Arne composed for the Drury Lane Theater and made three visits to Dublin (1742-1744, 1755-1756, 1758-1759) where he produced operas and his first oratorio. In 1759 Oxford University awarded him a D.Mus. Arne's opera *Artaxerxes* (1762) was composed in the Italian manner, using recitative instead of spoken dialogue between the arias or ensembles. Besides operas, two oratorios, and music for masques, plays, and pantomimes, Arne composed church music and orchestral, chamber, and keyboard music.

Although his work was overshadowed by that of his contemporary George Frederick Handel, Arne is still lauded by many experts as the foremost British composer of his time. He died one week before his sixty-eighth birthday and was buried at St. Paul's, Covent Garden.

Composer: ARLINGTON (*This is the day the Lord has made*), **642**

ARTHUR, JOHN W. (b. Mar. 25, 1922, Mankato, Minn.; d. Aug. 15, 1980, Palo Alto, Calif.) received both a B.A. and a B.Mus. from Gustavus Adolphus College, St. Peter, Minnesota, in 1944. He studied at Wartburg Theological Seminary, Dubuque, Iowa; completed his B.D. at Augustana Theological Seminary; and was ordained in 1946 as pastor of Zion Lutheran Church, Duquesne, Pennsylvania. In 1949 he received an M.A.Th. at Pittsburgh Theological Seminary (Pa.) and served Lutheran denominations in a variety of pastoral and teaching positions until his retirement in 1976 due to ill health. He served on many worship committees and published various liturgical and musical books for Lutheran worship.

Author: *Spirit of God, unleashed on earth*, **364**; *This is the feast of victory*, **476**

ATKINSON, FREDERICK COOK (b. Aug. 21, 1841, Norwich, England; d. Nov. 30, 1896, East Dereham, England) was a boy chorister at Norwich Cathedral and later was assistant to Zechariah Buck, organist and choirmaster. He received his B.Mus. at Cambridge University, England, in 1867 and served as organist/choirmaster at St. Luke's Church in Manningham, Bradford; at Norwich Cathedral (1881-1885); and at St. Mary's Parish Church in Lewisham after 1886. Atkinson composed a number of Anglican services, anthems, hymn tunes, and instrumental pieces.

Composer: MORECAMBE (*Spirit of God! descend*), **502**

AUGSBURGER, DAVID W. (b. Aug. 14, 1938, Delphos, Ohio), ordained in the Mennonite Church, is a graduate of Eastern Mennonite College and Seminary, Harrisonburg, Virginia, and Claremont School of Theology (Calif.) where he received a Ph.D. in Personality, Theology, and Therapy. For more than a decade, he was a radio spokesman for the Mennonite churches, with his productions winning ten awards for creative religious broadcasting. He has taught at seminaries in Illinois, Indiana, and Pennsylvania. In 1990 Augsburger joined the faculty of Fuller Theological Seminary, Pasadena, California, as professor of pastoral care and counseling.

He is the author of twenty books on pastoral counseling, marriage, conflict, and human relations. His most recent writings are *Sustaining Love, Pastoral Counseling Across Cultures*, and the caring series, beginning with the widely published *Caring Enough to Confront*. His feature articles have appeared in more than one hundred different periodicals. A diplomate of the American Association of Pastoral Counselors, Augsburger is active in teaching, therapy, consulting, and leading workshops internationally. His avocational pursuits include art, music, gardening, writing, cooking, and bicycling.

Translator: *Who now would follow Christ*, **535**

AUGUSTINE (see ST. AUGUSTINE)

BABCOCK, MALTBIE DAVENPORT (b. Aug. 3, 1858, Syracuse, N.Y.; d. May 18, 1901, Naples, Italy) graduated in 1875 from Syracuse University where he was a champion swimmer and baseball player, as well as a dynamic personality and leader. After finishing at Auburn Theological Seminary in 1882, Babcock was ordained as a Presbyterian minister and served his first church in Lockport, New York, followed by Brown Memorial Church in Baltimore, Maryland (1885-1899). He was called to Brick Presbyterian Church in New York City in 1899, succeeding Henry van Dyke as pastor, but Babcock died just eighteen months later on a cruise to the Holy Lands. A collection of his writings, *Thoughts for Every-Day Living* (1901), was published after his death.

Author: *This is my Father's world*, **154**

BACH, JOHANN SEBASTIAN (b. Mar. 21, 1685, Eisenach, Germany; d. July 28, 1750, Leipzig, Germany) was born into a musical family that supplied Thüringen, Germany, with a multitude of organists, town pipers, and members of court bands. Receiving his first musical education from his family, Bach was trained in the choir schools at Ohrdruf and Lüneburg, becoming the outstanding organist of his time. After a brief stint as organist in Arnstadt and Mühlhausen, his major positions were in Weimar (1708-1717) as court organist, Anhalt-Cöthen (1717-1723) as *Kapellmeister*, and in Leipzig (1723-1750) where he was cantor of St. Thomas Church until his death.

In his choral, instrumental, and keyboard music—both sacred and secular—Bach brought the musical forms of his time to their highest level of development. His settings of 371 Lutheran chorale melodies are models of four-voice harmonization.

A devout, orthodox Lutheran, Bach has been called the "Fifth Evangelist" because his faith permeated his music in such a way that many listeners have been drawn to Christian belief by his compositions.

Composer: FAITHFUL (*With happy voices singing*), **83**. Arranger: CHRIST LAG IN TODESBANDEN (*Christ Jesus lay*), **470**; ERMUNTRE DICH (*Break forth, O beauteous heavenly light*), **203**; HERZLICH TUT MICH VERLANGEN (*O sacred Head, now wounded*), **252**; JESU, MEINE FREUDE (*Jesus, priceless treasure*), **595**; LOBT GOTT, IHR CHRISTEN (*Let all together praise our God*), **213**; O GOTT, DU FROMMER GOTT (DARMSTADT) (*O God, thou faithful God*), **376**; SCHMÜCKE DICH, O LIEBE SEELE (*Soul, adorn thyself with gladness*), **473**; TONUS PEREGRINUS (*God, be merciful and gracious*), **424**; WERDE MUNTER (*Jesu, joy of man's desiring*), **604**

BAKER, HENRY WILLIAMS (b. May 27, 1821, London, England; d. Feb. 11, 1877, Monkland, Herefordshire, England) was educated at Trinity College, Cambridge, England (B.A., 1844; M.A., 1847). He was ordained in 1844 and became vicar of Monkland in 1851, holding this position until his death.

He was editor-in-chief of *Hymns Ancient and Modern* (1861) during the twenty years of preparation and contributed translations of Latin hymns and a number of original ones to this eminent collection. This book grew out of the Oxford movement, spearheaded by Baker and John Henry Newman. This was an effort to revive the best of the liturgy, and to this end old Latin texts with their Gregorian chants were researched. A good many of the proponents of the Oxford movement became Catholic priests, and though Baker retained his status as an Anglican, he never married because he believed in the celibacy of the clergy.

Author: *O God of love, O Power of peace*, **368**; *The King of love my shepherd is*, **170**. Translator: *Of the Father's love begotten*, **104**

BAKER, THEODORE (b. June 3, 1851, New York, N.Y.; d. Oct. 13, 1934, Dresden, Germany) first trained for a business career but then turned to music. He studied at the University of Leipzig where his doctoral dissertation (1881 or 1882) was the first serious study of the music of the Native North American. Baker returned to New York City in 1891 to become literary editor and translator for G. Schirmer, Inc. He published *A Dictionary of Musical Terms* (1895) and *Baker's Biographical Dictionary of Music* *and Musicians* (1900, 1905). He retired in 1926 and lived in Germany until his death.

Translator: *Christ, we do all adore thee,* **105**; *Lo, how a Rose e'er blooming,* **211**; *We gather together,* **17**

BARBAULD, ANNA LAETITIA (b. June 20, 1743, Kibworth-Harcourt, England; d. Mar. 9, 1825, Newington Green, England) was the daughter of a dissenting (meaning he was not of the Church of England) minister, John Aiken. He provided her with a literary background for her future interests in writing. She married Rochmont Barbauld, a Unitarian clergyman of French extraction, and they established a boarding school in Palgrave, Suffolk. In 1781 she published her *Hymns in Prose for Children,* which was translated into French, Spanish, and Italian. Barbauld wrote twenty-one hymns, six of which are still in use in Unitarian hymnals. Her collected works were published in London in 1825.

Author: *Lord, should rising whirlwinds,* **92**; *Praise to God, immortal praise,* **91**

BARCLAY, MARGARET (b. 1932) served as an English translator on the staff of the World Council of Churches from 1947 to 1953. After 1954 she did similar work in Luxembourg for the High Authority of the European Coal and Steel Community, which is a branch of the Common Market. She is a fellow of the Institute of Linguists in London, the British association of professional translators and interpreters. Barclay translated several other German hymns and a Chinese hymn for *Cantate Domino* (1951), a hymnbook sponsored by the World Student Christian Federation.

Translator: *Each morning brings us,* **645**

BARCLAY, WILLIAM (b. Dec. 5, 1907, Wick, Scotland; d. Jan. 24, 1978, Glasgow, Scotland) was educated at the University of Glasgow and the University of Marburg, Germany. Ordained in the Church of Scotland in 1933, he served for thirteen years as a parish minister in Renfrew. In 1946 he returned to academia as a lecturer at Trinity College in Glasgow. From 1963 until his retirement in 1974, he was professor of divinity and biblical criticism at the University of Glasgow. A prolific writer, Barclay published many scholarly works but is best known for his popular writings, especially his series of Daily Study Bible commentaries. Barclay took part in the preparation of the New English Bible (1961, 1970) and published his own colloquial translation of the New Testament (1968). In Scotland he was also known for his radio and television broadcasts. *The New York Times* once called him a "bustling and humorous Scot."

Author: God of guidance, quicken your Holy Spirit, **725**

BARING-GOULD, SABINE (b. Jan. 28, 1834, Exeter, England; d. Jan. 2, 1924, Lew Trenchard, England) led a richly varied life as clergyman, author of fiction, poet, composer of hymn texts and tunes, translator, editor, and folksong collector. He spent his early life mostly in Germany and France. He studied at Clare College, Cambridge, and was ordained in 1864.

From 1864 to 1867, Baring-Gould was curate of Horbury parish near Wakefield where he met Grace Taylor; they married in 1868. At Horbury he conducted Sunday services in a tiny apartment, two rooms stacked one above the other. He comments that the "hymns were performed somewhat laggingly, as the singing had to bump down the stairs, fill the kitchen, and one strain of the tune after another came up irregularly through the chinks in the floor. . . . The notes from the stair also jostled" (Bailey 1950).

Baring-Gould became perpetual curate of Dalton, near Thirsk, in 1867 and rector of East Mersea, Colchester, in 1871. In 1881, after succeeding his father as lord of the manor in the estate of Lew Trenchard, Devon, he took on the position and duties of rector. The ninety-three principal works of this prolific writer include writings on religion, travel, fiction, poetry, history, and biography. Writing without a secretary, he explains his prodigious output this way: "I stick to a task when I begin it." Baring-Gould edited two important collections of folk songs and is the author of the well-known hymn texts "Onward Christian soldiers" and "Now the day is over."

Author: *The angel Gabriel*, **180**

BARNBY, JOSEPH (b. Aug. 12, 1838, York, England; d. Jan. 28, 1896, London, England) became a chorister in the choir of Yorkminster when he was seven, was an organist there at age twelve, and choirmaster at age fourteen. Educated at the Royal Academy of Music, London, he held positions of organist/choirmaster at four churches before occupying the position at St. Anne's, Soho. There Barnby started the annual performances of Bach's *Passion According to St. John* with orchestral accompaniment. He served as musical adviser to Novello and Company (1861-1876), music leader at Eton College, England (1875-1892), and principal of the Guildhall School of Music. A fellow of the Royal School of Music, he was knighted in 1892. Barnby's compositions include numerous services, anthems, part-songs, and vocal solos. His 246 hymn tunes, which he did not name, were published in one volume in 1897. Barnby edited five hymnals, the most important of which was *The Hymnary* (1872).

Composer: ADORO (ST. CHRYSOSTOM) (*Jesus, my Lord, my God, my all*), **533**; LAUDES DOMINI (*When morning gilds the skies*), **644**; SANDRINGHAM (*O perfect Love*), **624**

BARTHÉLÉMON, FRANÇOIS HIPPOLYTE (b. July 27, 1741, Bordeaux, France; d. July 23, 1808, London, England), born of an Irish mother and French father, served briefly in the Irish brigade but left military life to study music on the continent. His musical career began in England in 1765 when he became a professional violinist and conductor of the Vauxhall Gardens orchestra (1770-1776). He was closely associated with Franz Joseph Haydn during the master's sojourn in London. Barthélémon composed many instrumental works, primarily sonatas and concertos for violin, plus works for organ, a method for piano and one for harp, and many songs and dramatic pieces. He was a member of Swedenborgian Church.[1]

Barthélémon also set music to Thomas Ken's "Awake, my soul, and with the sun." On the subject of that tune, Thomas Hardy contributed a poem in 1921 to the *Times* of London on the anniversary of Barthélémon's death.[1]

Composer: BALERMA (*Help us to help each other*), **362**

1. Hardy's poem is quoted in *The Hymnal 1940 Companion* (3rd rev. ed.), pages 109-110.

BARTHOLOMEW, WILLIAM (b. Sept. 6, 1793, London, England; d. Aug. 18, 1867) was a libretto translator who, for some years, wrote English translations for music originally set to other languages. He did this for Mendelssohn from 1841 to 1847. He was, reportedly, a violinist and painter, as well as a writer.

Translator: *Cast thy burden upon the Lord*, **586**

BARTLETT, LAWRENCE FRANCIS (b. 1933, Sydney, Australia) studied at North Sydney Technical High School where he was the school choir accompanist and wrote arrangements for the choir. He received his diploma from the Sydney Conservatorium of Music in 1953 and served as assistant director of music at the King's School, Parramatta (1952-1957). From 1958 to 1960, he was a tutor in church music at Ridley College, Melbourne, where he then studied theology (Th.D., 1963). Ordained in 1961, he has served as curate and music director of St. Andrew's Cathedral in Sydney (1962-1968) and rector of St. Thomas's, Enfield (1968-1975). He was named rector of St. Michael's Parish and canon of St. Andrew's Cathedral in 1975.

The composer of several hymn tunes, Bartlett was an Anglican representative on the committee that prepared *The Australian Hymn Book* (1977).

Composer: HALLGRIM (*Before the cock crew twice*), **243**; HILARY (*Awake, awake, fling off the night*), **448**

BARTON, BERNARD (b. Jan. 31, 1784, London, England; d. Feb. 19, 1849, Woodbridge, England), known as the "Quaker poet," received his schooling from a Society of Friends institution in Ipswich. After trying his hand at several different careers, Barton in 1810 accepted a position in a Woodbridge bank as a clerk, a job he held for the rest of his life. Barton, a friend of Byron, Charles Lamb, and Sir Walter Scott, published several collections of poetry and prose, among them *Devotional Verses* (1826) and *Household Verses* (1849).

Author: *Lamp of our feet*, **312**

BASIL (see ST. BASIL)

BAYLER, LAVON (b. Jan. 17, 1933, Sandusky, Ohio) grew up in parsonages in Ohio and Iowa. She earned degrees at the University of Northern Iowa, Cedar Falls (B.A., 1955), and Eden Theological Seminary, Webster Groves, Missouri (B.D., 1959), and has studied at Lancaster Theological Seminary (Pa.). Her career in pastoral ministry in the United Church of Christ (UCC) began in her native Ohio where she was ordained in 1959 and served as co-pastor of four congregations. Between 1964 and 1979, she was pastor/associate pastor of three UCC congregations in Illinois. Since 1979 she has been a conference minister in the UCC's Illinois Conference, first for the Northern Association and now—after reorganization—for the fifty-two congregations forming the Fox Valley Association, with offices in DeKalb. She has been active in issues of civil rights, peace, and conservation. Among her publications are four volumes of lectionary-based worship resources, all published by The Pilgrim Press: *Fresh Winds of the Spirit* (1986; and Book 2, 1992), *Whispers of God* (1987), and *Refreshing Rains of the Living Word* (1988) for lectionary years A, B, and C, respectively. Another series is in progress.

Author: Call a solemn assembly, **666**; With all your saints across the generations, **672**

BAYLY, ALBERT FREDERICK (b. Sept. 6, 1901, Bexhill on Sea, Sussex, England; d. July 26, 1984, Chichester, England) was trained to be a shipbuilder at the Royal Dockyard School, Portsmouth, but he sought another profession when work on warships ran contrary to his emerging pacifist views. He attended London University, earning his B.A. and graduating with honors. In 1925 he started studying for the ministry at Mansfield College, Oxford University, England.

Beginning his pastoral ministry in 1928, Bayly served Congregational parishes in Northumberland, Lancashire, and East York until his retirement in 1972. His numerous poems and hymns have been published in four small volumes: *Rejoice, O People* (1950), *Again I Say Rejoice* (1967), *Rejoice Always* (1971), and *Rejoice in God* (1977). In 1968 Westminster Choir

College made him an honorary fellow, and he was further honored in his native country at a special service in Westminster Abbey in 1978.

Author: *Fire of God, undying Flame*, **129**; *Lord of the home*, **490**; *Lord, whose love in humble service*, **369**; *What does the Lord require*, **409**; *When the morning stars together*, **34**

BECHLER, JOHANN CHRISTIAN (b. Jan. 7, 1784, on island of Oesel in Baltic Sea; d. 1857, Germany) came to Pennsylvania in 1806 and was named one of the first professors in the newly established Moravian Theological Seminary at Nazareth the following year. In 1812 he was made a deacon and moved to Philadelphia where he preached in English. A pastorate at New Dorp, Staten Island, followed in 1814. He served as principal of Nazareth Hall boys' school from 1818 to 1822 when he moved to Lititz, Pennsylvania, to become pastor of the congregation and principal of Linden Hall School for Girls. Prior to his return to Europe in 1836 to serve the church in Russia, he spent several years (1829-1836) in Salem, North Carolina, where he was made bishop in 1835. In addition to his leadership in ministry and education, Bechler was a noted musician, playing cello and bassoon and composing much sacred music.

Composer: BECHLER (*Sing hallelujah, praise the Lord*), **67**

BEDDOME, BENJAMIN (b. Jan. 23, 1717, Henley-in-Arden, Warwickshire, England; d. Sept. 3, 1795, Bourton-on-the-Water, Gloucestershire, England), the son of a Baptist clergyman, was a surgeon's apprentice in Bristol before moving to London. There in 1739 he joined the Baptist church on Prescott Street. Upon being called to the ministry by this church, Beddome began preaching in 1740 at Bourton where he served as pastor until his death in 1795. In 1770 he earned an M.A. from Providence College (R.I.). His usual practice was to write a hymn every week to follow his Sunday sermon. More than fifty of his hymns were included in Rippon's *Selection of Hymns* (1787). A posthumous collection of *Hymns adapted to Public Worship or Family Devotions, now first Published from the Manuscripts of the late Rev. B. Beddome, M.A.* (1817) contains some eight hundred works. James Montgomery, who included twenty-six of Beddome's hymns in his *Christian Psalmist* (1825), commended the author's output as embodying one central idea, "always important, often striking, and sometimes ingeniously brought out" (Julian 1907).

Author: *If Christ is mine*, **331**

BEDE, THE VENERABLE (b. 673, Jarrow, England; d. May 26, 735, at Jarrow or Wearmouth, England) was a monk heralded as the chief European scholar of his time. His literary works included translations of the scriptures into Anglo-Saxon. His *Ecclesiastical History of the English*

Nation (731) lists all of his works, which include *A Book of Hymns* in several sorts of meter or rhyme. Of these hymns, eleven or twelve are believed to be his.

Author: *Sing we triumphant hymns*, **287**

BEERY, ADALINE HOHF (b. Dec. 20, 1859, Hanover, Pa.; d. Feb. 24, 1929, Elgin, Ill.) grew up in Pennsylvania, Maryland, Iowa, and Illinos. She attended Mount Morris College Academy (Ill.; 1881-1882). Three years later she was called to Huntingdon, Pennsylvania, where she served as editor of the *Young Disciple* and other publications of the Church of the Brethren. She and William Beery married in 1888.

During her lifetime she wrote hundreds of poems, many of which were included in a volume titled *Poems of a Decade*. She was the only woman to contribute to *Two Centuries of the Church of the Brethren—Bicentennial Addresses*, published in 1908. She was musically talented as well and is credited with several musical settings in William Beery's *Gospel Chimes* (1889).

Author: *Lo, a gleam from yonder heaven*, **591**

BEERY, WILLIAM (b. Apr. 8, 1852, near Bremen, Ohio; d. Jan. 28, 1956, Elgin, Ill.), though a sickly child, lived to be more than one hundred years old. He taught in the public schools of Ohio before attending Juniata College, Huntingdon, Pennsylvania, where he received his degree in 1882. He taught music at Juniata while a student, continuing until 1885. He returned to Juniata College as head of the music department in 1888, the same year he and Adaline Hohf were married. The Beerys moved to Elgin in 1910 where both were employed by Brethren Publishing House.

Beery's earliest musical works date from around 1878, and two of his tunes were printed in the *The Brethren's Hymnal* (1879). He assisted in compiling the 1901 and 1925 hymnals for the Brethren and in editing other songbooks. His musical output totaled more than one hundred works. Beery's last published tune was a setting of the text "I will not be afraid," written in 1948 at age ninety-six.

Composer: HUNTINGDON (*Take my hand and lead me, Father*), **601**; JOHN NAAS (*Savior of my soul*), **549**; JUNIATA (*Lo, a gleam from yonder heaven*), **591**

BEETHOVEN, LUDWIG VAN (b. Dec. 16, 1770, Bonn, Germany; d. Mar. 26, 1827, Vienna, Austria), universally recognized as one of the greatest of all composers, brought the grand Viennese classical style of Haydn and Mozart to its culmination and provided the transition to nineteenth-century Romantic music. Born into a musical family, Beethoven left his native city of Bonn in 1792 for Vienna where he lived for the remainder of his life. He studied composition in Bonn with Neefe and in Vienna with Haydn, Schenk, Albrechtsberger, and Salieri. Beethoven soon earned a reputation in Vienna as a composer and virtuoso pianist, although, due to his increasing deafness, he was forced eventually to give up performing in public. Acclaimed as a composer of symphonies, string quartets, concertos, piano sonatas, and many other compositions, he also wrote sacred works, of which the most important is the *Missa Solemnis*. Beethoven's compositions have been the source for several hymn tunes.

Composer: HYMN TO JOY (*Joyful, joyful, we adore thee*), **71**

BELL, MAURICE FREDERICK (b. Sept. 3, 1862, London, England; d. ca. 1931), active as both a musician and priest, received his B.A. (1884) and M.A. (1887) from Oxford University. His most significant position was as vicar of London's St. Mark's Church at Regent's Park. Bell contributed to *The English Hymnal* (1906), and in 1909 he brought out *The Art of Church Music*. Some sources give his date of death as 1947.

Translator: *The glory of these forty days*, **225**

BENDER, JAN OSKAR (b. Feb. 3, 1909, Haarlem, Holland), of German/Dutch parentage, moved to Lübeck, Germany, in 1922 after his father's death. His education took him to Leipzig, Amsterdam, and Lübeck where he studied with Karl Straube and Hugo Distler. In 1935 he received a degree in church music. From 1934 to 1960, Bender was organist/choirmaster of several churches in Germany, including St. Michael's Church, Lüneburg (1953-1960), where J. S. Bach had once been a choirboy.

In 1960 Bender moved to the U.S., teaching organ and composition at Concordia Teachers College, Seward, Nebraska (1960-1965), followed by a tenure at Wittenberg University, Springfield, Ohio (1965-1976). After returning to Germany for three years, he came to the U.S. again as visiting professor at Valparaiso University (Ind.); Gustavus Adolphus College, St. Peter, Minnesota; and Lutheran Theological Southern Seminary, Columbia, South Carolina. In 1983 he retired to Hanerau in Holstein, Germany.

Bender was a prolific composer, with his Opus Nos. 1-90 containing more than fifteen hundred single settings and organ works published in Germany and the United States. His honors include a doctorate from Concordia Teachers College and the Canticum Novum award from Wittenberg University. In 1975 he was made a fellow of the Hymn Society of the United States and Canada.

Composer: EARTH AND ALL STARS (*Earth and all stars*), **47**

BENSON, LOUIS FITZGERALD (b. July 22, 1855, Philadelphia, Pa.; d. Oct. 10, 1930), considered a great scholar of English hymnody, studied law at the University of Pennsylvania, Philadelphia. After practicing law for seven years, he decided to enter the ministry and attended Princeton

Theological Seminary (N. J.). In 1886 Benson was ordained as a Presbyterian minister and served the Church of the Redeemer, Germantown (Philadelphia), for six years. He resigned this position to become an editor for various hymnals of the Presbyterian Church. His significant publications, in addition to the hymnals he edited, include *The English Hymn—Its Development and Use in Worship* (1915) and the collection of his *Hymns, Original and Translated* (1925). He contributed his extensive hymnological library to Princeton Theological Seminary.

Author: *For the bread*, **477**

BERG, CAROLINE V. SANDELL (b. Oct. 3, 1832, Fröderyd, Sweden; d. July 27, 1903, Stockholm, Sweden), daughter of a Lutheran pastor, was in frail health as a girl. She was very close to her father, and in 1858 she accompanied him on a boat trip to Göteborg (Gothenburg), but the two of them never reached their destination. The ship gave a sudden lurch, her father fell overboard, and he drowned as she watched. She found comfort in her writing, publishing fourteen hymns that same year and 650 hymns in her lifetime. Sandell became known as "the Fanny Crosby of Sweden," as her writing was imbued with the evangelistic revival then sweeping northern Europe.

In 1867 she married C. O. Berg, a Stockholm merchant, but continued to sign her hymns "L. S." (Lina Sandell). Much of the popularity of her hymns came through the musical settings of Oscar Ahnfelt, a "spiritual troubadour" of his day. She once said that "Ahnfelt has sung my songs into the hearts of the people" (Gealy, Lovelace, Young 1970). Ahnfelt's collections, which consisted mostly of Sandell's texts, were published with financial help from Jenny Lind, a famous Swedish soprano.

Author: *Children of the heavenly Father*, **616**

BERGEN, ESTHER CATHRYN KLAASSEN (b. June 18, 1921, Morden, Manitoba) received her education at the Mennonite Collegiate Institute, Gretna, Manitoba (1941) and the Normal School in Winnipeg. After teaching in elementary schools in southern Manitoba for four years, she studied music at the Mennonite Brethren Bible College (MBBC), Winnipeg, graduating in 1950. The following year she taught music and harmony at MBBC. In 1952 she married Menno Bergen, a graduate of Canadian Mennonite Bible College (CMBC), Winnipeg, where she also worked as registrar and bookkeeper. The couple served in Mexico with the General Conference Mennonite Board of Missions (1956-1968) and in ministry for churches in Alberta and Saskatchewan where Esther was involved with choirs and instrumental groups.

Bergen first tried her hand at translation at MBBC, rendering Stainer's *Crucifixion* into German. Some years later she translated about 150 songs from German to English for the English version of the *Mennonite Brethren*

Hymnbook (1960). Most of her work has been in German/English translation and includes Sunday school materials, songs for the Mennonite Brethren "Gospel Light Hour," and work for Mennonite World Conferences in 1978 and 1990.

In 1984 the Bergens retired to Winnipeg where they are members of Bethel Mennonite Church.

Translator: *For God so loved us*, **167**; *The Lord is King*, **69**; *We are people of God's peace*, **407**. Adapter: *Blessed are the persecuted*, **230**

BERNARD OF CLAIRVAUX (see ST. BERNARD OF CLAIRVAUX)

BERTHIER, JACQUES (b. June 27, 1923, Auxerre, Burgundy, southeastern France) is the son of Genevieve Parquin, a former organist at the Cathedral of Auxerre, and Paul Berthier, an organist, composer, and writer. Jacques Berthier studied Gregorian chant, harmony, composition, and organ at Cesar Franck School in Paris. There he worked with Guy de Lioncourt, a disciple and nephew of Vincent d'Indy. In 1946 he married de Lioncourt's daughter, and all four of their children became musicians.

Berthier met Father Joseph Gelineau at Cesar Franck School in 1946 and was trained by him in the composition of liturgical pieces in French. About this same time, the brothers of Taizé asked Berthier to compose some suitable pieces for their community. The style of Berthier's music, which "follows that of ancient music and the Gregorian chant," is well suited to the composition of post-Vatican II religious music with vernacular texts. His works have often been commissioned for large gatherings and special events (Handbook to *Worship III*, pre-publication manuscript).

Author/composer: *O Christe Domine Jesu*, **113**. Composer: *Alleluia*, **101**; *Dona nobis pacem Domine*, **346**; *Eat this bread*, **471**; GLORIA III (*Gloria*), **204**; *Jesus, remember me*, **247**; *Jubilate Deo omnis terra*, **103**; TAIZÉ KYRIE (*Kyrie*), **152**; *Nada te turbe*, **562**; *O Lord, hear my prayer*, **348**; *Our Father who art in heaven*, **554**; *Stay with me*, **242**; UBI CARITAS (*Ubi caritas et amor*), **452**; VENI SANCTE SPIRITUS (*Veni Sancte Spiritus*), **298**

BIANCO DA SIENA (b. Anciolina, Italy; d. ca. 1434, Venice, Italy), in the preface to Bianco's *Laudi Spirituali* (edited by Telesforo Bini, 1851), is described as an ardent young convert to the Jesuits at Siena in 1367. This religious order is a group of laymen following the rule of St. Augustine. One writer has said, "[Bianco da Siena's] poems have an almost sensual quality in their expression of the love of the soul for God" (*The Hymnal 1940 Companion*, 1951 ed.).

Author: *Come down, O Love divine*, **501**

BILLINGS, WILLIAM (b. Oct. 7, 1746, Boston, Mass.; d. Sept. 26, 1800) apparently had a very minimal basic education. When Billings was fourteen, his father died and he was apprenticed to a tanner. There is scant information about his early musical education, but he likely attended singing schools in the Boston area and acquired most of his musical skills on his own by studying the compositions of other authors, including the noted English psalmist William Tans'ur.

Billings began teaching singing schools in 1769, giving instruction in Providence, Rhode Island, and Boston and Stoughton, Massachusetts. The Stoughton Musical Society, organized in 1786 and still in existence, was the result of one of Billings' singing schools. His financial fortunes began to decline in the 1780s, but he continued as a music teacher and tanner until his death. He wrote more than 340 compositions and published a number of collections, including *The Singing Masters' Assistant* (1778), *The Psalm Singer's Amusement* (1781), *Suffolk Harmony* (1786), and *The Continental Harmony* (1794).

Author/Composer: *When Jesus wept, the falling star* (WHEN JESUS WEPT), **234**

BIXEL, JAMES W. (b. Nov. 7, 1913, Bluffton, Ohio) studied music at Bluffton College (1935) and received the M.M. degree from Cincinnati Conservatory (Ohio). He spent various summers in music study, and from 1970 to 1971, he studied with Gottfried von Einem in Vienna, Austria. From 1941 to 1945, he served in Civilian Public Service. He taught music theory and piano at Bethel College in North Newton, Kansas (1947-1959); he taught music in the Aspen, Colorado, public school system (1959-1960); and he taught music theory and piano at Bluffton College (1960-1979).

Bixel has been a choral director most of his professional life and has conducted several opera productions at Bethel and Bluffton Colleges. His compositions, 1939 to the present, cover a wide range: hymn tunes, anthems, solo vocal works, piano works, incidental music, operas, and operettas. *Four Parables*, *Love Is Come Again*, and *The Road to Emmaus* are three choral works, and *The Dance of the Kobzar* (1989) is an opera depicting scenes from the life of John P. Klassen (1888-1975), a professor of art at Bluffton College.

Composer: BIXEL (*O God, great womb*), **155**; REJOICE IN GOD (*Rejoice, rejoice in God*), **313**

BLISS, PHILIP PAUL (b. July 9, 1838, Clearfield County, Pa.; d. Dec. 29, 1876, near Ashtabula, Ohio) worked on a farm and in lumber camps in his boyhood and always showed a keen interest in music. His earliest musical training was under J. G. Towner and W. B. Bradbury. In 1860 Bliss became an itinerant music teacher during the winter months and attended the Normal Academy of Music in Geneseo, New York, for several summers. In 1863 Bliss sent his first song to Root and Cady, music publishers in Chicago, who sent him a flute in payment. For the next four years, Bliss was associated with that company as a composer.

In 1874, with the encouragement of D. L. Moody, Bliss launched a career as a singing evangelist, accompanied by his wife, Lucy. They traveled extensively throughout the Midwest and southern U.S. in association with evangelist D. W. Whittle. Just two years later, Bliss and his wife were en route to an engagement at Moody's Tabernacle in Chicago when their train broke through a bridge that spanned a sixty-foot chasm. The train was consumed in flames. Bliss survived the fall but died in a desperate attempt to save his wife.

Bliss wrote many successful gospel songs for George F. Root's collections and helped compile numerous Sunday school and gospel songbooks up to the time of his death.

Author: *I will sing of my Redeemer*, **344**. Author/Composer: *Man of sorrows* (MAN OF SORROWS), **258**. Composer: VILLE DU HAVRE (*When peace, like a river*), **336**

BODE, JOHN ERNEST (b. Feb. 23, 1816, St. Pancras, London, England; d. Oct. 6, 1874, Castle Camps, Cambridge, England) studied at Eton College, Charterhouse in London, and Christ Church, Oxford, where he was the first recipient of the Hertford Scholarship in 1835. He remained at Oxford as a tutor for seven years. Ordained in 1843, Bode became rector at Westwell, Oxfordshire, in 1847. From 1860 until his death, he ministered at the country parish of Castle Camps, but he was also well known as a literary figure. His published poetical collections include *Ballads from Herodotus* (1853), *Short Occasional Poems* (1858), and *Hymns for the Gospel of the Day, for Each Sunday and the Festivals of Our Lord* (1860).

Author: *O Jesus, I have promised*, **447**

BOMBERGER, HAROLD Z. (b. May 13, 1918, Lebanon County, Pa.) earned degrees at Elizabethtown College (Pa.; A.B., 1943); Bethany Theological Seminary, Oak Brook, Illinois (B.D., 1946); and Lutheran Theological Seminary (St.M., 1960). He also studied at Westminster Theological Seminary. Ordained in 1940, Bomberger has served the Church of the Brethren in pastorates at Allentown, Pennsylvania; Westminster, Maryland; and McPherson College (Kan.). He also has been secretary of the Eastern Region and executive of the Atlantic Northeast District. Since retirement he has had six interim pastorates and has been involved in the Church of the Brethren's evangelism program. His considerable international experience includes special courses at several universities, a preaching exchange mission to Great Britain, a visit to churches in Nigeria and Ecuador, and an archaeological dig in Israel. Among other offices in church and church-related organizations, he has served as moderator of the Church of the Brethren's Annual Conference and president of the Kansas Council of Churches.

Bomberger received a citation for seventeen years on the Mennonite Mental Health Services Board, an honorary doctorate from Bethany Theological Seminary, and the 1993 Peacemaker of the Year award from the Brethren Peace Fellowship, Atlantic Northeast District. Once a contributing editor of *Gospel Messenger*, he has made numerous contributions to other church publications, including *We Gather Together* (Brethren Press 1979), a collection of worship resources. His home now is Mt. Gretna, Pennsylvania.

Author: Eternal Lord, as we leave this place, **768**

BONAR, HORATIUS N. (b. Dec. 19, 1808, Edinburgh, Scotland; d. July 31, 1889, Edinburgh) came from a family whose ministry in the Church of Scotland spanned more than two centuries. After studying at the University of Edinburgh, he followed the family profession as a minister, was ordained in 1837, and moved to Kelso where he served the North Parish. The Church of Scotland split in 1843, but Bonar stayed at Kelso, serving the Free Church organization and becoming co-editor of a newspaper published in that church's interest. A scholar in the field of biblical prophecy, he also edited *The Journal of Prophecy* for twenty-five years. He received the D.D. degree from Aberdeen in 1853, served as pastor of Chalmers Memorial Free Church, Grange, Edinburgh, and was elected moderator of the General Assembly of his denomination in 1883.

Bonar's hymns, some of which were written spontaneously on scraps of paper on train journeys, are included in his books: *Songs for the Wilderness* (1843), *The Bible Hymn Book* (1845), *Hymns, Original and Selected* (1846), *Hymns of Faith and Hope* (1857, 1861), *The Song of the New Creation* (1872), and *Hymns of the Nativity* (1879). At his death a memorial volume of his hymns was published anonymously.

It is said that Bonar's gift of expression cracked through the heavy-handed Calvinism of nineteenth-century Scotland, so that "the massive theology of the Reformation . . . breaks into deep and tender melody, a crystal river from the rock" (Bailey 1950).

Author: *Blessing and honor and glory,* **108**; *Here, O my Lord, I see thee,* **465**; *I heard the voice of Jesus say,* **493**; *Jesus, sun and shield art thou,* **466**; *O Love of God,* **326**

BONHÖFFER, DIETRICH (b. Feb. 4, 1906, Breslau, now Wroclaw, Poland; d. Apr. 9, 1945, Flossenburg concentration camp, Bavaria) was a German Lutheran pastor and inspiring theologian. He studied in Berlin under Adolf von Harnack and was influenced by Karl Barth. After studying at Union Theological Seminary, New York City (1930-1931), Bonhöffer taught systematic theology at Berlin University. In 1933, in protest against anti-Jewish legislation in Germany, he moved to London where he ministered to German congregations and warned ecumenical gatherings about the dangers of Naziism.

In 1935 Bonhöffer returned to Germany to head a theological college at Finkenwalde affiliated with the anti-Nazi German Confessing Church. In 1939 he returned briefly to a lectureship at Union Theological Seminary but resigned a few weeks later when Germany invaded Poland. Dismayed that he was safe while fellow Christians in Germany were risking resistance to Hitler, Bonhöffer returned to Germany against the advice of his friends. There he struggled to mesh his pacifist convictions with the growing resistance movement. In 1942 he met Bishop G. K. A. Bell in Sweden to disclose plans for Hitler's overthrow and to seek help from the Allied Forces. Bonhöffer was arrested on April 5, 1943, imprisoned for two years, and then hanged as the Allies overran Germany.

His own faith having been held to the fire and tested for integrity, Bonhöffer sought to liberate "the gospel from the Western tradition which clothes it in metaphysical and individualistic religion, with patronizing dogmas and privileged institutions, giving access neither to the suffering Christ nor to the modern world" (Bethge 1968). Some of Bonhöffer's books that appeared posthumously in English translations include *The Cost of Discipleship* (1948), *Letters and Papers from Prison* (1953), *Life Together* (1954), and *Prisoner for God* (1954).

Author: *By gracious powers*, **552**

BORTNIANSKY, DIMITRI STEPANOVICH (b. Oct. 28, 1751, Glukhov, Ukraine; d. Oct. 10, 1825, St. Petersburg, Russia) entered the imperial choir school at age eight and was educated there under Baldassare Galuppi, an Italian composer who was court musician at St. Petersburg. He later studied with Galuppi in Venice, Italy, returning to St. Petersburg in 1779 to become director of the Imperial Chapel Choir. His collected works in ten volumes, edited by Peter Tchaikovsky, contain more than one hundred vocal compositions: hymns, various choruses, sacred concertos, a Mass, and a liturgy, in addition to three extant operas and some instrumental music. Some of his church music also has appeared in modern English and American editions.

Composer: ST. PETERSBURG (*O Power of love*, **593**; *'Tis not with eyes of flesh we see*, **571**); VESPER HYMN (attrib.) (*Now, on land and sea descending*), **655**; THE GREAT PROKEIMENON (*Who is so great a God*), **62**

BOURGEOIS, LOUIS (b. ca. 1510, Paris, France; d. ca. 1561) first became known in 1539 when three of his four-voice *chansons* were published. He is chiefly remembered for contributing melodies to the Calvinist *Genevan Psalter*. For fifteen years he was John Calvin's chief musician, adapting French secular melodies and plainsong, as well as composing new melodies for the new metrical French psalms, set into poetry from the

Hebrew by Clément Marot and Theodore de Beze. He also published the first French music teaching manual on singing and sight-reading (1550).

Even though Bourgeois was authorized by Calvin to work on psalm tunes and was a highly regarded music teacher, his work was viewed with suspicion by the Genevan authorities who imprisoned him in 1551 for having "changed the tunes of some printed psalms" without license. Calvin stepped in to obtain his release the next day, but a volume of Bourgeois' tune "improvements" was burned because the new melodies "disoriented the faithful." His work was later accepted, and some of it has survived for more than four hundred years.

Bourgeois was last heard of in 1561 when he published harmonizations of all the psalm melodies then in use. More extensive information on Bourgeois is available in standard musical reference works.

Composer: GENEVA 42 (FREU DICH SEHR) (*As the hart with eager yearning*, **500**; *Comfort, comfort, O my people*, **176**); GENEVA 124 (OLD 124th) (*We would extol thee*), **74**; OLD HUNDREDTH (*All people that on earth do dwell*, **42**; *Be present at our table, Lord*, **457**; *Praise God from whom*, **119**)

BOWIE, WALTER RUSSELL (b. Oct. 8, 1882, Richmond, Va.; d. Apr. 23, 1969, Alexandria, Va.), a Phi Beta Kappa scholar at Harvard University, Cambridge, Massachusetts, received his B.A. in 1904 and his M.A. the following year. He was ordained to the Episcopal priesthood in 1909, one year after earning a B.D. from Virginia Theological Seminary. He pastored Emmanuel Church, Greenwood, Virginia (1908-1911); St. Paul's Church, Richmond, Virginia (1911-1923); and Grace Church, New York City (1923-1939).

Turning from pastoring to academia, Bowie was professor of practical theology at Union Theological Seminary (1939-1950). While in that post, he served on the committee that produced the Revised Standard Version of the Bible in 1946. He was professor of homiletics at the Protestant Episcopal Theological Seminary (formerly Virginia Theological Seminary), Alexandria, from 1950 to 1955. He received honorary doctorates from Richmond College (Va.), Virginia Theological Seminary, and Syracuse University (N. Y.). For a number of years, he was editor of the *Southern Churchman*, as well as author of numerous books. He also has the distinction of being one of a few American poets whose hymns have found a place in British as well as American hymnals.

Author: *Oh, holy city seen of John*, **320**

BOWMAN, JOHN DAVID (b. Apr. 8, 1945, Lima, Ohio) grew up in Johnstown, Pennsylvania, where his father was pastor of Roxbury Church of the Brethren. He attended La Verne College (now University of La Verne, Calif.); Bridgewater College (Va.); St. Mary's College of St. Andrew's University, Scotland; and Bethany Theological Seminary, Oak Brook, Illinois. He earned a B.A. from Bridgewater (1967) and both an

M.Th. (1972) and D.Min. (1982) from Bethany. During his pastoral ministry, he has served congregations in Virginia, Scotland, Maryland, Indiana, and Pennsylvania. After twenty-seven years of pastoring, Bowman aspires to minister through the medium of video.

Author/Composer: *Anoint us, Lord* (ANOINT US, LORD), **631**

BOWRING, JOHN (b. Oct. 17, 1792, Exeter, England; d. Nov. 23, 1872, Claremont, Exeter, England), one of the most brilliant and versatile men of his time, was born of Puritan parents. At fourteen he left school to help his father, who made woolen goods. Through that business, much of it conducted in Spain and China, Bowring became interested in the study of languages. By the time he was sixteen, he was proficient in German, Dutch, Spanish, Italian, and Portuguese. By the end of his life, he had studied two hundred languages and was able to converse in one hundred. He translated works into an astounding number of languages and dialects, published at least thirty-six volumes on a wide variety of subjects, and served in Parliament (1835-1837, 1841-1849) and in a variety of diplomatic posts, including governor of Hong Kong. He was knighted by Queen Victoria in 1854.

Bowring's later diplomatic career was marred by controversy and insensitivity to indigenous concerns, especially in China. His poetry, however, was written early in his life, during his zealous advocacy of social reform and before his ascent on the British imperialist power ladder. Although Bowring was Unitarian, he was associated with the branch of Unitarianism that believes "Christ is all we know of God." His devotional poetry was published in two volumes: *Matins and Vespers with Hymns and Occasional Devotional Pieces* (1823) and *Hymns: as a Sequel to Matins* (1825).

Author: *In the cross of Christ I glory*, **566**

BRADBURY, WILLIAM BATCHELDER (b. Oct. 6, 1816, York, Maine; d. Jan. 7, 1868, Montclair, N.J.) at age seventeen entered the Boston Academy (Mass.) where he was influenced by Lowell Mason and Sumner Hill. He became an organist, singing-school teacher, composer, piano manufacturer, and compiler of many church music and song collections. Through these activities he had a significant influence on the church music of his time. Living most of his life in Boston and New York City, Bradbury had a hand in publishing fifty-nine collections of sacred and secular music and helped introduce music into New York public schools.

His views on church music carefully delineated the roles of both the choir and congregation. Though he believed it the "privilege and duty of *all* to unite in singing as an act of worship," he asserts that the choir, made up of those "possessing more musical talent than the rest," should be set apart, leading the congregation in singing as well as performing "new and beautiful music . . . with as much taste and skill . . . as they can command." The people of the congregation need not aspire, he writes, to "art or musical effect," but should sing "simply and solely as an act of worship before their Maker" (*The Hymnal 1940 Companion*, 1951 ed.).

Composer: BACA (*Come, gracious Spirit*), **303**; BRADBURY (*Savior, like a shepherd lead us*), **355**; HE LEADETH ME (*He leadeth me*), **599**; JESUS LOVES ME (*Jesus loves me*), **341**; OLIVE'S BROW (*'Tis midnight, and on Olive's brow*), **241**; SWEET HOUR (*Sweet hour of prayer*), **11**; WOODWORTH (*Just as I am, without one plea*), **516**; SOLID ROCK (*My hope is built on nothing less*), **343**

BRADSTREET, ANNE DUDLEY (b. ca. 1612, Northampton, England; d. Sept. 16, 1672, Andover, Mass.) came with the Puritans to the Massachusetts Bay Colony from England in 1630. After living in Boston, Newtown (Cambridge), and Ipswich, she, together with her husband and eight children, finally settled in Andover sometime around 1644 or 1645. Her poems were published in London without her knowledge in 1650, and a second edition (corrected by the author) was published in Boston in 1678. Recognized as one of the earliest poets in the colonies, her best known collection of poems was *The Tenth Muse Lately Sprung Up in America* (1650).

Author: *As spring the winter doth succeed*, **568**

BRADY, NICHOLAS (b. Oct. 28, 1659, Bandon, Ireland; d. May 20, 1726, Richmond, Surrey, England) was educated at Westminster School; went to Christ Church, Oxford, England; and then to Trinity College, Dublin, Ireland. Among his various positions, he was chaplain to the king in London and afterward was rector at Stratford-on-Avon, England (1702-1705). Besides his famous collaboration with Nahum Tate in the *New Version of the Psalms of David* (1696), his publications include several volumes of sermons.

Compiler: *O come, loud anthems let us sing*, **68**

BRÉBEUF, JEAN DE (b. Mar. 25, 1593, Conde-sur-Vire, Lower Normandy; d. Mar. 16, 1649, Saint-Ignace, Québec) was a Jesuit priest and missionary to the Hurons in the early seventeenth century. Said to be a descendant of William the Conqueror and King Louis of France, Brébeuf entered the Jesuit novitiate in Rouen, France, in 1617, and in 1619 he became a secondary school teacher. He taught at the college in Rouen from 1620 to 1621 and entered the priesthood at Pontoise in 1622, taking his final vows in 1630. Brébeuf stayed at Rouen as a steward of the college until 1625 when he was chosen for the mission field in New France and sailed to Québec.

In the summer of 1626, he traveled some eight hundred miles by canoe from Québec to Huron country where he lived among the Bear tribe. Brébeuf left a valuable written account of this trip and an early description of the Huron Indians. He returned to France, but by the time he came back to Huron country in 1634, European viruses had decimated two-thirds of the Huron population. The missionaries were despised, and Brébeuf and other priests suffered relentless persecution. The Iroquois, in particular, set out to annihilate missionaries and Brébeuf was captured, taken to Saint-Ignace, tortured, and put to death. Brébeuf's work, however, served as a basis for future mission work among the neighboring tribes.

Author: *'Twas in the moon of wintertime,* **190**

BRIDGES, MATTHEW (b. July 14, 1800, Malden, Essex, England; d. Oct. 6, 1894, Sidmouth, Devon, England) was educated in the Church of England and began his literary career in 1825 with the publication of the poem "Jerusalem Regained." This was followed in 1828 by a book, *The Roman Empire under Constantine the Great,* which examines the origin of papal superstitions. Influenced by the Oxford movement (initiated by Anglicans to recover some pre-Reformation Catholic liturgy) and John Henry Newman, Bridges converted to Roman Catholicism in 1848. He spent a number of years in Canada but returned to England where he lived out his final years at the guest house of the Convent of the Assumption in Sidmouth.

Bridges' hymns appeared first in *Hymns of the Heart* (1847) and in *The Passion of Jesus* (1852). They were disseminated in the U.S. through Henry Ward Beecher's *Plymouth Collection* (1855).

Author: *Crown him with many crowns* (sts. 1,3-5), **116**

BRIDGES, ROBERT SEYMOUR (b. Oct. 23, 1844, Walmer, Kent, England; d. Apr. 21, 1930, Boar's Hill, Berkshire, England) was educated at Eton College and Corpus Christi College, Oxford. He studied medicine at St. Bartholomew's Hospital, London (M.B., 1874), and became a physician there and also at the Great Northern Hospital. Meanwhile, he wrote poetry and in 1882 gave up medical practice due to ill health. He settled in Yattendon, Berkshire, where he married and devoted himself to literature.

In his first volume, *Shorter Poems* (1873), he proved himself an unusual and distinctly gifted poet. In 1913 King George V appointed Bridges poet laureate. Bridges continued to write and publish until 1929 when his most famous volume, *Testament of Beauty,* appeared.

Bridges also cultivated an interest in hymnody. His *Yattendon Hymnal* (1899, 1920), an elegant contribution, is considered a paragon of artistry in hymn selection—and in printing style. As a hymnal compiler and writer, he was fussy and unforgiving of inferior texts. As a poet, however, he surprisingly rendered hymn texts subservient to tunes. "I do not find that an occasional disagreement between accent of words and music offends me," he writes.

> A fine tune is an unalterable artistic form, which pleases in itself and for itself. . . . The words are better suited if they fit in with all the quantities and accents of the tune, but it is almost impossible and not necessary that they should. Their mood is what the tune must be true to; . . . the enormous power that the tune has of enforcing or even of creating a mood is the one invaluable thing of magnitude, which overrules every other consideration. (Oyer 1980)

Bridges' own translations were carefully prepared with particular tunes in mind. His other works in this field include *A Practical Discourse on Some Principles of Hymn Singing* (1899) and *About Hymns* (1911).

Translator: *Ah, Holy Jesus*, **254**; *Jesu, joy of man's desiring*, **604**; *Come, O Creator Spirit, come*, **27**

BRIGGS, GEORGE WALLACE (b. Dec. 14, 1875, Nottingham County, England; d. Dec. 30, 1959, Hindhead, Surrey, England), whose formal education was at Emmanuel College, Cambridge, contributed his literary gifts to Christian education. In his earlier years, he was curate in Yorkshire, chaplain in the Royal Navy, tutor in a theological school, vicar, and rector. From 1927 to 1934, he was canon of Leicester Cathedral and canon of Worcester from 1934 until his retirement in 1956.

Briggs' hymnwriting began gradually in his local church positions where he wrote many hymns for his Sunday school children. He played a major part in the production of *Prayers and Hymns for Use in Schools* (1927), published by Leicester County. His hymn tunes are included in worship books such as *The Daily Service, Songs of Praise* (1925) and *Songs of Praise for Boys and Girls* (1929). He also wrote liturgical services for children, as well as single prayers, one of which was used in 1941 when Franklin D. Roosevelt and Winston Churchill met on the HMS *Prince of Wales* to declare the Atlantic Charter. He was a founder of The Hymn Society of Great Britain and Ireland and was considered by hymnologist Erik Routley to be the most prolific of successful hymnwriters in the twentieth century.

Author: *Christ is the world's true light*, **334**

BRIGHTBILL, ALVIN FRANZ (b. Jan. 4, 1903, Lebanon, Pa.; d. Feb. 28, 1976, North Manchester, Ind.) was educated at Elizabethtown College (Pa.; B.S., 1923; B.A., 1925); Bethany Bible School, now Bethany Theological Seminary, Oak Brook, Illinois (B.D., 1927; D.D., 1944); and Northwestern University, Evanston, Illinois (B.Mus., 1931; M.Mus., 1933), where he studied conducting with Frederick Stock, who was then conductor of the Chicago Symphony. For more than thirty years, Brightbill taught church music, fine arts in religion, and speech at Bethany Theological Seminary

(Chicago and Oak Brook), the Brethren school of theology. In 1956 he began a stint at Chicago Theological Seminary teaching speech and was later honored posthumously when the Alvin F. Brightbill Speech Laboratory was named for him.

Brightbill was hymnology editor and a contributor for *The Brethren Hymnal* (1951). He served on the executive committee of the Hymn Society of America and the National Council of Churches Commission on Worship and the Arts and as chairman of church music for the National Federation of Music Clubs. Between 1934 and 1959, he served often on the Church of the Brethren Music and Worship Committee, and he led preaching and church music workshops in Brethren congregations throughout the nation. His expansive and dramatic style made him a popular song leader at Brethren conferences, where he had a knack for eliciting choral refinement even from these large assemblies. Brethren musician Nancy R. Faus writes:

> While he accomplished much, Brightbill is best remembered waving his strong hands in front of several thousand worshipers . . . inspiring them to sing from their hearts. His deep voice would lead the people to the last phrase, followed by an "amen" that resounded once, twice, three times, until the congregation appeared to be lifting off toward heaven. The "Alvin Brightbill School of Music" may never have been built of stone or wood, but it is an alma mater in the hearts of those who sang hymns in the mid-twentieth century. (Faus 1993)

Author: I believe in God, the giver of grain, **717**. Composer: BOUNDING HEART (*Lift up your hearts*), **602**

BRISTOL, LEE HASTINGS, JR. (b. Apr. 9, 1923, Brooklyn, N.Y.; d. Mar. 11, 1979, Syracuse, N.Y.), a businessman, administrator, educator, and musician with a broad range of interests, earned his A.B. in 1947 at Hamilton College, Clinton, New York. Bristol was a licentiate in organ at Trinity College of Music, London (1947). He did graduate work as well in Geneva, Switzerland, at the Institute of International Studies and the Conservatoire de Musique (1947-1948). In addition, he received honorary doctorates from eleven colleges and universities.

From 1948 to 1962, Bristol held a variety of positions at the Bristol-Myers Company, New York City. He was president of Westminster Choir College, Princeton, New Jersey, from 1962 to 1969 and was named president emeritus in 1976. He served on the Joint Commission on Church Music of the Episcopal Church as vice-chairperson and executive secretary. A fellow of the Royal School of Church Music and the Hymn Society of America, Bristol was a member and trustee of numerous civic organizations and foundations. He composed anthems and other sacred music, authored many articles and books, and was general editor of the

Joint Commission's *Hymnal Supplement, Songs for Liturgy,* and *More Hymns and Spiritual Songs* (1971).

Composer: DICKINSON COLLEGE (*The church of Christ, in every age*), **403**

BRODE, RICHARD DAVID (b. May 29, 1963, Harrisburg, Pa.) grew up in Harrisburg First Church of the Brethren where he was a music leader following his graduation in 1985 from Lebanon Valley College, Annville, Pennsylvania. Although his degree was in mathematics, he supplemented his course work with music theory and composition and was an active instrumentalist. His compositions include a piece for organ called "Resurrection," which premiered in 1985 at Lebanon Valley College.

In 1992 Brode received his M.A.Th. from Bethany Theological Seminary, Oak Brook, Illinois. During his seminary years, he was organist for Faith Inspirational Choir and the New Horizons Youth Choir at Chicago First Church of the Brethren where he served as summer pastor.

Composer: HUMMEL STREET (*Shepherd of tender youth*), **480**; NEW BEGINNINGS (*This is a day of new beginnings*), **640**

BROKERING, HERBERT (b. May 21, 1926, Beatrice, Neb.), whose father was also a Lutheran minister, was educated at Wartburg College and Seminary, Dubuque, Iowa, and at Trinity Seminary, Columbus, Ohio (B.D., 1950). He also received a master's degree in child psychology from the University of Iowa, Iowa City (1947). Brokering took advanced study in religious education at the University of Pittsburgh (Pa.) and in theology at the University of Kiel and the University of Erlangen in Germany.

In addition to pastorates in Pennsylvania, New York, and Texas, Brokering's diverse career has included positions with the Lutheran World Federation, the World Council of Churches (European workcamp), the University of Iowa Lutheran Student Association, and the American Lutheran Church. Since 1970 he has been freelancing in creative worship, his work ranging from consulting to part-time professor appointments.

A prolific author, Brokering has written texts for hymns, anthems, and cantatas, as well as thirty-three books. Among these is *Pilgrimage to Luther's Germany,* co-authored with his close friend and Yale University scholar Roland Bainton. Their other collaborations include co-directing the film *Where Luther Walked* and conducting tours to significant Reformation sites.

Author: *Earth and all stars,* **47**

BROOKE, STOPFORD AUGUSTUS (b. Nov. 14, 1832, Glendoen, near Letterkenny, Donegal, Ireland; d. Mar. 18, 1916, Four Winds, Surrey, England) studied at Trinity College, Dublin (B.A., 1856; M.A., 1858).

While there he won the Downes Prize and the Vice-Chancellor's Prize for English verse. After his ordination he was curate of St. Matthew's, Marylebone (1857-1859); curate of Kensington (1860-1863); chaplain at the British Embassy in Berlin, 1863-1865; minister of St. James' Chapel, York Street, London, 1866-1875, and of Bedford Chapel, 1876. In 1872 he was appointed chaplain to Queen Victoria.

Though a popular preacher in London, he left the Anglican Church in 1880 because of his liberal views and remained independent from denominational ties. Besides a number of books on English literature, a book of poems, and a collection of sermons, he published *Christian Hymns* (1881), a collection of 269 works for use by his congregation. He did not copyright any of his hymns, believing all hymns should be available for use free of charge.

Author: *Let the whole creation cry,* **51**

BROOKS, PHILLIPS (b. Dec. 13, 1835, Boston, Mass.; d. Jan. 23, 1893, Boston, Mass.) attended the Boston Latin School and received his A.B. from Harvard University in 1855. Following a brief, unsuccessful teaching career, he decided to prepare for the ministry at the Episcopal Theological Seminary in Alexandria, Virginia. He was ordained in 1859 and became one of America's most gifted and magnetic preachers. His tall and imposing figure in the pulpit was balanced by his sense of humor and winning personality, especially with children.

Brooks served two parishes in Philadelphia before being called to Trinity Church in Boston, where he preached his first sermon in October of 1869. Many of his sermons were published and are still widely read. Brooks was well traveled and preached in England on many occasions. He died suddenly, only two years after being named bishop of Massachusetts.

Author: *O little town of Bethlehem,* **191**

BROWNE, SIMON (b. 1680, England; d. 1732, Shepton Mallet, England) studied for the ministry under John Moore and subsequently served an independent congregation in Portsmouth, England, until 1716. A pastorate in Old Jewry, London, followed, where he was a neighbor of Isaac Watts. Although Browne suffered severe depression and delusions after accidentally killing a highway robber, he was a competent writer and translator. His works include children's stories, hymns, and a volume of sermons. He published more than twenty volumes.

Author: *Come, gracious Spirit,* **303**

BRÜCKNER, HERMAN H. M. (b. Mar. 11, 1866, Grundy County, Iowa; d. Jan. 25, 1942, Beatrice, Neb.) followed in the footsteps of his father, a

Lutheran pastor, studying at Wartburg Seminary, Dubuque, Iowa, and being ordained to the ministry in 1888. He served pastorates in Illinois, Michigan, Kentucky, Wisconsin, and Iowa. While residing for fifteen years in Iowa City, he earned an M.A. degree at the University of Iowa (1917). During World War I, he taught at Wartburg Seminary, preparing German-speaking pastors to preach in English. In 1926 he accepted a professorship at Hebron College (Neb.), from which he retired as professor emeritus in 1941. He continued his academic education at the state universities of Nebraska and Wisconsin and was awarded an honorary D.D. degree by Wartburg Seminary in 1938. The *American Lutheran Hymnal* contains seventy-two of his translations from German and French, as well as five original hymn texts.

Translator: *Take thou my hand, O Father*, **581**; *O Power of love*, **593**

BRUMBAUGH, WILBUR E. (b. Dec. 11, 1931, near Carrollton, Ohio; d. Oct. 25, 1977, Washington, D.C.) graduated from Kent State University (Ohio) in 1953 and from Bethany Theological Seminary, Oak Brook, Illinois, in 1957. He pastored congregations in California and Oregon. From 1960 to 1964, he was employed by Brethren Press as assistant editor of Christian education publications and served as managing editor of both the Church of the Brethren *Leader* and *Messenger* (1964-1972). From 1973 until his tragic death in a theater fire, he edited heritage materials and coordinated worship ministries for the denomination. Though a writer and editor by profession, Brumbaugh is also remembered for his tunes, nine of which appear in *The Brethren Songbook* (1974).

Composer: MINE ARE THE HUNGRY (*Brothers and sisters of mine*), **142**; O GOD OF MYSTERY (*O God of mystery and might*), **130**; ROHRER (*Bread of life*), **455**

BRUNK, JOHN DAVID (b. Mar. 13, 1872, Harrisonburg, Va.; d. Feb. 5, 1926, Elkhart, Ind.), a significant leader in music of the (Old) Mennonites during the first quarter of the twentieth century, studied at the New England Conservatory of Music, Boston, and at the American Conservatory, Chicago. He taught at Bridgewater College (Va.) and at Goshen College (Ind.) from 1906 to 1914.

Besides teaching music, he dedicated himself to hymn editing and composition. Always interested in promoting good hymn singing, he authored *Educational Vocal Studies*, a kind of singing-school book in the nineteenth-century tradition for church music leaders. He edited the following hymnals: *Church and Sunday School Hymnal* (1902), its *Supplement* (1911), *Life Songs* (1916), and *Church Hymnal* (1927, co-edited with S. F. Coffman).

Brunk composed his hymns in styles compatible with then-current Mennonite singing, patterning them after chorales, psalm tunes, Lowell Mason types, and Sunday school and gospel songs. A chromatic,

Victorian style can be seen in his "In thy holy place" (Oyer 1980) and even the tune name WATTS reflects his inspiration for "Before Jehovah's aweful throne."

Composer: *In thy holy place we bow*, **2**; WATTS (*Before Jehovah's aweful throne*), **18**

BUDRY, EDMOND L. (b. Aug. 30, 1854, Vevey, Switzerland; d. Nov. 12, 1932, Vevey) studied theology at Lausanne, Switzerland, and was then pastor at Cully from 1881 to 1889. He was pastor of the Free Church at Vevey for the next thirty-five years, retiring in 1923. In addition to writing original hymns in French, he translated German, English, and Latin texts into French.

Author: *Thine is the glory*, **269**

BURLEIGH, WILLIAM HENRY (b. Feb. 2, 1812, Woodstock, Conn.; d. Mar. 18, 1871, Brooklyn, N.Y.) started his literary career as a journeyman printer and contributor to various periodicals, using his media access as a platform for his passionate anti-slavery and temperance convictions. In Pittsburgh, Pennsylvania, he published the *Christian Witness* and the *Temperance Banner*, then moved to Hartford, Connecticut, to edit the abolitionist paper *Christian Freeman*, later known as *Charter Oak*. Burleigh's writing and oratory earned him enemies, but he persisted. He finished out his career as harbor master in New York City.

Burleigh's volume of *Poems* (1841) warranted reprinting in 1871. His wife, a Unitarian minister, wrote a biographical sketch for that book. Although he was an American Unitarian, his hymns are used more extensively in other denominations and are better known in England.

Author: *Lead us, O Father*, **359**

BURNAP, UZZIAH C. (b. 1834, Brooklyn, N.Y.; d. 1900, Brooklyn), a seller of dry goods in New York City, also studied at the University of Paris and graduated with a music degree. He was considered a very competent organist and noted improviser. Burnap served the Reformed Church in Brooklyn Heights for thirty-seven years. For his denomination he edited *Hymns of the Church* (1869) and *Hymns of Prayer and Praise* (1871). He also gave editorial assistance to *Hymns and Songs of Praise* (1874). Some of his more popular tunes are WIDER WAY, BOSTON, and SCHELL.

Arranger: SERENITY (*Immortal Love, forever full*), **629**

BUTLER, HENRY MONTAGU (b. 1833, Gayton, Northamptonshire, England; d. 1918, Cambridge, England) studied at Harrow School and Trinity College, Cambridge, becoming a fellow there in 1855. In 1856 he became private secretary to William Francis Cooper and also served as secretary to the royal commission for rebuilding the National Gallery. After traveling for a year, he became a curate at Great St. Mary's, Cambridge. In 1859 he was elected headmaster at Harrow School, a position he held for twenty-six years, modernizing both curriculum and facilities. He introduced the study of science, which at that time was regarded suspiciously as "godless."

Butler was named dean of Gloucester Cathedral (1885) and master of Trinity College (1886) where he stayed until his death. His publications include the biographical work *Ten Great and Good Men*, a collection of essays titled *Some Leisure Hours of a Long Life*, as well as several books of sermons.

Author: *Lift up your hearts*, **602**

BYRNE, MARY ELIZABETH (b. July 1, 1880, Dublin, Ireland; d. Jan. 19, 1931, Dublin) was educated at the Dominican Convent in Dublin and the University of Ireland. She specialized in the historic Gaelic language and was a researcher for the Board of Intermediate Education in Ireland. Assisting in compiling the catalogue of the Royal Irish Academy, she also was a contributor to the *Old and Mid-Irish Dictionary* and *Dictionary of the Irish Language*.

Translator: *Be thou my vision*, **545**

CAMERON, CATHERINE (b. Mar. 27, 1927, St. John, New Brunswick) was naturalized as a U.S. citizen in 1965. Following her studies at McMaster University (B.A. in English literature, 1949) and the University of Southern California (M.S., 1970; Ph.D., 1971, sociology), she joined the faculty of the University of La Verne, (Calif.) as professor of social psychology. Now an emeritus, she is a specialist in the area of family dynamics, researching, writing, and speaking in that field. She is married to Stuart Oskamp, professor of social psychology at the Claremont graduate school (Calif.), and has two children and three grandchildren.

Author: *God, who stretched*, **414**

CAMPBELL, JANE MONTGOMERY (b. 1817, London, England; d. Nov. 15, 1878, Bovey Tracey, Devon, England) is known for her English translations of several German hymns. Trained in music and language, she assisted her father, an Anglican priest, as a music teacher at his parish school. In 1861 she translated C. S. Bere's *Garland of Song, or an English Liederkranz* and in 1869 Bere's *Children's Choral Book*. Campbell also authored a textbook titled *A Handbook for Singers* for her classes.

Translator: *We plow the fields and scatter*, **96**

CAMPBELL, ROBERT (b. Dec. 19, 1814, Trochraig, Ayrshire, Scotland; d. Dec. 29, 1868, Edinburgh, Scotland) was a lawyer and active church layman. As a student at the University of Glasgow, he was keenly interested in theology but decided on a profession in law, which he pursued at the University of Edinburgh. Raised Presbyterian, he later joined the Episcopal Church of Scotland, becoming very committed to the education of poor children.

With his extensive classical training, he began a series of translations of Latin hymns in 1848. Many of these, plus a few of his original hymns, were published in *Hymns and Anthems for use in the Holy Services of the Church within the United Diocese of St. Andrew's, Dunkeld, and Dunblane* (1850), often referred to as the "St. Andrew's Hymnal."

Translator: *At the Lamb's high feast*, **262**

CARR, BENJAMIN (b. Sept. 12, 1768, London, England; d. May 24, 1831, Philadelphia, Pa.), after early musical studies with Charles Wesley, Samuel Wesley, and Samuel Arnold, left his native England in 1793 to settle in North America where, together with his father and brother, he continued the family tradition as a successful music publisher in Philadelphia, New York City, and Baltimore.

A notable composer, writer, publisher, and organist, Carr established the Musical Fund Society of Philadelphia in 1820. His Philadelphia publishing firm printed the *Musical Journal for the Piano Forte*, *Music Journal for the Flute or Violin*, Carr's *Musical Miscellany in Occasional Numbers*, and *The Gentleman's Amusement*, while the Baltimore interest published the first edition of "The Star Spangled Banner."

Carr composed both sacred and secular music. One of his operas, *The Archers*, is thought to be among the first American works in that genre. His sacred works include the *Masses, Vespers, Litanies, Psalms, Anthems and Motets* (1805) and *A Collection of Chants and Tunes for the Episcopal Churches of Philadelphia* (1816).

Arranger: SPANISH CHANT (*Come, divine Interpreter*), **302**

CASWALL, EDWARD (b. July 15, 1814, Yately, Hampshire, England; d. Jan. 2, 1878, Edgbaston, Birmingham, England), son of the vicar at Yately, was educated at Marlborough and Brasenose College, Oxford. Ordained in the Anglican Church in 1839, he was later caught up in the Oxford movement and its recovery of Roman Catholic liturgy. In 1847 Caswall resigned his pastorate to join the Roman Catholic Church. Upon the death of his wife in 1849, he became a priest, entering the Oratory of St. Philip Neri at Edgbaston under John Henry Newman. A minister to the poor and a sensitive poet, he is chiefly remembered for his 197 translations of Latin hymns from the *Roman Breviary* and other sources. These translations are collected in *Lyra Catholica* (1849).

Translator: *At the cross, her vigil keeping,* **245**; *I love thee, Lord,* **605**; *Jesus, the very thought of thee,* **588**; *When morning gilds the skies,* **644**

CENNICK, JOHN (b. Dec. 12, 1718, Reading, Berks, England; d. July 4, 1755, London, England), a prolific author of some five hundred hymns, was a denomination-hopper. Born to Quaker parents, he was raised in the Church of England, later converted to Methodism, and for the last decade of his brief life joined the Moravians.

In 1740 John Wesley helped Cennick get a job as a teacher at the Kingswood School near Bristol. While there he became a lay preacher and, after a falling out with Wesley, eventually became a disciple of George Whitefield. In 1749, four years after joining the Moravian Church, Cennick was ordained as a deacon. Though he followed doctrine erratically, his piety and devotion to ministry were unquestioned.

Most of Cennick's hymns appear in four collections published between 1741 and 1754: *Sacred Hymns for the Children of God, Sacred Hymns for the Use of Religious Societies, A Collection of Sacred Hymns,* and *Hymns to the Honor of Jesus Christ.*

Author: *Be present at our table, Lord,* **457**

CHANDLER, JOHN (b. June 16, 1806, Witley, Surrey, England; d. July 1, 1876, Putney, England) was educated at Corpus Christi College, Oxford (B.A., 1872; M.A., 1830). He was ordained deacon in 1831 and priest in 1832, succeeding his father as patron and vicar of Witley in 1837. He was one of the earliest and most successful modern translators of Latin hymns. His first volume, *The Hymns of the Primitive Church, now first Collected, Translated and Arranged* (1837), contains one hundred hymns, most of them ancient, with a few additions from the *Paris Breviary* of 1736. Four years later he republished this volume with a slight variation in the title.

Translator: *Christ is our cornerstone,* **43**; *On Jordan's banks the Baptist's cry,* **183**

CHAPIN, AARON (b. 1753, probably in Springfield, Mass.; d. 1838) was the son of Edward Chapin (1724-1800), a fourth-generation descendant of Samuel Chapin who emigrated from England to the colonies in 1636. The Chapin home resonated with music, with both parents practicing and encouraging it with their five sons, four of whom became singing-school teachers. Aaron, the older brother of Lucius and Amzi (see biographies following), was a cabinetmaker, and for a while Amzi was an apprentice in his shop.

Aaron was not as enthusiastic about Andrew Law's shaped-note method, which Amzi and Lucius encouraged in their teaching. Blessed with good health and a fine singing voice, Aaron was musically active even in his eighties.

Composer: GOLDEN HILL (*In lonely mountain ways*), **560**

CHAPIN, AMZI (b. Mar. 2, 1768, Springfield, Mass.; d. Feb. 19, 1835, Northfield, Ohio), a younger brother of Lucius and Aaron, taught numerous singing schools in the Shenandoah Valley of Virginia and in North Carolina. Tunes credited to Lucius or Amzi include NINETY-THIRD, TWENTY-FOURTH, VERNON, ROCKINGHAM, and ROCKBRIDGE, the latter two named for counties in the Shenandoah Valley.

Amzi lived in Connecticut from 1783 to 1791 and was a cabinetmaker with his brother Aaron. Then he went with the newly married Lucius to Virginia. Amzi conducted his first singing school in Staunton, Virginia, in late 1791. He took his singing schools further south to North Carolina the next year, before setting out for Kentucky in 1795. There he continued the singing schools and assisted Lucius and his family when they arrived in 1797. Amzi retired from farming and moved in 1831 to Northfield where he lived in declining health until his death.

James W. Scholten (*The Chapins: A Study of Men and Sacred Music West of the Alleghenies*, 1795-1842) credits seven tunes to Lucius and Amzi, but definite attributions remain questionable.

Composer: PRIMROSE (*This is a story full of love*), **315**

CHAPIN, LUCIUS (b. Apr. 25, 1760, Springfield, Mass.; d. Dec. 24, 1842, Cincinnati, Ohio) was a noted composer of folk hymn tunes and a well-known singing-school teacher who migrated to Pennsylvania and then to the South. He spent most of his later years in Virginia and Kentucky.

Lucius served in the Continental Army until 1780, participating in the battle at Saratoga and suffering frostbite during the winter of 1777-1778 at Valley Forge, Pennsylvania. From 1782 to 1787 he taught singing schools in New England and probably left for Virginia in 1789. He became a member of Lexington Presbyterian Church (Va.) in 1791. In 1797 he moved to Kentucky where he taught singing schools and was a partner with his brother Amzi in a mill. In 1836 or 1837, Lucius and his wife moved to Cincinnati where he died in 1842.

Composer: PRIMROSE (*This is a story full of love*), **315**

CHATFIELD, ALLEN WILLIAM (b. Oct. 2, 1808, Chatteris, Cambridgeshire, England; d. Jan. 10, 1896, Much-Marcle, Herefordshire, England) had a distinguished career as a student at Charterhouse School and Trinity College (B.A., 1831). Ordained in the Church of England in 1832, he was vicar of two parishes, Stotfold, Bedfordshire (1833-1847), and Much-Marcle, Herefordshire (1847 until his death). He published sermons, a *Litany*, the *Te Deum*, and other parts of the Anglican liturgy in Greek verse. He also published *Songs and Hymns of Earliest Greek Christian Poets, Bishops, and Others, Translated into English Verse* (1876).

Translator: *Lord Jesus, think on me*, **527**

CHISHOLM, THOMAS OBEDIAH (b. July 29, 1866, Franklin, Ky.; d. Feb. 29, 1960, Ocean Grove, N.J.) attended a small rural school, then took over as its teacher at age sixteen. He assumed the editorship of *The Franklin Favorite*, a weekly newspaper, when he was twenty-one. In 1893 he experienced a conversion at a revival meeting headed by Henry Clay Morrison, founder of Asbury College and Theological Seminary, Wilmore, Kentucky. Morrison persuaded Chisholm to move to Louisville to edit the *Pentecostal Herald*.

In 1903 Chisholm was ordained to the Methodist ministry and briefly held a pastorate at Scottsville, Kentucky, but poor health prompted him to move his family to Winona Lake, Indiana, where he began selling insurance. He relocated to Vineland, New Jersey, in 1916, retired in 1953, and finished his life at the Methodist Home for the Aged in Ocean Grove. Chisholm drafted more than twelve hundred poems; at least eight hundred have been published and many set to music.

Author: *Great is thy faithfulness*, **327**

CHIU, EVELYN SAU-YEE (b. Oct. 19, 1957, Hong Kong) studied psychology. From 1983 to 1989, she worked with her husband, David, in the planting of Saskatoon Chinese Mennonite Church in Saskatchewan. They now reside in Abbotsford, British Columbia.

Translator: *Now go forward*, **399**

CHRISTIERSON, FRANK VON (b. Dec. 25, 1900, Lovisa, Finland) came to the U.S. in 1905 with his parents and five siblings. A graduate of Stanford University (Calif.; B.A. in psychology), he directed youth work in California for three years before entering San Francisco Theological Seminary. He was ordained to the Presbyterian ministry following his graduation in 1929 and served fourteen years as minister of Calvary Presbyterian Church in Berkeley, California. Under the auspices of the Presbyterian Board of National Missions, he began two new churches in North Hollywood and Citrus Heights, both in California.

After retiring in 1965, he served several interim pastorates in Nevada and northern California and is now pastor emeritus at First Presbyterian Church of Roseville, near Sacramento. He has also been moderator of the

San Francisco and Los Angeles presbyteries and vice-moderator of the synod of California, Utah, and Nevada.

Christierson began writing hymns during his pastorate at Berkeley. In 1939 one of his texts was chosen as the official hymn of the San Francisco Golden Gate International Exposition. He has been published in *Monday Morning* magazine for Presbyterian ministers and in recent hymnals of seven major denominations. The collection *Make A Joyful Noise* (1987) contains 114 hymns and 15 poems and meditations from his pen. Eighteen of these have been published by the Hymn Society of the United States and Canada, which named him a fellow of the society in 1982.

Author: *As saints of old*, **386**

CLAASSEN, SARA (b. May 6, 1935, Beatrice, Neb.) teaches a bilingual kindergarten in Houston, Texas. She prepared the Spanish translation of this hymn for use in her church, the Church of the Redeemer, in Houston.

Translator (Spanish): *I am the Bread of life*, **472**

CLARK, ALDEN H. (b. 1878; d. 1960) was a Congregational missionary for nearly thirty years in India where he founded the Nagpada Neighborhood House in Bombay. Later, he returned to Boston, to serve as secretary for India, Ceylon, the Philippines, Spain, and Mexico for the American Board of Commissioners for Foreign Missions.

Translator: *Heart and mind, possessions, Lord*, **392**

CLARKE, JEREMIAH (b. ca. 1669; d. Dec. 1, 1707, London, England) received his early musical training as a chorister in the Chapel Royal under John Blow. His positions were: organist (1692-1695), Winchester College; organist (1695), vicar-choral (1699), and master of the choristers (1703), St. Paul's Cathedral; and organist (with William Croft, 1704), Chapel Royal. He also served as Queen Anne's music master. Poet and hymn critic Robert Bridges remarks that "his tunes are beautiful, and have the plaintive grace characteristic of his music and melancholy temperament. . . . they are truly national and popular in style, so that their neglect is to be regretted" (Stulken 1981).

Devastated in love, Clarke took his own life in his home in St. Paul's Churchyard and was buried in the New Crypt of St. Paul's. His compositions include many anthems, psalm tunes, and songs, as well as dramatic, instrumental, and keyboard music.

Composer: BISHOPTHORPE (*Make music to the Lord most high*), **73**

CLAUDIUS, MATTHIAS (b. Aug. 15, 1740, Reinfeld near Lübeck, Germany; d. Jan. 21, 1815, Hamburg, Germany), the son of a Lutheran pastor, studied theology at the University of Jena, but a chest illness, coupled with the rationalistic bent at the university, prompted him to study law and languages instead. Attuned to the writings of William Shakespeare and Isaac Newton, Claudius became literary editor in 1771 of *Der Wandsbecker Bote* (The Wandsbeck Messenger), a paper that sought to bring cultural refinement to commoners.

A few years after his marriage, Claudius became a commissioner of Agriculture and Manufactures of Hesse-Darmstadt in 1776 but resigned just a year later after re-evaluating his life. His acquaintance with Goethe and association with a group of free-thinking philosophers had cooled his religious outlook, but his severe illness prompted another about-face and reaffirmation of faith. He returned to Wandsbeck and edited the *Bote* with new Christian fervor.

In 1788 the crown prince of Denmark appointed him auditor of the Schleswig-Holstein Bank at Danish Altona (near Hamburg) where he stayed until 1813 when he was forced to flee during the Napoleonic wars. Claudius returned in time to spend his last days in his daughter's home in Hamburg.

Though Claudius had an unconventional background for hymnwriting and none of his written works were actually designed for church use, his writings have a Christian tone that reflects his faith.

Author: *We plow the fields and scatter*, **96**

CLAUSNITZER, TOBIAS (b. probably Feb. 5, 1619, Thum, near Annaberg, Saxony; d. May 7, 1684, Weiden, Upper Palatinate), a Lutheran pastor, studied at several universities before earning his M.A. from the University of Leipzig in 1643. In 1644 he became chaplain to the Swedish army at Leipzig during the Thirty Years War. In this capacity he preached the thanksgiving sermon at St. Thomas Church in 1645 when Queen Christina assumed the Swedish throne. He also preached a thanksgiving sermon for General Wrangel's army at Weiden on January 1, 1649, following the signing of the Peace of Westphalia. Clausnitzer then became the first pastor of the newly established parish there, which included the towns of Weiden and Pergstein. In addition to this position, he later became a member of the consistory and inspector of the district.

Two other Clausnitzer hymns in English use are "Lord Jesus! may thy grief and pain" and "We all believe in one true God."

Author: *Blessed Jesus, at your word*, **13**

CLAYTON, WILLIAM (b. July 17, 1814, Penwortham, Lancashire, England; d. Dec. 4, 1879, Salt Lake City, Utah) became a Mormon in England where he served as a missionary from 1837 to 1840. Immigrating to the

U.S., he first lived in Nauvoo, Illinois, and was Joseph Smith's private secretary until Smith's death in 1844. Then in 1846 Clayton joined the Brigham Young party heading for Salt Lake City. A pioneer and writer, he was also a musician, playing in a local brass band in Illinois and participating in the first Salt Lake Theatre orchestra as a violinist.

Author: *Come, come, ye saints*, **425**

CLEMENS, PHILIP K. (b. June 7, 1941, Lansdale, Pa.) grew up in the Franconia Mennonite Conference (Mennonite Church), graduated from Christopher Dock Mennonite High School in Lansdale, and married Nancy Musselman. After music studies at Goshen College (Ind.; 1963), he received graduate degrees from Goshen College Biblical Seminary (1966); the School of Sacred Music, Union Theological Seminary, New York City (1968); and a doctorate in church music from the School of Music, Northwestern University, Evanston, Illinois (1975).

After teaching two years at Eastern Mennonite College, Harrisonburg, Virginia, Clemens joined the music faculty at Goshen College where he taught organ, music theory, church music, and black music studies (1970 to 1986). In 1976 he founded the Goshen College Jazz Band and directed it until 1986. Ordained in 1986, he served College Mennonite Church, Goshen, as associate minister through October 1995. In November 1995 he became pastor of Beaverdam Mennonite Church, Corry, Pennsylvania.

Clemens composes music for congregation, choir, organ, brass, and jazz band. He has published *An Irish Blessing* (for choir), *Short Hymn-Tune Arrangements for Organ*, and *Choosing a Church Organ*. Clemens also works in the areas of worship and spirituality and has helped develop the Association of Mennonites in the Arts.

Composer: CHRISTOPHER DOCK (*Creating God, your fingers trace*), **168**; JOYFUL DARK (*Joyful is the dark*), **233**

CLEMENT OF ALEXANDRIA (b. ca. 170; d. ca. 220) was a great teacher of the early Christian era associated with the Gnostics (from the Greek for "knowledge"). The great intellectuals of the day clustered around Alexandria, with its tremendous library and "schools" of the world's philosophical systems. Clement headed one of these schools, teaching that Greek philosophy was a "handmaid" of Christianity and focusing on Jesus as the *Logos* (Word) of God.

Except for his activities at Alexandria, very little is known about this scholar after he was driven from the city under the persecution of Emperor Eseptimius Severus. Clement, whose given name was Titus Flavius Clemens, is thought to have written ten works. Of these, his treatise *The Instructor*, also known as *The Tutor*, was the source of the hymn "Shepherd of tender youth."

Author: *Shepherd of tender youth*, **480**

CLEPHANE, ELIZABETH CECILIA (b. June 18, 1830, Edinburgh, Scotland; d. Feb. 19, 1869, Melrose, Scotland), a sheriff's daughter, was a member of the Free Church of Scotland. After her father's death, the family moved to Melrose, near the home of Sir Walter Scott. In spite of ill health, she was known for her humanitarian work among the poor who gave her the name "Sunbeam." She is also the author of the hymn "The ninety and nine," made famous by Ira Sankey.

Author: *Beneath the cross of Jesus*, **250**

CLEVELAND, JUDGE JEFFERSON (b. Sept. 21, 1937, Elberton, Ga.; d. June 20, 1986, Washington, D.C.) graduated *summa cum laude* from Clark College, Atlanta, Georgia, and with highest honors from Illinois Wesleyan University, Bloomington. He received his doctoral degree from Boston University (Mass.). Cleveland taught at Claflin College, Orangeburg, South Carolina; Langston University (Okla.); Jarvis Christian College, Hawkins, Texas; University of Massachusetts, Boston; and Wesley Theological Seminary, Washington, D.C.

Cleveland, who despite his first name was not a judge, employed his special expertise in African American music to co-edit and contribute to the United Methodist *Songs of Zion* hymnbook (1981). During the same year, he toured the U.S. and Africa as teacher, performer, and lecturer; then he made a similar tour of Europe in 1984. He also served as a consultant to the General Board of Discipleship of the United Methodist Church.

Arranger: MARTYRDOM (*Father, I stretch my hands to thee*), **529**

CLOCK (KLOCK), LEENAERDT (fluorished ca. 1600) was a Mennonite preacher who moved from Germany to Holland around 1590. He was a prolific author of devotional hymns, but his work was sometimes criticized because he was so fond of writing in acrostics, forcing the initial lines of his stanzas into a form that, when read together, give the name of a person. Of 435 hymns, 398 are written this way. Clock also published an important book of prayers (*A Formulary of Several Christian Prayers*), a standard upon which later Mennonite prayer literature has been built. As a proponent of audible prayers, he was at odds with those who favored silent prayer.

Author: *O Gott Vater*, **33**; *Our Father God, thy name we praise*, **32**; Almighty, merciful, and loving Father, **787**

COBER, KENNETH LORNE (b. July 12, 1902, Dayton, Ohio) was brought up in Puerto Rico by missionary parents and then attended Bucknell University, Lewisburg, Pennsylvania, and Colgate Rochester Divinity School, Hamilton, New York. He served the American Baptist denomination as a local pastor and as an administrator on the state level in New York, Rhode Island, and Connecticut before becoming executive director of the Division of Christian Education, American Baptist Convention, from 1953 to 1970. He is author of a number of books on Christian education, including *The Church's Teaching Ministry* (1964); he served on the joint committee for the *Hymnbook for Christian Worship* (1970). Cober retired to Penney Farms, Florida.

Author: *Renew your church*, **363**

COFFIN, CHARLES (b. 1676, Buzancy, France; d. June 20, 1749, Paris, France) attended Duplessis College, University of Paris. He began teaching at the College of Dormans, Beauvais, in 1701, becoming principal there in 1713. After serving as rector of the University of Paris from 1718 to 1723, he returned to his position as principal at Beauvais. He was the leading Latin author in France and wrote more than one hundred hymns. A collection of his Latin poems was first published in 1727, followed in 1736 by his *Hymni Sacri*. The *Paris Breviary* (1736), which sought to improve the literary quality of Latin hymns, included many of Coffin's texts. In 1755 his collected poems were published in two volumes by Lenglet of Paris.

Author: *On Jordan's banks the Baptist's cry*, **183**

COFFIN, HENRY SLOANE (b. Jan. 5, 1877, New York, N.Y.; d. Nov. 25, 1954, Lakeville, Conn.) graduated from Yale University, New Haven, Connecticut (A.B., 1897; M.A., 1900). He studied at New College, Edinburgh, Scotland; the University of Marburg, Germany; and Union Theological Seminary, New York City (B.D., 1900). Ordained in 1900, he spent the first five years of his ministry at Bedford Park Presbyterian Church. During the next twenty-one years, he served Madison Avenue Presbyterian Church, New York City, while also teaching practical theology and hymnody at Union Theological Seminary. In 1926 he became president of the seminary, serving in that capacity until his retirement in 1945. He was elected moderator of the Presbyterian Church (USA) in 1943. During his lifetime he received fourteen honorary degrees. He was co-editor of *Hymns of the Kingdom* (1910) and the author of numerous books on contemporary issues facing the church.

Translator: *O come, O come, Immanuel* (sts. 5-6), **172**

COFFMAN, SAMUEL FREDERICK (b. June 11, 1872, near Dale Enterprise, Va.; d. June 28, 1954, Vineland, Ontario) was the second son of John S. Coffman, known among the Mennonites as one of the earliest evangelists of the nineteenth century and later assistant editor of the *Herald of Truth*. In his youth S. F. ran errands and learned a number of jobs at the publishing house, continuing to work in the book-binding department after his graduation from Elkhart High School (Ind.).

Coffman began teaching Sunday school when he was thirteen. After baptism at age fifteen, he became even more involved in teaching and other activities of the church. In 1894 he served in the Mennonite mission in Chicago with M. S. Steiner and attended Moody Bible Institute where he learned the analytical method of Bible study that he used in teaching and writing throughout his life.

He was ordained in 1895 and soon was assisting some of the smaller congregations in the Vineland, Ontario, area (around Niagara). With his wife, Ella Mann Coffman, he raised five children and lived most of the remainder of his life there. He was ordained a bishop in 1903.

For the larger church, Coffman was responsible for beginning short-term Bible schools, the first one at Kitchener, Ontario, in 1907. He was Bible study editor of the *Christian Monitor* for its entire existence, from 1909 to 1953, and contributed many articles to other church periodicals. He was a member of the music committee of the (Old) Mennonite General Conference from its beginning in 1911 until 1947, serving as hymn editor during the production of the *Supplement to the Church and Sunday School Hymnal* (1911), *Life Songs* (1916), *Life Songs No. 2* (1938), and *Church Hymnal* (1927).

Author: *In thy holy place we bow*, **2**

COLE, JOHN (b. 1774, Tewkesbury, England; d. Aug. 17, 1855, Baltimore, Md.) emigrated from England with his family and settled in Baltimore in 1785. He claimed that he was self-taught in music, though he may have attended local singing schools to acquire some basic musical knowledge. In the War of 1812, he served in the Maryland militia, where he played clarinet in a band. From 1822 until 1839, he operated a music store in Baltimore along with his publishing business, which included the publication of secular sheet music. During his lifetime Cole compiled about thirty collections of tunebooks, including some printed in his own shop. His collections include *The Beauties of Psalmody* (1797), *Sacred Harmony* (1799), *The Seraph* (ca. 1827), *Union Harmony* (ca. 1829), and *Laudate Dominum* (1846). His *Devotional Harmony* (1814) contains mostly his own compositions.

Composer: GENEVA (*When all thy mercies, O my God*), **72**

COLE-TURNER, RONALD S. (b. Dec. 22, 1948, Logansport, Ind.) spent most of his childhood in northeastern Ohio, the son of a Christian and Missionary Alliance Church minister and a Mennonite mother. He attended Wheaton College (Ill.) where he met his wife, Rebecca Cole. After graduating from Wheaton (1971) and Princeton Theological Seminary (N.J.; M.Div., 1974; Ph.D. in systematic theology, 1983), he was ordained by the United Church of Christ and served two pastorates in New York. He was campus minister at Michigan Technological University, Houghton, from 1982 to 1985 when he joined the faculty at Memphis Theological Seminary (Tenn.) where he teaches theology.

Cole-Turner has written numerous articles, many on the relationship of genetics and science to religion, that have been published in both scientific and religious publications. He also has authored a book on the subject: *The New Genesis: Theology and the Genetics Revolution.*

Author: *Child of blessing, child of promise,* **620**

COLLER, PERCY E. B. (b. 1895, Liverpool, England) was a choirboy in the cathedrals of Liverpool and Oxford. At age fifteen he was appointed sub-organist of Liverpool Cathedral and obtained his education at Liverpool University. After serving in the British army during World War I, he was organist/choirmaster at St. Peter's Church, Mount Royal, Montréal, Québec.

Composer: ST. JOAN (*Christ is the world's true light*), **334**

COLLINS, HENRY (b. 1827, Barningham, Darlington, England; d. 1919, St. Bernard's Abbey, Coalville, North Leicester, England) received his M.A. from Oxford in 1854, having been ordained in the Church of England the year before. He entered the Roman Catholic Church in 1857 and in 1860 joined the Cistercian Order, becoming a Trappist monk in St. Bernard's Abbey. Known as "Father Augustine," he was also chaplain to the Cistercian nuns at Staplehill, Dorset, from 1882 to 1913. Most of his writings are biographical or historical and relate to Roman Catholic topics. He compiled *Hymns for Schools and Missions* (1854), to which he contributed two hymns, both written while he was an Anglican.

Author: *Jesus, my Lord, my God, my all,* **533**

COLLYER, ROBERT (b. Dec. 8, 1823, Keighly, Yorkshire, England; d. 1912, New York, N.Y.), a blacksmith by trade, came to the U.S. in 1850 and set up shop in Shoemakersville, Pennsylvania. He was also a Methodist preacher with little formal schooling and read voraciously to increase his education. He later entered the Unitarian ministry.

In 1859 Collyer went to Chicago as supervisor of a Unitarian agency for helping the needy. He stayed in Chicago to pastor and in 1866 was made minister of the newly built Church of the Messiah. Although this church was one of the buildings that survived the great Chicago fire of 1871, the church members relocated it out of the isolated, blackened area and rebuilt it, dubbing the new structure Second Church of the Messiah.

Collyer was a popular lecturer, outstanding preacher, and author of numerous books. In 1879 he accepted a call to Church of the Messiah in New York City where he remained until his retirement.

Author: *Unto thy temple, Lord, we come*, **4**

COLVIN, THOMAS STEVENSON (b. Apr. 16, 1925, Glasgow, Scotland) first studied engineering at Royal Technical College of Glasgow. After military service he enrolled as a divinity student at Trinity College, Glasgow; became a member of the Iona Community; and in 1954 was ordained as a minister in the Church of Scotland.

During his years as a missionary serving the Church of Central Africa Presbyterian in Malawi and Ghana, Colvin collected folk melodies and hymns, which the Iona Community members helped spread throughout Europe. These hymns were published in *Free to Serve* (1969) and *Leap My Soul* (1976), which are brought together in *Fill Us with Your Love* (1983). In 1976 Colvin returned to London and became pastor of Sydenham United Free Church. He has since served as consultant with the Christian Council of Malawi, with special interest in the work of the churches as they assist refugees from Mozambique. He returns to Africa frequently.

Author/Arranger: *God sends us the Spirit* (NATOMAH), **293**

CONKEY, ITHAMAR (b. May 15, 1815, Shutesbury, Mass.; d. Apr. 30, 1867, Elizabeth, N.J.), of Scottish ancestry, was a talented musician. After serving Central Baptist Church of Norwich, Connecticut, as organist and choirmaster, he moved to New York City in 1850. There he had a successful career as a bass soloist, both at Calvary Episcopal Church and in numerous oratorios. From 1861 until his death, he was director and bass soloist of the quartet/choir of Madison Avenue Baptist Church.

Composer: RATHBUN (*In the cross of Christ I glory*), **566**

CONVERSE, CHARLES CROZAT (b. Oct. 7, 1832, Warren, Mass.; d. Oct. 18, 1918, Highwood, N.J.) began studying music at Leipzig Conservatory in 1855 and returned to the U.S. in 1859 to study at Albany Law School (N.Y.) where he received his LL.B. in 1861. In 1895 Rutherford College (N.C.) conferred on him the degree of LL.D.

In addition to his successful law practice in Erie, Pennsylvania, Converse edited and compiled Sunday school hymnbooks and became a partner in the Burdette Organ Company. Besides writing hymn tunes, he composed overtures, songs, oratorios, several string quartets and quintets, and two symphonies. He sometimes used the pen names of Reden, Nevers, or Revons.

Composer: ERIE (CONVERSE) (*What a friend we have in Jesus*), **574**

COOTE, CONSTANCE HEADLAM (b. Dec. 30, 1844, England; d. Aug. 16, 1936, Tunbridge Wells, Kent, England) is an obscure biographical subject. In 1897 she married a minister, Algernon Coote, who became the eleventh baronet and thus titled the Reverend Sir Algernon. For a time they lived at Ballyfin, Ireland, where Rev. Coote died in 1899. Mrs. Coote returned to Tunbridge Wells where she had lived prior to her marriage.

Author: *In the quiet consecration*, **461**

COPES, VICAR EARLE (b. Aug. 12, 1921, Norfolk, Va.) earned his degrees from Davidson College (N.C.; B.A., 1940) and Union Theological Seminary, New York City (S.M.M., 1944; B.D., 1945). From 1946 to 1949, he was minister of music at Highland Park Methodist Church, Dallas, Texas. He was professor of organ and church music at Hendrix College, Conway, Arkansas (1949-1956), and at Cornell College, Mount Vernon, Iowa (1956-1958).

After those stints in the academic world, he edited the Methodist monthly magazine *Music Ministry* from 1958 to 1967. As teacher and editor, he sought to foster higher standards for church music among Methodists and ecumenically.

Copes later headed the organ and church music department at Birmingham-Southern College (Ala.) before moving to Ohio where he was minister of music at Christ United Methodist Church in Kettering (1973-1986), also teaching part time at Wright State University in Dayton. Copes is retired but maintains status as an ordained elder in the West Ohio Conference of the United Methodist Church.

A composer of anthems, he served as a special consultant for *The Methodist Hymnal* (1966) and contributed a number of original tunes and harmonizations to that collection.

Composer: KINGDOM (*For the bread*), **477**

CORBEIL, PIERRE DE (d. June 3, 1221 or 1222) attended the Academy of Paris when he was ten years old. He served as archdeacon of York and of Evreux and was assistant to the bishop of Lincoln. He became bishop of Cambrai in 1199 and archbishop of Sens a year later.

Composer: ORIENTIS PARTIBUS (*Christian, do you hear the Lord?*, **494**; *Lord, should rising whirlwinds*, **92**)

COWPER, WILLIAM (b. Nov. 15, 1731, Berkhampstead, Hertfordshire, England; d. Apr. 25, 1800, East Dereham, Norfolk, England) was a son of the chaplain to King George II. His mother, a descendant of the poet John Donne, died when William was six years old; he was still composing lines to her memory when he was an old man. Although he studied law at Westminster School and was called to the bar in 1754, he never practiced.

It is said he paled at the thought of the routine examination for clerkship in the House of Lords. Plagued by bouts of depression throughout his life, he attempted suicide, believing he was condemned by God.

Cowper pulled out of his illness for a productive period of nineteen years when John Newton befriended him in Olney. *Olney Hymns* (1779), a product of his collaboration with Newton, contains sixty-seven of his hymns. Cowper was a highly regarded poet of his day, recognized for his translation of Homer (1791) and his poem "The Task" (1785). Belying his melancholy feelings, Cowper's work is replete with sensitivity and tenderness.

Author: *Christian, do you hear the Lord?*, **494**; *Heal us, Immanuel, here we are*, **375**; *Oh, for a closer walk with God*, **520**; *Sometimes a light surprises*, **603**

COX, FRANCES ELIZABETH (b. May 10, 1812, Oxford, England; d. Sept. 23, 1897, Headington, England) was one of the major translators of German chorales. Baron Bunsen, the ambassador of Prussia to England, helped Cox select hymns to translate. Her work appears in two volumes: *Sacred Hymns from the German* (1841) and its revision, *Hymns from the German* (1864).

Translator: *Sing praise to God who reigns*, **59**

CRANMER, THOMAS (b. July 2, 1489, Aslacton, Nottinghamshire, England; d. Mar. 21, 1556, Oxford, England), the first Protestant archbishop of Canterbury, was educated at Cambridge University. At Cambridge he was married briefly (his wife died in childbirth) before becoming ordained. Amid the religious ferment of that time, he rejected papal supremacy early on and abandoned the belief in transubstantiation by 1538. He caught the attention of Henry VIII when he appeared to be sympathetic to the king's attempt to have his marriage annulled. The king made him archdeacon of Taunton and a royal chaplain and sent him abroad on diplomatic missions. In Germany Cranmer secretly married a niece of a Lutheran reformer (not until much later was he able to acknowledge her publicly). He was consecrated as the archbishop of Canterbury in 1533 and soon pronounced the king's first marriage void, his second valid.

While religious reformation under Henry's reign was limited (one innovation was the placement of the English Bible in parish churches), Cranmer oversaw significant reforms after Edward VI's accession to the throne. His most notable work was the production of the first Book of Common Prayer and its revision in 1552, more Protestant than the original. Edward's successor, Mary I, temporarily restored the old religious order, including recognition of papal authority. Cranmer was imprisoned, tried, and sentenced to death for having acquiesced in a plot to block Mary's accession. Under pressure, he recanted some of his former beliefs. Nonetheless, he was burned at the stake, at which time he reversed his recantation.

Translator: Most holy God, the source of all good, **742**

CRIPE, MERVIN A. (b. May 3, 1919, Goshen, Ind.) studied at Purdue University, West Lafayette, Indiana; Bridgewater College (Va.; B.S., 1947); and Bethany Theological Seminary, Oak Brook, Illinois (M.Div., 1950). Having grown up in the Church of the Brethren, he entered Civilian Public Service when he was drafted in 1941; he served for the duration of World War II in soil conservation, wildlife research, and dairy management. Ordained in 1948, Cripe was pastor of three Church of the Brethren congregations in the course of full-time ministry: Swan Creek, near Wauseon, Ohio; Eel River, near North Manchester, Indiana; and Brook Park, Ohio, where he was given pastor-emeritus status. Cripe has been active in Church of the Brethren leadership as a member of the district board in each of the three districts where he was pastor, as district moderator twice, as district board chairman a number of times; he also represented the respective districts on their standing committees for Annual Conference from time to time. Since retirement in 1981 he has had fourteen interim pastorates. His worship resources have been published in Church of the Brethren bulletins, *Messenger* magazine, and elsewhere. Currently, he and his wife divide their time between Sebring, Florida, and North Manchester, Indiana.

Author: O God, we come seeking you, **671**

CROFT, WILLIAM (bapt. Dec. 30, 1678, Nether Ettington, Warwickshire, England; d. Aug. 14, 1727, Bath, England) was a chorister in the Chapel Royal under John Blow and, in time, became one of the most influential English hymn composers. From 1700 to 1711, he was the organist at the church of St. Anne's, Soho, London; and in 1704, Croft and Jeremiah Clarke were sworn in as joint organists of the Chapel Royal. When Clarke died four years later, Croft was named sole organist. In 1708 he followed Blow as organist at Westminster Abbey and as master of the children and composer at Chapel Royal. In 1713 he received a D.Mus. from Oxford University and, with others, founded the Academy of Vocal Musick in 1725.

His psalm tunes, published in *The Divine Companion* (1707) and *Supplement to the New Version* (1708), mark the transition from the older Genevan and French psalm tunes to the newer English hymnody. He also composed anthems and services, of which the burial service in *Musica Sacra* is considered the classic setting of the Anglican ritual.

Composer: ST. ANNE (*O God, our help in ages past*), **328**

CROLY, GEORGE (b. Aug. 17, 1780, Dublin, Ireland; d. Nov. 24, 1860, Holborn, England) was educated at Dublin University (M.A., 1804; LL.D., 1831). After being ordained in the Anglican Church in 1804, he minstered in Ireland until about 1810 when he moved to London. There he devoted himself to writing biographical, historical, scriptural, and poetic literature, both serious and humorous, but always with a conservative bent. In 1835 Lord Brougham, a Whig patron and relative, provided Croly a yoked pastorate in London, one congregation at St. Stephen's in the city's slum section in Walbrook and the other at Bene't Sherehog. His magnetic, evangelical preaching revived the St. Stephen's parish, which had been closed for one hundred years. He prepared a hymnal for his congregations, *Psalms and Hymns for Public Worship* (1854), with the majority of the hymns bearing his initials. Croly died suddenly on a public street in Holborn. "Spirit of God" is the only one of his hymns to survive.

Author: *Spirit of God! descend*, **502**

CROSBY, FANNY JANE (b. Mar. 24, 1820, Putnam County, N.Y.; d. Feb. 12, 1915, Bridgeport, Conn.) was blinded at six weeks of age because of improper treatment for an eye infection. She began writing verse at the age of eight. Crosby studied at the New York City School for the Blind where she later taught. Because of her poetic gift, she attracted the attention of prominent personalities, including U.S. presidents.

At age thirty-eight, she married Alexander Van Alstyne, a blind musician. Although they were offered financial help, they chose to live in the poorer sections of New York City, giving away what they considered superfluous resources.

A prolific writer, Crosby penned texts for the minstrel songs and cantatas of George F. Root and published several books of secular verse. She is known as "the queen of gospel song" and wrote nearly nine thousand hymns, of which approximately three thousand were published, primarily by the Biglow and Main Company. Her hymns were set to music by the prominent gospel musicians of her time—Bradbury, Doane, Lowry, Sankey, and Kirkpatrick—but under more than two hundred different pseudonyms.

Crosby was also a capable singer, organist, and harpist, as well as a vital devotional speaker and Christian counselor to many people. She lived much of her life in New York City and was a lifelong Methodist. A complete biography is available: *Fanny Crosby*, by Bernard Ruffin (United Church Press 1976).

Author: *A wonderful Savior is Jesus*, **598**; *Blessed assurance*, **332**; *God of our strength*, **36**; *I am thine, O Lord*, **505**; *Jesus, keep me near the cross*, **617**; *Jesus, thou mighty Lord*, **115**; *Praise him, praise him*, **100**; *To God be the glory*, **102**

CROSSMAN, SAMUEL (b. ca. 1624, Bradfield Monachorum, England; d. Feb. 4, 1683 or 1684, Bristol, England) was educated at Pembroke College, Cambridge, from which he graduated in the arts and earned his B.D. in 1660. He was among the few who wrote English hymn paraphrases of scripture before those of Isaac Watts. He was one of two thousand ministers ejected from their churches in 1662 for participating in a movement to make the *Book of Common Prayer* acceptable to both Anglicans and Puritans. Soon afterward he conformed and became one of the king's chaplains. He was named dean of Bristol Cathedral in 1683, shortly before his death.

Author: *My song is love unknown*, **235**

CROUCH, ANDRAÉ (b. 1945, Los Angeles, Calif.), performing with his group, Andraé Crouch and the Disciples, was "discovered" by gospel pioneer Ralph Carmichael. Since then, Crouch has done vocal arranging for many performers, including Michael Jackson and Madonna; Crouch performed with Jackson at the 1988 Grammy Awards. Crouch is the recipient of six Grammy Awards and three Dove Awards, gospel music's equivalent of the Grammy.

Crouch was gospel historian for the Steven Spielberg film adaptation of Alice Walker's *The Color Purple*, and he wrote, adapted, arranged, and conducted choirs for all gospel segments of the film. For his efforts Hollywood voters nominated him for a 1985 Hollywood Oscar for best original score.

As a gospel artist, Crouch performed to sell-out audiences at Carnegie Hall in 1975 and 1978. He is also the first gospel artist to perform at New York City's famed Radio City Music Hall, the Sydney Opera House in Australia, and the Royal Albert Hall in London. He has traveled to forty countries, and his songs have been translated into twenty different languages, as well as numerous African dialects.

Author/Composer: *Soon and very soon*, **611**

CRÜGER, JOHANN (b. Apr. 9, 1598, Gross-breesen bei Guben, Prussia; d. Feb. 23, 1662, Berlin, Germany) began his education in Guben and continued at Jesuit College of Olmütz and at the poetry school in Regensburg. Though extensive travel and his job as a tutor made his formal schooling sporadic, he also studied theology at the University of Wittenberg.

In 1622 he became cantor of the Lutheran St. Nicholas's Church, Berlin's most important cathedral. During his forty years there, he established its famous choir. His prominent collection of chorales, *Praxis Pietatis Melica* (1644), spurred the evolution of seventeenth-century Lutheran hymnody. Republished more than forty times, Crüger themes, not surprisingly, have been used in many compositions of Bach and other Protestant composers.

Composer: GRÄFENBURG (NUN DANKET ALL') (*Lamp of our feet*, **312**; *Spirit divine, inspire our prayers*, **30**); HERZLIEBSTER JESU (*Ah, holy Jesus*), **254**; JESU, MEINE FREUDE (*Jesus, priceless treasure*), **595**; NUN DANKET ALLE GOTT (*Now thank we all our God*), **85, 86**; SCHMÜCKE DICH, O LIEBE SEELE (*Soul, adorn thyself with gladness*), **473**

CRULL, AUGUST (b. Jan. 26, 1845, Rostock, Germany; d. Feb. 17, 1923, Milwaukee, Wis.), a Lutheran pastor and educator, attended Concordia colleges at St. Louis, Missouri, and Fort Wayne, Indiana, and Concordia Seminary, St. Louis. He lived for a while in Milwaukee where he was assistant pastor of Trinity Church and director of the Lutheran high school. Later he became pastor of the Lutheran church in Grand Rapids, Michigan, and from 1873 to 1915, he was professor of German at Concordia College, Fort Wayne. Crull authored a German grammar book, edited a devotional book in German, and enjoyed a reputation as a distinguished hymnologist and German-hymn translator.

Translator: *Abide, O dearest Jesus*, **426**

CUMMINGS, WILLIAM HAYMAN (b. Aug. 22, 1831, Sidbury, Devonshire, England; d. June 6, 1915, London, England), as a choirboy at St. Paul's Cathedral in London, sang the alto arias for the 1846 premiere of *Elijah*, directed by its composer, Felix Mendelssohn. He became a renowned soloist, performing in Europe and the U.S., and was a vocal teacher at the Royal Academy of Music in London. He was principal at the Guildhall School of Music, from which he retired in 1911.

Arranger: MENDELSSOHN (*Hark! the herald angels sing*), **201**

CURTIS, CHRISTINE TURNER (b. 1891, Abington, Mass.; d. 1961) graduated from Wellesley College (Mass.) in 1913. From that time on, she was enveloped in the literary world, working in the advertising departments of two New York City publishers—and later doing editorial work for Ginn and Company, Boston. She was a member of the Congregational Church of North Abington and a trustee of the public library there. Her published works include the novel *Amarilis* (1927) and a collection of poems for children, *Nip and Tuck* (1931).

Author: *As the hart with eager yearning*, **500**

CUTTS, PETER WARWICK (b. June 4, 1937, Birmingham, England) received a B.A. in music from Clare College, Cambridge (1961), and added an M.A. in 1965. He also completed a B.A. in Theology from Mansfield College, Oxford (1963). He has held teaching posts in the music and religious studies departments of two colleges in Huddersfield. Since 1968 Cutts has been a lecturer in music at Bretton Hall College, Wakefield, Yorkshire. He has held various organist positions and has been a tutor/counselor of students. In recent years he has been director of music at St. John's United Methodist Church, Watertown, Massachusetts, and at Andover-Newton Theological School, Newton, Massachusetts.

Composer: BRIDEGROOM (*Like the murmur of the dove's song*), **29**

DAMON (or **DAMAN**), **WILLIAM** (b. ca. 1540, Liege, Belgium; d. ca. 1591, London, England) moved to England in 1562 and seems to have been a musician in the household of Lord Buckhurst (Thomas Sackville). In 1579 he became one of Queen Elizabeth's musicians and was organist of the Chapel Royal for the rest of his life. He is best known for his harmonizations of psalm tunes then in common use. These were published in 1579 under the following title: "*The Psalmes of David in English Meter with Notes of foure partes set unto them by Guilielmo Damon, for John Bull, to the use of the godly Christians for recreating themselves in stede of fond and unseemly Ballades.* At London, printed by John Daye. Cum privilegio."

Editor/Source: SOUTHWELL (*Lord Jesus, think on me*), **527**

DARWALL, JOHN (b. January 1731, Haughton, Staffordshire, England; d. Dec. 18, 1789, Walsall, England) studied at Brasenose College, Oxford, receiving his B.A. in 1756. After ordination he became curate of St. Matthew's Church in Walsalland and later its vicar, a position he held for the remainder of his life. Besides two volumes of piano sonatas, Darwall composed three manuscript volumes of tunes for all 150 psalms of the *New Version* by Nahum Tate and Nicholas Brady. Not confining his work to music and religion, he also wrote a pamphlet about the American Revolution called "Political lamentations . . . ."

Composer: DARWALL'S 148th (*Christ is our cornerstone*, **43**; *Rejoice, the Lord is King*, **288**)

DAUERMANN, STUART (b. Sept. 15, 1944) is one of the founding members of the organization Jews for Jesus. Raised in a conservative Jewish home, he has been a Christian since college days. Seeking to contribute to the body of Christ through his music, Dauermann has been composing music in a Jewish idiom since the mid-1960s, hoping it "will make the church more aware of and comfortable with its Jewish roots." He attended the Manhattan School of Music (N.Y.), receiving his B.A. in music theory and a master's degree in music education.

Composer: THE TREES OF THE FIELD (*You shall go out with joy*), **427**

DAVIES, SAMUEL F. (b. Nov. 3, 1723, Summit Ridge, New Castle, Del.; d. Feb. 4, 1761, Princeton, N.J.) was educated in Chester County, Pennsylvania, under the tutelage of Samuel Blair. The Presbyterian minister William Robinson financed Davies' education by contributing the money he received for preaching a series of evangelistic services.

Davies was licensed to the ministry by the presbytery of New Castle in 1745. In 1753 he went to England to raise funds for the College of New Jersey at Princeton (now Princeton University). Upon his return he completed his M.A. and in 1759 was appointed president of the college, succeeding Jonathan Edwards. During Davies' brief tenure, the standard for the bachelor's degree was raised, as were the requirements for admission. He died of pneumonia in 1761, presumably in Princeton. Davies was considered a great pulpit orator, and "for fifty years after his death, his sermons were more widely read than those of any of his contemporaries" (*Dictionary of American Biography*).

Author: *Great God of wonders*, **149**

DAVISSON, ANANIAS (b. Feb. 2, 1780, Virginia; d. Oct. 21, 1857, Rockingham County, Va.) is best known as the compiler and printer of the famous *Kentucky Harmony*, produced in several editions between 1816 and 1826. Besides publishing this and other shaped-note tunebooks, Davisson contributed some of his own tunes to these collections. He was Presbyterian and strongly promoted the singing-school tradition in the southern U.S. He was active in the Harrisonburg, Virginia, area and is buried just east of there.

Composer: TENDER THOUGHT (*Lord, thou hast searched me*), **556**

DAW, CARL PICKENS, JR. (b. 1944, Louisville, Ky.), a Baptist pastor's son, is the eldest of four children. He lived in Tennessee before going to Rice University, Houston, Texas, where he majored in English. He received his Ph.D. in 1970 from the University of Virginia, Charlottesville. During his college years, Daw became an Episcopalian. He taught at the College of William and Mary, Williamsburg, Virginia, for eight years, leaving there to study for the ministry at the University of the South, Sewanee, Tennessee, from 1978 to 1981. Through his associations in the seminary, he became a member of the text committee for *The Hymnal 1982* (Episcopal). Following seminary graduation he was an assistant pastor for three years in Virginia where he wrote "O day of peace" and "Like the murmur of the dove's song." In 1984 he became vicar-chaplain of St. Mark's Chapel in Storrs, Connecticut, a small parish that also ministers to the University of Connecticut. Then he gave up his chaplaincy to try community life at Community of Celebration, Aliquippa, Pennsylvania, a residential religious order centered on daily community worship and music/worship outreach. Daw is known especially for his outstanding psalm paraphrases and for his expertise in sculpting words into vivid images.

Author: *God the Spirit, Guide and Guardian*, **632**; *How shallow former shadows*, **251**; *Let all creation bless the Lord*, **61**; *Like the murmur of the dove's song*, **29**; *My soul proclaims with wonder*, **181**; *O day of peace*, **408**; *O God, who gives us life*, **483**. Translator: *Sleepers, wake*, **188**

DAWNEY, MICHAEL WILLIAM (b. Aug. 10, 1942, Ilford, Essex, England) received his education at Durham University and Lincoln College, Oxford University. At the London International Film School he worked with Richard Arnell. Dawney has lectured at several colleges, including Trinity and All Saints' at Leeds and University College, Cork. Among his publications are *Ten New Hymnals in Praise of God* (1982) and three collections of folk songs that he edited.

Composer: BAY HALL (*Come and give thanks to the Giver*), **57**

DEARMER, PERCY (b. Feb. 27, 1867, Kilburn, Middlesex, England; d. May 29, 1936, Westminster, London, England) studied at Westminster School and at Christ Church, Oxford. He also studied abroad. Ordained as an Anglican priest in 1892, he was curate in several parishes prior to his fourteen-year stint as vicar of St. Mary the Virgin, London. Under his leadership, St. Mary became noted for the beauty of its liturgy and music.

Dearmer was chaplain to the British Red Cross in Serbia during World War I. From 1919 until his death, he was professor of ecclesiastical art, King's College, London, and became canon of Westminster in 1931.

A well-versed hymnodist, Dearmer surrounded himself with the musical stars of the Anglican Church in his day. As general editor for *The English Hymnal* (1906), he secured Ralph Vaughan Williams as music editor. Martin Shaw, his organist at St. Mary, joined Dearmer and Vaughan Williams in editing *Songs of Praise* (1925), *Oxford Book of Carols* (1928), and *Enlarged Songs of Praise* (1931). As a hymn text writer, Dearmer authored *Songs of Praise Discussed* with Archibald Jacob (1933) and *The English Carol Book* with Martin Fallas Shaw.

Dearmer was not limited in his interests, his expertise, or his energy. His other books include treatises on ecclesiastical history, public worship, ministers' manuals, and travel in Normandy. He was also a Christian socialist and served as secretary of the London chapter of the Christian Social Union (1891-1912).

Author: *Thou true Vine, that heals*, **373**. Translator: *Father, we praise thee*, **650**. Adapter: *I love thee, Lord*, **605**

DECIUS, NICOLAUS (b. ca. 1485, Hof, Upper Franconia, Bavaria; d. ca. 1546) was also known as Nicolaus à Curia, von Hofe, or Hovesch, because German family names were not yet firmly fixed. He studied at a Latin school in Hof and received a B.A. in 1506 at the University of Leipzig and later the M.A. in 1523 from Wittenberg University where he studied Reformation theology.

He became a monk and educator, serving first as prior of the Benedictine nunnery at Steterburg near Wolfenbüttel in 1519; then as rector of the lyceum in Hanover in 1522; and finally as master in the St. Katherine and Egidien School in Braunschweig, by that time a Reformation city.

Attracted to Martin Luther's teachings, Decius anticipated Luther's first hymnal by one year when he wrote Low German versions of the *Gloria in excelsis*, the *Sanctus*, and the *Agnus Dei*, all parts of the Catholic liturgy. At Luther's recommendation, Decius was made assistant pastor at St. Nicholas Church, Stettin, where he served until 1527.

Decius's capabilities as a musician (harpist) eventually influenced his career, and he became cantor in Bartenstein, south of Königsberg, and a teacher in the village's Latin school. Then in 1540, despite Decius's sympathy with Calvinism, the open-minded Margrave Albrecht invited him to become the senior pastor and assistant cantor in Königsberg. Three years later Decius moved to the Calvinist community at Mühlhausen and trained his successor there. After 1546 no biographical information is known.

Author/Composer: *All glory be to God on high* (ALLEIN GOTT IN DER HÖH), **122**; *O Lamb of God all holy* (O LAMM GOTTES), **146**

DECKER, JOACHIM (b. ca. 1575, Hamburg, Germany; d. Mar. 15, 1611, Hamburg) was a German organist and composer whose father, Eberhard Decker, was cantor for the city of Hamburg for forty-six years. Joachim was organist of the Nikolaikirche in Hamburg from 1596 (or possibly 1593) until his death, but none of his organ compositions survives. Thirty of his four-part chorale settings, intended for congregational singing with organ accompaniment, appear in the *Melodeyn Gesangbuch* (Hamburg 1604). Seven of these settings are preserved in *Organum*, i/26-7 (Lippstadt 1950) and one in the *Antigua Chorbuch*, i (Mainz 1951). Continuing the family tradition, Decker's son Johann was organist at Hamburg Cathedral.

Arranger: CHRISTE, DU LAMM GOTTES (*O Christ, the Lamb of God*), **153**

DERSTINE, M. GERALD (b. May 17, 1948, Harrisonburg, Va.) did undergraduate work at Hesston College (Kan.); Millsaps College, Jackson, Mississippi; and Goshen College (Ind.; B.A. in music education, 1970). His professional experience includes teaching choral and general music in Topeka, Kansas; writing and performing songs as a member of two bands based in Aspen, Colorado (1972-1979); and serving as a staff songwriter at MCA Music, Nashville, Tennessee (1982-1990). Since his move to Nashville in 1980, he has used the professional name J. D. Martin. Eleven of his songs have become top-ten country hits. He is now a staff songwriter at Warner-Chappell Music, Nashville.

Author/Composer: *Jesus, Rock of ages,* **515**

DEXTER, HENRY MARTYN (b. Aug. 13, 1821, Plympton, Mass.; d. Nov. 13, 1890, Boston, Mass.) was educated at Yale University, New Haven, Connecticut, receiving his degree in 1840, and at Andover Theological Seminary (Mass.), graduating in 1844. A Congregationalist minister, Dexter held pastorates in Manchester, New Hampshire, and in Boston. He was also an author and editor and left the ministry in 1867 to edit *The Congregationalist and Recorder*.

Translator: *Shepherd of tender youth,* **480**

DIX, WILLIAM CHATTERTON (b. June 14, 1837, Bristol, England; d. Sept. 9, 1898, Cheddar, Somerset, England), son of a surgeon, was educated in the schools of Bristol. He pursued a career in business, becoming manager of a marine insurance company in Glasgow, Scotland. As one of the few lay hymnwriters, he wrote a number of Christmas and Easter carol texts, as well as other literary works for contemporary magazines. His publications include *Hymns of Love and Joy* (1861), *Altar Songs, Verses on the Holy Eucharist* (1867), *Vision of All Saints* (1871), and some metrical settings of Greek and Abyssinian (Ethiopian) hymns.

Author: *As with gladness men of old,* **218**; *What Child is this,* **215**

DOAN, GILBERT EVERETT, JR. (b. Sept. 14, 1930, Bethlehem, Pa.) was educated at Harvard University, Cambridge, Massachusetts (B.A., 1952); Lutheran Theological Seminary, Philadelphia, Pennsylvania (B.D., 1955); University of Pennsylvania, Philadelphia (M.A., 1962); and Princeton Theological Seminary (N.J.; A.B.D., 1984). He was awarded an honorary doctorate by Wagner College, Staten Island, New York, in 1984. Doan was a campus pastor in Philadelphia from 1955 to 1961 and then became the northeastern director of National Lutheran Campus Ministry. Since November 1984 he has been pastor of the Lutheran Church of the Holy Communion in Philadelphia. From 1967 to 1978, Doan chaired the text committee of the Inter-Lutheran Commission on Worship, the group that produced the 1978 *Lutheran Book of Worship*. He is the author of many published books, articles, sermons, and reviews on the subjects of campus ministry and Lutheran church life.

Translator: *All glory be to God on high,* **122**

DOANE, GEORGE WASHINGTON (b. May 27, 1799, Trenton, N.J.; d. Apr. 27, 1859, Burlington, N.J.) was educated at Union College in Schenectady, New York, and General Theological Seminary in New York City. Doane had a distinguished career. He became an Episcopal deacon in 1821 and was ordained in 1823. A year later he was appointed a professor at Trinity College, Hartford, Connecticut. In 1828 he moved to Boston where he became assistant rector of Trinity Church; he was named rector there in 1830. In 1832, when he was just thirty-three, he was appointed bishop of New Jersey, a position he held for the rest of his life.

Influenced by the Oxford movement in England, Doane prepared the initial North American edition of John Keble's *The Christian Year . . .* in 1834. Many of Doane's hymn texts are included in his *Songs by the Way, Chiefly Devotional* (1824), which subsequently appeared in two more editions. His son comments: "My father's poetical writings were simple necessities. He could not help them. His heart was so full of song. . . . And with his heart so full of it, nothing ever touched it but it pressed some out" (Bailey 1950). All of his works were published posthumously in four volumes.

Author: *Thou art the way*, **339**

DOANE, WILLIAM HOWARD (b. Feb. 3, 1832, Preston, Conn.; d. Dec. 24, 1915, South Orange, N.J.) attended Woodstock Academy where he conducted the school choir at age fourteen. In his youth he worked with his father in a cloth manufacturing business and later became head of a large woodworking machinery plant in Cincinnati, Ohio, where he was a respected civic leader and an active Baptist layman.

By avocation he was a composer of songs, cantatas, and ballads, both secular and sacred. He wrote more than 2,200 gospel tunes, frequently collaborating with Fanny Crosby, and edited more than forty songbooks. The Crosby/Doane hymns received frequent exposure through the popular evangelism team of D. L. Moody and Ira D. Sankey.

Composer: DOANE (*Jesus, thou mighty Lord*), **115**; GOD OF OUR STRENGTH (*God of our strength*, **36**; I AM THINE (*I am thine, O Lord*), **505**; NEAR THE CROSS (*Jesus, keep me near the cross*), **617**; TO GOD BE THE GLORY (*To God be the glory*), **102**

DOCK, CHRISTOPHER (b. Germany; d. 1771, near Morristown, N.J.) emigrated from Europe to North America about 1714. By 1718 he had begun teaching in an elementary school in a Mennonite community on the Skippack River, north of Germantown, Pennsylvania. In 1728 he left teaching for farming but returned to the classroom a decade later. From 1738 until his death, he taught three days a week at Skippack and Salford. A respected educator, Dock wrote a school management treatise (*Schul-Ordnung*) in 1750 at the request of Johann Christoph Sauer I, his Brethren contemporary. Although Dock requested that it not be published in his lifetime, he later permitted its publication in 1770 by Christopher Sauer II, one of his former pupils.

Dock passed on his artistic interests to his classes, using a "note-board" (a small blackboard with musical staves) to teach music, and introduced them to the art of *fraktur* (decorative lettering). Some examples of his work are preserved by the Historical Society of Pennsylvania and in the Schwenkfelder Library in Pennsburg, Pennsylvania.

Dock contributed articles to Sauer's *Geistliches Magazien* (Spiritual Magazine), including his "Rules of Conduct" and several hymns. Five of his hymns were included in *Kleine Geistliche Harfe* (1803), the earliest North American Mennonite hymnal. It is said that Dock died in his classroom—on his knees in prayer for his students.

Author: *O little children, gather*, **489**

DODDRIDGE, PHILIP (b. June 26, 1702, London, England; d. Oct. 26, 1751, Lisbon, Portugal) was the youngest of twenty children, of whom only two survived infancy. His parents, a London merchant and the daughter of a Lutheran minister, both died before Philip was thirteen. He refused an offer by the duchess of Bedford to train for the priesthood in the Church of England. Instead, like Isaac Watts, he opted for ministry training at the Nonconformist academy at Kibworth. He pastored at Kibworth and Northhampton, serving the latter as minister and academy head for twenty-two years. His nearly four hundred hymns circulated in manuscript form and were lined out as congregations sang. Showing "unusual social and missionary concern for their time" (Hustad 1978), they were published in 1755, four years after Doddridge's death.

Doddridge aroused the ire of his friends and ecclesiastical contemporaries by sympathizing with the revivalists George Whitefield and John Wesley, preachers then on the periphery of eighteenth-century English church life. Doddridge died of tuberculosis in Lisbon, where he had gone for a rest from his energetic lifestyle.

Author: *Awake, my soul*, **609**; *Great God, we sing*, **639**; *Hark! the glad sound*, **184**

DORAN, CAROL (b. Nov. 11, 1936, Philadelphia, Pa.) studied music and organ at West Chester State University (Pa.; B.S.) and the Eastman School of Music at the University of Rochester (N.Y.; M.M. and D.M.A.). Since 1975 she has been on the faculty of Colgate Rochester Divinity School/Bexley Hall/Crozer Theological Seminary, Hamilton, New York, where she is associate professor of church music and director of community worship and the pastoral music program.

Doran is active in the Association of Anglican Musicians, the American Guild of Organists, and the Hymn Society of the United States and Canada. She has contributed to the publications of these organizations; served on the editorial advisory board for the *Compan-*

ion to Hymnal 1982; and has been guest lecturer at numerous conferences, institutes, and workshops. Doran is a frequent collaborator with text writer Thomas Troeger, and her hymn tunes appear in a number of contemporary denominational and ecumenical hymnals published in the U.S. and England.

Composer: AUTHORITY (*Silence! frenzied, unclean spirit*), **630**; CHRISTPRAISE RAY (*O praise the gracious power*), **111**; FALCONE (*Wind who makes all winds*), **31**; FIRST COMMAND (*If all you want, Lord*), **512**; LIBERATION (*How buoyant and bold the stride*), **394**; WORDLESS (*Through our fragmentary prayers*), **347**

DORSEY, THOMAS ANDREW ("GEORGIA TOM") (b. 1899, Villa Rica, Ga.; d. Jan. 23, 1993, Chicago, Ill.), a blues singer, pianist, and gospel songwriter whose father was a revivalist preacher, moved in 1910 to Atlanta, Georgia, where he was influenced by local blues pianists. During World War I, he studied at the Chicago College of Composition and Arranging and became an agent for Paramount Records.

In 1923 his skill as a pianist, composer, and arranger earned him a place in Les Hite's Whispering Serenaders. Soon after, Dorsey formed his own Wildcats Jazz Band, which led to the development of his illustrious career. As a young man, he wavered between religious and secular music, playing Atlanta bordellos and parties threatened with police raids. Although his first gospel song "Someday, Somewhere" was published in 1921 in the collection *Gospel Pearls*, it was not until the early 1930s that Dorsey moved totally to gospel music. Then his tunes became so popular that songs in that genre were simply called "Dorseys" (*Christian Century*, Mar. 3, 1993).

After a religious conversion connected with an admonition to abandon "the devil's music," he pioneered the first gospel choir at the Ebenezer Baptist Church of Chicago in 1931. The following year he founded, with Sallie Martin, the National Convention of Gospel Choirs and Choruses and also started the first outlet for printed black American gospel music, the Thomas A. Dorsey Gospel Songs Publishing Company. His most successful gospel song was "Precious Lord, take my hand" (1932). Becoming best known for his compositions, Dorsey toured with Mahalia Jackson and Roberta Martin.

The "father of gospel music," Dorsey was considered the most influential personality in the gospel song movement. He was also the first African American to be voted into the National Music Hall of Fame. "[Dorsey] was able to take the anxieties, joys and aspirations of the poor, rejected and often uneducated African-American population and express them in lyrics that not only captured the very essence of the Christian movement but also spoke for each Christian as if he or she were making a personal statement" (*Christian Century*, Mar. 3, 1993).

Author/Adapter: *Precious Lord, take my hand*, **575**

DÖVING, CARL (b. Mar. 21, 1867, Norddalen, Norway; d. Oct. 2, 1937, Chicago, Ill.) came to North America from Norway as a young man, completing his education at Luther College, Decorah, Iowa, and at Luther Seminary, St. Paul, Minnesota. Döving pastored Lutheran churches in Minnesota and Brooklyn, New York. Late in his career he did missionary work in Chicago. Because of his command of languages, Döving was selected for the committee responsible for publishing the English-language *The Lutheran Hymnary* of 1913. He translated more than thirty German and Scandinavian hymns and texts into English for that hymnal.

Translator: *Built on the Rock,* **309**

DRAPER, WILLIAM HENRY (b. Dec. 19, 1855, Kenilworth, Warwickshire, England; d. Aug. 9, 1933, Clifton, Bristol, England) studied at Cheltenham College and Keble College, Oxford. Ordained in 1880, Draper served as curate, vicar, and rector at several churches before becoming Master of the Temple in London (1919-1930). Besides translating many Greek and Latin hymn texts into English, he published a number of books, including *The Victoria Book of Hymns* (1897), *The Way of the Cross* (1925), and *Hymns for Tunes by Orlando Gibbons* (1925).

Translator: *All creatures of our God and King,* **48**

DRURY, MIRIAM (b. 1900, California; d. 1985, Pasadena, Calif.) was a church organist in her youth, and when she married a Presbyterian minister, she continued her study of and interest in music wherever her husband's career took them: Shanghai, China; Edinburgh, Scotland; Moscow, Idaho; and San Francisco, California. She created both texts and tunes, some of which appear in *Hymns for Primary Worship* (1946) and other children's hymnals. Drury also won awards from the Hymn Society of America (now the Hymn Society of the United States and Canada), which published a number of her hymns. Following her husband's retirement from the faculty of San Francisco Seminary in 1963, they lived in Pasadena, California.

Author: *Become to us the living Bread,* **475**

DUBOIS, (FRANÇOIS CLEMENT) THÉODORE (b. Aug. 24, 1837, Rosnay, Marne, France; d. June 11, 1924, Paris, France), an organist, teacher, and composer, was a brilliant student at the Paris Conservatoire where he took first prizes in harmony, fugue, and organ. A winner of the Prix de Rome in 1861, he remained in Italy until 1866 when he returned to Paris, becoming choirmaster at Ste. Clothilde. There his cantata *The Seven Last Words of Christ* was first performed on Good Friday of 1867. He became choirmaster at La Madeleine in 1869 and was organist there from 1877 until 1896; meanwhile, he was appointed professor of harmony at the Conservatoire in 1871 and was the director from 1896 to 1905. His church music, suited to Catholic liturgies, was quite popular in its time.

Composer: *Christ, we do all adore thee,* **105**

DUCK, RUTH C. (b. Nov. 21, 1947, Washington, D.C.) graduated with honors from Southwestern-at-Memphis University (now Rhodes College), Tennessee (B.A. Christian Ed., 1969) and from Chicago Theological Seminary (M.Div., 1973), which also bestowed on her an honorary doctorate in 1983. She earned additional degrees at the University of Notre Dame, South Bend, Indiana (M.A.Th., 1987) and Boston School of Theology (Th.D., 1989).

Duck is noted for her work in worship, hymnody, and inclusive language. She has edited or co-edited the worship resources *Bread for the Journey* (1981), *Flames of the Spirit* (1985), and *Touch Holiness* (1989). She was co-editor of *Because We Are One People* (1974), one of the first inclusive-language hymn collections, and *Everflowing Streams: Songs for Worship* (1981).

Duck was ordained in the United Church of Christ in 1974. She pastored in Wisconsin (1975-1984), then served as interim minister and supply preacher in several churches in Massachusetts. In 1989 she became assistant professor of worship at Garrett-Evangelical Theological Seminary in Evanston, Illinois.

Author: *Lead on, O cloud of Presence,* **419**; *Praise God, the Source of life,* **95**; Grace unto you and peace, **659**; We gather as pilgrims on a journey, **661**; God of love and justice, we long for peace, **696**; Hidden God, in mystery and silence, **745**. Adapter: *O God of love, O Power of peace* (st. 1), **368**

DUDLEY-SMITH, TIMOTHY (b. Dec. 26, 1926, Manchester, England), the son of a schoolmaster, was brought up in Derbyshire, England, and educated at his father's preparatory school. He continued his studies at Pembroke College, Cambridge. Following training at Ridley Hall, Cambridge, he was ordained by the Church of England as deacon and priest in 1950 and 1951, respectively. His pastoral appointments include some years in Kent and work for the Church Pastoral Aid Society (1959-1972). He was appointed archdeacon of Norwich in 1973 and bishop of Tretford in 1981.

A poet from his youth, Dudley-Smith does most of his writing at the family vacation home in Cornwall.

With Michael Baughan he edited and compiled *Youth Praise 1 & 2*, which by 1973 had sold a million copies. He was founder and editor of the magazine *Crusade* and served on the committee for *Psalm Praise* (1973). His hymns appear in more than seventy hymnals published in Britain, the U.S., Canada, Australia, New Zealand, Africa, India, and

China. More than 150 of his hymn texts are published in two collections: *Lift Every Heart* (1984) and *Songs of Deliverance* (1988).

Author: *He comes to us as one unknown*, **498**

DUFNER, DELORES (b. Feb. 20, 1939, Buxton, N.D.) showed an early interest in music and poetry while attending a one-room school. She majored in music at The College of St. Benedict, St. Joseph, Minnesota, where she joined the Sisters of St. Benedict. She received her M.A. in liturgical music from DePaul University in Chicago and St. Joseph's College, Rensselaer, Indiana, in 1973. She also completed an M.A. in liturgy from the University of Notre Dame, South Bend, Indiana (1990).

Between these accomplishments she directed the office of worship for her diocese of St. Cloud, Minnesota, and more recently spent fifteen months as a liturgical music consultant in Victoria, Australia. Dufner has been commissioned to write numerous hymn texts, and some have been published. Others have been used at festivals, conventions, and dedication services.

Author: *Let the hungry come to me*, **464**

DURNBAUGH, HEDWIG T. (b. June 5, 1929, Vienna, Austria) is a professional language teacher, linguist, translator, and academic librarian. She received her university education in Vienna; Marburg, Germany; and at Northwestern University, Evanston, Illinois (M.A. in German literature and linguistics); and Rosary College, Chicago (M.A.L.S.).

Although Durnbaugh is a Lutheran, she is associated with the Church of the Brethren through her husband, church historian, Donald F. Durnbaugh. She is a member of the Hymn Society of the United States and Canada. She began writing poetic translations of Scandinavian hymns through her involvement in the European-based International Fellowship for Research in Hymnology (IAH), to whose board of directors she was elected in 1989. In addition to translating hymns, Durnbaugh has authored several articles on hymnody and a monograph, *The German Hymnody of the Brethren, 1720-1903*.

Arranger: KOMMT HER ZU MIR (*How pleasant is it*), **451**. Translator: *In the stillness of the evening*, **551**

DWIGHT, TIMOTHY (b. May 14, 1752, Northampton, Maine; d. Jan. 11, 1817, Philadelphia, Pa.) was the son of a merchant and the grandson of the Congregationalist preacher Jonathan Edwards. Schooled early by his mother, Timothy was a prodigy. He could read the Bible at age four; entered Yale College, New Haven, Connecticut, at thirteen; and graduated in 1769 at seventeen.

Although his intensive study apparently damaged his eyesight, Dwight was a tutor at Yale until 1775 when he was appointed chaplain in the Continental Army in 1777. On the way to becoming one of New England's most influential personages in education and theology, Dwight pastored the Congregational church in Fairfield, Connecticut, in 1783, and then joined the Yale theology faculty. He rose to the college presidency in 1795 and remained twenty-two years in that position; his piety and chapel preaching there wrought a religious revolution set against the backdrop of the colonial "free-thinkers" and French revolutionists.

At the request of the General Association of Connecticut, Dwight helped New England churches make the transition from pure psalmody to hymnody by revising Watts's *The Psalms of David* ... (1719). He added some of his own texts; his revision, known as *Dwight's Watts*, was published in 1800.

Author: *I love thy kingdom, Lord*, **308**

DYKES, JOHN BACCHUS (b. Mar. 10, 1823, Kingston-upon-Hull, England; d. Jan. 22, 1876, Ticehurst, Sussex, England) could play musical instruments by ear at an early age. By the time he was ten, he was playing the organ at his grandfather's church. He was educated at St. Catherine's College, Cambridge (1843-1847), where he was instrumental in founding the University Musical Society. He received an honorary D.Mus. from Durham University in 1861. He was ordained deacon and appointed curate of Malton, Yorkshire, in 1847. In 1849 he was named minor canon and, four months later, precentor (music director) of Durham. In 1862 he became vicar of St. Oswald's in Durham.

In 1860 Dykes sent several of his tunes—unsolicited—to W. H. Monk for the original edition of *Hymns Ancient and Modern*. All of them were accepted. Dykes published many sermons, anthems, and liturgical compositions, but he is best known for his hymn tunes, which total almost three hundred. The 1950 revised edition of *Hymns Ancient and Modern* contains thirty-one of his tunes, and "he remains of all the Victorian composers of hymn tunes the most representative and successful; his tunes are standard repertory . . . over one hundred years after their introduction" (Gealy, Lovelace, Young 1970).

Composer: BLAIRGOWRIE (*O young and fearless Prophet*), **374**; KEBLE (*Forth in thy name*), **415**; MELITA (*O Holy Spirit, making whole*, **300**; *Strong, righteous man of Galilee*, **540**); NICAEA (*Holy, holy, holy*), **120**; ST. AGNES (*Jesus, the very thought of thee*), **588**

EBER, PAUL (b. Nov. 8, 1511, Kitzingen, Bavaria; d. Dec. 10, 1569, Wittenberg, Germany) was, after Martin Luther, the finest of the Wittenberg poets. An equestrian accident in 1523 left him with a permanent disability; nevertheless, he studied with Luther and Philipp Melanchthon at the University of Wittenberg, graduating in 1536. In 1544 Eber became a Latin professor there and in 1557 a professor of Hebrew. Also in that year he became pastor of Castle Church, and in 1558 he followed Johannes Bugenhagen as minister of City Church and as superintendent of the district. The University of Wittenberg granted Eber the D.Div. in 1559.

Author: *When in the hour of deepest need*, **131**

EDGAR, MARY SUSANNE (b. May 23, 1889, Sundridge, Ontario; d. Sept. 17, 1973, Toronto, Ontario) studied at Havergal College and the University of Toronto. Also a graduate of the National Training School of the YWCA, New York City, she was associated with the YWCA of Canada in Montréal for many years. Edgar founded Camp Glen Bernard for Girls in northern Ontario in 1922. She published collections of poems and essays—*Woodfire and Candlelight* (1945), *Under Open Skies* (1955), and *A Christmas Wreath of Verse* (1965)— and also wrote a number of hymns, mostly for camping and ecumenical occasions.

Author: *God, who touches earth*, **511**

EDSON, LEWIS, SR. (b. Jan. 22, 1748, Bridgewater, Mass.; d. 1820, Woodstock, N.Y.), a blacksmith by trade, became a very active music teacher, conducting singing schools in New York, Massachusetts, and Connecticut. He was reputed to be a great singer himself. Due to conflicts with the British, members of the Edson family moved to the less populous area of western Massachusetts. Edson married in 1770, moved to New York in 1776, and settled in Woodstock in 1817. With Thomas Seymour he compiled *The New York Collection of Sacred Music*. He composed fuguing tunes—songs that use imitative techniques in the voicing—including BRIDGEWATER, GREENFIELD, and LENOX. Such tunes became popular in the South, as well as in Edson's own region, and were included in most of the early American singing-school books.

Composer: LENOX (*Lord of the worlds above*), **39**

EDWARDS, ROBERT LANSING (b. Aug. 5, 1915, Auburn, N.Y.) studied at Deerfield Academy, Princeton University (N.J.; B.A., 1937), and Harvard University, Cambridge, Massachusetts (M.A., 1938), where he continued working toward a Ph.D. in history. After World War II, in which he served as a captain of intelligence (1941-1946), he resumed his education at Union Theological Seminary, New York City (M.Div., 1949). He was ordained that same year and has served only two churches, both in Connecticut, since that time: First Congregational Church, Litchfield (1949-1956), and Immanuel Congregational Church, Hartford (1956-1980), where he is now pastor emeritus.

Edwards has been president and member of numerous ecumenical councils and committees. In 1968 he was a delegate of the United Church of Christ to the World Council of Churches (WCC) Assembly and three times was delegate to the International Congregational Council. His publications include three hymns, a book of Advent verse, *Nairobi Notebook* (an account of the Fifth Assembly of the WCC), and a biography of Bible scholar Horace Bushnell (1802-1876).

Author: *God, whose giving,* **383**

ELLERTON, JOHN (b. Dec. 16, 1826, London, England; d. June 15, 1893, Torquay, Devonshire, England) was educated at King William's College, Isle of Man, and Trinity College, Cambridge (B.A., 1849; M.A., 1854). After his ordination as deacon in 1850 and priest in 1851, he became curate at St. Nicholas's, Brighton, where he wrote hymns for children. Devoted to the education of the poor and working class, he took up the vicarage of Crewe Green, a congregation of poor mechanics, farmers, and laborers. There he compiled *Hymns for Schools and Bible Classes* (1859), for hymnody was another of his passions.

During the years he served the parish of Barnes, Surrey (1876-1884), Ellerton became involved in the work of the British SPCK (Society for Promoting Christian Knowledge), which published various hymnals. He made a number of contributions to the 1889 edition of *Hymns Ancient and Modern,* and in the latter half of the nineteenth century, he was consulted on the compilation of every major English hymnal. His biography, *John Ellerton, his life and writing on hymnody,* edited by Henry Housman, appeared in 1896.

Author: *Savior, again to your dear name,* **656**; *The day you gave us, Lord,* **652**

ELLINGSEN, SVEIN (b. July 13, 1929, Kongsberg, Norway) molded as a Norwegian Lutheran, studied at the Academy of Fine Arts in Oslo and abroad. An editor, educator, painter, and musician, he was assistant editor for the Norwegian Christian weekly paper *Vår Kirke* (1957-1963) and later, for many years, was art critic for the Christian daily newspaper *Vårt Land;* he also taught in the public schools. In recognition of his work as hymnologist and writer of hymns, in 1976 he received a government stipend for life.

Ellingsen began writing hymn texts in the late 1950s. Many were developed over a long period of time and some did not find their final form until the 1970s. Hope, quiet joyfulness in faith, and the presence of Christ in the sacraments are chief themes in Ellingsen's texts. Many hymns are doxological in nature and characterized by a pastoral care for those who suffer. Most of the texts have been set to music by contemporary Norwegian composers and have found their way into hymnal supplements and the new Norwegian hymnals, such as his own *Norsk Salmebok* (1985), *Metodistkirkens Salmebok* (Methodist 1987), and *Lovsyng Herren* (Baptist 1989). Many hymns are included in non-Norwegian hymnals as well. Besides hymnals, Ellingsen's hymns are gathered into three collections: two in Norwegian (*Noen må våke*, 1978, and *Det finnes en dyrebar rose*, 1989) and one in Norwegian and English (*Praises Resound!*, 1991, with translations by Hedwig T. Durnbaugh).

Author: *In the stillness of the evening*, **551**

ELLIOTT, CHARLOTTE (b. Mar. 18, 1789, Clapham, England; d. Sept. 22, 1871, Brighton, England), a member of the Church of England, was born and raised in refined, cultured, and evangelical Christian surroundings. Though early in her life she was a natural and cheerful person who wrote comic verse, at thirty-two she became an invalid for the rest of her life.

Elliott credited her spiritual conversion to her friendship with César Malan, an evangelist from Geneva. She turned to hymnwriting, and her texts ministered especially to the frail and sick. She edited and assisted in publishing a number of collections of hymns and poems, including *The Invalid's Hymn Book* (1836).

Author: *Just as I am, without one plea*, **516**

ELLIOTT, JAMES WILLIAM (b. Feb. 13, 1833, Warwick, England; d. Feb. 5, 1915, London, England) was a church musician for most of his life. His initial music education took place at Leamington where he was a chorister. Elliott was organist at Leamington, Heaton Hall, and Banbury before moving to London in 1862. His most significant position was as organist at St. Mark's, Hamilton Terrace, where he served from 1874 to 1909. Elliott assisted Sir Arthur Sullivan in the publication of *Church Hymns with Tunes* (1874).

Composer: CHURCH TRIUMPHANT (*Let God, who called the worlds*), **138**

ELLOR, JAMES (b. 1819, Droylsden, Lancashire, England; d. Sept. 27, 1899, Newburgh, N.Y.), music director at the Wesleyan Chapel in Droylsden near Manchester, was a hat maker and railroad construction worker. In 1843 he moved to the United States. Nearly blind for many years, he died at the home of his son in Newburgh.

Composer: DIADEM (*All hail the power of Jesus' name*), **285**

ELVEY, GEORGE JOB (b. Mar. 27, 1816, Canterbury, England; d. Dec. 9, 1893, Windelsham, Surrey, England), born into a musical family, was a boy chorister at Canterbury Cathedral, studied music with his brother Stephen, and attended the Royal Academy of Music, London. A skillful organist before age seventeen, Elvey played organ at Christ Church,

Magdalen, and at New College, Oxford. At nineteen he was appointed by King William IV as organist at St. George's Chapel, Windsor, the home church of England's royalty. His tenure lasted from 1835 to 1882. He received the B.Mus. from New College in 1838 and two years later the D.Mus., by special dispensation of the university chancellor. In 1871 he was knighted. Though his compositions were chiefly for the church, many of his anthems were published.

Composer: DIADEMATA (*Crown him with many crowns*), **116**; ST. CRISPIN (*Strong Son of God, immortal Love*), **488**; ST. GEORGE'S WINDSOR (*Come, ye thankful people*), **94**

ENGLE, STEVE (b. May 1, 1943, Waynesboro, Pa.) wrote his first church music and two school choir anthems while still a student in high school. He attended Manchester College, North Manchester, Indiana, and graduated from Juniata College, Huntingdon, Pennsylvania (B.A., 1966). While at Juniata he formed the New Century Singers, a folk group who gave numerous performances and cut several records over a two-year period. Following college he attended Bethany Theological Seminary, Oak Brook, Illinois (1966-1967), and served in Brethren Volunteer Service (1968-70) in southern California. Having returned to his hometown in Pennsyvania, Engle is a full-time ventriloquist, making hundreds of appearances in Pennsylvania, Maryland, Virginia, and West Virginia.

Several of his songs have appeared in *Singing for Peace* (1986) and *The Brethren Songbook* (1974). His stage musical *Saint Judas Passion* premiered in 1973 and has since been recorded and performed across the U.S.

Author/Composer: *Beyond a dying sun* (ENGLE), **323**

ENNS, LEONARD JACOB (b. Feb. 2, 1948, Winnipeg, Manitoba) has been associate professor of music at Conrad Grebel College, University of Waterloo, Ontario, since 1977. He earned degrees in music from Canadian Mennonite Bible College, Winnipeg (1969); Wilfrid Laurier University, Waterloo, Ontario (1974); and Northwestern University, Evanston, Illinois, including a Ph.D. in music theory in 1982. Enns has written hymns, hymn-anthems, and instrumental and organ works. Three of his anthems—"Other Foundation" (1982), "Parables" (1986), and "Alleluia/Now Thank" (1989)—were commissioned for Mennonite conferences and celebrations.

He is an associate composer of the Canadian Music Centre, a member of the Canadian League of Composers, and associate member of the Manitoba Composers' Association, as well as the recipient of several awards, fellowships, and grants. Major performances of his compositions include *Songs of Innocence* (Winnipeg, 1984; Toronto, 1985; and Vienna, Austria, 1987); *The Sunne of Grace* (CBC broadcast, Toronto, 1987);

Sing for Joy! (Three Choirs Festival, Gloucester, England, 1986); *The Sun Beames of Thy Face* (Gloucester, 1987); and *Psalm Cyklus* (Winnipeg, 1990).

Composer: HEALER (*O Holy Spirit, Root of life*), **123**

ESCAMILLA, ROBERTO (b. Aug. 29, 1931, Sabinas, Mexico) is a graduate of both Parsons College and Iowa Wesleyan College, Mount Pleasant, Iowa. He also earned degrees from Perkins School of Theology, Dallas, Texas; Trinity University, San Antonio, Texas (M.A., 1963); Union Theological Seminary, New York City (S.T.M., 1967); and Vanderbilt University Divinity School, Nashville, Tennessee (D.Min., 1985). His extensive professional experience includes pastoring in the United Methodist Church, directing city ministries, and teaching in college.

Escamilla has traveled throughout South America, Europe, Canada, and the Holy Land, and has led preaching missions and retreats across the U.S. He has served numerous denominational and ecumenical boards and committees and is widely recognized as a public speaker for regional and national events. The author of *Prisoners of Hope* and other publications, Escamilla has edited *A Feast of Life, Celebremos I and II* (a collection of contemporary songs in bilingual editions), and *The Upper Room* (Spanish edition).

Translator: *Cantemos al Señor* (*Let's sing unto the Lord*), **55**

EVANS, DAVID (b. Feb. 6, 1874, Resolven, Glamorganshire, Wales; d. May 17, 1948, Rhosllanerchrugog, near Wrexham, Denbighshire, Wales), a distinguished Welsh musician, studied at Arnold College; Swansea University College, Cardiff; and Oxford University (England; D.Mus., 1859). After serving as organist/choirmaster at Jewin Street Welsh Presbyterian Church, London, he was professor of music from 1903 to 1939 at the University College, Cardiff, where he organized a large music department. He was also a senior professor at the University of Wales.

Evans was an outstanding judge for the National Eisteddfod (a Welsh competitive festival in the arts, especially singing) and from 1916 to 1921 was the editor of the Welsh periodical *Y Cerddor* (The Musician). He was music editor for *The Church Hymnary* (rev. ed., 1927) and the Welsh Methodist hymnal *Llyfr Tonau ac Emynau* (1929). Evans composed cantatas, anthems, services, and hymn tunes, many under the pseudonym Edward Arthur. Evans died shortly after leading a singing festival at Rhosllanerchrugog.

Arranger: O QUANTA QUALIA (*Here from all nations*), **296**

EVEREST, CHARLES WILLIAM (b. May 27, 1814, East Windsor, Conn.; d. Jan. 11, 1877, Waterbury, Conn.) graduated in 1838 from Trinity College, Hartford, Connecticut, and was ordained in 1842. His entire ministry career was spent at the Episcopal church in Hamden, Connecticut (1842-1873), but he was also an agent for the Society for the Increase of the Ministry. His *Visions of Death and Other Poems* (1833) was published when he was nineteen years old. He also contributed texts to the original edition of *Hymns Ancient and Modern* (1861).

Author: *Take up your cross*, **536**

EVERETT, ASA BROOKS (b. 1828, Virginia; d. Sept. 1875, Nashville, Tenn.) was a noted composer, teacher, and songbook compiler. He studied music in Boston, Massachusetts, where he became familiar with the methods and materials of Lowell Mason, then spent four years in musical studies in Leipzig, Germany. With his brother and R. M. McIntosh, he taught music and trained teachers to use the "Everett System" for elementary school instruction. Reportedly, more than fifty teachers in southern and mid-Alantic schools were using this method prior to the Civil War in the U.S. They established the L. C. Everett (music) Company, located first in Richmond, Virginia, and later in Pennsylvania. Even with his European training and the influence of Lowell Mason, some of Everett's hymn tunes are styled after southern folk melodies.

Composer: MAGNIFICENCE (*Since o'er thy footstool*), **158**

EXCELL, EDWIN OTHELLO (b. Dec. 13, 1851, Stark County, Ohio; d. June 10, 1921, Louisville, Ky.), whose father was a German Reformed pastor, was a plasterer and bricklayer when he was a young man. His musical talent, however, made him a popular singing-school teacher. While leading music at a Methodist Episcopal revival service, he experienced a spiritual conversion and from then on focused on sacred music, studying with George F. and Frederick Root.

After moving to Chicago in 1883, Excell published gospel songbooks and became a well-known congregational song leader with evangelist Sam Jones. Excell died in Louisville while participating with Gypsy Smith in a city-wide revival.

Excell composed the music for more than two thousand gospel songs and published about ninety songbooks. The copyrights he left behind were combined with the music firm Biglow and Main to become the Biglow-Main-Excell Company.

Composer: *The Lord is in his holy temple*, **38**. Arranger: NEW BRITAIN (AMAZING GRACE) (*Amazing grace*), **143**

FABER, FREDERICK WILLIAM (b. June 28, 1814, Calverly, Yorkshire, England; d. Sept. 26, 1863, London, England) was educated at Shrewsbury and Harrow, receiving his advanced education at Balliol and University Colleges, Oxford. In 1842 he was ordained in the Church of England, becoming rector at Elton, Huntingdonshire, that same year.

Although raised in the strictest Calvinist tradition, Faber became an ardent follower of John Henry Newman while at Oxford and, like others inspired by the liturgy revival of the Oxford movement, joined the Roman Catholic Church in 1845. He was one of the founders of a religious community known as the "Wilfridians" (called by Faber's Catholic name, Wilfred), and in 1848 this group merged with the Oratory of St. Philip Neri where Newman was the superior. From 1849 until his death, the dynamic Faber was superior of a branch of this prayer community, or oratory, established in London.

Faber is remembered chiefly for his hymns, all published after he joined the Catholic Church. Having been exposed to the appealing hymns of John Newton and William Cowper in his youth, Faber meant to fill the gap of popular hymns to which Catholics had little access. His hymns total 150, intended to match the number of psalms. Most of them are in his *Hymns* (1862), and many are in various Roman Catholic collections.

Author: *Faith of the martyrs*, **413**; *There's a wideness in God's mercy*, **145**

FALK, JOHANNES DANIEL (b. Oct. 28, 1768, Danzig, Germany; d. Feb. 14, 1826, Weimar, Germany) was the son of a wigmaker. With a stipend from the town council, he studied classics and theology at the University of Halle. For several years he was a private tutor. He married in 1798 and settled in Weimar as a man of letters, developing acquaintances with Johann von Goethe (poet and dramatist), Johann von Herder (philosopher and writer), and Christopher Wieland (author). During this time Falk wrote a number of satirical works. He wrote very few hymns; *O du fröhliche* is his best known. He included it in his *Auserlesene Werke* (1819).

After the Battle of Jena (1806) in the Napoleonic Wars, Falk became a philanthropist, organizing field hospitals and later caring for destitute children. Along with a local court preacher, he founded the Society of Friends in Need and began the Refuge for poor children. In 1829 the Refuge became a public training school for neglected youth and was renamed Falk's Institute.

Author: *Oh, how joyfully* (st. 1), **209**

FALLERSLEBEN, HEINRICH AUGUST HOFFMAN VON (b. Apr. 2, 1798, Fallersleben, Hannover, Germany; d. Jan. 29, 1874, Corvey, Westphalia, Germany) is remembered as a philologist, poet, hymnwriter, and amateur composer. He studied at Helmstedt, Brunswick, and at the

University of Göttingen. He moved to Bonn in 1819. Having studied Dutch literature in Holland, he became a professor at Breslau, Germany, in 1835, a position he held until 1843 when he was dismissed due to his political views. Later he became librarian to Prince Lippe at Corvey.

Fallersleben was the author of *Geschichte der deutschen Kirchenlieder* (Hannover 1832; 2nd ed. 1854), which contains significant discoveries about the history of German hymns. He also edited *Schlesische Volkslieder mit Melodien* (1842) and *Deutsche Gesellschaftslieder des 16. und 17. Jahrhunderts* (1844). His original melodies, and especially his poems for children in *Kinderlieder* (1843), merited their wide popularity.

Author: *Fairest Lord Jesus* (st. 2), **117**

FARJEON, ELEANOR (b. Feb. 13, 1881, Westminster, London, England; d. June 5, 1965, Hampstead, London, England), who came from a family of literary and theatrical talent, was educated privately. Primarily known for her musical settings of nursery rhymes, she wrote some eighty works, including poems, novels, plays, music, and books for children. Her first book, *Nursery Rhymes of London Town*, was published in 1916. She was awarded the Carnegie Medal, the first Hans Christian Andersen Award, and the Regina Medal. Though she was not born into a Catholic family, she joined that church later, considering her faith to be part of a spiritual pilgrimage, rather than a conversion. She is the subject of a number of biographies, including one by her niece Annabel Farjeon (1987).

Author: *Morning has broken*, **648**

FARMER, JOHN (b. Aug. 16, 1836, Nottingham, England; d. July 17, 1901, Oxford, England) studied music at Leipzig Conservatory and followed a career as music educator, editor, and composer. After teaching music at Zürich, he taught at Harrow School from 1862 to 1885. He then became organist at Balliol College, Oxford, where he organized a series of choral concerts and the Balliol College Musical Society. His compositions were largely directed to the needs of his educational circles. He also edited *Hymns and Tunes for High Schools.*

Composer: FARMER (*Hail to the Lord's anointed*), **185**

FARRINGTON, HARRY WEBB (b. July 14, 1879, Nassau, British West Indies; d. Oct. 27, 1931, Asbury Park, N.J.) was a Methodist clergyman who pioneered in weekday Christian education. Orphaned in infancy, he was brought to Baltimore, Maryland, and did not find his relatives until many years later. He studied at Darlington Academy (Md.); Dickinson Seminary, Syracuse University (N.Y.; B.A., 1907); Boston University School of Theology (Mass.; S.T.B., 1910); and later, Harvard University, Cambridge, Massachusetts (M.A.). During World War I, Farrington was lauded as a physical educator for the French military. He later held pastorates in New York and New England and was director of education for the Methodist Church Welfare League (1920-1923). Farrington wrote numerous poems, books on American history, an autobiography of his youth, and twenty-nine hymns.

Author: *Strong, righteous man of Galilee*, **540**

FAWCETT, JOHN (b. Jan. 6, 1739 or 1740, Lidget Green, near Bradford, Yorkshire, England; d. July 25, 1817, Hebden Bridge, Yorkshire, England) was captivated in his teens by the preaching of the Calvinistic Methodist evangelist George Whitefield, but around age eighteen he joined a small Baptist church in Bradford and began a long and happy marriage, both with the Baptists and with his wife, Mary. After ordination in 1765, Fawcett served Baptist churches at Wainsgate, Yorkshire, and Hebden Bridge, pastorates where gifts of appreciation far outweighed monetary support. A self-sacrificing pair, the Fawcetts turned down at the last minute a call to a larger, more prosperous parish and remained at Wainsgate/Hebden Bridge fifty-four years. During a long period of his ministry, Fawcett conducted an academy for the training of Baptist ministers, but he declined an offer of the presidency of the Baptist Academy at Bristol. In 1811 Brown University, Providence, Rhode Island, conferred on him the D.D. degree.

An author of a number of prose works on practical religion, he is best known for his *Devotional Commentary on the Holy Scriptures*. He wrote more than 160 hymns, mostly suited for singing after his sermons. These hymns were published as *Hymns Adapted to the Circumstances of Public Worship and Private Devotion* (1782).

Author: *Bless'd be the tie that binds*, **421**

FEATHERSTON(E), WILLIAM RALPH (ROLF) (b. July 23, 1846, Montréal, Québec; d. May 20, 1873, Montréal, Québec), also listed as William Rolf Featherston, was a member of Wesleyan Methodist Church in Montréal, now St. James United Church.

Author: *My Jesus, I love thee*, **522**

FEDAK, ALFRED V. (b. July 4, 1953, Elizabeth, N.J.) earned degrees at Hope College, Holland, Michigan, and Montclair State College, Upper Montclair, New Jersey. He has been awarded both Fellowship and Choirmaster certificates from the American Guild of Organists and has gained national recognition as a composer of church music. Fedak has served churches in Michigan and New Jersey and is music director at Westminster Presbyterian Church in Albany, New York.

Composer: EARTHRISE (*God, who touches earth*), **511**

FEILLÉE, FRANÇOIS DE LA (see **LA FEILLÉE**)

FEITEN, DAN (b. Oct. 9, 1953, near Tokyo, Japan) is a publisher, composer, musical arranger, and pediatrician. In 1975 he co-founded the musical group Ekklesia, which performs in contemporary Christian style. With that ensemble of five, he is vocalist and principal guitarist. Educated at the University of Colorado, Boulder (1976) and its medical school (1983), Feiten resides with his family in Denver, Colorado.

Author/Composer: *Seed, scattered and sown* (EKKLESIA), **454**

FELICIANO, FRANCISCO F. (b. Feb. 19, 1941, Morong, Rizal, the Philippines) received his education at the University of the Philippines (music composition, 1967; M.M., 1972) and Yale University, New Haven, Connecticut (M.M.A., 1979; D.M.A., 1984). From 1973 to 1977, he participated in special studies in church music at the Berlinerkirchenmusikschule, Germany. Feliciano is co-director of the Asian Institute for Liturgy and Music. He treasures teaching, and many of his students, coming from different Asian countries, are now considered significant composers in their own lands.

As a conductor he has led such distinguished orchestras as the Moscow State Symphony Orchestra, the Chicago Symphony Orchestra, the Beijing Central Philharmonic Orchestra, and the New Zealand Symphony Orchestra. For eight years he was principal conductor of the Philippine Philharmonic Orchestra. His award-winning compositions encompass a range of styles—from songs and hymns to operas, ballets, and symphonic works. His opera *La Loba Negra* has been acclaimed as a "jewel" of Philippine music. His liturgical compositions are sung not only in his homeland, but in Asian churches and at international conferences in Europe and America.

Author/Composer: *See the splendor of the morning* (TINMINAGO), **268**; *Still, I search for my God* (WASDIN PANG IPAAD), **88**

FERGUSON, MANIE PAYNE (b. 1850, Carlow, Ireland) married T. P. Ferguson, an evangelist in the Wesleyan Holiness movement. Together they founded the Peniel Missions in 1886. By the beginning of the twentieth century, they had established a number of missions on the west coast of the U.S. and in Alaska, Hawaii, and Egypt. It was at their mission in Astoria, Oregon, that Haldor Lillenas, outstanding gospel songwriter of the Church of the Nazarene, was converted. The *Peniel Herald* was published at the Los Angeles headquarters of the missions. *Echoes from Beulah* (1913) is a collection of Ferguson's hymns.

Author: *Joys are flowing like a river*, **301**

FIKE, EARLE W., JR. (b. Jan. 28, 1930, Harrisonburg, Va.) earned degrees from Bridgewater College (Va.; B.A., 1951; L.H.D., 1972) and Bethany Theological Seminary, Oak Brook, Illinois (B.D., 1954; M.Th., 1964) and did postgraduate studies at Garrett Theological Seminary, Evanston, Illinois. Ordained to ministry in the Church of the Brethren in 1952, he has had pastorates in Chicago, as well as at Meyersdale, Elizabethtown College, and Huntingdon, all in Pennsylvania. His career has also included five years of teaching at Bethany Seminary, in the field of preaching and worship, and ten years as associate general secretary of the Church of the Brethren General Board. Now officially retired, he is a part-time associate pastor at Stone Church of the Brethren, Huntingdon. He has also served his denomination as moderator; vice-chair of the Bethany Theological Seminary Board; and chair of the committee that produced the pastor's manual, *For All Who Minister* (Brethren Press 1993). Other publications include *Please Pray with Me* (Brethren Press 1990) and articles in *Brethren Life and Thought*. He has received a distinguished alumnus award from Bridgewater College and a church service award from Juniata College, Huntingdon.

Author: Come, let us worship, for we are the people, **662**; Go in love, for love alone endures, **764**

FILITZ, FRIEDRICH (b. Mar. 16, 1804, Arnstadt, Thüringen, Germany; d. Dec. 8, 1876, München, Germany), received a Ph.D., lived in Berlin from 1843 to 1847, then spent the remainder of his life in München (Munich). With Ludwig Christian Erk, he published *Vierstimmige Choräle der vornehmsten Meister des 16. und 17. Jahrhunderts* (1845), one of the collections that revived the Reformation chorales after a decline in their use during the previous century. He was the editor of *Vierstimmiges Choralbuch* (1847), a book of four-part tunes for the *Allgemeine Gesang und Gebetbuch* of his friend and poet Christian K. J. von Bunsen. In 1853 Filitz also published *Über einige Interessen der älteren Kirchenmusik*.

Composer: WEM IN LEIDENSTAGEN (*Jesus, stand among us*), **25**

FILLMORE, JAMES HENRY (b. June 1, 1849, Cincinnati, Ohio; d. Feb. 6, 1936, Cincinnati, Ohio) was the eldest of seven children of A. D. Fillmore, himself a composer, singing-school instructor, songbook publisher, and ordained minister in the Christian Church. At age sixteen, after his father's death, young James conducted the singing-school engagements to help support the family. With his brothers he established Fillmore Brothers Music House, eventually a thriving publishing company in Cincinnati. They featured anthems, sheet music, a monthly periodical (*The Musical Messenger*), and numerous Sunday school collections. His son, Henry Fillmore (1881-1956), was a noted band director and composer of marches.

Composer: SING GLORY, HALLELUJAH (*Proclaim the tidings near and far*), **282**

FISCHER, WILLIAM GUSTAVUS (b. Oct. 14, 1835, Baltimore, Md.; d. Aug. 13, 1912, Philadelphia, Pa.) learned to sing and read music as a youth in his German-speaking church in Baltimore. Also in his youth, he studied music in the evenings while learning bookbinding at J. B. Lippincott's, Philadelphia. For ten years (1858-1868), he taught music at Girard College, then, with John E. Gould, established a retail piano business. Upon Fischer's retirement in 1898, his son took over the flourishing company.

As a song leader and conductor, he was in great demand at conventions and revivals. In 1876 Fischer directed a chorus of a thousand voices at the Moody and Sankey meetings in Philadelphia. Of his more than two hundred gospel songs, however, few remain in use today. In addition to the melody listed below, he wrote the music for "Lord Jesus, I long to be perfectly whole."

Composer: HANKEY (*I love to tell the story*), **398**

FISHER, NEVIN WISHARD (b. Nov. 15, 1900, Waynesboro, Pa.; d. Feb. 12, 1984, Sebring, Fla.), a noted Brethren teacher, pianist, and conductor, was a graduate of the Peabody Conservatory of Music, Eastman School of Music, Rochester, N.Y. (B.M., 1940), and Northwestern University, Evanston, Illinois (M.M., 1947). He served on the faculties of various colleges and universities, including McPherson College (Kan.), Bridgewater College (Va.), Elizabethtown College (Pa.), and Millersville University (Pa.). Fisher chaired the music department of Elizabethtown College for about fifteen years and remained active as a piano teacher and performer until his death at age eighty-three. He edited *The Brethren Hymnal* (1951) and authored two books on Brethren hymns and hymnwriters.

Composer: PRAISE AND PRAYER (*Jesus Christ, God's only Son*), **40**. Arranger: LAUDA ANIMA (ANDREWS) (*Praise, my soul, the God of heaven*), **63**

FLORY, GERTRUDE A. (b. 1862, Indiana; d. 1930, Windber, Pa.) lived for a time in La Porte, Indiana, and also in Virginia where her husband Isaac passed away. She was associated with the Hastings Street mission in Chicago for a while, then lived in Brethren retirement homes in Fostoria, Ohio, and Windber, Pennsylvania. She wrote extensively in her early years but is remembered for this one text set to music by William Beery.

Author: *Take my hand and lead me, Father*, **601**

FOLEY, JOHN B., S.J. (b. July 1939, Peoria, Ill.) studied piano from his childhood through his twenties and continued his musical training at Wichita State University (Kan.) and Washington University in St. Louis, Missouri. He studied composition at the Royal Conservatory of Music in Toronto, Ontario, and privately with Reginald Smith Brindle in London, as well as with Dominick Argento and Paul Fetler in Minneapolis, Minnesota. He holds a B.A. from Regis College, Denver, Colorado; master's degrees in theology and philosophy from St. Louis University (Mo.); and a Ph.L. in philosophy.

Since 1962 he has been a member of the Society of Jesus, known as the Jesuits, and was ordained to the priesthood in 1972. Foley has composed music most of his life, producing a distinguished catalogue of orchestral and chamber music, as well as four full-length musicals. Since 1970 he has been writing Roman Catholic liturgical music; and from 1972 to 1986, he collaborated with four other composers, known collectively as "The St. Louis Jesuits," in bringing out seven collections of liturgical music. With the others in this group, he received an honorary doctorate from the University of Scranton (Pa.) in 1980. Other numerous awards include citations from Regis College and St. Louis University.

Author/Composer: *Let the heavens be glad*, **187**; *O let all who thirst* (COME TO THE WATER), **495**

FORTUNATUS, VENATIUS HONORIUS (b. ca. 530, Ceneda, near Treviso, Italy; d. 609), a contemporary of Gregory the Great, was the leading Latin muse of his time and considered a genuine liturgical poet. After being trained in the conventions of court life at Metz, France, and other places, Fortunatus directed his literary ability to the work of God; he lived near the Abbey of the Holy Cross at Poitiers, France, which was founded by his friend Queen Radegunde. He entered the priesthood, becoming bishop of Poitiers in 599.

Legend envelops Fortunatus as it did the so-called Dark Ages when religious relics made their rounds as objects of healing and devotion. Fortunatus is said to have been cured of near blindness by anointing his eyes with lamp oil from the altar of St. Martin of Tours. Also inspired by legends about the cross of Christ and by the gift of a fragment of the holy wood, he wrote numerous poems in its honor. In addition, he was author of several biographies of saints.

Author: *Sing, my tongue, the song*, **256**

FOSDICK, HARRY EMERSON (b. May 24, 1878, Buffalo, N.Y.; d. Oct. 5, 1969, Bronxville, N.Y.) earned degrees from Colgate University, Hamilton, New York (A.B., 1900); Union Theological Seminary, New York City (B.D., 1904); and Columbia University, New York City (M.A., 1908). He also received numerous honorary degrees. In 1903 Fosdick was ordained as a Baptist clergyman and then pastored First Baptist Church of Montclair, New Jersey. From 1919 to 1926, he served First Presbyterian Church of New York City, but his liberal theological views forced his resignation.

In 1926 Fosdick was called to Park Avenue Baptist Church in New York City, which later became renowned as Riverside Church, the cathedral-like building made possible by funds from J. D. Rockefeller, Jr., who was an active layman there. The church was located close to several educational institutions and, at Fosdick's insistence, bordered low-income communities. Fosdick's influential tenure at Riverside Church continued until 1946. He also was on the faculty of Union Theological Seminary, teaching homiletics (1908-1915) and practical theology (1915 until his retirement). Fosdick's preaching reached a large radio audience through the Sunday afternoon program *National Vespers*.

As a chaplain in World War I, he won the admiration of the peace churches when, on Armistice Day 1933, he delivered his sermon "The Unknown Soldier," totally and unconditionally renouncing war. He authored many books including his autobiography, *The Living of These Days* (1956). His preaching ministry is summarized in *Riverside Sermons* (1958), published in honor of his eightieth birthday.

Author: *God of grace and God of glory*, **366**; *O God, in restless living*, **557**

FRANCIS OF ASSISI (see ST. FRANCIS OF ASSISI)

FRANCK, JOHANN (b. June 1, 1618, Guben, Brandenburg, Germany; d. June 18, 1677, Guben) was born into wartime, for the Thirty Years War was waged during his first thirty years. A result of continuing unrest after the Peace of Augsburg in 1555, the war was ignited by both political and religious tensions between the Holy Roman Empire and the rest of Europe. It engulfed the entire region of central Europe and Denmark and seared the character of many a hymn and hymnwriter.

Young Franck was adopted by his uncle when his father died; with his uncle's financial help, he then studied in Guben, Cottbus, Stettin, and Thorn. His law study at the University of Königsberg was cut short when he returned home in 1640 because his mother feared the invading armies and marauding soldiers. Nonetheless, Franck began practicing law in 1645 in Guben and became a magistrate and councillor in his hometown the year the Peace of Westphalia was signed (1648). By 1661 he was mayor. In 1671 he was appointed a deputy from Guben to the Landtag (Diet) of Lower Lusatia.

Franck wrote both religious and secular poetry. His religious poetry was heavily influenced by the pietist movement in the German Lutheran Church. This "revival" movement in Lutheranism did not deny orthodox or Lutheran beliefs but valued the believer's personal inner experience with Christ. "Christ as lover" was a characteristic theme in this era.

Franck published 110 of his collected hymns in *Teusche Gedichte, bestehend im Geistliches Sion* (1674); the two best known in English translation are those included here. Franck is rated by some as second only to his contemporary Paul Gerhardt as a hymnwriter.

Author: *Jesus, priceless treasure*, **595**; *Soul, adorn thyself with gladness*, **473**

FRANTZ, NADINE (DENA) PENCE (b. May 29, 1953, Hanford, Calif.) grew up in the Church of the Brethren in La Verne, California. She earned degrees at Manchester College, North Manchester, Indiana (B.A., 1976); Bethany Theological Seminary, Oak Brook, Illinois (M.Div., 1980); and the University of Chicago (Ph.D., 1990). Licensed to Church of the Brethren ministry in 1984, she served first as interim pastor of York Center Church of the Brethren, Lombard, Illinois, and then as pastor at College Community Mennonite Brethren Church, Clovis, California. In California she also taught part time at the Mennonite Brethren Biblical Seminary. Currently she lives in Richmond, Indiana, and teaches theology at Bethany Theological Seminary. She has also served the Church of the Brethren as convener of its Women's Caucus; as one of its representatives on the worship committee of The Hymnal Project; by writing articles on theology, ministry, and theological education for *Messenger* and *Brethren Life and Thought*; and by providing leadership in a number of church conferences focusing on women in ministry, as well as theology and feminism.

Author: As ______'s and _______'s community(ies) of faith, **797**

FRANZ, IGNAZ (b. Oct. 12, 1719, Protzau, Silesia; d. 1790), a noted German Catholic hymnologist and compiler, was educated in Glaz and Breslau. After his ordination in 1742, he became chaplain at Gross-Glogau. He was assessor in the apostolic vicar's office in Breslau from 1766, probably until his death. Among his ten published collections, the most significant are *Katholisches Gesangbuch* (ca. 1774), which includes forty-seven of his own hymns, and a tunebook (1778).

Translator (Latin to German): *Holy God, we praise thy name*, **121**

FRAYSSÉ, CLAUDE (b. July 31, 1941, Versailles, France) is professor (chair) of trombone and tuba at the National School of Music at Romans, France, and professor of musical education in the secondary school since 1974. Fraysse was a member and manager of a variety orchestra from 1960 to 1970; in this environment he developed his ability on the saxophone, accordion, concertina, and flute. As a singer and entertainer, he is noted as the author and performer of *Moi, je dors avec Nounours dans mes bras* (Me, I sleep with teddy bear in my arms). When touring, Fraysse associates and works with such artists as G. Becaud, Guy Bedos, Sim, Mouloudji, and Bill Coleman.

During the summer of 1973, Frayssé found the Christian faith through Alain Bergèse, a professor of classical guitar at the conservatory of music at Romans. Since 1973 Frayssé has turned his talents as musician, author, composer, and arranger to serving the people of God. He was a member of the Troubadours of Hope, later forming and directing the groups Nathaniel and Hope in Celebration. He has recorded the solo album titled *Resister* (To Withstand).

Author/Composer: *Je louerai l'Eternel* (*Praise, I will praise you, Lord*), **76**

FRAZIER, FRANCIS PHILIP (b. June 2, 1892, Santee, Neb.; d. Sept. 29, 1964, Yankton, S.D.), a Congregational clergyman and missionary, was also a third-generation, full-blooded Sioux. He studied at Santee Mission; Yankton Academy; Mt. Herman School; and Dartmouth College. After serving in the American Expeditionary Forces in France and Germany from 1917 to 1919, he studied at Oberlin College (Ohio; B.A., 1922); Garrett Seminary, Evanston, Illinois; and Chicago Theological Seminary (B.D., 1925). He received honorary degrees from Oberlin and Dartmouth.

Frazier's work as a Quaker missionary took him to the Kickapoo Indians in Oklahoma (1924-1932) and the Osage Indians in Hominy, Oklahoma (1947-1956). He was also superintendent of Native Churches in North Dakota (1932-1937); at Ponca Creek, South Dakota (1937-1943); the Los Angeles Indian Center (Calif.; 1943-1947); and the Standing Rock Indian Reservations (1956-1964). An extensive article about him was published in *Music Ministry*, June 1968, and a monograph on his life and work has been written by his wife, Susie M. Frazier.

Paraphraser: *Many and great, O God*, **35**

FREDERICK, DONALD R. (b. Jan. 13, 1917, near Nappanee, Ind.), born on a small farm in Elkhart County, Indiana, was educated in a one-room country school through eighth grade. As a high school vocal and instrumental musician, he won a medal in a national sousaphone solo contest in his senior year and was part of a boys' quartet known as the Farmland Four. He pursued music studies at Manchester College, North Manchester, Indiana (1939); Northwestern University, Evanston, Illinois (1950); Wichita State University (Kan.); and Kansas University. He also earned his B.D. from Bethany Theological Seminary, Oak Brook, Illinois, in 1946.

A former music supervisor and teacher in Ohio, Frederick was with the music department of McPherson College (Kan.) from 1946 until 1971. Since then he has maintained a small music-publishing business. He also has been minister of music at McPherson Church of the Brethren for various stints. A composer of more than one hundred published works, he may be best known for his prize-winning anthem "O Church of Christ, count well your charge," written for the 250th anniversary of the Church of the Brethren. He has served as Brethren Annual Conference music director six times.

Harmonizer: ENGLE (*Beyond a dying sun*), **323**

FREYLINGHAUSEN, JOHANN ANASTASIUS (b. Dec. 2, 1670, Gandersheim, Braunschweig, Germany; d. Feb. 12, 1739, Halle, Germany), the son of a merchant, attended the University of Jena. He was a private tutor in his hometown and pastor in Glauche and Halle. A compelling preacher and an author of hymns in the pietist tradition, he is best remembered for his influential and portly *Neues Geistreiches Gesangbuch*, which consists of two volumes (1704, 1714). Two years after his death, a combined edition was published, which augmented the number of hymns to nearly 850, with more than 150 tunes.

Editor/Source: *Oh, that I had a thousand voices*, **84**; AMSTERDAM (*Praise the Lord who reigns above*), **54**; MACHT HOCH DIE TÜR (*Fling wide the door, unbar the gate*), **186**

FRIEDELL, HAROLD W. (b. May 5, 1905, Jamaica, N.Y.; d. Feb. 17, 1958, Hastings-on-Hudson, N.Y.) studied music with David Williams, Clement B. Gale, and Bernard Wagenaar. He also pursued studies at General Theological Seminary and at the Juilliard School of Music, both in New York City. He served as organist/choirmaster at St. John's Church, Jersey City (N.J.; 1930-1939); Calvary Episcopal Church, New York City (1939-1946); and St. Bartholomew's Church, New York City (1946-1958). Friedell was professor of theory and composition at Union Theological Seminary, New York City, and Juilliard School of Music; he taught organ at Union as well. His compositions include instrumental, choral, and organ works.

Composer: *Day by day, dear Lord*, **569**

FUNK, JOSEPH (b. Apr. 6, 1778, Berks County, Pa.; d. Dec. 24, 1862, Singers Glen, Va.) was a noted Mennonite compiler of tunebooks, a singing-school teacher, and a publisher of both musical and non-musical materials in the Shenandoah Valley of Virginia. His first book, *Die Allgemein nützliche Choral-Music* (1816), was followed by *Genuine Church Music* (1832) in the four-shape notation of Little and Smith. With the printing of the fifth edition in 1851, the name of this collection was changed to *Harmonia Sacra* and the seven-shape system was used. After Funk's death his work and publications were continued by his sons, and later by his grandson Aldine S. Kieffer in Dayton, Virginia. The *New*

Harmonia Sacra, still in print, continues to be used in hymn sings in the Shenandoah Valley and Goshen, Indiana, perpetuating Funk's legacy.

Editor/Source: AWEFUL MAJESTY (*How wondrous great*), **126**; BIRMINGHAM (CUNNINGHAM) (*Filled with the Spirit's power*), **289**; CHAPEL (*If death my friend and me divide*), **608**; FARMINGTON (*And is the gospel peace and love*), **406**; FOUNDATION (BELLEVUE) (*How firm a foundation*), **567**; HANTS (*Give to the winds thy fears*), **561**; NEW CONCORD (*Oh, how happy are they*), **597**; RESIGNATION (*My Shepherd will supply my need*), **589**

FYOCK, JOAN ANNETTE (b. Aug. 31, 1938, Harrisburg, Pa.) graduated *magna cum laude* from Juniata College, Huntingdon, Pennsylvania (B.A. in music education, 1959), and the University of Michigan (M.M., 1961). She taught at the Toledo Museum of Art (Ohio) and in public schools in New Jersey and Pennsylvania; for fifteen years she was head of the music department of Linden Hall School for Girls, Lititz, Pennsylvania (1969-1984). She teaches voice and piano and has been director of music ministries at Lititz Church of the Brethren since 1984. Interested in composing since early childhood, she has published several anthems and composed a musical for children's choirs. She was a member of the music committee and research associate for *Hymnal: A Worship Book* (1992) as well as writer/compiler of this *Hymnal Companion*.

Composer: McRAE (*Where is this stupendous Stranger?*), **200**. Arranger: BEACH SPRING (*Holy Spirit, come with power*, **26**; *Lord, whose love in humble service*, **369**); CRADLE SONG (*Away in a manger*), **194**

GABARAÍN, CESÁREO (b. 1936, Hernani, Spain; d. 1991) became a parish priest in Antzuola upon completing his ecclesiastical studies, which included philosophy, moral theology, and post-graduate degrees in biblical theology, journalism, and musicology. Passionate about athletics, he played racquetball as a youth and spent summer vacations traveling with cyclists in the Tour de France. Accompanying them as friend and chaplain, he was called the "priest of the cyclists." Gabaraín also enjoyed a similar role with various soccer players in Madrid.[1]

During the last years of his life, he was a pastor at Our Lady of Snows parish in Madrid, dedicating himself at the same time to music and to youth ministry. Gabaraín's involvement with young people molded both his pastoring and his music into a contemporary and energetic style. Among his thirty-six recorded albums are *Jesus Nuestro Amigo, Un Joven Soy*, and *Madre De Los Jovenes*, which reflect his love and concern for young people. "Gabaraín was most admired for his good heart, his capacity for friendship, his deep spirituality, and his pastoral, priestly soul."[2] His swift terminal illness caused many to mourn his absence as a friend, musician, and good priest.

Author/Composer: *Tú has venido a la orilla* (*Lord, you have come to the lakeshore*) (PESCADOR DE HOMBRES), **229**; *Una espiga* (*Sheaves of summer*) (UNA ESPIGA), **460**

1. *Liturgia y Canción*, Vol. 3:1, 1991
2. *Liturgia y Canción*, Vol. 3:1, 1991

GABRIEL, CHARLES HUTCHINSON (b. Aug. 18, 1856, Wilton, Iowa; d. Sept. 15, 1932, Los Angeles, Calif.), raised on an Iowa farm, taught himself to play the family's reed organ. He began teaching in singing schools at age sixteen and became recognized as a teacher, church music director, and composer. A move to Chicago in 1895 brought him into music publishing circles; he joined the Rodeheaver-Hall Mack publishing firm in 1912. Gabriel edited nearly one hundred collections of gospel and Sunday school songs, cantatas, anthems, and choruses. "Charlotte G. Homer" was the pseudonym he sometimes used for the texts of his numerous compositions.

Author/Composer: *I stand amazed in the presence* (HOW MARVELOUS), **528**

GAITHER, GLORIA (b. Mar. 4, 1942, Battle Creek, Mich.) and **GAITHER, WILLIAM J.** (b. Mar. 28, 1936, Alexandria, Ind.) have become one of the most successful gospel songwriting teams of the latter twentieth century. Gloria graduated *cum laude* from Anderson College (now Anderson University, Ind.) in 1963 with majors in English, French, and sociology; she later did graduate work in English at Ball State University, Muncie, Indiana, and Anderson Theological Seminary. During her junior year of college, she filled in for a high school teacher who required emergency surgery, and there she met Bill Gaither, an English instructor who was transferred to the school that same day.

William Gaither, also educated at Anderson College (B.A., M.A. in English), taught at Alexandria High School for six years before devoting full time to Gaither Music Company. With strong teaching backgrounds, Bill and Gloria continue to be involved in education. Bill served on the board of trustees at Anderson University where Gloria has taught a course in songwriting.

Married in 1962, Bill and Gloria began touring local churches, making up two-thirds of the Bill Gaither Trio. The Gaithers have recorded forty-five albums, received two Grammys and dozens of Dove Awards (Gospel Music Association). Working collaboratively, they have written more than five hundred published songs and several musicals. Gloria is also the author of numerous books.

Author (Gloria)/Composer (William): *Gentle Shepherd, come and lead us* (GENTLE SHEPHERD), **352**. Authors (Gloria and William)/Composer (William): *God sent his Son* (BECAUSE HE LIVES), **345**

GAŁUSZKA, JACEK, O.P. (b. Jan. 8, 1965, Gorlice, Poland,) is a member of the Order of Preachers (the Dominicans). He works principally with the choir and orchestra of the Student's Chaplaincy and Dominican Friars, under the guidance of Zbigniew Bujarski from the Academy of Music in Krakow. Since 1986 he has been composing liturgical chant. Some of his compositions were presented during the Sixth World Day of Youth festivities in Czestochowa, Poland, in August 1991.

Composer: OTO SĄ BARANKI (*Who are these*), **270.** Arranger: OTO JEST DZIEŃ (*This is the day*), **58**

GARBER, ORA W. (b. May 5, 1903, Hanfield, Ind.; d. Oct. 17, 1981, Elgin, Ill.), a graduate of Manchester College, North Manchester, Indiana (B.A., 1927) and Hartford Seminary (Conn.; B.D., 1930; S.T.M., 1931), was a pastor in Kansas, Illinois, and Iowa until 1939. For the next thirty years, he was literary and book editor for Brethren Publishing House, Elgin, Illinois. Garber was co-compiler and co-editor of *The Brethren Hymnal* (1951). His interest in writing poetry and in translating German poetry, especially that of Brethren writers, created a body of nearly two hundred hymns—originals and translations.

Author: *'Tis not with eyes of flesh we see*, **571**. Translator: *Count well the cost*, **437**; *How pleasant is it*, **451**; *Jesus Christ, God's only Son*, **40**

GARDINER, WILLIAM (b. Mar. 15, 1770, Leicester, England; d. Nov. 16, 1853, Leicester) was an English hosiery manufacturer, amateur composer, and editor. He rubbed shoulders with major musical personalities of his day and introduced the practice of adapting their musical masterworks into hymn tunes. He even sent Joseph Haydn specialty stockings—with Haydn melodies interwoven in the design.

His most noteworthy publication is *Sacred Melodies from Haydn, Mozart, and Beethoven, Adapted to the best English Poets and appropriated to the use of the British Church* (2 vols., 1812, 1815, London). By 1838, four more volumes had been published.

Editor/Source: GERMANY (*Where cross the crowded ways*), **405**

GAST, MARY SUSAN (b. Oct. 27, 1945, Baroda, Mich.) earned degrees at Michigan State University, East Lansing (B.A., 1970), and Chicago

Theological Seminary (D.Min., 1975). "Growing up Catholic in a rural setting in the 1950s, pre-Vatican II," she says, "I heard the Word interpreted in ways that either ignored or bound me." Her transition to the United Church of Christ (UCC) began during seminary days when the man who would become her husband invited her to a service at his home church. Ordained in the United Church of Christ in 1975, she has served as a campus minister at Iowa State University, Ames; as pastor of two congregations in Michigan; and as associate conference minister of the UCC's Indiana-Kentucky Conference. Currently she is executive director of the UCC Coordinating Center for Women in Church and Society, Cleveland, Ohio. In 1980 she and her husband committed themselves to a couple of years of intense work for world-wide nuclear disarmament and established an educational ministry called the Southwest Michigan Riverside Project. They made presentations to thousands of people throughout the state and organized groups for peace study and action. Gast has written worship resources for various publications.

Author: We follow Christ who says, **758**

GASTOLDI, GIOVANNI GIACOMO (b. ca. 1556, Caravaggio, Italy; d. 1622) is best known for his late sixteenth- and early seventeenth-century publications of Italian secular vocal music, especially *canzonette* and *balletti*, which are light, dancing pieces with a fa-la-la refrain. Active at the church of Santa Barbara in Mantua from the 1570s until after the turn of the century, he was appointed *maestro di cappella* there in 1592, a position he held until 1608.

The last years of Gastoldi's career are clouded in obscurity, though it is thought he probably moved to Milan sometime after 1608. While he composed both sacred and secular compositions, his most influential works were the two books of *balletti* published in 1591 and 1594.

Composer: IN DIR IST FREUDE (*In thee is gladness*), **114**

GAUNTLETT, HENRY JOHN (b. July 9, 1805, Wellington, Shropshire, England; d. Feb. 21, 1876, Kensington, England) showed remarkable talent on the organ at an early age but, under family pressure, studied law and began practice in London in 1831. He did not abandon the organ, however. He played for a number of churches and in 1846 was chosen by Felix Mendelssohn to play the organ part in performances of the oratorio *Elijah* at Birmingham. His talents extended to organ design as well. In cooperation with organ-builder William Hill, Gauntlett added an independent pedal division, an important development for organ playing in England.

Mendelssohn acclaimed Gauntlett for his mastery of the organ and his music knowledge, and the archbishop of Canterbury awarded him the first honorary D.Mus. conferred by an archbishop in two hundred years. Gauntlett was not only an expert, but also prolific; he reportedly wrote ten thousand pieces.

Composer: ARDWICK (*Away with our fears*), **292**. Arranger: STUTTGART (*Child of blessing, child of promise*, **620**; *God, whose farm is all creation*, **391**; *Grant us, Lord, the grace*, **388**)

GEBHARDT, ERNST HEINRICH (b. July 12, 1832, Ludwigsburg, Württemberg, Germany; d. 1899) spent his childhood and adolescence in Württemberg, a center of pietist activity. He first studied to be an apothecary, but five years of farm work in Chile, coupled with a shipwreck and a spiritual awakening, spurred him instead to ministry in 1859. After study in Bremen, he pastored a number of congregations in the Methodist Church in Germany, with his longest stint at Karlsruhe from 1888 until his death in 1899. He also traveled extensively, doing evangelistic work in the U.S., England, and Switzerland. Gebhardt wrote hymns, translated more than fifty hymns from English into German, and compiled several songbooks.

Translator: *Oh, have you not heard*, **606**

GEISER, LINEA REIMER (b. June 3, 1936, Winnipeg, Manitoba) is a graduate of Goshen College (Ind.; B.A., 1957) and Associated Mennonite Biblical Seminaries, Elkhart, Indiana (M.Div., 1985). She began writing poetry as a young mother with three preschoolers and was a charter member of a poetry group in Orrville, Ohio, where she and her husband lived for twenty-one years. Soon her poems began to appear in various Mennonite and other periodicals. Being asked in 1975 to write children's Sunday school curriculum made use of her previous experience as an elementary schoolteacher and established her more firmly on a writing track. In 1979 she and her family moved to Goshen, Indiana, where she has been an active member of College Mennonite Church, serving a term on the worship commission, preaching on occasion, always working in children's education. Since 1988 Geiser has been a writer in the Church Relations Department at Mennonite Board of Missions, Elkhart. Over the years she has led many workshops for Sunday school teachers. In 1978 several of her poems earned for her the accolade of Ohio Poetry Day winner, and a series of her Advent poems has been set to music by Dennis Friesen-Carper ("A Blinding Light").

Author: He's coming, he's coming, **667**; May ground below, **682**; O God, for too long the world, **756**; Empower us to nurture those newborn, **761**

GERHARDT, PAUL (b. Mar. 12, 1607, Gräfenhainichen, near Wittenberg, Germany; d. May 27, 1676, Lübben, Germany) was educated at the Elector's school at Grimma (1622-1627) and at the University of Wittenberg (1628-1642) where, under the influence of Paul Röber and Jacob

Martini, he learned fully the purpose and use of hymnody. In 1643 he moved to Berlin where he wrote many "Occasional Poems," eighteen of which Johann Crüger included in *Praxis Pietatis Melica.*

Nearly half of Gerhardt's life was subject to the suffering of the Thirty Years War. He lost his wife and four of his five children. His formal ministry was another casualty—it was not until 1651 that he was appointed chief pastor at Mittenwalde, near Berlin. In 1657 he became deacon in St. Nicholas's Church, Berlin, where Crüger was choirmaster. Gerhardt was dismissed from his position in 1666 because of a theological controversy with a local Reformed politician, but he remained in Berlin until 1668 when he was appointed archdeacon at Lübben, the position he held until his death.

Gerhardt's collected poems appear in several editions. His writing represents a transition from the confessional to the pietist era; his work is more personal and intimate than that of his predecessors. James Mearns ranked Gerhardt next to Luther as "the most gifted and popular hymn-writer of the Lutheran Church." In the Lübben church there is a portrait of Gerhardt with an inscription that reads: "A theologian sifted in Satan's sieve" (a reference to his many trials and tribulations).

Author: *Give to the winds thy fears,* **561**; *Now all the woods are sleeping,* **657**; *O sacred Head, now wounded,* **252**; *Oh, how shall I receive thee,* **182**; *Spirit, come, dispel our sadness,* **290**

GEYER, JOHN BROWNLOW (b. May 9, 1932, Wakefield, Yorkshire, England) studied at Silcoates School in Wakefield. As a pacifist he spent 1951 to 1953 in national service engaged in farming. He then continued his education at Queen's College, Cambridge, and Mansfield College, interrupting tenure there to study under theologian Gerhard von Rad of Heidelberg in Germany. Geyer began keeping diaries when he was fifteen years old and used that rich source (more than fifty volumes) to write histories of his alma maters.

Ordained in 1959 to the ministry of the Congregational Union of Scotland, he was chaplain at the University of St. Andrew's in Fife, Scotland, for the next four years, then minister of the Congregational Church, Drumchapel, Glasgow (1963-1965). In 1965 he married Margaret Lochhead Young and turned to education, tutoring at Cheshunt College, Cambridge. In 1969 Geyer returned to pastoral ministry at Little Baddow Congregational Church, which affiliated with the United Reformed Church in 1972. Since 1980 he has been minister of Weoley Hill United Reformed Church, as well as chaplain to students of the Reformed tradition at the University of Birmingham and at Westhill College.

An Old Testament scholar, Geyer has published a commentary on *The Wisdom of Solomon* and articles in several journals. His hymns appear in a variety of contemporary and international hymnals.

Author: *We know that Christ is raised,* **443**

GIARDINI, FELICE DE (b. Apr. 12, 1716, Turin, Italy; d. June 8, 1796, Moscow, Russia) received musical training as a chorister at the Milan Cathedral and as a violin student of Somis. An outstanding violinist in the opera orchestras of Rome and Naples, he also gave concerts in Italy, Germany (1748), and London (1750). He lived in England (1752 to 1784) where he was a teacher, performer, conductor, and manager of the Italian Opera in London. He contributed four hymn tunes under commission for Martin Madan's *Collection of Psalm and Hymn Tunes* (1769), one of which remains in use.

A better performer than opera manager, Giardini suffered some reverses in his operatic career and went to Moscow in 1796. There, in less than three months, he died in poverty. He was a prolific composer of operas, string quartets, sonatas, and other pieces.

Composer: ITALIAN HYMN (*Come, thou Almighty King*), **41**

GIBBONS, ORLANDO (b. 1583, Oxford, England; d. June 5, 1625, Canterbury, England) at age twelve joined the choir at King's College, Cambridge, where his brother Edward was master of the choristers. At twenty-one he was appointed organist at the Chapel Royal, a position he held for the rest of his life. Gibbons received the B.Mus. from Cambridge in 1606 and the D.Mus. from Oxford in 1622. Esteemed as the outstanding organist of his day, he was given the position of organist for Westminster Abbey in 1623. Gibbons died from a stroke on Pentecost Sunday at Canterbury while he and the Chapel Royal were accompanying King Charles I to meet his new queen, Henrietta Maria of France. Gibbons was buried the next day in Canterbury Cathedral where his monument can be seen on the wall of the north side of the nave.

Gibbons' forty anthems and services appear in *Tudor Church Music IV*, edited by E. H. Fellowes. His sixteen hymn tunes for Wither's *Hymns and Songs of the Church* (1623) are considered among the finest of their kind.

Composer: SONG 13 (*Christ, from whom all blessings*, **365**; *Open are the gifts of God*, **255**); SONG 34 (*Christ, who is in the form of God*), **333**

GILLARD, RICHARD (b. Dec. 22, 1953, Malmesbury, Wiltshire, England) immigrated to New Zealand with his family in 1956. He is a computer operator and creative ministries coordinator for the charismatic Anglo-Catholic Parish of St. Paul's in central Auckland where he was formerly a member. Although nurtured in the Assemblies of God denomination, he now holds membership in the Willow Avenue Chapel (Brethren) fellowship. Gillard is a self-taught guitarist, having had no formal training in music. He and his family live on Auckland's North Shore in the suburb of Birkenhead.

Author/Composer: *Will you let me be your servant* (THE SERVANT SONG), **307**

GILMORE, JOSEPH HENRY (b. Apr. 29, 1834, Boston, Mass.; d. July 23, 1918, Rochester, N.Y.) had a multifarious career as a minister, newspaper editor, college professor, and author. A graduate of Phillips Academy, Gilmore received his college education from Brown University, Providence, Rhode Island, and his theological training from Newton Theological Seminary (Mass.). He held pastorates in Baptist churches in New Hampshire and New York. From 1868 until 1911, he taught at the University of Rochester (N.Y.) as a professor of English and logic. He was also private secretary to the governor of New Hampshire—his father. Included among his writings are *He Leadeth Me, and Other Religious Poems* (1877) and *Outlines of English and American Literature* (1905).

Author: *He leadeth me*, **599**

GLADDEN, WASHINGTON (b. Feb. 11, 1836, Pottsgrove, Pa.; d. July 2, 1918, Columbus, Ohio) graduated from Williams College in 1859. He was ordained in the Congregational Church in 1860, the year of his marriage. Over the next eleven years, Gladden served pastorates in New York and Massachusetts. Opting out of pastoring for three years, he edited the influential periodical *Independent*, but he returned to ministry at North Church in Springfield, Massachusetts, over an ethics disagreement with his senior editor. As an editor, Gladden had been outspoken and aggressive; during his tenure with the *Independent*, his editorials triggered the prosecution of the crooked politicians of Boss Tweed's Tammany Hall ring, who bilked the New York City treasury of millions of dollars.

From 1882 until his death, Gladden lived in Columbus, Ohio, where he was the controversial pastor of First Congregational Church for thirty-two years. He was never hesitant about applying the gospel of Jesus in social and economic realms, a trait that had people flocking to hear him speak, but it also earned him the disapproval of many church officials and politicians. He even took on the corporate giant Standard Oil and its head John D. Rockefeller, Sr., criticizing shady deals that turned Standard into a monopoly and Rockefeller into a millionaire.

A prolific author, Gladden wrote more than thirty books. He served as moderator of the National Council of Congregational Churches (1904-1907) and was awarded honorary doctorates by the University of Wisconsin, Madison; the University of Notre Dame, South Bend, Indiana; and Roanoke College, Salem, Virginia.

Author: *O Master, let me walk with thee*, **357**

GLÄSER, CARL GOTTHELF (b. May 4, 1784, Weissenfels, Germany; d. Apr. 16, 1829, Barmen, Germany) began his musical training with his father and continued at the Thomasschule in Leipzig, noted for its earlier association with J. S. Bach. Gläser studied law for a time but gave it up to teach piano and concentrate on violin with the Italian master Campagnoli. Later, in Barmen, he also taught voice and conducted choral groups. His compositions include motets, school songs, and piano works.

Composer: AZMON (*Oh, for a thousand tongues to sing*), **110**

GORDON, ADONIRAM JUDSON (b. Apr. 19, 1836, New Hampton, N.H.; d. Feb. 2, 1895, Boston, Mass.), a namesake of Baptist missionary Adoniram Judson, graduated from Brown University, Providence, Rhode Island (1860) and was a noted editor, author of hymn texts, and composer. He pastored Clarendon Street Baptist Church in Boston and edited *The Service of Song for Baptist Churches* (1871) and *The Vestry Hymn and Tune Book* (1872). His earlier compilation, *The Coronation Hymnal* (1860), included four of his tunes and eleven of his hymns. Gordon was a trustee of Newton Theological Seminary and served on Brown University's Board of Fellows. He received an honorary D.D. from Brown University in 1878. Gordon also edited *The Watchword* and authored several books.

Composer: GORDON (*My Jesus, I love thee*), **522**

GOSS, JOHN (b. Dec. 27, 1800, Fareham, Hants, England; d. May 10, 1880, London, England), the son of an organist, became a chorister in the Chapel Royal at age eleven. After studying with Thomas Attwood and singing in the chorus at Covent Garden Theatre, he was organist at Stockwell Chapel (1821-1824); St. Luke's Church, Chelsea (1824-1838); and then succeeded Attwood as organist of St. Paul's Cathedral, London. He was also professor of harmony at the Royal Academy of Music and wrote a textbook, *An Introduction to Harmony and Thoroughbass*, which had thirteen editions. In 1856 he was appointed one of the composers to the Chapel Royal; he was knighted the same year he retired (1872).

Other than two overtures and the musical drama *The Serjeant's Wife* (1827), which ran more than one hundred nights, Goss composed only glees and sacred music, which was heralded for its "union of solidity and grace." He published psalmody, chants, canticles, anthems, and hymns.

Composer: BENEDIC ANIMA (*Jesus came—the heavens adoring*, **297**; *Praise, my soul, the King of heaven*, **65**)

GOTTSCHALK, LOUIS MOREAU (b. May 8, 1829, New Orleans, La.; d. Dec. 18, 1869, Tijuca, Brazil) ranks as one of the first North American musicians to achieve an international reputation, both as a virtuoso pianist and as a composer. As a child prodigy, his early training took place in New Orleans. In 1842 he went to Paris, France, where (though denied admission to the Paris Conservatoire) he studied piano with Charles Hallé and Camille Stamaty and composition with Pierre Maleden. Gottschalk traveled throughout Europe, the U.S., the Caribbean, and South America presenting piano recitals, often featuring his own compositions. His music, imbued with New World elements, includes orchestral works and numerous popular compositions for piano.

Composer: MERCY (*Holy Spirit, Truth divine*), **508**

GOUDIMEL, CLAUDE (b. ca. 1505, Besançon, France; d. Aug. 27 or 28, 1572, Lyons, France) was studying at Paris University in 1549 when his *chansons* (songs) first appeared in print in 1551. He was first a proofreader with the publisher Nicolas du Chemin and then became du Chemin's partner (1552-1555). At some point, he transferred his affiliation from Roman Catholicism to the Protestant French Huguenot Church, but he was composing psalm settings even before his conversion, because Catholics and Protestants alike used the psalms until they came under a Catholic ban.

Goudimel's most prolific years were in the 1550s when he published most of his *chansons*, psalms, motets, odes, and masses. From 1557 to about 1567, he lived in the Huguenot city of Metz where he worked with poet-dramatist Louis des Masures on his first complete psalter (1564). Goudimel's last known correspondence is dated August 23, 1572, from Lyons. He was a victim of the Roman Catholic persecutors in the St. Bartholomew's Day massacres the next week, leaving his third psalter of part motets unfinished. Goudimel is noted primarily for his psalm settings in both polyphonic and homophonic styles.

Arranger: GENEVA 42 (FREU DICH SEHR) (*As the hart with eager yearning*, **500**; *Comfort, comfort, O my people*, **176**); GENEVA 124 (OLD 124th) (*We would extol thee*, **74**); LES COMMANDEMENS DE DIEU (*Bread of the world*), **469**

GOULD, JOHN EDGAR (b. 1822, Bangor, Maine; d. Mar. 4, 1875, Algiers, Algeria) lived primarily in New York City and Philadelphia, Pennsylvania, where he operated music stores. He composed psalm and hymn tunes, published music books, and was a choral conductor. Some of his publications include *The Modern Harp*, issued with Edward L. White (1846); *Harmonia Sacra* (1851); and *Songs of Gladness for the Sunday School* (1869). The latter includes more than fifty of Gould's tunes. He died suddenly on a tour of southern Europe and North Africa, a trip he had taken because of ill health. Appropriately, the evening before his departure, he sat at the piano and played "Jesus Savior, pilot me," for which he had composed the music.

Composer: RESURRECTION (*Lift your glad voices*), **275**

GOUNOD, CHARLES FRANÇOIS (b. June 18, 1818, Paris, France; d. Oct. 18, 1893, Saint-Cloud, France) was a celebrated French composer who came from a family of artists. He gained his early musical training from his mother and his classical education at the Lycee Saint-Louis. In 1836 he began studying counterpoint and composition at the Paris Conservatoire and won the Grand Prix de Rome in 1839 for his musical dramatic scene "Fernand." Because of his success, he stayed in Rome to study and compose music during the early 1840s.

Upon returning to Paris, Gounod became organist and *maitre de chapelle* of the church of the Mission Etrangeres. Meanwhile, he took up theology but decided against becoming a priest. He spent five years in London as an eminent composer and conductor and founded a choir called by his name, which was later to become the Royal Choral Society. In the latter part of his life, Gounod became absorbed with religious mysticism and his compositions consisted of large sacred oratorios, including *The Redemption* (1882), written for a festival performance in Birmingham, England. His catalogue of compositions includes an extensive list of operas, orchestral works, masses, oratorios, church music, songs (including "Ave Maria"), piano solos, and chamber music.

Composer: LUX PRIMA (*Christ, whose glory fills the skies*), **216**

GRABER, DAVID (b. Nov. 22, 1942, near Wayland, Iowa) attended Hesston College (Kan.) and Goshen College (Ind.; B.A., 1965). He completed his M.M. at the University of Iowa, Iowa City, in 1970. After teaching at Iowa Mennonite School, Kalona, and in several public schools in Indiana and Iowa, he moved to the Cheyenne reservation in Montana where he became a music teacher in 1973. His interest in Native American hymnody was sparked by James Shoulderblade, who led Cheyenne hymns at the evening services in Birney, Montana.

From 1978 to 1984, Graber lived in Kansas where he was a member of New Creation Fellowship in Newton. That congregation provided a stipend that freed him to work on collecting and editing the Cheyenne hymnal, *Tsese-Ma'heone-Nemeotȯtse* (1982). In 1984 he was called back to Montana to do similar work with the indigenous hymns of the Crow people. Volume I of these hymns was completed in 1991. He continues his work in public school music as a band director.

Translator: *Ehane He'ama* (*Father God, you are holy*), **78**; *Jesus A, Nahetotaetanome* (*Jesus Lord, how joyful you have made*), **9**

GRAHAM, SANDRA E. (b. Nov. 9, 1954, Hartford, Conn.) grew up in Vermont in the United Church of Christ (UCC). By age ten she had decided she wanted to become a minister. At age eighteen she moved with her husband to Missouri to work for a year and a half in a mission program. Next came study at the University of New Mexico, Albuquerque (B.A., 1977), and the United Theological Seminary of the Twin Cities, New Brighton, Minnesota (M.Div., 1981). During the years in Minnesota, she and her husband pastored two rural United Methodist churches. After seminary, she spent eight years as pastor of a small, struggling UCC church in Milwaukee, Wisconsin, where she became involved in outreach programs for the urban poor and developed her skills in liturgical writing. Near the end of her tenure there, she received a fellowship to attend Harvard University, Cambridge, Massachusetts, for one semester. This experience led to graduate work in psychology at Marquette University, Milwaukee (Ph.D., 1992). Still residing in Milwaukee, she is an assistant professor of psychology at Alverno College and a psychotherapist working with pastoral/spiritual issues and with women. She is a founding board member of a shelter for the homeless in Milwaukee and has received an award for outstanding urban ministry.

Author: Watch! Wait! The day of God is at hand, **664**

GRANT, DAVID (b. 1833; d. 1893) was a prominent businessman and amateur musician who lived in Aberdeen, Scotland. He was a friend of William Carnie, editor of *The Northern Psalter*. Grant is associated with the hymn tunes CRIMOND and RALEIGH.

Arranger: CRIMOND (*The care the eagle gives her young*, **590**; *The Lord's my shepherd*, **578**)

GRANT, JOHN WEBSTER (b. June 27, 1919, Truro, Nova Scotia) attended Pictou Academy, then received his B.A. *magna cum distinctione* from Dalhousie University in Halifax, Nova Scotia. After graduate study at Princeton University (N.J.), he completed his M.A. at Dalhousie in 1941. He received a Certificate in Theology from Pine Hill Divinity Hall in Halifax two years later and earned his Ph.D. at Keble College, Oxford, England, in 1949.

Grant's academic career includes teaching systematic theology and church history in such diverse places as Nova Scotia, British Columbia, and India where he was visiting professor at United Theological College of South India and Ceylon for a year. He was editor (1959) and editor-in-chief (1960-1963) of *The Ryerson Press*. Grant returned to teaching at Emmanuel College in Ontario as professor of church history (1963-1984), retiring as professor emeritus.

Among Grant's achievements and awards are several honorary doctorates. He has been involved at the highest levels of ecumenical consultations, and he helped prepare the lectionary of the United Church of Canada and the *Hymn Book* (1971), a joint venture of the United Church of Canada and the Anglican Church of Canada. He has written ten books, including *God Speaks . . . We Answer* (1965), *The Church in the Canadian Era* (1972), and *Moon of Wintertime* (1984); articles for books and professional journals; and hymn translations, which appear in collections in Canada, the U.S., and Australia.

Translator: *O Holy Spirit, by whose breath*, **291**

GRANT, ROBERT H. (b. 1779, Bengal, India; d. July 9, 1838, Dalpoorie, India), the son of Charles Grant, a director of the East India Company, was educated at Magdalene College, Cambridge, England (B.A., 1801; M.A., 1804). He was admitted to the bar in 1807, elected to Parliament in 1818, and appointed advocate general in 1832. In 1833 he presented to Parliament a resolution for Jewish emancipation, which was adopted. In 1834 he was knighted and appointed governor of Bombay, India.

Grant was the author of twelve hymns that appeared in the *Christian Observer* and H. V. Elliot's *Psalms and Hymns* (1835). These were published posthumously by his brother as *Sacred Poems* (1839).

Author: *O worship the King*, **66**

GREEN, FRED PRATT (b. Sept. 2, 1903, Roby, near Liverpool, England), a clergyman and poet, attended Rydal School, Colwyn Bay. After working four years in his father's leather manufacturing business, he turned to the Wesleyan Methodist ministry in 1924. Green developed his literary interests at Didsbury Theological College, Manchester, then began pastoral work in 1928 as chaplain at Hunmanby Hall, a girls' school. There he wrote his first hymn and also met his future wife, Marjorie Dowsett, who taught French at the school.

During his pastoral career, Green led churches in Yorkshire and London. He was superintendent of the Dome Mission in Brighton (1947-1952), one of the largest congregations in Great Britain, and was chairman of the district of York and Hull (1957-1962). He returned to local ministry at London's Sutton Trinity Church, serving there until his retirement in 1969. Since then he has resided in Norwich.

Fred Pratt Green did not begin to write poetry until he was in his forties and did not write hymns, with a few exceptions, until past the age of sixty. His poetry is collected in *This Unlikely Earth* (1952), *The Skating Parson* (1963), and *The Old Couple* (1976); in anthologies such as the *Oxford Book of Twentieth Century English Verse*; and in periodicals such as *The New Yorker*. His work first appeared in the *Methodist School Hymn Book* (1950) and *Hymns and Songs* (supplement to the *Methodist Hymn Book*, 1969). They were then picked up by nearly all denominational hymnals, including *Cantate Domino*, the international hymnal of the World Council of Churches. His collected works have been published in *Hymns and Ballads of Fred Pratt Green* (1982), *Later Hymns and Ballads and Fifty Poems* (1989), and *The Last Lap* (1991).

A longtime member of The Hymn Society of Great Britain and Ireland, Green has been commissioned to write hymns for a number of special occasions, including the centenary of the bells in St. Paul's Cathedral, London, and Queen Elizabeth's Silver Jubilee in 1977.

Discussing his craft, Green writes: "Coming to hymn-writing after experience as a poet, I have learned to distinguish between these two activities. One writes poetry to please oneself, one writes hymns as a servant of Christ and his Church. Only one thing matters: that the hymn shall be right for use in worship" (Stulken 1981).

Author: *For the fruit of all creation*, **90**; *How clear is our vocation, Lord*, **541**; *O Christ, the healer*, **379**; *The church of Christ in every age*, **403**; *This is the threefold truth*, **335**; *When in our music God is glorified*, **44**; *Whom shall I send?*, **633**. Translator: *Break forth, O beauteous heavenly* (sts. 2 and 3), **203**; *By gracious powers*, **552**

GREEN, JOSEPH FRANKLIN (b. June 6, 1924, Waco, Tex.), a Southern Baptist pastor and editor, was educated at Texas Wesleyan College, Fort Worth (B.S.); Baylor University, Waco, Texas (M.A.), and Southwestern Baptist Theological Seminary, Fort Worth (Th.D.). After service in the U.S. Army (1943-1946), Green was ordained and held pastorates in Texas and Colorado. In 1954 he began editorial work with Broadman Press in Nashville, Tennessee, later becoming product development coordinator in the Broadman Products Department, Baptist Sunday School Board. His books include *The Heart of the Gospel* and *Biblical Foundations for Church Music*. Green has written concise hymn interpretations for *The Church Musician* and other Southern Baptist publications, as well as hymn and anthem texts and numerous articles and curriculum pieces. Though retired in 1979, he has continued pastoring and editing.

Adapter: *Come, come, ye saints*, **425**

GREGORY I, POPE, surnamed **THE GREAT** (b. ca. 540, Rome, Italy; d. 604, Rome) came from a devout Roman family, active in public service. In his early years, he was a superlative student and became a member of the Senate. Soon after he was thirty, he became *praetor* (magistrate) of Rome, but later he renounced this position and gave himself (and his inherited fortune) to the monastic life. He reluctantly became pope in 590 and sent missionaries to all parts of the Roman empire, including England, where his administrative prowess firmly entrenched papal authority.

It is the name of Gregory that is attached to the ancient liturgical chant of the Roman Catholic Church (Gregorian chant). However, his connection with its composition and performance has been magnified beyond fact in a tradition that began nearly three hundred years after his death. With regard to the liturgy and its chant, Gregory probably was more efficient as an administrator interested in regulating and organizing the ritual of the Roman church (Hoppin 1978) than in personally creating new liturgical forms.

Author (attrib.): *Father, we praise thee*, **650**; *The glory of these forty days*, **225**

GREGORY, PAUL R. (b. Dec. 19, 1920, Chapman Quarries, Pa.) earned a B.S. in chemical engineering from Lehigh University, Allentown, Pennsylvania, and did graduate work at Yale University and Yale Divinity School, New Haven, Connecticut. He has received honorary doctorates from International Christian University, Tokyo, Japan; from Eden Theological Seminary, Webster Groves, Missouri; and from Tohoku Gakuin University, Japan.

Gregory retired in 1986 after eleven years as general secretary of the mission division of the United Church Board for World Ministries. He also held the post of East Asia secretary for twenty-nine years. Prior to this he had been a missionary for two years in Hunan Province, China, and nine years in Japan. He now lives in Lancaster, Pennsylvania, and continues as president of the Japan International Christian University Foundation, having served many years as vice-chairman of the Foundation for Theological Education in Southeast Asia.

Translator: *In lonely mountain ways*, **560**

GREGORY, PHILIP E. (b. 1886, London, England; d. 1974) came to the United States after his graduation from Queen's Park College, London, in 1907. Ordained in 1909, he had a long term of service as a Congregational pastor in the midwestern U.S. and later at Laguna Beach, California. Prior to his retirement in 1956, Gregory served the denomination in a number of leadership positions.

Author: *Jesus, friend so kind and gentle*, **621**

GRIEVE, NICHOL JAMES (b. 1868, Sunderland, England; d. June 20, 1954, Liverpool, England) was educated at the University of Edinburgh, Scotland, and the Theological College of the Presbyterian Church of England, in London. Ordained in 1894, he ministered in Presbyterian churches at Newbiggen-by-the-Sea and in Liverpool. He was on the editorial committee of *The Church Hymnary* (rev., 1930) and published *The Scottish Metrical Psalter of 1650: A Revision* (T&T Clark 1940).

The 1650 Scottish psalter had been in continuous use in Presbyterian churches since its publication. Grieve began his work on the metrical psalter because of increasing discontent over the poetic quality of the 1650 psalter. Grieve's work, which he called an "experiment," was not authorized by the Presbyterian Church, but he hoped it would prod the church to undertake a full revision. Sources consulted in the U.S. do not indicate whether Grieve's hope for a church-approved revision of the *Scottish Psalter* ever occurred. His work has made its way into other hymnals, however, suggesting that perhaps his "experiment" did serve as such a revision.

Adapter: *We would extol thee*, **74**

GRINDAL, GRACIA (b. May 4, 1943, Powers Lake, N.D.) spent her early years in North Dakota and Oregon. She earned a bachelor's degree from Augsburg College, Minneapolis, Minnesota (1965); spent a year in Oslo, Norway; and completed the M.F.A. at the University of Arkansas (1969).

During a tenure of teaching poetry and writing courses at Luther College, Decorah, Iowa (1968-1984), she received her M.A.Th. (1983) from Luther Northwestern Theological Seminary in St. Paul Minnesota. She is now associate professor there, teaching pastoral theology and ministry.

Grindal's poems and articles have appeared in numerous publications, including *The Hymn, Lutheran Women*, and *Christian Century*. She was on the text committee of the commission that produced the 1978 *Lutheran Book of Worship* and has been a consultant to other denominational hymnal committees.

Author: *The kingdom of God*, **224**. Translator: *Fling wide the door, unbar the gate*, **186**; *Out of the depths I cry to you*, **133**

GRISSO, LILLIAN E. (b. Feb. 16, 1889, Laketon, Ind.; d. Jan. 24, 1974, North Manchester, Ind.) was educated at Manchester College, North Manchester (B.A., 1915); Illinois (Cook County) Training School for Nurses (1916); and Bethany Bible School (B.D., 1925). After teaching in public schools in Indiana (1905-1917), she was a missionary to India from 1917 to 1958. On the mission field, she was a practical nurse, evangelist, and teacher in girls' schools at Anklesvar and Vyara. She co-authored a social studies textbook and compiled *Heritage of Devotion*, a collection of Brethren devotional writings. After retirement she lived in Mexico, Indiana.

Translator: *Savior of my soul*, **549**

GRUBER, FRANZ XAVER (b. Nov. 25, 1787, Unterweizberg, Austria; d. June 7, 1863, Hallein, Austria) was born near Hochburg in Upper Austria. Gruber learned the linen-weaving trade from his father, a poor man who discouraged his son's music studies in favor of a more lucrative career. Nevertheless, Gruber secretly studied organ and violin. He taught at the Roman Catholic school at Arndorf while also playing the organ at St. Nicholas church in nearby Orndorf. For the last thirty years of his life, he was headmaster at Berndorf and organist at Hallein, near Salzburg.

Composer: STILLE NACHT (*Silent night, holy night*), **193**

GRUNDTVIG, NIKOLAI FREDERIK SEVERIN (b. Sept. 8, 1783, Denmark; d. Sept. 1, 1872, Vartov, Denmark), the greatest of nineteenth-century Danish hymnwriters, graduated from the University of Copenhagen in 1803. While tutoring and then teaching at a boys' school, he started writing poetry and developed an interest in Danish history and literature, as well as Nordic mythology. The son of a Lutheran pastor, he filled in at the church when his father got ill, but he was denied ordination after his trial sermon betrayed his intense opposition to the then-current rationalistic theology. Grundtvig made an earnest self-examination, which reportedly caused a temporary nervous breakdown. He was eventually ordained in 1811 but, nonetheless, denied a parish and the right to confirm his own children.

Despite the setbacks, Grundtvig won popularity through his preaching—and even more through his hymns and poetry. His hymnal, *Sangvärk til den Danske Kirke* (1837), was well received, and in 1839 he was completely restored to a pastorate in Vartov. He used story and song to teach language and history, and in 1844 he began founding residential folk schools, open to wealthy and poor alike. The trend spread to Sweden, Finland, and Norway, earning him the appellation "father of the folk high school in Scandinavia." His political influence rose and in 1848, as a member of the constitutional assembly of Denmark, he helped establish a constitutional monarchy.

In the latter part of his life, Grundtvig's beliefs and work were finally vindicated; his golden jubilee as a pastor was attended by representatives from all segments of church and state and other Scandinavian countries.

Author: *Bright and glorious is the sky*, **219**; *Built on the Rock*, **309**

GURNEY, DOROTHY FRANCES BLOMFIELD (b. Oct. 4, 1858, London, England; d. June 15, 1932, Kensington, London), with a family history of Anglican clergy, married Gerald Gurney in 1897, a former actor who was ordained in the Church of England. They became Roman Catholic in 1919. She wrote and published two volumes of poems, including this well-known verse:

> The kiss of the sun for pardon,
> The song of the birds for mirth;
> One is nearer God's heart in a garden
> Than anywhere else on earth.

Author: *O perfect Love*, **624**

GUTIÉRREZ-ACHON, RAQUEL (b. May 5, 1927, Central Preston, Oriente, Cuba) is a graduate of the Instituto Santiago and the Conservatorio Provincial, Santiago de Cuba, Oriente, Cuba. She also has earned degrees from Martin College and George Peabody College for Teachers, both in Tennessee. Known as a researcher in Hispanic hymnody, she has been a consultant for the Hispanic hymnal of the Protestant Episcopal Church and was involved in the publication of *Celebremos II* (1983) and *The United Methodist Hymnal* (1989).

Translator: *Tú has venido a la orilla* (*Lord, you have come to the lakeshore*), **229**

HAGEN, FRANCIS FLORENTINE (b. Oct. 30, 1815, Salem, N.C.; d. July 7, 1907, Lititz, Pa.), a musically talented youth, was playing the pipe organ by the age of twelve. By adulthood he had learned to play many musical instruments but loved the violin. Hagen attended school in his native Salem, leaving there in 1829 to study at Nazareth Hall Academy and the Moravian Theological Seminary at Nazareth (Pa.), from which he graduated in 1835. He taught at the boys' school in Salem (1835-1837) and at Nazareth Hall (1837-1844).

Ordained in the Moravian church in 1844, Hagen returned to Wachovia as pastor at Bethania, Friedland, and Friedberg, meanwhile providing music instruction at the girls' boarding school in Salem. In 1854 he once again moved north, becoming pastor at York, Pennsylvania (1854-1861); member of the provincial elders conference at Bethlehem, Pennsylvania (1861-1867); and pastor at New Dorp, Staten Island, New York (1867-1870). Hagen spent five years in mission work in New York City before assuming a pastorate in Harmony, Iowa, in 1875. After an accident caused a permanent hip injury, he retired from pastoring and devoted much of his time to composing. In addition to anthems and hymns, Hagen wrote several extended works, including an orchestral overture and a cantata for soloists, choir, and orchestra. He lived his final years in Pennsylvania with his son Ernest, who was pastor at York and then Lititz.

Composer: HAGEN (*Morning Star, O cheering sight*), **214**

HAMBLEN, STUART (b. Oct. 20, 1908, Kellyville, Tex.; d. Mar. 8, 1989, Los Angeles, Calif.) began his career in 1926 as a country/western singer, composer, and radio/movie personality in Abilene, Texas, where he became radio broadcasting's first singing cowboy. After recording four songs for the Victor Talking Machine Company (the forerunner of RCA Victor), Hamblen set out for Los Angeles where he went on the air as "Cowboy Joe" and also became a member of the original Beverly Hillbillies, radio's first popular, western singing group.

In 1931, and for twenty-one years thereafter, Hamblen stayed atop the charts with his radio programs *King Cowboy and His Woolly West Review*, *Stuart Hamblen and His Lucky Stars*, and *Covered Wagon Jubilee*. His movie credits included westerns with John Wayne, Gene Autry, and Roy Rogers.

During his long span on radio, Hamblen composed western songs, many of which are still being recorded today: "Texas Plains," "My Mary," "Golden River," "Walkin' My Fortune," and "Ridin' Old Paint." His classic "It Is No Secret" has been translated into more than fifty languages, and "This Ole House" took the 1954 Song of the Year award. In addition, Hamblen was inducted into the country/western Hall of Fame in 1970, took the prestigious Pioneer Award in 1972 (first country/western singer on radio), and in 1976 received his star on Hollywood Boulevard.

Married for more than fifty-five years, Hamblen and his wife, Suzy, lived on a horse ranch near Los Angeles where he produced his nationally syndicated *Cowboy Church of the Air* radio program.

Author/Composer: *They that wait upon the Lord,* **584**

HAMM, MARILYN HOUSER (b. June 26, 1951, Decatur, Ind.), a Geneva, Indiana, native, graduated from Goshen College (Ind.; B.A., 1974), then studied piano performance at the Royal Conservatory of Music in Toronto, Ontario, and hymnology with Mary K. Oyer in Goshen. Immersed in the musical life of the Mennonites, she chaired the music committee for *Hymnal: A Worship Book* (1992) and the songbook committee for the 1990 Mennonite World Conference. She has been co-pastor with her husband, Ray, of the Altona Mennonite Church (Manitoba) where she is also minister of music and worship.

Hamm composes, arranges, conducts, and teaches music and has contributed arrangements to this hymnal, as well as to its *Accompaniment Handbook.*

Author/Composer: *Come and see,* **20**. Composer: CANDLE (*Woman in the night*), **223**. Arranger: EKKLESIA (*Seed, scattered and sown*), **454**; *Jesus, Rock of ages,* **515**; KINGSBORO (*Here, O my Lord, I see thee*), **465**

HANAOKA, NOBUAKI (b. Dec. 25, 1944, Saga, Japan) was raised in Osaka and Tokyo. He completed graduate work at Kanto Gakuin University School of Theology in Yokohama, after which he finished his M.Div. at Crozer Theological Seminary, Chester, Pennsylvania. Hanaoka was called to the Japanese Baptist Church in Seattle, Washington. Then in 1975 he did further advanced study at Graduate Theological Union, Berkeley, California. In succeeding years he pastored Buena Vista United Methodist Church in Alameda, California; Pine United Methodist Church in San Francisco, 1979-1991; and is now at Japanese United Methodist Church in Sacramento, California.

During his college years, Hanaoka faced the difficult decision of choosing either theology or music. Though he chose to pursue theology, his love for music has remained strong, and he particularly enjoys writing hymns in traditional Japanese style.

Author: *Praise the Lord,* **52**

HANDEL, GEORGE FREDERICK (b. Feb. 23, 1685, Halle, Germany; d. Apr. 14, 1759, London, England) had to convince his businessman father that his innate skill was worthy of musical training. When George impressed a duke with his organ playing, the elder Handel consented to arrange study with Wilhelm Friedrich Zachau, the organist of the Liebfrauenkirche in Halle. In 1697 Handel became assistant organist at the Halle Cathedral and in 1702 entered the university to study law, but he left a year later for Hamburg to join the opera house as a violinist and, later, harpsichordist. It was here that his first opera, *Almira*, was produced. He spent a few years in Italy composing, but in 1712 he settled for the rest of his life in England, where Italian opera was all the rage.

After almost thirty years as an opera composer and producer/director, Handel turned to oratorio. Of his nineteen oratorios, *Messiah* (1742) has justifiably received countless professional and amateur performances. In this and his other works of this type, Handel set the standard for English choral music for the next two centuries. He also composed many other choral, orchestral, instrumental, and keyboard works. As an acquaintance of the Wesleys, he wrote a few hymn tunes for Charles Wesley's texts. Several other tunes also have been derived from his opera and oratorio music, including ANTIOCH, which Lowell Mason crafted for "Joy to the world."

Composer: CHRISTMAS (*Awake, my soul*), **609**; JUDAS MACCABEUS (*Thine is the glory*), **269**

HANKEY, CATHERINE (b. 1834, Clapham, England; d. May 9, 1911, London, England) was christened Arabella Catherine but was known as Kate or Katherine. Her father, banker Thomas Hankey, was a member of the Anglican evangelical "Clapham Sect" (associated with William Wilberforce), a group that lobbied for the abolition of slavery in England. Through her father's influence, Kate got caught up in religious and social work. She began teaching Sunday school as a schoolgirl herself, and at eighteen she organized a Bible class for shop girls in London.

A trip to Africa ignited her interest in the mission fields; in later years she donated all the income from her writings to this cause. "I love to tell the story" and "Tell me the old, old story" appear in *The Old, Old Story* (1866). Her collection of poems, *Heart to Heart* (1870), was reprinted in several editions.

Author: *I love to tell the story*, **398**

HARKNESS, GEORGIA ELMA (b. Apr. 21, 1891, Harkness, N.Y.; d. Aug. 30, 1974, Claremont, Calif.), a leading theologian of her generation, received a B.A. from Cornell University, Ithaca, New York, and her graduate degrees (M.A., M.R.E., Ph.D.) from Boston University. She also studied at Harvard University, Cambridge, Massachusetts; Yale Divinity School, New Haven, Connecticut; and Union Theological Seminary, New York City.

Ordained in the Methodist ministry, she was a professor of theology and the philosophy of religion at Elmira College (N.Y.); Mount Holyoke College, South Bradley, Massachusetts; and Garrett School of Theology, Evanston, Illinois. At Garrett she was the first woman in the United States to be named full professor at a theological seminary. Tenures at Pacific School of Religion, Berkeley, California, and the Japanese International Christian University rounded out her academic career. Harkness traveled extensively, was a member on the Methodist Commission on World Peace, and authored thirty-seven books, three of which are collections of her poems and prayers.

Author: *God of the fertile fields*, **390**

HARLOW, SAMUEL RALPH (b. July 20, 1885, Boston, Mass.; d. Aug. 21, 1972, Northampton, Mass.) received his A.B. from Harvard University, Cambridge, Massachusetts; his M.A. from Columbia University, New York City; and his Ph.D. from Hartford Theological Seminary (Conn.). In 1912 he earned a diploma in theology from Union Theological Seminary, New York City, and was ordained as a Congregational minister. From 1912 to 1922, he was chaplain and chairman of the sociology department at International College, Smyrna, Turkey. After 1923 he was on the religion faculty at Smith College, Northampton, Massachusetts, where he lived until his death. In addition to these major positions, Harlow served the YMCA as religious director during World War I, the Student Volunteer Movement for the Near East, and the American Board of Commissioners for Foreign Missions. He was author of a number of books on Christian topics and wrote several hymns, including "O Church of God triumphant."

Author: *O young and fearless Prophet*, **374**

HARRISON, RALPH (b. Sept. 10, 1748, Chinley, Derbyshire, England; d. Nov. 4, 1810, Manchester, Lancashire, England), whose father was a free-church pastor, studied at Warrington Academy. In Manchester he was organist and, later, pastor at Cross Street Chapel (Independent) and taught classics at Manchester Academy, a boys' school. He published books on English grammar and geography and edited *Sacred Harmony* (2 vols., 1784, 1791), which included several of his psalm tunes.

Arranger: ARLINGTON (*This is the day the Lord has made*), **642**

HASSLER, HANS LEO (b. Oct. 25, 1564, Nürnberg, Germany; d. June 8, 1612, Frankfurt am Main, Germany), like many musicians of the time, came from a family of organists and composers. He was influenced, however, by a teacher who was a pupil of Lassus and went to Venice, Italy, where he was a fellow student of Giovanni Gabrieli. Both studied with Andrea Gabrieli, a famed organist of St. Mark's Cathedral.

Hassler brought the polychoral sacred style and the Italian madrigal to Germany. Although he wrote many masses and works in Latin, he also wrote *Psalmen* and *Kirchengesänge*, both elaborate, fugal settings and simpler versions of the chorale melodies. Upon his return to Germany, Hassler was the private organist of Octavian Fugger in Augsburg from 1585 until his patron died in 1600. Later he held positions in Prague, Czechoslovakia (where he also built musical clocks), Nürnberg, and Dresden. At the time of his death from tuberculosis, he was *Kapellmeister* to the Saxon Court.

Composer: HERZLICH TUT MICH VERLANGEN (*O sacred Head, now wounded*), **252**

HASTINGS, THOMAS (b. Oct. 15, 1784, Washington, Conn.; d. May 15, 1872, New York, N.Y.), the son of a physician/farmer, moved with his family at the age of twelve to Clinton, New York. He was an albino and very nearsighted; nevertheless, he taught himself music and became an outstanding choral conductor and music teacher. From 1823 to 1832, he edited *The Western Recorder*, a weekly in Utica, New York, which he used as a springboard for his articles on improving church music. In 1832, at the invitation of twelve churches, he moved to New York City and there assisted in developing their music for worship.

With Lowell Mason he promoted European standards for church and public school music. In addition to writing more than six hundred texts and a thousand hymn tunes, he compiled and edited fifty volumes, beginning with the *Utica Collection* in 1816 (later called *Musica Sacra*). With Mason he published *Spiritual Songs for Social Worship* (ca. 1832) and, with William Bradbury, the influential *Mendelssohn Collection*. The University of the City of New York conferred upon Hastings the honorary Doctor of Music in 1858. Perhaps he is best remembered for his tune TOPLADY ("Rock of ages").

Author: *Come, ye disconsolate* (st. 3), **497**. Composer: RETREAT (*Great God, the giver of all good*), **458**

HATCH, EDWIN (b. Sept. 4, 1835, Derby, England; d. Nov. 10, 1889, Oxford, England) was educated at King Edward's School in Birmingham and at Pembroke College, Oxford (B.A., 1857). Though his parents were not part of the Church of England (i.e., Nonconformist), he was ordained as an Anglican priest in 1859. He soon moved to Canada where he was professor of classics at Trinity College in Toronto and later the rector of a high school in Québec. In 1867 he returned to Oxford where he held several appointments. Hatch was widely acclaimed as a lecturer, especially on church history; his famous Bampton Lectures on "The Organization of the Early Christian Churches" were delivered in 1880, and in 1888 he gave the Hibbert Lectures on "The Influence of Greek Ideas and Usages upon the Christian Church." His distinguished scholarship was enhanced by his creativity, sincerity, and piety.

Author: *Breathe on me, breath of God*, **356**

HATTON, JOHN (b. ca. 1710, Warrington, England; d. December 1793, St. Helen's, England), known as "John of Warrington," resided in St. Helen's in the township of Windle, Lancashire, on Duke Street. It is for this one tune he is remembered. His funeral was held at Presbyterian Chapel of St. Helen's on December 13, 1793, reportedly after a stagecoach accident.

Composer (attrib.): DUKE STREET (*From all that dwell below the skies*, **49**; *Jesus shall reign*, **319**)

HAUGEN, MARTY (b. Dec. 30, 1950, Zumbrota, Minn.) graduated in 1973 from Luther College, Decorah, Iowa, with a B.A. in psychology and a minor in music. At St. Paul Seminary School of Divinity/College of St. Thomas (Minn.), he continued his education in liturgy and pastoral studies, receiving his M.A. in 1991. From 1974 to 1985, he served as music director at two Roman Catholic parishes in the Minneapolis area, then was composer-in-residence at Holden Village, an ecumenical retreat center administered by the Lutheran Church in Chelan, Washington.

Since 1985 he has been a freelance composer and leads workshops for church musicians. Haugen is a member and composer-in-residence at Mayflower Congregational Church (United Church of Christ) in Minneapolis.

Author/Composer: *Healer of our every ill*, **377**; *Here in this place* (GATHER US IN), **6**; *Shepherd me, O God*, **519**; *We give thanks unto you*, **161**; *You are salt for the earth* (BRING FORTH THE KINGDOM), **226**. Composer: SHANTI (*We walk by faith*), **570**

HAUSMANN, JULIE KATHARINA (b. 1825 or 1826, Riga, Latvia; d. Aug. 15, 1901, Wössö, Estonia), from a German family, lived in Latvia where her father was a teacher at the local high school. Hausmann was tutored privately, but her work was complicated by migraine headaches. For a period of time, she was a governess for private families. When her father became a town councillor, he also moved the family up the social ladder to aristocracy, and they changed their name to von Hausmann.

After her mother's death in 1859, Hausmann cared for her ailing father until his death in 1864. She then moved to southern France to live with a younger sister. In 1870 they visited another sister in St. Petersburg where they worked together in the St. Anna school and pension house.

Her publications include a devotional book, *Hausbrot*, and poetry in several volumes under the title *Maiblumen, Lieder einer Stillen im Lande* (May flowers, songs of a quiet one in the land). The latter was collected by a friend and sent to a pastor in Berlin. Hausmann agreed to its publication only if it would appear without her name, and all proceeds went to a hospital and orphanage in Hong Kong.

Author: *Take thou my hand, O Father*, **581**

HAVERGAL, FRANCES RIDLEY (b. Dec. 14, 1836, Astley, Worcestershire, England; d. June 3, 1879, Caswell Bay, Wales) was the youngest child of clergyman William Henry Havergal. She began writing at age seven and her work appeared in the magazine *Good Words*. Due to frail health, her education was sporadic. Still, she became proficient in several languages and continued writing for thirty-five years.

Havergal was also a natural musician; a brilliant pianist; and a singer with a pleasing, well-trained voice. Sought after as a concert soloist, she believed that her mission was "singing for Jesus" and sang nothing but sacred music after 1873. Although she composed music, she is best remembered for her hymn texts with their themes of faith, consecration, and service.

Author: *I am trusting thee, Lord Jesus*, **564**; *Lord, speak to me*, **499**; *Take my life*, **389**

HAVERGAL, WILLIAM HENRY (b. Jan. 18, 1793, Chipping, Wycombe, Buckinghamshire, England; d. Apr. 19, 1870, Leamington, Warwick, England), the father of Frances Havergal, studied at Merchant Taylor's School and St. Edmund's Hall, Oxford (B.A., 1815; M.A., 1819). Ordained in 1817 as an Anglican priest, he held two pastorates before becoming rector of Astley, Worcestershire, in 1829. That same year he was seriously injured when thrown from a carriage. Unable to continue in pastoral work, he turned to composing and publishing church music.

Years later Havergal was well enough to resume active ministry and served the parishes of St. Nicholas, Worcester; Shareshill near Wolverhampton; and Worcester Cathedral where he became honorary canon. In 1867 he retired from the ministry and lived in Leamington until his death. His published works include a reprint of Ravenscroft's *Whole Booke of Psalms* (1844), *Old Church Psalmody* (1847), and *A History of the Old Hundredth Psalm Tune, with specimens* (1854). *A Hundred Psalm and Hymn Tunes*, all of which he composed, was published in 1859.

Arranger: WINCHESTER NEW (*On Jordan's banks the Baptist's cry*, **183**; *Ride on, ride on in majesty*, **239**)

HAWEIS, THOMAS (b. ca. 1734, Cornwall, England; d. Feb. 11, 1820, Bath, England) was first apprenticed to a physician, then studied theology at Cambridge University. Though an Anglican clergyman, he sympathized with the Methodists and corresponded with John Newton. After a stint with Martin Madan at Lock Hospital in London, he pastored All Saints Church in Aldwinkle, Northampshire, for fifty-six years. During some of that time, he was also chaplain to Lady Huntingdon in Bath. Interested in interdenominational missions as well, Haweis helped organize the London Missionary Society in 1795.

He received recognition for his ability as a musician and was acclaimed as a prolific author. Haweis's most significant publications include *A History of the Church, A Commentary on the Holy Bible,* and *Original Music Suited to the various Metres.*

Composer: RICHMOND (*Thou art the way*), **339**

HAWKS, ANNIE SHERWOOD (b. May 28, 1835, Hoosick, N.Y.; d. Jan. 3, 1918, Bennington, Vt.) was for many years a member of Hanson Place Baptist Church, Brooklyn, New York, where her pastor, Robert Lowry, discovered and encouraged her gift for hymnwriting. Although she wrote about four hundred texts, it is for this one in *Hymnal: A Worship Book* (1992) that she is best remembered. She and her husband, Charles H. Hawks, married in 1857. She died at the Vermont home of her daughter.

Author: *I need thee every hour*, **555**

HAY, EDYTH HILLERY (b. Oct. 28, 1891; d. 1943, Indiana) was a student of J. Henry Showalter who recognized her as "a musically gifted young woman." A member of the committee for the 1925 Church of the Brethren hymnal, she wrote and composed many hymns that were published in songbooks compiled by Showalter. She was the daughter of Lemuel and Aloretta (Nihart) Hillery and married James Hay.

Author/Composer: *Lord, with devotion we pray* (HILLERY), **79**

HAYDN, FRANZ JOSEPH (b. Mar. 31, 1732, Rohrau, Austria; d. May 31, 1809, Vienna, Austria) was born in a small village southeast of Vienna, not far from the Hungarian border. He became a choirboy at St. Stephen's Cathedral in Vienna and remained there until his voice changed. After a time of musical freelancing, he was placed in charge of the total music program in the court of the Esterházy family in Eisenstadt from 1761 until his death in 1809. This position provided Haydn the financial security and musical resources to produce his tremendous output of compositions.

A genius of the classical period of music, he visited England twice in the 1790s. There he was honored by both the public and royalty. Oxford University conferred on him an honorary Mus.D. in 1791. His works include at least 104 symphonies and 83 string quartets, two well-known oratorios (*The Creation*, 1798, and *The Seasons*, 1801), piano sonatas, folk song arrangements, and concertos, many of which have been combed by tunebook editors and adapted for hymnody.

Hayden was a deeply religious man and closed each of his manuscripts with the words *Laus Deo* or *Soli Deo Gloria.* Although he composed six hymn tunes for William Tattersall's *Improved Psalmody* (1794), it is the tune listed here and CREATION ("The spacious firmament on high"), derived from his other works, that are best known.

Composer: AUSTRIAN HYMN (*Glorious things of thee are spoken*), **619**

HAYDN, JOHANN MICHAEL (b. Sept. 14, 1737, Rohrau, Austria; d. Aug. 10, 1806, Salzburg, Austria), like his older brother Franz Joseph, was a boy soprano at St. Stephen's Cathedral in Vienna (ca. 1745). His professional career began in 1757 when he was appointed *Kapellmeister* to the bishop at Grosswardein. Five years later he was a court musician and concertmaster to Archbishop Sigismund von Schrattenbach in Salzburg where he stayed until his death. During this time (1781), he was also musical director to Archbishop Hieronymous at the Cathedral, a position Wolfgang Amadeus Mozart had held just before him.

He, too, was considered a devout and respected Christian and initialed all of his manuscripts "O.a.M.D. gl." (*Omnia ad Majorem Dei Gloriam*). Between 1783 and 1800, he composed approximately one hundred musical works for the Catholic Church. When German was revived as a language acceptable for worship, Haydn composed a number of works in that language for congregational and choir performance. In 1804 he was invited to membership in the Royal Swedish Academy of Music. Like Mozart his last work was a requiem Mass, which Haydn also failed to complete before his death.

Composer: DIE SACH' IST DEIN (*The work is thine, O Christ*), **396**

HEAP OF BIRDS, JOHN (b. 1894, Oklahoma; d. 1966) was given the Indian name of his grandfather, *Mo'e'hane Oxhaestozese* (Many Magpies), translated Heap of Birds, when he was enrolled in school. Like his father, Alfrich, whom he succeeded in 1922 as head of the Heap of Birds family, he sang hymns with Plains Indian melodies. Many of the hymns attributed to him in *Tsese-Ma'heone-Nemeotȯtse* (Cheyenne Spiritual Songs) were contributed by his family members who continued the oral tradition.

Working with Mennonite missionary J. B. Ediger, Heap of Birds led worship services and helped the Cheyenne people of Thomas, Oklahoma, form a congregation and build a chapel, known as the Deer Creek (Indian) Church (*Tsese-Ma'heone-Nemeotȯtse,* 1982). In later years he became an itinerant preacher, wandering as far as Montana, teaching his own hymns and other hymns from the oral tradition of the Cheyenne Christians.

Author: *Jesus A, Nahetotaetanome* (*Jesus Lord, how joyful you have made*), **9**

HEBER, REGINALD (b. Apr. 21, 1783, Malpas, Cheshire, England; d. Apr. 3, 1826, Trichinopoly, India) was educated at Brasenose College, Oxford, and was named a fellow of All Souls' College in 1805. Ordained in 1807, he was rector of his family's parish at Hodnet, Shropshire, until 1823. In that year he was made bishop of Calcutta, with responsibility for all of India, but he died there suddenly, just three years later, at the age of forty-two.

Heber's own hymnwritings appeared in the *Christian Observer*, beginning in 1811. Noting the successful hymn-singing of the Baptists and Methodists, he began to collect texts appropriate for each Sunday of the Christian year. Though his collection did not receive official church approval, it ushered in a new era in English hymnody, paving the way for hymns coming out of the later Oxford movement. Published by his widow shortly after his death, *Hymns Written and Adapted to the Weekly Service of the Church Year* (1827) was of marked quality both literarily and lyrically, and its new organization helped introduce hymn singing to the Anglican Church in a way that unified the weekly scripture readings, music, and sermons.

Author: *Bread of the world*, **469**; *Hail the bless'd morn*, **221**; *Holy, holy, holy*, **120**

HEDGE, FREDERICK HENRY (b. Dec. 12, 1805, Cambridge, Mass.; d. Aug. 21, 1890, Cambridge) was sent to study in Germany at age thirteen. He returned four years later to be educated at Harvard University, Cambridge, from which he graduated in 1825. Ordained as a Unitarian minister in 1829, Hedge served churches in Maine, Rhode Island, and Massachusetts. During his fifteen-year Unitarian Church tenure in Brookline, Massachusetts, he was also professor of ecclesiastical history at Harvard, later being appointed professor of German as well. Associated with the transcendental movement, Hedge was a contributor to the *Christian Examiner* for a number of years. As a scholar of German literature, Hedge's other publications include *Prose Writers of Germany* and *Hymns for the Church of Christ* (1853), compiled with F. D. Huntington.

Translator: *A mighty fortress* is our God, **165**

HEERMANN, JOHANN (b. Oct. 11, 1585, Raudten, Silesia; d. Feb. 17, 1647, Lissa, Posen), the fifth child of a poor furrier, was the only one to survive. When Johann suffered a serious childhood illness, his mother vowed that if he lived she would somehow see that he was trained for the ministry. He studied at the secondary schools in Breslau and Brieg—and for a brief time at the University of Strassburg, becoming a teacher. His mother's dream for him was realized when an eye infection compelled him to forsake teaching. In 1611 he was made a deacon at Koeben where he eventually became pastor.

Heermann's setbacks did not conclude with his youth. He has been described as a "German Job among hymn text writers," for Heermann's writings are best understood by knowing what he suffered. His first wife died before bearing any children. The son of his second wife became a preacher but suffered a debilitating throat disease and subsequently converted to Catholicism. When the son returned to the faith of his father, he was poisoned by the Jesuits who had converted him earlier. In the midst of these personal crises, Heermann three times lost all his personal property to marauding armies during the Thirty Years War. Despite these setbacks and threats to his own safety, his hymns reflect a deep spiritual serenity. In the words of German writer Lieselotte von Eltz-Hoffmann: "Pain became a spring of poetry in which his tears were turned into pearls" (Eltz-Hoffmann 1980).

Author: *Ah, holy Jesus,* **254**; *O God, thou faithful God,* **376**

HEMY, HENRI FREDERICK (b. Nov. 12, 1818, Newcastle-on-Tyne, England; d. 1888, Hartlepool, Durham, England), a son of German parents, was organist at St. Andres' Roman Catholic Church of Newcastle. Years later he taught music at Tynemouth and then became professor of voice and piano at St. Cuthbert's College in Durham. He was the author of the *Royal Modern Tutor for the Pianoforte* (1858), a piano method that continued through many editions. Hemy also edited *Crown of Jesus Music* (1864), which was composed of four parts containing Latin hymns, chants, benediction services, and masses. This collection enjoyed wide usage in Roman Catholic churches.

Composer: ST. CATHERINE (*Faith of the martyrs,* **413**; *God of the earth, the sky, the sea,* **53**)

HERBERT, GEORGE (b. Apr. 3, 1593, Montgomery Castle, England; d. February 1633, Bemerton, Wiltshire, England), who learned to play the lute and viol, grew up in a home where psalm-singing was a regular activity and musicians such as John Bull and William Byrd were known to visit. He was an exceptional student, educated at Westminster School and Trinity College, Cambridge, where he received his B.A. in 1611, an M.A. in 1615, and became a major fellow of the college that same year. About 1626 he was ordained as an Anglican priest and appointed to the parish at Leighton Bromswold. He became rector of the country parish of Foughleston, Bemerton (near Salisbury), in 1630.

Single-minded and pious, the man known as "holy Mr. Herbert" once said, "We live in an age that hath more need of good examples than precepts" (Bailey 1950). He dedicated his life to being a good example, and his poetry reflects his "mystic sainthood." He gave his most famous work *The Temple* to his friend Nicholas Ferrar just three weeks before Herbert died of consumption, instructing Ferrar that if he thought his poems might do good to "any dejected poor soul," they should be printed; otherwise he should burn them (Summers 1967). The poems—marked by simple, ordinary speech and crafted with dignity—were not destroyed, and though they lay in obscurity for some hundred years after publication, a number of them are in present-day hymnals.

Author: *Come, my Way, my Truth, my Life,* **587**

HERKLOTS, ROSAMOND ELEANOR (b. June 22, 1905, Masuri, North India; d. July 21, 1987, Bromley, Kent, England), the daughter of British parents, was educated at Leeds Girls' High School and Leeds University. She was a teacher for a time but resigned to take a secretarial position. After more than twenty years as secretary to a prominent neurologist, she worked in London in the main office of the Association for Spina Bifida and Hydrocephalus.

Author: *Forgive our sins as we forgive*, **137**

HERMANN, NICOLAUS (b. ca. 1485; d. May 3, 1561, Joachimsthal, Bohemia) was a church musician in Joachimsthal where, for most of his career, he served the local Lutheran church as organist, cantor, and choirmaster, as well as teaching in the town's Latin School. His close association with his pastor, Johann Mathesius, inspired him to write hymns. Hermann wrote both the text and music for his chorales, most of which were intended for the use of the children in the school. The majority of Hermann's nearly two hundred hymns were published in two collections: *Die Sonntags Evangelia über das gantze Jahr* (1560) and *Die Historien von der Sintflut* (1562).

Author/Composer: *Let all together praise our God* (LOBT GOTT, IHR CHRISTEN), **213**. Composer: LOBT GOTT, IHR CHRISTEN (*If Christ is mine*), **331**

HERR, AMOS (b. Feb. 23, 1816, Lancaster County, Pa.; d. June 19, 1897, Lancaster County) resided all his life on the farm where he was born. A son of Bishop Christian Herr, he was ordained to the ministry in 1850 or 1851 and, like most nineteenth-century Mennonite ministers, was also a farmer. He was one of the first to preach in English, convinced that if the church wanted to hold young people who were being educated in English, it would be necessary to preach to them in English as well. His interest in the development of Sunday schools complemented his "liberal" preaching conviction. Still, "his comprehensive understanding of the word of God, his fluency as a speaker, his deep sympathies coupled with his warm social qualities, his devoted friendship, and affectionate love toward all made him a general favorite among all classes of people."[1] Until the time of his death, Herr had active charge of Brick Church (now Willow Street Mennonite Church) and also the Strasburg and New Providence meetings.

Author/Composer: *I owe the Lord a morning song* (GRATITUDE), **651**

1. *Herald of Truth*, July 15, 1897, Vol. 34, No. 14

HERRESTHAL, HARALD (b. 1944) holds the chair for church music at the Norwegian Academy of Music in Oslo. He is a scholar, composer, writer, educator, and performing organist both in Norway and abroad. When the original text of *I de sene timers stillhet* (In the stillness of the evening) was selected for the official hymnal of the Norwegian Lutheran Church, *Norsk Salmebok* (1985), his melody and arrangement were chosen from among several compositions for this text.

Composer: I DE SENE TIMERS STILLHET (*In the stillness of the evening*), **551**

HERSHBERGER, MARTHA BUCKWALTER (b. Feb. 27, 1927, Hesston, Kan.), growing up in a minister's family, participated in many aspects of church life and worship, including singing. Together with her five siblings, she presented music programs in other churches. Her first compositions were *a cappella* arrangements for her sisters' trio and quartet.

In 1948 Hershberger graduated from Hesston College with a degree in elementary education. She married and taught one year (all eight grades) and later took additional courses in church music, choral conducting, and piano pedagogy. She taught piano for six years.

Beginning in 1961 Hershberger organized both junior and adult choirs at Whitestone Mennonite Church in Hesston. Her choral directing career, first at Hesston and later in Harper, Kansas, has spanned almost thirty years. She has continued composing for the church choirs she directed. She still enjoys singing, playing the piano, attending concerts, and arranging music.

Arranger: HOW MAJESTIC IS YOUR NAME (*O Lord, our Lord, how majestic*), **112**

HEWITT, ELIZA EDMUNDS (b. June 28, 1851, Philadelphia, Pa.; d. Apr. 24, 1920, Philadelphia) was a lifelong resident of Philadelphia where she was active in Olivet Presbyterian Church and, later, Calvin Presbyterian Church. She graduated from Girls' Normal School as valedictorian of her class, then taught school for a short period of time. She faced some serious physical limitations early in life (she was injured by one of her students), but as her health improved, she taught Sunday school classes and contributed literary works to *Sunday-school Helps* and other children's church papers. In addition to the hymn included here, other popular texts include "When we all get to heaven," "More about Jesus would I know," and "There is sunshine in my soul today." The music for the latter two was written by outstanding musician and music leader John R. Sweney, who read some of her writing and asked for contributions to his publications. She also wrote many texts for such composers as William J. Kirkpatrick and J. H. Hall.

Author: *For Christ and the church*, **416**

HEWITT, JAMES (b. June 4, 1770, England; d. Aug. 2, 1827, Boston, Mass.) in his youth went to sea, but he also played in the court orchestra in London before moving to North America in 1792. He settled in New

York City and became a leading composer of his time. Hewitt's reputation as conductor, composer, and publisher spread as early as 1805 to Boston, where he and his family moved in 1811. He was also organist at Trinity Church, Boston, but his career kept him traveling between Boston and New York City as well as to southern cities, including Charleston, South Carolina, and Augusta, Georgia. He died of facial cancer.

Hewitt published at least 639 compositions, mostly by British composers, but some works by Handel, Haydn, and Mozart. He also published about 160 original compositions, including instrumental and keyboard works, ballad operas, and other stage works, songs, and, in particular, seven hymns in his collection *Harmonia Sacra* (Boston 1812). His own setting of "The Star-Spangled Banner" never caught on.

Editor/Source: CHRISTMAS (*Awake, my soul*), **609**

HEWS, GEORGE (b. Jan. 6, 1806, Weston, Mass.; d. July 6, 1873, Boston, Mass.) was a Boston area music teacher and singer. He sang tenor in the Handel and Haydn Society chorus and was its vice-president from 1854 to 1858. He established a piano manufacturing company in 1840 and was granted several patents for mechanism improvements. Hews was an organist at Brattle Street Church and also composed instrumental and secular vocal works, in addition to hymn tunes.

Composer: HOLLEY (*Here in our upper room*), **450**

HIBBARD, ESTHER (b. Sept. 23, 1903, Tokyo, Japan), a missionary teacher to Japan with the United Church of Christ, spent her first ten years in Tokyo where her father was student secretary of the YMCA. They returned to the U.S. in 1913, traveling by train through Siberia. Hibbard did her undergraduate work at Mount Holyoke College, South Hadley, Massachusetts, and earned her master's degree in English at the University of Wisconsin.

She returned to Japan as a career missionary in 1929, under the auspices of the Congregational Mission Board, and taught at Doshaissha Christian High School for Girls. Along with other Americans, she was evacuated in 1941 for the duration of World War II. For the next five years, Hibbard took up doctoral study in oriental civilizations at the University of Michigan, where she also taught conversational Japanese in the Army Specialized Trainees' Program. Then in 1946 she returned to Japan where missionaries were warmly welcomed at the Doshaissha Junior College for Women. When the school became a four-year women's college of liberal arts in 1948, Hibbard became its first dean. She resigned for her furlough in 1949 but returned as a professor until her retirement in 1968.

Hibbard remained in Japan for another five years, teaching at the coeducational college Tohoku Gakuin (Northeast College), affiliated with the Evangelical and Reformed Church. In 1973 she left Japan to retire at Pilgrim Place in Claremont, California. In addition to her translations of Japanese hymns, Hibbard has done research in Ulysses motifs in Japanese literature.

Translator: *Ah, what shame I have to bear,* **531**; *In this world abound scrolls,* **316**

HILLER, PHILIPP FRIEDRICH (b. Jan. 6, 1699, Mühlhausen, Germany; d. Apr. 24, 1769, Steinheim, Germany), the son of a pastor, attended the clergy training schools at Denkendorf and Maulbroon and graduated from the University of Tübingen (M.A., 1720). Hiller was a clerical assistant for a time and a private tutor in Nürnberg until he landed a pastoral post at Neckargröningen near Marbach in 1732. He moved on to Mühlhausen in 1736 and Steinheim in 1748. During his third year at Steinheim, he lost his voice and was forced to employ an assistant to deliver his sermons.

Hiller's 1,075 hymns are representative of the period of chorale writing identified by Carl Schalk as the period of Pietism (ca. 1675-ca. 1750) when the pietistic movement reached its peak in Europe. Hymns of personal devotion elevated by now to an art form by Paul Gerhardt and Johannes Franck were finding their way back into congregational worship.

Hiller's hymns first appeared in *Paradiss-Gärtlein . . . in teutsche Lieder* (Nürnberg). His *Geistliches Liederkästlein* (1762) ran through two series (second in 1767); each volume included one hymn for every day of the year.

Author: *What mercy and divine compassion,* **524**

HILLERT, RICHARD WALTER (b. Mar. 14, 1923, Granton, Wis.) received his B.S. in education in 1951 from Concordia College, River Forest, Illinois. He earned both the M.M. (1955) and D.Mus. (1968) in composition from Northwestern University, Evanston, Illinois. He also studied composition with Matthew N. Lundquist, Anthony Donato, and Goffredo Petrassi, the latter at the Berkshire School of Music, Tanglewood, Massachusetts.

Hillert has been director of music at a number of churches in the midwestern U.S. prior to and in addition to his music professorship at Concordia College (now Concordia University). Employed by the school since 1959, he teaches music theory, composition, and twentieth-century music literature and directs graduate studies in church music.

As assistant editor of *Church Music* magazine from its inception in 1966 until 1980, Hillert contributed numerous articles to that journal and other publications. His more than three hundred published compositions include choral music, hymns and carols, chamber music, and works for keyboard and other instruments. He was a member of the liturgical music committee for the *Lutheran Book of Worship* (1978).

Composer: FESTIVAL CANTICLE (*This is the feast of victory*), **476**. Arranger: NARODIL SE KRISTUS PÁN (*Let our gladness have no end*), **198**

HODGES, EDWARD (b. July 20, 1796, Bristol, Gloucestershire, England; d. Sept. 1, 1867, Clifton, Gloucestershire, England) was educated at Cambridge University (D.Mus., 1825). He served as organist at both Bristol and Clifton. After moving to Canada in 1838, he became organist of the Toronto Cathedral (Ont.). A year later Hodges settled in New York City as organist at St. John's Episcopal Church (1839-1846) and at Trinity Church (1846-1863). He then returned to England for his retirement years.

Hodges composed anthems and hymn tunes, as well as some books on church music. The U.S. Library of Congress received his music library and manuscripts in 1919.

Arranger: HYMN TO JOY (*Joyful, joyful, we adore thee*), **71**

HOFFMAN, ELISHA ALBRIGHT (b. May 7, 1839, Orwigsburg, Pa.; d. Nov. 25, 1929, Chicago, Ill.) was born in Schuylkill County, Pennsylvania, the son of a minister in the Evangelical Association. He was musically talented, and his home background exerted a profound influence on his interest in sacred music. Hoffman wrote his first composition when he was eighteen; from then on he published more than two thousand works during his lifetime. He attended Union Seminary of the Evangelical Association and pastored Congregational and Presbyterian churches in Illinois and Michigan. He became the first music editor for Hope Publishing Company in 1894 and assisted in editing and compiling approximately fifty songbooks.

Author: *Breathe upon us, Holy Spirit*, **28**; *Lord, I am fondly, earnestly longing*, **514**

HOLBROOK, JOSEPH PERRY (b. 1822, near Boston, Mass.; d. 1888) is best known as a compiler and editor of *Songs for the Church* (1862) and *Songs for the Sanctuary* (1865), which he edited for Charles S. Robinson, and the *Methodist Hymnal* (1878) with Eben Tourjee.

Composer: BISHOP (*Teach me, O Lord*), **487**

HOLDEN, OLIVER (b. Sept. 18, 1765, Shirley, Mass.; d. Sept. 4, 1844, Charlestown, Mass.) was a carpenter by trade. He moved at age twenty-one to Charlestown to help rebuild the city after it was burned by the British in the battle of Bunker Hill. He served as a justice of the peace, was successful in real estate dealings, served six terms in the state legislature (1818-1833), and operated a music store. Holden was a versatile man—a Puritan minister, tunebook editor and compiler, music teacher, and composer. The small pipe organ on which he played and composed is now at the Bostonian Society in the Old State House.

Composer: CORONATION (*All hail the power of Jesus' name*), **106**

HOLSINGER, GEORGE B. (b. 1857, Bedford County, Va.; d. Nov. 22, 1908, Astoria, Ill.) attended music schools during the summer and served as head of the music department at Bridgewater College in Virginia. In 1898 he became music editor for Brethren Publishing House in Elgin, Illinois, and remained in that post until his death in 1908. Holsinger is quoted as saying: "As a rule I compose music from the inspiration received from the first reading of the poetry" (Garrett, Beery 1924). He died in Astoria, Illinois, where he had gone to direct an institute in sacred music.

Composer: BE THOU OUR GUIDE (*On the radiant threshold*), **649**

HOPKINS, EDWARD JOHN (b. June 30, 1818, Westminster, London, England; d. Feb. 4, 1901, London) became a chorister at the Chapel Royal when he was eight. His career positions as church organist/choirmaster began in 1834, culminating after fifty-five years at Temple Church, London. He was professor of organ at the Royal Normal College for the Blind at Norwood and gave organ recitals until he was seventy-eight years old. He was known as a master of service playing and accompanying. Hopkins was a noted scholar and a prolific composer of church music. He was a founder of the Royal College of Organists in 1864 and Trinity College of Music in 1872. Hopkins served as music editor for the hymnals of several denominations. He was honored with a D.Mus. degree from the archbishop of Canterbury in 1882 and from Trinity College, Toronto, Ontario, in 1886.

Composer: *My God, my God, why*, **248**; ELLERS (*Lead us, O Father*, **359**; *Savior, again to your dear name*, **656**)

HOPKINS, JOHN HENRY, JR. (b. Oct. 28, 1820, Pittsburgh, Pa.; d. Aug. 14, 1891, near Hudson, N.Y.) demonstrated talents in music, poetry, and art. He graduated from the University of Vermont, Burlington, in 1839—in 1845 he took his M.A. as well—and worked as a reporter in New York City while studying law. After earning his M.A., he went on to graduate from General Theological Seminary, New York City (1850) where he became the first instructor in church music (1855-1857). Ordained in 1872, he pastored in Plattsburg, New York, and Williamsport, Pennsylvania, until 1887. He was an artist out of an artistic household, designing stained-glass windows as well as founding and editing *Church Journal* (1853-1868).

Hopkins was a leader in the development of hymnody in the Episcopal Church during the mid-nineteenth century. He is probably best known as the author and composer of the Christmas carol "We three kings." His *Carols, Hymns, and Songs* (1863) reached its fourth edition in 1883.

Composer: *Like Noah's weary dove,* **496**

HOPKIRK, JAMES (b. 1908, Toronto, Ontario; d. 1972) received a B.Mus. from the University of Toronto and the associate certificate of the Canadian College of Organists. His positions as organist/choirmaster included St. Matthias Church, Toronto (1929-1937); Church of the Ascension, Hamilton, Ontario (1937-1939); and St. James Church, Vancouver, British Columbia (1939-1942), when he resigned to become a volunteer in the Canadian army. In 1946 he resumed his organist/choirmaster career at St. Thomas Church, St. Catharine's, Ontario. As a member of the musical advisory committee, he prepared for publication all musical material submitted for the revision of *The Book of Common Praise,* the hymnbook of the Church of England in Canada. He also contributed several original compositions and arrangements.

Composer: BELLWOODS (*O day of God, draw nigh*), **370**

HORN, JOHANN (b. ca. 1490, Domaschitz, near Leitmeritz, Bohemia; d. Feb. 11, 1547, Jungbunzlau, Bohemia), whose surname was Roh in Bohemian, called himself Cornu in Latin and Horn in German. Ordained as a priest in 1518, he received an appointment to preach at the Bohemian Brethren's community at Jungbunzlau. He was made an elder in 1529 and consecrated bishop at the synod of Brandeis in 1532, a position he held until his death. He prepared a Czech hymn collection, published in Prague in 1541, and edited the second German hymnbook of the Bohemian Brethren, *Ein Gesangbuch der Brüder im Behemen und Merherrn . . .* (Nürnberg 1544). The latter includes several of his texts and tunes.

Composer: AVE VIRGO VIRGINUM (GAUDEAMUS PARITER) (*Come, ye faithful, raise the strain,* **265**; *We are people of God's peace,* **407**)

HORST, JOHN L. (b. Aug. 18, 1938, Scottdale, Pa.) is the son of a Mennonite pastor and Herald Press editor. Horst graduated from Eastern Mennonite College (EMC), Harrisonburg, Virginia, in 1960 with a double major in mathematics and music. He later pursued graduate studies in physics at the University of Virginia, Charlottesville, returning to EMC to teach math and physics. Horst is a member of Park View Mennonite

Church, Harrisonburg, and sustains a strong avocational interest in singing, composition, and synthesizer.

Composer: TRUSTING MERCY (*From time beyond my memory*), **484**

HORSTMANN, JULIUS HENRY (b. Mar. 16, 1869, Naperville, Ill.; d. February 1954) was educated at Northwestern College (later called North Central College), Naperville; Elmhurst College (Ill.); and Eden Theological Seminary, Webster Groves, Missouri. He was ordained to the ministry in 1891. During his years as a pastor in Indiana and Texas, Horstmann wrote occasional poems for friends and relatives. He edited publications for the Evangelical Synod of North America from 1906 until his retirement in 1939. This translation, along with twelve others, was included in the Evangelical Synod's *Christian Hymns* (1908).

Translator: *The work is thine, O Christ*, **396**

HOSMER, FREDERICK LUCIAN (b. Oct. 16, 1840, Framingham, Mass.; d. June 7, 1929, Berkeley, Calif.), educated at Harvard University, Cambridge, Massachusetts, was a Unitarian minister who held pastorates in Congregational churches in Massachusetts and Illinois and in Unitarian churches in Ohio, Missouri, and California. Outstanding among Unitarian hymnologists, Hosmer edited *Unity Hymns and Carols* (1880) with W. C. Gannett and J. V. Blake. Fifty of his hymns appear in *The Thoughts of God in Hymns and Poems*, published with Gannett in 1885.

Author: *O Lord of life, wherever they be*, **635**

HOW, WILLIAM WALSHAM (b. Dec. 13, 1823, Shrewsbury, England; d. Aug. 10, 1897, Leenane, County Mayo, Ireland), an English clergyman educated at Wadham College, Oxford, was ordained in 1847. He was a beloved pastor, serving in Kidderminster, Whittingdon, and Oswestry as curate, rector, and rural dean, respectively. In 1865 he was chaplain of the English Church in Rome, Italy, and in 1879 was named bishop of Bedford, serving the slum section in East London; there he became known as the "poor man's bishop" for his work on behalf of the destitute. He also earned the nickname "the omnibus bishop," because he always took public transportation. In 1888 he became the first bishop of Wakefield.

He was also joint editor of *Church Hymns* (1871), published by the Society for Promoting Christian Knowledge (SPCK), of which Arthur Sullivan was music editor. How's other publications include *Psalms and Hymns* (1864), which he compiled with Thomas B. Morell, and *Daily Family Prayers for Churchmen*. He was honored with D.D. degrees from the archbishop of Canterbury in 1879 and from Oxford in 1886. His fifty-four hymns, published separately, include "O Jesus, thou art standing" and "O Word of God incarnate." They appear in a collected edition,

Poems and Hymns (1881). He once said, "A good hymn should be like a good prayer—simple, real, earnest, and reverent" (Bailey 1950).

Author: *For all the saints*, **636**; *We give thee but thine own*, **384**

HOYLE, RICHARD BIRCH (b. Mar. 8, 1875, Cloughfold, England; d. Dec. 14, 1939, London, England) attended Regent's Park College in London (1895-1900) and then was a Baptist pastor in various churches in England for twenty-six years. Later he worked with the YMCA and for a while was editor of its publication, *The Red Triangle*. It was during this time he translated about thirty French hymns into English. Hoyle came to the U.S. in 1934, teaching for two years at Western Theological Seminary in Philadelphia, Pennsylvania. After his return to England, he became pastor of the Baptist church in Kingston-upon-Thames.

Translator: *Thine is the glory*, **269**

HUBMAIER (HUEBMÄR), BALTHASAR (b. ca. 1480, Friedberg, Bavaria; d. Mar. 10, 1528, Vienna, Austria), an Anabaptist theologian and martyr, was educated at the Latin school in Augsburg and the University of Freiburg. He received his baccalaureate degree in 1510 and was ordained to the priesthood that same year. He continued his studies at the University of Ingolstadt (D.Th.), then taught theology there before assuming the prestigious post of pastor and chaplain at the cathedral in Regensburg.

While pastoring in Waldshut, he began to embrace some of the concepts of the Swiss Reformation and, after a brief return to Regensburg, openly championed the cause. Back at Waldshut, he began conducting services in German, spoke out against abuses of the Mass and the worship of images, and abolished laws on fasting. During this time he married Elisabeth Hügeline. Hubmaier's defense of adult baptism, *Vom christlichen Tauf der Gläubigen*, is considered one of the most eloquent. He and sixty others of his parish were baptized by Wilhelm Reublin on Easter of 1525.

Persecution of the reformers forced Hubmaier and his wife to flee Waldshut on December 5, 1525, but in Zürich, Switzerland, he was captured and, under duress, recanted his position. Although he recanted, he remained in prison until he managed to escape a year later. Hubmaier became a leading figure in Nikolsburg, Moravia, but after King Ferdinand of Austria acquired control of Moravia, Hubmaier and his wife were again arrested and held at Kreuzenstein Castle. This time, even when tortured on the rack, he held firm, and on March 10, 1528, he was burned at the stake for heresy and insurrection. His wife was martyred three days later. Hubmaier's extensive writings have been of lasting influence.

Author: *Rejoice, rejoice in God*, **313**; Father, I have sinned against heaven, **693**

HUFFAKER, PERRY LEE (b. Mar. 28, 1902, Decatur, Ill.; d. Apr. 3, 1982, Greenville, Ohio) was the adopted son of Harrison and Alice Thompkins Huffaker. As a junior choir singer, the mischievous Perry reportedly was the bane of his director, but he developed into one of the leading musicians of the Church of the Brethren. He graduated from Manchester College, North Manchester, Indiana (B.A., 1923) and Northwestern University, Evanston, Illinois (B.M., 1933), then attended Bethany Theological Seminary, Oak Brook, Illinois, for two years.

Huffaker chaired the music committee for *The Brethren Hymnal* (1951), in which nine of his hymn tunes appear. He led camp music, seminars, and oratorios—and nine times directed the music for the Brethren Annual Conference. After teaching for twelve years in public schools of Indiana, Huffaker became assistant pastor and minister of music at Hagerstown Church of the Brethren (Md.), followed by pastorates in Spring Run and Pine Glen, Pennsylvania; West Milton, Ohio; Pine Creek, Indiana; and Pleasant Valley, Ohio.

Composer: PINE GLEN (*Move in our midst*), **418**

HUFFMAN, NELSON THOMAS (b. Nov. 4, 1901, Rileyville, Va.; d. Feb. 14, 1992, Bridgewater, Va.) was a popular choral director and vocal soloist in the Church of the Brethren and in his local community. He received his undergraduate degree from Bridgewater College and did advanced musical studies at Peabody Conservatory of Music, Baltimore, Maryland, as well as at the Cincinnati Conservatory of Music (Ohio). Later he earned an M.M. from Northwestern University, Evanston, Illinois.

Huffman was professor of music at Bridgewater College for forty years (1925-1965), teaching voice and directing college choral groups and ensembles while developing the department's facilities as its chairman. He was a distinguished tenor soloist, and after his retirement, Huffman founded the Rockingham Male Chorus, which he directed between 1966 and 1987, giving five hundred concerts throughout the eastern region of the U.S. He was also choir director at Bridgewater Church of the Brethren. In various years he also was called upon to direct the Brethren Annual Conference choirs. In 1976, Bridgewater College awarded him an honorary D.Mus. He composed and arranged a number of anthems, vocal solos, and songs.

Author/Composer: *Hear thou our prayer, Lord,* **23**

HUGHES, JOHN (b. 1873, Dowlais, Wales; d. May 14, 1932, Llantwit Fardre, Pontypridd, Wales) spent most of his life at Llantwit Fardre. At age twelve he began working as a "door boy" at a local mine (the Glyn Colliery). Later he became an official in the traffic department of the Great Western Colliery Company. Hughes was a lifelong member of Salem Baptist Church, succeeding his father as a deacon and precentor (music director). He composed two anthems, many Sunday school marches, and numerous hymn tunes.

Composer: CWM RHONDDA (*God of grace and God of glory*, **366**; *Guide me, O thou great Jehovah*, **582**)

HUIJBERS, BERNARD (b. July 24, 1922, Rotterdam, Holland) was a member of the Society of Jesuits order in the Netherlands. Like Jelineau in France, he was a leader of the movement that introduced the use of the vernacular and changes into liturgy in Holland. In the mid-1960s after Vatican II, Huijbers, along with hymnwriter Huub Oosterhuis, moved out of the "ivory tower" campus setting to help revitalize worship in local parishes, especially at Dominicus Church in Amsterdam. The church, now under civil rather than Roman authority, has become a self-determined community with lay presiders—both women and men—whose "catholic focus" has returned to the basic roots of covenant and Judeo-Christianity.

Huijbers visited the United States several times just before his retirement in the mid-1970s when he felt he had contributed all he could to Catholicism. He had already left the priesthood and married a Dutch woman, and together they moved to southern France. His more recent writings are influenced by the new physics, bringing radical insights into traditional theology.

Arranger: KOMT NU MET ZANG (*What is this place*), **1**

HULL, ASA (b. 1828, New York, N.Y.; d. ca. 1908) studied music in Boston and in 1848 became an organist/choirmaster in Watertown, Massachusetts. Later he was a music merchant and publisher in Philadelphia. He composed many hymn tunes and published at least seventeen gospel songbooks and hymnals between 1861 and 1898.

Composer: THE BEAUTIFUL RIVER (*Oh, have you not heard*), **606**

HULL, ELEANOR HENRIETTA (b. Jan. 15, 1860, Manchester, England; d. Jan. 13, 1935, London, England) was an avid promoter of Irish literature and Gaelic culture. In 1899 she founded the Irish Text Society, which she served as secretary. The author of several books on Irish literature and history, she was president of the Irish Literary Society of London.

Versifier: *Be thou my vision*, **545**

HURD, BOB (20th c.), assistant professor of philosophy and systematic theology at St. Patrick's Seminary, Menlo Park, California, and talented composer of liturgical music, has given numerous workshops and concerts across the country. His trips to Central America and involvement in Hispanic ministry have inspired him in his most recent bilingual compositions. Hurd's writings have appeared in *Worship, Liturgy,* and *Today's Liturgy.*

In recent years his workshops have focused on the congregation's role in liturgy and bilingual celebrations. His published albums are *Roll Down the Ages, In the Breaking of the Bread, Each Time I Think of You, Everlasting Your Love, Behold the Cross,* and the latest, in gospel style, *Alleluia, Give the Glory!*

Composer: *Oyenos, mi Dios,* **358**

HUSBAND, JOHN JENKINS (b. 1760, Plymouth, England; d. Mar. 19, 1825, Philadelphia, Pa.), prior to his immigration to the U.S. in 1809, was a choirboy at Westminster Abbey, then clerk at Surrey Chapel. At age forty he settled in Philadelphia where he was a clerk at St. Paul's Protestant Episcopal Church. A highly respected music teacher, Husband led singing schools and devised "an improved mode of teaching music," which appeared as part of Andrew Adgate's *Philadelphia Harmony.*

Composer: REVIVE US AGAIN (*We praise thee, O God*), **99**

HUXHOLD, HARRY NORMAN (b. Dec. 21, 1922, Oak Park, Ill.) studied at Concordia College, Milwaukee, Wisconsin; Concordia College, River Forest, Illinois; and Concordia Seminary, St. Louis, Missouri. Huxhold received his B.A. in 1944 and M.Div. in 1947. After additional study in social and industrial relations and in theology, he earned his D.Min. from Christian Theological Seminary, Indianapolis, Indiana, in 1972.

Since 1947 Huxhold has been a Lutheran pastor in Wisconsin, Illinois, and Minnesota, but he also was a child welfare worker and high school religion instructor in the Chicago area. He turned to campus ministry at the University of Minnesota (1960-1965) and since then has been pastor of Our Redeemer Church, Indianapolis.

Huxhold has been a member of numerous church and community boards and committees and in 1973 was guest lecturer in homiletics at Christian Theological Seminary, Indianapolis. He is widely published in journals, books, and pamphlets—among them *The Church in Our House* (1971), *Power for the Church in the Midst of Chaos* (1972), *Followers of the Cross* (1985), *Twelve Who Followed* (1987), and *About the Prophets* (1990).

Author: *Hear us now, O God our Maker,* **626**

IDLE, CHRISTOPHER MARTIN (b. Sept. 11, 1938, Bromley, Kent, England) was educated at Eltham College, St. Peter's College, Oxford (B.A. 1962), and Clifton Theological College, Bristol. In 1965 he was ordained to ministry in the Church of England and wrote his first published hymn texts while serving as curate of St. Mark's Church,

Barrow-in-Furness. Thirteen of his twenty years of ministry were spent in inner London as rector of Limehouse.

Since 1989 Idle has been rector of seven linked Suffolk villages. A supporter of the peace movement, he was once jailed for nonviolent civil disobedience in objection to nuclear weapons. He writes extensively on Christian topics for newspapers and periodicals and has served on the editorial committees for *Psalm Praise* (1973) and *Hymns for Today's Church* (1982). Most of his ninety published hymn texts are Bible-based paraphrases.

Author: *Eternal Light, shine in my heart,* **518**; *Here from all nations,* **296**; *I will sing the Lord's high triumph,* **261**; *Lord, you sometimes speak,* **594**; *Make music to the Lord most high,* **73**

IONA COMMUNITY, THE, SCOTLAND, is an ecumenical community of women and men, founded in 1938 by George MacLeod, an inner-city pastor who wanted to train ministers who could understand and serve working-class people. To accomplish that purpose, he took a half-dozen young ministers and a half-dozen craftsmen to the remote island of Iona (off the western Scottish coast) to rebuild a thousand-year-old historic abbey. The restored abbey became the center of a community devoted to peace, justice, work, and a new economic order, along with celebrative worship.

Today the community consists of two hundred men and women who live mainly in Britain but also reside in Africa, Australia, India, and North America. Like the Taizé community in France, Iona attracts thousands of travelers who come to experience the spiritual life, the unity of worship, and the work to which the community is devoted.

Wild Goose Publications, the publishing division of the Iona Community, produces songbooks and tapes, as well as worship resources.

Author: O living Christ, come to us, **677**

IRELAND, JOHN NICHOLSON (b. Aug. 13, 1879, Bowdon, Cheshire, England; d. June 12, 1962, Rock Mill, Washington, Sussex, England) received his musical training at the Royal College of Music, London (1893-1897), studying composition with C.V. Stanford. As an organist/choirmaster, he established himself among the leading English composers of his generation with some of the finest English songs. Ireland's compositions span fifty years and encompass most performance media, including the score for the film *The Overlanders* (1946-1947). His church music includes settings for Communion and for morning and evening services, a motet, and eight hymn tunes.

Composer: LOVE UNKNOWN (*My song is love unknown*), **235**

IRVINE, JESSIE SEYMOUR (b. 1836, Dunothar, Scotland; d. 1887, Crimond, Scotland) was the daughter of a clergyman. She accompanied her father to his pastorates in Peterhead and Crimond. Her melody cited below is the only Scottish psalm tune known to have been composed by a woman.

Composer: CRIMOND (*The Lord's my shepherd,* **578**; *The care the eagle gives her young,* **590**)

ISAAC, HEINRICH (b. ca. 1450, Flanders; d. Mar. 26, 1517, Florence, Italy), one of the eminent Netherlandic composers of the Renaissance, is distinguished for his large collection of music (offices) composed for the liturgical year. Known as the *Choralis Constantinus,* it was completed after Isaac's death by his pupil Ludwig Senfl.

Isaac was an eclectic, itinerate musician who was court organist and director of music in Florence for the Medici family, one of whose sons became Pope Leo X. In Vienna and Innsbruck, he was court composer to Emperor Maximilian I. As a skillful international composer of his time, Isaac assimilated into his work music trends current throughout Europe. He wrote masses, motets, and *chansons* in the Netherlandic style, *frottolas* in the Italian style, and *lieder* in the German style.

Composer: O WELT, ICH MUSS DICH LASSEN (*Now all the woods are sleeping*), **657**

ISELE, DAVID CLARK (b. Apr. 25, 1946, Harrisburg, Pa.) was educated at Oberlin College (Ohio; B.M. in voice and education); Southern Methodist University, Dallas, Texas (M.M. and M.S.M. in organ and sacred music); and Eastman School of Music, Rochester, N.Y. (D.M.A. in composition). While at the University of Notre Dame, South Bend, Indiana (1973-1979), he was assistant professor of music and composer-in-residence. Isele began the school's first accredited, mixed singing ensemble, the Notre Dame Chorale. Since 1979 he has been teaching at the University of Tampa in Florida. He is also organist and music director of Sacred Heart Catholic Church. In the midst of these duties, he composes music, conducts clinics and workshops, and serves as a guest composer and performer upon request. G.I.A. Publications has released two recordings of his service music: *Song of Sunday* and *Song of David.*

Composer: *The sacrifice you accept, O God,* **141**

IVERSON, DANIEL (b. Sept. 26, 1890, Brunswick, Ga.; d. Jan. 3, 1977, Asheville, N.C.), a Presbyterian pastor and evangelist, studied at the University of Georgia; Moody Bible Institute, Chicago; Columbia Theological Seminary, New York City; and the University of South Carolina. He was ordained in 1914 and held pastorates in Georgia as well as in the Carolinas. Iverson organized Shenandoah Presbyterian Church in

Miami, Florida, serving as its pastor from its inception in 1927 until his retirement in 1951. He simultaneously helped organize seven other Presbyterian churches in the Miami area. In 1962 he settled near Asheville, North Carolina, and continued to do supply preaching in various churches there.

Author/Composer: *Spirit of the living God*, **349**

JABUSCH, WILLARD F. (b. Mar. 12, 1930, Chicago, Ill.) is chaplain for Catholic students at the University of Chicago and director of Calvert House. He earned a M.A.Th. from the University of St. Mary of the Lake; a master's degree in English from Loyola University, Chicago; and a Ph.D. in speech from Northwestern University, Evanston, Illinois. In addition he trained in music at the Chicago Conservatory of Music and studied English at the University of London.

Jabusch has also been a parish priest and has taught at all his alma maters except for Northwestern. He has written magazine articles, as well as more than forty hymn tunes and eighty texts, including "The King of glory comes," sung to a traditional Israeli melody.

Author: *From the depths of sin*, **136**

JACKSON, ROBERT (b. 1842, Oldham, Lancashire, England; d. 1914, Oldham) was a composer, conductor, and organist, and studied at the Royal Academy of Music. His first appointment was as organist of St. Mark's, Grosvenor Square, London. For some time Jackson was a member of Sir Charles Halle's orchestra in Birmingham and was conductor of the Oldham Music Society. In 1868 he took over as organist and choirmaster at St. Peter's in Oldham, a position his father had held for forty-eight years. He remained there for forty-six years, creating a father-son tenure of almost a century.

Composer: TRENTHAM (*Breathe on me, breath of God*), **356**

JACOBI, JOHN CHRISTIAN (b. 1670, Thüringen, Germany; d. Dec. 14, 1750, London, England), about whom little is documented, was keeper of the Royal German Chapel, St. James Palace, London, for forty-two years. His translations appear in two collections that include hymn tunes with thorough bass: *A Collection of Divine Hymns, Translated from the High Dutch* (1720) and its revision, *Psalmodia Germanica, or a Specimen of Divine Hymns* (ca. 1722). He was buried at Church of St. Paul's, Covent Garden.

Translator: *Spirit, come, dispel our sadness*, **290**

JACOPONE DA TODI (b. early 13th c., Todia, Umbria, Italy; d. 1306, Todia), also known as Jacobus de Benedictis and Jacopone di Benedetti, came from a noble family and led a high-brow lifestyle until his young wife was killed by the collapse of a stage. Jacopone withdrew from secular life and joined the Order of St. Francis as a lay brother (tertiary) for the rest of his life. He took his acts of penance to such extremes that he was sometimes considered crazy. "An earnest humourist," wrote Archbishop Trench, "he carried the being a fool for Christ into everyday life. The things . . . he did, some [were] morally striking enough, others mere extravagances and pieces of gross spiritual buffoonery" (Julian 1907). His zealous opposition to the religious abuses of his time provoked Pope Boniface VIII enough to have him repeatedly imprisoned.

His dramatic poems, called *laude,* were in Italian or Latin and glorified poverty, denounced the excesses of the church, or revered the mother of Jesus. Besides the present poem, the most famous Latin work attributed to him is *Cur mundus militat sub vana gloria* (possibly by Walter Mapes).

Author (attrib.): *At the cross, her vigil keeping,* **245**

JAMES, MARY DAGWORTHY YARD (b. Aug. 10, 1810; d. 1883) was a close friend of Phoebe Palmer, mother of hymnwriter Phoebe Palmer Knapp. Palmer's husband, a minister, preached at Ocean Grove, New Jersey, during the summer; after the Palmers left around September, James would continue preaching there through October. She contributed articles to *Guide to Holiness* and authored at least five books. Of these, *The Soul Winner: A Sketch of Edmund J. Yard . . .* (1883) appeared in two English versions, as well as in one Norwegian-Danish translation. Some of her hymns were translated into Norwegian; two, "My body, soul, and spirit" and "O, this uttermost salvation," have become well known in Norway. Her son J. H. James, a minister, authored her biography, *The Life of Mrs. Mary James* (1886).

Author: *In the rifted Rock I'm resting,* **526**

JANUS (JAHN), MARTIN (b. ca. 1620; d. ca. 1682, Silesia) lived in Silesia (today near the Polish-Czech border) where he received his license in theology and became precentor (music director) of two churches at Sorau. About 1653 he was appointed rector of the Evangelical School at Sagen and precentor of the church near Eckersdorf gate. In 1664 he became pastor at Eckersdorf but was expelled by the imperial edict of 1668 by which evangelical pastors and teachers were driven out of the realm. It was reported that he then became music director at Ohlau.

Author: *Jesu, joy of man's desiring,* **604**

JANZEN, JACOB H. (b. Mar. 19, 1878, Steinbach, Ukraine; d. Feb. 16, 1950, Waterloo, Ontario) grew up in the Mennonite colony of Molotschna in the Ukraine and there, in 1906, was ordained to the ministry. Through private study he obtained a teaching certificate. His teaching career in the colony was interrupted by a year of university study in Germany and two years of service in Mennonite forestry camps during World War I. While he was opposed to the self-defense units organized by some Mennonites during the Russian Revolution and Civil War, Janzen acted as chaplain for the Mennonite soldiers serving in the White Army, spending a whole winter in the Crimea. In 1921 the Communist government forced him to choose between ministry and teaching; thereafter, he concentrated on preaching to the colony congregations and representing the interests of the Mennonites to the government. In 1924 he settled in Waterloo, Ontario, where he was active in organizing his fellow (and succeeding) Russian Mennonite immigrants into congregations. In 1926 he was ordained as *Altester* (elder), a bishoplike position. Except for a brief period as head of the Girls' Home in Vancouver, British Columbia, and elder of the United Mennonite Church in British Columbia, he remained in Waterloo until his death. Janzen is also remembered as a traveling evangelist and pioneer Mennonite writer (his writings include stories, poetry, and plays). Bethel College, North Newton, Kansas, where he often lectured, awarded him an honorary doctorate for his leadership in the General Conference Mennonite Church.

Author (attrib.): How can we discern our errors, O God?, **781**

JANZEN, JEAN WIEBE (b. Dec. 5, 1933, Langham, Saskatchewan) was educated in the U.S., studying at Tabor College, Hillsboro, Kansas; Grace College, Winona Lake, Indiana; and Fresno Pacific College (Calif.; 1968). Later she received her M.A. in creative writing from California State University, Fresno. Her publications include poems in various magazines and journals, along with the collection *Words for the Silence*. She teaches poetry writing at Fresno Pacific College and Eastern Mennonite University, Harrisonburg, Virginia, as well as serving as poet-in-the-classroom in local public schools. She and her husband, a pediatrician, are members of College Community Church (Mennonite Brethren) in Clovis, California.

Author: *Come and give thanks to the Giver*, **57**; *From the hands*, **97**; *I cannot dance, O Love*, **45**; *Mothering God, you gave me birth*, **482**; *O Holy Spirit, Root of life*, **123**. Adapter: *How lovely is your dwelling*, **171**; *I long for your commandments*, **543**; *O bless the Lord, my soul*, **80**

JARMAN, THOMAS (b. 1776, Clipston, Northamptonshire, England; d. 1861, Clipston, England) as a youth joined the choir of the Baptist chapel in the small village where he lived. As a young man, he began writing hymn tunes and anthems and later spent some time at Leamington where he "exercised his musical gifts in Methodist circles" (Thomson 1967).

Composer: LYNGHAM (*Oh, for a thousand tongues to sing*), **81**

JENKS, STEPHEN (b. Mar. 17, 1772, Glocester, R.I.; d. June 5, 1856, Thompson, Ohio) was a noted singing-school teacher, compiler of tunebooks, and composer. He taught in New England and New York, and as a composer he followed the style of New England composers of the latter eighteenth century, cultivating the fuguing-tune style of William Billings, Daniel Read, and others. He compiled ten collections of music for singing schools and composed about 125 musical works for these publications.

Jenks moved to Ohio in 1829 and continued to compose until 1850. His published collections include *The New-England Harmonist* (1799), *The Delights of Harmony* (1804), *The Christian Harmony* (1811), and *The Harmony of Zion* (1814). NORTH SALEM, LIBERTY, and EVENING SHADE are three of his tunes still in use.

Composer: RESIGNATION (JENKS) (*All praise to our redeeming Lord*), **21**

JOB, RUEBEN P. (b. Feb. 7, 1928, Jamestown, N. D.) is a graduate of Westmar College, Le Mars, Iowa (B.A., 1954), and Evangelical Theological Seminary (B.D., 1957). He also received a number of honorary degrees. His early career was divided between Methodist pastorates in Illinois and North Dakota and a chaplaincy in the U.S. Air Force Reserves (with one year of active duty in France). Since 1965 his work has been in church administration and publications in Ohio, Tennessee, South Dakota, and Iowa. He was editor at Tidings (a Methodist press) and world editor at The Upper Room (an ecumenical press). His administrative experience has included eight years as bishop in Des Moines, Iowa. He was also an adjunct faculty member at Vanderbilt Divinity School, Nashville, Tennessee, for five years. Since 1992 he has served on the Board of Discipleship, The Upper Room, in Nashville. In the 1980s Job chaired the revision committee for *The United Methodist Hymnal* (1989). Among his numerous publications are *A Guide to Prayer for All God's People* and *A Guide to Prayer for Ministers and Other Servants*, both co-authored with Norman Shawchuck (The Upper Room, 1990 and 1992, respectively).

Author: Lord God, in whom I find life, **724**

JOHN OF CHRYSOSTOM (see ST. JOHN OF CHRYSOSTOM)

JOHN OF DAMASCUS (see ST. JOHN OF DAMASCUS)

JOHNSON, CHRISTOPHER (b. Dec. 17, 1962, Congleton, Cheshire, England) is a freelance composer/arranger based in London's West End. Raised in Staffordshire, he began his musical training at Huddersfield Polytechnic, receiving his B.A. in music with honors. He studied at London's Guildhall School of Music and Drama, specializing in film and television music, and later worked with film composers Malcolm Williamson (Master of the Queen's Musicke) and Wilfred Josephs (score composer for the BBC-TV series *I Claudius*).

Since leaving the Guildhall, Johnson has dabbled in a variety of musical styles, from classical to popular, arranging music for the BBC Concert Orchestra, Cliff Richard, and BBC television and radio. Other credits and commissions include studying at the London International Film School; writing scores for both British and American television; and writing a new orchestral overture to the popular musical by Jimmy and Carol Owens, *The Witness*.

As music assistant at All Souls Church, Langham Place, Johnson regularly leads services, conducting the sixty-member orchestra and choir. He also travels nationwide, directing workshops and seminars on music in worship. When he is not composing, arranging, or conducting, he can be found at the piano of one of London's top hotels.

Composer: CLEVELAND (*Lord, you sometimes speak*), **594**

JOHNSON, DAVID N. (b. June 28, 1922, San Antonio, Tex.; d. Aug. 2, 1987, Tempe, Ariz.) studied music in his hometown at Trinity University, San Antonio. He received his graduate education from Syracuse University (N.Y.), earning both an M.Mus. and Ph.D. As an organist and composer, he held positions at St. Olaf College Northfield, Minnesota; Syracuse University; Trinity Episcopal Church in Phoenix, Arizona; and Arizona State University, Tempe. In addition to his published compositions, the majority of which are church works for organ or choir, Johnson authored two organ manuals: *Instruction Book for Beginning Organists* and *Organ Teacher's Guide*.

Composer: TYRANT HEROD (*O Christ, the healer*), **379**

JOHNSON, JOHN ROSAMOND (b. Aug. 11, 1873, Jacksonville, Fla.; d. Nov. 11, 1954, New York, N.Y.) was a composer, actor, singer, and director of plays. He was the younger brother of poet James Weldon Johnson ("The Creation" and "Go Down Death"), with whom he collaborated in writing a number of songs. The younger Johnson studied at the New England Conservatory of Music and, for a brief time, in Europe. He also received an honorary master of arts degree from Atlanta University (Ga.). He was a private music teacher, music supervisor of the Jacksonville public schools (1896-1908), as well as musical director of Oscar Hammerstein's Grand Opera House in London and the Music School

Settlement in New York City. He also composed piano pieces, songs, and musicals and arranged more than 150 spirituals.

As an actor Johnson made his debut in the first African American play to open on Broadway. Later he appeared in leading roles, including the original casts of *Porgy and Bess* (1935) and *Cabin in the Sky* (1940). He described his *Rolling Along in Song* (1937) as "a chronological survey of American Negro music" (Logan, Winston 1982). His other publications included four important books on African American spirituals.

Author/Composer: *Lift every voice and sing* (ANTHEM), **579**

JOHNSTON, JULIA HARRIETTE (b. Jan. 21, 1849, Salineville, Ohio; d. Mar. 6, 1919, Peoria, Ill.), at the age of six, moved with her family to Peoria, Illinois, where her father was pastor of First Presbyterian Church until his death in 1864. Julia remained in Peoria as a Christian educator; there she was a longtime Sunday school teacher and superintendent. She authored lesson materials for David C. Cook Publishing Company, Elgin, Illinois. Her books include *School of the Master* (1880), *Bright Threads* (1897), *Indian and Spanish Neighbors* (1905), and *Fifty Missionary Heroes* (1913). She also wrote about five hundred hymn texts, which were set to music by a number of composers.

Author: *Marvelous grace of our loving Lord*, **151**

JONCAS, (JAN) MICHAEL (b. Dec. 20, 1951, Minneapolis, Minn.) majored in English at St. Thomas College, St. Paul, Minnesota (B.A., *magna cum laude*, 1975). He studied liturgy at the University of Notre Dame, South Bend, Indiana (M.A., 1978), and systematic theology at St. Paul Seminary. Ordained as a Roman Catholic priest in 1980, he was associate pastor of Church of the Presentation of the Blessed Virgin Mary, Maplewood, Minnesota (1980-1984), and was education director/campus minister of the Newman Center at the University of Minnesota in Minneapolis (1984-1987). Joncas received his S.L.L. (*summa cum laude*, 1989) and S.L.D. (1991) from the Pontifical Liturgical Institute at Collegio S. Anselmo in Rome. He has been assistant professor of theology at the University of St. Thomas and parochial administrator of St. Cecilia's Parish in St. Paul since 1991.

Joncas is a popular lecturer and writer, as well as musician. His recordings are *On Eagle's Wings* (1979), *Every Stone Shall Cry* (1982), *No Greater Love* (1988), and *Come to Me* (1990). He also helped edit the Catholic folk hymnal *Gather* (1988).

Author/Composer: *And I will raise you up* (ON EAGLE'S WINGS), **596**

JONES, GRIFFITH HUGH (b. 1849, Llanberis, Wales; d. 1919, Rhiwddolion, Wales) was the son of the music director at Capel Coch in Llanberis, a post his father held for sixty years. The younger Jones received some of his musical training from the pastor of the chapel, Rev. John Roberts, who recognized the lad's talents. Jones became both pupil and teacher at Dolbadarn, subsequently serving as assistant master at Aberystwyth. From 1869 onward he was schoolmaster at the elementary school in Rhiwddolion where he developed sight-singing classes and choirs. He was also a judge at Eisteddfodau.

Composer: LLEF (*Babylon streams received our tears*), **134**

JOSEPH, GEORG (17th c.) was a musician in the chapel of the prince-bishop of Breslau, Germany, during the second half of the seventeenth century. He published five volumes of songs on the texts of Johann Scheffler between 1657 and 1668. Of the 205 tunes in these volumes, it is believed that Joseph wrote 185 and that most of these were adaptations of secular tunes.

Composer (attrib.): ANGELUS (WHITSUN HYMN) (*At evening, when the sun had set*), **628**

JOSEPH, JANE MARION (b. 1894, London, England; d. 1929, London) attended Norland Place School; St. Paul's Girls' School; Brook Green; and Girton College, Cambridge. Having composed music from early childhood, she later studied composition under Gustav T. Holst, a hymn composer who was director of music at St. Paul's Girls' School (1905-1934).

Joseph herself became musical director at Eothen Girls' School, Caterham, and was active in various music festivals and competitions. She was a gifted composer whose promise was cut short by her early death.

Translator: *On this day earth shall ring*, **192**

JUDSON, ADONIRAM (b. Aug. 9, 1788, Malden, Mass.; d. Apr. 12, 1850, at sea, Bay of Bengal) studied at Brown University, Providence, Rhode Island, and Andover Theological Seminary (Mass.). In 1812, as one of the first North American missionaries, Judson and his wife sailed for India, representing the Congregational foreign missions board. During this voyage, while studying the New Testament, Judson became convinced of the validity of baptism by immersion and was so baptized upon his arrival in Calcutta. Forced by the British to leave India in 1813, he settled in Burma where he was imprisoned many months because of Burmese-British conflict. Judson completed a translation of the Bible into Burmese in 1834 and later assembled a Burmese-English dictionary.

Author: *Come, Holy Spirit, Dove divine*, **445**

KAAN, FRED (FREDERIK HERMAN) (b. July 27, 1929, Haarlem, Holland), the son of nominal Christians, did not attend church with any regularity until his late teens. He joined the Netherlands Reformed Church in 1947. Kaan made his way to England and studied theology at Western College, Bristol, and Bristol University (B.A., 1954).

Ordained to the Congregational ministry a year later, Kaan served churches at Barry, South Wales (1955-1963), and Plymouth, England (1963-1968). In 1970 he became an executive secretary of the newly formed World Alliance of Reformed Churches, based in Geneva, Switzerland. While there, he was also a member of the World Council of Churches editorial committee that produced the ecumenical hymnal *Cantate Domino.*

Although he returned to England in 1978, Kaan retained his connections with the international church. Focusing on language in hymnody, he earned a Ph.D. from Geneva Theological College in 1984. His hymn texts have appeared in *Psalm Praises* (1968) and *Break Not the Circle* (1975). *The Hymn Texts of Fred Kaan* (1985) contains 140 of his hymns and translations.

Author: *For the healing of the nations,* **367**; *God of Eve and God of Mary,* **492**; *Today I live,* **607**

KAUFMAN, FRIEDA (b. 1883, near Basel, Switzerland; d. 1944) came to Halstead, Kansas, with her parents. Although she attended Bethel College, North Newton, Kansas, she graduated from a nursing course in Cincinnati, Ohio. For many years she was associated with Bethel Deaconess Hospital, Newton, Kansas, as both sister-in-charge of the hospital (1908-1943) and superintendent. She was also instrumental in planning for a home for the aged affiliated with the hospital. These two institutions owe their high standards of Christian service to her devotion and the generosity of her rare gifts. Kaufman was likewise endowed with unusual literary and artistic abilities, which she used in translating several English hymns from their German origins.

Translator: *What mercy and divine compassion,* **524**

KARAY TRIPP, DIANE (b. Aug. 9, 1954, Holland, Mich.) was raised in Elkhart, Indiana. Her call to writing came from a fifth grade teacher with this comment: "Some day you will write a book." Her call to ministry came later. The two calls have coalesced in a career devoted to a scholarly study of worship and to writing prayers that speak to the people of today. She earned degrees at Indiana University (A.B., 1975); Chicago Theological Seminary (M.Div., 1979); and the University of Notre Dame, South Bend, Indiana (M.A. in liturgical studies, 1987). Ordained in 1980 as a minister of the Presbyterian Church (USA), she is now a freelance writer and independent scholar, residing in Wolcottville, Indiana. Author of *All the Seasons of Mercy* (Westminster Press 1987), a book of prayers, Karay Tripp served as an editorial consultant for the *Book of Common Worship* (1993), the service book of her denomination and the Cumberland Presbyterian Church. Her poetry has appeared in various periodicals, including *Purpose*, a Mennonite Church publication, and in a volume titled *New Christian Poetry*, edited by Alwyn Marriage (Collins 1990). Her articles have appeared in four periodicals: *Worship, Studia Liturgica, Celebration*, and *Liturgy*. She is a member of the international Societas Liturgica.

Author: This is the day that the Lord has made, **668**; Savior of the earth's children, **734**

KEBLE, JOHN (b. Apr. 25, 1792, Fairford, Gloucester, England; d. Mar. 29, 1866, Bournemouth, England), the precocious son of a vicar, received his A.B. with honors from Corpus Christi College, Oxford, when he was just eighteen. By the time he was twenty-one, Keble had his M.A. from Oriel College. He was ordained in 1815 and remained at Oriel College as a tutor and examiner while serving local country churches over a five-year period. In 1827 his religious poetry was published anonymously and titled *The Christian Year: Thoughts in verse for the Sundays and Holidays throughout the Year*. It became a classic and achieved many editions, arriving on the North American scene in 1834.

In 1833 Keble preached his famous Assize Sermon at Oxford University, to which John Henry Newman credited the start of the Oxford movement, the drive to revitalize liturgy in the British churches by recovering ancient Latin texts and tunes. Unlike many others in the movement, Keble remained with the Church of England, and in 1836 he became vicar of the church at Hursley, a village near Winchester. He held this position until the end of his life. Profits from *The Christian Year . . .* went to restoring the church at Hursley. Keble's published works include volumes of sermons and essays. Almost all of his hymns are derived from his longer poems.

Author: *Sun of my soul*, **654**

KELLER, MATTHIAS (b. Mar. 20, 1813, Ulm, Würtemberg, Germany; d. Oct. 13, 1875, Boston, Mass.) displayed musical ability at an early age. He studied at Stuttgart and at sixteen became first violinist in the Royal Chapel, where he stayed five years. During this time he also began to compose and later developed his technical skill by studying harmony and counterpoint in Vienna, Austria. Keller was bandmaster for the Third Royal Brigade for seven years before leaving Europe in 1846, immigrating to the U.S. and Philadelphia. There he played violin in the orchestras of the Walnut Street Theater and the Chestnut Street Theater. After moving to New York City, Keller entered a contest to compose an "American

Hymn." He won the first prize of $500 with AMERICAN HYMN set to his own "Speed our republic, O Father on high!" but spent all the money, plus money that his brother had saved to buy a house, to present the piece at a grand concert. The concert earned $42 (Stulken 1981).

Keller later moved to Boston where his song was played more frequently, including at a special ceremony at the State House in 1865 when the tune was performed by Gilmore's band at the request of the governor. Keller composed more than one hundred songs, many of them sacred. A year before his death, he gathered together his literary works and published *Keller's Poems.*

Composer: AMERICAN HYMN (*Blessing and honor and glory*), **108**

KELLY, THOMAS (b. July 13, 1769, Kellyville, County Queens, Ireland; d. May 14, 1855, Dublin, Ireland) attended Trinity College, Dublin (B.A., 1789). Although he planned to be a lawyer, he responded instead to a call to ministry and was ordained as an Anglican clergyman in 1792. His evangelical preaching roused the ire of more orthodox authorities, however, and he was summarily ousted from the Church of England. He went independent and, with his own money, started churches at Athy, Portarlington, and Wexford. A brilliant scholar, Kelly was author of 765 hymns published in *A Collection of Psalms and Hymns* (1800), *Hymns on various passages of Scripture* (1804; 7th ed., 1853), and *Hymns not before published* (1815; 5th ed., 1820).

Author: *Look, you saints*, **286**

KEN, THOMAS (b. July, 1637, Little Berkhampstead, Hertfordshire, England; d. Mar. 19, 1710 or 1711, Longleat, Wiltshire, England), orphaned as a child, grew up in the household of writer/outdoorsman Izaak Walton, who was married to Ken's sister. Ken was educated at Winchester and Oxford, and after his ordination in 1662, his extraordinary life began its twists and turns. After several years of being a curate and a chaplain, Ken returned to Winchester in 1669, serving for the next decade at the cathedral, the college, and as Bishop's chaplain. During this time he prepared his *A Manual of Prayers for Use of the Scholars of Winchester College* (1674), which achieved later editions. Ken was a chaplain to queens and kings (Mary, wife of William II, and Charles II) but found himself frequently at odds with them in matters of conscience. When Charles II was about to bring his mistress, Nell Gwyn, to Winchester, Ken objected to the king's request to lodge her in his home. To make the plan impossible, Ken renovated his house, timing the dismantling of the roof with the royal visit. Nell Gwyn was forced to sleep elsewhere (Reynolds 1990).

Ken was also chaplain with the fleet to Tangier under Lord Dartmouth. He then became bishop of Bath and Wells in 1685. In 1688 Ken was one of seven bishops imprisoned in London Tower for refusing to read James II's Declaration of Indulgence. He was later tried and acquitted. After the revolution in 1691, Ken resigned as bishop rather than take the oath of allegiance to William III. He retired to the home of Lord Weymouth at Longleat. His poetry was published in four volumes in 1721.

Author: *All praise to thee, my God,* **658**; *Praise God from whom,* **118, 119**

KENNEDY, BENJAMIN HALL (b. Nov. 6, 1804, Summer Hill, near Birmingham, England; d. Apr. 6, 1889, near Torquay, Devon, England) was a prominent educator, clergyman, hymnwriter, compiler, and translator. He completed his formal education at St. John's College, Cambridge, where he was a fellow from 1828 to 1836. In additon to writing hymns, he authored textbooks for Latin study. Two of his major publications are *Psalter, or the Psalms of David in English Verse* (1860) and *Hymnologia Christiana, or Psalms and Hymns Selected and Arranged in the Order of the Christian Seasons* (1863).

Translator: *Ask ye what great thing I know,* **337**

KERR, HUGH THOMPSON (b. Feb. 11, 1872, Elora, Ontario; d. June 27, 1950, Pittsburgh, Pa.) was educated at the University of Toronto, Ontario, and Western Theological Seminary, Pittsburgh. Ordained in the Presbyterian Church, he held pastorates in Kansas and Illinois prior to his longest tenure at Shadyside Presbyterian Church, Pittsburgh (1913-1946) where he participated in some of the earliest religious radio broadcasting. In 1930 he was moderator of the General Assembly of the Presbyterian Church (USA) and was chairman of committees for *The Presbyterian Hymnal* (1933) and the *Presbyterian Book of Common Worship*.

Author: *God of our life,* **486**

KETHE, WILLIAM (d. ca. 1594), whose life and death are largely a mystery, was said to be a Scotsman. He was among those in exile in Frankfurt, Germany, and Geneva, Switzerland, from 1555 to 1559, during the persecution under the Catholic "Bloody Mary." It is uncertain, according to the *Brieff discours off the trouble begonne at Franckford* (1575), whether he was one of those who remained in Geneva to work on the English-language Geneva Bible of 1560 and the Psalms. He did, however, serve as chaplain to the British troops in 1563 and 1569. He is thought to have been vicar of Childe Okeford, Dorsetshire, from 1561 to 1593, though early records no longer exist (Julian 1907). Twenty-five of his psalms are included in the Anglo-Genevan Psalter of 1561. Most of those were in unusual meters, and only Psalm 100 was retained in the Scottish Psalter of 1650. His date of death is given as early as 1593 and as late as 1608.

Author: *All people that on earth do dwell,* **42**

KIMBALL, JACOB (b. Feb. 15, 1761, Topsfield, Mass.; d. July 24, 1826, Topsfield) may have taken his musical cues from his father, a blacksmith, who was a song leader in the local meetinghouse. Kimball served in the colonial army during the battles of Lexington and Bunker Hill, playing the fife or drum. He graduated from Harvard University, Cambridge, Massachusetts, in 1780, and was a schoolmaster in Ipswich and Topsfield. Later he studied law and passed the bar exams in New Hampshire, but he did not become a lawyer. During the early 1790s, he taught singing schools at Marblehead and at Danvers. Kimball wrote some 120 compositions and compiled *The Rural Harmony* (1793) and *The Essex Harmony* (1800); the former included only his works.

Composer: PLAINFIELD (*O Spirit of the living God*), **361**

KINGO, THOMAS HANSEN (b. Dec. 15. 1634, Slangerup, Denmark; d. Oct. 14, 1703) was known as the first great Danish hymnwriter. Although from a family of weavers, Kingo studied Danish literature in the home of a school rector. At the University of Copenhagen, he studied theology and, after completing his degree in 1658, became a private tutor. Kingo was ordained in 1661 and ministered in the parishes of Vedby and Slangerup. In 1669 he received an M.A. and married Sille Lambertsdotter the same year. In 1677 Kingo was consecrated bishop of Odense and made a member of the Danish nobility in 1679. Kingo was given an honorary Th.D. in 1682.

Kingo collected hymns indigenous to Denmark and promoted their use over translated hymns. He published a hymnal in two parts called *Aandeligt Sjunge Chor* (1673, 1681) and in 1683 was commissioned by King Christian V to compile a hymnal for use in the Danish Church. After several efforts by different people, a committee finished the hymnal in 1699; it contained eighty-five hymns by Kingo.

This *Kirkepsalmebog* (church hymnal), one of the foundational books of Danish folk culture, included hymn texts as well as gospel lessons for the church year. Popularly known as "Kingo's Hymnal," this book was set in the *Evangeliebog* (gospel book) format (Grindal, n.d.). It was used devotionally in the home and church for more than one hundred years.

Author: *All who believe and are baptized*, **436**

KIRBYE, GEORGE (b. ca. 1565; d. October 1634, Bury St. Edmunds, England) may have been a native of Suffolk where he lived most of his life. His name was first mentioned in 1592 when he contributed to Est's *Whole Booke of Psalmes*. He furnished more harmonizations of tunes in that collection than any other composer except for John Farmer. Kirbye composed a number of madrigals and poetic and musical forms of fourteenth-century Italy, revived in the sixteenth century. One of them, for six voices, appears in *The Triumphs of Oriana* (1601), a collection of madrigals for Queen Elizabeth.

Arranger: WINCHESTER OLD (*While shepherds watched*), **196**

KIRK, JAMES M. (b. June 18, 1854, Flushing, Ohio; d. July 11, 1945) was raised by Methodist parents and accepted Christ at a young age. In 1887 he associated himself with the recently founded Christian and Missionary Alliance. Under those auspices Kirk and his wife established the Gospel Mission in his hometown in 1907. He was a member of The Ohio Quartet, which often was called on to sing at conventions and other meetings of the Christian and Missionary Alliance. Kirk also wrote both texts and tunes of a number of gospel songs.

Arranger: *Joys are flowing like a river*, **301**

KIRKPATRICK, WILLIAM JAMES (b. Feb. 27, 1838, Duncannon, Pa.; d. Sept. 20, 1921, Germantown, Pa.), the son of Irish immigrants, learned to play several instruments under the tutelage of his father, a well-known music teacher in Mifflin, Juniata, Cumberland, and Perry Counties in Pennsylvania. In 1854, William, only in his mid-teens, left home to study music and learn a trade. In February of 1855, he joined the Methodist Episcopal Church on Wharton Street in Philadelphia and devoted himself to sacred music. His first collection of songs, *Devotional Melodies*, was published when he was just twenty-one. His career as a prolific gospel songwriter was already launched.

After serving as a fife major in the U.S. Civil War, Kirkpatrick ventured into the furniture business (1866-1878). He devoted himself full time to music after his wife's death in 1878. He performed as a cellist, became a member of the Harmonia Society and the Handel and Haydn Music Society, directed convention and camp-meeting singing, composed considerably, and served as music director and organist of Ebenezer and Grace Methodist Episcopal Churches in Philadelphia. In 1880 he began his music publishing collaborations with John R. Sweney, H. L. Gilmore, John H. Stockton, and J. Howard Entwistle. In the years that followed, Kirkpatrick helped publish more than eighty gospel song collections.

Composer: PRAISE JEHOVAH (*Praise the Lord, sing hallelujah*), **50**; CRADLE SONG (Away in a manger), **194**; FOR CHRIST AND THE CHURCH (*For Christ and the church*), **416**; KIRKPATRICK (*A wonderful Savior is Jesus*), **598**; TRUST IN JESUS (*'Tis so sweet to trust in Jesus*), **340**

KITCHIN, GEORGE WILLIAM (b. Dec. 7, 1827, Suffolk England; d. Oct. 13, 1912, Durham, England), son of a clergyman, was educated at Ipswich Grammar School; King's College School and College; and Christ Church, Oxford. He later tutored at Oxford. For eleven years (1883-1894), he was dean of Winchester Cathedral until in 1894 he became dean of Durham

Cathedral. In 1909 he was named chancellor of Durham University. He published many books on archaeology, biography, and history.

Author: *Lift high the cross*, **321**

KLAASSEN, WALTER (b. May 27, 1926, Laird, Saskatchewan) taught at Bethel College, North Newton, Kansas, and at Conrad Grebel College, Waterloo, Ontario, from 1960 to 1987. In addition to publishing books and articles on Anabaptist history and theology, he has served several churches as a short-term pastor. Klaassen and his wife, Ruth Strange, have retired to Vernon, British Columbia.

Translator: *Heart with loving heart united*, **420**

KNAPP, PHOEBE PALMER (b. Mar. 9, 1839, New York, N.Y.; d. July 10, 1908, Poland Springs, Maine) was the daughter of a Methodist evangelist. She showed early musical talent as a singer and composer of children's songs. At age sixteen she married Joseph Fairfield Knapp, a successful businessman and founder of the Metropolitan Life Insurance Company. After her husband died in 1891, Knapp donated much of her $50,000 annual income to charity, but she still had enough resources to entertain in her elegant Hotel Savoy apartment in New York City, where she housed a large pipe organ.

She composed more than five hundred gospel songs, of which only this one and "Open the gates of the temple" remain in common use. Both are settings for texts by Fanny J. Crosby, a close friend and also a member of John Street Methodist Church in New York City.

Composer: BLESSED ASSURANCE (*Blessed assurance*), **332**

KNAPP, WILLIAM (b. ca. 1698 or 1699, Wareham, Dorsetshire, England; d. September 1768, Poole, Dorsetshire, England), though born in England, probably was of German descent. For thirty-nine years he was parish clerk at St. James Church, Poole, where he led the responses and announced the hymns. Little else is known about him, because in 1762 a fire destroyed records at the parish where he was born. Knapp published two collections, *A Sett of New Psalm Tunes and Anthems* (1738) and *New Church Melody* (1753). Knapp was buried September 26, 1768, near the old town wall.

Composer: WAREHAM (*Great God, we sing*, **639**; *O God, your constant care*, **481**)

KNEPPER, WILHELM (b. 1691, Germany; d. ca. 1743, Pennsylvania), a weaver by trade, joined the Brethren in Solingen, Germany. On February 1, 1717, he and six others were imprisoned at Düsseldorf for their beliefs. During his years in prison, Knepper wrote about four hundred hymns.

In 1720 a merchant from Elberfeld contacted representatives of the Dutch government, who interceded on behalf of the group, securing their release on November 20. After a three-day journey, they were welcomed warmly at Krefeld, especially among the Mennonites.

The Brethren moved on to the Netherlands, and the record of Knepper's marriage to Veronica Bloom in Friesland in 1723 is one of the few documentations of the group's presence there. In 1729 the Kneppers were among those who sailed with Brethren leader Alexander Mack from Rotterdam on the ship *Allen*, arriving in the religious haven of Philadelphia in September of that year.

Author: *How pleasant is it*, **451**

KNIGHT, GERALD HOCKEN (b. July 27, 1908, Cornwall, England; d. Sept. 16, 1979, London, England) became assistant organist at Truro Cathedral when he was fourteen. He earned the B.Mus. at Peterhouse, Cambridge, and attended the Royal College of Music, London. From 1937 to 1952, he was organist of Canterbury Cathedral and from 1952 to 1972 was director of the Royal School of Music. As a notable musician and educator at the Royal School, he did much to raise the quality of Anglican church music.

Arranger: ASH GROVE *(Sent forth by God's blessing)*, **478**

KOCHER, CONRAD (b. Dec. 16, 1786, Ditzingen, Germany; d. Mar. 12, 1872, Stuttgart, Germany) moved to St. Petersburg, Russia, in his late teens to be a private tutor. Influenced by the musical works of Mozart and Haydn and his friendship with Muzio Clementi, he decided to pursue a career in music. He studied in St. Petersburg and Rome; and with his formal study completed, Kocher established a school for the study of church music in Stuttgart in 1821. Motivated by his study of Palestrina and his interest in four-part singing, he was at the head of the early nineteenth-century reform of church music in Germany. From 1827 until 1865, he was organist/choirmaster of the collegiate church in Stuttgart. In 1852 he was honored with a doctorate from the University of Tübingen.

Besides publishing a treatise on church music, *Die Tonkunst in der Kirche* (1823), Kocher composed two operas, an oratorio, and chorale tunes.

Composer: DIX (*As with gladness men of old*, **218**; *For the beauty of the earth*, **89**)

KOIZUMI, ISAO (b. Nov. 3, 1907, Osaka, Japan), a prominent Japanese hymnologist, was also an economics professor at his alma mater, the Osaka University of Commerce (1932-1942). He was a church organist for a time and then appointed minister of music at the U.S. Far East Air Forces (FEAF) Chapel Center in Tokyo in 1951. He worked at many FEAF chapels in the Tokyo area until 1972. Annually, at the Christmas season, he directed joint American and Japanese choruses and orchestra in singing Handel's *Messiah.*

In 1967 Koizumi became a director of the Christian Music Seminary, Tokyo. Throughout his career, he composed and arranged many hymn tunes for both *The Hymnal 1954* and *The Sunday School Hymnal* (1954) of the United Church of Christ in Japan (UCCJ), for which he was music editor. He also served as a member of the music committee of *The Hymnal II 1967.* Besides his contributions to hymnals, Koizumi's publications include *Companion to The Hymnal 1954,* Vol. II, as well as many treatises on the hymn tunes. His published music includes works for organ, Palestrina's *Pieces* (1956), two volumes of *Songs for Children* (1940, 1943), *Songs of the Bible* (1960), and *Songs Old and New* (1978). In 1991 Koizumi won an official commendation from the Christian Literature Society of Japan.

Composer: TOKYO (*Here, O Lord, your servants gather*), **7**

KOLB, ABRAM BOWMAN (b. Nov. 10, 1862, near Kitchener, Ontario; d. Mar. 15, 1925) studied at the Toronto Normal School and taught in public schools in Michigan and Ontario. In 1886 he connected with John F. Funk's Mennonite Publishing Company in Elkhart, Indiana, and later became Funk's son-in-law. He was assistant editor (1886-1897) and editor (1897-1904) of *Herald of Truth* and did considerable translating between German and English.

Active in church music, he was a choral director at Elkhart Institute, which later became Goshen College. An intriguing sidelight is that Kolb and Funk, whose ancestors Dielman Kolb and Bishop Henry Funk translated *Martyrs' Mirror* into German in the mid-1700s, collaborated to translate the same book into English more than a century later.

Author/Composer: *Christ who left his home in glory* (CHRIST IS RISEN), **283**

KÖNIG, JOHANN BALTHASAR (b. 1691, Waltershausen, Germany; d. March 1758, Frankfurt am Main, Germany) is known primarily as the compiler of one of the most exhaustive chorale collections published in eighteenth-century Germany, the *Harmonischer Liederschatz, oder Allgemeines evangelischen Choral-Buch* (Frankfurt 1738). He acquired his musical education as a choirboy in Frankfurt and later sang under the famous Georg Philipp Telemann at Frankfurt's St. Catherine's Church, eventually becoming the music director there in 1719.

Composer: O DASS ICH TAUSEND ZUNGEN HÄTTE (*Oh, that I had a thousand voices*), **84**

KOYZIS, DAVID THEODORE (b. 1955, Oak Park, Ill.) gleaned his interest in hymnody and poetry from his father, who was born on the island of Cyprus and wrote poems in both English and his native Greek. The younger Koyzis was educated at Bethel College, St. Paul, Minnesota, and the Institute for Christian Studies, Toronto, Ontario. In 1986 he received his Ph.D. from the University of Notre Dame, South Bend, Indiana. He has been a member of the political science faculty of Redeemer College, Ancaster, Ontario, since 1987.

Versifier: *Christ, who is in the form of God,* **333**

KOZAK, PAT, C.S.J. (b. Jan. 24, 1947, Cleveland, Ohio) entered a Roman Catholic religious order, the Congregation of the Sisters of St. Joseph (at its mother house in Cleveland), immediately after high school. She has earned degrees at St. John College, Cleveland (B.S., 1969); St. Louis University (Mo.; M.A., 1978); and the Pacific School of Religion, Berkeley, California (D.Min., 1991). She spent ten years as a teacher in elementary and secondary schools and then worked for ten years in vocation/formation in her religious community, orienting women before and after their joining the order. In her doctoral program, she pursued a special interest in ritual and adult faith development. During these years she lived and worked at the Holy Family Center in Pleasant Hill, California, a center for fostering personal and spiritual growth. Since completing her doctorate, she has been co-director of this center—working in spiritual direction, facilitating small groups, leading retreats, planning prayer and ritual for various groups, and exploring women's spirituality. She is co-author of a book of worship services, *More Than Words* (see Schaffran).

Author: God of all life, we thank you, **680**

KREMSER, EDWARD (b. Apr. 10, 1838, Vienna, Austria; d. Nov. 26, 1914, Vienna) became chorusmaster of the Vienna *Männergesangverein* (male chorus) in 1869. In addition to several operettas, he composed numerous works for piano, voice, and chorus. His *Sechs altniederländische Volkslieder* for male chorus and orchestra (1877) propelled these six anonymous Dutch folk songs into popular use—and thence into hymnals. He published two volumes of *Wiener Lieder und Tänze* (1912, 1913).

Arranger: KREMSER (*We gather together*), **17**

KROPF, MARLENE (b. Jan. 8, 1943, McMinnville, Ore.) grew up in Oregon, studied at Oregon College of Education, Monmouth (B.A., 1965; M.A.T., 1968), and began a career as a high school English teacher in the Oregon public school system. In a two-year stint of service under Mennonite Central Committee, Kropf taught English in a government secondary school in Kingston, Jamaica. Writing for church periodicals and organizations during these years of teaching undoubtedly prepared her for a midlife career shift when she moved to Elkhart, Indiana. There she enrolled at the Associated Mennonite Biblical Seminaries (earning an M.Div. in 1988) and began working on issues of congregational education and worship and spirituality with the Mennonite Board of Congregational Ministries (MBCM). Presently, Kropf spends much of her work time writing and conducting seminars on worship and spirituality. Over the years at MBCM, she has developed and edited a variety of worship resources, and she frequently leads worship in conference and retreat settings. For the past eight years, she has also taught part time at the Elkhart seminary. Serving on the Hymnal Council and its worship committee of *Hymnal: A Worship Book* was, she says, one of the most satisfying experiences of her life. She currently writes bimonthly columns on worship and prayer for *Builder* and *The Mennonite* and is co-author of a book titled *Praying with the Anabaptists* (Faith and Life Press 1994).

Author: Our lives are cluttered, Lord Jesus, **695**; Because of God's great love for you, **706**; Spirit of peace, quiet our hearts, **729**; Savior God, through your grace we hold, **757**

LA FEILLÉE, FRANÇOIS DE (d. ca. 1780) was a French theorist who likely lived in or near Poitiers around 1750. He is noted for his *Methode nouvelle pour apprendre parfaitement les regles du plainchant et de la psalmodie* (Poitiers 1748), which appeared nine times in four editions up to 1784. This treatise gives directions regarding the use of expression in chanting: "The same text should be sung more slowly on a solemn feast-day than on normal days, but otherwise the immediate contents of the text should determine the manner of singing: prayers are to be sung 'devoutly and sadly,' narrative texts 'without any passion but with good pronunciation' " (Sadie 1980). An 1808 edition of the treatise by Aynes contained some melodies not found in the earlier editions.

Adapter: O QUANTA QUALIA (*Here from all nations*), **296**

LAFFERTY, KAREN (b. Feb. 29, 1948, Alamogordo, N.M.) completed a B.Mus.Ed. at Eastern New Mexico University, Portales, in 1970. In 1971 she turned her talents from playing and singing in dinner houses and hotel lounges to a ministry through Maranatha! Music, an outreach of her home church, Calvary Chapel of Costa Mesa, California.

Invitations to sing in other countries kindled Lafferty's calling to world evangelism, and in 1980 she pioneered Musicians for Missions (MFM), under the umbrella of Youth with a Mission, to train and mobilize other Christian musicians. Based in Amsterdam, Holland, she and the MFM teams aim to "fill the world with God's music" through concerts, recordings, and seminars in the U.S., Europe, and South Africa.

Author/Composer: *Seek ye first the kingdom of God* (SEEK YE FIRST), **324**

LANDSBERG, MAX (b. 1845, Berlin, Germany; d. 1928, Rochester, N.Y.) was educated privately by his father, Meyer Landsberg, rabbi of Hildesheim. Later he attended the Universities of Göttingen, Breslau, Berlin, and Halle (Ph.D., 1886). From 1866 to 1871, he taught at a seminary for Jewish teachers in Hannover. In 1870 he became a rabbi and in 1871 was called to Temple Berith Kodesh, Rochester, New York, a position he held for thirty-four years. In 1911 he was elected president of the New York State Conference of Charities and Correction. He acquired a reputation for serious scholarship and devoted service to both Jewish and Gentile communities.

Translator: *The God of Abraham praise*, **162**

LANIER, H. GLEN (b. Dec. 12, 1925, Welcome, N.C.; d. Sept. 9, 1978, Statesville, N.C.) received his A.B. from High Point College (N.C.) and the M.Div. from Duke Divinity School, Durham, North Carolina, with further study at Yale Divinity School, New Haven, Connecticut. As a United Methodist minister, he served pastorates in Wilkesboro and Statesville, North Carolina.

Lanier authored more than a thousand poems, many of which appear in two published volumes: *The Seasons of Life* (1960) and *Three Dozen Poems for Christians* (1967). Some seventeen of his hymn texts have been published by the Hymn Society of the United States and Canada, including the bicentennial hymn "America, my homeland fair" (*The Hymn*, July 1977).

Author: *O God, your constant care*, **481**

LATHBURY, MARY ARTEMISIA (b. Aug. 10, 1841, Manchester, N.Y.; d. Oct. 20, 1913, East Orange, N.J.), the daughter of a Methodist pastor, taught drawing and painting. She also wrote children's verse and prose, which were published in various magazines and Sunday school periodicals. She was an editor for the Methodist Sunday School Union and in 1885 founded the Look-Up Legion, a Methodist youth movement.

Lathbury also assisted Bishop John H. Vincent in the promotion of the Chautauqua Assembly from its beginnings in western New York. She did much writing in connection with these popular summer spiritual renewal retreats and became known as Chautauqua's poet laureate.

Author: *Break thou the bread of life*, **360**

LAWES, HENRY (b. December 1595, bapt. Jan. 5, 1596, Dinton, Wiltshire, England; d. Oct. 21, 1662, London, England) was a noted composer who was especially adept at setting poetic texts. He studied music under John Cooper and became a member of the Royal Chapel. Lawes composed music for masques, a popular form of entertainment that developed around a masked dance. He composed one such masque for his friend John Milton's *Comus*, first performed at Ludlow Castle in 1634. Laws contributed settings to George Sandys' collection of psalm paraphrases (1637-1638), and in 1648 he published *Choice Psalms*, which included both his work and compositions by his brother William (1602-1645). Other music by Lawes was included in John Playford's *Select Musical Ayres* (1652 and later) and *Treasury of Music* (1669). He fell into disfavor during Oliver Cromwell's rule but was reinstated to his court posts with the restoration of Charles II, for whose coronation he composed the anthem "Zadok the Priest." Others of his sacred works were included in various choirbooks, and his settings of Psalms 9, 10, and 34 may be found in a number of hymnals. Lawes is buried at Westminster Abbey.

Composer: PSALM 9 (*As spring the winter doth succeed*), **568**

LAYRITZ (LAYRIZ), FRIEDRICH (b. Jan. 30, 1808, Nemmersdorf, Franconia, Germany; d. 1859, Unterschwaningen, Franconia, Germany) was educated at Erlangen and Leipzig. He became a private tutor at the theological seminary of Erlangen in 1833. Layritz was a pastor in Hirschlag, at St. Georgen near Bayreuth, and in Unterschwaningen near Ansbach. A "prominent advocate of the restoration of the rhythmic form of chorale melodies" (*The Hymnal 1982 Companion*), he published numerous books of melodies and four-part chorale settings, among them a four-volume collection, *Kern des deutschen Kirchengesangs* (Nordlingen 1844-1855).

Author: *Lo, how a Rose e'er blooming* (st. 3), **211**

LEASURE, MARNA J. (b. Oct. 18, 1934, Middletown, Ohio) graduated from Miami University, Oxford, Ohio (B.S. in education, 1956), and Marshall University, Huntington, West Virginia (M.A., 1972), with additional graduate study at the University of Houston (Tex.) in the Kodaly approach to music. Because of numerous moves made by her family, Leasure has been minister of music in Ohio, Kentucky, and Texas, and has served fourteen denominations, feeling "very privileged to have had that rewarding experience." She has taught music in both public and parochial schools, including St. Francis Episcopal Day School, Houston (1978-1987), and St. Agnes Parochial School, Louisville, Kentucky, since 1988.

Author/Composer: *Awake, arise, O sing a new song*, **56**

LEHMAN, BRADLEY P. (b. July 27, 1964, Goshen, Ind.) concentrated on music and mathematics at Goshen College (Ind.; B.A., 1986), where he was the first music graduate with harpsichord as his principal instrument. While at Goshen he studied church music with Mennonite musicians Philip Clemens and Mary Oyer. He continued in graduate study at the University of Michigan, Ann Arbor, in early keyboard performance and musicology. Lehman is a member of Waterford Mennonite Church, Goshen, and has been organist at Plymouth United Church of Christ, Goshen, and University Reformed Church, Ann Arbor.

Composer: FIRSTFRUITS (*For the fruit of all creation*), **90**; HEALING HEM (*By Peter's house*), **378**; MOUNTAIN PEAK (*Christ upon the mountain peak*), **232**; OYER (*Prince of peace, control my will*), **534**; STORM (*Holy Spirit, Storm of love*), **132**; WHISPER (*Open, Lord, my inward ear*), **140**

LEONI, MEYER (b. 1751; d. 1797, Kingston, Jamaica), also listed as "Meier Leoni" or "Meyer Lyon," sang in various theaters and synagogues of London, England, including the Great Synagogue, Duke's Palace (1768-1772). He was unsuccessful in opera because he lacked acting ability. In 1787 he accepted the position of cantor with the Ashkenazic (German and English) Jewish congregation in Kingston, serving there until his death.

Transcriber: LEONI (*The God of Abraham praise*), **162**

LEW, TIMOTHY T'ING FANG (b. 1892, Wenchau, Chekiang, China; d. Aug. 5, 1947, Albuquerque, N.M.), one of China's outstanding educators and authors, was educated in China and the U.S. He received degrees from Columbia University, New York City (M.A. and Ph.D.); Yale University, New Haven, Connecticut (B.D.); and Oberlin College (Ohio; S.T.D.). He also studied at Union Theological Seminary in New York City, taught Christian education, and lectured widely at a number of North American colleges from 1926 to 1928.

Lew chaired the commission that prepared the Chinese Union hymnbook, known as *Hymns of Universal Praise* (1936), and also co-edited the *Union Book of Common Prayer* used by four Protestant Chinese denominations. He served as delegate to the World Council of Churches in 1927, 1937, and 1939. From 1936 to 1941, he was a member of the national legislative body of the Chinese government. In 1941 and again in 1947, he lived in the U.S. and was teaching at the University of New Mexico, Albuquerque, at the time of his death.

Author: *O Bread of life, for sinners broken*, **468**

LEWIS, HOWELL ELVET (b. Apr. 14, 1860, Conwil Elvet, Carmarthenshire, Wales; d. Dec. 10, 1953, Penarth, Glamorganshire, Wales), after attending Carmarthen Presbyterian College, held a number of pastorates in Congregational churches in Wales and England. In 1904 he became the minister of Welsh Tabernacle, King's Cross, London, a post he held until 1940. In his later years he was almost blind but continued preaching until he was ninety-one. Lewis was honored with doctorates from the University of Wales, and in 1948 the Order of the Companion of Honour was bestowed upon him. He was noted throughout Wales and beyond as a preacher, writer, and hymnologist. He was one of the early members of The Hymn Society of Great Britain and Ireland and served on the editorial committee that prepared the *The Congregational Hymnary* (1916).

Author: *Lord of light, your name outshining*, **410**

LILLENAS, HALDOR (b. Nov. 19, 1885, Bergen, Norway; d. Aug. 18, 1959, Calif.) came to the U.S. in 1887 and received his education at Pacific Bible College. He was awarded an honorary doctorate by Olivet Nazarene College, Kankakee, Illinois. Active in the Church of the Nazarene, Lillenas was an elder for twelve years, a pastor for fifteen years, and a singing evangelist for ten years. He was also a music editor and pub-lished much of his own music. His songs include "Jesus will walk with me," "Wonderful peace," "The garden of my heart," and "I know a name." He was a member of the American Society of Composers, Authors and Publishers (ASCAP).

Author/Composer: *Wonderful grace of Jesus* (WONDERFUL GRACE), **150**

LINDEMAN, LUDVIG MATHIAS (b. Nov. 28, 1812, Trondheim, Norway; d. May 23, 1887, Oslo, Norway) was the most gifted member of a prominent Norwegian musical family. His father taught him piano, organ, and theory. Although young Ludvig assisted his father as organist of the cathedral in Trondheim, he planned to study theology, since his father discouraged music as a profession (Stulken 1981). In 1833, after finishing his liberal arts course, he attended the seminary located in Christiania, Oslo. During his seminary studies, however, he played the cello in a theater orchestra and served as substitute organist for his brother at *Vor Frelsers Kirke* (Our Savior's Church). In 1840 Lindeman succeeded his brother in this position, which he held until his death in 1877. During his long tenure, Lindeman became the outstanding organ virtuoso of his time, as well as professor of singing and church music at the seminary where he had studied. The school he founded in 1883 with his son Peter became the first music conservatory in Oslo.

Lindeman composed hymn tunes, songs, choral and instrumental works, chamber music, and organ works. He is remembered primarily for his hymn tunes, his collections of folk music, and his revision of the Lutheran hymnbook. Of the nearly two thousand folk melodies he collected between 1840 and 1867, six hundred were published, many in his three-volume *Older and Newer Norwegian Mountain Melodies*, issued between 1853 and 1867. Through his editorial work with hymn tunes and chorales, it is generally agreed that Lindeman infused new life into Norwegian church music.

Composer: KIRKEN DEN ER ET GAMMELT HUS (*Built on the Rock*), **309**

LINDEMANN, JOHANN (b. ca. 1550, Gotha, Thüringen, Germany; d. ca. 1634,[1] Gotha, Germany), the son of a burgess, earned his M.A. at the University of Jena (1570). Early in the 1570s he became a cantor at Gotha and held this position until his retirement with a pension in 1631. Lindemann composed sacred songs, both texts and music, and in 1598 published three volumes of Christmas and New Year's songs.

Author: *In thee is gladness*, **114**

1. Although the *Hymnal Companion to the Lutheran Book of Worship* gives his date of death as Nov. 6, 1631, James Mearns states that "in 1634 Lindemann was a member of the new Council at Gotha" (Julian 1907).

LINT, CONRAD GILLIAN (b. May 19, 1834, Meyersdale, Pa.; d. June 18, 1918, Meyersdale) worked in his father's blacksmith shop and learned the trade. In 1855 he was married, baptized into the Church of the Brethren, and elected a deacon, in that order. That same year he became elder of the churches in Somerset County, Pennsylvania. Just one week after his election as deacon, he was advanced to the first degree of the ministry, and from that time on, he devoted himself to the further preparation and practice of pastoral work. Before long, he was among the most capable and popular preachers in his county. Besides loving music, he was a good singer, song leader, music teacher, and composer of hymns.

Composer: FELLOWSHIP (*May the grace of Christ our Savior*), **423**

LITTLEDALE, RICHARD FREDERICK (b. Sept. 14, 1833, Dublin, Ireland; d. Jan. 11, 1890, London, England) received his undergraduate and graduate degrees at Trinity College, Dublin, then was ordained a priest in 1857. He was a curate in two churches from 1856 until 1861 when, due to chronic ill health, he had to confine his work to writing. He wrote and published nearly fifty works in the fields of theology, history, liturgy, and hymnology. A "man of unusually wide knowledge," he was also a zealous Anglican, which made him a "formidable adversary in controversy" (*The Hymnal 1940 Companion*, 1951 ed.). He drew controversy when he counseled against a return to Roman Catholicism, though he was a part of the Oxford movement. Like John Keble, he remained an Anglican.

Littledale was a frequent contributor to various periodicals and translated hymns from seven different languages: Greek, Latin, Syriac, German, Italian, Danish, and Swedish. He compiled *Carols for Christmas and Other Seasons* (1863) and, with James Edward Vaux, prepared the *Priest's Prayer Book* (1864), *The People's Hymnal* (1867), and *The Altar Manual* (1863-1877).

Translator: *Come down, O Love divine*, **501**

LOCKWOOD, GEORGE FRANK IV (b. Apr. 3, 1946, Tacoma, Wash.) began music training under the tutelage of his mother, an accomplished organist and choir director. He studied voice, French horn, and piano in elementary and high school and then attended Indiana University, where he majored in music education with a concentration in horn (B.M.E., 1968).

During the year and a half he spent as a missionary in Costa Rica, Lockwood developed an interest in the new Hispanic music emerging from both Catholic and Protestant musicians in Latin America following Vatican II. Lockwood has translated some thirty new Hispanic hymns and led workshops on new Hispanic hymnody and translation. He has been consultant for *The United Methodist Hymnal* (1989) and *Celebremos: Segundo Parte* (Hispanic United Methodist hymnal supplement, 1983).

In 1981, after teaching music and selling life insurance in Chicago and Los Angeles, Lockwood earned a D.Min. from the School of Theology in Claremont, California. He has since served both Anglo and Hispanic United Methodist churches in Arizona and Southern California. As a pastor in Tucson in 1986, he was active in the sanctuary movement, protecting Guatemalan and Salvadoran refugees, and was under house arrest during an ensuing federal trial, because he refused to testify against fellow church workers. On both personal and denominational levels, he promotes racial and ethnic inclusiveness.

Translator: *Cantemos al Señor* (*Let's sing unto the Lord*), **55**; *En medio de la vida* (*You are the God within life*), **537**; *Niño lindo* (*Child so lovely*), **207**; *Tú has venido a la orilla* (*Lord, you have come to the lakeshore*), **229**; *Una espiga* (*Sheaves of summer*), **460**

LOEWEN, HARRIS J. (b. Sept. 6, 1953, Vancouver, British Columbia) is a vocal soloist, composer, choral conductor, and teacher. A graduate of the University of British Columbia, Vancouver (B.Mus., 1976), and the University of Iowa, Iowa City (M.A., 1985; D.M.A., 1994), he earned degrees in choral conducting, performance, and pedagogy and also studied at Canadian Mennonite Bible College, Winnipeg, Manitoba, and Associated Mennonite Biblical Seminaries, Elkhart, Indiana. Loewen is both a poet and musician and has been teaching fine arts at Brock University, St. Catherines, Ontario, since 1987. He is currently director of ensembles at Brock, conductor of the Niagara Vocal Ensemble, and music director of the Etobicoke Centennial Choir. He co-edited *Great Trek I Songbook* (1981) and *Assembly Songs* (1983) and was a member of the text committee for *Hymnal: A Worship Book* (1992).

Author: *O God, great womb,* **155**; Gracious God, hear our confession, **703**. Author/Composer: *New earth, heavens new* (ALEXANDRA), **299**. Arranger: FROM THE DEPTHS (*From the depths of sin*), **136**. Translator: *Oh, how joyfully*, **209**; *The word of God is solid ground*, **314**. Adapter: *I sing with exultation*, **438**

LONGFELLOW, SAMUEL (b. June 18, 1819, Portland, Maine; d. Oct. 3, 1892, Portland) was educated at the Portland Academy and at Harvard

University, Cambridge, Massachusetts, where he earned the B.A. in 1839 and a degree in theology in 1846. As a Unitarian minister, he served churches in Massachusetts, New York, and Pennsylvania. In his editing of several hymn collections, he remolded some Calvinistic and Trinitarian hymns into a more Unitarian theology. He also wrote a biography of his famous brother, Henry Wadsworth Longfellow. A final collection of his literary works, Hymns and Verses, was published two years after his death.

Author: *God of the earth, the sky, the sea,* **53**; *Holy Spirit, Truth divine,* **508**; *Now, on land and sea descending,* **655**

LORENZ, EDMUND SIMON (b. July 13, 1854, near Canal Fulton, Ohio; d. July 11, 1942, Dayton, Ohio) grew up speaking both German and English because his father was a missionary to German immigrants in northern Ohio. He was educated at Otterbein University, Union Biblical Seminary, and Yale Theological Seminary. He also did further study at the University of Leipzig, Germany. He served for two years (1884-1886) as pastor of High Street United Brethren Church in Dayton, Ohio, and briefly as president of Lebanon Valley College in Annville, Pennsylvania. In 1888 his health gave way under the strain of his study and the demands of the pastorate and the college presidency. During a lengthy recovery, he turned to music. In 1890 Lorenz began publishing music in Dayton; significant publications included the monthly music periodicals *The Choir Leader* (1894) and *The Choir Herald* (1897). First known as Lorenz and Company, today's Lorenz Publishing Company has become a major publisher of church music. In addition to composing hymn tunes and gospel songs, Lorenz also wrote a number of books, including *Practical Church Music,* published by Revell in 1909.

Composer: GOD IS LOVE (*Come, let us all unite to sing*), **12**

LOVELACE, AUSTIN COLE (b. Mar. 26, 1919, Rutherfordton, N.C.), one of North America's outstanding leaders in church music, is a noted teacher, composer, author, organist, and music director. Educated at High Point College (N.C.; A.B., 1939) and Union Theological Seminary School of Sacred Music, New York City (S.M.M., 1941; S.M.D, 1950), he served as minister of music in leading Methodist and Presbyterian churches in North Carolina, Nebraska, Illinois, Colorado, and Texas. He has taught at Garrett Theological Seminary, Evanston, Illinois; Union Theological Seminary; Iliff School of Theology, Denver, Colorado; and Temple Buell College, Denver. Sacred choral music, organ works, and hymn tunes are among his more than seven hundred compositions. His publications include *The Organist and Hymn Playing* (1962), *The Anatomy of Hymnody* (1965), and *Hymn Notes for Church Bulletins* (1987). Lovelace co-authored

Music and Worship in the Church (1960, rev., 1976) and the Methodist *Companion to the Hymnal* (1970).

Versifier: *Jesus, we want to meet*, **10**. Composer: MUSTARD SEED (*The kingdom of God*), **224**

LOWRY, ROBERT (b. Mar. 12, 1826, Philadelphia, Pa.; d. Nov. 25, 1899, Plainfield, N.J.), as a youth of seventeen, joined the Baptist Church. He attended Bucknell University, Lewisburg, Pennsylvania (B.A., 1854; M.A., 1857), later becoming a member of the faculty and chancellor of the board. The university conferred on him an honorary doctorate in 1875.

Lowry's gift for preaching was on par with his later popularity as a gospel songwriter. He pastored in West Chester and Lewisburg, Pennsylvania; New York City; and Plainfield, New Jersey. In 1868 he succeeded William B. Bradbury as editor of Sunday school songbooks for the New York-based company of Biglow and Main. With William H. Doane, Lowry edited a number of tunebooks to which both men contributed numerous songs. These collections include *Bright Jewels, Glad Refrain*, and *Royal Diadem*.

Author/Composer: *Low in the grave he lay* (CHRIST AROSE), **273**; (Attrib.) *My life flows on* (HOW CAN I KEEP FROM SINGING), **580**; *O worship the Lord* (BEAUTY OF HOLINESS), **124**; *Shall we gather at the river* (BEAUTIFUL RIVER), **615**. Composer: NEED (*I need thee every hour*), **555**; WE'RE MARCHING TO ZION (*Come, we that love the Lord*), **14**

LUTHER, MARTIN (b. Nov. 10, 1483, Eisleben, Saxony, Germany; d. Feb. 18, 1546, Eisleben), the son of a miner, received his education at Magdeburg, Eisenach, and the University of Erfurt (M.A., 1505). He joined the Augustinian convent at Erfurt where he resided for three years. After he was ordained in 1507, Luther began teaching at the University in Wittenberg. In 1511 a visit to Rome aroused his ire at corrupt practices in the church. These issues were brought to a climax for Luther when a Dominican friar came to Wittenberg selling indulgences (favors of God for money). On October 31, 1517, Luther nailed ninety-five theses to the door of the Wittenberg Castle Church, protesting such abuses. This eventually led to his break with Rome and clarified the Reformation movement in Germany. Further details on Luther and the Reformation are available in standard reference works.

Though Luther himself was trained in music, he employed a cantor, Johann Walther, to be his musical scribe. They spent late nights in Luther's study composing and adapting music. Luther walked the floors playing melodies on his piccolo while Walther wrote down notes until Luther was satisfied that the melody "matched the mouth and heart of the common people," earning him the title "liberator of congregational hymnody" (Erik Routley's appellation).

Luther wrote about thirty-seven congregational hymns and paraphrases. Although he has been credited with composing some chorale tunes, his greater contribution has been in the adaptation of music for worship. Reflecting his attitude toward music, Luther wrote:

> I am strongly persuaded that after theology, there is no art that can be placed on a level with music; for besides theology, music is the only art capable of affording peace and joy of the heart. . . . A proof of this is that the devil, the originator of sorrowful anxieties and restless troubles, flees before the sound of music almost as much as before the Word of God. (Dearmer, Jacob 1933)

Author: *Christ Jesus lay,* **470**; *From heaven above to earth I come,* **205**. Translator: *Savior of the nations, come,* **173**. Author/Composer: *A mighty fortress* is our God (EIN FESTE BURG), **165, 329**; *Out of the depths I cry to you* (AUS TIEFER NOT), **133**. Composer (attrib.): ERHALT UNS, HERR (*The glory of these forty days,* **225**; *When Christ's appearing,* **217**)

LYNCH, THOMAS TOKE (b. July 5, 1818, Dunmow, Essex, England; d. May 9, 1871, London, England) was educated at Islington and attended Highbury Independent College but withdrew before graduating. He served as minister of several churches in London and the surrounding area between 1847 and 1871. In 1862 he opened Mornington Church on Hampstead Road where he remained until his death.

As theological students and others were drawn by the freshness and spirituality of his preaching, the influence of Lynch's ministry reached beyond his small congregations. His theology evoked considerable controversy, however, especially with his book of poetry called *The Rivulet.* The controversy came to a head when he turned a bouquet of flowers into the theme of a Sunday sermon, attracting criticism of his "non-doctrine scheme." He responded in gentleness, saying, "We must conquer our foes by suffering them to crucify us rather than by threatening them with crucifixion." The criticism seemed to affect his fragile health, though, and might have hastened his death (Dearmer, Jacob 1933). In addition to writing poetry, Lynch also wrote the music for at least twenty-five of his hymn texts.

Author: *Gracious Spirit, dwell with me,* **507**

LYTE, HENRY FRANCIS (b. June 1, 1793, Ednam, Scotland; d. Nov. 20, 1847, Nice, France), born of English parents near Kelso, Scotland, was educated at Portora Royal School, Enniskillen, Ireland, as a charity student, since he was orphaned early. He went on to graduate from Trinity College, Dublin, in 1814, but a year later he abandoned his plans for a medical career and became a priest in the Church of England. In 1823, after short stints in several parishes, he was named perpetual curate of the newly formed parish at Lower Brixham, a small fishing village in Devonshire. Suffering from asthma and tuberculosis in his later years,

Lyte preached his farewell sermon to his congregation in September 1847 and traveled to the south of France upon the advice of his physician. He died shortly after his arrival in Nice.

Besides his much-loved hymns, Lyte published a number of books: *Tales on the Lord's Prayer in Verse* (1826); *Poems, Chiefly Religious* (1833); and *Spirit of the Psalms* (1834).

Author: *Abide with me*, **653**; *Praise, my soul, the God of heaven*, **63**; *Praise, my soul, the King of heaven*, **65**

MACDUFF, JOHN ROSS (b. May 23, 1818, Bonhard, Perthshire, Scotland; d. Apr. 30, 1895, Chislehurst, Kent, England), a pastor and writer, studied at the Universities of Edinburgh, Glasgow, and New York, receiving the honorary D.D. from each institution. In 1842 he was ordained in the Church of Scotland and held pastorates on Forfarshire and Perthshire before serving Sandyford Parish, Glasgow. Declining a royal appointment to the Glasgow Cathedral, MacDuff ceased his pastoral work in 1871 to devote full time to writing. He moved to Chislehurst where he wrote many devotional books, including *The Faithful Promise* and *Morning and Night Watches*. He was a member of the hymnal committee for the Church of Scotland and also wrote thirty-one hymns that were included in *Altar Stones* (1853) and *The Gates of Praise* (1876). He was a staunch advocate of the pre-millennial view of the coming of Christ, a theme reflected in some of his hymns.

Author: *Christ is coming! Let creation*, **295**

MACK, ALEXANDER, JR. (b. Jan. 25, 1712, Schwarzenau, Germany; d. Mar. 20, 1803, Germantown, Pa.), the youngest son of one of the founders of the Church of the Brethren, was baptized at the age of sixteen, probably in Holland. After his father's death, he entered the Ephrata Cloister for ten years, but he returned to the Brethren and was called to the ministry in 1748. Mack was an elder for more than fifty years. He is noted as the greatest Brethren leader of colonial North America and the person who gave the church its first written historical account of the Brethren in Pennsylvania. A weaver by trade and a prodigious writer of letters, he also wrote hymns. His friend and fellow pastor, Christopher Sauer II, printed five different books of his poetry.

Author: *Jesus Christ, God's only Son* (*Bless, O Lord, this church*), **40**

MACK, ALEXANDER, SR. (bapt. July 27, 1679, Schriesheim, Germany; d. Feb. 15, 1735, Germantown, Pa.) was baptized in the local Reformed Church where his father, Johann Philip Mack, was elder and an influential and respected member of the Schriesheim town council. Young Mack was educated in the local schools and worked at the family mill and vineyards. When his eldest brother died in 1689, Alexander took over as miller and stayed in Schriesheim until after his marriage to Anna Margarethe Kling (1701) and the birth of their first two sons.

Mack became involved in the Pietist movement about 1705. The following year he sold his half of the family mill to his brother, freeing him to travel, preach, and teach with Ernst Christoph Hochmann, a noted radical Pietist. On an August evening in 1706, while Hochmann was leading a service at the Mack home, civil authorities arrived to disperse the meeting. That same night the Mack family packed their belongings and fled to Schwarzenau, a haven for religious dissidents. There, two years later, after much prayer and Bible study, eight believers were baptized by trine immersion in the River Eder. Mack, who had become spokesman for the group, was baptized first, and he baptized the rest in turn.

In the years that followed, the congregation grew to more than two hundred members. After 1715, however, economic conditions in the area took a downturn and even Mack's inheritance, which had been thrown into a common pot, was depleted.

In 1720 forty Brethren families continued their pilgrimage to the province of Friesland in the Netherlands. Conditions there were not much better, and in 1729 about half the group, with Mack at the helm, sailed from Rotterdam to Philadelphia, Pennsylvania. Mack became elder of the Germantown congregation, which had been established by Peter Becker in 1723. Mack died at the age of fifty-five and was buried at Germantown.

Author: *Count well the cost*, **437**; Now may the Lord Jesus bless your soul, **766**

MACKAY, WILLIAM PATON (b. May 13, 1839, Montrose, Scotland; d. Aug. 22, 1885, Portree, Scotland) was a physician, educated at the University of Edinburgh. He practiced medicine until, feeling called to the ministry, he was ordained and appointed pastor of Prospect Street Presbyterian Church of Hull in 1868. He was the author of a number of hymns, seventeen of which appeared in *Praise Book*, compiled by W. Reid in 1872.

Author: *We praise thee, O God*, **99**

MAKER, FREDERICK CHARLES (b. 1844, Bristol, England; d. 1927, Bristol) was a chorister in the local cathedral but became part of the Free Church (Nonconformist) movement. He was organist at several churches, including Redland Park Congregational Church from 1882 until he retired in 1910. A music professor at Clifton College for twenty years, Maker also was conductor of the Bristol Free Choirs Association for a period of time. Besides hymn tunes, he composed a number of anthems and a cantata, *Moses in the Bulrushes.*

Composer: REST (WHITTIER) (*Dear Lord and Father of mankind*), **523**; ST. CHRISTOPHER (*Beneath the cross of Jesus*), **250**

MALAN, HENRI ABRAHAM CÉSAR (b. July 7, 1787, Geneva, Switzerland; d. May 18, 1864, Vandoeuvres, Switzerland) authored nearly a thousand hymns, composing his own tunes for many of them. He was embroiled in controversy for much of his professional life as a minister, because he opposed the established church. After receiving his education from the College of Geneva, he became an ordained pastor in 1810; later, after fervently embracing Calvinism, he attained fame as a popular evangelist, preaching to large crowds in Switzerland, France, Belgium, England, and Scotland.

A prominent figure in the development of French Protestant hymnody, Malan also published the hymn collection *Chants de Sion* in 1841.

Composer: HENDON (*Ask ye what great thing I know*, **337**; *Take my life*, **389**)

MAMBULA, JABANI P. (b. 1935, Giwa Higi, Uba District, Nigeria), a member of the Margi tribe, was baptized in 1947 by John Grimley. After studying in the schools of Lassa, he took teacher training courses at Waka (1954-1956), Gindiri (1959-1960), and Zaria (1962-1965). In 1968 he became an ordained Brethren minister in Nigeria. His B.A. (1972) is from Bayaro College, Kano, though he also studied missiology twenty years later.

Mambula is an experienced educator. He has been headmaster and vice-principal at Waka Secondary School (1968-1969); principal at Waka Teachers College (1972-1976); and provost at Borno College of Basic Studies (1976-1978). Government posts have opened to him as well. He was assistant chief inspector of education at Borno State (1978-1979); then he was state commissioner for Health, Agriculture, and Community Development (1979-1983). Since 1985 he has been general secretary of the Fellowship of Churches of Christ in Nigeria (TEKAN).

The author and composer of many Christian songs, Mambula once served as choirmaster of Waka Secondary School. Through the years he has written articles on education for secular sources and on the family and faith for Christian publications.

Composer: *Our Father who art in heaven*, **351**

MANN, ARTHUR HENRY (b. May 16, 1850, Norwich, Norfolk, England; d. Nov. 19, 1929, Cambridge, England) was trained in the choir at Norwich Cathedral and could already play the cathedral service when he was eight years old (*The Hymnal 1940 Companion*, 1951 ed.). He earned his B.Mus. (1874) and D.Mus. (1882) at New College, Oxford, and then was organist at several churches before he went to King's College Chapel, Cambridge, as a choir director. He was considered incomparable in this position, which he held for fifty-three years. He composed many hymn tunes, anthems, and organ works and was also an authority on the music of Tallis and Handel. He was the music editor for Charles D. Bell's *The Church of England Hymnal* (1895).

Composer: ANGEL'S STORY (*O Jesus, I have promised*), **447**

MANN, NEWTON M. (b. Jan. 16, 1836, Cazenovia, N.Y.; d. July 25, 1926, Chicago, Ill.) received his only formal education at Cazenovia Seminary. A Unitarian minister, he pastored in Wisconsin, New York, and Nebraska. He published a number of scholarly works, especially in the field of sacred scripture, tracing the history of Jewish and Christian literature. Besides his translation of the *Yigdal*, the fourteenth-century metrical rendition of the Hebrew creed, he wrote many poems on religious or philosophic themes.

Translator: *The God of Abraham praise* (*Praise to the living God*), **162**

MANZ, FELIX (b. ca. 1498, Zürich, Switzerland; d. Jan. 5, 1527, Lake Zürich) was a founder—and first martyr—of the original Swiss Brethren congregation in Zürich. Manz gained a thorough knowledge of Latin, Greek, and Hebrew and became an enthusiastic and regular member of Ulrich Zwingli's Bible classes when Zwingli arrived in Zürich in 1519. Later, Manz and his associates broke with Zwingli on issues concerning the abolition of tithes, the Mass, and the right to practice adult baptism. In addition, the Swiss Brethren refused to have their children baptized.

Manz, a well-educated and eloquent man, devoted himself wholeheartedly to persistent and courageous efforts to live out his Anabaptist faith, resulting in repeated arrests, imprisonments, and escapes. This pattern continued until his final imprisonment in the Wellenberg jail; on January 5, 1527, he was sentenced to death by drowning. In this form of execution, "the executioner . . . shall tie [the victim's] hands, put him in a boat, take him to the lower hut, there strip his bound hands down over his knees, place a stick between his knees and arms, and thus push him into the water and let him perish . . . " (*The Mennonite Encyclopedia* 1957). As Manz was bound and taken from Wellenberg to the Limmat River, he cheerfully praised God in a loud voice and assured the people following the grim procession that he was dying for the truth. As he went into the water, he sang in a loud voice, "*In manus tuas, Domine, commende spiritum meum*" (Into your hands, Lord, I commend my spirit, Luke 23:46). Though Manz left no published works, it has been shown by W. Schmid that Manz wrote the *Protestation und Schutzschrift* of December 1524, a defense of Anabaptism addressed to the Zürich Council.

Author: *I sing with exultation*, **438**

MARK, ARLENE MARTIN (b. July 30, 1931, Maugansville, Md.) grew up in a Conservative Mennonite congregation that frowned on education beyond the eighth grade, but she dared to dream of college for herself—a dream realized when she first attended Eastern Mennonite College, Harrisonburg, Virginia, and then finished her B.A. at Goshen College (Ind.; 1955). As she and her husband moved about for his medical training, she taught school in several states. More recently she trained in and taught English as a second language in Goshen and Elkhart, Indiana. After moving to Elkhart in 1962, she took courses in worship and liturgy whenever possible at Associated Mennonite Biblical Seminaries, Elkhart, and the University of Notre Dame, South Bend, Indiana. Beginning around 1980, as a worship leader in her congregation, she was inspired to study worship even more seriously. Among the worship materials she has published is a booklet titled *Worship Resources* (Mennonite Publishing House 1982); another collection is in progress. Mark has also conducted workshops on worship. She has been a member and officer of numerous church, educational, and civic organizations, including Goshen College's Board of Overseers, the General Board of the Mennonite Church, and Mennonite Health Services.

Author: Liberating God, your Son taught us, **732**

MARLATT, EARL BOWMAN (b. May 24, 1892, Columbus, Ind.; d. June 13, 1976, Winchester, Ind.), the son of a Methodist minister, was educated at DePauw University, Greencastle, Indiana (B.A., 1912), and Boston University (Mass.; S.T.B., 1922; Ph.D., 1929), with additional study at Oxford University, England, and the University of Berlin, Germany. From 1925 to 1945, he taught religion and religious literature at Boston University, eventually becoming dean of the School of Theology. In 1946 he went to Southern Methodist University, Dallas, Texas, as professor of philosophy of religion at the Perkins School of Theology. Following his retirement in 1957, Marlatt was curator of the Treasure Room and Hymn Museum of the Interchurch Center, New York City (1960-1962). A member of the executive committee of the Hymn Society of the United States and Canada, Marlatt also had several books of poetry published.

Adapter: *Angels we have heard on high*, **197**

MARSHALL, JANE MANTON (b. Dec. 5, 1924, Dallas, Tex.) was educated at Southern Methodist University (SMU), Dallas (B.M., 1945; M.M., 1968), where she has also served on the English, music, and seminary faculties. Since 1974 she has taught choral conducting and music theory at the Perkins School of Theology, SMU. She was organist and choir director at several churches in Texas, including Northaven United Methodist Church in Dallas where she and her husband, Elbert, are members.

Her published works include anthems for adults, youth, and children's choirs, and her hymn tunes have appeared in both denominational and ecumenical collections.

In addition to holding membership in numerous professional organizations, she is a church music clinician, a contributor to church music journals, and a member of the editorial committees of numerous hymnbooks. In 1974 she received an award from the Southern Baptist Church Music Conference for distinguished service.

Author/Composer: *What gift can we bring* (ANNIVERSARY SONG), **385**. Composer: ANDERSON (*Holy Spirit, gracious Guest*), **542**; HEARTBEAT (*Today I live*), **607**; JACOB (*Eternal Light, shine in my heart*), **518**; SURPRISE (*Sometimes a light surprises*), **603**

MARTIN, GEORGE WILLIAM (b. Mar. 8, 1828, London, England; d. Apr. 16, 1881, Wandsworth, London, England), like many British church musicians, began his music training as a choir member in St. Paul's Cathedral. His first professional position was professor of music at Normal College for Army Schoolmasters. From 1845 to 1853, he was resident music master at St. John's Training College, Battersea, London. There he also became organist of Christ Church when it opened in 1849. Besides being an effective and highly esteemed conductor of choral societies, he edited *The Journal of Part Music* (1861-1862). He composed glees, madrigals, and part-songs and also arranged popular oratorios for the public to purchase at a low cost. Martin was a victim of broken health and died a pauper at Bolingbroke House Hospital. His hospital bills were paid by a man who admired Martin's work.

Composer: LEOMINSTER (pronounced Lem'inster) (*Make me a captive, Lord*), **539**

MARTIN, STEPHANIE (b. Mar. 29, 1962, Ontario) received her education from Wilfrid Laurier University, Waterloo, Ontario (B.Mus., 1984), and the University of Toronto (Ont.; M.A. in musicology, 1989). She has had private instruction in organ, harpsichord, voice, and historical wind instruments. Martin has lectured at the University of Guelph, Ontario; the University of Waterloo's Conrad Grebel College; and the University of Toronto. She has been director of music or organist for Anglican, Roman Catholic, and United Church of Canada parishes, as well as Waterloo Lutheran Seminary. Her choral directing experience includes the Toronto Mennonite Children's Choir (1984-1986) and Massey College Choir of the University of Toronto (1987-1991). Since 1988 she has been harpsichordist with the Arbor Oak Trio, which specializes in performances of baroque music on historical musical instruments.

Martin's compositions include motets, canticles, hymns, anthems, and incidental music for the theater, including a one-act opera commissioned for Laurelville Mennonite Church Center, a camp and retreat setting near Mount Pleasant, Pennsylvania.

Composer: DORKING (*Prayer is the soul's sincere desire*), **572**

MASON, LOWELL (b. Jan. 8, 1792, Medfield, Mass.; d. Aug. 11, 1872, Orange, N.J.) received his first musical instruction from local teachers and musicians. By age sixteen he was leading the village choir and conducting singing schools. In 1812 Mason moved to Savannah, Georgia, where he worked in a bank while studying harmony and composition. While there he compiled a tunebook modeled on the *Sacred Melodies* of William Gardiner. Mason's book appeared in 1821 as the *Boston Handel and Haydn Society Collection of Church Music* and became one of the most significant collections in North American hymnody.

Prompted by the book's success, Mason moved in 1827 to Boston where he became president of the Handel and Haydn Society and director of the choir of Bowdoin Street Church. He eventually resigned his positions to launch a full-time music instruction program for children. Mason became a premier music educator on the North American scene, founding the Boston Academy of Music in 1832 and establishing institutes for training music teachers. He was thus called the "father" of public school music education. He advocated European methods of teaching music by well-known composers; he twice visited Europe to study and lecture, bringing the Pestalozzian method of music instruction back to the U.S.

In addition, Mason composed numerous hymn tunes and compiled many collections of music for singing schools, churches, and singing societies. One of the most famous of his tunebooks was *Carmina Sacra*, which went through thirteen editions between 1841 and 1860 and is estimated to have sold more than 500,000 copies. His extensive library is now housed at the School of Music at Yale University, New Haven, Connecticut.

Composer: ANTIOCH (*Joy to the world*), **318**; BEALOTH (*I love thy kingdom, Lord*), **308**; BOYLSTON (*A charge to keep I have*), **393**; HAMBURG (*When I survey the wondrous cross*), **259**; NASHVILLE (*I'll praise my Maker*), **166**; OLIVET (*My faith looks up to thee*), **565**; ZERAH (*To us a Child of hope is born*), **189**. Arranger: AZMON (*Oh, for a thousand tongues to sing*), **110**; DENNIS (*Bless'd be the tie that binds*), **421**; MENDEBRAS (*O day of rest and gladness*), **641**

MASSIE, RICHARD (b. June 18, 1800, Chester, England; d. Mar. 11, 1887, Pulford Hall, Coddington, Cheshire, England) came from an ancient Cheshire family and was the oldest of twenty-two children in a clergyman's family. In 1834 Massie married Mary Ann Hughes, who died seven years later. Living in substantial wealth with two estates, Massie wrote and published skillful translations of German hymns by Spitta, Gerhardt, Luther, and others. Many of these were published in his two-volume *Lyra*

Domestica (1860, 1864). Massie was also a devoted gardener who is said to have cultivated an outstanding rock garden, a rarity in his day.

Translator: *Christ Jesus lay*, **470**

MATHESON, GEORGE (b. Mar. 27, 1842, Glasgow, Scotland; d. Aug. 28, 1906, North Berwick, Scotland), although he became blind by age eighteen, was one of the most brilliant students of his day, attending Glasgow Academy and Glasgow University (B.A., 1861; M.A., 1862). Licensed to the ministry in 1866, Matheson was an outstanding Presbyterian pastor of his time, serving churches in Glasgow, Argyllshire, and Edinburgh. It is said that he compensated for his blindness by developing his memory; he would dictate his Sunday sermon to his sister. After she read it back to him twice, he could preach it word for word.

As a scholar who could write in a simple literary style, Matheson penned books of verse, theology, and devotional material. His verse was published in the volume *Sacred Songs* (1890).

Author: *Make me a captive, Lord*, **539**; *O Love that will not let me go*, **577**

MCAFEE, CLELAND BOYD (b. Sept. 25, 1866, Ashley, Mo.; d. Feb. 4, 1944, Jaffrey, N.H.) graduated from Park College, Parkville, Missouri (1884) and then continued his education at Union Theological Seminary. He returned to Park College where his father was a founder and five of his siblings were working. He taught there and also served as pastor and director of the choir at the college church. McAfee was pastor of 41st Street Presbyterian Church in Chicago (1901-1904) and Lafayette Presbyterian Church in Brooklyn (1904-1912). From 1912 to 1930, he taught systematic theology at McCormick Theological Seminary. He also served his denomination as secretary of the Foreign Mission Board. Upon retirement he moved to New Hampshire where he continued to preach, teach, and write.

Author/Composer: *There is a place of quiet rest* (McAFEE), **5**

MCGRANAHAN, JAMES (b. July 4, 1840, near Adamsville, Pa.; d. July 7, 1907, Kinsman, Ohio), a prominent figure in the nineteenth-century evangelistic movement in the U.S., had only a limited formal education, but he developed his musical skills and by age nineteen was teaching music. He attended Bradbury's Music School in Geneseo, New York, for a brief period of time and led music conventions and singing schools in Pennsylvania and New York in association with J. G. Towner. McGranahan studied under George F. Root, eventually becoming one of the teachers at Root's musical institutes in Somerset, Pennsylvania (1875), and Towanda, Pennsylvania (1876) (Reynolds 1976).

After the sudden death of P. P. Bliss in 1876, McGranahan became the song leader for the evangelist Daniel W. Whittle, traveling with him throughout the U.S. and England. McGranahan was the first to use men's choirs in the meetings and compiled a number of male chorus and gospel song collections. He was associated with Ira D. Sankey and George C. Stebbins in the publication of *Gospel Hymns*, Nos. 3, 4, 5, and 6.

Composer: EL NATHAN (*I know not why God's wondrous*), **338**; *I will praise the Lord*, **109**; MY REDEEMER (*I will sing of my Redeemer*), **344**; NONE BUT CHRIST (*O Christ, in thee my soul*), **510**

MCKINNEY, BAYLUS BENJAMIN (b. July 22, 1886, Heflin, La.; d. Sept. 7, 1952, Bryson City, N.C.) was on the faculty of the School of Sacred Music, Southwestern Baptist Theological Seminary, Fort Worth, Texas (1919-1932). When the seminary was forced to cut back on faculty during the Depression, McKinney took a position as assistant pastor of Travis Avenue Baptist Church in Fort Worth. In December 1935 he took over as music editor, and later secretary, of the newly organized Church Music Department for the Baptist Sunday School Board, Nashville, Tennessee. In this position he compiled and published several hymn collections, including the 1940 *Broadman Hymnal*, and edited the periodical *The Church Musician*.

From 1918 to 1935, he was music editor for Robert H. Coleman, an independent publisher of hymnals and gospel songbooks. This was a most prolific period for McKinney, who wrote both words and music for about 150 gospel songs; he composed tunes, as well, for more than a hundred texts by other authors. McKinney was awarded the D.Mus. in 1942 from Oklahoma Baptist University, Shawnee. He died in an automobile accident as he and his wife were returning home from a church music leadership week in North Carolina.

Author/Composer: *Blessed Savior, we adore thee* (GLORIOUS NAME), **107**

MEDEMA, KEN (b. Dec. 7, 1943, Grand Rapids, Mich.) studied music therapy at Michigan State University, East Lansing, concentrating on performance skills in piano and voice. He received his bachelor's degree in 1965 and a master's in 1969. Both he and his wife, Jane Smith, are music therapists. Medema began composing as an adjunct to his therapy work.

In 1973, soon after his first recording, *Fork in the Road*, was released, he turned to composing, recording, and performing contemporary Christian songs full time. Blind from birth, Medema understands the importance of inclusiveness; he incorporates the challenges of justice and peace into his songs. His eclectic musical style ranges from classical to rock, from ballads to blues. He is a dynamic and popular performer, especially with young people, and is adept at on-the-spot composing. His performance schedule has taken him across North America and to

Australia, Africa, and Europe. He now resides in San Francisco where he is a member of Dolores Street Baptist Church.

Author/Composer: *Lord, listen to your children* (CHILDREN PRAYING), **353**

MEDLEY, SAMUEL (b. June 23, 1738, Cheshunt, Hertfordshire, England; d. July 17, 1799, Liverpool, Lancashire, England), the son of a schoolteacher, served as a midshipman in the Royal Navy and was wounded in 1759 off Port Lagos. Upon his return home, he experienced a conversion after reading a sermon by Isaac Watts. Medley joined Eagle Street Baptist Church, London, and eventually became pastor of Baptist churches in Watford and Liverpool. He was especially successful in the latter where he remained from 1772 until 1799. His hymns were printed in magazines and in collections published in the last fifteen years of the eighteenth century. Some are included in *A Memoir* (1833), written by his daughter Sarah.

Author: *I know that my Redeemer lives*, **277, 279**

MEINEKE, CHRISTOPHER (a.k.a. CHARLES) (b. May 1, 1782, Germany; d. Nov. 6, 1850, Baltimore, Md.), thought to be the son of the Oldenburg organist Karl Meineke, immigrated to North America in the early 1800s. Settling in Baltimore, he became the organist at St. Paul's Episcopal Church and was active in local music societies. Meineke spent 1817 to 1819 in Vienna, Austria, where he met Beethoven.

Meineke composed a substantial amount of piano music, as well as sacred compositions and songs. Among his best-known church works are a *Te Deum*, a Mass, and *Music for the Church* (1844), which includes more than sixty psalm and hymn tunes.

Composer: *Glory be to the Father*, **127**

MENDELSSOHN, FELIX (b. Feb. 3, 1809, Hamburg, Germany; d. Nov. 4, 1847, Leipzig, Germany), whose full name was Jakob Ludwig Felix Mendelssohn-Bartholdy, was a grandson of the eminent Jewish philosopher Moses Mendelssohn. Felix's father was an affluent banker, and his mother was a woman of culture who nurtured her son's musical ability early on. When the family moved to Berlin in 1811, they converted to Lutheranism and added the name Bartholdy. Felix studied music with the best teachers in Berlin. When he was nine years old, he made his first public appearance as a pianist and two years later began to compose regularly.

Every two weeks the Mendelssohn family hosted musical gatherings that were attended by noted musicians, at which many of young Felix's compositions had their first hearings. In 1823 he received as a Christmas present from his grandmother a manuscript copy of J. S. Bach's *Passion According to St. Matthew*. In 1829, he conducted the first performance of that work after the composer's death, leading to a nineteenth-century revival of interest in Bach's music.

Mendelssohn's professional reputation as a composer was established with the performance of his overture to *A Midsummer Night's Dream* in 1826, when he was seventeen. His compositions represent almost every genre except opera. Of particular interest to church-music aficionados are his sacred choral works, oratorios, and organ works, as well as some hymn tunes that have been adapted from his secular compositions. Mendelssohn was also a noted conductor, pianist, organist, educator, and administrator who traveled widely. He died when he was just thirty-eight. For more detailed information, see standard musical references.

Composer: BIRMINGHAM (MENDELSSOHN) (*Cast thy burden upon the Lord*), **586**; HEAVENLY LOVE (*In heavenly love abiding*), **613**; MENDELSSOHN (*Hark! the herald angels sing*), **201**. Arranger: MUNICH (*I believe in you, Lord Jesus*), **440**; NUN DANKET ALLE GOTT (*Now thank we all our God*), **86**

MENTZER, JOHANN (b. July 27, 1658, Jahmen, near Rothenburg, Silesia; d. Feb. 24, 1734, Chemnitz, near Bernstadt, Saxony, Germany) studied theology at Wittenberg, Germany. In 1691 he became the pastor at Merzdorf, and two years later he moved to Hauswolde, near Bischofswerde. In 1696 he went to Chemnitz for the remainder of his life.

Mentzer was one of a group of pietistic hymnwriters that included Johann Christoph Schwendler, Henriette Catherine von Gersdorf, and Nicolaus Ludwig von Zinzendorf; Mentzer was a friend and neighbor to all of them. Mentzer himself wrote thirty-four hymns.

Author: *Oh, that I had a thousand voices*, **84**

MERCER, WILLIAM (b. 1811, Barnard Castle, Durham, England; d. Aug. 21, 1873, Leavy Greave, Sheffield, England) was educated at Trinity College, Cambridge (B.A., M.A.). He was appointed to the parish of St. George's, Sheffield, where he ministered for thirty-three years, from 1840 until his death in 1873. With James Montgomery and John Goss, Mercer edited *The Church Psalter and Hymn Book . . .* (1854), to which he contributed several translations and paraphrases of Latin and German hymns. For many years this collection was the most widely used and influential hymnbook in the Church of England.

Translator: *O come, all ye faithful* (st. 2), **212**

MIDDLETON, JESSE EDGAR (b. Nov. 3, 1872, Pilkington Township, Ontario; d. May 27, 1960, Toronto, Ontario) enjoyed a successful career as a journalist, holding positions with the *Montréal Herald*, the Toronto *Mail and Empire*, and *The Saturday Night*. He also served Centennial United Church of Toronto as a choirmaster for almost four decades.

Moreover, Middleton was an accomplished author of poetry, plays, novels, and nonfiction books.

Translator: *'Twas in the moon of wintertime*, **190**

MIDGLEY, ROBERT H. (b. Oct. 10, 1921, Worcester, Mass.) earned degrees at Northeastern University, Boston, Massachusetts (B.A., 1944) and Andover-Newton Theological School (Mass.; M.Div., 1947). He grew up in Westboro, Massachusetts, where he was confirmed in the Congregational Church (later United Church of Christ [UCC]). The youth minister there, he says, "planted the seeds of a ministerial calling," which bore fruit in Midgley's forty years of pastoral ministry in the UCC—in Wyoming, South Dakota, Wisconsin, Illinois, and Hawaii. He was also influenced by the death of his best high school friend from leukemia, which "was the beginning of a lifelong belief in resurrection theology—that out of life's 'crucifixions' come, by the grace of God, new growth, new healing, new opportunity." He experienced this process in the death of a daughter from leukemia and in many pastoral-care situations. Another formative experience was a three-month mission to Japan where he participated in a mentoring program for young pastors. He has been involved in denominational and conference leadership in the UCC and has served as a trustee at two colleges, one of which made him a trustee emeritus. Now retired, he lives in Kimball, Nebraska.

Author: God of resurrection and life, **747**

MILGROVE, BENJAMIN (b. 1731; d. 1810) was likely organist and/or precentor (music director) at the Countess of Huntingdon's Chapel in Bath, England. He also owned a shop in the city and was one of the financial proprietors for John Wesley's chapel in New King Street, Bath.

Composer: MT. EPHRAIM (*Create my soul anew*), **3**

MILLER, EDWARD (b. 1735,[1] Norwich, England; d. Sept. 12 or 13, 1807, Doncaster, Yorkshire, England) was an author, composer, and organist. The son of a stonemason and paver, Miller was apprenticed to his father's occupation but ran away from home to study music at Lynn with the renowned music historian Charles Burney. For a time Miller was a flutist in George Frederick Handel's orchestra and was awarded the D.Mus. from Cambridge University in 1786.

Miller's longest tenure, however, was as organist for fifty-one years (1756-1807) at Doncaster Parish Church. Among his most important publications were *The Psalms of David Set to New Music* (1774), *Elements of Thorough-bass and Composition* (1787), *The Psalms of David* (1790), *Thoughts on the Present Performance of Psalmody* (1791), *The Psalms of Watts and Wesley for three voices for the use of Methodists* (1801), and *Sacred Music* (1802).

Arranger: ROCKINGHAM OLD (*Unto thy temple, Lord, we come*), **4**

1. Some sources give his date of birth as 1731; however, Hayden and Newton in their *British Hymn Writers and Composers: A Check-List* cite the date listed above.

MILMAN, HENRY HART (b. Feb. 10, 1791, London, England; d. Sept. 24, 1868, London) was educated at Dr. Burney's, Greenwich; at the reputable Eton College, and at Brasenose College, Oxford (B.A., 1814; M.A., 1816; B.D. and D.D., 1849). Millman's excellence in poetry and drama was evident early in life; he wrote *Apollo Belvedere* in 1812, winning a prestigious poetry prize for it and for a number of his other essays. His literary acumen later extended to theology and history; he put out a history of the Jews, a history of early Christianity, and a history of Latin Christianity. His translations from Sanskrit are also considered significant.

Ordained in 1816, Milman served as vicar at St. Mary's; professor of poetry, Oxford University (1821-1831); rector of St. Margaret's; and canon of Westminster from 1835 to 1849 when he became dean of St. Paul's Cathedral. During his time at St. Paul's, the great services under the dome began.

Thirteen of Milman's hymns were published in his friend Reginald Heber's *Hymns* (1827) and later in his own *Selection of Psalms and Hymns* (1837).

Author: *Ride on, ride on in majesty*, **239**

MOE, DANIEL (b. Nov. 2, 1926, Minot, N.D.), indulging his "very strong sense" of wanting to compose church music, has published more than forty works for orchestra, chorus, and chamber groups. In retirement he plans to work on some larger pieces in addition to providing leadership for Key Chorale, a semi-professional ensemble that he and his wife founded.

Moe completed his B.A. at Concordia College, Minnesota; the M.A. at the University of Washington, Seattle; and Ph.D. at the University of Iowa, Iowa City. He did further study at Hamline University in Germany and the Aspen School of Music in Colorado. The recipient of numerous awards and fellowships, Moe was honored with a D.Mus. from Gustavus Adolphus College, St. Peter, Minnesota.

Moe began his teaching career at the University of Denver, Colorado (1953-1959), after which he became director of choral music at the University of Iowa. He later developed a nationally recognized graduate program in choral literature and conducting at Iowa before joining the Oberlin Conservatory (Ohio) faculty in 1972. At Oberlin, in addition to teaching, he conducted three vocal ensembles, including the 250-voice

Musical Union, one of America's oldest musical societies. For twenty years he led the Oberlin College Choir to continued critical acclaim across the U.S. Moe is known for his work as a leading choral clinician, composer, and conductor. He authored two widely used books: *Problems in Conducting* and *Basic Choral Concepts.*

Composer: CITY OF GOD (*O Jesus Christ, may grateful hymns*), **404**

MOHR, JOSEPH (b. Dec. 11, 1792, Salzburg, Austria; d. Dec. 5, 1848, Wagrein, Austria) was a choirboy at Salzburg Cathedral where Mozart had served a generation before. Raised by the village vicar because his father was often on the road as a mercenary soldier, Mohr was educated at the university and ordained to the Roman Catholic priesthood in 1815. It was during his short assignment as assistant priest of St. Nicholas Church in Oberndorf (1817-1819) that he wrote his famous carol. He served several other parishes, the last two being at Hintersee (1828) and Wagrein (1837) where he remained until his death.

Though it is said that Mohr penned other sacred music, nothing more is known of it. "Silent night," however, is enshrined on a wall of the Oberndorf church; a bronze relief shows Mohr looking out on a group of singing children, with Franz Gruber playing his guitar accompaniment in the background.

Author: *Silent night, holy night*, **193**

MONK, WILLIAM HENRY (b. Mar. 16, 1823, London, England; d. Mar. 1, 1889, London), trained by private tutors, began his career as a church organist at age eighteen. He served numerous London churches and, in 1852, was named organist at St. Matthias Church, Stoke Newington, London. He remained in that post for the rest of his life. At the same time, he taught at King's College, London; the School for the Indigent Blind; the National Training School for Music; and Bedford College.

Monk, a leading hymnologist of his day, is noted for his work as music editor for the first three editions of *Hymns Ancient and Modern* (1861, 1875, 1889). For the 1861 edition alone, he arranged fifty tunes and composed fifteen others. In addition to his work on that historic hymnal, he was editor of *The Parish Choir* from 1840 to 1851. He received an honorary doctorate from Durham University in 1882.

Composer: EVENTIDE (*Abide with me*), **653**. Arranger: DIX (*As with gladness men of old*, **218**; *For the beauty of the earth*, **89**); ELLACOMBE (*Hosanna, loud hosanna*, **238**; *I sing the mighty power of God*, **46**); VICTORY (*The strife is o'er*, **263**; *O Lord of life, wherever they be*, **635**)

MONSELL, JOHN SAMUEL BEWLEY (b. Mar. 2, 1811, St. Columb's, Londonderry, Ireland; d. Apr. 9, 1875, Guildford, England) was educated at Trinity College, Dublin (B.A., 1832; LL.D., 1865). He was ordained in

1834 and was a pastor of churches in Ireland and England. Monsell became rector of St. Nicholas's Church, Guildford, in 1870, then died a few years later in a construction accident at the church when it was being rebuilt. He wrote more than three hundred hymns and published eleven volumes of poetry. "We are too distant in our praises," he writes. A deeply devout man, he was convinced that hymns should be "fervent and joyous" (Parry, Routley 1953).

Author: *I hunger and I thirst*, **474**; *Sing to the Lord of harvest*, **98**; *Worship the Lord in the beauty*, **220**

MONTGOMERY, JAMES (b. Nov. 4, 1771, Irvine, Ayrshire, Scotland; d. Apr. 30, 1854, Sheffield, York, England) was the son of the only Moravian minister in Scotland. In 1778 he started school but made little progress and was dismissed in 1787 due to his preoccupation with writing poetry. After being apprenticed to a baker, Montgomery settled in Sheffield in 1792 and worked for the newspaper, the Sheffield *Register*. Later he became editor and owner of the paper, changing its name to the Sheffield *Iris*.

A "fearless social leader," Montgomery spoke out against the slave trade and for civil rights. He was jailed twice for printing his views—he had "the temerity to reprint a song celebrating the fall of the Bastille" at the height of the French Revolution (Adams 1984). Shortly after his release, his report of the quelling of a riot in Sheffield landed him behind bars again for "seditious libel."

Montgomery was also embroiled in a controversy concerning the singing of hymns in the Church of England, the outcome of which resulted in the publication of Thomas Cotterill's hymnal, *Selection of Psalms and Hymns* (1819). Some of Montgomery's own work appears in that hymnal. In all, he wrote more than four hundred hymns and delivered lectures on poetry in Sheffield and at the Royal Institute, London. He was a staunch supporter of foreign missions and the British Bible Society. Ranked in popularity with Wesley, Watts, Newton, and Cowper, he was considered the most important Moravian hymnwriter in the nineteenth century.

Author: *Go to dark Gethsemane*, **240**; *Hail to the Lord's anointed*, **185**; *Lord, teach us how to pray aright*, **350**; *O bless the Lord, my soul*, **80**; *Prayer is the soul's sincere desire*, **572**; *Shepherd of souls, refresh* (sts. 3-4), **456**; *Songs of praise the angels sang*, **60**

MOORE, THOMAS (b. May 28, 1779, Dublin, Ireland; d. Feb. 25, 1852, Chittoe, Wiltshire, England), not to be confused with Sir Thomas More, was educated in private schools and attended Trinity College, but since he was Roman Catholic, he was not allowed to graduate. He studied law at Middle Temple in London and, after completing his studies in 1804, went to Bermuda as registrar in the Admiralty Court. Boredom prompted him to think of returning to England, so he hired a deputy to take over his responsibilities. This deputy proved to be less than trustworthy, embezzling funds for which Moore was responsible. Moore took refuge in Virginia and New York until the situation could be rectified, finally returning to London after touring the U.S. and Canada. He was very popular in London society, both because of his literary notoriety and his refined social graces.

Moore published a number of books and collections of poetry. The appearance of *Irish Melodies* (1807-1809), in which a number of his texts were set to tunes by John Stevenson, won him the title of the "National Lyrist of Ireland." Better known as the poet of "Believe me, if all those endearing young charms" and "The last rose of summer," Moore's connection with hymnwriting rests on thirty-two of his texts in *Sacred Songs, Duets, and Trios* (1816), set to popular tunes of the day. He also published *Tales of the Fudge Family* (under a pseudonym); *Poems by the Late Thomas Little* (1801); and *Memoirs, Journal, and Correspondence* (1855). In 1830 he edited the *Life and Letters of Lord Byron*. Moore's *Collected Works* were published in 1866.

Author: *Come, ye disconsolate* (sts. 1-2), **497**

MORISON, JOHN (b. 1749, Cairnie, Aberdeenshire, Scotland; d. June 12, 1798, Canisbay, Caithness, Scotland) studied at the University of Aberdeen, earning an M.A. in 1771. The *Edinburgh Weekly Magazine* published his early poems under the pen name "Musaeus." After teaching for a period of time, he became a minister at Canisbay, Caithness, in 1780. That same year he was appointed an editor on the committee that produced *Scottish Paraphrases* (1781), a revision of the 1745 collection. These paraphrases introduced new hymnody to the Scottish churches, which, at the time, used only psalms or texts with scriptural bases. Morison contributed seven original paraphrases. The collection was never approved by the General Assembly but was "allowed to be used" (Loewen, Moyer, Oyer 1983).

Author: *To us a Child of hope is born*, **189**

MORLEY, JANET (b. Aug. 6, 1951, near Birmingham, England) grew up in Claygate, Surrey, England. She earned degrees at New Hall College, Cambridge University (B.A. in English, 1972), and King's College, University of London (B.A. in biblical studies, 1985). She has worked as executive secretary for the British Council of Churches Community of Women and Men. Since 1985 she has been an adult education adviser at Christian Aid, London. She has also served on the executive committee and as chairwoman of Women in Theology. Publications include *Celebrating Women* (Movement for the Ordination of Women/Women in Theology 1986), *All Desires Known* (Morehouse Publishing 1988), *Bread* *of Tomorrow: Praying with the World's Poor* (SPCK/Christian Aid 1992), and *Companions of God: Praying for Peace in the Holy Land* (Christian Aid 1994).

Author: O God, you withdraw from our sight, **676**; God our healer, whose mercy, **723**; God of community, whose call, **736**; God our lover, in whose arms we are held, **740**; God our creator, you have made us, **744**; God our security, who alone can defend us, **760**; O Eternal Wisdom, O Vulnerable God, **782**

MORNINGSTAR, DIANNE HUFFMAN (b. Apr. 30, 1944, Timberville, Va.), born in the Shenandoah Valley of Virginia, was educated at Bridgewater College (Va.); the American Conservatory of Music in Chicago; and Westminster Choir College, Princeton, New Jersey. She taught in the public schools of Elmhurst, Illinois, and Elizabethtown, Pennsylvania, as well as at Messiah College, Grantham, Pennsylvania. Beginning at age thirteen, she has been an organist in Virginia, Illinois, and Pennsylvania churches. She is also an energetic choir leader and a favorite of junior choirs. Since 1989 she has served as minister of music at Trinity United Methodist Church in New Cumberland, Pennsylvania.

Composer: STRANGERS NO MORE (*For we are strangers no more*), **322**

MORSE, KENNETH I. (b. May 30, 1913, Altoona, Pa.), son of Herman V. and Sadie Bennett Morse, grew up Brethren and graduated from Juniata College, Huntingdon, Pennsylvania, and Pennsylvania State University (M.A., English lit.). In 1951 he was awarded an honorary doctorate by Juniata College. Further formal study was taken at Princeton University and Bethany Biblical Seminary (now Bethany Theological Seminary, Richmond, Indiana).

After teaching public school, he joined the editorial staff of Brethren Publishing House in Elgin, Illinois, as youth editor; in 1950 he was named editor of *Gospel Messenger*. In 1971 Morse became the book editor for Brethren Press while continuing as associate editor of *Messenger* until his retirement in 1978. A poet and worship specialist known for his soft-spoken wisdom, Morse served on the hymnal committees for both *The Brethren Hymnal* (1951) and *Hymnal: A Worship Book* (1992). His earliest poetry dates from 1937.

Author: *Bread of life*, **455**; *Brothers and sisters of mine*, **142**; *For we are strangers no more*, **322**; *Move in our midst*, **418**; *O God of mystery and might*, **130**; He was the Son of God, **714**; Gracious God, we thank you for gifts, **750**. Translator: *Je louerai l'Eternel* (*Praise, I will praise you, Lord*), **76**

MOSEMANN, JOHN H. (b. Aug. 6, 1907, Lancaster, Pa.; d. Feb. 25, 1989, Goshen, Ind.) graduated from Elizabethtown College (Pa.) in 1932 and was ordained to ministry in the (Old) Mennonite Church the following year. From 1934 to 1939, he and his wife, Ruth L. Histand, were missionaries in Tanganyika Territory (now Tanzania); they were among the first missionaries to be sent to Africa by the Eastern Mennonite Board of Missions and Charities. Health problems prevented them from returning to the mission field after a furlough. During World War II, Mosemann served two years as an administrator in Civilian Public Service. Thereafter, he earned two seminary degrees: at Eastern Baptist, Philadelphia (B.D., 1945) and at Princeton (N.J.; Th.M., 1948). In the major phase of his career, he taught at Goshen College Biblical Seminary (Ind.; 1946-1955) and was a pastor in the Goshen area (1947-1975), serving for three years at Yellow Creek Mennonite Church and twenty-five years at College Mennonite Church. In retirement Mosemann worked as church relations director at Goshen College and as conference minister of Indiana-Michigan Mennonite Conference. He was president of two major organizations in his denomination: Mennonite Board of Missions (1948-1971) and Indiana-Michigan Mennonite Conference (1976-1979).

Author: You have offered your child, **791**; These persons now presented to you, **794**; As God's Spirit calls and the church commissions, **796**; We accept your confession of failure, **800**

MOTE, EDWARD (b. Jan. 21, 1797, London, England; d. Nov. 13, 1874, Southwark, London, England), although he grew up without religious training, was influenced as a youth by the preaching of John Hyatt at Tottenham Court Road Chapel. Mote became a successful cabinetmaker and a devoted churchman, settling in Southwark, a suburb of London. He wrote more than a hundred hymns that were published in his *Hymns of Praise, A New Selection of Gospel Hymns, Combining All the Excellencies of Our Spiritual Poets, with Many Originals* (1836). The title of this collection has been cited as the first use of the term "gospel hymn," though its contents are primarily hymns of praise. In 1852, at age fifty-five, Mote became a Baptist minister, serving the church at Horsham, Essex, for the next twenty-one years. One story has it that members of his congregation so appreciated his efforts to get them a church building that they offered him the deed to the property. He turned down the gift, saying: "I do not want the chapel, I only want the pulpit; and when I cease to preach Christ, then turn me out of that" (Reynolds 1990).

Author: *My hope is built on nothing less,* **343**

MOULTRIE, GERARD (b. Sept. 16, 1829, Rugby, England; d. Apr. 25, 1885, Southleigh, England), the son of an Anglican clergyman, was also the great-grandnephew of General William Moultrie, who was elected governor of South Carolina in 1785 and after whom Fort Moultrie was named. Gerard studied at Rugby School and Exeter College, Oxford (B.A., 1851; M.A., 1856). Following his ordination to the Anglican priesthood, he held several chaplaincies, then became vicar of Southleigh in 1869 and warden of St. James College, Southleigh, in 1873.

Moultrie's publications include *Hymns and Lyrics for the Seasons and Saints' Days of the Church* (1867) and the preface to *Cantica Sanctorum* (1880). Moultrie's reputation rests mainly on his excellent translations of Greek, Latin, and German hymns.

Translator: *Let all mortal flesh keep silence,* **463**

MOWBRAY, DAVID (b. May 1, 1938, Wallington, Surrey, England) studied at Fitzwilliam House, Cambridge, and the University of Bristol. He was ordained in 1963 and has served parishes at Northampton, Watford, Broxbourne, and Wormley. Since December 1991 he has been vicar of St. Matthew's, Darley Abbey, Derby.

Author: *Let God, who called the worlds,* **138**; *Lord of our growing years,* **479**

MOYER, J. HAROLD (b. May 6, 1927, Newton, Kan.) was educated at Bethel College, North Newton, Kansas (A.B., 1949); George Peabody College, Nashville, Tennessee (M.A., 1951); and the University of Iowa, Iowa City (Ph.D., 1958). A composition major in his graduate studies, Moyer was honored as Kansas Composer of the Year in 1971 and received the ASCAP (American Society of Composers, Authors and Publishers) Composer Award in 1988. Numerous musical groups have commissioned his works, both choral and instrumental. As a music educator, he has taught music theory, music history, and piano at several colleges, including Freeman Junior College (S.D.) and Goshen College (Ind.; 1957-1959). Since 1959 he has been a member of the faculty of his alma mater, Bethel College, where he is professor of music.

Composer: FAITH (*I sought the Lord*), **506**; NEWTON (*Lord of our growing years*), **479**; THE WORD OF GOD (*The word of God is solid ground*), **314**; WALNUT (*My soul proclaims with wonder*), **181**. Arranger: BOUND FOR THE PROMISED LAND (*On Jordan's stormy banks I stand*), **610**; COMMUNION (*Hark! the glad sound*), **184**; NEW CONCORD (*Oh, how happy are they*), **597**; RESIGNATION (*My Shepherd will supply my need*), **589**; SOCIAL BAND (*My dear Redeemer and my Lord*), **547**; WARUM BETRÜBST DU DICH, MEIN HERZ (*Who now would follow Christ*), **535**; ZION'S PILGRIM (*O thou, in whose presence*), **559**

MUHLENBERG, WILLIAM AUGUSTUS (b. Sept. 16, 1796, Philadelphia, Pa.; d. Apr. 6, 1877, New York, N.Y.) was the great-grandson of the Lutheran Church's patriarch, Henry M. Muhlenberg. He graduated from the University of Pennsylvania, Philadelphia, in 1814, and was ordained into the Episcopal Church, serving parishes in Lancaster, Pennsylvania; Flushing, Long Island; and New York City. He founded a boys' school, the Flushing Institute (1828), and St. Paul's College on Long Island (1838), becoming president of the latter. Muhlenberg established St. Luke's Hospital in New York City where he worked as pastor and superintendent from 1858 until his death. Near the end of his life, the hospital chaplain came to his bedside to pray for his recovery. Muhlenberg has been quoted as saying: "Let us have an understanding about this. You are asking God to restore me and I am asking him to take me home. There must not be a contradiction in our prayers, for it is evident that he cannot answer them both" (Ryden 1959).

Author: *Like Noah's weary dove*, **496**; *Since o'er thy footstool*, **158**

MURRAY, M. ANDREW (b. June 25, 1942, Roanoke, Va.) has earned degrees from Bridgewater College (Va.; B.A. in sociology, 1964) and Bethany Theological Seminary, Oak Brook, Illinois (M. Div., 1968; D. Min., 1980). After pastoring for three years at Peace Church of the Brethren, Portland, Oregon, he joined the faculty of Juniata College, Huntingdon, Pennsylvania, where he has taught religion, been campus minister, and, since 1987, directed the Baker Institute for Peace and Conflict Studies.

Murray has been a consultant and lecturer on peace studies at educational institutions across the U.S., from Columbia University in New York City to the University of Hawaii. He is in demand as a presenter for churches, camps, and conferences for many denominations. He is currently a member of the United Nations/International Association of University Presidents (IAUP) Commission on Arms Control Education and director of the International Seminar on Arms Control and Disarmament, which is sponsored by the United Nations Office of Disarmament Affairs, the IAUP, and the Baker Institute.

As a folk composer and musician, Murray has helped develop five albums of original songs that bring to life the stories of Brethren heroes, as well as emphasizing peace and justice concerns. In his music ventures, he collaborates with his wife, Teresa, who is also a musician; they are much in demand as concert performers.

Author: *Lord, bless the hands*, **93**

MURRAY, ROBERT (b. Dec. 25, 1832, Earltown, near Truro, Nova Scotia; d. Dec. 10, 1909, Halifax, Nova Scotia) began writing poetry at age ten. He was educated at the Free College, Halifax, of which he became a governor in later years. As an ordained minister in the Presbyterian Church in Canada, Murray was noted for his great literary skills. His abilities eventually landed him the editorship of *The Presbyterian Witness*, a position he held for fifty years. He also was recognized for his efforts to unite the various Presbyterian groups in Canada but died before the union took place. *The Hymnary* (1872), used by the United Church of Canada (which includes Presbyterian, Congregational, Methodist, and other groups), contains the Canadian national hymn "Our loved dominion bless" and "From ocean unto ocean," both by Murray.

Author: *Lord, thou dost love*, **387**

MURRAY, TERESA ROBINSON (b. Dec. 15, 1943, Long Island, N.Y.) attended Bridgewater College (Va.; B.S. in Music Ed., 1965) where she specialized in piano, organ, voice, and choral conducting. At Westminster Choir College, Princeton, New Jersey, she received an M.M. in organ performance with honors in 1984. She has done additional work in organ with Leonard Raver of the Juilliard School, New York City; Harold Vogel of the North German Music Academy; and Joan Lippincott at Westminster Choir College.

Murray was a music teacher in the Illinois public school system and organist, pianist, and choir director for numerous churches representing seven denominations. She is currently minister of music at Stone Church of the Brethren, Huntingdon, Pennsylvania; she has taught organ and piano at Juniata College, Huntingdon. With her husband, Andy, she has produced five record albums, consisting mostly of original pieces with a Brethren twist, beginning with *Summertime Children* (1973). Their most recent contribution is *Just As I Am* (1991). Together the Murrays have performed their original music for colleges, churches, and conferences in at least eighteen states.

Composer: *Lord, bless the hands,* **93**

NAAS, JOHN (JOHANNES) (b. 1669, Nordheim, Germany; d. May 12, 1741, Amwell, N.J.) was a Brethren minister in the Marienborn area of Germany. When the Brethren were expelled from that region in 1715, he moved his family to Krefeld where he served as an elder. John Naas is well known to Brethren young people as the subject of the children's book *The Tall Man,* which tells the story of his gentle but adamant refusal to serve the king of Prussia as a bodyguard.

In 1733 Naas moved to colonial America and settled in Amwell where he played a vital role in developing a congregation and also helped establish several new churches in Pennsylvania. *Die Kleine Harfe* (1792) includes some of his hymns; other texts were subsequently used in other Brethren hymnbooks.

Author: *Savior of my soul,* **549**

NÄGELI, JOHANN GEORG (b. May 26, 1768 or 1773, Wetzikon, Switzerland; d. Dec. 26, 1836, Zürich, Switzerland) is listed in some sources as Hans rather than Johann. Born at Wetzikon, near Zürich, he studied composition with Johann David Brüning. The music publishing company he established in his hometown in 1792 was renowned for its publication of some significant first editions, including Ludwig von Beethoven's sonatas. Nägeli's application of the principles of Pestalozzi to music instruction drew the attention of Lowell Mason, who utilized the same methods in the U.S. In addition to this work as a music publisher, editor, and pioneer music educator, Nägeli composed vocal and instrumental works.

Composer: DENNIS (*Bless'd be the tie that binds*), **421**

NAUMANN, JOHANN GOTTLIEB (b. Apr. 17, 1741, Blasenitz, near Dresden, Germany; d. Oct. 23, 1801, Dresden), the son of a peasant farmer, was an organist by age twelve. He attended the *Kreuzschule* and became a choirboy in the Royal Chapel at Dresden. In 1757 he was chosen to accompany the Royal Chapel's master chamber musician to Hamburg and to Italy where he studied music with Tartini and Padre Martini. Naumann returned to Dresden in 1763 as court composer of sacred music for the ruling family. From 1765 to 1768 he again spent time in Italy, composing and producing operas in Palermo, Venice, and Padua. Called to Sweden to reorganize the opera there, Naumann traveled on to Copenhagen where a lavish production of his opera *Orpheus og Euridice* brought the offer of a post at the Danish court. He declined and was rewarded upon his return to Dresden with a promotion and handsome salary. In addition to operas, Naumann's compositions include oratorios, masses, and other church music.

Composer (attrib.): *Amen*, **381**

NAYLOR, RUTH EILEEN BUNDY (b. Sept. 3, 1934) grew up in a Quaker home in southeastern Ohio. Her marriage in 1954 interrupted her study at Bluffton College (Ohio), but she returned later to finish her B.A. in English in 1971. From there she earned her M.A. from Bowling Green State University (Ohio; 1976) and did additional graduate work in clinical pastoral education in Fort Wayne, Indiana, and a two-year program at Shalem Institute for Spiritual Formation, Washington, D.C.

Naylor has taught junior high and high school English in Ohio. Since 1984 she has pastored at First Mennonite Church of Bluffton. As a poet and writer, she is frequently called upon as a workshop leader in both Mennonite and ecumenical settings. Her publications include more than a hundred poems, plus devotionals and articles that have appeared in at least twenty different religious magazines, including *Christian Century*, *The Mennonite*, *Christian Herald*, *The Lutheran*, and *Pegasus* (National Poetry Press).

Translator: *Rejoice, rejoice in God*, **313**

NEALE, JOHN MASON (b. Jan. 24, 1818, London, England; d. Aug. 6, 1866, East Grinstead, Sussex, England) was educated by private tutors before enrolling in Trinity College, Cambridge. Even as a student, he became a noted writer of sacred poetry and also was involved with the Oxford movement, an effort to revitalize worship. Neale was ordained in 1841 and given a position at a small parish in Sussex, but he lived in Madeira for a time because of his chronic lung disease. In 1846 he was appointed warden of Sackville College, a home for indigent old men in East Grinstead. In disfavor with the ecclesiastical hierarchy because of his "high church" views, Neale was made a caretaker rather than a chaplain. He established the nursing Sisterhood of St. Margaret, devoted to the care of women and girls.

Neale was an excellent scholar in Greek and Latin and a gifted poet. Many of his translations of early Christian hymns are considered more beautiful and meaningful than the originals. Despite his significant contribution to English hymnody, most of the recognition accorded him during his lifetime came from outside his own country. He received an honorary degree from Trinity College, Hartford, Connecticut, and in 1860 the Metropolitan of Russia presented him with an inscribed copy of an ancient liturgy.

Translator: *All glory, laud, and honor*, **237**; *Come, ye faithful, raise the strain*, **264, 265**; *Good Christian friends, rejoice*, **210**; *O come, O come, Immanuel* (sts. 1-4), **172**; *O sons and daughters, let us sing*, **274**; *Of the Father's love begotten*, **104**; *That Easter day with joy was bright*, **281**; *When Christ's appearing* (sts. 2-5), **217**

NEANDER, JOACHIM (b. 1650, Bremen, Germany; d. May 31, 1680, Bremen), a major hymnwriter of the German Reformed Church, has been called the "Paul Gerhardt of the Calvinists." A brilliant but undisciplined scholar, he reveled in the rebellious student life. When he was twenty, he went with two friends to hear the pietist preacher Theodore Under-Eyck, but he only intended to criticize and make fun. Instead, he found himself moved by the preaching—"the fools who came to scoff remained to pray."

Following his conversion Neander became a tutor at Frankfurt and Heidelberg, and in 1674, at age twenty-four, he was appointed rector of the Latin School of Düsseldorf. Through his students he met and was influenced by the pietists P. J. Spener and J. J. Schütz. A few years later, his passion for pietist practices put him at odds with his employers, and he was suspended briefly from his position at the Calvinist school. In 1679 he accepted an invitation to be an assistant to Under-Eyck, but he was never ordained. Neander was teased by his Bremen contemporaries, who called him the "five preacher," because he was allowed to preach only in that time slot since he was not ordained. A few months later he lost his health to tuberculosis and was dead at the age of thirty.

Amid the turbulence caused by his pietist spirituality, Neander found solace and respite in God's creation. Hiking in the mountains near Mettmann, he discovered a cave from which he had a spectacular view over Düsseldorf. The valley below his "secret" cave later was named for him—Neanderthal. But it was not so private a spot as he might have believed. It was there, in 1856, that the remains of a man believed to be six thousand years old were found. That monumental discovery has become known as Neanderthal man.

During Neander's brief life, he wrote sixty hymns plus tunes for a number of these. His works were published in *Geistreiche Bundes-und-danck-lieder* and *Alpha und Omega, Joachimi Neandri Glaub-und Liebesübung* (1680).

Author: *Praise to the Lord, the Almighty*, **37**. Composer: UNSER HERRSCHER (NEANDER) (*Christ is coming! Let creation*, **295**; *Open now thy gates of beauty*, **19**)

NEUMARK, GEORG (b. Mar. 16, 1621, Langensalza, Thüringen, Germany; d. July 18, 1681, Weimar, Germany) composed both hymn texts and tunes, usually when he was suffering or destitute. When he finally secured a position as tutor for a prominent family, he wrote the text and music of his most famous hymn "If thou but suffer God to guide thee" as an expression of gratitude for his change in fortune. Eventually, Neumark was able to study law at the University of Königsberg (1643-1648). After holding various positions in several European cities, he ultimately settled in Weimar where he served the duke as court poet, librarian, register, and secretary.

Author/Composer: *If you but trust in God* (WER NUR DEN LIEBEN GOTT LÄSST WALTEN), **576**

NEWBOLT, MICHAEL ROBERT (b. 1874, Dymock, Gloucestershire, England; d. Feb. 7, 1956, Bierton, Buckinghamshire, England), educated at St. John's College, Oxford, was ordained to the Anglican priesthood in 1900. He served churches in Wantage and Iffley, then became principal of Missionary College in Dorchester (1910-1916). He spent the next eleven years as perpetual curate in Brighton, followed by nineteen years as canon of Chester Cathedral. In 1946 he was licensed to officiate in Oxford.

Reviser: *Lift high the cross*, **321**

NEWTON, JOHN (b. July 24, 1725, London, England; d. Dec. 21, 1807, London) at age eleven went to sea with his father, a shipmaster. The younger Newton served in the Royal Navy as a midshipman and then as master of a slave-trade ship for six years. By his own confession, he led a contemptible life, but he was deeply influenced by reading *The Imitation of Christ* by Thomas à Kempis which, with the experience of a stormy night at sea, led to his conversion.

In 1755 Newton left the sea to become tide surveyor at Liverpool where he studied Hebrew and Greek to prepare for ordination. Here he also came under the guidance of George Whitefield and the Wesleys. At first refused ordination by the archbishop of York, Newton was offered a post at Olney in 1764 as curate, and the bishop of Lincoln ordained him. During his sixteen years at Olney, he and William Cowper published *Olney Hymns* (1779) for "the promotion of the faith and comfort of sincere

Christians." Its 349 hymns (283 by Newton and 66 by Cowper) are divided into three books: "On Select Passages of Scripture," "On Occasional Subjects," and "On the Rise, Progress, Changes, and Comforts of the Spiritual Life." It was in print for one hundred years.

Newton was later rector at St. Mary's Woolnoth in London. The epitaph he wrote, which is on a plain white marble tablet near the vestry door of the church, reads:

> John Newton, Clerk
> Once an infidel and libertine
> A servant of slaves in Africa:
> Was by the rich mercy of our Lord and Saviour
> Jesus Christ
> Preserved, restored, pardoned,
> And appointed to preach the Faith
> He had laboured long to destroy.
> Near XVI years at Olney in Bucks
> And XXVII years in this church.[1]

Author: *Amazing grace*, **143**; *Glorious things of thee are spoken*, **619**; *May the grace of Christ our Savior*, **423**

1. A fuller biographical sketch is in Haeussler's *The Story of Our Hymns*, 1952.

NEWTON, JOHN (bapt. Sept. 1, 1802, Nottingham, England; d. July 4, 1886, Nottingham) attended Castle Gate Congregational Chapel, Nottingham, in early life, but in 1824 he joined Zion Chapel where he reorganized the choir. Originally a lacemaker, he changed professions about 1830 because of a depression in that trade. He moved to Beeston, Nottinghamshire, where he became choirmaster of the Wesleyan Chapel. Returning to Nottingham some four years later, he served as choirmaster at Parliament Street Chapel (Methodist New Connexion) until 1842. Newton published several collections of hymn tunes. Through his association with the Nottingham Choral Society, he began composing oratorios.

Composer: SOVEREIGNTY (*Great God of wonders*), **149**

NICHOLSON, SYDNEY HUGO (b. Feb. 9, 1875, London, England; d. May 30, 1947, Ashford, Kent, England) was educated at Rugby School, New College, Oxford (M.A., D.Mus.), and studied under Charles V. Stanford at the Royal College of Music, London. In 1908 he became organist of Manchester Cathedral and, in 1918, organist of Westminster Abbey. He resigned, however, in 1928 to become warden of the School of English Church Music (now the Royal School of Church Music), which he founded for the training of church musicians.

Nicholson edited a number of publications in the field of English church music, particularly the 1916 supplement to *Hymns Ancient and Modern* and its shortened music edition of 1939. He was the first layman to hold the chair of the proprietorship (1938-1947). He summarized his experiences in the book *Quires and Places where they sing* (1932). Nicholson was knighted in 1938 for his contributions to English hymnody.

Composer: CRUCIFER (*Lift high the cross*), **321**

NICOLAI, PHILIPP (b. Aug. 10, 1556, Mengeringhausen, Waldeck, Germany; d. Oct. 26, 1608, Hamburg, Germany), the son of a Lutheran pastor, attended the University of Erfurt in 1575 and the University of Wittenberg in 1576, completing his studies in 1579. He assisted his father in preaching at Mengeringhausen, then continued with pastorates at Herdecke (1583), Niederwildungen (1586), and Altwildungen (1588). He found himself in nearly constant and vociferous controversy with Catholics, not an uncommon predicament in the late Reformation era. When Nicolai pastored in Unna, in Westphalia (1596), he had similar altercations with the Calvinists, especially over the interpretation of the Lord's Supper sacraments. While at Unna he also survived a terrible epidemic of bubonic plague and fled an invasion of Spaniards on December 27, 1598, returning in April 1599. In April 1601 Nicolai was elected chief pastor of St. Katherine's Church at Hamburg where he served until his death. He was widely respected as a popular preacher and hymnwriter. Two of his works have been dubbed the "king and queen of chorales."

Author/Composer: *How brightly beams the morning* (WIE SCHÖN LEUCHTET DER MORGENSTERN), **222**; *Sleepers, wake* (WACHET AUF), **188**

NISHIMURA, SUGAO (b. 1871, Japan; d. 1964, Japan) became a Christian as a young man in Matsuyama on the island of Shikoku, Japan. He developed Jonan Boys' School as an educational opportunity for youngsters who had to work during the day and had no chance to attend the regular schools. In the years after child labor disappeared, he saw his school develop from a night school into a fine daytime high school with night classes for adults. He was principal of the school until age eighty-two.

Author: *In lonely mountain ways*, **560**

NIX-ALLEN, VEROLGA (b. 1933, Philadelphia, Pa.), a Germantown high school music major, tested and won the first out-of-state, four-year music scholarship ever offered by the board of education. After two years at the New England Conservatory of Music, she transferred to Oberlin Conservatory of Music (Ohio; B.Mus.Ed.). Later she earned an M.Mus. She returned to Philadelphia to teach in the public school music division for twenty years.

Nix-Allen is a member of New Covenant Church of Philadelphia and Salem Baptist Church, Jenkintown. She has conducted church and festival choirs and is the founder, arranger, and musical director of the twenty-voice Intermezzo Choir. She holds membership in numerous professional organizations, including the Hymn Society and NANM (National Association for Negro Musicians). Nix-Allen has been the recipient of many awards and citations and was selected as co-editor with J. Jefferson Cleveland of the supplementary hymnal *Songs of Zion*. This collection, the first African American songbook published by the United Methodist Church, has sold well in excess of two million copies. She has composed, arranged, and published more than 150 songs.

Arranger: *Father, I stretch my hands to thee*, **529**

NOEL, CAROLINE MARIA (b. Apr. 10, 1817, London, England; d. Dec. 7, 1877, London), the daughter of an English clergyman and poet, started writing hymns at age seventeen, but due to poor health and competing interests, laid down her pen for twenty years. In the last twenty-five years of her life, she resumed writing, and in 1861 a collection of her work was published as *The Name of Jesus and Other Verses for the Sick and Lonely*. The posthumous edition of 1878 contains seventy-eight pieces.

Author: *At the name of Jesus*, **342**

NORTH, FRANK MASON (b. Dec. 3, 1850, New York, N.Y.; d. Dec. 17, 1935, Madison, N.J.) earned the B.A. and M.A. from Wesleyan University, Middletown, Connecticut, and was ordained in the Methodist Episcopal Church in 1872. From 1872 to 1892, he served Methodist pastorates in Florida, New York City, and Connecticut. For the next twenty years (1892-1912), he was corresponding secretary of the New York City Mission and Church Extension Society and editor of the *Christian City*. From 1912 to 1924, he was secretary of the Methodist Board of Foreign Mission, as well as president of the Federal Council of Churches of Christ in America (1916-1920).

North was a minister well acquainted with the seamy side of city life. Though this modest man claimed he was not a hymnwriter, a number of his special-occasion hymns were published. Several of these, along with memorial addresses, are gathered in a commemorative volume issued by his many friends shortly after his death.

Author: *Where cross the crowded ways*, **405**

NOWACKI, SHEILAGH PORTO (b. Sept. 12, 1947, Greenville, S.C.) spent her early years in New York and Pennsylvania. She received her nursing degree from Reading Hospital School of Nursing (Pa.) in 1968 and attended Goshen College (Ind.) for one year. She and her husband are both nurses at Methodist Hospital in Indianapolis, Indiana, where they also are active in Indianapolis Christian Fellowship. Although not trained in music theory, Nowacki has sung in choirs since the age of twelve and studied voice at various times since 1983.

Composer: OBEY MY VOICE (*Obey my voice*), **163**

OAKELEY, FREDERICK (b. Sept. 5, 1802, Shrewsbury, England; d. Jan. 29, 1880, London, England) was educated at Christ Church, Oxford, and ordained in 1826. He served at Lichfield Cathedral, Whitehall, and at Margaret Chapel (1839) where Richard Redhead was organist. A leader in the Oxford movement in the Church of England, Oakeley translated Latin hymns to "offset the influence of evangelical hymnody" (*The Hymnal 1940 Companion*, 1951 ed.). Like others in the movement who were intent on recovering the best of ancient liturgy, he eventually joined the Roman Catholic Church and was re-ordained. In 1852 Oakeley was appointed canon of Westminster, London.

Translator: *O come, all ye faithful* (sts. 1,3-4), **212**

OKEYO, SAMUEL C. OCHIENG' (20th c., Kenya), a teacher in the secondary schools in Kenya, graduated from Kenyatta University with a B.Mus. and has pursued graduate work at Manchester, England. Many of his compositions have been written for and published by the Catholic Church of Kenya.

Composer: NASADIKI (*I believe in God*), **330**

OLEARIUS, JOHANNES (b. Sept. 17, 1611, Halle, Germany; d. Apr. 24, 1684, Weissenfels, Germany) studied at the University of Wittenberg (M.A., 1632; D.D., 1643). Prior to 1637 Olearius lectured in philosophy at his alma mater. From 1637 to 1680, he served the court at Halle, and from 1680 to 1684, he held similar clergy positions at the court in Weissenfels.

Olearius was a proficient and productive author, writing several books and compiling a collection of hymns in 1671 known as the *Geistliche Singe-Kunst*, considered the best collection of German hymns at that time. Olearius contributed 302 original hymns to this mammoth 1,207-hymn publication. In addition to his large hymn collection, Olearius also published devotional books and a commentary on the Bible.

Author: *Comfort, comfort, O my people*, **176**

OLSON, ERNST WILLIAM (b. Mar. 16, 1870, Skåne, Sweden; d. Oct. 6, 1958, Chicago, Ill.) immigrated to the U.S. when he was five. The family settled in Nebraska and later moved to Texas. He graduated from Augustana College, Rock Island, Illinois, in 1891 and became editor of several Swedish-language weekly publications. After five years as office editor for the Engberg-Holmberg Publishing Company in Chicago, he accepted a similar position with the Augustana Book Concern (Lutheran) where he remained for more than thirty years until he retired in 1949.

Noted for his writing skills in both English and Swedish, Olson received a prize for Swedish poetry (1922) and an honorary doctorate from his alma mater (1926). *A History of the Swedes in Illinois* is among the several books he authored. Four of his original hymn texts and twenty-eight translations were included in the *Augustana Hymnal* (1925), and he served as a member of the hymnal committee for the Lutheran *Service Book and Hymnal* (1958).

Translator: *Children of the heavenly Father,* **616**

OLSON, HOWARD S. (b. July 18, 1922, St. Paul, Minn.) attended Gustavus Adolphus College, St. Peter, Minnesota (B.A.); Augustana Seminary, Rock Island, Illinois (M.Div.); and Hartford Seminary Foundation (Conn.; Ph.D.). In his forty-two-year ministry in Tanzania, Olson was a theologian, linguist, and hymnologist. He edited the *Africa Theological Journal* for many years and is now professor emeritus of Lutheran Theological Seminary in Makumira, Tanzania, where he taught for twenty-four years.

In linguistics, Olson published the first and only analysis of Kinyaturu in the Girwana dialect, titled *The Phonology and Morphology of the Rimi Language.* In addition, he authored and published *Jifunze Kiyunani,* a text for teaching Koine Greek in Kiswahili.

In the field of hymnology, Olson was director of music research at the seminary. He has written numerous articles on ethnic music and has published books of hymns in English and Kiswahili. In his African publications, he used his Tanzanian *nom de plume,* Mudimi Ntandu.

Translator: *Christ has arisen,* **267**; *To go to heaven,* **513**

OLUDE, ABRAHAM TAIWO OLAJIDE (b. July 16, 1908, Ebute-Metta, Lagos, Nigeria; d. 1986) was trained as a teacher and minister at Wesley College, Ibadan, and studied journalism at a training school in Minodola. While he was a student in 1925, Olude became interested in the use of indigenous African music in worship. Since that time he has been a leader in replacing European hymnody with African tunes and instruments in both choir and congregational singing. From 1937 to 1950, Olude toured Nigeria with his own choir to demonstrate the use of this folk music, as well as hymns he had written in that idiom. He also wrote dramas and music for use in the schools and was a pastor and district superintendent. Among his honors, Olude received the Order of the Niger and was awarded an honorary D.Mus. by the University of Nigeria in 1967.

Author/Composer: *Jesus, we want to meet,* **10**

OOSTERHUIS, HUUB (b. Nov. 1, 1933, Amsterdam, Holland) was a member of the Jesuit order in the Netherlands. With Bernard Huijbers he was instrumental in introducing the vernacular into the liturgy of the Roman Catholic Church in Holland. In the mid-1960s, after Vatican II, while Huijbers was working to revitalize the worship of the Dominicus parish, Oosterhuis was similarly involved in the Amsterdam Student Church. As they worked in these sister churches, Oosterhuis and Huijbers developed a more informal musical style, and their creative work from that period still influences liturgical worship in Amsterdam.

In 1980 Oosterhuis established the Association for Liturgy and Learning, a move that recommitted the Amsterdam Student Church to its biblical roots. At this center, investigation and inquiry in the areas of politics, art, and the church are grounded in biblical perspective.

In more recent years, his writing has turned from hymnody to other forms and themes, especially social justice.

Author: *What is this place,* **1**

OWEN, WILLIAM, called **PRYSGOL** (b. 1814, Bangor, Caernarvonshire, Wales; d. 1893) was the son of a laborer in the Penrhyn slate quarries. He grew up singing in the quarries, and those who heard him were convinced he would be a great musician. He wrote his first tune when he was eighteen, setting it to a popular hymn text. But the Welsh were traditionalists, and he was criticized severely for meddling with a traditional text/tune combination. So he began composing his tunes for new texts. Volume 2 of *Y Perl Cerddorol* (The Pearl of Music) contains both hymn tunes and anthems composed by Owen.

Composer: BRYN CALFARIA (*Look, you saints*), **286**

OXENHAM, JOHN (b. Nov. 12, 1852, Manchester, England; d. Jan. 24, 1941, London, England), whose real name was William A. Dunkerly, was a prolific author of more than forty novels and some twenty-five collections of poetry and prose. His first book of poetry, *Bees in Amber*, launched him as a poet, with nearly 300,000 copies issued.

After completing his education at Victoria University in Manchester, Oxenham traveled throughout Europe and North America as a businessman, an occupation he eventually gave up in order to pursue full time the writing he had learned to love. During World War I, he published his *Hymns for Men at the Front*, an immense success. He was a member of Ealing Congregational Church in London where he taught a Bible class and was a deacon. Many of his works, especially those written after 1921, are strongly religious in nature.

Author: *In Christ there is no East or West,* **306**

OYER, MARY K. (b. Apr. 5, 1923, Hesston, Kans.) has been the Mennonites' leading hymnologist in the second half of the twentieth century. She has music degrees from Goshen College (Ind.; B.A., 1945) and the University of Michigan, Ann Arbor (M.Mus., 1948; D.Mus.A., 1958). She has done post-doctoral studies in Africa (1969-1995); in Europe (1960, 1964); in Scotland with Erik Routley (1963-1964); and at the University of California at Los Angeles (1968) and Northwestern University, Evanston, Illinois (1975).

Oyer was a professor of music/humanities at Goshen College (1945-1987) and is a professor of church music at Associated Mennonite Biblical Seminaries, Elkhart, Indiana (1989-1996). She also has taught at Kenyatta University, Kenya (1980-1981, 1985-1986); Canadian Mennonite Bible College, Winnipeg, Manitoba (1985); and Great Plains Seminary, Newton, Kansas, and Bethel College, North Newton, Kansas (both in 1992).

Named a fellow of the Hymn Society of the United States and Canada (1989), Oyer has received many awards, including an honorary doctorate from Christian Theological Seminary, Indianapolis, Indiana (1992) and a Lilly Faculty Fellowship (1979-1980) for work in the Kenya National Archives. She researched, wrote, and edited much of *The Mennonite Hymnal* (1969), a joint effort of the (Old) Mennonites and the General Conference Mennonite Church. She wrote *Exploring the Mennonite Hymnal: Essays* (1980) and co-authored *Exploring the Mennonite Hymnal: Handbook* (1983). She chaired The Hymnal Project (1984-1986) and represented the Mennonite Church on this hymnal's music committee (1984-1989), editing the 150-number *Hymnal Sampler* (1989).

Oyer has led singing at dozens of Mennonite conferences and has visited several hundred congregations since the late 1960s, usually to introduce new hymns and hymnals—and to share new musical insights from her fifteen trips to Africa.

An accomplished cellist, Oyer often plays chamber music during her visits to Africa. She has lectured on hymnody in Kenya, Japan, Sweden, and Canada. While acknowledging she is blessed with perfect pitch in leading singing, Oyer says she derives much greater joy in being able to help a congregation "create a beautiful musical phrase." She believes music—and hymns in particular—"are very important to people; music and poetry are essential to our spiritual life. There's a kind of release and relief when we sing. Hymns involve the whole person: the spiritual, the emotional, the theological, the social. Hymns function in so many different ways." Now in her mid-70s, Oyer has no plans to retire; her work is too fulfilling.

PALESTRINA, GIOVANNI PIERLUIGI DA (b. ca. 1525, Palestrina, Italy; d. Feb. 2, 1594, Rome, Italy) may have received his first music training at Santa Maria Maggiore as a choirboy, but little is known about his early life. A document dated October 28, 1544, indicates his appointment as organist at the cathedral of San Agapito in the town of Palestrina.

He was married in 1547 to Lucrezia Gori, and shortly afterward the bishop of Palestrina, Cardinal Giovanni Maria del Monte, was elected pope, assuming the name Julius III. He called Palestrina to Rome and became his most powerful patron. The composer dedicated his first book of masses (1554) to him.

Palestrina's musical positions included *maestro* of the Cappella Guilia of St. Peter's, Rome; *maestro* of the Cappella Sistina, the pope's official musical chapel (in spite of his being married); and *maestro di cappella* of the great church, St. John Lateran. His compositions include 104 securely attributed masses, 375 motets, at least 65 hymns, 35 Magnificat settings, and more than 140 madrigals. He was buried in a chapel of St. Peter's. More detailed information may be found in musical reference works.

Composer: VICTORY (*O Lord of life, wherever they be*, **635**; *The strife is o'er*, **263**)

PALMER, RAY (b. Nov. 12, 1808, Little Compton, R.I.; d. Mar. 29, 1887, Newark, N.J.) attended Phillips Academy and Yale University, New Haven, Connecticut, from which he graduated in 1830. He ministered at Central Congregational Church in Bath, Maine (1835-1850), and First Congregational Church of Albany, New York. After retiring from ministry in 1865, Palmer served with distinction until 1878 as corresponding secretary for the American Congregational Union.

Author: *My faith looks up to thee*, **565**

PARKER, ALICE (b. Dec. 16, 1925, Boston, Mass.) earned a B.A. from Smith College, Northampton, Massachusetts, and an M.S. from the Juilliard School, New York City, with honorary doctorates from Hamilton College, Clinton, New York, and Macalester College, St. Paul, Minnesota. In 1982 she received the Smith College Medal for "filling countless lives with song." Parker arranged music for the Robert Shaw Chorale from 1948 to 1967; from 1951 to the present, she has composed, conducted, and led seminars. A church music clinician and teacher of choral arranging and composition, Parker has been associated with the Mennonite Church Center and Westminster Choir College, Princeton, New Jersey. With a special flair for arranging early American tunes, she has been awarded grants from the National Endowment for the Arts and ASCAP (American Society of Composers, Authors and Publishers), in addition to receiving numerous commissions for musical compositions.

Composer: APPLE TREE (*The tree of life*), **509**; MAGDEBURG (*I cannot dance, O Love*), **45**; *Grace to you and peace*, **24**. Arranger: AWEFUL MAJESTY (*How wondrous great*), **126**; BEAUTIFUL FLOWER (*O little children, gather*), **489**; DETROIT (*Forgive our sins as we forgive*), **137**; HANTS (*Give to the winds thy fears*), **561**; O SANCTISSIMA (*Oh, how joyfully*), **209**; O WALY WALY (*When love is found*), **623**; SHOUT ON, PRAY ON (*I know that my Redeemer lives*), **277**; STAR IN THE EAST (*Hail the bless'd morn*), **221**; VRUECHTEN (*This joyful Eastertide*), **276**;

WONDROUS LOVE (*What wondrous love is this*), **530**. Translator: *O little children, gather*, **489**

PARKER, EDWIN POND (b. Jan. 13, 1836, Castine, Maine; d. May 28, 1925, Hartford, Conn.) attended Bowdoin College, Brunswick and Bangor Theological Seminary (both in Maine). He was pastor of Center Church (Congregational) of Hartford for fifty years. Also a musician, Parker composed and arranged many tunes. He wrote at least two hundred hymns after his fifty-sixth birthday and was editor or compiler of a number of hymnals.

Arranger: MERCY (*Holy Spirit, Truth divine*), **508**

PARRY, CHARLES HUBERT HASTINGS (b. Feb. 27, 1848, Bournemouth, England; d. Oct. 7, 1918, King's Croft, Rustington, England), whose father was a decorative artist, was educated at Eton College and at Exeter College, Oxford. He passed the examination for a B.Mus. at Oxford while still a student at Eton. Because his father opposed a musical career, Parry became a businessman with Lloyd's of London, but after three years he turned again to his music. In 1883 he became professor of composition and lecturer in music history at the Royal College of Music, London. Eleven years later he was its director, a position he held until his death.

A man of broad interests and talents (amateur scientist, diarist, drama critic, yachtsman, expert in many games), Parry was a master writer on musical subjects and a prolific composer in most musical media. His largest body of composition is in the area of church music and choral works, both unaccompanied and with orchestra.

Composer: INTERCESSOR (*By gracious powers*), **552**; JERUSALEM (*O day of peace*), **408**; REPTON (*He comes to us as one unknown*, **498**; *How clear is our vocation, Lord*, **541**)

PARRY, JOSEPH (b. May 21, 1841, Merthyr Tydfil, Glamorganshire, Wales; d. Feb. 17, 1903, Cartref, Penarth, Wales) was born into a poor family; he was working in the local iron foundry by age ten. In 1854 the family immigrated to the U.S. and settled in Danville, Pennsylvania. Parry's music study began in a class organized by fellow Welsh ironworkers. Encouraged by his mother, he attended a music school in Geneseo, New York, during the summer of 1861. Returning to Wales, he won prizes at several Eisteddfod contests: Swansea (1863), Llandudno (1864), and Chester (1866). So impressed were the members of the Eisteddfod Council that they raised funds to finance his study at the Royal Academy of Music (1868-1871). There he studied composition with William S. Bennett and voice with Manuel Garcia. He received both the B.Mus. and D.Mus. from Cambridge University in 1871 and 1878, respectively.

For a brief time (1871-1873), Parry returned to Danville where he conducted a private music school. Upon his return to Wales, he became professor of music at the universities in Aberystwyth (1873-1879) and Cardiff (1888-1903). In 1896 he was awarded 600 pounds by the Welsh Eisteddfod in recognition of his great service to Welsh music. Parry wrote operas, cantatas, oratorios and other choral works, some instrumental music, and more than four hundred hymn tunes.

Composer: ABERYSTWYTH (*Jesus, lover of my soul*), **618**

PATRICK, SAINT (see ST. PATRICK)

PAYNE, ERNEST ALEXANDER (b. Feb. 19, 1902, London, England; d. Jan. 14, 1980) was an English Baptist minister, ordained in 1928. A leader in wider Baptist circles, he was vice-president of the Baptist World Alliance from 1965 to 1970. From 1968 to 1975, he served as president of the World Council of Churches.

Translator: *Our Father God, thy name we praise*, **32**

PEACE, ALBERT LISTER (b. Jan. 26, 1844, Huddersfield, England; d. Mar. 14, 1912, Liverpool, England), a child prodigy, became organist of the parish church of Holmfirth, Yorkshire, at age nine. Educated at Oxford University (B.Mus. 1870; D.Mus. 1875), he made a career of playing the organ, serving a number of churches before settling at Glasgow Cathedral (1879-1897) and St. George's Hall in Liverpool (from 1897 until his death).

In 1865, the Church of Scotland withdrew its ban on the use of organs in public worship. This gave Peace many opportunities to play opening recitals on new organs in Scotland. Besides being a music editor of *The Scottish Hymnal* (1885), *Psalms and Paraphrases with Tunes* (1886), and *The Scottish Anthem Book* (1891), he published cantatas, service music, organ pieces, and hymn tunes.

Composer: ST. MARGARET (*O Love that will not let me go*), **577**

PEACEY, J. R. (JOHN RAPHAEL) (b. July 16, 1896, Hove, Sussex, England; d. Oct. 31, 1971, Brighton, Sussex, England) was the youngest of ten children, whose mother died when he was two and whose father was a bishop in the Church of England. After serving in the British army in World War I, Peacey studied theology at Selwyn College, Cambridge, graduating with honors in 1921.

His career in ministry took him to Wellington College as assistant master; to Selwyn College, Cambridge, as chaplain; and to India where he headed Bishop Cotton School in Simla and Bishop's College in Calcutta. In 1945, at the close of World War II, Peacey returned to England with his family, settling in Bristol where he was appointed canon of the Cathedral (1945-1966).

Peacey retired in 1967 to the Brighton area; it was only then that he took up hymnwriting. In the four years before his death, he completed eighteen texts, five of which were published in *100 Hymns for Today* (1969), a supplement to *Hymns Ancient and Modern*. Since then, his hymns have been included in several supplements and denominational hymnals. Many of Peacey's hymns not previously published are in *Go Forth for God* (1991), an anthology published by Hope Publishing Company on the twentieth anniversary of his death.

Author: *Awake, awake, fling off the night*, **448**; *Filled with the Spirit's power*, **289**

PEACHEY, JANET (b. 1953, Zürich, Switzerland) grew up in Washington, D.C., attending First Mennonite Church of Hyattsville, Maryland. At the time of her birth, her father was doing dissertation research in Switzerland on the Anabaptists of the sixteenth century. She received a B.Mus. in composition from Catholic University of America in 1976. The next two years she was a Fulbright scholar in composition and conducting in Vienna, Austria. While there, she conducted performances of her orchestral works: *Sinfonietta* (1981) and *The Temptation of Jesus in the Wilderness* (1983). She also performed her *Piano Sonata* in a broadcast on Austrian radio in 1981.

Now a resident of Washington, D.C., Peachey chairs the music theory department at Duke Ellington School of the Arts and Washington Conservatory of Music and also teaches composition at the American University Preparatory Division.

Composer: MOTHERING GOD (*Mothering God, you gave me birth*), **482**

PEARSALL, ROBERT L. (b. Mar. 14, 1795, Clifton, Gloucestershire, England; d. Aug. 5, 1856, Wartensee, Lake Constance, near Rohrschach, Germany) came from an ancient Gloucestershire family. He was educated at home and at Lincoln's Inn for a career in law, which he practiced only four years. Blessed with an innate musical ability, Pearsall produced a cantata, *Saul and the Witch of Endor*, when he was just thirteen.

After suffering a slight stroke in 1825, Pearsall moved to Mainz where he started serious study of music with Joseph Panny. In 1830 he moved to Karlsruhe, living there for thirteen years, continuing his music study and indulging his interest in archaeology as well. In 1843 he purchased the castle of Wartensee, overlooking Lake Constance, and lived there until his death.

Pearsall kept contact with friends in England, but he was more influenced by the German music of his day than English. Nestled in the heart of Catholic Germany, he also turned to Roman Catholicism and called himself de Pearsall. He composed madrigals, part-songs, hymns, psalm settings, anthems, and music for Roman Catholic and Anglican liturgies. Some of his letters on sacred music were edited for *The Musical Quarterly* and *The Musical Times*.

Arranger: IN DULCI JUBILO (*Good Christian friends, rejoice*), **210**

PENNEFATHER, WILLIAM (b. Feb. 5, 1816, Dublin, Ireland; d. Apr. 30, 1873, London, England), born of titled parents, was educated at Westbury College, near Bristol, and Trinity College, Dublin. He was ordained in 1841, served Anglican churches in Ireland, and moved to England where he later founded the Mildmay Religious and Benevolent Institution. This was a center for religious work in East London at Barnet, and later at Mildmay, where Pennefather introduced an order of deaconesses. His hymn texts, only a few of which bear dates, were written mainly for the Barnet and Mildmay Conferences and were first published in leaflets. His pamphlet *Hymns Original and Selected* appeared in 1872 and contains twenty-five of his texts. Of Pennefather's hymns, Julian has written that they "possess much beauty and earnest simplicity" (Julian 1907).

Author: *Jesus, stand among us,* **25**

PERRONET, EDWARD (b. 1726, Sundridge, Kent, England; d. Jan. 2, 1792, Canterbury, England), a descendant of French Huguenots from Switzerland, studied for the ministry in the Church of England. After becoming disenchanted with the established church, he associated with the Wesleys and Methodism. But when John Wesley insisted that Methodist ministers should send their parishioners to local Anglican congregations for the Lord's Supper, Perronet claimed the right to administer the elements himself. He aroused Wesley's ire as well with his satire on the established church, *The Mitre*.

Perronet left to become the minister of an independent church in Canterbury where he remained for the rest of his life. He was the author of many hymns and poems, most of which were published anonymously.

Author: *All hail the power of Jesus' name,* **106, 285**

PERRY, MICHAEL ARNOLD (b. Mar. 8, 1942, Beckenham, Kent, England) was educated at Ridley Hall, Cambridge; London University (B.D., 1964); and Southampton University (M.Phil., 1974). Ordained to the ministry in the Church of England in 1965, he has served parishes in St. Helen's; Southampton; and Eversley, Hampshire. Many of his hymn texts appear in *Hymns for Today's Church* (1982), for which he served as a member of the editorial committee. Other hymnals he helped edit include *Psalm Praise* (1973), *Carols for Today* (1986), and *Psalms for Today* (1990). He has organized many hymn festivals in England, and, through his work with the publishing company Jubilate Hymns, Ltd., he has formed a network of writers who support and encourage one another.

Author: *Bless'd be the God of Israel*, **174**; *From time beyond my memory*, **484**

PETTMAN, CHARLES EDGAR (b. Apr. 20, 1866, Dunkirk, Kent, England; d. 1943, London, England) was an organist in London, a composer, and an editor. His special interest was in old French and Spanish carols, many of which he arranged for the early volumes of *The University Carol Book*.

Composer: LOVE INCARNATE (*Love came down at Christmas*), **208**

PIERPOINT, FOLLIOTT SANDFORD (b. Oct. 7, 1835, Bath, England; d. Mar. 10, 1917, Newport, England) was educated at Queen's College, Cambridge University. After his graduation in 1857, he was master of the classics at Somersetshire College for a time. He resided in Babbicombe, Devonshire, and other locations, occasionally teaching the classics. Pierpoint published several volumes of verse and was a contributor to *Lyra Eucharistica* (a collection of hymns for Communion) and Neale's *The Hymnal Noted*.

Author: *For the beauty of the earth*, **89**

PILCHER, CHARLES VENN (b. June 4, 1879, Oxford, England; d. July 4, 1961, Sydney, Australia) was educated at Charterhouse School (1892-1898) and received degrees from Hertford College, Oxford (B.A., 1902; M.A., 1905; B.D., 1909; and D.D., 1921). Ordained in the Church of England in 1903, he was curate of St. Thomas's, Birmingham, until 1905 when he was named chaplain to the bishop of Durham. In 1906 Pilcher moved to Canada where he taught Greek, Old Testament literature, and New Testament language and literature at Wycliffe College, Toronto, Ontario, over the course of three decades. During this period he also served several churches as minister and song leader. A skilled musician, he played the bass clarinet in the Toronto Symphony Orchestra for ten years.

In 1936 Pilcher was consecrated bishop of Sydney, Australia, and served in that office for twenty years. Also an outstanding Icelandic scholar, he translated *Passion Hymns of Iceland* (1913), *Icelandic Meditations on the Passion* (1923), and *Icelandic Christian Classics* (1950). He contributed several hymn translations and tunes to the *Canadian Book of Common Praise* (1938) and was secretary to the committee that prepared an Australian *Supplement to the Book of Common Praise*. Pilcher contributed thirteen hymns and fourteen tunes to that supplement.

Translator: *Before the cock crew twice*, **243**

PJETURSSON, HALLGRIM (b. 1614, Holar, Iceland; d. 1674, Sourby, Iceland) was the son of a bell-ringer at the cathedral. He was sent to Copenhagen to apprentice to a blacksmith. There, Pjetursson was chosen to re-instruct a group of refugees in the faith. Among these thirty-four people, who had been taken captive and sold into slavery in Algiers, Algeria, was Gudred, a woman sixteen years his senior. Although her husband was still living, she and Pjetursson fell in love, returned to Iceland together, and, after her husband's death, were married. The Lutheran Church acknowledged his penitence, and he was ordained. It was during his pastorate at Sourby on the Whalefirth that Pjetursson began writing his fifty hymns on the Passion of Christ. He died of leprosy in 1674 (Milgate 1982).

Author: *Before the cock crew twice*, **243**

POLACK, WILLIAM GUSTAVE (b. Dec. 7, 1890, Wausau, Wis.; d. June 5, 1950, St. Louis, Mo.), writer, editor, administrator, and theologian, was educated at Concordia College, Fort Wayne, Indiana, and Concordia Seminary, St. Louis, Missouri. Ordained in 1914, he succeeded C. A. Franck, first editor of the *Lutheran Witness*, as pastor of Trinity Lutheran Church, Evansville, Indiana. In 1925 Polack became professor of theology at Concordia Seminary, later chairing the department of historical theology there.

In 1929 Polack was named chair of the Missouri Synod Lutheran Committee on Hymnology and Liturgics and organized the intersynodical committee that prepared *The Lutheran Hymnal* (1941). Three of his hymn texts and nine translations are included in that collection. His *Handbook to the Lutheran Hymnal* (1942; rev., 1947, 1958) is still a valuable hymnological tool. He was also on the editorial staff of the *Lutheran Witness* (1925-1950) and the *Concordia Junior Messenger* (1928-1939). His other publications include books of poetry, collections of hymns, and works on church history. He was honored with the D.D. by Valparaiso University (Ind.) in 1942.

Translator: *Christ is arisen*, **271**

POLLARD, ADELAIDE ADDISON (b. Nov. 27, 1862, Bloomfield, Iowa; d. Dec. 20, 1934, New York, N.Y.), born Sarah Addison Pollard, chose the name Adelaide. She was educated in Denmark, Iowa, and Indiana, and at the Boston School of Oratory (Mass.). In the 1880s she lived in Chicago where she taught public speaking in several girls' schools. She became well known as a traveling Bible teacher and taught for eight years at the Missionary Training School in New York City (Christian and Missionary Alliance).

Finally fulfilling a lifelong dream to be a missionary, Pollard spent a few months in mission work in Africa prior to the outbreak of World War I; during the war years, she was transferred to Scotland. Although she was in poor health most of her life, she continued her speaking engagements until she was seventy-two. She wrote a number of hymns, but only this one survives.

Author: *Have thine own way*, **504**

POSTLETHWAITE, R. DEANE (b. Mar. 16, 1925, Concordia, Kan.; d. Oct. 7, 1980, Annandale, Minn.) was a graduate of the University of Kansas, Lawrence (B.A., 1947; M.A., 1948); Union Theological Seminary (M.Div., 1956); and the United Theological Seminary of the Twin Cities, New Brighton, Minnesota (D.Min., 1979). After a three-year stint teaching political science at Baker University in Baldwin City, Kansas, he was ordained as a Methodist deacon (1956) and elder (1958) and pastored churches in Kansas, New York, and Minnesota. His last pastorate was at Minnehaha United Methodist Church in Minneapolis where he served from 1972 until his death. Postlethwaite's hymns, written from his pastor/poet perspective, intertwine daily life with worship.

Author: *The care the eagle gives her young*, **590**

POTT, FRANCIS (b. Dec. 29, 1832, Southwark, England; d. Oct. 26, 1909, Speldhurst, England) was educated at Brasenose College, Oxford (B.A., 1854; M.A., 1857). Ordained in 1856, he was a curate until becoming rector at Norhill, Ely, in 1866. Deafness forced his resignation in 1891, after which he turned to research and translation of Latin and Syriac hymns. His interest in musical chant is revealed in his collection *Hymns fitted to the Order of Common Prayer, and Administration of the Sacraments and other Rites and Ceremonies of the Church, according to the Use of the Church of England, To which are added Hymns for Certain Local Festivals* (1861), which was reprinted several times. Pott assisted in preparing the original edition of the important hymnal *Hymns Ancient and Modern* (1861).

Translator: *The strife is o'er*, **263**

PRAETORIUS, MICHAEL (b. Feb. 15, 1571, Creuzburg, Thüringen, Germany; d. Feb. 15, 1621, Wolfenbüttel, Germany) began his career as *Kapellmeister* at Lüneburg. In 1604 he became organist for the duke of Brunswick at Wolfenbüttel, later becoming his *Kapellmeister* and private secretary. A prolific and distinguished composer, Praetorius was a leading innovator in the new instrumental concertate style (antiphonally grouped instruments) at the beginning of the seventeenth century. His music encyclopedia *Syntagma Musicum*, a sort of performance guide for church musicians, became a foremost description of early baroque musical practice.

In his many sacred and secular works, Praetorius made use of every development in harmony and polyphony up to his time. His *Musae Sioniae* (The Muses of Zion) comprises nine volumes of sacred music published from 1605 to 1616. Volumes VI, VII, and VIII are devoted entirely to congregational hymns in simple four-voice harmony. He died on his fiftieth birthday.

Arranger: ES IST EIN ROS' (*Lo, how a Rose e'er blooming*), **211**

PREISWERK, SAMUEL (b. Sept. 19, 1799, Rümlingen, Switzerland; d. Jan. 13, 1871, Basel, Switzerland) studied at the Universities of Basel and Erlangen. He was appointed a curate at Benken and preached at the Basel Orphanage. In 1829 he tutored in Hebrew at the Basel Mission House and from 1830 to 1832 served a pastorate at Muttenz. For the next three years, he taught at the Evangelical Theological Institute in Geneva, then returned to Basel, first as deacon (1840) and later as pastor (1843) at St. Leonhardt Church. He accepted the chair of Hebrew and Old Testament exegesis at the University of Basel in 1845. Preiswerk's preaching, writing, and scholarship brought him recognition and leadership of the Swiss Reformed Church. In 1859 he was made superintendent of Basel, the highest dignitary at the cathedral. Sixteen of his hymns appear in *Evangelischer Liederkranz* (1844) and nine in Knapp's *Evangelischer Liederschatz* (1850).

Author: *The work is thine, O Christ*, **396**

PRICE, FRANK W. (b. 1895, China; d. 1974) was a missionary to China for thirty years. In 1952 he returned to the U.S. after three years of detention imposed by the new Communist regime. He worked at Union Theological Seminary, New York City, as director of the Missionary Research Library until 1961, after which he lived in Lexington, Virginia. Price translated twenty-three hymns from the Chinese hymnal *Hymns of Universal Praise* (1936) and published them separately in the booklet *Chinese Christian Hymns* (1953).

Translator: *Fount of love, our Savior God*, **354**; *O Bread of life, for sinners broken*, **468**

PRICHARD, ROWLAND HUGH (b. Jan. 14, 1811, Graienyn, near Bala, North Wales; d. Jan. 25, 1887, Holywell, Wales), grandson of the bard Rowland Huw Prichard, was a textile worker. He lived most of his life in Bala where he was a precentor (music director) and composer of tunes that found their way into Welsh periodicals. He was just twenty when he composed the ever popular HYFRYDOL. In 1844 he published *Cyfaill y Cantorion* (The Singer's Friend), which includes most of his tunes. In 1880 he moved to Holywell where he worked for the Welsh Flannel Manufacturing Company as an assistant loom tender.

Composer: HYFRYDOL (*Come, thou long-expected Jesus*, **178**; *God the Spirit, Guide and Guardian*, **632**; *God, whose giving*, **383**; *Hear us now, O God our Maker*, **626**)

PROULX, RICHARD (b. 1937, St. Paul, Minn.), already composing at age eight, received his musical training at the McPhale College of Music and the University of Minnesota. He has studied organ with Arthur Jennings and Rupert Sircom; composition with Theodore Ganshaw and Gerald Bales; and choral conducting with Robert Shaw and Roger Wagner—and at the Columbus Boychoir School in Princeton, New Jersey.

As a composer, Proulx (pronounced "pru") has written more than 250 works, ranging from piano, solo voice, chorus, organ, and orchestra to television commercials, documentary films, and two operas: *The Pilgrim* (1978) and *Beggars Christmas*.

Proulx is as ecumenical in his church work as he is in his musical endeavors. He was in demand as an editorial consultant for recent hymnals put out by the Episcopalians, the Methodists, and the Catholics, and has served both Episcopal and Roman Catholic parishes in Minnesota and Washington. He was a founding member of the Conference of Roman Catholic Cathedral Musicians and also served twelve years as a member of the Standing Commission on Church Music of the Episcopal Church. Since 1980 he has been organist/director of music at the Cathedral of the Holy Name in Chicago where he has firmly established the cathedral as an influential presence in the musical life of the city.

Arranger: JERUSALEM (*O day of peace*), **408**; KONTAKION (*Oh, blessed are the poor in spirit*), **231**. Composer: *Amen,* **643**

PRUDENTIUS, (MARCUS) AURELIUS CLEMENS (b. 348, northern Spain; d. ca. 410) practiced law and served in several judicial positions before becoming a monk at age fifty-seven. His decision to enter the monastery was motivated in part by his desire to atone for the "worldly" exploits of his younger years. He devoted himself to writing religious poetry and theology. His hymns rank with those of Ambrose for artistry and theological integrity.

A gifted poet, Prudentius wrote at a time when Christianity was under attack in Spain; it was thought to be an anti-intellectual, backward, and uncultured religion. This social condition stimulated Prudentius to produce his best work. He wrote hymns, which were didactic in nature, primarily for devotional purposes, usually one hundred lines or more in length, in various classical meters. None of his hymns has come through the centuries of common use in complete form. Selected lines and stanzas were used in breviaries (books for daily prayer) in Spanish, Roman, and British monastic communities. His *Cathemerinon* (Christian Day) contains twelve hymns for the hours of the day; *Peristephanon* (Crowns of the Martyrs) contains fourteen hymns. These two hymn collections and *Psychomachia* (The Spiritual Combat) were widely read during the Middle Ages.

Prudentius apparently spent time in Rome in 405. Where he died is unknown. Most sources set his death around 410 or 413.

Author: *Of the Father's love begotten*, **104**

PULKINGHAM, BETTY CARR (b. 1928, Burlington, N.C.) received a B.S. in music, *magna cum laude*, from the University of North Carolina, Greensboro, in 1949, and did graduate studies in music theory at the Eastman School of Music in Rochester, New York. Her professional career includes four years as instructor in the School of Fine Arts at the University of Texas, Austin; choral music direction at Austin High School; continuous periods of private piano training and direction of church choirs; and the composition and arranging of hymns, anthems, mass settings, and psalm settings. She is also a founding member of Community of Celebration, Aliquippa, Pennsylvania.

Since 1975 Pulkingham has been researching and developing resources for Christian worship and nurture. In this capacity she has co-edited four songbooks (*Sound of Living Waters, Fresh Sounds, Cry Hosanna,* and *Come Celebrate*); authored two books (*Little Things in the Hands of a Big God* and *Sing God a Simple Song*); and helped produce more than forty recordings for Community of Celebration. Pulkingham is particularly successful in blending traditional, classical musicianship with the folk arts in a manner that draws congregations into a profound and lively experience of worship.

Arranger: THE SERVANT SONG (*Will you let me be your servant*), **307**

PURDAY, CHARLES HENRY (b. Jan. 11, 1799, Folkestone, Kent, England; d. Apr. 23, 1885, London, England) had a varied musical career as a vocalist (he sang at the coronation of Queen Victoria), teacher, lecturer, conductor, and publisher. He was a reformer in music copyright laws and authored *Copyright, a Sketch of Its Rise and Progress* (1877). Purday was for many years precentor (music director) at Scottish Church in Westminster, London. He published *The Sacred Musical Offering* (1833), *A Few Directions for Chanting* (1855), and *A Church and Home Tune Book* (1857). He also composed many popular songs and contributed to the first edition of Grove's *Dictionary of Music and Musicians* (1878-1879).

Composer: SANDON (*God of our life*), **486**

RAHUSEN, REINHARD (b. Aug. 23, 1735, Hamburg, Germany; d. Mar. 8, 1793) studied at the University of Leiden. An exceptionally successful preacher and pastor, he served Mennonite congregations in northern

Holland and Germany: Enkhuizen (1760-1763), Leer (1763-1785), and Hamburg (1785-1793). He was also a prolific writer in both Dutch and German; his publications include sermons and smaller catechetical and devotional works.

Author: Blessed are you, O God. You made bread, **785**

RANKIN, JEREMIAH EAMES (b. Jan. 2, 1828, Thornton, N.H.; d. Nov. 28, 1904, Cleveland, Ohio) studied at Middlebury College (Vt.) and Andover Theological Seminary (Mass.), from which he graduated in 1854. In 1855 he was ordained in the Congregational Church and held prominent pastorates in New York, Vermont, Massachusetts, New Jersey, and Washington, D.C., where he was pastor of First Congregational Church for fifteen years. An arresting speaker with a deeply resonant voice, Rankin was later president of Howard University, Washington, D.C., beginning in 1899. He published many gospel songbooks, including *Gospel Temperance Hymnal* (1878); *Gospel Bells* (1880); and *German-English Lyrics, Sacred and Secular* (1897).

Author: *God be with you*, **430, 431**

REDHEAD, RICHARD (b. Mar. 1, 1820, Harrow, Middlesex, England; d. Apr. 27, 1901, Hellingly, Sussex, England), a career organist and choir director, was educated at Magdalene College, Oxford University, where he received a B.Mus. in 1871. In 1839 he became organist of Margaret Street Chapel, London, where he conducted daily choral services. Redhead continued in this post in the newly erected All Saints' Church, also on Margaret Street, from 1859 to 1864. At that time he went to St. Mary Magdalene Church, Paddington, where he served for thirty years. A number of his musical compositions were published, including at least eighty hymn tunes. As an Oxford-movement sympathizer and co-editor (with Frederick Oakeley) of the plainsong hymnal *Laudes Diurnae* (1843), he became a leader in the revival of Gregorian music.

Composer: REDHEAD NO. 76 (GETHSEMANE) (*Go to dark Gethsemane*, **240**; *Gracious Spirit, dwell with me*, **507**). Arranger: ORIENTIS PARTIBUS (*Christian, do you hear the Lord?*, **494**; *Lord, should rising whirlwinds*, **92**)

REDNER, LEWIS HENRY (b. December 1830 or 1831,[1] Philadelphia, Pa.; d. Aug. 29, 1908, Atlantic City, N.J.) started selling real estate while he was in his teens and later established his own firm. Besides running a very successful business, he was organist and superintendent of the Sunday school at Holy Trinity Episcopal Church. Under his nineteen-year tenure, church school attendance swelled from thirty-six to more than a thousand. His rector, Phillips Brooks, destined to become a magnetic preacher in Boston, collaborated with him to produce "O little town of Bethlehem" for a children's Christmas program.

Composer: ST. LOUIS (*O little town of Bethlehem*), **191**

1. His birth dates are given in different sources as either December 15, 1830, or December 14, 1831.

REED, ANDREW (b. Nov. 27, 1787, London, England; d. Feb. 25, 1862, London) was the son of a watchmaker and Congregational lay preacher. He was educated at Hackney College and ordained in the Congregational ministry in 1811. This same year he became pastor of New Road Chapel, St. George's-in-the-East, London, a tenure lasting until 1861. Under his leadership the church grew out of its building and into the new Wycliffe Chapel, built in 1831. During a visit to North American churches in 1834, Reed was awarded the D.D. by Yale University, New Haven, Connecticut. He also helped found the London Orphan Asylum, the Asylum for Fatherless Children, the Asylum for Idiots, the Infant Orphan Asylum, and the Hospital for Incurables.

His *Hymn Book* (1817; enlarged ed., 1825), which includes twenty-one of his own hymns, was a supplement to Watts's *Psalms and Hymns*. These collections were superseded by Reed's *Hymn Book prepared from Dr. Watts's Psalms and Hymns and Other Authors, with some Originals* (1842). The hymns by Reed, plus twenty by his wife, appear in the *Wycliffe Chapel Supplement* (1872).

Though Reed left behind a number of hymnbooks, he could not be persuaded to write an autobiography. "I was born yesterday," he said, "I shall die tomorrow, and I must not spend today telling what I have done, but in doing what I may for him who has done all for me" (McKim 1993).

Author: *Spirit divine, inspire our prayers*, **30**

REED, EDITH MARGARET GELLIBRAND (b. Mar. 31, 1885, Islington, Middlesex, London, England; d. June 4, 1933, Barnet, Herefordshire, England) was educated at St. Leonard's School, St. Andrew's; the Guildhall School of Music; and the Royal College of Organists where she was an associate. She provided editorial help to Percy Scholes in publishing *The Music Student* and *Music and Youth* (also called *Piano Student*). From 1923 to 1926, she edited *Panpipes*, a music magazine for children. Reed wrote two mystery plays for Christmas and *Story Lives of the Great Composers*.

Translator: *Infant holy, Infant lowly*, **206**

REINAGLE, ALEXANDER ROBERT (b. Aug. 21, 1799, Brighton, England; d. Apr. 6, 1877, Kindlington, Oxford, England) belonged to a family of musicians. His grandfather was one of the king's trumpeters, his father was a fine cellist and organist, and his uncle was Alexander Reinagle, who settled in the U.S. as a conductor, composer, and teacher. Alexander Robert Reinagle was the organist of St. Peter's Church, East Oxford, from 1821 to 1853. Besides composing a number of sacred pieces, he also wrote and compiled instruction books for violin and cello. He published two collections of hymn tunes, one in 1836 and the other in 1840.

Composer: ST. PETER (*In Christ there is no East or West*), **306**

REMPEL, JOHN DONALD (b. Apr. 14, 1944, Waterloo, Ontario) earned a B.A. in history at the University of Waterloo in 1966 (he resided at Conrad Grebel College there) and went on to study at Associated Mennonite Biblical Seminaries, Elkhart, Indiana, where he received an M.Div. in 1974. A year of voluntary service followed seminary. In the early 1970s, he pursued theological studies for two years in West and East Berlin. In 1973 he returned to Conrad Grebel College where he served as lecturer, dean of students, and chaplain. During this period he spent a sabbatical year in the Philippines and completed a Th.D. (1987) at the University of Toronto. Since 1989 he has been the minister at Manhattan Mennonite Fellowship in New York City, adjunct assistant professor at Seminary of the East (Conservative Baptist), and Mennonite Central Committee's liaison officer at the United Nations. He is secretary of the New York City Council of Mennonite Churches and a member of the North American Academy of Liturgy. Rempel served on The Hymnal Project's Hymnal Council and its worship committee. Rempel has written extensively on worship, including *Planning Worship* (Herald Press 1992). Beginning with his active opposition to the Vietnam War, his concern about justice has informed his focus on worship.

Author: Speak to all the world of the Child, **755**; O God, you brooded over the water, **779**; All-powerful God, grant ____ the fullness, **780**; Lord Jesus, we have knelt before each other, **783**; Blessed are you, O God. You set aside, **790**; Maker of galaxies and planets, **792**; O God, Sovereign of the universe, **803**. Translator/Adapter: We declare anew our covenant, **775**; How can we discern our errors, O God?, **781**; Almighty, merciful, and loving Father, **787**. Translator: *Heilig, heilig, heilig* (*Holy, holy, holy*), **75**; Father, I have sinned against heaven, **693**; Blessed are you, O God. You made bread, **785**

REYNOLDS, WILLIAM MORTON (b. Mar. 4, 1812, Fayette County, Pa.; d. Sept. 15, 1876, Oak Park, Ill.), who was a college professor, college president, and priest, received his education at Jefferson College, Canonsburg, Pennsylvania, and from the theological seminary at Gettysburg (Pa.). After an academic career at Pennsylvania College (1833-1850); Capital University, Columbus, Ohio (1850-1853); and Illinois State

University, Normal (1857-1860), he was a priest in the Protestant Episcopal Church, serving congregations in Warsaw (1865-1871) and Oak Park (1872-1876), both in Illinois.

Reynolds was a translator and editor, and in 1851 he edited *Hymns, Original and Selected, for Public and Private Worship, in the Evangelical Lutheran Church.* He also founded a journal, *Evangelical Review.*

Translator: *Savior of the nations, come* (sts. 1-2), **173**

REZA, MARY FRANCES (20th c.) is a graduate of the University of New Mexico, Albuquerque, and also has studied at the University of Guadalajara, Mexico, and Catholic University, Washington, D.C. She is involved in Hispanic music and liturgy as a teacher, choir director, and composer. With her talent and dynamic personality, she has helped bring new life and depth to many bilingual parishes and Hispanic groups. She is director of the Office of Worship and Liturgical Music for the archdiocese of Santa Fe, New Mexico.

Translator: *Oyenos, mi Dios,* **358**

RICCIUTI, GAIL ANDERSON (b. Oct. 31, 1948, Longview, Wash.) earned degrees at the University of Puget Sound, Tacoma, Washington (B.A., 1970), and Princeton Theological Seminary (N.J.; M.Div., 1973) and received an honorary doctorate from Keuka College, Keuka Park, New York (1979). Since her ordination in 1973, she has served as pastor in three Presbyterian churches in Ohio and New York. Currently she is co-pastor of Downtown United Presbyterian Church in Rochester, New York. She also serves as adjunct faculty in homiletics at Colgate Rochester Divinity School.

Ricciuti has been active in church-wide and regional Presbyterian bodies and has been preacher for various conferences and theological institutes. In 1977 she was the first clergywoman and youngest person ever to preside at a General Assembly of the United Presbyterian Church (USA). In 1978 she represented the United Presbyterian Women at the 50th Anniversary Jubilee Celebration of Korean Presbyterian Women in Seoul and was the first woman to preach at a Sunday morning worship service in the Korean Presbyterian Church. From 1983 to 1990 she was chairperson of the Shalom Education Fund, an arm of the Presbyterian Peace Fellowship. In 1993 she was named to the Wall of Fame at the National Women's Hall of Fame, Seneca Falls, New York. She is co-author of *Birthings and Blessings: Liberation Worship for the Inclusive Church,* 2 vols. (Crossroad/Continuum Publishing Co., 1991, 1993).

Author: In company with your faithful people, **795** (last three lines)

RICHARD OF CHICHESTER (see ST. RICHARD OF CHICHESTER)

RIMBAULT, EDWARD FRANCIS (b. June 13, 1816, London, England; d. Sept. 26, 1876, London, England) studied music with his father, Stephen Francis Rimbault, William Crotch, and Samuel Wesley. He later earned a Ph.D. from Göttingen University in Germany. This distinguished organist, composer, author, and editor refused a professorship in music at Harvard University, Cambridge, Massachusetts, but received an honorary degree from there nonetheless, as well as from Stockholm and Göttingen. In addition to his own music and his editions of works prepared by earlier composers, he published several books, among them two volumes on the organ and a biography of J. S. Bach.

Arranger: RUTHERFORD (*O God, in restless living*), **557**

RINCKART (RINKART), MARTIN (b. Apr. 23, 1586, Eilenburg, Saxony, Germany; d. Dec. 8, 1649, Eilenburg), the son of a cooper (barrel maker), attended St. Thomas's School in Leipzig where J. S. Bach would later be organist and choirmaster. In 1602 Rinckart began his studies of theology at the University of Leipzig. Included among his many writings was a cycle of dramas on the Reformation, written to celebrate the centennial of that event in 1617. In 1610 Rinckart became an instructor in music and Latin at the Eisleben *Gymnasium* (high school), as well as cantor of St. Nicholas Church and later deacon at St. Anne's. After serving as pastor at Erdeborn, he became archdeacon in 1617 at Eilenburg where he remained for thirty-two years. Throughout the Thirty Years War, he ministered to the refugees who fled to that walled town. The overcrowded city succumbed to the plague in 1637, and thousands died, including his wife. Since he was the only clergyman remaining in the city, he conducted more than four thousand funerals that year, sometimes forty or fifty a day. Exhausted and prematurely aged, he died in 1649, the year after the peace treaty signing where his hymn was sung. He is remembered as one of the great German pietist writers whose unshakable faith was tested in intense suffering.

Author: *Now thank we all our God*, **85, 86**

RIPPON, JOHN (b. Apr. 29, 1751, Tiverton, Devon, England; d. Dec. 17, 1836, London, England) enjoyed great success as a Baptist minister and author of hymns. He prepared for ministry at the Baptist College of Bristol. In 1773 Rippon turned an interim pastorate at London's Baptist Church in Carter Lane into a tenure of sixty-three years, concluding only with his death in 1836. A specialist on the hymns of Isaac Watts, Rippon's most significant collections are the *Selection of Hymns from the Best Authors, Intended as an Appendix to Dr. Watts' Psalms and Hymns* (1787) and his *Selection of Psalms and Hymn Tunes from the Best Authors* (1791).

Reviser: *All hail the power of Jesus' name*, **106, 285**

RIST, JOHANN (b. Mar. 8, 1607, Ottensen, near Hamburg, Germany; d. Aug. 31, 1667, Wedel, Germany), a clergyman, poet, and musician whose gifts were evident in boyhood, began his schooling in Hamburg and Bremen. He was the son of a Lutheran pastor and seemingly destined for the ministry from his birth. He entered the University of Rinteln in 1626 and remained there only a short time, but his interest in hymnology was sparked by one of his theology professors, Josua Stegmann. While tutoring students at the University of Rostock, Rist studied Hebrew, mathematics, and medicine. In 1633 he became a tutor for the family of a lawyer at Heide in Holstein; there he met his future wife. They were married in 1635 and settled in Wedel, a small town on the Elbe near Hamburg where Rist was appointed pastor.

The Thirty Years War cost him his personal property, including his scientific and musical instruments, but he declined calls to pastor other parishes, choosing to stay in Wedel where he was also the congregation's physician and where he wrote poetry that gradually brought him recognition. He authored some 680 hymns and spiritual songs, covering the entire range of theology. Most of these hymns, intended for private devotions, were published in six collections between 1641 and 1656. At one time more than two hundred of his hymns were in common use in Germany; today, however, few appear in hymnals.

Rist also founded the Hamburg song school, for which he secured many of the finest song composers of the time. As a result he influenced the evolution of German song and the musical taste of the people. He was named poet laureate by Emperor Ferdinand III in 1644 and raised to the rank of nobility in 1653.

Author: *Break forth, O beauteous heavenly*, **203**

ROBINSON, PAUL MINNICH (b. Jan. 26, 1914, Denver, Colo.) grew up in Ohio and Pennsylvania, then went to Juniata College, Huntingdon, Pennsylvania, and Princeton Theological Seminary (N.J.). He was later awarded honorary doctorates by Juniata College and Bridgewater College (Va.). Robinson became a pastor in the Church of the Brethren, serving in the Ambler, Pennsylvania, and Hagerstown, Maryland, congregations, and was moderator of the 1956 Annual Conference of the Church of the Brethren, the highest elected office of the denomination. He also chaired the worship committee for *The Brethren Hymnal* (1951). An educator as well as a pastor, he was president of Bethany Biblical Seminary (now Bethany Theological Seminary in Richmond, Indiana) from 1953 to 1975. Upon retirement he returned to the pastorate at Crest Manor in South Bend, Indiana.

Author: *Here in our upper room*, **450**

ROBINSON, ROBERT (b. Sept. 27, 1735, Swaffham, Norfolk, England; d. June 9, 1790, Showell Green, Warwickshire, England) was apprenticed to a barber as a teenager. But after hearing the preaching of George Whitefield, he was converted to Christianity, studied for the ministry, and was ordained to serve Methodism. Robinson was a popular preacher, and in later life he was a pastor in churches of other denominations, including the Baptist Church. He also ran a farm for a time to support his very large family. During the last twenty years of his life, he wrote several books, including a history of the Baptists. He died "soft, suddenly, and alone," as was his wish (Stulken 1981).

Author: *Come, thou fount*, **521**

ROOP, EUGENE F. (b. May 11, 1942, South Bend, Ind.) earned degrees at Manchester College, North Manchester, Indiana (B.S., 1964); Bethany Theological Seminary, Oak Brook, Illinois (M.Div., 1967); and Claremont Graduate School (Calif.; Ph.D., 1972). He also has studied at Harvard Divinity School, Cambridge, Massachusetts; Cambridge University (England); and the University of California at Santa Barbara. Although the Church of the Brethren congregations of his youth had a strong formative influence, Roop assumed that his work for the church would be in lay leadership. While in college, however, he was challenged by his home pastor in Fort Wayne, Indiana, to consider pastoral ministry as a vocation. Between 1963 and 1967, Roop held part-time or interim pastorates in Indiana, Maryland, and Pennsylvania; in 1967 he was ordained. His career took a turn toward academia in 1970 when he began teaching at Earlham School of Religion, Richmond, Indiana. Since 1977 he has been at Bethany Theological Seminary, first on the teaching faculty (in 1987 becoming the Wieand Professor of Biblical Studies), now as president. His pastoral ministry continues in numerous engagements to preach and conduct Bible study, both inside and outside the Church of the Brethren. In 1989 he was instructor of a travel seminar to the Middle East. He has been a member of many Church of the Brethren and ecumenical committees, as well as civic and professional organizations. While his many writings are mostly in the areas of biblical commentary, stewardship, and peace, Roop has contributed worship resources to Church of the Brethren and ecumenical publications. He has authored a book of prayers, *Heard in Our Land* (Brethren Press 1991).

Translator: Have mercy on me, O God, **818**

ROSAS, CARLOS (b. Nov. 4, 1939, Linares, Nuevo León, Mexico) is music director and liturgy coordinator at San Juan de los Lagos Catholic Church in San Antonio, Texas, a position he has held since 1970. After studying music and liturgy at a religious seminary in Monterrey, Mexico, and a stint as a hotel bellboy, he married and moved to San Antonio to practice what he had learned in the seminary.

Rosas continued his studies at the Instituto de Liturgia, Música y Arte Cardenal Dario Miranda in Mexico City; at San Antonio College; and at the Mexican American Cultural Center, San Antonio. At the latter he has served as music director, liturgy coordinator, and recruiter. He writes, leads workshops, and speaks on music and liturgy throughout the western United States. Rosas is an internationally known composer of religious Hispanic music. His works include: *Diez Canciones para la Misa* (Ten Songs for the Mass), *Misa a la Virgen de San Juan* (Mass of the Virgin of San Juan), and *Gracias Señor* (Thank You, Lord). His hymn *San Antonio y Roman Cantan* was sung for Pope John Paul II's visit to San Antonio in 1987.

Author/Composer: *Cantemos al Señor* (*Let's sing unto the Lord*) (ROSAS), **55**

ROSS, JIMMY R. (b. Aug. 8, 1935, Augusta County, Va.) grew up in the Church of the Brethren in the Shenandoah Valley of Virginia. The church was central in the life of his family (singing was especially important), and his home congregation had its beginnings on the front porch of their house. He earned degrees at Bridgewater College (Va.; B.A., 1959) and Bethany Theological Seminary, Oak Brook, Illinois (M.Div., 1970; D.Min., 1983). For his very early decision to become a pastor, Ross credits excellent pastoral leadership and strong support in his congregation and church district during his growing-up years. Ordained to Church of the Brethren ministry in 1957, he has been a pastor for almost forty years in or near the following towns: Stuarts Draft, Virginia; Hagerstown, Maryland; and Logansville and Lititz, Pennsylvania. He has served more than a decade at Lititz Church of the Brethren. Ross has also served his denomination as district conference moderator and as a speaker at Annual Conference. He was a member of the Hymnal Council and co-chair of its worship committee.

Author: We came to worship. We go now to serve, **763**

ROSSETTI, CHRISTINA GEORGINA (b. Dec. 5, 1830, London, England; d. Dec. 29, 1894, London) was the daughter of an Italian refugee who taught Italian at Kings College, London. Her grandfather published her first verses when she was twelve. She studied with her brother, the pre-Raphaelite poet and painter, Dante Gabriel Rossetti, "who chose her, because of the grave religious beauty of her features, to be the model of the Virgin in his Ecce Ancilla Domini" (*The Hymnal 1940 Companion*, 1951 ed.). For some time she assisted her mother in a small day school in North London.

The real events of her life were spiritual and emotional, surviving in her poetry. Under the thumb of her famous brother, Rosetti's writing may have been somewhat bleached out and objectified by his "determined revising, editing, and interpreting." Nonetheless, her later prose devotional writings were widely read, and she is the subject of a number of biographies.

Author: *Love came down at Christmas,* **208**

ROUTLEY, ERIK REGINALD (b. Oct. 31, 1917, Brighton, Sussex, England; d. Oct. 8, 1982, Nashville, Tenn.) is considered one of the foremost hymnologists of his time and a major influence on North American church musicians. He earned degrees at Lancing College, Sussex; Magdalen and Mansfield Colleges, Oxford; and Oxford University (B.A., 1940; M.A., 1943; B.D., 1946; Ph.D., 1952). His doctoral dissertation (1957) became a well-used book, *The Music of Christian Hymns* (1981). In 1943 Routley was ordained as a Congregational minister and pastored in England and Wales from 1943 to 1974. For a portion of this time, he was a lecturer in church history at Mansfield College, as well as its chaplain, director of music, and librarian.

After ten visits and lecture tours to the U.S., Routley moved permanently in 1975, settling in Princeton, New Jersey, where he was professor of church music and director of the chapel choir at Westminster Choir College. He immediately became a leader of national importance in the field of church music, authoring more than thirty-five books and hymn texts, composing numerous hymn tunes, and editing many hymnals. Perhaps his most unusual work is *Christian Hymns: An Introduction to Their Story* (1980), a six-hour cassette recording.

Routley was memorialized in Leaver and Litton's *Duty and Delight, Routley Remembered* where he was described as "a fine pianist and organist, given to frequent laughter, deeply committed to pastoral care, 'incandescently' swift as a typist, and 'perpetually awestruck'; devoting all his energy and skill . . . so that thanks to his testimony we might look past him and see what he had seen."

Author: *All who love and serve your city,* **417**

ROWAN, WILLIAM P. (b. Nov. 30, 1951, San Diego, Calif.) is a graduate of the University of Michigan, Ann Arbor, and Southern Illinois University, Carbondale. He has earned graduate degrees in organ and harpsichord performance, as well as an undergraduate degree (1973) in music history and piano performance. He has published more than thirty-five hymns, anthems, and organ works. His hymn settings have been sung at festivals throughout the U.S., Great Britain, and Europe and are included in a variety of recent hymnals.

Rowan has been director of music ministries at St. Cyril of Jerusalem Parish, Taylor, Michigan (1979-1986) and Holy Trinity Chapel, Eastern Michigan University, Ypsilanti (1986-1988). He presently directs music at

St. Mary Cathedral in Lansing, Michigan, and is liturgical music consultant for the diocese of Lansing. He is a founding member of the Huron Valley Chapter of the Hymn Society of America and is listed in the International *Who's Who in Music.*

Composer: MANY NAMES (*God of many names*), **77**

ROWLANDS, WILLIAM PENFRO (b. 1860, Maenclochog, Pembrokeshire, Wales; d. Oct. 22, 1937, Swansea, Glamorganshire, Wales), a schoolteacher and conductor of the Morriston United Choral Society, was considered among the finest musicians in South Wales. Later he served as precentor (music director) of Tabernacle Congregational Church in Morriston. He composed both anthems and hymn tunes.

Composer: BLAENWERN (*What a friend we have in Jesus*), **573**

ROWTHORN, JEFFERY WILLIAM (b. Apr. 9, 1934, Newport, Gwent, Wales), after his national service in the British Royal Navy, studied Russian, German, Persian, and Arabic at Cambridge University, England, where he received a B.A. and M.A. He later earned a B.Lit. from Oxford, and in 1961 he completed his M.Div. at Union Theological Seminary, New York City. Rowthorn further prepared for the ordained ministry at Cuddesdon Theological College, Oxford. Ordained in 1963, he pastored three years in Southeast London (1962-1965) and another three in Garsington, Oxford.

His academic career includes several "firsts." In 1968 he joined the faculty of Union Theological Seminary and became its first chaplain; then he went to Yale University, New Haven, Connecticut (1973), as a founding member of the Institute of Sacred Music. During his fourteen years at Yale, he was also the first chapel minister. Then he became the first holder of the Bishop Percy Goddard Chair (pastoral theology and worship) at Berkeley Divinity School (Calif.). In 1987 Berkeley conferred on him a D.Div. the same year he was consecrated as bishop of Connecticut.

Rowthorn has edited a hymnal supplement and co-edited, with Russell Schulz-Widmar, *A New Hymnal for Colleges and Schools* (Yale 1992). He also put out a two-volume collection of litanies (*The Wideness of God's Mercy*), has written hymns, and has lectured extensively in liturgics and hymnody. In 1988 Bishop Rowthorn became a U.S. citizen.

Author: *Creating God, your fingers trace*, **168, 325**

RUNYAN, WILLIAM MARION (b. Jan. 21, 1870, Marion, N.Y.; d. July 29, 1957, Pittsburg, Kan.) was already playing the organ for church services when he was twelve years old. The son of a Methodist minister, Runyan also was ordained and served as a pastor in several churches in Kansas, eventually becoming an evangelist for the Central Kansas Methodist Conference for two decades. Later, he was affiliated with John Brown University, Siloam Springs, Arkansas, and the Moody Bible Institute in Chicago. He also was an editor for the *Christian Workers' Magazine* and worked with Hope Publishing Company, a prominent church music firm. Runyan did not write his first gospel hymn until 1915 when he was forty-five. He retired in 1948, receiving an honorary doctorate from Wheaton College (Ill.) that same year.

Composer: FAITHFULNESS (*Great is thy faithfulness*), **327**

RUPP, ANNE NEUFELD (b. Mar. 5, 1932, near Boissevain, Manitoba), whose father was a pastor, studied at Canadian Mennonite Bible College, Winnipeg, Manitoba; the Royal Conservatory of Music, Toronto, Ontario; Bethel College, North Newton, Kansas; and Associated Mennonite Biblical Seminaries, Elkhart, Indiana. She primarily took various degrees in education and music. She taught school in Mexico and has been a piano teacher for many years. After marrying Kenneth Rupp in 1966, she and her husband served numerous Mennonite churches in Oklahoma, Nebraska, Indiana, and Kansas over the following two decades. She was ordained in 1976.

Throughout the years Rupp has spent considerable time writing and has had articles published in some twenty different periodicals. Since 1988 she has been employed at Meadowlark Homestead, a rehabilitation center for people with long-term mental illness. At Meadowlark she is coordinator of education and rehabilitation. She also has chaplaincy responsibilities in addition to directing a day program that includes curriculum writing and teaching.

Author: *Holy Spirit, come with power*, **26**; O God, our offerings proclaim, **749**

RUSBRIDGE, ARTHUR EWART (b. 1917, Reading, England; d. 1969) graduated from St. John's, Oxford, in 1939, and was a fellow of the Royal College of Organists. He taught for four years at Monmouth School before becoming director of music at Mill Hill School. He left that post in 1948 to become classics master and director of music at Bristol Grammar School. Rusbridge was a member of the music advisory committee for *The Baptist Hymn Book* (1962). That collection contains seven of his arrangements and his tune HORFIELD, named for the Baptist church where he served as choirmaster. He also was a contributor to *The Baptist Hymn Book Companion* and had a leading role in the development of the Baptist Music Society.

Arranger: W ŻŁOBIE LEŻY (*Infant holy, Infant lowly*), **206**

RUSSELL, ARTHUR TOZER (b. Mar. 20, 1806, Northampton, England; d. Nov. 18, 1874, Southwick, Brighton, England) was the son of a Congregational clergyman, educated at St. Saviour's School, Southwark; Merchant Taylors' School, London; and Manchester College, York (1822-1824). In 1825 he won the Hulsean Prize during his freshman year at St. John's College, Cambridge.

Ordained in 1829, Russell was curate of Great Gransden, Hunts; vicar of Caxton (1830-1852); Whaddon (1852-1866); St. Thomas's, Toxteth Park, Liverpool (1866-1867); Wrackwardine Wood, Shropshire (1867-1874); and Southwick, Brighton, where he died after a long illness.

Russell's study of St. Augustine's writings prompted him to turn from his high-church views to those of a moderate Calvinist. He was thus a critic of the Oxford movement and its attempt to reclaim the best of early Latin worship and its "high" liturgy. He wrote prolifically, including about 140 hymns, many of which appear in his *Hymns for Public Worship* (1848). His translations are considered as "on the whole . . . vigorous and strong" (Julian 1907).

Translator: *O Lamb of God all holy,* **146**; *Oh, how shall I receive thee,* **182**; *Let all together praise our God,* **213**

RYGH, GEORGE ALFRED TAYLOR (b. Mar. 21, 1860, Chicago, Ill.; d. July 16, 1942, Northfield, Minn.) graduated from Luther College, Decorah, Iowa (1881) and continued at Luther Seminary and Capital University, Columbus, Ohio. He successfully divided his career between ministry and teaching. Rygh held pastorates in Maine (1880-1889), North Dakota (1890-1891), Chicago (1899-1910), and Minneapolis, Minnesota (1920-1930). His teaching positions were at Wittenberg Academy (1889-1890); the University of North Dakota, Grand Forks (1891-1895); Mount Horeb, Wisconsin (1895-1898); and St. Olaf College, Northfield, Minnesota (1910-1913). After retirement Rygh lived in Northfield.

He was a productive editor and translator, providing translations for the *The Lutheran Hymnary* (1913) and editing the *American Lutheran Survey* and the *Lutheran Herald*. In recognition of his achievements, Rygh was awarded an honorary doctorate by Newberry College (S.C.) in 1917.

Translator: *All who believe and are baptized,* **436**

ST. AUGUSTINE (b. Nov. 13, 354, Tagaste, Numidia, North Africa; d. Aug. 28, 430, Hippo, North Africa), considered the greatest thinker among the Western church fathers, was born to a Christian mother and a pagan father; he was neither baptized nor received much Christian instruction as a child. In his youth he studied Latin literature and became interested in philosophy. During study at Carthage, he had a son by a mistress and became a proponent of the heretical Manichaeism. After teaching in Tagaste and Carthage for a total of ten years, he went to Rome and then to Milan, establishing schools at both places. Various influences led to his conversion to Christianity in 386. Along with his son, he was baptized the following year. Shortly thereafter he returned to Africa and devoted his life to service for God. In Tagaste he sold the estate inherited from his father and gave the money to the poor, keeping only a house which he turned into a monastery. He had not intended to become a priest, but in 391 he was ordained in the nearby city of Hippo, not a Christian stronghold. A few years later, he became bishop of Hippo. Augustine wrote extensively, setting forth philosophical and theological doctrines and defending the faith against heresy. See standard reference works for full accounts of his life and work.

Author: Come Lord, work upon us, **675**; Almighty God, in whom we live and move, **737**

ST. BASIL (b. ca. 329, Caesarea, Cappadocia [now Kayseri, Turkey]; d. Jan. 1, 379, Caesarea), one of the church fathers, was born into a distinguished family that had been Christian since the days of persecution. He received a literary education, studying at Caesarea, Constantinople, and Athens. Back home he began a secular career as a teacher of rhetoric. Sources differ on the order of the next two events in his life: his tour of the monasteries of Egypt and other Middle Eastern lands, and his establishment of a monastic settlement. Around 364 he was ordained as a priest to assist Eusebius, bishop of Caesarea; he succeeded Eusebius upon his death in 370. As bishop, Basil founded hospitals, homes for the poor, and hospices for travelers. He also became known for combating the heresy of Arianism, which denied that Jesus and the Father were one. His many writings—on monasticism, theology, and canon law—have been influential in Eastern Christianity and beyond. Tradition generally attributes to Basil a series of eucharistic prayers known as The Liturgy of St. Basil. This liturgy is still in use in the Eastern Church today.

Author (attrib.): Lord, our God, great, eternal, wonderful, **699**

ST. BERNARD OF CLAIRVAUX (b. ca. 1091, Les Fontaines, near Dijon, France; d. Aug. 20, 1153, Clairvaux, France) was the son of the knight Tecelin (or Tesselin) and is said to have inherited a deeply religious nature from his mother. He was educated at Chatillon and entered the Cistercian monastery at Citeaux around 1112. As an eminent spiritual leader with a magnetic personality, he was sent in 1115, at age twenty-four, to found the monastery of Clairvaux where he remained as abbot until his death. He was canonized in 1174.

Bernard had both political and religious influence; he kindled Europe to a second crusade (1146), which ended in disaster, and he effected the downfall of Peter of Abelard, the influential intellectual and theologian.

In addition to Bernard's political feats, he was an eloquent preacher and intense poet. His writing was characterized by mystic imagery and fervent piety. The authenticity of Bernard's hymns has been doubted, but Archbishop Trench, the great authority on Latin hymnody, expressed certainty that all hymns attributed to Bernard are authentic except *Cur mundus militat*. Of these hymns Trench writes: "They bear profoundly the stamp of his mind, being only inferior in beauty to his prose" (Julian 1907).

Author: *Jesus, the very thought of thee*, **588**

ST. FRANCIS OF ASSISI (b. ca. 1182, Assisi, Italy; d. Oct. 4, 1226, Assisi, Italy), perhaps the most venerated of the saints, established the monastic order of Franciscans. He was born wealthy, but after a serious illness, he single-mindedly dedicated his life to "Lady Poverty" and to Jesus Christ. He was banished from his family for selling off his father's warehouse inventory to raise funds to rebuild a church where he first heard the voice of Jesus.

St. Francis was a charismatic leader, attracting devoted followers by preaching throughout Italy of simplicity, repentance, and hope. His legendary love for nature and animals is beautifully expressed in "All creatures of our God and King."

Francis's singing and hymns, among the earliest metrical songs written in the Italian vernacular, were part of his itinerate mission. He is quoted as saying, "Is it not in fact true that the servants of God are really like jugglers, intended to revive the hearts of men and lead them into spiritual joy?" (Bailey 1950). See standard reference works for full accounts of his life and work.

Author: *All creatures of our God and King*, **48**; (Attrib.) Lord, make me an instrument, **733**

ST. JOHN CHRYSOSTOM (b. ca. 347, Antioch, Syria; d. Sept. 14, 407, Comana, Pontus [both sites in modern Turkey]), one of the church fathers, was born into a Christian family and, despite education for a career in law, chose the life of a hermit-monk. Poor health forced him to return to Antioch where he was ordained and served as a priest for twelve years, acquiring a reputation as a great preacher—hence his name Chrysostom, which means "golden mouth." In 398 he reluctantly became the archbishop of Constantinople. Concerned about social justice, he criticized the wealthy and, in so doing, angered them. In 403, in a conspiracy with the empress, the archbishop of the rival see of Alexandria called a synod that declared John deposed. The emperor banished John from the city, soon recalled him, and finally banished him permanently the next year. John died on a forced march from one place of confinement to another. Although his authorship is unsubstantiated, the most frequently used eucharistic service in the Eastern Orthodox Church is called The Liturgy of St. John Chrysostom.

Author (attrib.): Almighty God, you have given us grace, **728**

ST. JOHN OF DAMASCUS (b. ca. 675, Damascus, Syria; d. ca. 749) was born into wealth. His father was financial adviser to the caliph who built the "Dome of the Rock," the mosque erected over the ruins of Solomon's temple. He was educated primarily by Cosmas, an Italian monk who arrived in Damascus as a slave by way of a pirate ship.

John was a theologian and hymnwriter, one of the last early fathers of the Eastern Church. Spurning his inherited job with the caliph, he gave away all his possessions and went to live and work at the monastery of St. Sabas near Jerusalem. A powerful administrator and writer as well, he succeeded in salvaging Christian images and artwork in a time when they were suppressed on the grounds that pictures promoted idolatry. It was his contribution to hymnody, though, that paralleled that of Gregory I (Gregorian chant) in its influence of Eastern Orthodox liturgy. John of Damascus is remembered chiefly for his canons, which were then a very new form. A canon in Greek hymnody is a "series of odes, usually eight, sometimes nine, threaded on an acrostic" (Dearmer 1933). John's best-known work is the Easter canon or "Golden Canon."

Author: *Come, ye faithful, raise the strain,* **264, 265**

ST. PATRICK (b. ca. 389, near the lower Severn River, England; d. 461) acquired a Roman and Christian education. When he was about sixteen, he was abducted by Irish raiders and held captive the following six years in Ireland. During this time he was converted to Christianity and, upon his escape, entered the Church. In 432, he became the second missionary bishop to Ireland where he is credited with organizing the Irish church and was a zealous adversary of the still-prevalent Druid customs. His two important writings are *Confessions* and *Letter to Coroticus.* An exceptional biography on this Irish saint is *The Life of St. Patrick and His Place in History* by John B. Bury (1905).

Author: *Christ be with me,* **442**; *I bind unto myself today,* **441**

ST. RICHARD OF CHICHESTER (b. 1197, Droitwich, Worcester, England; d. 1253, Dover, England) was born Richard Wycke. He was educated at Oxford, Paris, and Bologna and appointed to a series of important posts in academia and the church, becoming chancellor of Oxford University in 1235 and chancellor of Canterbury in 1237. After further study at Orlean, he was consecrated bishop of Chichester in 1245, over the opposition of Henry III. Noted for his strict adherence to church discipline and defense of the church, Richard was canonized by Pope Urban IV in 1262.

Author: *Day by day, dear Lord,* **569**

ST. TERESA DE JESUS (see SANTA TERESA DE JESUS)

SAMMIS, JOHN H. (b. July 6, 1846, Brooklyn, N.Y.; d. June 12, 1919, Los Angeles, Calif.) at age twenty-three moved to Logansport, Indiana, where he was a businessman and an active Christian layman. Later he left his business to be a YMCA secretary. Subsequently, he felt called to the ministry and took theological training at Lane and McCormick Seminaries. In 1880 he was ordained in the Presbyterian Church, serving pastorates in Iowa, Indiana, Michigan, and Minnesota. In 1901 he moved to California where he was on the faculty of the Bible Institute of Los Angeles until his death.

Author: *When we walk with the Lord*, **544**

SANGLE, KRISHNARAO RATHNAJI (b. 1834, Ahmednagar, near Bombay, India; d. 1908), though raised in a Hindu family, received much of his early schooling from Christian missionaries. In spite of opposition from his family, he was baptized in 1860 and devoted the rest of his life to teaching and evangelism. He became headmaster of the Girls' School in Ahmednagar. Skilled in English and Sanskrit, Sangle was the author of more than one thousand hymns and poems. He was also a musician, a gardener, and an excellent weaver.

Author: *Heart and mind, possessions, Lord*, **392**

SANTA TERESA DE JESUS (b. Mar. 28, 1515, Avila, Spain; d. Oct. 4, 1582, Alba de Tormes, Spain) was the second of nine children born to Don Alonso Sanchez and his second wife, Beatriz Davila y Ahumada. Beatriz died when Teresa was thirteen years old. Teresa was a vain girl who had seen and tasted much of what life had to offer. At fifteen Teresa boarded at the Augustinian convent of St. Mary of Grace for eighteen months until she became ill and was taken to her sister's home. After she returned to her father's house about a year later, she announced her plans to return to the convent. Her father and other family members resisted, unable to imagine the fun-loving young woman living as a cloistered nun. Nonetheless, she entered the Carmelite Convent of the Incarnation in 1536 and made her profession in 1537.

The first twenty years of Teresa's stay in the convent were very difficult, physically as well as spiritually. She was ill for several years, even paralyzed at times. She also struggled to find a way of communicating deeply with God, certain that her difficulty meant she had not completely turned from the world. Her trials finally gave way to a life of prayer, both mental and mystical. Teresa's commitment to this prayer life of words, visions, and ecstasy led to a reform in the Carmelite order and, in 1562, a new convent at Avila—St. Joseph's. There, on the order of her confessor, she wrote three works: her autobiography (1565), *The Way of Perfection* (1566), and *The Interior Castle* (1577). She also produced a number of other smaller works during those years, most notably *Foun-*

dations (1576). She became good friends with John of the Cross, a Jesuit, and helped start other reformed Carmelite convents.

Teresa was not first and foremost a hymnwriter; rather, she wrote to nurture the prayer life of her nuns. Her writings, though, are filled with short prayers and exclamations of praise that are being set to music by the Taizé community in France. (For more information on Taizé, see "Alleluia," **101**.)

Canonized as a saint in 1622, Teresa is commemorated each year on October 15.

Author: *Nada te turbe*, **562**

SAPTAYAADI (b. ca. 1950, Java, Indonesia) graduated from Wiyata Wacana School of Theology in 1972. His wife, Darmini, also graduated from Wiyata Wacana, and the family lives in her home village, Banyutowo, founded in 1870 by the famous Javanese evangelist Ibrahim Tunggul Wulung. Rev. Saptayaadi is pastor of the Tanjungrejo Congregation of Evangelical (Mennonite) Church of Java, situated along the shores of the Java Sea in the Muria area of north central Java.

Author/Composer: *O Prince of peace*, **15**

SATEREN, LELAND BERNHARD (b. Oct. 13, 1913, Everett, Wash.), son of a Lutheran clergyman and educator, earned his B.A. in 1935 from Augsburg College, Minneapolis, Minnesota, and his M.A. in 1943 from the University of Minnesota. While at the university, he was music director for its radio station KUOM. Since then he has received a number of honorary degrees and awards. Sateren taught music in public schools, followed by three years in Civilian Public Service as educational director. He then began teaching at Augsburg College where he was chairman of the music department and director of the Augsburg choir from 1950 to 1973. In 1979, the year Sateren was named professor emeritus, the governor of Minnesota declared February 3 to be "Leland B. Sateren Day."

Sateren has been a leading educator in choral music: conducting choral workshops (also in Norway and Sweden), adjudicating contests, organizing festivals, and lecturing at various choral schools and music institutes. He is the author of major studies of choirs and choral music and has contributed articles to professional journals. He served on the Inter-Lutheran Commission on Worship from 1967 to 1978 and has been a member of several professional organizations, including the Hymn Society of the United States and Canada and the Music Educators National Conference. Sateren has also written more than three hundred choral compositions and published many works for treble voices, including *Cantate Domino*.

Composer: REGWAL (*As saints of old*), **386**

SCHAFFRAN, JANET, C.D.P. (b. Dec. 28, 1945, Detroit, Mich.) earned degrees at LaRoche College, Pittsburgh, Pennsylvania (B.A., 1972), and Seattle University (Wash.; M.A., 1979) and a certificate in clinical pastoral education (1993) at Allegheny General Hospital, Pittsburgh. In 1963 she entered a Roman Catholic religious order, the Congregation of the Sisters of Divine Providence, whose mother house is located in Allison Park, Pennsylvania. In her life as a Catholic sister, she has been a primary school teacher; a religious education coordinator; a campus minister at Walsh University, Canton, Ohio; and a chaplain at Allegheny General Hospital. Currently she lives in Pittsburgh and works in pastoral care at Forbes Hospice. She is also the director of lay membership in her religious community, a group of more than fifty people—men and women, married and single—who make a commitment of a year at a time and meet for meals, prayer, education days, and retreats. With Sister Pat Kozak, C.S.J., Sister Schaffran has authored a book of worship services written in inclusive language and focusing on such matters as spirituality, creation, and justice: *More Than Words* (Crossroad/Continuum Publishing Company 1988).

Author: God of all life, we thank you, **680**

SCHALK, CARL FLENTGE (b. Sept. 26, 1929, Des Plaines, Ill.) holds degrees from Concordia College, River Forest, Illinois (B.S. in Ed., 1952); the Eastman School of Music, Rochester, New York (M.Mus., 1958); and Concordia Seminary, St. Louis, Missouri (M.A.R., 1965). He has received honorary degrees from Concordia College, Seward, Nebraska, and Concordia College, St. Paul, Minnesota, and was named a fellow of the Hymn Society of the United States and Canada in 1992.

After a three-year tenure at Zion Lutheran Church, Wausau, Wisconsin (1952-1958), Schalk directed music for the International Lutheran Hour (1958-1965). Since 1965 he has been a church music professor at Concordia University, River Forest, Illinois. Schalk has been a lecturer and clinician at church music workshops and pastoral conferences, edited *Church Music Magazine* (1966-1980), and served on the committee that prepared the *Lutheran Book of Worship* (1978). Since 1964 he has been on the music editorial advisory committee of Concordia Publishing House; he has also served on various boards and committees of professional music organizations. Schalk's choral compositions are widely used, and his hymn tunes and settings have had similarly broad appeal for a range of denominational hymnals. A writer as well, Schalk has published music handbooks, books on music history and hymnody, and helps for pastors working with church musicians.

Composer: NOW (*Now the silence*), **462**

SCHEFFLER, JOHANN ANGELUS SILESIUS (b. 1624, Breslau, Silesia; d. July 9, 1677, Breslau, Silesia) was the son of a Polish nobleman forced to leave his homeland because of his Lutheran beliefs. He was educated as a strict Lutheran, studying at the universities in Strassburg, Leyden, and Padua (Ph.D. and M.D., 1648). Upon his return to Silesia, he was appointed personal physician to the duke of Württemberg-Oels.

During this time his spiritual leanings tended toward the mystical, and no one would publish his earliest hymns. In 1652 Scheffler resigned his post and became acquainted with the Jesuits in Breslau and, through them, with the writings of the medieval mystics. The following year, he joined the Roman Catholic Church and took the name Angelus, after a Spanish mystic. In 1661 he entered the order of St. Francis and was ordained priest, his "mystic physician" days behind him. He retired to the monastery of St. Matthias in 1671 and died there in 1677.

His most important hymnal is *Heilige Seelenlust . . .* (1657), published in three books containing 123 hymns arranged according to the Christian year, and a fourth book of thirty-two hymns. His hymn texts appear in a number of Lutheran hymnbooks and were especially admired by Zinzendorf, who included seventy-nine of them in his 1727 Moravian collection.

Author: *Morning Star, O cheering sight*, **214**

SCHEIN, JOHANN HERMANN (b. Jan. 20, 1586, Grünhain, Saxony, Germany; d. Nov. 19, 1630, Leipzig, Germany), a distinguished composer and notable precursor of the late baroque German musical style, was a choirboy in Dresden and later studied law at the University of Leipzig. His first important musical position was as *Kapellmeister* to the court at Weimar; then, in 1615 or 1616, he assumed the post in Leipzig as cantor at St. Thomas's Church (where Bach would later preside). He remained there for the rest of his life. Schein's most significant collection of church music is the *Cantional*, first published in 1627 and again in an expanded second edition in 1645.

Composer: MACH'S MIT MIR (*Count well the cost*), **437**

SCHLONEGER, FLORENCE (b. Apr. 24, 1947, Newton, Kan.) did her undergraduate study at Hesston College (Kan.) and Goshen College (Ind.; B.A., 1969), after which she and her husband, Weldon, did a two-year stint with Mennonite Central Committee as schoolteachers in Newfoundland. Following six years in Louisville, Ohio, her husband decided to study at Associated Mennonite Biblical Seminaries, Elkhart, Indiana, and she too began to consider pastoral ministry as a vocation and took courses there. Back in Ohio, at Columbus, she studied at Trinity Lutheran Seminary (eventually earning an M.T.S. in 1991). In 1984 she became co-pastor with her husband at Bethel Mennonite Church, West

Liberty, Ohio (she was ordained in 1988). In working out her identity as a pastoring woman, she found some clinical pastoral education in Ohio hospitals especially helpful. Since 1991 she and her husband have been co-pastors at Meadows Mennonite Church (General Conference), Chenoa, Illinois, where she divides her time equally between preaching and planning worship. Among her publications is a book of historical fiction for children (*Sara's Trek*, Faith and Life Press, 1981), about the immigration of a Russian Mennonite girl to Canada.

Author: May the body and blood of Christ, **784**

SCHMOLCK, BENJAMIN (b. Dec. 21, 1672, Brauchitzchdorf, Silesia, Germany; d. Feb. 12, 1737, Schweidnitz, Silesia, Germany), the son of a Lutheran pastor, preached his first sermon from his father's pulpit when he was sixteen. A patron of the church was so moved that he provided the monies for Schmolck to study theology at the University of Leipzig for three years. There, under the influence of Johannes Olearius, he was tutored in "a warm and living practical Christianity, but Churchly in tone and not Pietistic" (Julian 1907).

Schmolck became his father's assistant and was ordained in 1701. He married the daughter of a merchant in 1702 and later that year was appointed deacon of the Friedenskirche at Schweidnitz where he stayed the rest of his life. During the counter-Reformation, and according to the terms of the Peace of Westphalia (1648), this was the only Lutheran church allowed in the district, and the three clergymen assigned there were responsible for the inhabitants in more than thirty-six villages. In time he became the primary pastor and continued to preach until 1735, although he suffered a series of paralytic strokes beginning in 1730.

Schmolck had begun to write poetry while a student at Leipzig and was eventually crowned poet laureate. The most popular hymnwriter of his time, he was sometimes compared to Johann Rist and Paul Gerhardt. Of his more than nine hundred hymns, the earlier works are considered the best.

Author: *Open now thy gates of beauty*, **19**

SCHOLEFIELD, CLEMENT COTTERILL (b. June 22, 1839, Edgbaston, England; d. Sept. 10, 1904, Godalming, London, England) was a clergyman as well as a self-taught musician and composer of hymn tunes. The youngest son of a member of Parliament, he earned his M.A. at St. John's College, Cambridge. Following ordination in 1867, his positions included St. Peter's, South Kensington, when Arthur Sullivan was organist there; chaplain of prestigious Eton College (1880-1890); and vicar of Holy Trinity, Knightsbridge.

Composer: ST. CLEMENT (*The day you gave us, Lord*), **652**

SCHOP, JOHANN (b. ca. 1590; d. ca. 1665, Hamburg, Germany) was probably born in the vicinity of Hamburg near the end of the sixteenth century. By 1615 he was a court musician at Wolfenbüttel, with special talent on the lute, violin, and trombone. In 1615 he moved to Copenhagen; after 1621 he became director of municipal music in Hamburg and organist of St. James Church. Schop composed much occasional court music but is now remembered chiefly for his chorale tunes, having contributed some of them to Johann Rist's *Himmlische Lieder* (1641), as well as to other collections.

Composer: ERMUNTRE DICH (*Break forth, O beauteous heavenly*), **203**; WERDE MUNTER (*Jesu, joy of man's desiring*), **604**

SCHRADER, JACK (JOHN ALBERT) (b. July 16, 1942, St. Louis, Mo.) majored in voice and organ at Moody Bible Institute, Chicago (1964), then received his B.Mus.Ed. from the University of Nebraska, Lincoln (1966), with a major in voice. Following his ordination in the Evangelical Free Church of America in 1975, Schrader became minister of music in several local churches. Since 1978 he has worked at Hope Publishing Company, Carol Stream, Illinois, a major U.S. church music publishing firm, and is now executive editor with responsibilities in both the editorial department and recording divisions.

An experienced recording-studio musician, Schrader also has been an arranger, composer, conductor, vocalist, and organist/pianist. He directs a forty-voice male chorus, as well as the Hope Chorale, the recording choir of Hope Publishing Company. He conducts numerous church music workshops throughout the year and has established a national reputation as a choral clinician.

Composer: ACCLAMATIONS (*This is the threefold truth*), **335**

SCHUBERT, FRANZ PETER (b. Jan. 31, 1797, Himmelpfortgrund, near Vienna, Austria; d. Nov. 19, 1828, Vienna, Austria), an inspired melodist and master of the German *lied* (art song), studied violin with his schoolmaster father and piano with his brother, Ignaz. He also took lessons in piano, organ, singing, and theory from local choirmaster Holzer. In 1808 he joined the Vienna Imperial Court chapel choir and entered a training school for court singers. There he studied with the organist Wenzel Kuzicka and the composer Antonio Salieri.

Schubert began composing in school, writing for piano, chamber ensembles, and orchestra. He eventually became a teacher in his father's school, all the while composing prolifically and easily throughout his brief life. In 1815, when he was eighteen, he composed around 140 songs, eight of which were written in a single day.

In 1817 Schubert left teaching to compose and perform full time. He usually lived with one or another of his friends, performing his own music in coffeehouses and friends' homes. Except for a few summers as a private tutor to the two daughters of Count Johann Esterházy, he always lived on the edge of poverty. His health began to decline in 1823, but his composing continued unabated up to his death.

In addition to more than six hundred art songs, Schubert wrote piano works, church music, chamber music, symphonies, stage music, operas, and other choral and vocal works. Despite the brevity of his life, Schubert is ranked with the greatest composers in all forms except operas and concertos.

Composer: *Heilig, heilig, heilig* (*Holy, holy, holy*), **75**

SCHULZ (SCHULTZ), JOHANN ABRAHAM PETER (b. Mar. 31, 1747, Lüneburg, Germany; d. June 10, 1800, Schwedt, Germany), an organist and conductor, also composed operas, instrumental works, and church music. In his youth he studied in Berlin with the noted theorist Kirnberger and traveled to France, Italy, and Austria as keyboard teacher and accompanist to the Polish Princess Sapieha. From 1776 to 1787, he held positions as *Kapellmeister* and was director in public and private theaters.

During this time Schulz's fame spread through his dramatic incidental music and his carefully crafted folk songs. His work came to the attention of the king of Denmark, and Schulz accepted his invitation to be court music director (1787-1795). When the royal palace burned, his lungs were damaged in his attempt to rescue valuable music archives. Wracked by pneumonia, Schulz returned to Germany, where he died.

Schulz was at his best as a composer of songs and was among the first to give folk songs an artistic quality. Many of these were published in the Göttingen *Musenalmanach* and Voss's *Almanach*. He also published *Lieder im Volkston bey dem Klavier zu singen* (1782), containing forty-eight songs, with two editions following.

Composer (attrib.): WIR PFLÜGEN (*We plow the fields and scatter*), **96**

SCHULZ-WIDMAR, RUSSELL E. (b. July 29, 1944, Harvard, Ill.) was launched into church music by the excellent program at his congregation, St. John's Lutheran Church in Hebron, Illinois. He received degrees from Valparaiso University (Ind.; B.Mus., 1966); Union Theological Seminary, School of Sacred Music, New York City (S.M.M., 1968); and University of Texas at Austin (D.M.A., 1974). In 1970 he became co-director of music (with his wife, Suzanne) at University United Methodist Church in Austin. Four years later he joined the faculty of Episcopal Theological Seminary of the Southwest, Austin, where he is adjunct professor of church music. He was also visiting lecturer in church music at Austin Presbyterian Theological Seminary from 1975 to 1991.

Schulz-Widmar, who chaired the music committee for *The Hymnal 1982* (Episcopal), was president of the Hymn Society of the United States and Canada from 1988 to 1990. He has published many articles on hymnody, the hymnal *Songs of Thanks and Praise* (1980), and more than one hundred compositions. He co-edited *A New Hymnal for Colleges and Schools* (Yale 1992) with Jeffery Rowthorn.

Author: *Your love, O God, has called us,* **625**

SCHUMANN, ROBERT ALEXANDER (b. June 8, 1810, Zwickau, Saxony, Germany; d. July 29, 1856, Endenich, near Bonn, Germany), the son of a bookseller and publisher, was raised in a literary atmosphere and started composing at the age of seven. He began studying law in 1828 at the University of Leipzig to please his mother but eventually turned to a musical career.

Schumann studied piano with Friedrich Wieck and later married Wieck's daughter, Clara. She became an accomplished pianist who introduced and popularized Schumann's music. Schumann's own piano career ended when he permanently injured a finger experimenting with a mechanical finger-strengthening device. Consequently, he concentrated on composition and musical criticism by founding a journal, *Die Neue Zeitschrift für Musik*. He also was the driving force in the public recognition of Chopin and Brahms. Schumann, however, also suffered increasing mental instability and even tried to drown himself. In 1854 he was committed to an asylum where he spent the remainder of his life.

Schumann was a prolific composer of piano and vocal works, but his orchestral and chamber works are also significant. His music is an ideal expression of nineteenth-century romanticism. See standard reference works for full accounts of his life and work.

Composer/Source: CANONBURY (*Lord, speak to me*), **499**

SCHUTTE, DANIEL L. (b. Dec. 28, 1947, Neenah, Wis.) earned a B.S. in philosophy and letters, St. Louis University, Missouri (1973); an M.Div., Jesuit School of Theology, Berkeley, California (1979); and a Master of Liturgical Theology, Graduate Theological Union, Berkeley (1980). He was awarded an honorary doctorate by the University of Scranton (Pa.) in 1980. Once a Jesuit priest, he served the Pine Ridge Indian Reservation in South Dakota, as well as teaching high school music and theology. On the college level he has been director of liturgy at Marquette University, Milwaukee, Wisconsin. Now a layman, he is director of music at Our Lady of Lourdes parish in Milwaukee.

Author/Composer: *Here I am, Lord,* **395**

SCHÜTZ, HEINRICH (b. Oct. 8, 1585, Köstriz, Germany; d. Nov. 6, 1672, Dresden, Germany) stands as the most eminent composer in seventeenth-century Germany. After university studies in law at Marburg,

Schütz traveled to Venice (then center of the music world) where he mastered the Italian musical style in his studies with Giovanni Gabrieli (1609-1612). He thus imported the Italian style to his native Germany. In 1617 he became *Kapellmeister* to the Saxon Court at Dresden, a position he held for the rest of his life, except for stints as a musician at the courts of Copenhagen, Hannover, and Brunswick during the turmoil of the Thirty Years War.

Schütz was a very productive church music composer. After his wife of six years died, he turned frequently to the Psalms, setting some of Cornelius Becker's psalm paraphrases. Among Schütz's most important collections are *Psalmen Davids* (a.k.a. the Becker Psalter, 1619), *Cantiones sacrae* (1625), two volumes of *Kleine geistliche Konzerte* (1636, 1639), three volumes of *Symphoniae sacrae* (1629, 1647, 1650), *Geistliche Chormusik* (1648), and three Passions.

Composer: *How lovely is your dwelling*, **171**; *I long for your commandments*, **543**

SCHÜTZ, JOHANN JACOB (b. Sept. 7, 1640, Frankfurt am Main, Germany; d. May 22, 1690, Frankfurt, Germany) studied law at Tübingen and established his practice in Frankfurt. He was a close friend of Philipp J. Spener, who sparked a movement in the German Lutheran Church that became known as Pietism. In later years Schütz became a separatist, leaving the Lutherans in 1686 for the lifestyle advocated by the Pietists: personal spiritual development through devotions, Bible study, and prayer. His *Christliches Gedenckbüchlein* was published in Frankfurt in 1675.

Author: *Sing praise to God who reigns*, **59**

SCHWEDLER, JOHANN CHRISTOPH (b. Dec. 21, 1672, Krobsdorf, Silesia, Germany; d. Jan. 12, 1730, Niederwiese, Silesia) wrote hymns copiously, the bulk of which were published in his *Die Lieder Mose und des Lammes, oder neu eingerichtetes Gesang-Buch* (1720). Following study at the University of Leipzig, he spent most of his career as a minister in a church at Niederwiese, near Grieffenberg, where his preaching was renowned. He was a pastor from 1701 until his death; he also was instrumental in establishing an orphanage at Niederwiese.

Author: *Ask ye what great thing I know*, **337**

SCOTT, CLARA H. (JONES) (b. Dec. 3, 1841, Elk Grove, Ill.; d. June 21, 1897, Dubuque, Iowa), at age fifteen, attended the first musical institute in Chicago in 1856, conducted by C. M. Cady. She began teaching music at the Ladies' Seminary in Lyons, Iowa, in 1859, two years before her marriage to Henry Clay Scott. Horatio R. Palmer encouraged her writing and published many of her songs in his collections. *Royal Anthem Book* (1882) was the first collection of anthems to be published by a woman.

Scott never knew the success of her "Open my eyes." While visiting Dubuque, Iowa, she was killed when she was thrown from a buggy pulled by a runaway horse.

Author/Composer: *Open my eyes, that I may see* (OPEN MY EYES), **517**

SCOTT, ROBERT BALGARNIE YOUNG (b. July 16, 1899, Toronto, Ontario; d. Nov. 1, 1987, Toronto, Ontario) was educated at Knox College, Galesburg, Illinois (B.D.) and the University of Toronto (B.A., M.A., Ph.D). Following a year of study in Europe, Scott was ordained in 1926 in the United Church of Canada. After a two-year pastorate, he became professor of Old Testament at Union College, Vancouver, British Columbia. In Montréal, Québec, he filled similar positions at United Theological College (1931-1948) and McGill University (1948-1955) before joining the faculty of Princeton University (N.J.; 1955-1965). There he chaired the religion department for the two years preceding his retirement.

Scott wrote two books on biblical subjects, including *The Relevance of the Prophets* (1945); he co-authored *Towards the Christian Revolution* with Gregory Vlastos. He was president of the Fellowship for a Christian Social Order for four years and also wrote a number of hymns related to the concerns of that organization.

Author: *O day of God, draw nigh,* **370**

SCRIVEN, JOSEPH MEDLICOTT (b. Sept. 10, 1819, Seapatrick, County Down, Ireland; d. Aug. 10, 1886, Bewdley, Rice Lake, Ontario) was educated at Addiscombe Military College and at Trinity College, Dublin (B.A., 1842). Denied a military career because of poor health, Scriven immigrated to Canada when he was twenty-five, just after his fiancée drowned the night before their wedding. In Ontario he taught school at Woodstock and Brantford. As a member of the Plymouth Brethren, he gave much of his life and goods in voluntary humanitarian service. In 1855 he was again deprived of marriage when his bride-to-be died after a short illness. In later years he suffered physically, financially, and emotionally. Scriven drowned in Rice Lake in 1886, but no one knows for certain whether it was an accident or suicide. In 1920 a monument to his memory was erected near Rice Lake; it is engraved with the stanzas of "What a friend we have in Jesus."

Author: *What a friend we have in Jesus,* **573**

SEARS, EDMUND HAMILTON (b. Apr. 6, 1810, Sandisfield, Mass.; d. Jan. 16, 1876, Weston, Mass.) graduated from Union College, Schenectady, New York (1834) and Harvard Divinity School, Cambridge, Massachusetts. Although he was ordained a Unitarian minister, his preaching reflected his belief in the divinity of Christ. He served various pastorates in the Boston area, did editorial work on *Monthly Religious Magazine*, and wrote a number of religious books. The few hymns he wrote were true treasures.

Author: *It came upon a midnight clear*, **195**

SEDDON, JAMES EDWARD (b. Aug. 24, 1915, Omskirk, Lancashire, England; d. Sept. 19, 1983, London, England) was trained in music at London College of Music and Trinity College, London, earning associate degrees from both institutions. He studied for the ministry at the Bible Churchmen's Theological College (now Trinity College) in Bristol and was curate in three parishes of the Church of England during the war years (1939 to 1945). After World War II, Seddon was a missionary to Morocco, spending five years each in Tangier and Marrakesh. Upon his return to England, he became home secretary of the Bible Churchmen's Missionary Society, followed by service in the Church of England before he retired in 1980.

Seddon wrote about thirty hymns in English, a number of them on the topic of missions. While in Morocco he wrote several hymns in Arabic. Seddon was a member of the committees that prepared *Psalm Praise* (1973) and *Hymns for Today's Church* (1982).

Author: *How good a thing it is*, **310**

SEDULIUS, COELIUS (flourished ca. 450) was probably born in Rome, Italy. All that is known of his personal life is derived from two letters that he wrote to Macedonius. These reveal that his early years had been devoted to heathen literature and that he was converted to Christianity later in life. Asterius, who was consul in 494, collected the writings of Sedulius after his death. Sedulius's works include both prose and poetry, among them *Carmen Paschale*, a poem that encompasses the whole gospel story.

Author: *When Christ's appearing*, **217**

SEERVELD, CALVIN (b. 1930, Bayshore, N.Y.) studied at Calvin College, Grand Rapids, Michigan; the University of Michigan; the Free University of Amsterdam; Basel University, Switzerland (where he was a student of Karl Jaspers and Karl Barth); and the University of Rome. He has taught philosophy at Bellhaven College, Jackson, Mississippi, and Trinity College, Palos Heights, Illinois. Since 1972 he has been a senior member in philosophical aesthetics at the Institute for Christian Studies in Toronto, Ontario. His publications include *The Greatest Song: In Critique of Solomon* (1967) and *Rainbows for the Fallen World: Aesthetic*

Life and Artistic Task (1980). He was on the committee for revising the *Psalter Hymnal* (1987), a combination psalter/hymnal which contains nineteen psalms that Seerveld versified, as well as eighteen of his hymn texts, two translations, and two hymn tunes.

Versifier: *Babylon streams received our tears*, **134**

SEISS, JOSEPH AUGUST (b. Mar. 18, 1823, Graceham, Frederick County, Md.; d. June 20, 1904, Philadelphia, Pa.) was born into the German Moravian community of Graceham, was educated in Moravian schools, and was confirmed in the Moravian Church at eighteen. His father and bishop did not support his interest in ministry; nevertheless, he studied privately with a Moravian pastor. Seiss entered Pennsylvania College, Gettysburg, in 1839 with the help of some Lutheran pastors. In 1842 he was licensed in the Evangelical Lutheran Synod in Virginia (ordained in 1848) and ministered in three congregations between 1844 and 1858. Then he was pastor at St. John's Lutheran Church for sixteen years and Church of the Holy Communion until he retired.

Seiss was a prolific writer and editor, focusing on education, Lutheran liturgy, and hymn collections. His best-known works are *The Last Times* (1856), *The Evangelical Psalmist* (1859), *The Assassination of a President* (1865), *Ecclesia Lutherana* (1868), *Lectures on the Gospels* (1868-1872), and *Lectures on the Epistles* (1885).

Translator: *Fairest Lord Jesus* (st. 4), **117**

SELTZ, MARTIN LOUIS (b. Dec. 20, 1909, near Gibbon, Minn.; d. Oct. 5, 1967, St. Paul, Minn.), both a pastor and musician, graduated from Concordia College, St. Paul (1928), and Concordia Seminary, St. Louis, Missouri (1934). He was an instructor at Concordia College from 1928 to 1932. Following a brief stint as vicar in New Jersey, Seltz pastored Lutheran churches in Minnesota, Iowa, and Illinois for thirty-three years. He directed choral unions in Minnesota and Iowa and for three summers (1932-1934) served as music director of Lutherland in Pennsylvania. He was editor of *The North Star Song Book* (1945, 1956) and was active in the Lutheran Church-Missouri Synod in various districts, as well as a member of the Commission on Worship. From 1965 until his death in 1967, Seltz was a member of the Inter-Lutheran Commission on Worship.

Translator: *O Savior, rend the heavens*, **175**; *Savior of the nations, come* (sts. 3-4), **173**

SHAW, MARTIN FALLAS (b. Mar. 9, 1875, London, England; d. Oct. 24, 1958, Southwold, England) studied composition at the Royal College of Music with C. V. Stanford. After years of varied musical activities, he became organist at St. Mary's, Primrose Hill (1908-1920), and St. Martin's in the Fields (1920-1924); he was director of church music for the diocese of Chelmsford (1935-1945). Shaw composed orchestral and choral works, chamber music, cantatas, and songs. He edited various Anglican hymnals with George Wallace Briggs, Percy Dearmer, and Ralph Vaughan Williams and wrote *Principles of English Church Music Composition* (1921). It has been stated that Shaw's most influential pieces were those for congregational use, including the hymn tunes LITTLE CORNARD and MARCHING. In 1929 he wrote his autobiography, *Up to Now*.

Composer: PURPOSE (*God is working his purpose out*), **638**. Arranger: BUNESSAN (*Morning has broken*), **648**; ROYAL OAK (*All things bright and beautiful*), **156**; SLANE (*Be thou my vision*), **545**

SHAW, ROBERT LAWSON (b. Apr. 30, 1916, Red Bluff, Calif.) is one of the eminent North American choral conductors of the twentieth century. Religious conviction has always been central for Shaw, and he studied at Pomona College, Claremont, California (1934-1938), intending to be a minister. There he conducted the glee club, and his choral work attracted the attention of Fred Waring who secured Shaw to organize and conduct the Fred Waring Glee Club. Later Shaw formed his own Collegiate Chorale; the group, based in New York City, sang a varied repertoire until 1954.

In 1946 Shaw conducted the NBC Symphony Orchestra and several times prepared symphonic choral groups for its celebrated conductor, Arturo Toscanini. Shaw directed the choral departments of the Juilliard School, New York City, and the Berkshire Music Center at Tanglewood, Massachusetts, from 1945 to 1948. In 1948 he founded the Robert Shaw Chorale, which toured internationally and recorded extensively under his direction until it disbanded in 1967.

Also interested in orchestral conducting, Shaw honed his skills as the director of the San Diego Symphony summer concerts (1953-1958) and as associate conductor with George Szell of the Cleveland Symphony (Ohio; 1956-1967), for whom he formed an adjunct chorus. After developing yet another symphony-related chorus in Atlanta, Georgia, Shaw retired in 1988 with the titles "music director emeritus" and "conductor laureate." Thereafter, he directed the new institute named in his honor at Emory University, Atlanta.

Shaw has made outstanding contributions to choral music, both *a cappella* and symphonic. Details about his conducting repertoire and activities appear in standard musical references.

Arranger: O SANCTISSIMA (*Oh, how joyfully*), **209**

SHAWCHUCK, NORMAN (b. May 13, 1935, Elgin, N.D.) earned degrees at Jamestown College (N.D.; B.A., 1965); Garrett Theological Seminary, Evanston, Illinois (M.Div., 1969); and Northwestern University, Evanston (Ph.D., 1974). An ordained minister of the United Methodist Church since 1965, Shawchuck is the president of Shawchuck & Associates, Ltd., in Leith, North Dakota, which specializes in management consulting, research, and training seminars for religious organizations. He has served on the doctoral faculty of McCormick Theological Seminary, Chicago, for nearly twenty years and as an adjunct faculty member in the doctoral programs at Trinity Evangelical Divinity School, Deerfield, Illinois, for eighteen years, teaching in the fields of religious leadership and spirituality. He is a research scholar on the faculty of the School of Industrial Engineering at Northwestern University and a Senior Beeson Fellow at Asbury Theological Seminary, Willmore, Kentucky. Among his numerous publications are *A Guide to Prayer for All God's People* and *A Guide to Prayer for Ministers and Other Servants,* both co-authored with Rueben P. Job. Shawchuck is a contributing editor to *Leadership: A Practical Journal for Church Leaders.*

Author: Lord God, in whom I find life, **724**

SHEETS, DOROTHY HOWELL (b. July 3, 1915, Mendham, N.J.) was born into a musical family; her father tutored her in piano when she was five. Following her graduation from the Peabody Conservatory of Music, Sheets earned an Associate of the American Guild of Organists certification while serving as organist/choir director in several churches in New Jersey.

After a stint with the U.S. Navy during World War II, Sheets took the M.S.M. degree at the School of Sacred Music at Union Theological Seminary, New York City, and was elected a fellow of Trinity College, London. Involved with music ever since, she has been a college organist, a church organist, a minister of music at Samuel Lutheran Church, and music teacher at Muskegon Community College (Mich.). Now in retirement, she is devoting more time to composition.

Composer: BINGHAM (*Lord, our Lord, your glorious name*), **157**

SHELLY, PATRICIA JOYCE (b. Dec. 21, 1951, Chicago, Ill.), daughter of a minister, grew up in three different church families in Iowa, Ohio, and Kansas. She earned her B.A. from Bethel College, North Newton, Kansas (1976), and both her M.Div. (1980) and Ph.D. in biblical interpretation (1992) from the Iliff School of Theology, Denver, Colorado. Shelly began composing in 1970 when she learned to play the guitar. She says that her "sense of Christian 'folk' or informal music was shaped by extensive church camp experience as well as singing and playing guitar during college years." She was ordained in 1985 and has been associate pastor of First Mennonite Church, Denver, Colorado, as well as guest lecturer, preacher, worship leader, and music leader in a variety of conference, workshop, camp, and church settings. She is assistant professor and campus minister at her alma mater, Bethel College.

Author/Composer: *There are many gifts* (MANY GIFTS), **304**

SHENK, SARA WENGER (b. May 7, 1953, Nazareth, Ethiopia) pastors Immanuel Mennonite Church, Harrisonburg, Virginia. Her educational experience includes studies at Wheaton College (Ill.) and Eastern Mennonite College, Harrisonburg (B.A., English education, 1975); Fuller Theological Seminary, Pasadena, California; Garrett-Evangelical Theological Seminary, Evanston, Illinois (M.T.S., 1986); and the University of Zagreb (Yugoslavia). She served on a study/service commission to the former Yugoslavia under the auspices of Mennonite Central Committee (1977-1983 and 1986-1989). During those years she was a regular columnist for Yugoslavian church publications and a frequent speaker/teacher at church-sponsored seminars in that region. In addition to numerous articles on church and family dynamics, she has authored three books: *And Then There Were Three: An Ode to Parenthood* (1985), *Why Not Celebrate!* (1987), and *Coming Home* (1992).

Translator: *Living and dying with Jesus*, **550**

SHEPPARD, FRANKLIN LAWRENCE (b. Aug. 7, 1852, Philadelphia, Pa.; d. Feb. 15, 1930, Germantown, Pa.) graduated from the University of Pennsylvania, Philadelphia, in 1872 at the head of his class and was a charter member of the university's chapter of Phi Beta Kappa. He moved to Baltimore, Maryland, to take charge of a foundry, which was part of his father's stove and heater company. Sheppard was raised in the Episcopal Church and was even elected a vestryman, but after his move to Baltimore, he joined Second Presbyterian Church and became its music director. Sheppard became a member and, later, president of the Presbyterian Board of Publication and Sabbath-School Work. His efforts influenced construction of the denominational headquarters (the Witherspoon Building) in Philadelphia. He served on the hymnal committee for *The Presbyterian Hymnal* (1911) and edited the Presbyterian Sunday school songbook *Alleluia* (1915).

Composer: TERRA BEATA (*This is my Father's world*), **154**

SHERWIN, WILLIAM FISKE (b. Mar. 14, 1826, Buckland, Mass.; d. Apr. 14, 1888, Boston, Mass.) studied under Lowell Mason in Boston and later taught at the New England Conservatory of Music. For some time he was a musical editor for the music publishing firms Century and Company and Biglow and Main. Because of his special abilities in working with amateur singers, this Baptist layman was chosen by Methodist John H. Vincent to be director of the musical program at the Chautauqua Assembly in western New York from 1874 to 1888. His long tenure there attests to his reputation as an outstanding organizer and director of amateur choruses.

Composer: BREAD OF LIFE (*Break thou the bread of life*), **360**

SHIVELY, JONATHAN ADIN (b. Nov. 13, 1967, Lancaster, Pa.) learned to appreciate music as a form of worship and praise as he grew up in Lancaster Church of the Brethren. He graduated from Elizabethtown College (Pa.; B.A. in music, 1990) and from Bethany Theological Seminary, Oak Brook, Illinois (M.Div., 1993). A composer, choral leader, and vocalist, he currently is pastor of Pomona Fellowship (Brethren) in southern California.

Composer: GRACIOUS GIFT (*O God, who gives us life*), **483**

SHOWALTER, J. HENRY (b. Nov. 2, 1864, Singers Glen, Va.; d. Nov. 29, 1947, West Milton, Ohio) came from a very musical family. The Showalters were the first in the community to have an organ, and music teachers, writers, and publishers regularly visited their home (Statler, Fisher 1959). Like his father, John A. Showalter, J. Henry became a noted singing-school teacher. He studied music in Chicago, began teaching in singing schools about 1882, and was especially active teaching music in schools and churches between 1894 and 1910. He edited or co-edited about fifty different musical publications. These included books on voice, harmony and composition, and rudiments of music, as well as hymnals and gospel songbooks. He was a member of the committee for *The Brethren Hymnal* (1901), and a number of his hymn tunes appear in Brethren hymnals.

Composer: RICHES OF GRACE (*Oh, how wondrous the grace*), **147**; SHOWALTER *(Breathe upon us, Holy Spirit)*, **28**. Arranger: HILLERY *(Lord, with devotion we pray)*, **79**

SILCHER, FRIEDRICH (b. June 27, 1789, near Schorndorf, Württemberg, Germany; d. Aug. 28, 1860, Tübingen, Germany), after a period of teaching and conducting in Ludwigsburg and Stuttgart, was named director of music at the University of Tübingen in 1817. During his forty-three years there, he founded the university's Choral Society, earned a Ph.D., and published numerous works. He is remembered primarily for his *Sammlung deutscher Volkslieder* (Collection of German Folk Songs). This twelve-volume collection includes arrangements for one or two voices and for male chorus. Silcher's other published works include the *Württemberg Choralbuch*, three small collections of hymns for children dated 1841 and 1843, and a church music history titled *Geschichte der evangelischen Kirchengesänge* (1844).

Composer: SO NIMM DENN MEINE HÄNDE (*Take thou my hand, O Father*), **581**

SIMONS, MENNO (b. 1496, Witmarsum, the Netherlands; d. Jan. 31, 1561, Wüstenfelde, near Oldesloe, Holstein, Germany) became the leader of the Anabaptist movement in the Netherlands at a point when it was in danger of losing its original peaceful, biblical foundations. Raised a

Roman Catholic, he was ordained a priest at Utrecht in 1524. During his second year as a priest, he began to read the Bible and was torn between the authority of the Bible and that of the church. He became known for his evangelical preaching, which he based on scripture. After a decade of soul-searching, he left Roman Catholicism in 1536 and joined the Anabaptist movement. He was baptized soon thereafter. Called by a small group of believers to become their leader, Simons assumed the office of elder. Thus he began an "underground" life, always on the move, not being able to stay even six months in any one place. The authorities offered a sizable reward for his capture, and two people who had sheltered him were executed.

Apparently, by 1544 Simons was married and had small children. It was not until late in 1554 that he found shelter at Wüstenfelde, the estate of Bartholomeus von Ahlefeldt. There his books were printed, he revised earlier writings, and he began new works. His writings are filled with biblical quotations, evidence of his intensive study of the Bible as the foundation for his theology and practices, which were both Christ-centered and congregation-centered. Most significant was his *Foundation-Book* (*Dat Fundament des Christelycken leers* 1539, 1540). In the matter of church discipline, Simons mediated between those who held strict and lenient interpretations, leaning toward more rigid views later in his life. More extensive information on Simons, who has been the subject of more biographies than any other Anabaptist leader, may be found in *The Mennonite Encyclopedia*, Vol. III.

Author/Source: *We are people of God's peace*, **407**; Lord Jesus, blind I am, **700**

SIMPSON, ROBERT (b. Nov. 4, 1790, Glasgow, Scotland; d. July or August 1832, Greenock, Scotland) was well educated and a weaver by trade. For a time he led the singing in Wardlaw's Congregational Church in Glasgow and, in 1823, he became precentor (music director), as well as session clerk of the East Parish Church, Greenock. In 1823 music became his profession. He died during a cholera epidemic (*The Hymnal 1940 Companion*, 1951 ed.).

Arranger: BALERMA (*Help us to help each other*), **362**

SLEETH, NATALIE ALLYN WAKELEY (b. Oct. 29, 1930, Evanston, Ill.; d. Mar. 21, 1992, Denver, Colo.), the only child of musical parents, began piano lessons at the age of four. She received a B.A. in music from Wellesley College (Mass., 1952) and married soon after. Because her husband was a homiletics professor, they lived in university communities in Nashville, Tennessee; Dallas, Texas; Evanston; and Denver for the thirty-three years of their marriage, until his death in 1985.

While in Dallas, Sleeth studied choral arranging with Lloyd Pfautsch at Southern Methodist University, which launched her composing career.

Her first published work was "Canon of Praise," released by Choristers Guild in 1969. At the time of her death, more than 150 of her compositions for church and school choirs had been published. Among Sleeth's best known anthems are "Jazz Gloria" and "Joy in the Morning" (1977), which was written for her husband's inauguration as president of West Virginia Wesleyan College, Buckhannon, West Virginia.

Sleeth's book *Adventures for the Soul* (1987) contains thirty-five of her inspirational poems and the stories behind them. Sleeth, who wrote both music and text for all her compositions, was the subject of the video *Words and Music* (Hope 1990). She received honorary doctoral degrees from West Virginia Wesleyan College in 1989 and Nebraska Wesleyan University, Lincoln, in 1990.

Author/Composer: *Go now in peace* (GO NOW IN PEACE), **429**; *In the bulb there is a flower* (PROMISE), **614**

SLOUGH, REBECCA J. (b. Sept. 11, 1952, Cherry Point, N.C.) grew up in the Church of the Brethren in Elkhart, Indiana. After one year as a piano performance major at Indiana University at South Bend, Indiana, Slough transferred to Goshen College (Ind.), where she received a B.A. in education in 1978. During her years at Goshen College, she worked in nearby Elkhart at Oaklawn Center in a program for emotionally handicapped children. At age twenty-three she joined the Mennonite Church. Slough continued her studies at the Associated Mennonite Biblical Seminaries, Elkhart (M.Div., 1982), and the University of Notre Dame, South Bend (M.A. in liturgical studies, 1983). In 1983 she began working on the worship committee of The Hymnal Project. The following year she moved to El Cerrito, California, to do doctoral work at Graduate Theological Union. After receiving her Ph.D. (in liturgics and anthropological linguistics) in 1989, she became managing editor of *Hymnal: A Worship Book.* Upon completion of The Hymnal Project in 1992, Slough became a pastor at First Mennonite Church of San Francisco. In August 1994 she joined the faculty at Bethany Theological Seminary, Richmond, Indiana, as associate professor of congregational studies and field education. A member of the Hymn Society of the United States and Canada (serving on its editorial advisory committee, 1991-1993) and the North American Academy of Liturgy, she has led workshops and published a number of articles on the subject of worship.

Author: Come, Child of Bethlehem, **678**; Transforming God, you come to us, **735**

SMART, CHRISTOPHER (b. Apr. 11, 1722, Shipbourne, Kent, England; d. May 21, 1771, London, England) won prizes as a scholar and poet at Pembroke College, Cambridge. By 1742 he was also a scholar of the university and three years later was teaching philosophy.

Although a great scholar, Smart was undisciplined. He fell into debt and eventually lost his position at Cambridge in 1749, whereupon he moved to London to work as a journalist. He married, and his poems on religious subjects earned him the annual Seatonian Prize of Cambridge five years running (1750-1755). His charm won over a distinguished circle of friends, including Samuel Johnson, Fanny Burney, David Garrick, and William Hogarth. But his mind began to slip, and he became a public nuisance in expressing his religious convictions, kneeling ostentatiously for prayer in streets, parks, and assembly rooms. In 1756 he was committed to a madhouse and spent the rest of his life in and out of asylums and debtors prisons. He died in prison.[1]

Smart's works include *A Song of David* (1763), *Jubilate Agno* (Rejoice in the Lamb, written 1759-1763), *Hymns and Spiritual Songs for the Fasts and Festivals of the Church of England* (1765), *Parables of our Lord . . . set into familiar verse* (1768), and *Hymns for the amusement of children* (1765). *Jubliate Agno* was first published in 1939 and a portion was set by Benjamin Britten as a festival cantata for choir and organ titled *Rejoice in the Lamb.*

Author: *To God, with the Lamb*, **125**; *Where is this stupendous Stranger?*, **200**

1. Smart's biography was written by Edward G. Ainsworth and Charles E. Noyes, 1943.

SMART, HENRY THOMAS (b. Oct. 26, 1813, London, England; d. July 6, 1879, London) was the last descendant in a line of musicians beginning with George Smart in the eighteenth century. Henry, however, was apprenticed to a lawyer, even though he studied music with his father. His musical heritage proved stronger than the legal profession, and he became a self-taught organist, noted for his improvisations. He served with distinction in several churches in Lancashire and London and put his early prowess in mechanical drawing to use in designing organs for the cities of Glasgow, Scotland, and Leeds, England.

Smart composed services, anthems, and organ pieces—and even published collections of sacred choral music— but he also encouraged congregational singing. To that end he edited two hymnals: *Psalms and Hymns for Divine Worship* (1867) and *The Presbyterian Hymnal* (1875). In 1864 his eyesight failed and he thereafter dictated his compositions to his daughter.

Composer: COLDREY (*Jesus, sun and shield art thou*), **466**; LANCASHIRE (*Lead on, O cloud of Presence*), **419**; REGENT SQUARE (*For the healing of the nations*), **367**

SMITH, DAVID (b. Apr. 23, 1933, London, England) was educated at the University of London (B.A., 1950). He served in the military for five years in the Middle East and Europe. After a period of full-time teaching, he has been working almost exclusively since 1960 as a translator. His publications include books, articles, and papers on a wide range of subjects translated from French, Dutch, and German. He also authored a number of books for young people, including *Winston Churchill* (1963) and *Discovering Flight* (1966).

Translator: *What is this place*, **1**

SMITH, DEBORAH (b. Mar. 3, 1958)—see article on Michael W. Smith.

Author: *Great is the Lord*, **87**

SMITH, HENRY PERCY (b. 1825, Malta; d. Jan. 28, 1898, Bournemouth, Hampshire, England) was educated in England, earning bachelor's and master's degrees from Balliol College, Oxford University. In 1850 he was ordained a priest in the Church of England and served a number of churches, including Eversley in Hamptonshire; St. Michael's in Surrey; and Christ Church in Cannes, France. His last appointment was at the Cathedral of Gibraltar in 1892. Little is known of his life as a musician.

Composer: MARYTON (*Come, Holy Spirit, Dove divine*, **445**; *O Master, let me walk with thee*, **357**)

SMITH, MICHAEL W. (b. Oct. 7, 1957, Kenova, W.Va.) has already established himself as a songwriter and Christian music performer. He grew up with music, singing in church choirs and learning to play the piano. In 1978 he moved from West Virginia to Nashville and worked odd jobs, including playing with nightclub bands, until he joined the gospel group Higher Ground. Later that same year, 1980, his songwriting was "discovered" by Paragon Music, and he was offered a position as staff writer. When his contract with Paragon expired, he joined newly formed Meadowgreen Music, a gospel division of Tree International. Smith met his wife, Debbie, then a nursing student, in 1981, and discovered, just after they were married, that she was the poet he'd been searching for to complement his musicianship. He encouraged her to write lyrics, and together they wrote all the songs on the album *The Michael W. Smith Project*. He defines his music as "top 40; rock 'n' roll gospel; worship songs."

Author/Composer: *Great is the Lord* (GREAT IS THE LORD), **87**; *O Lord, our Lord, how majestic* (HOW MAJESTIC IS YOUR NAME), **112**

SMITH, ROBERT ARCHIBALD (b. Nov. 16, 1780, Reading, Berkshire, England; d. Jan. 3, 1829, Edinburgh, Scotland) as a child was already proficient on both violin and cello. Though he was also a composer, performer, and teacher, he spent most of his professional career as a church musician. In 1807 he became choir director of Abbey Church in Paisley; from 1823 until his death he served as precentor (music director) at St. Edinburgh's St. George's Church, a notable position in the absence of instruments. Smith edited and compiled two important collections of church music: *Sacred Music sung at St. George's Church* and the six-volume *Scottish Minstrel.*

Arranger: MARTYRDOM (*Alas! and did my Savior bleed?*), **253**

SMITH, WALTER CHALMERS (b. Dec. 5, 1824, Aberdeen, Scotland; d. Sept. 20, 1908, Kinbuck, Perthshire, Scotland) was educated at the University of Aberdeen and New College, Edinburgh. He was ordained in the Free Church of Scotland in 1850 and served churches in London, Glasgow, and Edinburgh over the next forty-four years, the last being the influential Free High Church of Edinburgh (1876-1894). In 1893 he was moderator of the Free Church of Scotland.

Anything Smith was reluctant to express in the pulpit came out in his poetry, which he described as "the retreat of his nature from the burden of his labors" (Stulken 1981). Among his numerous published works are *Hymns of Christ and the Christian Life* (1867) and *Poetical Works* (1902). Julian describes his hymns as "rich in thought and vigorous in expression" (Julian 1907).

Author: *Immortal, invisible, God only wise*, **70**

SMITH, WILLIAM FARLEY (b. 1941, Durham, N.C.) graduated from Manhattan School of Music (B.A. and M.A.) and Columbia University (Ed.M. and Ed.D.), both in New York City, and completed music therapy certification at New York University. Smith was a teacher for twenty-three years with the New York City Board of Education and has also taught at Montclair State College, Upper Montclair, New Jersey. He is a faculty member of Drew University, Madison, New Jersey, where he completed a religious studies certification. Smith received a fellowship grant from the Boston Symphony Orchestra (Mass.) and has traveled, lectured, and performed in Europe, West Africa, the West Indies, and North America for the Harlem Opera Company and the United Methodist Church.

Recognized as a scholar of slave songs, Smith has had articles published in numerous periodicals and served as African American ethnic consultant/arranger/historian/composer for *The United Methodist Hymnal* (1989).

Arranger: LATTIMER (*This little light of mine*), **401**; TURNER (*I am leaning on the Lord*), **532**; STAND BY ME (*When the storms of life are raging*), **558**

SPAETH, HARRIET REYNOLDS KRAUTH (b. Sept. 21, 1845, Baltimore, Md.; d. May 5, 1925, Philadelphia, Pa.) attended Girls' School in Philadelphia, but it is not recorded whether she studied beyond high school. In 1879 she became the second wife of Adolph Spaeth, a professor at Lutheran Theological Seminary (Mount Airy, Pa.). One of their children, Sigmund, became well known as a lecturer, writer, and music critic.

Besides caring for a large household, Spaeth was organist at St. Stephen's Church in West Philadelphia. She edited the *Lutheran Church Book with Music* (1872) and provided hymn translations for other hymnals. She also translated *The Deaconess and Her Works and Pictures from the Life of Hans Sachs* and wrote biographies of both her husband, Adolph, and her father, Charles Porterfield Krauth, an eminent Lutheran clergyman and educator. In addition to being a musician and writer, Spaeth was a humanitarian, working at the Mary J. Drexel Home, Lankenau Hospital, and the Lutheran Orphans' Home in Germantown (Philadelphia).

Translator: *Lo, how a Rose e'er blooming* (st. 3), **211**

SPAFFORD, HORATIO GATES (b. Oct. 20, 1828, North Troy, N.Y.; d. Oct. 16, 1888, Jerusalem, Jordan) lived his early years in New York and later moved to Chicago where he developed a successful law practice. He was an active Presbyterian layman and served as a director and trustee for the Presbyterian Theological Seminary of the Northwest (now McCormick).

Spafford's life seemed dogged by tragedy. Having invested heavily in real estate, he lost most of his fortune in the Chicago fire of 1871, and two years later four of his daughters died in a shipwreck. A son died of scarlet fever in 1880.

Leaving a church that had grown wary of the family's repeated misfortune, the Spaffords followed up their interest in biblical archaeology and settled in Jerusalem in 1881, founding the American Colony there. This Christian mission was truly ecumenical in its ministry—aiding Jews, Muslims, and Christians, and later functioning as a haven during two world wars. Spafford's remaining daughter, Bertha Spafford Vester, gives an account of their extraordinary experiences in her book *Our Jerusalem* (1977).

Author: *When peace, like a river*, **336**

SPEE, FRIEDRICH VON (b. Feb. 25, 1591, Kaiserswörth, Germany; d. Aug. 4, 1635, Trier, Germany) went to Köln's Jesuit high school, entered the Jesuit order in 1610, and was ordained a priest in 1621. He was a tutor in the Jesuit colleges at Paderborn, Würzburg, and Peine (1613-1624), then returned to Köln in 1630 as a professor of theology. His last years were spent in Trier where he died from a fever.

Spee was an important and prolific author of sacred poetry. His most significant collection of poems is the *Trutz Nachtigal, oder Geistlichs-Poetisch Lust-Waldlein*, completed the year before his death. It was published posthumously at Köln in 1649.

Author: *O Savior, rend the heavens*, **175**

STAINER, JOHN (b. June 6, 1840, London, England; d. Mar. 31, 1901, Verona, Italy) was in the choir at St. Paul's Cathedral as a boy and became a church organist by age fourteen. Educated at Oxford University, Stainer was appointed organist at Magdalen College when he was twenty. In 1872 he succeeded John Goss as organist of St. Paul's Cathedral. A capable choirmaster, Stainer made St. Paul's choir one of the best in England, retiring only when his eyesight failed in 1888. In that same year he was knighted by Queen Victoria. He returned to Oxford as professor of music, remaining there until his death.

Stainer was editor of numerous hymn collections, including *The Church Hymnary* (1898) and *Christmas Carols Old and New* (1871), co-edited with Henry Ramsden Bramley, which was part of a carol-singing revival. He published textbooks on music theory and organ. He also wrote more than 150 hymn tunes, as well as anthems, cantatas, and oratorios, the best known of which is his *Crucifixion*.

Arranger: THE FIRST NOEL (*The first Noel, the angel did say*), **199**

STANFORD, CHARLES VILLIERS (b. Sept. 30, 1852, Dublin, Ireland; d. Mar. 29, 1924, St. Marylebone, London, England), a music prodigy, heard one of his compositions performed at the Dublin Royal Theatre before he was ten. In 1870 he attended Queens' College in Cambridge, was appointed organist of Trinity College (1873-1892), and graduated with honors (B.A., 1874; M.A., 1877). From 1874 to 1876, he studied composition in Germany with Carl Reinecke and Friedrich Kiel. In 1883 he became professor of composition and orchestral playing at the Royal College of Music, London, and professor of music at Cambridge, retaining both positions until his death.

Stanford taught such musical giants as Walford Davies, Gustav T. Holst, and Ralph Vaughan Williams. When Vaughan Williams once turned in an under-par composition, Stanford dismissed it with the curt remark, "All rot, my boy" (Foss 1974). He also conducted choruses and orchestras at many British music festivals. Besides writing several books on music, he composed symphonies, operas, and cantatas, and his settings of Irish melodies helped to revive an interest in Irish folk music. More information is available in standard musical reference books.

Composer: ENGELBERG (*We know that Christ is raised,* **443**; *When in our music God is glorified,* **44**). Arranger: ST. PATRICK (*I bind unto myself today*), **441**

STEAD, LOUISA M. R. (b. ca. 1850, Dover, England; d. Jan. 18, 1917, Penkridge, near Umtali, Southern Rhodesia) moved to the U.S. in 1871 and lived with friends in Cincinnati, Ohio. At age nine she was converted, and, later, at a camp meeting in Urbana, Ohio, she dedicated her life to missionary service. Due to poor health, she was not sent out at that time.

It was not until after her husband drowned trying to rescue a child off Long Island, New York, that she went to South Africa with her daughter, Lily. There she served in the Cape Colony for fifteen years and married Robert Wodehouse, a native of South Africa. In 1895 they returned to the U.S., for she was still in frail health. He became a Methodist minister, and when her health improved they returned to the Methodist mission at Umtali, Southern Rhodesia, serving there from 1901 until she retired in 1911. Her daughter, who had also become a missionary in the region, cared for her mother in her last illness. Steade was buried near the Mutambara Mission.

Author: *'Tis so sweet to trust in Jesus*, **340**

STEBBINS, GEORGE COLES (b. Feb. 26, 1846, East Carlton, N.Y.; d. Oct. 6, 1945, Catskill, N.Y.), raised on a farm in Orleans County, New York, developed an interest in music when he attended a singing school at age thirteen. He studied music in Buffalo and Rochester, both in New York, before moving to Chicago at twenty-three to work for Lyon & Healy Music Company. While in Chicago he also served as director of music at First Baptist Church. In 1874 he went to Boston where he was music director at Clarendon Street Baptist Church and later at Tremont Temple. For twenty-five years, beginning in 1876, Stebbins teamed up with Dwight L. Moody (and other evangelists) as song leader, composer, and co-compiler of gospel song collections.

Following the death of P. P. Bliss in 1876, Stebbins joined James McGranahan and Ira Sankey in editing and compiling the third through the sixth editions of *Gospel Hymns*. In the autumn of 1890, he traveled with his wife and son to India to work with English-speaking people in that country. In great demand as soloists, they held song services in several Indian cities as well as in the Holy Lands and Europe on their return trip.

Composer: ADELAIDE (*Have thine own way*), **504**

STEELE, ANNE (b. 1716, Broughton, Hampshire, England; d. Nov. 11, 1778, Hampshire) spent her whole life in Broughton where her father was a timber merchant and lay pastor at the Baptist church. She was in delicate health from childhood and deeply affected by the loss of her fiancé, who drowned accidentally only a few hours before their wedding.

Although she wrote 144 hymns, 34 metrical psalms, and 30 poems, she allowed none to be published until 1760 when they appeared in two volumes in *Poems on Subjects chiefly Devotional* under the pen name "Theodosia." It was more than a century after sixty-two of her hymns were included in the *Bristol Baptist Collection* (1769) that the number of her hymns published in hymnals—and the frequency with which they were sung—placed her at the forefront of Baptist hymnwriters. Her complete works were reprinted by Daniel Sedgewick in 1863.

Author: *And is the gospel peace and love*, **406**

STEGMANN, JOSUA (b. Sept. 14, 1588, Sülzfeld, near Meiningen, Germany; d. Aug. 3, 1632, Rinteln, Germany), a Lutheran pastor, teacher, and author, attended the University of Leipzig. After earning the M.A. there in 1611, he stayed to teach philosophy part time and finished his D.D. in 1617. That same year he was appointed to three positions: superintendent of the district of Schaumburg, pastor at Stadthagen, and first professor of the *Gymnasium* (high school) at Stadthagen. When the *Gymnasium* became a university and moved to Rinteln in 1621, Stegmann moved with it.

Stegmann himself became a refugee in 1623 when his work was disrupted by the Thirty Years War. He returned to Rinteln two years later and became supervisor of the Lutheran clergy in Hesse-Schaumburg. When the emperor's Edict of Restitution came in 1629, Benedictine monks moved to Rinteln and claimed they were the rightful professors of the university, insisting that the lands used to pay the professors' stipends be transferred to them. Stegmann's home was searched by soldiers to seize his salary, and in July 1632 the monks forced him into a public debate, then planted hecklers to harass him. The burden of repeated injustices is believed to have destroyed his health and eventually killed him. Many of Stegmann's hymns likely are adaptations of older hymns. Of the sixty-one published in 1630, thirty-six are believed to be his own.

Author: *Abide, O dearest Jesus*, **426**

STENNETT, SAMUEL (b. 1727, Exeter, England; d. Aug. 25, 1795, London, England) was born into a family prominent in the Seventh Day Baptist Church of England. Like his father he became a Baptist minister, assisting his father at the church in Little Wild Street, London. When his father died in 1758, Stennett succeeded him as pastor and held the position the rest of his life.

In 1767 Stennett was called to Sabbatarian Baptist Church where his grandfather had served for twenty-three years. Although Stennett did not accept the call, he did preach there every Saturday morning for twenty years. Stennett was a prominent Nonconformist (not of the Church of England) and champion of religious freedom, which meant his exclusion from any university. However, at age thirty-six, he was awarded an honorary doctorate by King's College, Aberdeen, Scotland, in recognition of his scholarship. A number of his sermons have been printed, as well as thirty-eight hymns he contributed to the 1787 *Selection of Hymns . . .*, published by his friend John Rippon.

Author: *On Jordan's stormy banks I stand*, **610**

STEURLEIN (STEURLIN), JOHANN (b. July 5, 1546, Schmalkalden, Germany; d. May 5, 1613, Meiningen, Germany) was the son of the first Lutheran pastor of Schmalkalden. He became town clerk of Wasungen in 1575, government clerk at Weimar in 1588, then imperial notary and poet laureate in 1604. Steurlein was a talented and successful amateur composer, with several books of sacred and secular songs, psalms, and motets to his credit.

Composer: WIE LIEBLICH IST DER MAIEN (*Sing to the Lord of harvest*), **98**

STEVENSON, JOHN ANDREW (b. November 1761, Dublin, Ireland; d. Sept. 14, 1833, Headfort House) was an Irish composer who lived chiefly in Dublin where he directed the choral music at St. Patrick's Cathedral. He started out as a choirboy in Christ Church Cathedral, Dublin. From 1775 to 1780, he sang in the choir of St. Patrick's where in 1783 he became a vicar-choral; he assumed a similar post at Christ Church in 1800. In 1814 he was the first to become organist and music director of the castle chapel. Stevenson was awarded the D.Mus. from Dublin University in 1791 and was knighted in 1803. He composed works for the stage, an oratorio, and numerous glees and songs. Some of his service music and anthems were published in 1825. He is best known for his collection of *Irish Melodies* (1807-1809), set to words by Thomas Moore, and *A Selection of Popular National Airs* (1818).

Arranger: VESPER HYMN (*Now, on land and sea descending*), **655**

STONE, SAMUEL JOHN (b. Apr. 25, 1839, Whitmore, Staffordshire, England; d. Nov. 19, 1900, Charterhouse, England) was educated at Charterhouse and at Pembroke College (B.A., 1862; M.A., 1872). He was ordained in 1862; was curate at Windsor until 1870; and then became vicar in 1874 at St. Paul's, Haggerston, succeeding his father. In 1890 Stone became rector of All Hallows on the Wall, London, a post he held until his death.

Stone, with his "muscles of a prize-fighter," made his pastoral rounds on a tricycle—before bicycles became the vogue. He was a fundamentalist who was also a fighter, both literally and figuratively, and he took unkindly to theories of evolution and the advances of biblical criticism. Some of his hymns, including "The church's one foundation," were written to address what he considered attacks on Anglican dogma. Even some of his poetry was a sarcastic reaction to the new sciences and philosophies of his day. At the same time, he was a champion of the poor and weak, and this combination of Christian chivalry and pugnacity comes through in his many hymns, about which Julian says, "[T]he greater part are strongly outspoken utterances of a manly faith, where dogma, prayer, and praise are interwoven with much skill" (Bailey 1950).

Author: *The church's one foundation*, **311**

SUITOR, M. LEE (b. Feb. 4, 1942, San Francisco, Calif.) grew up in San Francisco where he was a choirboy at Grace Episcopal Church. Later, as a bass, he sang in the Roger Wagner Chorale in Los Angeles and the Atlanta Symphony Chorus under Robert Shaw. He attended the University of Redlands in California, earning both a B.A. (music) and B.Mus. (organ) in 1965. After receiving the M.S.Mus. from the School of Sacred Music at Union Theological Seminary (1968), New York City, Suitor held positions at several colleges and universities, including Rocky Mountain College, Billings, Montana; the State University of New York at Binghamton; and the University of Utah, Salt Lake City. Concurrently, he served in various ecclesiastical positions as consultant and organist.

From 1973 to 1979, he was a full-time church musician at St. Luke's Episcopal Church, Atlanta. A member of the American Guild of Organists, Suitor's performing career gradually drew to a close after he sustained an injury in 1985. Turning to composing, he has received commissions for extensive works from both General and Union Theological Seminaries in New York City and for shorter pieces from other individuals and institutions.

Composer: CORNISH (*Your love, O God, has called us*), **625**. Composer/Arranger: KINGSBORO (*Here, O my Lord, I see thee*), **465**

SULLIVAN, ARTHUR SEYMOUR (b. May 13, 1842, Bolwell Terrace, Lambeth, England; d. Nov. 22, 1900, Westminster, England) began his musical career singing in the choir in the Royal Chapel under Thomas Helmore. There he developed a strong interest in church music and had his first anthem published at age fifteen; however, few of his later compositions were sacred in nature. He continued his studies with Sterndale Bennett and John Goss at the Royal Academy of Music and Leipzig Conservatory (1858-1861) where he was a fellow student with Edvard Grieg.

From 1861 to 1872, Sullivan was organist at St. Michael's, Chester Square, and St. Peter's, Cranley Gardens. In 1866 he was appointed professor of composition at the Royal Academy. He was honored with doctorates from Cambridge and Oxford Universities, received the French Legion of Honor in 1878, and was knighted by Queen Victoria in 1883.

This is the "Sullivan" of the famed Gilbert and Sullivan duo who collaborated on such internationally recognized operettas as *H.M.S.*

Pinafore (1878) and *Mikado* (1885). The melodies of his operettas, however, are very different in style from his hymn tunes. He was also music editor of *The Hymnary* (1872) and *Church Hymns with Tunes* (1874). In the preface to the latter, he states that he was "not a believer in arranging hymns from popular works" and denied a number of requests to make hymn adaptations of melodies from the operettas (*The Hymnal 1940 Companion*, 1951 ed.).

Composer: ST. KEVIN (*Come, ye faithful, raise the strain*), **264**. Arranger: LEOMINSTER (pronounced Lem'inster) (*Make me a captive, Lord*), **539**

SUPPE, GERTRUDE C. (b. Nov. 6, 1911, Los Angeles, Calif.) studied at Pomona College, Claremont, California (B.A., 1933), and Claremont Graduate School (M.A., 1934). Prior to her marriage, she taught in the public schools for a short time. Her interest in the field of worship for Hispanic churches was sparked by a class she took in 1976. Since that time she has developed a computer database of virtually all Hispanic church music in current use. Her translations appear in *Celebremos II* (1983) and *The United Methodist Hymnal* (1989).

Translator: *Tú has venido a la orilla* (*Lord, you have come to the lakeshore*), **229**

SWAIN, JOSEPH (b. 1762, Birmingham, England; d. 1796), an orphan at an early age, became an apprentice to an engraver in London. In 1783 he was baptized by John Rippon and later ordained to the Baptist ministry. In 1791 he became pastor of a mission in Walworth, London, which, in the last five years of his life, grew to a church of two hundred members. Swain wrote several books of poetry and a collection of 129 hymns titled *Walworth Hymns, by J. Swain, Pastor of the Baptist Church Meeting there* (1792).

Author: *O thou, in whose presence*, **559**

SWERTNER, JOHN (b. Sept. 12, 1746, Haarlem, Holland; d. Mar. 11, 1813, Bristol, England) compiled the 1789 English Moravian hymnbook. Although he wrote a few hymn texts, he is remembered primarily for his German-to-English translations of the hymns of Gregor, Zinzendorf, and others. In addition to his interest in poetry, Swertner was also an artist. As a Moravian clergyman, he served the Fairfield, Dublin, and Bristol congregations in England and Ireland.

Author: *Sing hallelujah, praise the Lord*, **67**

SYNESIUS OF CYRENE (b. ca. 375, Cyrene, near modern Benghazi, Libya; d. ca. 414) came from a city famous in ancient times for its philosophers and artists. Synesius lived in Cyrene when it was on the edge of ruin, however. His wealthy parents claimed descent from Spartan kings, and their son exhibited a true nobility, both in intellect and in character. In 383 he went to study under the female philosopher Hypatia at Alexandria where he became an enthusiastic Neoplatonist. Upon his return to Cyrene in 397, he was sent to head an embassy to the imperial court from the cities of the Pentapolis. A friend of Augustine of Hippo, Synesius became a Christian about the year 401 and married a Christian wife in 403. When he was elected bishop of Ptolemais in 409 or 410, he was so popular that he could set his own terms—he kept his wife, along with a few dissenting views about the church.

Author: *Lord Jesus, think on me,* **527**

TALLIS, THOMAS (b. ca. 1505, Leicestershire, England; d. Nov. 23, 1585, Greenwich, England) was the "father" of English cathedral music, but we know little about his birth and childhood. He was an exceptional musician who survived the religious upheavals of the sixteenth-century English monarchy, composing for both Catholic and Protestant courts. Tallis was organist at Waltham Abbey at the time of its dissolution in 1540, at which time he was then appointed gentleman of the Chapel Royal where he served more than forty years, some of the time as organist. While he was joint organist with William Byrd there, both were given a monopoly on all music printed in England during the reign of Elizabeth I.

The majority of Tallis's choral compositions were composed for Latin and English services. Besides his service music, his contribution to hymnody consists of nine tunes in four-part harmony written for Archbishop Parker's *The whole Psalter translated into English Metre, which contayneth an hundred and fifty Psalmes . . . .* Eight were psalm tunes (the ninth was a setting of the hymn *Veni Creator Spiritus*—Come, Holy Ghost),[1] with a table indicating which tunes were most appropriate with certain psalms. The preface indicates the style of each tune.

> The nature of the eight tunes:
> The first is meek: devout to see,
> The second is sad: in majesty.
> The third doth rage: and roughly brayeth.
> The fourth doth fawn: and flattery playeth,
> The fifth delighteth: and laugheth the more,
> The sixth bewaileth: it weepeth full sore,
> The seventh treadeth stout: in forward race,
> The eighth goeth mild: in modest pace.

Composer: TALLIS' CANON (*All praise to thee, My God,* **658**; *O God of love, O Power of peace,* **368**); THE THIRD MELODY (*How shallow former shadows*), **251**

1. All nine tunes, with their original four-part harmonizations, are reprinted in Leonard Ellinwood's article, "Tallis' Tunes and Tudor Psalmody," in *Musica Disciplina,* II (1948).

TAN'SUR, WILLIAM (b. ca. Nov. 6, 1706, Dunchurch, Warwickshire, England; d. Oct. 7, 1783, St. Neots, England) is listed in the baptismal records of Dunchurch for November 6, 1706, as "William Tanzer, son of Edward and Joan Tanzer"; beyond that, little is known of his early life. He was a traveling music teacher who settled in St. Neots as a bookseller. His theoretical books and tune collections were important during his time and include *New Musical Grammar* (1746), which became *Elements of Musick Displayed* (1772) and was still in print as late as 1829. *Compleat Melody or Harmony of Zion* (1734), his earliest tunebook, also underwent a title change, becoming *Royal Melody Compleat* in 1755. Some selections from it appear in the collection *American Harmony*, published in Boston in 1767.

Source: BANGOR (*Alone thou goest forth*), **244**

TAPPAN, WILLIAM BINGHAM (b. Oct. 24, 1794, Beverly, Mass.; d. June 18, 1849, West Needham, Mass.) was a man of various talents—poet, minister, clockmaker, and teacher. He was an apprentice to a clockmaker, then moved to Philadelphia where he established his own business and later became a teacher. Tappan published ten volumes of his own poetry and writing, including *Poetry of Life, New England and Other Poems*, and *Poetry of the Heart*. He worked for the American Sunday School Union until 1826, lived several years in Cincinnati, Ohio, but returned to Philadelphia in 1834. In 1838 he moved to Boston where he was licensed to preach in 1841. He died of cholera in 1849.

Author: *'Tis midnight, and on Olive's brow*, **241**

TARRANT, WILLIAM GEORGE (b. 1853, England; d. 1928) was pastor of Wandsworth Unitarian Christian Church, near London. He was editor of *The Inquirer* (1888-1897) and *The Essex Hall Hymnal* (1890; rev., 1902) and was highly regarded as a hymnologist.

Author: *With happy voices singing*, **83**

TATE, NAHUM (b. 1652, Dublin, Ireland; d. Aug. 12, 1715, Southwark, London, England), the son of an Irish minister who spelled his name Faithful Teate, was educated at Trinity College, Dublin. Tate wrote primarily for the stage, adapting others' works; his only successful dramatic adaptation was a version of Shakespeare's *King Lear*, which at his hands got a happy ending. He was appointed poet laureate in 1692 and royal historiographer in 1702. Tate is remembered, however, for the *New Version of the Psalms of David* (1696), on which he collaborated with Nicholas Brady. This alternative to the psalter of Sternhold and Hopkins (the "old" version) was yet another attempt by sixteenth-century poets to exercise their creativity within the restrictive dictates of the "established church." Though his book was used extensively for many decades, Tate never achieved greatness as a poet and died a pauper.

Author: *While shepherds watched*, **196**. Compiler: *O come, loud anthems let us sing*, **68**

TENNYSON, ALFRED (b. Aug. 6, 1809, Somersby, Lincolnshire, England; d. Oct. 6, 1892, Aldworth, England) was the son of a clergyman. In 1828 he entered Trinity College, Cambridge, but was so frustrated with "the narrowness and dryness of college instruction" that he left in 1831 without completing a degree (Bailey 1950). In 1850, after the publication of *In Memoriam*, he succeeded William Wordsworth as national poet laureate. In 1859 his popular *Idylls of the King* was published. Thirty years later he wrote "Sunset and Evening Star." Although he never wrote hymns, some of his work has been adapted to that medium. He felt hymnwriting was a difficult art to which he wasn't suited.

Tennyson was endowed with what sometimes might be thought an odd combination—a poetic soul and immense physical strength. He could "bend horseshoes, and once he picked up an injured pony and carried it in his arms" (Reynolds 1990). As his literary eminence increased, he was offered but declined a baronetcy in 1873. In 1884 he was elected to the peerage, becoming Lord Tennyson. He was buried in Westminster Abbey.

Author: *Strong Son of God, immortal Love*, **488**

TERSTEEGEN, GERHARD (b. Nov. 25, 1697, Mörs, Westphalia; d. Apr. 3, 1769, Mühlheim, Rhenish Prussia), destined by his parents for the ministry, was instead apprenticed to his brother-in-law, who was a merchant, because his father's death in 1703 left insufficient funds to finance theological schooling. He eventually became a silkweaver and was so generous to the poor that he ate only one small meal a day. This deprivation is thought to have brought on severe mental and spiritual depression that lasted five years.

In 1724 Tersteegen made a new covenant with God, signed in his own blood, and began to speak at prayer meetings. He opened his house to other seekers, and it became a retreat center known as "The Pilgrim's Cottage." A mystic himself, he finally gave up his trade and devoted himself entirely to prayer, preaching, visiting the poor, translating the work of medieval mystics, writing devotional material, and carrying on voluminous correspondence. Working outside the Reformed Church tradition, Tersteegen is remembered as one of Germany's great spiritual leaders and hymnists, even though he was restricted from preaching for twenty years because of a law against private religious gatherings. He translated or paraphrased many

French and Latin classics into German and wrote 111 hymns, about 50 of which have been translated into English.

Author: *God is here among us*, **16**; *O Power of love*, **593**

TESCHNER, MELCHIOR (b. 1584, Fraustadt, Silesia; d. Dec. 1, 1635, Oberprietschen, Posen) in 1609 was appointed to the post of cantor at Zum Kripplein Christi Lutheran Church in Fraustadt. He also taught in the parish school until 1614 when he moved to nearby Oberprietschen to serve as pastor. Teschner survived the plague of 1613 that claimed two thousand lives in Fraustadt alone, but he died in a Cossack raid years later. Both his son and grandson followed him in his pastorate.

Composer: ST. THEODULPH (VALET WILL ICH DIR GEBEN) (*All glory, laud, and honor*, **237**; *Oh, how shall I receive thee*, **182**)

THEODULPH OF ORLEANS (b. ca. 750, probably Spain; d. Sept. 18, 821, Angers), born into a noble family, became abbot of a monastery in Florence, Italy. Well educated and a born leader, he attracted the notice of Charlemagne, who in 1781 brought him to France where he charmed the intellectuals of the court. He was appointed abbot of Fleury and bishop of Orleans. With the king's backing, Theodulph established schools in connection with the monasteries in the area, as well as "free" schools for the poor. After Charlemagne died in 818, Theodulph was accused of conspiring with King Bernard of Italy against Louis I. He was imprisoned at Angers and, contrary to the legend surrounding the writing of this hymn, apparently died in prison, possibly from poison (see the article on "All glory, laud, and honor," **237**) .

Author: *All glory, laud, and honor*, **237**

THIMAN, ERIC HARDING (b. Sept. 12, 1900, Ashford, Kent, England; d. Feb. 13, 1975, London, England) was a British organist and composer who was mostly self-taught before becoming a fellow of the Royal College of Organists in 1921. In 1927, after studying with Harold Darke, he earned the D.Mus. from London University.

Thiman (pronounced Tee-man) was organist/choirmaster at Park Chapel Congregational Church, London (1928-1957), professor of harmony at the Royal Academy of Music (1931-1975), and director of music and organist at City Temple, London (1957-1975). In 1938 he was named examiner to the Royal Schools of Music and, in 1952, joined the music faculty of London University, eventually becoming dean there.

Besides receiving recognition as a recitalist in England, South Africa, Australia, and New Zealand, Thiman was cited by hymnologist Erik Routley as the first significant church composer in the Congregationalist tradition. His cantatas, anthems, services, unison numbers, and part-songs, as well as piano and organ music, are all distinguished by craftsmanship. His music, however, is also accessible to amateur musicians of modest capabilities. *The Last Supper* (1930), *The Parables* (1931), and *The Temptations of Christ* (1952) are among his sacred cantatas.

Composer: MILTON ABBAS (*God of the fertile fields*), **390**

THOMAS À KEMPIS (b. ca. 1380, Kempen, near Düsseldorf, Germany; d. 1471, Zwolle, Holland), whose surname was Hammerken, was born to peasant parents. When he was twelve, he attended a "poor-scholars' house" connected with a community known as the Brethren of the Common Life in Deventer. There he was known as Thomas from Kempen (Latin, *à Kempis*). At age eighteen, he was admitted to the brotherhood and a year later joined the new monastery at Mount St. Agnes, near Zwolle. In 1407 he took his vows, was ordained a priest in 1413, and became a sub-prior in 1425. He stayed at Mount St. Agnes until his death, writing and editing several biographies, tracts, and hymns. He probably edited and compiled the classic devotional *The Imitation of Christ* (1471), which contains the aims of his community, a lay fellowship devoted to Christian service as exemplified by Christ.

Author: (Attrib.) *O love, how deep, how broad*, **236**; Most gracious God, protect us from worry, **730**

THOMPSON, WILL LAMARTINE (b. Nov. 7, 1847, East Liverpool, Ohio; d. Sept. 20, 1909, New York, N.Y.), educated at Mount Union College, Alliance, Ohio, and Boston Conservatory of Music, continued his studies in Leipzig, Germany. After a music publisher in Cleveland turned down some of his songs because they were too expensive at one hundred dollars, he instead established his own successful music publishing firm of Will L. Thompson and Company, with offices in East Liverpool, Ohio, and Chicago. He wrote numerous sacred and secular songs and became known as "the bard of Ohio" (Hustad 1978). The well-known revival team of Moody and Sankey used many of his hymns in their meetings.

Author/Composer: *Softly and tenderly Jesus is calling* (THOMPSON), **491**

THRELFALL, JEANNETTE (b. Mar. 24, 1821, Blackburn, Lancashire, England; d. Nov. 30, 1880, Westminster, England), the daughter of a wine merchant, became an orphan when she was quite young. She also suffered two serious accidents that left her an invalid. Despite these difficulties, Threlfall outwardly expressed cheerfulness and hope in her poems, as well as in her life. Many of her hymns and poems were published in *Woodsorrel, or Leaves from a Retired Home* (1856) and *Sunshine and Shadow* (1873).

Author: *Hosanna, loud hosanna,* **238**

THRING, GODFREY (b. Mar. 25, 1823, Alford, Somerset, England; d. Sept. 13, 1903, Shanley Green, Surrey, England) received his B.A. in 1845 from Balliol College, Oxford. After his ordination in the Church of England, he held several ministerial positions. In 1858 he followed his father as a pastor in Alford. In 1876 he became prebendary (a clergyman paid by an endowment from the state) of East Harptree in Wells Cathedral, a position he held until his retirement.

Thring's hymns are included in many hymnals, including several collections of his own: *Hymns and Other Verses* (1866), *Hymns Congregational and Others* (1866), and *A Church of England Hymn Book, adapted to the daily services of the Church throughout the year* (1880), the revised edition of which is known as *The Church of England Hymn Book* (1882).

Author: *Jesus came—the heavens adoring,* **297**; *Crown him with many crowns* (st. 2), **116**

THRUPP, DOROTHY ANN (b. June 20, 1779, London England; d. Dec. 14, 1847, London) was the daughter of an Anglican clergyman, but little else is known about her. She wrote hymns for children, often under pseudonyms. Her own compilation, *Hymns for the Young,* which she edited for the Religious Tract Society, first appeared around 1830; all the hymns in it were published anonymously.

Editor/Source: *Savior, like a shepherd lead us,* **355**

TIDDEMAN, MARIA (b. 1837; d. ca. 1911, Croyden, England), daughter of a Church of England minister, received her musical training at Oxford University. She is known to have composed hymn tunes, songs, part-songs, and anthems. Her date of death is given in various sources as 1911, 1913, and 1915.

Composer: IBSTONE (*I hunger and I thirst*), **474**

TINDLEY, CHARLES ALBERT (b. July 7, 1851, Berlin, Md.; d. July 26, 1933, Philadelphia, Pa.), a noted African American Methodist pastor whose parents were slaves, learned to read and write at age seventeen by pure determination. He then moved to Philadelphia where, working as a hod carrier and church custodian, he attended night school and took a correspondence course from the Boston School of Theology. He was ordained into the Methodist ministry; joined the Delaware Conference in 1885; and held pastorates in Delaware, Maryland, and New Jersey.

After presiding as elder of the Wilmington District (1899-1902), Tindley became pastor at Calvary Methodist Episcopal Church in Philadelphia where he had been custodian years earlier. Calvary was later renamed Tindley Temple Methodist Church, recognizing his highly successful ministry there. The church leadership was internationally diverse, including African Americans, Italians, Jews, Germans, Norwegians, Mexicans, and Danes. This self-educated man, who spoke six languages, was close friends with Frederick Douglass and Harriet Tubman, euologized Booker T. Washington, and had received an audience with Franklin D. Roosevelt.

Tindley wrote many gospel songs, both texts and tunes, including "I'll overcome some day" (1901), which later birthed the famous civil rights song "We shall overcome." He has been honored as the "father of black gospel music" with a permanent exhibition at the Smithsonian Institution. William Farley Smith categorized Tindley's hymns this way: "Whereas the slave's song was the historical preservation of slave culture in America's Southland, Tindley's hymns are historical commentary on the plight of free-Blacks in turn-of-the-century American northern industrialized cities."

Author/Composer: *When the storms of life are raging* (STAND BY ME), **558**

TISSERAND, JEAN (d. 1494, Paris, France), a preaching friar in the Franciscan order in Paris, founded an order for penitent women. He is thought to be the author of a worship history that commemorated members of his order martyred in Morocco in 1220. He is remembered for his Latin hymns, including *O filii et filiae* (O sons and daughters), which was published posthumously.

Author: *O sons and daughters, let us sing*, **274**

TITTLE, ERNEST FREMONT (b. Oct. 21, 1885, Springfield, Ohio; d. Aug. 3, 1949, Evanston, Ill.) earned degrees at Ohio Wesleyan University, Delaware (A.B., 1906) and Drew Theological Seminary (B.D., 1908) and received five honorary doctorates. After serving as pastor in a series of Methodist churches in Ohio, he was called in 1918 to First Methodist Church in Evanston where he remained until his death.

For many years, because of his outspoken pacifism and "socialist" statements, he was a controversial figure. In 1924 he was denied the honor of preaching the baccalaureate sermon at Northwestern University, because that year's class objected to his having invited a convicted World War I evader to speak to his youth group. In 1932 he created a sensation at the general conference of the Methodist Church by introducing a resolution to bar the denomination from ever meeting in a city where hotels practiced racial discrimination (the adopted resolution was considered damaging to the impending merger of the northern and southern branches of Methodism). According to *The New York Times*, Tittle became "one of America's foremost pulpit orators," as seen in his appointment as the 1932 lecturer on preaching at Yale University, New Haven, Connecticut, and in the annual demand for his preaching on other prestigious campuses. He held lectureships at six additional schools and was active in national and international ecumenical organizations.

Author: O God, you rule the world from end to end, **692**

TOOLAN, SUZANNE (b. 1927, Lansing, Mich.), after moving to California, studied organ with Richard Key Biggs, whom she assisted at St. Paul's Church in Los Angeles. Through Lucienne Gourdon Biggs at St. Paul's, she was introduced to working with boys' choirs and became involved in high school choral music at Villa Cabrini Academy in Burbank. She also was organist and choir director at St. Ambrose Church in Hollywood. Upon completion of her B.A. at Immaculate Heart College in Hollywood, she entered the Sisters of Mercy, Burlingame, California. She studied composition at Michigan State University, East Lansing, and liturgy at the University of Notre Dame, South Bend, Indiana. She received an M.A. in music at San Francisco State University.

In recent years Toolan has taught music at Mercy High School, Burlingame, directing her outstanding choral groups at events throughout the area. She has served on worship and liturgy commissions for the archdiocese of San Francisco and conducted workshops across California and beyond. She is also director of Mercy Center, a spirituality and conference center in Burlingame. Some of her hymns are recorded in two albums: *Living Spirit* (1971) and *Keeping the Festival* (1979).

Author/Composer: *I am the Bread of life* (I AM THE BREAD OF LIFE), **472**; *Two fishermen* (LEAVE ALL THINGS BEHIND), **227**

TOURJÉE, LIZZIE SHOVE (b. 1858; d. 1913), the daughter of Eben Tourjée who founded the New England Conservatory of Music, Boston, was educated at Newton, Massachusetts, and attended Wellesley College (Mass.) for one year. She married Franklin Estabrook in 1883; beyond that, little is known of her life.

Composer: WELLESLEY (*There's a wideness in God's mercy*), **145**

TOWNER, DANIEL BRINK (b. Mar. 5, 1850, Rome, Pa.; d. Oct. 3, 1919, Longwood, Mo.) received his early musical training from his father, J. G. Towner, who was a noted teacher and singer. He continued musical study with John Howard, George F. Root, and George J. Webb and became a music director in his own right, serving Methodist Episcopal churches in New York, Ohio, and Kentucky. In 1885 he joined the evangelism team headed by Dwight L. Moody, touring with revival teams until 1893, when he was made director of the music department of Moody Bible Institute, Chicago. In this position, which he held until his death, Towner exerted great influence in music among churches in the evangelical tradition. He received the honorary D.Mus. from the University of Tennessee in 1900.[1]

Towner is credited with more than two thousand gospel songs. He also compiled fourteen songbooks and hymnals and wrote textbooks on music theory and practice. As his life was immersed in music, so was his death; he died leading singing in an evangelistic meeting in Longwood, Missouri.

Composer: MARVELOUS GRACE (*Marvelous grace of our loving Lord*), **151**; TRUST AND OBEY (*When we walk with the Lord*), **544**

1. Towner is the subject of an unpublished thesis by Perry Carroll, written at New Orleans Baptist Theological Seminary, La.

TROEGER, THOMAS HENRY (b. Jan. 30, 1945, Suffern, N.Y.) was educated at Yale University, New Haven, Connecticut, where he majored in English (B.A., *cum laude*, 1967), and Colgate Rochester Divinity School (N.Y.; B.Div., 1970). Ordained as a Presbyterian minister in 1970, he was associate minister of New Hartford Presbyterian Church, New York, before joining the faculty of Colgate Rochester Divinity School/Bexley Hall/Crozer Theological Seminary, Hamilton, New York, in 1977 as a preaching professor. Since 1991 he has been at Iliff School of Theology, Denver, Colorado, teaching homiletics.

Troeger has written numerous books and articles on preaching, worship, and theology. As a professional flutist, he finds that music provides many materials and metaphors for his work. His *New Hymns for the Lectionary* (1986) and *New Hymns for the Life of the Church* (1991), created in partnership with tune writer Carol Doran, have given expression to many of the concerns of our time through contemporary hymnody.

Author: *How buoyant and bold the stride*, **394**; *If all you want, Lord*, **512**; *O praise the gracious power*, **111**; *Silence! frenzied, unclean spirit*, **630**; *Through our fragmentary prayers*, **347**; *Wind who makes all winds*, **31**

TROUTBECK, JOHN (b. ca. 1832, Blencowe, Cumberland, England; d. Oct. 11, 1889, London, England) was educated at Oxford University (B.A., 1856; M.A., 1858). Ordained in the Church of England, he was music leader at Manchester Cathedral and a chaplain to the queen. He also was secretary to the New Testament Revision Committee (1870-1881). As an outstanding translator for Novello and Company, London, Troutbeck worked on texts of operas, oratorios, anthems, and vocal solos from German, French, and Italian. Among the collections he edited were the *Manchester Psalter* (1867) and the *Westminster Abbey Hymn Book* (1883).

Translator: *Break forth, O beauteous heavenly* (st. 1), **203**

TRUEBLOOD, DAVID ELTON (b. Dec. 12, 1900, Pleasantville, Iowa; d. Dec. 20, 1994, Lansdale, Pa.), the son of a farmer and a member of the Society of Friends (Quakers), is known as an outstanding educator and author. He attended William Penn College, Oskaloosa, Iowa (A.B., 1922); Brown University, Providence, Rhode Island; Hartford Theological Seminary (Conn.); Harvard University, Cambridge, Massachusetts (S.T.B., 1926); and Johns Hopkins University, Baltimore, Maryland (Ph.D., 1934). He taught philosophy at Guilford College, Greensboro, North Carolina (1927-1930); Haverford College (Pa.; 1933-1936); Earlham College, Richmond, Indiana (1946-1966); and was chaplain and professor of religion at Stanford University, Palo Alto, California (1936-1945). Trueblood earned many honorary degrees and awards and is listed in *Who's Who in America*, *Who's Who in Religion*, and in *Contemporary Authors*. His books have been widely read and cited. He is the subject of a biography by James R. Newby, but he wrote his own autobiography as well, *While It Is Day . . .* (1974).

Author: *God, whose purpose is to kindle*, **135**

TUCKER, FRANCIS BLAND (b. Jan. 6, 1895, Norfolk, Va.; d. Jan. 1, 1984, Savannah, Ga.) was educated at the University of Virginia, Charlottesville, and the Virginia Theological Seminary (B.D., 1920; D.D., 1944). F. Bland Tucker was ordained an Episcopal priest in 1920 and served pastorates in Virginia; Washington, D.C.; and Georgia. Praised as an outstanding writer, he was a member of the committee that compiled the Episcopal *Hymnal 1940* and was a consultant to the text committee for *The Hymnal 1982* (also Episcopal). Both hymnals contain a number of his hymns and translations, several of which have achieved wider usage.

Translator: *Alone thou goest forth*, **244**

TWEEDY, HENRY HALLAM (b. Aug. 5, 1868, Binghamton, N.Y.; d. Apr. 11, 1953, Brattleboro, Vt.) was related to Governor William Bradford through his mother. He was educated at Phillips Andover Academy and trained for the Congregational ministry at Yale University, New Haven, Connecticut; Union Theological Seminary, New York City; and the University of Berlin, Germany. Ordained in 1898, he pastored congregations in New York and Connecticut. Then in 1909 he became professor of practical theology at Yale Divinity School where he continued as professor emeritus following his retirement in 1937. In addition to writing several books, Tweedy edited the hymnal *Christian Worship and Praise* (1939), in which six of his texts appear, all set to familiar tunes.

Author: *O Holy Spirit, making whole*, **300**; *O Spirit of the living God*, **361**

TWELLS, HENRY (b. Mar. 13, 1823, Ashted, near Birmingham, England; d. Jan. 19, 1900, Bournemouth, England) attended King Edward's School in Birmingham, St. Peter's College in Cambridge (B.A., 1848; M.A., 1851), and Oxford University (M.A., 1853). He was ordained as an Anglican priest in 1850. Twells held both ecclesiastical and academic positions throughout his long and distinguished career from 1851 to 1890. Closely associated with the important collection *Hymns Ancient and Modern* (1861), he helped prepare the original edition, contributed six hymns to the *Appendix* (1868), and was an editor of the supplement to its revised edition (1889).

Author: *At evening, when the sun had set*, **628**

VAJDA, JAROSLAV J. (b. Apr. 28, 1919, Lorain, Ohio) is the son of a Lutheran pastor and grandson of Czechoslovakian immigrants. After graduation from Concordia Junior College, Fort Wayne, Indiana (1938), he worked in the steel mills for a year to make money to attend Concordia Theological Seminary in St. Louis, Missouri. From 1945 to 1963, he served four churches in Pennsylvania and Indiana, two of them bilingual (English and Slovak). He edited both *The Lutheran Beacon* (1959-1963) and *This Day* magazine (1963-1971). From 1971 until his retirement, he was book editor and developer for Concordia Publishing House in St. Louis.

Vajda began translating and writing poetry when he was sixteen. It was not until the late 1960s that he ventured into the area of hymnody with "Now the silence." His collected hymns, carols, and songs are published in *Now the Joyful Celebration* (1987). In 1988 he was made a fellow of the Hymn Society of the United States and Canada, with many hymn credits to his name.

Author: *Go, my children*, **433**; *Now the silence*, **462**. Translator: *If you but trust in God* (st. 2), **576**

VAN DYKE, HENRY (b. Nov. 10, 1852, Germantown, Pa.; d. Apr. 10, 1933, Princeton, N.J.) was an eminent preacher, scholar, professor, and diplomat. He studied at Brooklyn Polytechnic Institute (N.Y.; 1869); Princeton University (B.A., 1873; M.A., 1876); and Princeton Theological Seminary (1877). He also did a year of study abroad. He was ordained in the Presbyterian Church, but served a Congregational church in Rhode Island before becoming pastor of Brick Presbyterian Church in New York City (1883-1899). Haeussler praises the "beautiful diction, arresting style, depth of scholarship, breadth of view, and fearless convictions which characterized his sermons" (Haeussler 1952).

In 1899 Van Dyke traded his pulpit for a lectern in English literature at Princeton University, teaching for twenty-three years; during this time Woodrow Wilson, as university president, came to know him well. When Wilson was elected U.S. president, he appointed Van Dyke United States

Minister to the Netherlands and Luxembourg in 1913, a position he held until 1916. In 1917 Van Dyke became a Navy chaplain, serving the remainder of World War I.

Van Dyke received a doctorate from Oxford University, England, in 1917, as well as honorary doctorates from several U.S. universities. In 1923 he retired, dedicating the last decade of his life exclusively to literary work. He chaired the committee of the Presbyterian *Book of Common Worship* (1905) and aided in its 1932 revision. Of his approximately twenty-five books, perhaps the best known is *The Story of the Other Wise Man* (1896). A list of Van Dyke's publications is included in his biography, published in 1935 by his son.

Author: *Joyful, joyful, we adore thee,* **71**

VANSTONE, WILLIAM HUBERT (b. May 9, 1923, Mossley, Manchester, England) earned degrees at Balliol College, Oxford (B.A., 1948); St. John's College, Cambridge (where he was a Westcott honors scholar, B.A., 1949); and Union Theological Seminary, New York City (S.T.M., 1950). Ordained in 1951 as a priest in the Church of England, Vanstone's pastoral assignments took him to St. Thomas Halliwell (1950-1955) and Kirkholt (1955-1976). From 1959 to 1978, he was chaplain to the bishop of Manchester, as well as honorary canon of Manchester Cathedral (1968-1976). Vanstone became canon residentiary of Chester Cathedral in 1978 and a preacher at Canterbury Cathedral in 1984. His writings include *The Statue of Waiting* (1982) and *Love's Endeavour, Love's Expense* (1977), which won the Collins Religious Book Prize.

Author: *Open are the gifts of God,* **255**

VAUGHAN WILLIAMS, RALPH (b. Oct. 12, 1872, Down Ampney, England; d. Aug. 26, 1958, London, England), hailed as "the greatest English composer since Purcell" (Young 1993), received early training in piano, theory, and violin and began his formal education at Charterhouse. His advanced musical studies were done at the Royal College of Music, London, and at Trinity College, Cambridge, where he received a B.Mus. in 1894, a B.A. (history) in 1895, and a D.Mus. in 1901. He studied composition with C. H. H. Parry and C. V. Stanford at the Royal College; with Max Bruch in Berlin; and with Maurice Ravel in Paris. He was organist/choirmaster at St. Barnabas Church in London (1896-1899), then a medic during World War I, after which he was appointed professor of composition at the Royal College of Music. Since he lived on an inherited income, his official position at the Royal College was part time, freeing his schedule for his prolific composing, which he continued to the day of his death.

Vaughan Williams completed nine symphonies, works for chorus and orchestra, five operas, ballets, film music, chamber music and songs, plus a few organ preludes and piano pieces. In 1903 he began to collect English folk songs, writing down texts and tunes by hand, accumulating eight hundred in ten years. He was music editor of *The English Hymnal* (1906); he co-edited *Songs of Praise* (1925, 1931) and *The Oxford Book of Carols* (1928) with Martin Shaw and Percy Dearmer. In these collections he arranged a number of English folk tunes for hymn settings and composed fifteen original hymn tunes, several of which have gained wide acceptance and set a standard for twentieth-century hymns. Complete accounts of Vaughan Williams' life and work are available in standard musical references.

Composer: DOWN AMPNEY (*Come down, O Love divine*), **501**; KING'S WESTON (*At the name of Jesus*), **342**; RANDOLPH (*God be with you*), **430**; SINE NOMINE (*For all the saints*), **636**; THE CALL (*Come, my Way, my Truth, my Life*), **587**. Arranger: FOREST GREEN (*All beautiful the march of days*), **159**; HYFRYDOL (*Come, thou long-expected Jesus*, **178**; *God the Spirit, Guide and Guardian*, **632**; *God, whose giving*, **383**; *Hear us now, O God our Maker*, **626**); KINGSFOLD (*I heard the voice of Jesus say*), **493**; LASST UNS ERFREUEN (*All creatures of our God and King*), **48**; PLEADING SAVIOR (*Thou true Vine, that heals*), **373**

VERDUIN, LEONARD (b. Mar. 9, 1897, South Holland, Ill.) grew up in the Christian Reformed Church. His grandparents had been involved in the *Afscheiding*, the secession from the state church of the Netherlands in 1834. Verduin writes: "It was this repudiation of the society-wide church that made me more or less akin to the Mennonites and the Anabaptist movement." In fact, at the time of Verduin's birth, his father was reading Baptist literature and decided not to have his son christened (he succumbed, however, about three years later). Verduin earned degrees at Calvin College (A.B.) and Seminary (Th.B.), Grand Rapids, Michigan, and the University of Michigan (A.M. in history). He served the Christian Reformed Church for many years, first as pastor of a congregation in South Dakota and then as chaplain at the University of Michigan until retirement in 1962. In 1966, under an exchange program, he lectured in all of South Africa's seminaries on the subject of church-state relations. He has contributed frequently to the *Reformed Journal* and has published a number of books, including a translation of *The Complete Works of Menno Simons* (Herald Press 1956). In his nineties he wrote a book-length manuscript on the First Amendment—to a large degree a product of the same thought system from which the Anabaptist movement also grew, he says.

Translator: Lord Jesus, blind I am, **700**

VORIES, WILLIAM MERRILL (b. Oct. 28, 1880, Leavenworth, Kan.; d. May 7, 1964, Omi-Hachiman, Japan) became interested in missionary work while still a student in high school. In 1905, six months after earning his architectural degree from Colorado College, Colorado Springs, he went to Japan to teach English under the auspices of the International YMCA. He stipulated that he earn his own living, as Apostle Paul had done in his missionary journeys.

As the first Christian missionary to the predominantly Buddhist province of Omi-Hachiman, Vories experienced hostility and opposition. Although he lost his teaching position at the end of the first year, he persevered, helping establish schools, a hospital, library, business ventures, and one of the finest architectural firms in Japan.

Through his friendship with A. A. Hyde of the Mentholatum company, he developed a combination work/study program for teenage girls too poor to attend high school. While earning money in the factory, they were able to complete the four-year course in five years (Gingerich 1959).

In 1919 Vories married the daughter of a Japanese nobleman, and she guided the development of the School Foundation. Before World War II, he became a citizen of Japan, and in 1958 he was honored by the mayor of Omi-Hachiman with the title of "Honorable Citizen No. 1." His alma mater had conferred on him the LL.D. in 1930.

Author: *Let there be light, Lord God,* **371**

VULPIUS, MELCHIOR (b. ca. 1560, Wasungen, Thüringen, Germany; d. August 1615, Weimar, Germany) was the Lutheran cantor at Weimar from approximately 1602 until his death in 1615. He was buried in Weimar on August 7, 1615, but most of the other details surrounding his life are clouded in obscurity. He left behind a great number of chorale tunes, however, as well as a setting of the *Passion According to St. Matthew.* His collections include the *Cantiones Sacrae* (1602, 1604), which contains most of his original chorale melodies; the *Kirchengesänge und geistliche Lieder* (1604); the *Canticum beatissimae* (1605); and *Ein schön geistlich Gesangbuch* (1609).

Composer: CHRISTUS, DER IST MEIN LEBEN (*Abide, O dearest Jesus*), **426**; GELOBT SEI GOTT (*Become to us the living Bread*, **475**; *O sons and daughters, let us sing*, **274**); LOBT GOTT DEN HERREN (*All who believe and are baptized*, **436**; *Let all creation bless the Lord*, **61**). Arranger: NUN KOMM, DER HEIDEN HEILAND (*Fire of God, undying Flame*, **129**; *Savior of the nations, come*, **173**)

WADDELL, CHRYSOGONUS (b. 1930, Corregidor, the Philippines) is organist, choirmaster, and liturgist at Gethsemani Abbey in Kentucky. He studied composition at Philadelphia Conservatory of Music (Pa.) with Vincent Persichetti (1948-1950). Waddell entered Gethsemani Abbey in 1950, was ordained in 1958, and did further study in Rome in the 1960s. He is the author of numerous articles and editions of medieval liturgical books.

Author/Composer: *Jesus took a towel* (JESUS TOOK A TOWEL), **449**

WADE, JOHN FRANCIS (b. ca. 1711; d. Aug. 16, 1786, Douay, France) was a devout Englishman who lived in the Roman Catholic center of Douay in northern France where many English religious and political dissidents found refuge. There he taught church music and made manuscript copies of Gregorian chants and other musical works, especially for Catholic chapels and families. His collected manuscripts are found in the 1751 volume *Cantus Diversi pro Dominicis et Festis per annum*, which is preserved at Stonyhurst College in Lancashire, England.

Author/Composer: *O come, all ye faithful* (ADESTE FIDELES), **212**

WALLACE, BILL (W. L.) (20th c.), a New Zealander, is a Methodist minister, hymnwriter, poet, and sculptor. Committed to serving in poor neighborhoods, he also was part of the formation of one of the first non-hierarchical team ministries in New Zealand, which came about when Methodist and Presbyterian congregations established an experimental union.

Author: *Why has God forsaken me?*, **246**

WALLACE, WILLIAM VINCENT (b. June 1, 1814, Waterford, Ireland; d. Oct. 12, 1865, Chateau de Bages, France), of Scottish ancestry, took his earliest musical training from his father. Inspired by the violin artistry of Paganini, he became a master violinist. At age fifteen, he played his first concert in Dublin and then toured the world as a performer. Wallace's compositions include seven operas that have had popular acclaim in France, a cantata, many piano pieces, and tunes set to four hymns of John Keble. When his eyesight failed, he ceased composing and retired to the Pyrenees.

Composer: SERENITY (*Immortal Love, forever full*), **629**

WALTHER (WALTER), JOHANN (b. 1496, Gotha, Thüringen, Germany; d. Apr. 24, 1570, Torgau, Saxony, Germany) was among the earliest Lutheran composers and a friend of Martin Luther. Originally named Blankenmüller, he took the name of a citizen who adopted him when he was a penniless choirboy. In 1524 Walther was a bass singer in the Saxon court of Frederick the Wise at Torgau, the same year he spent three weeks in Luther's home in Wittenberg adapting music for the German Mass. The celebration of this Mass in 1525 was a momentous watershed in the Reformation, since it so clearly departed from the tradition of the Roman Church, which used Latin exclusively. Meanwhile, Walther was also preparing his *Geystliche gesangk Buchleyn*, for which Luther wrote a preface. The book went through many editions.

In 1525 Walther became *Kapellmeister* to Johann of Saxony in Dresden, and in 1534 he took the job of cantor at the school in Torgau. In 1548 he moved on as *Kapellmeister* to Moritz of Saxony and in 1554 received a pension and retired to Torgau.

Walther published several collections, the final one being *Das christliche Kinderlied Dr. Martin Luthers* (Martin Luther's Christian Children's Song, 1566), which includes several of his hymn texts and musical settings. Walther is remembered chiefly for his compositions and adaptations of old melodies into chorale tunes.

Arranger: ALL MORGEN IST GANZ FRISCH (*Each morning brings us*), **645**

WALTON, JAMES GEORGE (b. Feb. 19, 1821, Clitheroe, Lancashire, England; d. Sept. 1, 1905, Bradford, Yorkshire, England) edited *Plainsong Music for the Holy Communion Office* (1874), which includes his adaptation of Henri F. Hemy's tune ST. CATHERINE.

Arranger: ST. CATHERINE (*Faith of the martyrs*, **413;** *God of the earth, the sky, the sea*, **53**)

WALWORTH, CLARENCE AUGUSTUS (ALPHONSUS) (b. May 30, 1820, Plattsburg, N.Y.; d. Sept. 19, 1900, Albany, N.Y.) graduated in 1838 from Union College, Schenectady, New York, and in 1841 was admitted to the bar. Though he was first a Presbyterian, in 1845 he prepared for the Episcopal ministry at General Theological Seminary, New York City. Influenced by the Oxford movement to revitalize liturgy in England, he was ordained a Roman Catholic priest and helped found the Paulist Order in the U.S., at which time he took the name Alphonsus. In 1866 he became rector of St. Mary's in Albany, remaining there until he died. He wrote *The Oxford Movement in America* (1895), which tells of his conversion to Roman Catholicism, and *Andiatorocte . . . and Other Poems* (1888). He was reportedly a powerful preacher who was blind the last ten years of his life.

Translator: *Holy God, we praise thy name*, **121**

WARD, PAMELA (b. 1946, Nelson, Lancashire, England) was ordained to the United Reformed Church ministry in 1972 and has served parishes in Hull, Leeds, and Erdington (Birmingham). In addition to the tune listed below, she has written a setting for another of Fred Kaan's texts "The church is like a table."

Composer: PENHILL (*God of Eve and God of Mary*), **492**

WARE, HENRY, JR. (b. Apr. 21, 1794, Hingham, Mass.; d. Sept. 25, 1843, Framingham, Mass.), the son of a Unitarian clergyman and teacher, completed his education at Harvard University, Cambridge, Massachusetts, in 1812 and was appointed to the faculty of Exeter Academy (N.H.).

He became a Unitarian minister and pastored Second Unitarian Church in Boston. In 1829, due to declining health, he was given an assistant pastor—Ralph Waldo Emerson. A year later Ware moved on to teach "pulpit eloquence" and pastoral care at Cambridge Theological School (1830-1842). He was also editor of the *Christian Disciple*, later renamed the *Christian Examiner*. His works were published in four volumes by Chandler Robbins in 1847.

Author: *Lift your glad voices*, **275**

WARING, ANNA LAETITIA (b. Apr. 19, 1823, Plas-y-Velin, Neath, Glamorganshire, Wales; d. May 10, 1910, Clifton, Bristol, England), though raised in the Society of Friends (Quakers), developed an appreciation for the sacraments of the Anglican Church, which she joined in 1842. Waring started writing hymns when she was in her teens and over the next twenty years completed thirty-nine texts. In her study of Old Testament poetry, she dispensed with translations by learning Hebrew. She was active in social service, visiting in the prisons of Bristol and serving in the "Discharged Prisoner's Aid Society." Among her publications are *Hymns and Meditations* (1850) and *Additional Hymns* (1858).

Author: *In heavenly love abiding*, **613**

WARKENTIN, LARRY R. (b. Aug. 14, 1940, Reedley, Calif.) was an honors student at Immanuel Academy in Reedley and at Tabor College, Hillsboro, Kansas (B.A., 1962, music education). He earned his M.A. in music composition from California State University, Fresno, in 1964, and the D.M.A. with an emphasis in church music from the University of Southern California, Los Angeles, in 1967.

In 1967 he was employed at Fresno Pacific College where he now chairs the humanities division. He also teaches music theory and composition, along with directing music in several area churches. Warkentin has composed numerous hymns, anthems, cantatas, chamber works, and a piano concerto. His symphonic essay *Koinonia* was performed at the Mennonite World Conference in Wichita, Kansas (1978). Warkentin represented the Mennonite Brethren Church as an observer-participant with the music committee of *Hymnal: A Worship Book* (1992).

Composer: CLOVIS (*From the hands*), **97**; LOVELLE (*Wonder of wonders*), **622**; MICAH (*What does the Lord require*), **409**; RYAN (*When grief is raw*), **637**

WARNER, ANNA BARTLETT (b. ca. 1822, Long Island, N.Y.; d. Jan. 22, 1915, Constitution Island, near West Point, N.Y.) lived on Constitution Island in the Hudson River with her father and sister, Susan, also an author who sometimes went by the name Elizabeth Wetherell. Anna's birthdate ranges from 1820 to 1827 in various sources. She wrote several novels using the pseudonym "Amy Lathrop" and published *Hymns of the Church Militant* (1858) and *Wayfaring Hymns, Original and Translated* (1869). In addition to the well-known "Jesus loves me," Warner wrote "We would see Jesus, for the shadows lengthen." She conducted Bible classes with her sister for the cadets at the military academy at West Point. Later, the family home was willed to the academy. When Warner died she was buried with military honors.

Author: *Jesus loves me,* **341**

WATT, LAUCHLAN MACLEAN (b. Oct. 24, 1867, Grantown, Inverness-shire, Scotland; d. Sept. 11, 1957, Loch Carron, Ross-shire, Scotland), a clergyman in the Church of Scotland, received his M.A., B.D., and honorary D.D. from the University of Edinburgh. After doing missionary and social work, he was ordained in 1896 and served large churches in Turriff, Alloa, Tullibody, Edinburgh, and Glasgow. During World War I, he was a chaplain in France and in Flanders. A scholar of Gaelic history, Watt lectured in Australia, New Zealand, the U.S., and at various universities in Scotland. He authored many devotional books and received a number of professional honors before retiring in 1934. Watt survived both his wife, Jenny Hall Reid, and their son, Hector.

Author: *I bind my heart this tide,* **411**

WATTS, ISAAC (b. July 17, 1674, Southampton, England; d. Nov. 25, 1748, Stoke Newington, England), the eldest of nine children born of Nonconformist (not of the Church of England) parents, was frail and sickly all his life, but brilliant. A woman who once fell in love with his poetry dissuaded his ardor with the remark, "I only wish I could say that I admire the casket as much as I admire the jewel" (Bailey 1950). Watts never married, but instead honed his intellectual and literary gifts, learning Greek, Hebrew, and Latin before he was fifteen. Offered the opportunity to study for the Anglican priesthood, he declined, studying instead at the Nonconformist academy at Stoke Newington, near London (1690-1694). Returning home at age twenty, he wrote many of his best-loved hymns during the next two years.

Watts spent the following six years at Stoke Newington as tutor to the son of Sir John Hartopp, an eminent Puritan. But he also studied theology and philosophy so intensely that he nearly broke his delicate health. Nonetheless, Watts was ordained and in 1702 was appointed pastor of Mark Lane Independent Chapel in London where he had been assistant pastor since 1699.

During a serious illness in 1712, Watts was invited to convalesce at the home of Sir Thomas Abney, and he stayed with the household as tutor and chaplain for the rest of his life. There he maintained a correspondence with contemporary religious leaders and wrote some sixty books on various subjects, including *Logic*, which became a standard textbook at Oxford University. The University of Edinburgh awarded him the D.D. in 1728. Nine years after suffering a paralyzing stroke, Watts died at the Abney home and was buried at Bunhill Fields. A monument to his memory was placed in Westminster Abbey.

Often acclaimed the "father of English hymnody," Watts was an independent spirit who tired of the steady diet of metrical psalms that were standard fare in the Church of England. Challenged by his father to "write one better," his vibrant poetry launched a new era in congregational hymnody. Using only a few basic meters and simple language, his work laid the hymn foundation for the likes of Charles Wesley and James Montgomery. His more than 750 hymns are contained in seven collections, the most noted of which are *Hymns and Spiritual Songs* (1707, 1709), *Divine and Moral Songs for Children* (1715), and *The Psalms of David, Imitated in the Language of the New Testament* (1719).

Author: *Alas! and did my Savior bleed?*, **253**; *Before Jehovah's aweful throne*, **18**; *Come, we that love the Lord*, **14**; *Create my soul anew*, **3**; *From all that dwell below the skies*, **49**; *Great God, how infinite art thou*, **82**; *How wondrous great*, **126**; *I sing the mighty power of God*, **46**; *I'll praise my Maker*, **166**; *Jesus shall reign*, **319**; *Joy to the world*, **318**; *Lord, I have made thy word*, **317**; *Lord of the worlds above*, **39**; *My dear Redeemer and my Lord*, **547**; *My Shepherd will supply my need*, **589**; *O bless the Lord, my soul*, **600**; *O come, loud anthems let us sing* (refrain), **68**; *O God, our help in ages past*, **328**; *Teach me the measure of my days*, **485**; *This is the day the Lord has made*, **642**; *When I survey the wondrous cross*, **259, 260**

WEAVER, CAROL ANN (b. May 6, 1948, Harrisonburg, Va.), undergirded by the heritage of four-part *a cappella* singing in the Mennonite churches in the Shenandoah Valley, studied composition, music theory, and piano performance at Indiana University, Bloomington, completing a doctorate in 1981. She taught music education at Eastern Mennonite College, Harrisonburg (1972-1976); Mennonite Brethren Bible College at Winnipeg, Manitoba (1976-1980); and Wilfrid Laurier University in Waterloo, Ontario. Weaver became a permanent member of the faculty of Conrad Grebel College/University of Waterloo where she teaches courses in composition, theory, popular music, jazz, and women in music.

As a composer, Weaver's work is a blend of styles from avant-garde to jazz, from lyric to dramatic. She has also produced a choral Mass and an extended work for choir and orchestra titled *Rejoice*. Two of her chamber pieces, *Algonquin Night* and *Algonquin Dawn*, have been broadcast on CBC national FM radio. *Jericho*, her children's music drama, premiered in 1979; the benediction appears in this hymnal.

She is a member of the Canadian Music Centre and the Association of Canadian Women Composers.

As a pianist, Weaver has performed solo in the U.S. and Canada, as well as with her husband, mandolinist Lyle Friesen. Together, they are known as Mooncoin.

Author/Composer: *With all my heart I offer* (BENEDICTION), **432**

WEBB, BENJAMIN (b. Nov. 28, 1819, Addle Hill, Doctors' Commons, London, England; d. Nov. 27, 1885, London) attended Trinity College, Cambridge (B.A., 1842; M.A., 1845). He was ordained as an Anglican priest in 1843 and had several church positions through 1851. In 1862 he became vicar of St. Andrew's in London, a position he retained until his death. Under his leadership the church gained a reputation for the quality of its music.

In 1881 Webb became editor of the *Church Quarterly Review* and jointly authored *The Hymnary* with W. Cooke (1870-1872). Webb was also one of the editors of *The Hymnal Noted* (1851), as well as of the Burntisland reprint of the *Sarum Missal* (1861-1863).

Translator: *O love, how deep, how broad*, **236**; *Sing we triumphant hymns*, **287**

WEBB, GEORGE JAMES (b. June 24, 1803, Rushmore Lodge, Wiltshire, England; d. Oct. 7, 1887, Orange, N.J.) obtained his training in music and organ under the tutelage of Alexander Lucas at Salisbury Cathedral. After his tenure as church organist at Falmouth, Webb immigrated in 1830 to Boston where he played the organ at Boston's Old South Church. He was there for nearly forty years. He taught with Lowell Mason at the newly established Boston Academy of Music and was president of Boston's famous Handel and Haydn Society. Webb spent the last seventeen years of his life in Orange.

Although he was well respected as a choral director and voice teacher, Webb also composed anthems and hymns and edited and published several important collections of music, some in collaboration with Mason. Among the most significant were *The Massachusetts Collection of Psalmody* (1840), *The American Glee Book* (1841), *The Psaltery* (1845), *The National Psalmist* (1848), and *Cantica Laudis* (1850).

Composer: WEBB (*Bless'd be the God of Israel*), **174**

WEBBE, SAMUEL, SR. (b. 1740, London, England; d. May 25, 1816, Gray's Inn, London) at age eleven was apprenticed to a cabinetmaker, but after his training, he supported himself by copying music for a dealer and drew the attention of Carl Barbandt, an organist who offered him lessons. In 1776 he got the job of organist at both the Portuguese and the Sardinian embassy chapels, two of the best positions in London for a Roman Catholic organist at the time. Eventually he became a teacher in his own right; *Laity's Directory* (1793) advertised that Webbe would "give instruction gratis every Friday evening at seven o'clock to such young gentlemen as present themselves to learn the church music" (*The Hymnal 1940 Companion*, 1951 ed.). His compositions include masses, motets, antiphons, and part-songs.

Composer: CONSOLATOR (*Come, ye disconsolate*), **497**

WEBSTER, BRADFORD GRAY (b. Oct. 30, 1898, Syracuse, N.Y.; d. Oct. 25, 1991, Bloomsburg, Pa.) attended Amherst College (Mass.) and graduated from Boston University School of Theology in 1925. He was a Methodist minister in New York State from 1935 until he retired in 1964. His twin sister also followed a church vocation, becoming a missionary to South America. Webster was active in numerous civic groups and church organizations from the local to the national level. A collection of his poems was published in 1987 under the title *Songs in the Night*.

Author: *O Jesus Christ, may grateful hymns*, **404**

WEISSEL, GEORG (b. 1590, Domnau, near Königsberg, East Prussia; d. Aug. 1, 1635, Königsberg) was the son of Johann Weissel, mayor of Domnau. Weissel studied mainly at the University of Königsberg and briefly at Wittenberg, Leipzig, Jena, Strassburg, Basel, and Marburg. In 1614 he became rector of the school at Friedland, near Domnau, but resigned three years later to resume his study of theology. Finally finishing his university work, he became pastor of the newly built Altrossgart Church in Königsberg from 1623 until his death. Weissel wrote about twenty hymns, mostly for festivals of the Christian year.

Author: *Fling wide the door, unbar the gate*, **186**

WENGER, MARION R. (b. Mar. 23, 1932, Elkhart, Ind.), a graduate of Goshen College (Ind.; B.A., 1958) and Ohio State University, Columbus (M.A., 1961; Ph.D., 1969), was a German Government Scholar at the University of Heidelberg. As professor of German at Goshen College (Ind.; 1963-1987), Wenger also headed the foreign language department and chaired the humanities division. He has been program director and mentor to North American college students studying abroad, taught English as a second language (ESL) courses, and helped prepare ESL teachers. He has been a language and cultural training specialist for corporations associated with international conglomerates.

Wenger has worked with the United Bible Societies in translations training and quality control. With the exception of this hymn, his translations have been published anonymously.

Translator: *I sing with exultation*, **438**

WESLEY, CHARLES (b. Dec. 18, 1707, Epworth Rectory, England; d. Mar. 29, 1788, Marylebone, London, England) is considered the great hymnwriter of the Wesleys. The eighteenth child born to Samuel and Susanna Wesley and the youngest son, he attended Westminster School and was supported by his older brother Samuel until he was chosen as a king's scholar, which provided him free education and board. In 1726 he received a scholarship to attend Christ Church, Oxford, and completed his degree three years later. He was part of the Holy Club whose extremely systematic approach to Christian living earned the group the name "Oxford Methodists."

Just after Wesley was ordained in 1735, his brother John persuaded him to sail to Savannah, Georgia, as a missionary. There he hired on as private secretary and chaplain to General James Oglethorpe, but he returned to England the next year, disenchanted with life in the New World. He was very much influenced, however, by some Moravians who had been on the outbound trip and by Count Zinzendorf and other Moravians he met in London in 1737. Thus, in the spring of 1738, he "found rest to his soul"—he was converted. He then began his life as a traveling preacher with his brother John, riding horseback to West England, Wales, and Ireland, powerfully preaching personal salvation to underprivileged classes and enduring persecution instigated by the Anglican clergy. Even so, Charles never disavowed the Anglican Church. After he married in 1749, his wife frequently accompanied him in his work. Finally, after 1756, he stayed closer to the central ministry base in Bristol until he moved his family to London in 1771. Wesley died in 1788 and was buried in Marylebone Churchyard, London.

As an itinerant preacher, Charles Wesley learned to write hymns anytime, anywhere and is credited with some 6,500 hymns. With his brother John, he produced fifty-six hymnbooks and hymn tracts over fifty-three years. Considering the quantity and quality of his work, Charles Wesley must be considered one of the great hymnwriters of all time.

Author: *A charge to keep I have*, **393**; *All praise to our redeeming Lord*, **21**; *Author of life divine*, **467**; *Away with our fears*, **292**; *Christ, from whom all blessings*, **365**; *Christ the Lord is risen today*, **280**; *Christ, whose glory fills the skies*, **216**; *Come away to the skies*, **284**; (Attrib.) *Come, divine Interpreter*, **302**; *Come, O thou Traveler unknown*, **503**; *Come, thou long-expected Jesus*, **178**; *Father, I stretch my hands to thee*, **529**; *Forth in thy name*, **415**; *Hark! the herald angels sing*, **201**; *Help us to help each other*, **362**; *If death my friend and me divide*, **608**; *Jesus, lover of my soul*, **618**; *Love divine, all loves excelling*, **592**; *Oh, for a thousand tongues to sing*, **81, 110**; *Oh, how happy are they*, **597**; *Open, Lord, my inward ear*, **140**; *Praise the Lord who reigns above*, **54**; *Rejoice, the Lord is King*, **288**

WESLEY, JOHN BENJAMIN (b. June 17, 1703, Epworth, Lincolnshire, England; d. Mar. 2, 1791, London, England), son of the Anglican clergyman Samuel Wesley and his wife, Susanna, was rescued from a fire in the rectory when he was a small child. His mother felt it was a sign that he was saved for God's work. Considered the greatest religious leader of the eighteenth century and "father" of Methodism, John Wesley studied at Charterhouse and received his degrees from Christ Church, Oxford (B.A., 1724; M.A., 1726-1727). He was ordained in 1728 and was curate to his father from 1727 to 1729. He tutored the next six years at Lincoln College, Oxford.

In 1735 John sailed with his brother Charles to Savannah, Georgia, under General James Oglethorpe, as resident minister for the Society for the Propagation of the Gospel. On board ship he met a group of Moravians who influenced his ministry, and shortly after returning to England in 1737, he had a spiritual "heart-warming" at a Moravian meeting on Aldersgate Street. As a result, he devoted his life to preaching the gospel to the poor. In 1739 Wesley converted an old foundry in London into a chapel that, in retrospect, is considered the birthplace of Methodism.

John Wesley, less known as a hymnwriter than his brother Charles, nevertheless wrote twenty-seven hymns and translated thirty others from German, especially from the Moravian tradition. His *Collection of Psalms and Hymns*, published in 1737 at Charleston, South Carolina, was his first hymnal and the first hymnal printed in the New World. His subsequent collections, issued every few years for the rest of his life, have provided the core of English hymnody for more than two hundred years.

Author: *Author of life divine*, **467**. Translator: *Give to the winds thy fears*, **561**. Adapter: AMSTERDAM (*Praise the Lord who reigns above*), **54**

WESLEY, SAMUEL SEBASTIAN (b. Aug. 14, 1810, London, England; d. Apr. 19, 1876, Gloucester, England), a grandson of Charles Wesley, became a chorister of the Chapel Royal when he was ten. He was a musical prodigy, having composed an oratorio, *Ruth*, at age eight. By sixteen he already held a position as organist. His career included posts in five parish churches and four in the cathedrals of Hereford, Exeter, Winchester, and Gloucester. His tenures were short due to his dissatisfaction with the miserable treatment the musical services received from the clergy, but it is also said that he accepted or rejected positions depending on their proximity to good fishing holes. Wesley was an avid fisherman but also one of the hardest workers for reform in cathedral music. He received both the B.Mus. and D.Mus. from Oxford University in 1839.

Wesley was the outstanding organist of his time and the greatest English church musician between Henry Purcell (1659-1695) and Charles V. Stanford (1852-1924). He composed services, psalm settings, anthems and glees, as well as music for organ, piano, and voice. Most of his 130 hymn tunes are included in *The European Psalmist* (1872), which contains more than 730 tunes. In general, his hymn tunes have been neglected unjustly.

Composer: AURELIA (*The church's one foundation*), **311**; *Lead me, Lord*, **538**

WESTENDORF, OMER (b. Feb. 24, 1916, Cincinnati, Ohio) has earned both the bachelor's and master's degrees in music from the University of Cincinnati. At age twenty he became organist/choirmaster of St. Bonaventure Church, remaining there for forty years. He directs the Bonaventure Choir, a freelance chorale heard in concert, on television, and in recordings. For a short while, he also directed the Bishop's Choir at the Basilica of the Assumption, Covington, Kentucky, and has taught music in several schools in Cincinnati.

Westendorf founded the World Library of Sacred Music in 1950, an organization that has had great impact on music in American Catholic churches. As a soldier in World War II, he did some Christmas shopping in Maastricht, Holland, before visiting the Frauenkirche and its marvelous pipe organ. When he arrived at his quarters, he realized his packages were missing. Westendorf returned to the church to learn that one of the choir members had taken his misplaced parcels home for safekeeping. From that choir member he received not only his missing gifts but also information about some new mass settings. After his release from the army, he sent for copies of the music to disseminate in the U.S. More orders from a number of countries and a visit to Europe in 1950 to seek out additional sources launched World Library Publications. Westendorf served as chairman and president until his resignation in 1976. Since that time he has continued consulting, lecturing, and conducting seminars on liturgical music.

In addition to his liturgical research, Westendorf has written more than one hundred hymns and compiled four hymnbooks, including *People's Mass Book* (1964, 1971), the first such book in the vernacular to be published following Vatican II. Among his other publications are *Music Lessons for the Man in the Pew* (1965) and his latest collection of forty hymns, *Hear Us, Lord.*

Author: *Sent forth by God's blessing*, **478**. Translator: *Where charity and love prevail*, **305**

WHALUM, WENDELL PHILLIPS (b. 1932; d. 1987), after studying at Morehouse College, Atlanta, Georgia, and taking his Ph.D. at the University of Iowa, Iowa City, headed the music department at Morehouse. He was both an author and a conductor and directed the glee club at Morehouse. Whalum was a leading African American choral clinician.

Arranger: GUIDE MY FEET (*Guide my feet*), **546**

WHELPTON, GEORGE (b. May 17, 1847, Redbourne, England; d. Nov. 25, 1930, Oxford, Ohio), a choral director and music editor, came to the U.S. in 1851. At sixteen he enlisted in the Union Army where he was an assistant pharmacist. His only musical training was at the Lake Chautauqua School of Music, western New York, with Horatio R. Palmer and for a brief time with a private teacher in Boston. From 1903 to 1925, he was a choral director in Buffalo, New York. For a while he worked for the Century Publishing Company, New York City, and then the A. S. Barnes Company. Among the compilations Whelpton edited are *Hymns of Worship and Service* and *The Church Hymnal*.

Composer: DISMISSAL (*Lord, let us now depart in peace*), **428**

WHISTON, CHARLES FRANCIS (b. Nov. 16, 1900, Yarmouth, Nova Scotia; d. June 1, 1992, Carmel, Calif.) moved to New England in early childhood. He received degrees from Trinity College, Hartford, Connecticut (B.A., 1926); Harvard University, Cambridge, Massachusetts (M.A., 1927); Episcopal Theological School (B.D., 1930); General Theological Seminary, New York City (S.T.D., 1951); Church Divinity School of the Pacific, Berkeley, California (D.D., 1968). After ordination to the priesthood in the Episcopal Church, he sailed for China to do mission work; during his eight years there, he taught at Central China College, Wuchang. In 1938 he returned to the U.S. to become rector of St. Stephen's in Middlebury, Vermont, and lecturer at Middlebury College. A few years later, he became vicar of St. John's in Ashfield, Massachusetts. From 1945 until retirement in 1968, he was professor of moral theology at the Church Divinity School of the Pacific. The school awarded him professor emeritus status in systematic theology after he did part-time teaching in that field for a number of years during retirement. As a result of his seven-year study of prayer, funded by the Lilly Endowment, he concluded that Christians need to be taught to pray. Subsequently, he conducted retreats and schools of prayer throughout the U.S. and published several books on the subject.

Adapter: Come, Holy Spirit. Come as Holy Fire, **762**

WHITE, BENJAMIN FRANKLIN (b. Sept. 20, 1800, Spartanburg, S.C.; d. Dec. 5, 1879, Atlanta, Ga.) helped his brother-in-law William Walker compile the eminent collection *Southern Harmony*, but White received no publication credits. He moved to Georgia in 1840 and with Elisha King published *Sacred Harp*, which continues to be used as a singing-school book for southern music festivals, as well as for groups of shaped-note aficionados throughout the U.S. It is in this collection, printed in Philadelphia, Pennsylvania, in 1844, that the tune BEACH SPRING is attributed to White. Besides these noteworthy projects, White also edited a local county newspaper; served in the Georgia militia; was appointed a court clerk in 1858; and was elected mayor of Hamilton, Georgia, in 1865.

Composer: BEACH SPRING (*Holy Spirit, come with power*, **26**; *Lord, whose love in humble service*, **369**)

WHITESHIELD, HARVEY (b. ca. 1860, Oklahoma; d. 1941), known among his people as *Heskovetseso* (Little Porcupine), was among the first Cheyenne chosen to study at the Carlisle Institute (for Native Americans) in Pennsylvania. After his return, Whiteshield assisted Rodolphe Petter in work with the Cheyenne language and taught at the school operated by General Conference Mennonites at Cantonment, Oklahoma. Whiteshield contributed greatly to his people as a preacher and singer. His hymns are still remembered among the Cheyenne in Montana where he made several visits.

Author: *Ehane He'ama (Father God, you are holy)*, **78**

WHITTIER, JOHN GREENLEAF (b. Dec. 17, 1807, Merrimac River Valley, near Haverhill, Mass.; d. Sept. 7, 1892, Hampton Falls, N.H.), often called "the Quaker poet," was brought up in rural poverty. Through hard work as a shoemaker and teacher, he saved enough to attend Haverhill Academy for two academic seasons. Around this same time, he acquired Robert Burns' *Poems* and also began to write verse.

An antislavery agitator, Whittier became an editor, working on *American Manufacturer* (1828), *New England Review* (1830), and *Pennsylvania Freeman* (1836), subsequently joining the staff of the abolitionist paper *National Era* in 1847. During his career he continued to write verse and was justly regarded as one of the great poets of his time. He did not, however, consider himself a hymnwriter, "for the good reason that I know nothing of music." Raised in the silence of Quaker meetings, he acknowledges: "A good hymn is the best use to which poetry can be devoted, but I do not claim that I have succeeded in composing one" (Haeussler 1952).

Nevertheless, at least seventy-five centos (portions) from his poetry have blossomed into hymn texts. Some of his best-known poems are *Snowbound* (1866), *Our Master* (1866), *The Tent on the Beach* (1867), and *The Eternal Goodness*.

Author: *Dear Lord and Father of mankind*, **523**; *Immortal Love, forever full*, **629**

WHITTLE, DANIEL WEBSTER (b. Nov. 22, 1840, Chicopee Falls, Mass.; d. Mar. 4, 1901, Northfield, Mass.) was named for the statesman his father admired. He was a cashier for the Wells Fargo Bank in Chicago before he joined Company B of the 72nd Illinois Infantry during the U.S. Civil War. While lying wounded in a prison camp after the battle of Vicksburg, Whittle was converted. After the war he was promoted and for the rest of his life was known as "Major Whittle."

Upon his return to Chicago, he was treasurer of the Elgin Watch Company until 1873 when, under the influence of Dwight L. Moody, he left business to become an evangelist. His highly successful evangelistic work was enhanced by the succession of musicians associated with him:

P. P. Bliss, James McGranahan, and George C. Stebbins. Most of his hymns appear with the pseudonym "El Nathan."

Author: *I know not why God's wondrous*, **338**; *I will praise the Lord*, **109**

WICHERT, JOHANN (JOHN) J. (b. Oct. 1, 1897, Mariawohl, Ukraine; d. Nov. 12, 1983, St. Catharines, Ontario) grew up in the Mennonite colony of Molotschna in the Ukraine. Orphaned as a teenager, he moved in with his sister's family. After acquiring a teaching certificate at age seventeen, he taught in village schools, with a hiatus as a medic in the Crimea during World War I. When his brother-in-law died in 1922, he gave up teaching to help his sister's family (and remained with them until his marriage at age forty-seven). Having learned English through self-study and the help of a Jewish civil servant, he acted as a translator for various officials regarding Russian Mennonite immigration to Canada. He himself immigrated in 1925, settling in Ontario. After a year in construction work in Kitchener, Wichert moved to Vineland where he would serve as a minister in the Vineland United Mennonite Church from 1927 (he was ordained in 1928) until retirement in 1965. He taught at the Brethren in Christ's Ontario Bible School (now Niagara Christian College), Fort Erie (1943-1944). In 1944 he was ordained as *Altester* (elder, a bishop-like position) and assumed full-time ministry in his congregation. After World War II, Wichert and his wife, Maria Peters, went to Germany for a year to assist the Mennonites coming out of Russia. He served on the board of Mennonite Biblical Seminary (General Conference), Chicago, for many years and in a number of other church organizations as well. His emphases were missions and evangelism. He was one of the compilers of the *Gesangbuch der Mennoniten* (Faith and Life Press 1965).

Author: How can we discern our errors, O God?, **781**

WIEAND, ALBERT CASSEL (b. Jan. 17, 1871, near Wadsworth, Ohio; d. July 24, 1954, La Verne, Calif.) was one of the leading Brethren educators of the late nineteenth/early twentieth centuries. He joined the Chippewa, Ohio, congregation in 1884 and served as a minister there beginning in 1893. Educated at the then-nascent Brethren colleges of Juniata in Huntingdon, Pennsylvania, and McPherson (Kan.), he also studied at the University of Chicago and several other U.S. and German universities. Wieand was a teacher and administrator at Juniata and McPherson Colleges and eventually co-founded (with E. B. Hoff) Bethany Bible School (later Bethany Theological Seminary), now in Richmond, Indiana. He was Bethany's president from 1905 to 1932 and also helped establish Bethany Hospital.

Author: *On the radiant threshold*, **649**

WIEBE, ESTHER (b. Mar. 18, 1932, Plum Coulee, Manitoba) is associate professor of music at Canadian Mennonite Bible College, Winnipeg, where she began her employment in 1954. She is a prolific composer/arranger whose pieces have been heard in both the U.S. and Canada. These include the cantata *That They May Be One*, performed at Bethlehem '83, an inter-Mennonite conference in Pennsylvania, and *Crossroad*, a musical written for the centennial of Mennonite Collegiate Institute, Gretna, Manitoba, in 1989. She also has published six books of arrangements and compositions for church choirs and male choirs. Her husband, George, was a member of the music committee for *Hymnal: A Worship Book* (1992).

Composer: BAPTISM BY FIRE (*God, whose purpose is to kindle*), **135**. Arranger: O HEILAND, REISS DIE HIMMEL AUF (*O Savior, rend the heavens*), **175**; STENKA RAZIN (*In the quiet consecration*), **461**

WILE, FRANCES WHITMARSH (b. Dec. 2, 1878, Bristol Valley, N.Y.; d. July 31, 1939, Rochester, N.Y.) lived most of her life in Rochester and was self-educated for the most part. She was active in First Unitarian Church and involved in civic affairs; she also promoted women's rights and often contributed her poems to local newspapers. Her husband, Abram Wile, was a teacher and one-time secretary of the Young Men's Hebrew Association in Rochester. Later in life she devoted much time to the religious and philosophical pursuit of theosophy.

Author: *All beautiful the march of days*, **159**

WILES, VIRGINIA (b. Dec. 3, 1954, Flagstaff, Ariz.), the daughter of a Southern Baptist minister, grew up in parsonages in the Southwest. She studied at Oklahoma Baptist University, Shawnee; Texas Wesleyan College, Fort Worth (B.S., 1977); Northern Baptist Theological Seminary, Lombard, Illinois (M.A. in New Testament, 1982); and the University of Chicago (Ph.D. in New Testament, 1994). While teaching in an adjunct position at Bethany Theological Seminary, Oak Brook, Illinois (1982 to 1987), she joined the Church of the Brethren, attracted, she says, to its emphases on community and service. Since 1990 she has been assistant professor of religion at Muhlenberg College, Allentown, Pennsylvania. She is a frequent lecturer for adult education in congregations, and she has served on the Women's Caucus steering committee of the Church of the Brethren for several years. She is a member of the Society of Biblical Literature and the American Academy of Religion.

Translator: For we know that in all things God works, **849**

WILKES, JOHN B. (d. 1882) "is not to be confused with John Bernard Wilkes (1785-1869)," [1] who in other hymnal companions is cited with the same biographical information. And neither is he to be confused with

John Wilkes Booth who assassinated Abraham Lincoln in 1865! Each John Wilkes is listed as a contributor to *Hymns Ancient and Modern* (1861) and as the arranger of the tune MONKLAND, which was set to H. W. Baker's text "Praise, O praise our God and King" in that hymnal. Each has been listed as the organist at Monkland Church near Leominster, England, and therefore associated with Baker, the vicar there. However, this Wilkes "was evidently alive when the 1875 edition [of *Hymns Ancient and Modern*] was published."[2] Further documentation to resolve the confusion is scant.

Arranger: MONKLAND (*Songs of praise the angels sang*), **60**

1. *Historical Companion to Hymns Ancient and Modern*
2. *Historical Companion to Hymns Ancient and Modern*

WILLAN, HEALEY (b. Oct. 12, 1880, London, England; d. Feb. 16, 1968, Toronto, Ontario) started his distinguished musical career as a chorister at St. Saviour's Choir School, Eastbourne, and then held several positions as organist/choirmaster in and around London before being appointed to St. John the Baptist, Kensington, in 1900. In 1913 he left London to become head of the theory department at the Toronto Conservatory of Music. His longest tenures were as professor at the University of Toronto (1914-1961) and as choirmaster and organist at St. Mary Magdalene Anglican Church from 1921 until his death.

At St. Mary Magdalene he established a high-church musical tradition, emphasizing the use of plainsong and Renaissance music, genres in which he was expert. Willan was a prolific composer of choral and organ music, extending his creativity into improvisation, dramatic music, opera, symphonies, and a piano concerto. Known for his masterful technique and sense of humor, his influence as a church musician and teacher was extensive.

Arranger: WIE LIEBLICH IST DER MAIEN (*Sing to the Lord of harvest*), **98**.

WILLIAMS, AARON (b. 1731, London, England; d. 1776, London) was a clerk for London's Scottish Church and had a multifaceted career in music as a composer, publisher, engraver, and teacher. Williams is noted for compiling and publishing several collections during the 1760s and 1770s: *The Universal Psalmodist* (1763), *The Royal Harmony* (1766), *The New Universal Psalmodist* (1770), *Harmonia Coelestis* (6th ed., 1775), and *Psalmody in Miniature* (1778). The popularity of his music reached North America; some of his anthems were performed here, and *The Universal Psalmodist* was published in an American edition under the title *The American Harmony*.

Composer: ST. THOMAS (WILLIAMS) (*O bless the Lord, my soul*), **600**

WILLIAMS, PETER (b. Jan. 7, 1722, Llansadurnin, Carmarthenshire, Wales; d. Aug. 8, 1796, Llandyfeilog, Wales) received his education from the Carmarthen Grammar School where he was converted through the preaching of George Whitefield, ministerial associate of John and Charles Wesley. Ordained in 1744, Williams left the Anglican Church in 1746 to join the Methodist revival movement in Wales. After being branded a heretic by the Methodists, Williams established his own chapel in Carmarthen. Among his publications are a Welsh Bible, a Welsh hymnbook (1759), and *Hymns on Various Subjects* (1771).

Translator: *Guide me, O thou great Jehovah* (st. 1), **582**

WILLIAMS, ROBERT (b. ca. 1781, Mynydd Ithel, Anglesey, Wales; d. 1821, Mynydd Ithel), born blind, spent his life as a skilled basketmaker on the Welsh island of Anglesey. He had the musical gifts of a good voice, as well as a good ear and memory.

Composer: LLANFAIR (*Let the whole creation cry*), **51**

WILLIAMS, THOMAS JOHN (b. 1869, Ynysmeudwy, Glamorganshire, Wales; d. 1944, Llanelly, Wales), after studying music in Cardiff with David Evans, spent the rest of his life as an organist and choirmaster, serving two different churches in Llanelly: Zion Church (1903-1913) and Cafaria Church (1913-1944). Williams also composed church music, especially anthems and hymns.

Composer: EBENEZER (*Lord of light, your name outshining*), **410**

WILLIAMS, WILLIAM (b. Feb. 11, 1717, Cefn-y-Coed, Llanfair-ar-y-Bryn, Carmarthenshire, Wales; d. Jan. 11, 1791, near Llandovery, Wales), known as "the Isaac Watts of Wales" and "the sweet singer of Wales," was a traveling evangelist of the Welsh Calvinistic Methodist Church and the author of more than eight hundred hymns in Welsh and one hundred in English. His hymns were so popular that the texts were not only committed to memory, but became reading lessons for illiterate Welsh people.

The son of a prosperous Welsh farmer, Williams attended Llwynllwyd Academy (later called Presbyterian College) at Carmarthen for medical study. A sermon preached in 1738 by the evangelist Howell Harris led Williams to the ministry instead. He was ordained as a deacon in the Church of England and was a curate for three years, but when he applied to be priest he was turned down because of his evangelical views. So Williams left the established church to become an evangelist, traveling an average of 2,230 miles a year for forty-five years. "He possessed the warm heart and glowing imagination of a true Welshman," writes Josiah Miller, "and his sermons abounded with vivid picturing, and, always radiant with the presence of his divine Master, they produced an extraordinary effect on susceptible Welshmen" (Haeussler 1952).

Williams's Welsh hymns are collected in *Aleluia* (1745) and *Y Mor o Wydr* (*The Sea of Glass* 1762) and his English hymns in *Hosannah to the Son of David . . .* (1759) and *Gloria in Excelsis . . .* (1772). Williams also wrote two long poems: *Theomemphus* and *Golwg ar Deyrnas Crist* (A View of the Kingdom of Christ). Two other works appeared in 1768: *Three Men from Sodom and Egypt* and *The Crocodile of the River of Egypt*. Among the many elegies he wrote was a lengthy one on Whitefield (1771), but Williams is most remembered for his hymns.

Author/Translator: *Guide me, O thou great Jehovah,* **582**. Author: *Ndikhokele, O Jehova,* **583**

WILLIS, RICHARD STORRS (b. Feb. 19, 1819, Boston, Mass.; d. May 7, 1900, Detroit, Mich.), after his graduation in 1841 from Yale University, New Haven, Connecticut, spent six years in Germany studying composition with Felix Mendelssohn and others. Willis wrote a biography of Mendelssohn who had become a close friend. After several years as music critic for the *New York Tribune, The Albion,* and the *Musical Times,* Willis became an editor for a number of publications. In 1861 he moved to Detroit, Michigan, where he spent most of his later years.

Composer: CAROL (*It came upon a midnight clear*), **195**. Arranger: CRUSADERS' HYMN *(Fairest Lord Jesus)*, **117**

WILSON, HUGH (b. 1766, Fenwick, Ayrshire, Scotland; d. Aug. 14, 1824, Duntocher, Scotland) was apprenticed to his father as a shoemaker, studied mathematics and music in his spare time, and designed sundials as a hobby. By 1800 he moved to Pollokshaws, and later to Duntocher, to become a calculator and draftsman in the mills there. An active member of the Secession Church, he occasionally led the psalm singing and helped to establish the first Sunday school there. At the time of his death, he ordered all the manuscripts of his tunes and arrangements to be burned, and only those published previously survived.

Composer: MARTYRDOM (*Alas! and did my Savior bleed?*, **253**; *Father, I stretch my hands to thee,* **529**)

WILSON, LOIS M. (b. Apr. 8, 1927, Winnipeg, Manitoba) earned degrees at the University of Winnipeg (B.A., 1947; M.Div., 1965). Born two years after the founding of the United Church of Canada (UCC), she has had a long career in its service. From the time of her ordination in 1965 until 1980, Wilson worked in a team ministry with her husband. During this period she broke new ground as the first female president of the Canadian Council of Churches. In the ensuing years she achieved more firsts, becoming the first female moderator of the United Church of Christ and the first Canadian president of the World Council of Churches. In this phase of her career, she was also co-director of the Ecumenical Forum, responsible for training the overseas personnel of all Canadian churches; under a UCC scholarship, she did research in theology based on women's struggles, from which came two books. She has also published her memoirs, a book of devotional studies inspired by her world travels, and numerous articles on social justice and human rights. Among the many honors she has received are the Order of Canada, a United Nations peace prize, and eleven honorary doctorates. In retirement she is serving as chair of the Urban-Rural Mission (Canada), WCC; vice-president of Canadian Civil Liberties; and chancellor of Lakehead University, Thunder Bay, Ontario.

Author: The blessing of the God of Sarah, **770**

WINE, MARY STONER (b. 1885, near Ladoga, Ind.; d. 1959) was the daughter of Samuel D. and Lina Norris Stoner. She attended Manchester College, North Manchester, Indiana, graduating in 1909, and then served one year in a mission in Indianapolis, Indiana. In 1911 she married Grover L. Wine and became active in women's work of the Church of the Brethren. Two published collections of her work are *Patchwork and Rhythm* (1949) and *Altar Candles* (1956). Wine also wrote several religious plays, and three of her hymns are included in the *The Brethren Hymnal* (1951): "The riches of God are eternal," "I believe in thee, Lord Jesus," and "Love of God, eternal God."

Author: *I believe in you, Lord Jesus*, **440**

WINKWORTH, CATHERINE (b. Sept. 13, 1827, London, England; d. July 1, 1878, Monnetier, Savoy, France) is considered the foremost translator of hymns from German to English. A devout woman of considerable learning, her keen interest in education and social concerns led her to positions as governor of the Red Maids' School, Bristol, and secretary of the Clifton Association for the Higher Education of Women in 1870.

Winkworth's translations are largely responsible for the dissemination of German hymns in England. They appear in the two-part *Lyra Germanica* (1855, 1858) and the *Chorale Book for England* (1863). Her *Christian Singers of Germany* (1869) contains biographies of the hymnwriters. Further information on this noted translator is in standard hymnological resources.

Translator: *Blessed Jesus, at your word*, **13**; *Comfort, comfort, O my people*, **176**; *From heaven above to earth I come*, **205**; *If you but trust in God* (sts. 1,3-4), **576**; *In thee is gladness*, **114**; *Jesus, priceless treasure*, **595**; *Lord Jesus Christ, be present now*, **22**; *Now thank we all our God*, **85, 86**; *O God, thou faithful God*, **376**; *Open now thy gates of beauty*, **19**; *Praise to the Lord, the Almighty*, **37**; *Soul, adorn thyself with gladness*, **473**; *When in the hour of deepest need*, **131**

WITMER, EDITH M. (b. Oct. 28, 1902, Lancaster County, Pa.; d. June 19, 1982, Lancaster, Pa.), the daughter of Jacob S. and Mary Brubaker Witmer, was the last surviving member of her immediate family. As a college student in the early 1920s, she prepared for teaching with hopes of going into foreign missions. Since her health was not strong enough for the rigors of that work, she began teaching in the same high school where she had done her student teaching. Following a year of graduate school, Witmer taught at Goshen College (Ind.) until serious health problems prevented her from continuing. In her later years, she was a member of Lititz Mennonite Church (Pa.).

Author: *Teach me thy truth*, **548**

WITT, CHRISTIAN FRIEDRICH (b. ca. 1660, Altenburg, Germany; d. Apr. 13, 1716, Altenburg) studied music under Wecker in Nürnberg, was court *Kapellmeister* at Gotha, and returned to his hometown of Altenburg as *Kapellmeister*, a position he held until his death. Witt composed many dramatic and instrumental works, cantatas, and hymn tunes, most of which have been lost or misascribed; his *Passacaglia in D Minor* was attributed to J. S. Bach when it was published. At Gotha in 1715, Witt also compiled and published *Psalmodia Sacra*, a work that became one of the most prominent hymnals of his era.

Composer (or Arranger): STUTTGART (*Child of blessing, child of promise*, **620**; *God, whose farm is all creation*, **391**; *Grant us, Lord, the grace*, **388**)

WOODWARD, GEORGE RATCLIFFE (b. Dec. 27, 1848, Birkenhead, England; d. Mar. 3, 1934, St. Pancras, London, England) earned both his bachelor's and master's degrees at Caius College, Cambridge University. Ordained as a priest in 1875, he served in a series of clerical positions from 1874 to 1906. Woodward was a noted linguist and made numerous translations from Latin, Greek, and German. On his own, or in collaboration with Charles Wood, he edited a number of musical collections. He was editor of the *Cowley Carol Book for Christmas, Easter and Ascension Tide*, which appeared in three series: 1901, 1902, and 1919. His *Songs of Syon* (1904) is an excellent world-wide compendium of plainsong melodies and hymns and psalm tunes. In 1924 Woodward received the Lambeth D.Mus.

Author: *This joyful Eastertide*, **276**

WORDSWORTH, CHRISTOPHER (b. Oct. 30, 1807, Lambeth, England; d. Mar. 20, 1885, Harewood, Yorkshire, England) was the son of a scholarly clergyman and the nephew of the celebrated English poet William Wordsworth. He was educated at Winchester and Trinity College, Cambridge, where he was a brilliant student in both the classics and mathematics, earning an astounding number of awards by the time he graduated in 1830. Following graduation, he lectured in the classics at Trinity, was headmaster at Harrow (1836-1844), and became canon of Westminster Abbey (1844-1850). His stint as parish priest in the village of Stanford-in-the-Vale-cum-Goosey in Berkshire (1850-1869) put him in better touch with common folk before he eventually became bishop of Lincoln (1869-1885). He resigned just before his death.

Ever the pedagogue and scholar, Wordsworth wrote prolifically, including *A Commentary on the whole Bible* (1856-1870). His collection *The Holy Year . . .* (1862) contains hymns for every season and festival of the church year, many of which were written on scraps of paper during his travels. His hymns have a didactic quality founded on his contention that "it is the first duty of a hymn-writer to teach sound doctrine, and thus to save souls" (Julian 1907).

Author: *Holy Spirit, gracious Guest,* **542**; *O day of rest and gladness,* **641**

WREN, BRIAN ARTHUR (b. June 3, 1936, Romford, Essex, England) was educated at Oxford University with degrees in modern languages and theology; he earned his D.Phil. in 1968. Ordained in 1965, Wren was pastor of a Congregational church in Essex (1965-1970). For the next five years, he was adult education consultant to the British Council of Churches and Roman Catholic Church, focusing on issues of peace and justice. Following work with the student-based campaign Third World First, he began a freelance ministry as poet, theologian, and worship consultant. Wren's hymn texts appear in a majority of late twentieth-century denominational hymnals.

Inclusive language is a priority in Wren's poetry, as well as broader images for God and emphases on Christ's suffering love. He has maintained a connection with the Church of the Brethren as a visiting scholar at Bethany Theological Seminary, Oak Brook, Illinois (now in Richmond, Indiana), and has been a permanent resident of the U.S. since 1991.

Author: *Christ is alive! Let Christians sing,* **278**; *Christ is risen! Shout hosanna,* **272**; *Christ upon the mountain peak,* **232**; *God of many names,* **77**; *Holy Spirit, Storm of love,* **132**; *I come with joy to meet my Lord,* **459**; *Joyful is the dark,* **233**; *Let hope and sorrow now unite,* **634**; *This is a day of new beginnings,* **640**; *This is a story full of love,* **315**; *When grief is raw,* **637**; *When love is found,* **623**; *Woman in the night,* **223**; *Wonder of wonders,* **622**. Versifier: *Oh, how joyfully,* **209**

YAMAGUCHI, TOKUO (b. July 13, 1900, Tomie-cho, Nagasaki, Japan) studied theology at the Aoyama Gakuin Seminary, graduating in 1924. In his longest tenure as a Methodist pastor (1937-1979), he served Toyohashi Church, Aichi Prefecture (since 1941 part of the United Church of Christ in Japan). Since 1979 he has been its pastor emeritus. His publications include a translation of *The Journal of John Wesley* (1961). In 1983

Yamaguchi won an official commendation from the Christian Literature Society of Japan.

Author: *Here, O Lord, your servants gather*, **7**

YANG, ERNEST YIN-LIU (b. 1899, Wuxi, Jiangsu, China; d. 1984) graduated from St. John's University, Shanghai, and Guanghua University. Regarded as the eminent musicologist of China, he taught at Yanjing University, the National Conservatory of Music, and Jinling Women's University. Yang's two-volume history of the ancient music of China, *Zhongkuo Gudai Yinyue Shigao*, is his most important work. He was a member of the committee that prepared the interdenominational hymnbook *Pu-tian-sung-zan* (Universal Praise 1936). He also wrote, composed, translated, or arranged more than two hundred hymns (*Psalter Hymnal Handbook*).

Author/Arranger: *Fount of love, our Savior God* (MAN-CHIANG-HUNG), **354**

YIN-LAN, SU (b. 1915, Tientsin, China; d. 1937, Tientsin) graduated with honors from the music department of Yenching University in Peking (now Beijing) where she was a student of Bliss Wiant. Soon after her graduation, she married and returned to Tientsin. She gave birth to a son during the summer of 1937, just before the Japanese army of occupation bombed the area. The awful noise of the bombing and shelling literally frightened this sensitive woman to death.

Composer: SHENG EN (*O Bread of life, for sinners broken*), **468**

YODER, LAWRENCE MCCULLOH (b. Apr. 14, 1943, Mount Joy, Pa.) was a construction worker, silk weaver, and assembly-line worker before he finished his B.A. in history at Messiah College, Grantham, Pennsylvania, in 1966. Married that same year, he continued his studies at Associated Mennonite Biblical Seminaries, Elkhart, Indiana (M. Div., 1969). In 1976 he was the first to receive Messiah College's Young Alumnus Achievement Award.

The Yoders taught church history and English at the Wiyata Wacana Theological School in Pati (central Java, Indonesia) under the auspices of Mennonite Central Committee (1970-1979). While there Yoder helped research and write the histories of the Evangelical Church of Java and the Muria Christian Church of Indonesia (1985).

Upon the couple's return to the U.S., Yoder completed advanced studies in missiology. In 1983 he joined the faculty of Eastern Mennonite Seminary, Harrisonburg, Virginia, teaching in that field and directing the Center for Evangelism and Church Planting. He has written for numerous periodicals and authored sixteen articles published in *The Mennonite Encyclopedia*, Vol. V.

Translator: *O Prince of peace*, **15**

YODER, RUTH A. (b. Aug. 20, 1949, Grantsville, Md.), the daughter of a Mennonite minister, attended Catherman's Business School and worked in a number of bookkeeping/secretarial positions before she herself was called to ministry in the Mennonite Church in 1978. In 1985 she became the first woman to be ordained as a pastor in Allegheny Conference. During ten years as co-pastor (with her husband, Harold) of University Mennonite Church in State College, Pennsylvania, she took several Bible courses at Penn State University, which gave her an appetite for seminary study. Not long after adopting two children, both she and her husband enrolled at Associated Mennonite Biblical Seminaries (AMBS), Elkhart, Indiana; she graduated in 1990 with a Certificate in Theology. At AMBS she was a member of the seminaries worship committee. Since 1990 she and her husband have been co-pastors of Prairie Street Mennonite Church, Elkhart. She has also worked with her husband in youth ministry.

Author: Our God, we gather to worship you, **670**; Have mercy on us, O God, **690**

YODER, WALTER E. (b. Jan. 8, 1889, near Howe, Ind.; d. Oct. 30, 1964, Goshen, Ind.) was interested in music from an early age. When he was ten, a reed organ was delivered to his home, and Walter was soon taking lessons. After high school graduation and twelve weeks of study at Goshen College, he began to teach school in Lagrange County, Indiana. During those first years of teaching he continued his education with J. D. Brunk at Goshen College, completing his music teacher's certificate in 1913. Yoder was a dairy farmer and schoolteacher at Metamora, Illinois, until 1931 when he moved with his family to Goshen College to help develop its music department. Meanwhile, he completed a master's degree in music at Northwestern University, Evanston, Illinois, in 1937. Through his teaching and his connection with a majority of the twentieth-century Mennonite hymnals (*Life Songs*, 1916; *Church Hymnal*, 1927; *Life Songs No. 2*, 1938; *The Mennonite Hymnal*, 1969), he deeply influenced the vital tradition of Mennonite hymnody and hymn-singing.

Composer: GOSHEN (*Teach me thy truth*), **548**

YOUNG, JOHN FREEMAN (b. Oct. 30, 1820, Pittston, Maine; d. Nov. 15, 1885, New York, N.Y.) was educated at Wesleyan University, Middletown, Connecticut, and Virginia Theological Seminary, Alexandria. He was ordained a deacon in the Episcopal Church in 1845 and served churches and missions in Florida, Texas, Mississippi, Louisiana, and New York. Columbia College honored him with a doctorate in 1865.

Elected the second bishop of Florida in 1867, Young served in that capacity for eighteen years. During that time—the Reconstruction era after the U.S. Civil War—he established and re-opened several schools and missions in the South, trying to win back African Americans who had joined other churches. Meanwhile, his interest in architecture led to the construction of many distinctive churches, and his commitment to missions extended to Cuban immigrants in Key West (Stulken 1981). Energetic in every way, he also published *Hymns and Music for the Young* (1860-1861) and edited *Great Hymns of the Church* (1887), which was published posthumously.

Translator: *Silent night, holy night*, **193**

ZAREMBA, FELICIAN MARTIN VON KALINOWA (b. Mar. 15, 1794, Zaroy, Poland; d. May 31, 1874, Basel, Switzerland) was born into a family of Polish nobility. Orphaned at an early age, he was raised by an uncle. Zaremba expressed an interest in the diplomatic service and was educated at the University of Dorpat, an important center of German culture in Russia. He was already proficient in Polish, Russian, German, and French when he entered the university; there he learned Latin and Greek as well and earned his Ph.D. by age twenty-two.

Zaremba followed up his original goals, serving in the Russian foreign office where he specialized in maritime law and consular affairs. Then, urged by a friend to read the Bible, Zaremba decided to give up his job and go to Basel, known as a city of "learning, Christian piety, and missionary zeal" (Haeussler 1952). In 1821, after studying at the Basel Mission House, he was sent to evangelize the area of South Russia (the Caucasus and Armenian regions). He mastered Armenian and several local dialects, later translating the Bible and some school texts into the modern language. But when Czar Nicholas suppressed his work in 1835, Zaremba returned to Basel and became an itinerant preacher, working in Germany, Switzerland, and the Baltic region of Russia.

Author: *The work is thine, O Christ* (st. 3), **396**

ZERCHER, J. RANDALL (b. Dec. 9, 1940, Mount Joy, Pa.), whose great-grandfather Smith donated the land on which Messiah College was built in Grantham, Pennsylvania, moved to Colorado with his family at age two for the sake of his father's health. There the family, who had been Brethren in Christ, joined the Mennonite Church.

Zercher has earned the following degrees: B.A. in voice, Bethel College, North Newton, Kansas (1964); M.Sac.Mus. in composition, Union Theological Seminary, New York City, (1966); and D.Mus.A. in conducting, University of Missouri at Kansas City (1983). He has taught in the music departments at both Bethel and Hesston Colleges in Kansas. In addition, he was conductor of the Newton Community Orchestra (Kan.) and assistant conductor for the Wichita Symphony (Kan.).

Zercher has served Methodist, Presbyterian, Congregational, and Mennonite churches as a musician. Since 1989 he has directed and coordinated the graded choir and handbell program (involving ten choirs) at Westbury United Methodist Church, Houston, Texas. He also enjoys gardening, hiking, and travel.

Composer: UNION (*I bind my heart this tide*), **411**

ZEUNER, CHARLES HEINRICH CHRISTOPHER (b. Sept. 20, 1795, Eisleben, Saxony, Germany; d. November 1857, Philadelphia, Pa.) was born in Martin Luther's hometown. In 1824 he came to North America and settled in Boston where Lowell Mason recognized his musical gifts. Zeuner became organist at St. Paul's Cathedral; he was also organist for the Handel and Haydn Society (1830-1837), serving as its president for a brief time (1838-1839). In 1854 he moved to Philadelphia to become organist of St. Anne's Episcopal Church and Arch Street Presbyterian Church, but severe criticism of his playing led to a depression that ended in suicide. The height of Zeuner's career seems to be the printing of his *American Harp* in 1832. All but five of the tunes in the four-hundred-page volume were his own compositions. Mason and Webb used a number of his tunes in *The Psaltery* (1845).

Composer: MISSIONARY CHANT (*Let there be light, Lord God*), **371**

ZIEGLER, EDWARD KRUSEN (b. Jan. 3, 1903, near Royersford, Pa.; d. Oct. 31, 1989, Bridgewater, Va.) earned degrees at Bridgewater College (B.S., 1929) and Bethany Theological Seminary, Oak Brook, Illinois (B.D., 1947). In 1921, as a young schoolteacher (having passed a teachers' examination after a couple of terms at Elizabethtown College in Pennsylvania), he was ordained to ministry in the Church of the Brethren. After several early pastorates, he and his wife Ilda M. Bittinger, went to India as missionaries (1931-1939). Between 1940 and 1971, he was pastor of congregations in York, Pennsylvania; Bridgewater, Roanoke, and Oakton, Virginia; and Bakersfield, California.

During hiatuses from congregational ministry, Ziegler taught at Manchester College, North Manchester, Indiana, for two years and at Bethany Theological Seminary for a quarter; he was director of evangelism and rural church concerns on the denominational staff at Elgin, Illinois, for four years (1951-1955). He also served the Church of the Brethren as founding editor of *Brethren Life and Thought* (1955-1980), moderator of Annual Conference for a term (1959-1960), a member of various committees and boards, and a representative to the National Council of Churches and the World Council of Churches. After Ilda's death he married Mary

Vivolo, a former Catholic sister, who subsequently joined the Church of the Brethren.

Ziegler's publications include an autobiography and several books on worship, ministry, and evangelism. He received honorary doctorates from Bethany Theological Seminary in 1950 and Bridgewater College in 1981.

Author: Almighty God, Spirit of purity and grace, **691**; Eternal God, we give you thanks, **718**

ZINZENDORF, NICOLAUS LUDWIG VON (b. May 26, 1700, Dresden, Germany; d. May 9, 1760, Herrnhut, Saxony, Germany), a contemporary of Isaac Watts and the Wesleys, was born into wealthy nobility and studied at Halle (1710-1716) and the University of Wittenberg (1716-1719). While at Halle, he founded a student society called the Order of the Mustard Seed, dedicated to spreading the gospel of Christ. Although he wanted to be a minister, Zinzendorf studied law at Wittenberg to please his family. After traveling through Europe, he took a position as counsel in the government at Dresden, remaining in that post until 1727.

With his considerable fortune, Count Zinzendorf bought the Saxony estate of Berthelsdorf, intending to settle there and make it a center for Christian work. Beginning in 1722, he gave asylum to Protestant refugees from Moravia and others from Germany, building the village of Herrnhut for them on a portion of the estate.

In 1734 Zinzendorf was given a license to preach by the theological faculty of the University of Tübingen. He totally immersed himself in the growing community of Moravian Brethren and was consecrated a bishop in 1737. That same year he was banished from Saxony on a charge of false doctrine. He became a missionary for the Moravians, traveling to Switzerland, Holland, England, and the West Indies. In 1741 he landed in New York and proceeded to found congregations in the Pennsylvania cities of Bethlehem, Nazareth, Lancaster, Hebron, and York. In 1748 the ban from his homeland was rescinded. He spent his entire fortune on religious work and died a poor man, but the community he reorganized continues its strong missionary emphasis to this day.

Zinzendorf wrote more than two thousand hymns, the first at age twelve and the last only five days before his death. Of the few remaining in use today, probably the most widely known outside of Moravian circles is "Jesus, still lead on."

Author: *Heart with loving heart united*, **420**; *The Lord is King*, **69**

ZUNDEL, JOHN (b. Dec. 10, 1815, Hochdorf, Germany; d. July, 1882, Connstadt, Germany) was educated in Germany and served as organist at St. Anne's Lutheran Church in St. Petersburg (later Leningrad and now St. Petersburg again), Russia, and bandmaster of the Imperial House Guards. In 1847 he came to the U.S. as organist at First Unitarian

Church, Brooklyn, and St. George's, New York City. In 1850 Zundel began his thirty-year tenure at Plymouth Congregational Church, Brooklyn, where Henry Ward Beecher was pastor. This preacher/musician duo attracted great crowds to Plymouth Church, noted for its excellence in preaching, organ playing, and congregational singing. Together Zundel and Beecher eventually compiled a hymnbook for that congregation (*The Plymouth Collection* 1855). In 1880 Zundel retired and returned to Germany.

In addition to his collaboration with Beecher, Zundel's prolific editorial work includes *The Choral Friend* (1852) and *Christian Heart Songs* (1870).

Composer: BEECHER (*Love divine, all loves excelling*), **592**

ZWICK, JOHANNES (b. ca. 1496, Constanz, Switzerland; d. Oct. 23, 1542, Bischofszell, Thurgau, Switzerland), one of the outstanding hymn-text writers associated with the Swiss Reformation, studied at European universities in Basel, Freiburg, Paris, and Padua for a career in law. By 1518, however, Zwick had turned to the priesthood; in 1522 he became a parish priest at Riedlungen. After encountering difficulty because of his Lutheran leanings, he went back to Constanz as a town preacher in 1527. In 1542 Zwick was called to the pastorate in Bischofszell where he died only a few months later, a victim of the plague.

Author: *Each morning brings us*, **645**

SOURCES CITED AND SELECTED BIBLIOGRAPHY

Adam, Adolf. *The Liturgical Year: Its History and Its Meaning after the Reform of the Liturgy*. Pueblo Publishers, 1981.

Adams, Charles B. *Our Moravian Hymn Heritage*. Moravian Church in America, 1984.

Bailey, Albert Edward. *The Gospel in Hymns, Backgrounds and Interpretations*. Charles Scribner's Sons, 1950.

Bender, Urie A. *Four Earthen Vessels*. Herald Press, 1982.

Bethge, Eberhard. In *Encyclopaedia Britannica*. William Benton, Publisher, 1968.

Bowman, Paul H., ed. and comp. *The Adventurous Future*. The Brethren Press, 1959.

Bruppacher, Theophil. *Gelobet sei der Herr*. Verlag Friedrich Reihnardt AG, 1953 (tr. George Wiebe).

Byzantine Liturgy, The: A New English Translation of the Liturgies of St. John Chrisostom and St. Basil the Great. Russian Center, Fordham University, 1956.

Castle, Tony, comp. *The New Book of Christian Prayers*. Crossroad Publishing Co., 1986.

Cleveland, J. Jefferson, and William B. McClain. "A Historical Account of the Negro Spiritual," *Songs of Zion*. Abingdon Press, 1981.

Colvin, Tom. *Fill Us with Your Love*. Hope Publishing Co., 1983.

Common Lectionary: The Lectionary Proposed by the Consultation on Common Texts. The Church Hymnal Corporation, 1983.

Cone, James H. *The Spirituals and the Blues: An Interpretation*. Seabury Press, 1972.

Cross, F. L., and E. A. Livingstone, eds. *The Oxford Dictionary of the Christian Church*. Oxford University Press, 1974.

Daw, Carl P., Jr. *A Year of Grace*. Hope Publishing Co., 1990.

Dearmer, Percy, and Archibald Jacob, comps. *Songs of Praise (1931) Discussed*. Oxford University Press (London), 1933.

Dearmer, Percy R., Vaughan Williams, and Martin Shaw. *Oxford Book of Carols*. Oxford University Press (London), 1964.

Dictionary of American Biography, Vol. 3. Charles Scribner's Sons, 1943.

Diehl, Katharine Smith. *Hymns and Tunes—an Index*. The Scarecrow Press, Inc., 1966.

Dorsey, Thomas A. "The Birth of 'Precious Lord,' " *Guideposts*. October 1987.

Douglas, Charles Winfred. *A Brief Commentary on Selected Hymns and Carols*. The Church Pension Fund, 1936.

Douglas, Charles Winfred, Leonard Ellinwood, and others. *The Hymnal 1940 Companion*. The Church Pension Fund, 1949, 1951.

Dudley-Smith, Timothy. *Lift Every Heart: Collected Hymns 1961-1983 and some early poems*. Hope Publishing Co., 1984.

Durnbaugh, Donald, ed. *The Brethren Encyclopedia*. The Brethren Encyclopedia, Inc., 1983.

Durnbaugh, Donald. *European Origins of the Brethren*. The Brethren Press, 1958.

Durnbaugh, Donald. "The Lesson in History," *Brethren Adult Quarterly*, 73:2, 1958.

Durnbaugh, Hedwig T. "*Geistreiches Gesang-buch*, 1720—The First Brethren Hymnal." *The Hymn*, October 1991.

Durnbaugh, Hedwig T. *The German Hymnody of the Brethren, 1720-1903*. The Brethren Encyclopedia, Inc., 1986.

Ellinwood, Leonard. "Tallis' Tunes and Tudor Psalmody." *Musica Disciplina, II* (1948).

Eltz-Hoffmann, Lieselotte von. *Lob Gott getrost mit Singen (Die schönsten Kirchengesangbuchlieder und ihre Dichter)*. Quell Verlag Stuttgart, 1980.

Epstein, Dena J. *Sinful Tunes and Spirituals: Black Folk Music to the Civil War*. University of Illinois Press, 1977.

Eskew, Harry. "An Interview with Carl Daw." *The Hymn*, April 1989.

Esther, James R., and Donald Bruggink. *Worship the Lord*. Wm. B. Eerdmans Co., 1987.

Fanny Crosby, Memories of Eighty Years. 1906.

Farlander, Arthur, Leonard Ellinwood, et al. *The Hymnal 1940 Companion*. Church Pension Fund, 1951 ed.

Faus, Nancy Rosenberger. *The Importance of Music in Worship*. Brethren and Mennonite monograph, 1993.

Foss, Hubert. *Ralph Vaughan Williams: A Study*. Greenwood Press, 1974 (reprint of original publication, George G. Harrop and Co., Ltd., 1950).

Fox, Matthew, ed. *Hildegard of Bingen's Book of Divine Works with Letters and Songs*. Bear and Company, 1987.

Frost, Maurice. *Historical Companion to Hymns Ancient and Modern*. William Clowes and Sons, Ltd., 1962.

Garrett, Margueritte Garrett, and William Beery. *History and Message of Hymns*. The Brethren Press, 1924.

Gealy, Fred D., Austin C. Lovelace, and Carlton R. Young. *Companion to the Hymnal*. Abingdon Press, 1970.

Gilbert, Arthur. *The Passover Seder: Pathways through the Haggadah*. KTAV Publishing House, Inc., 1970.

Gingerich, Melvin. "The Omi Brotherhood." *Christian Living*, February 1959.

Green, Fred Pratt. *The Hymns and Ballads of Fred Pratt Green*. Hope Publishing Co., 1982.

Grindal, Gracia. "The Dano-Norwegian Tradition of Hymnody and its Development in America" (unpublished paper, no date).

Grout, Donald J. *A History of Western Music*, 3rd ed. W. W. Norton and Co., Inc., 1980.

Haeussler, Armin. *The Story of Our Hymns*, Eden Publishing House, 1952.

Hamm, Charles. "The Chapins and Sacred Music in the South and West." *Journal of Research in Music Education* (Fall 1960).

Hatchett, Marion. *Commentary on the American Prayer Book*. Seabury Press, 1981.

Hauge, Tormod. "Kristendomssyn og poetisk form i Svein Ellingsen's diktning." Thesis (equivalent of M.A.Th.). Oslo: Menighetsfakultetet, 1986. [Quotation translated by Hedwig T. Durnbaugh]

Havergal, Maria V. G. *Memorials of Frances Ridley Havergal*. Anson D. F. Randolph and Co., 1880.

Henderson, Frank, Stephen Larson, and Kathleen Quinn, eds. *Liturgy, Justice and the Reign of God: Integrating Vision and Practice*. Paulist Press, 1989.

Hinks, Donald R. *Brethren Hymn Books and Hymnals, 1720-1884*. Brethren Heritage Press, 1986.

Hitchcock, H. Wiley, and Stanley Sadie, eds. *The New Grove Dictionary of American Music*. Groves Dictionaries, 1986.

Hooper, Wayne, and Edward E. White. *Companion to the Seventh-day Adventist Hymnal*. Review and Herald Publishing Association, 1988.

Hoppin, Richard H. *Medieval Music: The Norton Introduction to Music History*. W. W. Norton and Co., Inc., 1978.

Hostetler, John A. *Amish Society*. Johns Hopkins University Press, 1963.

Hostetler, Lester. *Handbook to the Mennonite Hymnary*. General Conference of the Mennonite Church of North America, 1949.

Huck, Gabe, Gail Ramshaw, and Gordon Lathrop, eds. *An Easter Sourcebook*. Chicago, 1987.

Hughes, Charles W. *American Hymns Old and New: Notes on the Hymns and Biographies of the Authors and Composers*. Columbia University Press, 1980.

Hustad, Donald P. *Dictionary-Handbook to Hymns for the Living Church*. Hope Publishing Co., 1978.

Hymnal 1982 Companion, The, pre-publication manuscript.

Hymnal for the Hours. G.I.A. Publications, Inc., 1989.

Jackson, George Pullen. *Spiritual Folk-Songs of Early America*. Dover, 1964.

Jesus Christ—the Life of the World. World Council of Churches, 1983.

Job, Rueben P., and Norman Shawchuck. *A Guide to Prayer for Ministers and Other Servants*. The Upper Room, 1983.

Jones, Cheslyn, Geoffrey Wainwright, and Edward Yarnold, S.J., eds. *The Study of Liturgy*. Oxford University Press, 1978.

Julian, John, ed. *A Dictionary of Hymnology*. John Murray, 1907, reprinted Dover Publications, 1957.

Kaan, Fred. *Hymn Texts of Fred Kaan*. Hope Publishing Co., 1985.

Kennedy, Michael. *A Catalogue of the Works of Ralph Vaughan Williams*, rev. ed. Oxford University Press, 1982.

Klassen, William, and Walter Klaassen. *The Writing of Pilgram Marpeck*. Herald Press, 1978.

Kulp, Buchner, Fornacon. *Die Lieder Unserer Kirche*. Göttingen: Vandenhoeck and Ruprecht, 1958.

Leaver, Robin A., and James A. Litton, eds. *Duty and Delight: Routley Remembered*. Hope Publishing Co., 1985.

Lefevre, Wayne. " 'Morning Star' Composer." *The North American Moravian*, November 1978.

Leith, John H., ed. *Creeds of the Churches*, rev. ed. John Knox Press, 1973.

Loewen, Alice, J., Harold Moyer, and Mary Oyer. *Exploring the Mennonite Hymnal: Handbook*. Faith and Life Press, Mennonite Publishing House, 1983.

Logan, Rayford W., and Michael R. Winston. *Dictionary of American Negro Biography*. W. W. Norton and Co., Inc., 1982.

Lovelace, Austin C. *Hymn Notes for Church Bulletins*. G.I.A. Publications, Inc., 1987.

Lovell, John B., Jr. *Black Song: The Forge and the Flame*. Macmillan, 1972.

McClain, William B. *Come Sunday: The Liturgy of Zion*. Abingdon Press, 1990.

McCutchan, Robert Guy. *Our Hymnody: A Manual of the Methodist Hymnal, 1932*. Abingdon-Cokesbury Press, 1937.

McKim, LindaJo. *The Presbyterian Hymnal Companion*. Westminster/John Knox Press, 1993.

Manschreck, Clyde, comp. *Prayers of the Reformers*. Muhlenberg Press, 1958.

Melloh, John A., and William G. Storey. *Praise God in Song*. G.I.A. Publications, Inc., 1979.

Mennonite Encyclopedia, The: A Comprehensive Reference Work on the Anabaptist-Mennonite Movement. Mennonite Publishing House; Mennonite Publication Office; Mennonite Brethren Publishing House, 1957.

Milgate, Wesley. *Songs of the People of God*. Collins Liturgical Publications, 1982.

Morley, Janet. *All Desires Known*. Morehouse Publishers, 1988.

Morse, Kenneth I. Association for the Arts Newsletter. Brethren Press, Fall 1982.

Nelle, Wilhelm. *Schluessel zum Evangelischen Gesangbuch für Rheinland und Westfalen*. Gütersloh, 1918.

New Harvard Dictionary of Music, The. Harvard University Press, 1986.

Osbourne, Stanley L. *If Such Holy Song*. The Institute of Church Music, 1976.

Oxford Book of Carols, The. Oxford University Press, 1964.

Oyer, Mary. *Exploring the Mennonite Hymnal: Essays*. Faith and Life Press, Mennonite Publishing House, 1980.

Parry, Kenneth L., and Erik Routley. *Companion to Congregational Praise*. Independent Press Ltd., 1953.

Pfatteicher, Philip H. *Commentary on the Lutheran Book of Worship*. Augsburg Fortress, 1990.

Pilgrim Hymnal, The Pilgrim Press, 1958.

Pipkin, H. Wayne, and John H. Yoder. *Balthasar Hubmaier: Theologian of Anabaptism*, Herald Press, 1989.

Polack, William G. *The Handbook to the Lutheran Hymnal*. Concordia Publishing House, 1942.

Posner, Raphael, Uri Kaploun, and Shalom Cohen. *Jewish Liturgy*. Keter Publishing House Jerusalem Ltd., 1975.

Psalter Hymnal Handbook, pre-publication manuscript.

Putnam, Alfred. *Singers and Songs of the Liberal Faith*. Roberts Brothers, 1875.

Ramirez, William Obed. Letter written on behalf of Guillermo Cuellar, dated May 17, 1992.

Reed, Luther D. *The Lutheran Liturgy*. Muhlenberg Press, 1947.
Reynolds, William J. *Companion to Baptist Hymnal*. Broadman Press, 1976.
Reynolds, William J. *Songs of Glory*. Zondervan Books, 1990.
Robinson, Edward. *The Language of Mystery*. Trinity Press, 1990.
Ronander, Albert C., and Ethel K. Porter. *Guide to the Pilgrim Hymnal*. United Church Press, 1966.
Routley, Erik. *A Panorama of Christian Hymnody*. G.I.A. Publications, Inc., 1979.
Routley, Erik. *An English-Speaking Hymnal Guide*. Liturgical Press, 1979.
Routley, Erik, ed. *Rejoice in the Lord*. Wm. B. Eerdmans Publishing, 1985.
Routley, Erik. *The Music of Christian Hymns*. G.I.A. Publications, Inc., 1981.
Ryden, E. E. *The Story of Christian Hymnody*. Augustana Book Concern, 1959.
St. Augustine. *Confessions*. Translated by R. S. Pine-Coffine. Penguin Books, 1961.
Sadie, Stanley, ed. *New Grove Dictionary of Music and Musicians*. Macmillan Publishers, Ltd., 1980.
Sankey, Ira D. *My Life and the Story of the Gospel Hymns and of Sacred Songs and Solos*. Harper and Brothers, 1906.
Sleeth, Natalie. *Adventures for the Soul*. Hope Publishing Co., 1987.
Statler, Ruth B., and Nevin W. Fisher. *Handbook to Brethren Hymns*. The Brethren Press, 1959.
Stuhlmueller, Carroll, C.P. *Psalms 1*. Michael Glazier, Inc., 1983.
Stuhlmueller, Carroll, C.P. *Psalms 2*. Michael Glazier, Inc., 1983.
Stulken, Marilyn Kay. *Hymnal Companion to the Lutheran Book of Worship*. Fortress Press, 1981.
Summers, Joseph H., ed. *George Herbert: Selected Poetry*. The New American Library, 1967.
Taft, Robert, S.J. *The Liturgy of the Hours in East and West: The Origins of Divine Office and Its Meaning for Today*. The Liturgical Press, 1986.
Thomas à Kempis. *The Imitation of Christ*. Translated by William C. Creasy. Mercer University Press, 1989.
Thompson, Bard. *Liturgies of the Western Church*. Fortress Press, 1961.
Thomson, R. W., ed. *The Baptist Hymn Book Companion*, rev. ed. Psalms and Hymns Trust, 1967.
Trench, Richard Chenivix. *Sacred Latin Poetry*. MacMillan and Co., 1864.
Troeger, Thomas, and Carol Doran. *New Hymns for the Lectionary*. Oxford University Press, 1986.
Tsese-Ma'heone-Nemeototse (Cheyenne Spiritual Songs). Faith and Life Press, 1982.
Utechin, S. V. *Everyman's Concise Encyclopedia of Russia*. E. P. Dutton and Co., Inc., 1961.
Vajda, Jaroslav J. *Now the Joyful Celebration*. Morning Star Music Publishers, 1987.
Verduin, Leonard, tr., and J. C. Wenger, ed. *The Complete Writings of Menno Simons*. Herald Press, 1956.
Watson, Richard, and Kenneth Trickett, eds. *Companion to Hymns and Psalms*. Methodist Publishing House, England, 1988.
We Gather Together: Worship Resources for the Church of the Brethren. The Brethren Press, 1979.

Weiser, Arthur. *The Psalms: A Commentary*. Westminster Press, 1962.

Wenger, John Christian, ed. *The Complete Writings of Menno Simons*. Translated from the Dutch by Leonard Verduin. Mennonite Publishing House, 1956.

Werner, Eric. *The Sacred Bridge: Liturgical Parallels in Synagogue and Early Church*. Schocken Books, 1970.

Work, John Wesley. *Folk Songs of the American Negro*. Bonanza Books, 1940.

Worshiping Church, The (worship leader's ed.). Hope Publishing Co., 1990, 1991.

Wren, Brian. *Bring Many Names*. Hope Publishing Co., 1989.

Wren, Brian. *Faith Looking Forward*. Hope Publishing Co., 1983.

Wren, Brian. *Praising a Mystery*. Hope Publishing Co., 1986.

Young, Carlton R. *Companion to the United Methodist Hymnal*. Abingdon Press, 1993.

NUMERICAL INDEX OF HYMNS

78 Ehane he'ama (Father God, you are holy)
79 Lord, with devotion we pray
80 O bless the Lord, my soul
81 Oh, for a thousand tongues to sing
82 Great God, how infinite art thou
83 With happy voices singing
84 Oh, that I had a thousand voices
85 Now thank we all our God
86 Now thank we all our God
87 Great is the Lord
88 Still, I search for my God
89 For the beauty of the earth
90 For the fruit of all creation
91 Praise to God, immortal praise
92 Lord, should rising whirlwinds
93 Lord, bless the hands
94 Come, ye thankful people
95 Praise God, the Source of life
96 We plow the fields and scatter
97 From the hands
98 Sing to the Lord of harvest
99 We praise thee, O God
100 Praise him, praise him
101 Alleluia
102 To God be the glory
103 Jubilate Deo omnis terra
104 Of the Father's love begotten
105 Christ, we do all adore thee
106 All hail the power of Jesus' name
107 Blessed Savior, we adore thee
108 Blessing and honor and glory
109 I will praise the Lord
110 Oh, for a thousand tongues to sing
111 O praise the gracious power
112 O Lord, our Lord, how majestic (How majestic is your name)
113 O Christe Domine Jesu
114 In thee is gladness
115 Jesus, thou mighty Lord
116 Crown him with many crowns
117 Fairest Lord Jesus
118 Praise God from whom (DEDICATION ANTHEM)
119 Praise God from whom (OLD HUNDREDTH)
120 Holy, holy, holy
121 Holy God, we praise thy name
122 All glory be to God on high
123 O Holy Spirit, Root of life
124 O worship the Lord
125 To God, with the Lamb
126 How wondrous great
127 Glory be to the Father
128 Create in me a clean heart
129 Fire of God, undying flame
130 O God of mystery and might
131 When in the hour of deepest need
132 Holy Spirit, Storm of love
133 Out of the depths I cry to you
134 Babylon streams received our tears
135 God, whose purpose is to kindle
136 From the depths of sin
137 Forgive our sins as we forgive
138 Let God, who called the worlds
139 Far, far away from my loving father
140 Open, Lord, my inward ear
141 The sacrifice you accept, O God
142 Brothers and sisters of mine
143 Amazing grace
144 Kyrie eleison
145 There's a wideness in God's mercy
146 O Lamb of God all holy
147 Oh, how wondrous the grace
148 By the waters
149 Great God of wonders
150 Wonderful grace of Jesus
151 Marvelous grace of our loving Lord
152 Kyrie
153 O Christ, the Lamb of God
154 This is my Father's world
155 O God, great womb
156 All things bright and beautiful
157 Lord, our Lord, your glorious name
158 Since o'er thy footstool
159 All beautiful the march of days
160 God created heaven and earth
161 We give thanks unto you
162 The God of Abraham praise
163 Obey my voice
164 When Israel was in Egypt's land
165 A mighty fortress is our God
166 I'll praise my Maker
167 For God so loved us
168 Creating God, your fingers trace
169 I to the hills will lift my eyes
170 The King of love my shepherd is
171 How lovely is your dwelling
172 O come, O come, Immanuel
173 Savior of the nations, come
174 Bless'd be the God of Israel
175 O Savior, rend the heavens
176 Comfort, comfort, O my people
177 Creator of the stars of night

271 Christ is arisen
272 Christ is risen! Shout hosanna
273 Low in the grave he lay
274 O sons and daughters, let us sing
275 Lift your glad voices
276 This joyful Eastertide
277 I know that my Redeemer lives
278 Christ is alive! Let Christians sing
279 I know that my Redeemer lives
280 Christ the Lord is risen today
281 That Easter day with joy was bright
282 Proclaim the tidings near and far
283 Christ who left his home in glory
284 Come away to the skies
285 All hail the power of Jesus' name
286 Look, you saints
287 Sing we triumphant hymns
288 Rejoice, the Lord is King
289 Filled with the Spirit's power
290 Spirit, come, dispel our sadness
291 O Holy Spirit, by whose breath
292 Away with our fears
293 God sends us the Spirit
294 Dona nobis pacem Domine
295 Christ is coming! Let creation
296 Here from all nations
297 Jesus came—the heavens adoring
298 Veni Sancte Spiritus (Come, Holy Spirit)
299 New earth, heavens new
300 O Holy Spirit, making whole
301 Joys are flowing like a river
302 Come, divine Interpreter
303 Come, gracious Spirit
304 There are many gifts
305 Where charity and love prevail
306 In Christ there is no East or West
307 Will you let me be your servant
308 I love thy kingdom, Lord
309 Built on the Rock
310 How good a thing it is
311 The church's one foundation
312 Lamp of our feet
313 Rejoice, rejoice in God
314 The word of God is solid ground
315 This is a story full of love
316 In this world abound scrolls
317 Lord, I have made thy word
318 Joy to the world
319 Jesus shall reign
320 Oh, holy city seen of John
321 Lift high the cross
322 For we are strangers no more
323 Beyond a dying sun (I see a new world coming)
324 Seek ye first the kingdom of God
325 Creating God, your fingers trace
326 O Love of God
327 Great is thy faithfulness
328 O God, our help in ages past
329 A mighty fortress is our God
330 I believe in God (Nasadiki)
331 If Christ is mine
332 Blessed assurance
333 Christ, who is in the form of God
334 Christ is the world's true light
335 This is the threefold truth
336 When peace, like a river
337 Ask ye what great thing I know
338 I know not why God's wondrous grace
339 Thou art the way
340 'Tis so sweet to trust in Jesus
341 Jesus loves me
342 At the name of Jesus
343 My hope is built on nothing less
344 I will sing of my Redeemer
345 God sent his Son (Because he lives)
346 Dona nobis pacem
347 Through our fragmentary prayers
348 O Lord, hear my prayer
349 Spirit of the living God
350 Lord, teach us how to pray aright
351 Our Father who art in heaven
352 Gentle Shepherd, come and lead us
353 Lord, listen to your children
354 Fount of love, our Savior God
355 Savior, like a shepherd lead us
356 Breathe on me, breath of God
357 O Master, let me walk with thee
358 Oyenos, mi Dios
359 Lead us, O Father
360 Break thou the bread of life
361 O Spirit of the living God
362 Help us to help each other
363 Renew your church
364 Spirit of God, unleashed on earth
365 Christ, from whom all blessings
366 God of grace and God of glory
367 For the healing of the nations
368 O God of love, O Power of peace
369 Lord, whose love in humble service
370 O day of God, draw nigh
371 Let there be light, Lord God

GENERAL INDEX

Tune names are in all capital letters. Sources of hymns, tunes, and worship resources are in italics. Worship resource articles are indexed by first line. Page numbers of brief essays on liturgical terms are in bold face. Biographies and hymns occur in alphabetical order in this book and, therefore, are not indexed. See *Hymnal: A Worship Book* for other useful indexes.